M̲___

1212 Lake Shore Dr

Chicago, Ill -
60610

ELEMENTS OF INTERIOR DESIGN AND DECORATION

·SHERRILL WHITON

FOUNDER AND DIRECTOR OF THE NEW YORK SCHOOL
OF INTERIOR DESIGN FROM 1916 TO 1961.

Elements of
INTERIOR
DESIGN
and
DECORATION

SHERRILL WHITON

LATE DIRECTOR
THE NEW YORK SCHOOL OF INTERIOR DESIGN

J. B. LIPPINCOTT COMPANY

PHILADELPHIA   NEW YORK   TORONTO

1951 Edition

Reprinted September 1952
Reprinted June 1953
Reprinted November 1954
Reprinted June 1956

1957 Edition

Reprinted February 1959
Reprinted March 1960
Reprinted April 1961
Reprinted January 1962
Reprinted November 1962

1963 Edition

Reprinted February 1964
Reprinted October 1964
Reprinted May 1965
Reprinted June 1965
Reprinted April 1966
Reprinted January 1967
Reprinted May 1967
Reprinted December 1967
Reprinted March 1968
Reprinted November 1968
Reprinted May 1969
Reprinted February 1970
Reprinted July 1971
Reprinted August 1972
Reprinted February 1973

Library of Congress Catalog Card Number: 63–21060

ISBN: 0–397–47025–8
ISBN: 0–397–47026–6

Elements of Interior Design and Decoration incorporates many of the features of *Elements of Interior Decoration* by Mr. Whiton, copyright, 1944, 1937, by Sherrill Whiton.

Dedicated to the several thousand former students of the New York School of Interior Design, whose responsiveness and search for knowledge have made them, without their realization, co-authors of this book.

This above all; to thine own self be true,
And it must follow, as the night the day,
Thou canst not then be false to any man.

PREFACE

The plan of this book is simple. Its purpose is to guide the reader to an intelligent understanding of what is beautiful and useful in the design, furnishing, decoration, and equipment of all types of rooms.

Many books that have been written on similar subjects have had the superficial approach of showing numerous illustrations with detailed captional descriptions as a substitute for a thorough explanatory text. The purpose of this method has been to show material that may be used as a basis for imitation or reproduction. While there is ample need for such publications, the author of this book has made no attempt to compete with them. Original creative results can only be attained through logical reasoning based on the principles of design and common sense, and not by purloining the work of other artists and designers.

The arts today are much closer to the daily life of every individual than they were a generation ago. They have become an unavoidable and essential ingredient to living. Good design in every object of household use is today a requisite for sales appeal. With increasing facilities for travel, communication, and the exchange of goods and ideas, art in a sense has become international in scope and has had a more universal appeal. The world is perhaps on the threshold of an artistic awakening that should be a logical sequel to the material advantages gained by an industrial age. A study of the arts must be on a firm foundation to meet the broader understanding that the future will require.

The value in studying the decorative arts is not limited to its contribution toward creative effort or to the development of the imagination. A greater benefit is the cultural information that is acquired in the process. The roots of these arts entwine themselves around nearly all branches of human thought and activity, and an understanding of them will aid greatly in the development of one's ability to analyze, reason, and judge human affairs. Even if no direct professional preparation is anticipated an acquaintance with these subjects will nourish the spiritual enjoyments of life, in opening alluring vistas that have been previously screened. Its value is measureless as preliminary reading for the tourist who intends to visit art centers.

Many years of teaching by the author have proved conclusively that if a designer is to be worthy of this title, he must be saturated with every scrap of knowledge that records can furnish as to the circumstances that have actuated the growth of all ancient and modern types of art. He must be able to discern causes, influences, and results. Only with this information will his capacity to reason enable him to produce the best of his own period. It is more important to learn the principles of the arts of the past than to know the forms and details, and the former rather than the latter should serve as a pattern for the young designer. Such training requires a liberal study of related cultural subjects. A text of this length can provide little more than an introduction to such an approach, but the author will feel amply compensated if the material included in this book awakens further interest and sows the seeds of future research.

Part One is devoted to a description of the dominant influences and characteristics of the historical and modern exterior and interior architectural, furniture, and ornamental design. As the decorative arts are a branch of architecture, and the architectural styles have been fundamentally an outgrowth of structural developments, it has been thought advisable to trace briefly these structural changes, and it is hoped that the serious student will thoroughly absorb this portion of the text. Part Two gives a description of the most important of the associated arts, crafts, and trades that are used in contemporary decorative work, concerning which the decorator must acquire a connoisseurship. Part Three relates to the abstract elements of taste, design, composition, and color. The illustrations so far as possible are from authoritative original sources, authentic documents, and museum collections. By limiting himself to a study of such source material the student will be able to interpret and adapt the forms according to his own judgment and needs. A bibliography of textual and illustrative material is added at the end of each chapter for students who desire to pursue further research.

The first edition of this book was published in 1937 under the shorter title *Elements of Interior Decoration*. In subsequent printings much material was added. In the present edition, the title has been altered to include the word *Design*. The author believes this to be more comprehensive and descriptive of the new and greatly enlarged text, and more in keeping with the modern approach to the study of the subject. It is his hope that this rewriting will be as acceptable to the public as the former edition.

The author wishes to state that he by no means claims to be a final authority in all the branches of the decorative arts that are included. Rather, the book may be considered an assemblage of information that has been gleaned over a long period from the many authorities with whom he has come in contact, and to whom he wishes to express his sincere gratitude. Among these are the many gracious museum officials in Europe and America, librarians, authors of books, lenders of photographs, trade specialists, and designers and decorators whose imagination, taste, and ideals have contributed to the improvement in the homes of North America, South America, and Central America. He is particularly grateful to Louis Bouché, Mary L. Brandt, Marcel Breuer, William Breger, Ralph M. Chait, Inez Croom, Arthur U. Dilley, Curt Hasenclever, Nancy V. McClelland, George Nelson, Richard L. Neutra, Isabel Neves, Jens Risom, Harold R. Sleeper, E. Kennedy Torrington, Herbert L. Weissberger, Edward Wormley, and Frank Lloyd Wright; for the drawings made by Gilbert Werlé; and for the research and manuscript corrections of Dorothy Merrick.

The indulgence of the reader is asked for errors of fact or judgment that inadvertently may have been included in this volume.

SHERRILL WHITON

June, 1956

PREFACE TO THE THIRD EDITION

The Third Edition of Elements of Interior Design and Decoration maintains the tradition of periodic revisions which were undertaken by Sherrill Whiton from the publication of the First Edition in 1937 until his death in June, 1961. In this volume the editor has rewritten Chapter IX, extending and developing the subject of contemporary architecture. Moreover, as we find ourselves confronted more and more with problems and their solutions arising from recent developments in contemporary interior design, it seemed advisable to add a new chapter dealing exclusively with contemporary furniture.

The editor wishes to thank Susan and Stanley Salzman and Gilbert Werlé for their extensive co-operation in the preparation of this edition.

SHERRILL WHITON, JR.

June, 1963

FOREWORD

A page of an old book, tacked to the wall of a seaman's bethel in New England, admonishes its patrons to guard their conversation as follows:

> *Great minds discuss ideas*
> *Average minds discuss events*
> *Small minds discuss people.*

Ideas are the fathers of creative thoughts. Coming from the cosmos, they germinate in minds that vibrate in harmony with them. Their most fertile soil has been among people who hungered for them, and whose initiative made it possible to transmute them into reality. Among such, they have blossomed into the creations of genius of the scientific and artistic worlds. Through the organization of knowledge and reason Science has produced the useful as a means to an end, but Art has fed the spirit of man by rationalizing thought into sensuous forms and developing a language of the emotions. Posterity has measured the greatness of bygone races by their artistic achievements, and the intellectual level of individuals is appraised by their knowledge of these subjects and the relative importance they give them.

Artists and poets have given a meaning to life, and their sensitivities to human perplexities have made them the perpetuators of civilization. The masterpieces of philosophy, literature, architecture, music, sculpture, and painting remain to record the procedures and thoughts of former times. The ideals of the Athenians, the philosophy of the Jews, the zeal of the Middle Ages, and the Humanism of the Renaissance still cast their rays upon millions today.

> *All passes, Art alone*
> *Enduring stays to us.*
> *The Bust outlasts the throne,*
> *The Coin, Tiberius.*
> AUSTIN DOBSON

The progress of civilization implies the inheritance of tradition and an understanding of the ideals of those who have excelled in the past. To disregard arbitrarily one's predecessors is a transgression of intelligence, for paradoxically the more extensive the study of what has been done and thought, the greater will be one's inventiveness and creative originality. But an art is invigorated through its roots and not its blossoms, and esthetic sensitivity is developed through an analysis of the philosophical attitude of the masters rather than their productions. The great creators always have been in tune with their times, and today's artist cannot scorn similar influences. Rules cannot be universal, and although they serve well the young student and nonthinker, they are of little value to the mature artist or intelligent person. While the gift of genius eventually settles where Providence selects, talent in the beginner may be developed best by arousing his curiosity and his urge to investigate rather than by obliging him to listen to theories or the interpretation of facts. A person is not really educated until he has learned to think for himself, and the impulse to learn must be born within.

A large portion of history has been devoted to the struggles of the underprivileged for a greater share in the benefits of civilization. It is to the credit of modern times that in most civilized nations there is less spread between classes than ever before, but in this achievement, the democratization of culture has lagged. Industrialized man, obsessed by gadgets, often worships the gods who have produced them, and has permitted these to pilfer the real nutrition of his soul. Machine production has contributed to some extent to a cultural paralysis. The material gains of the masses have clouded the fact that such benefits are not an end in themselves, and man has been blinded in his perspective of the future. The true joys of life are not material, but come from a contented mind and an enrichment of the spirit to which only the arts can abundantly contribute. The average man is as yet only half-educated, being satisfied with superficial interests; and it has not yet become fashionable for him to be well informed in the arts. Propaganda and slogans have been the directives of his thought, and he refuses to think for himself. Individualism is feared, and too many are satisfied to act, think, and live like their neighbors. Many can earn a living, but having earned it, have not the capacity to enjoy it.

The mission of the decorative artist is obvious. He has a vast opportunity to contribute to the betterment of the world, by broadening the public appreciation of the arts and creating a greater realization of their value and use. He must never be satisfied with his work, for complacency leads to stagnation. He must be a free agent, independent of dictation by patron, state, or public. He can aid in establishing an aristocracy of the intellect, and teach the people to distinguish the true from the false. The submergence of individualism must be combatted; the procreative impulses of intellectual movements must be fathomed, and the inner meanings of art productions must be made clear. Man must be taught to see, and to feel and to think coherently for himself, and to follow his own reasoned preferences, even if they conflict with fashion and public opinion. Art should be an integrated part of the life of every individual, who must learn to use, understand, respect, and revere every object that has been produced by the honest efforts of an artist. Individuals should cultivate zealously an art sense, and a capacity for rational judgment, in which praise or disapproval of a work will be deferred until the artist's intentions are understood. Educational institutions may arouse enthusiasms, and train the artist in history, philosophy, and techniques; but the public must be made conscious of the value of the arts, and of the mental processes that are followed in their production. Only then will be established the ultimate in public taste, and a realization of the satisfactions that may be obtained from subjective interests. The decorative artist is in a position to contribute more to these ends than all the museums in the world.

In a more universal distribution of culture, there would be a broader demand for perfection in all the arts, an increase in both production and consumption, and a greater support of the artist who is imbued with integrity. All branches of art would evolve to produce a new Golden Age expressive of contemporary life. Man surrounded by beauty would be happier and less envious of others. Let us hope that the people of the Americas, having acquired a profusion of material conveniences, will carry onward the torch that lit the streets of Athens and the squares of Florence.

SUGGESTIONS TO TEACHERS

In teaching any branch of art, an instructor must maintain an approach well above the mental level of his students, in order to establish an inspirational appeal. The first essential is to accentuate the importance and value of the subject; the second is to interpret the subject in as interesting a manner as possible. The average student reacts strongly to an element of surprise created by an association of ideas, and by an analysis of cause and effect. Facts alone are lifeless, unless there is a sequence of thought and an interrelationship is obvious. Few beginners realize why the fall of Constantinople in 1453 was the start of residential architecture in Europe, or know why the arts of Spain were so greatly influenced by Columbus' voyages, or why the revocation of the Edict of Nantes revolutionized the industries of France and England. The layman seldom looks upon Paul Revere as other than a celebrated patriot and night rider, but when told that he produced some of the finest American silverware, curiosity is immediately aroused. When causes and results are examined, art becomes vitalized, enthusiasm is developed, basic principles unfold, and imagination commences to bud.

In comparing the 20th century trend in the decorative arts with that of former movements, it is probable that an esthetic progression will continue for many years to come. In spite of its merits to date, there is much to be perfected, and there are many persons who neither understand, nor have willingly accepted the style. The design, decoration, and furnishings of the major portion of American homes will probably, for a long time, continue to be inspired by the historic periods. As architecture is the parent of decoration, a knowledge of its history, structural evolution, and details is essential, and it is important to understand the principles from which it has been conceived. Contemporary exterior and interior architectural designs, though differing in appearance from those of former styles, are produced by the same principles that have been the basis of all great art periods, and a knowledge of these principles is the first requirement of the creative artist. The elements of pure design, expression of structure, suitability of material to its use, contrast and variety, avoidance of monotony, pleasure of surprise, the establishment of unity, and evidence of taste will always remain the foundation stones of good design, regardless of style or period.

In addition to the study of history and abstract principles, a professional designer should be trained technically in the use of the pencil, pen, and brush, as the best means of developing an understanding of form, proportion, and color. The value of knowing how to produce and interpret sketches and working drawings is unquestioned, but such training can be obtained only through hours of patience over a drawing board, under the constant supervision of an instructor. This text is intended to develop the imagination of the student, to show the reasons how the arts of the past have been evolved, and how, by the application of the same processes and principles, the arts of the future may be produced. This knowledge is basic for the designer to enable him to understand design procedures, but the teaching of the techniques necessary to present his ideas on paper is outside the limits of this volume.

Many laymen little realize the breadth and dignity of the art of interior decoration or its intimacy with daily life. The subject is often superficially approached as a study of color schemes, draperies, and furniture arrangement, and is considered of importance only to the sophisticated dilettante. Such a contracted view is quite erroneous and fails to indicate an understanding of the more profound psychological sides of the subject, and the advantages of its application even in the most humble of circumstances.

One cannot create a spark of imaginative genius in another individual, but if the spark exists, an intelligent instructor may nurture it to a flame that eventually may grow by itself. A proper sequence and balance of thought is necessary in the presentation of the subject. The arrangement as indicated in the Table of Contents in this book confirms a method of presentation that has been used successfully by the author for many years.

The Introduction should be fully understood by the student before he proceeds to Part One. Assuming 18 weeks to a school semester with one hour per week given to the study of interior decoration, there is ample material in Part One to cover a single semester, if outside reading, research, and tracing are included. Parts Two and Three, comprising Chapters X to XXIV, may cover a second semester's work. If the subject becomes a major study and additional hours per week are allotted, the time for covering the text may be proportionately shortened. An unlimited amount of outside work may be given to the student, if desired. As a rule, greater fascination develops as the student proceeds and realizes how certain principles may be applied to his own home or surroundings, frequently with little effort or cost.

Notebooks may be kept with sketches or tracings of period patterns, decorations, architecture, furniture, and decorative accessories. It is also advisable to have each student keep a scrapbook in which may be inserted pictures of rooms or objects that may be cut from magazines or newspapers, and in which may be placed samples of colors, fabrics, or schemes worked out at home or in class.

For the benefit of schools, teachers, or students who may have a small fund available for the purchase of reference books, the list given on page xvii of authoritative and inexpensive publications is recommended. For more extensive research in source material volumes, many of which are only available in art libraries, a bibliography is given at the end of each chapter.

It is also recommended that certain magazines on the decorative arts be subscribed to either by the art department of a school or by the students individually. Subscription prices vary and there may be frequent changes or additions in the list given below. Information should be obtained from the publishers. Among those recommended are:

American Home. 300 Park Ave., New York City.
House and Home, Time & Life Bldg., Rockefeller Center, New York.
House and Garden. 420 Lexington Ave., New York City.
House Beautiful. 572 Madison Avenue, New York City.
The Architectural Forum, Time & Life Bldg., Rockefeller Center, N. Y.
Antiques. 601 Fifth Avenue, New York City.
Interiors, 18 East 50th Street, New York City.
Interior Design, 151 East 50th Street, New York City.
(The last two publications are for the trade only.)

For schools furnished with projection lanterns, slides may be rented from the Metropolitan Museum of Art and the Museum of Modern Art, New York City. A nominal charge is made for sending a set of about fifty slides covering any branch of the fine and decorative arts, but arrangements should be made in advance for this service. Full information is obtainable by writing to the Lantern Slide Departments of the museums. The Metropolitan Museum also lends photographs, textiles, and other art objects. In schools where regular courses in decoration are given, it is advisable to own a collection of slides, textiles, and other necessary illustrative materials.

No greater aid is available to the student of interior decoration and the decorative arts than that offered by the many museums throughout the country. If at all possible, students should make group tours to the nearest museums and by prearrangement avail themselves of the official guidance offered by most of these organizations.

Among the museums and public collections may be recommended:

Baltimore, Md.
Baltimore Museum of Art
Boston, Mass.
The Museum of Fine Arts
Cambridge, Mass.
William Hayes Fogg Art Museum
Chicago, Ill.
Art Institute of Chicago
Cincinnati, Ohio
Cincinnati Museum of Art
Taft Museum
Dayton, Ohio
Dayton Art Institute
Denver, Colo.
Denver Art Museum
Detroit, Mich.
Detroit Institute of Arts
Hartford, Conn.
Wadsworth Atheneum, Avery and Morgan Memorials
Kansas City, Mo.
William Rockhill Nelson Gallery
Minneapolis, Minn.
Minneapolis Art Institute
Monticello, Va.
Thomas Jefferson's Residence
Mount Vernon, Va.
Washington's Residence
New Haven, Conn.
Gallery of Fine Arts, Yale University
New York, N. Y.
Brooklyn Institute of Arts and Sciences
The American Museum of Natural History
The Cooper Union Museum of Decorative Arts
The Frick Collection

The Hispanic Society of America
The Metropolitan Museum of Art
The Museum of Modern Art
The Museum of the American Indian
The Museum of the City of New York
Omaha, Nebr.
Joslyn Memorial
Pasadena, Calif.
The Huntington Museum
Philadelphia, Penna.
Independence Hall
Philadelphia Museum of Art
Pittsburgh, Penn.
Carnegie Institute
Pittsfield, Mass.
Berkshire Museum
Providence, R. I.
Museum of the Rhode Island School of Design
Rochester, N. Y.
Memorial Art Gallery
St. Louis, Mo.
The City Art Museum
Salem, Mass.
The Essex Institute
The House of Seven Gables
Seattle, Wash.
Seattle Art Museum
Shelburn, Vermont
Shelburn Colonial Museum
Sturbridge, Mass.
Colonial Village
Toledo, Ohio
The Toledo Museum of Art
Washington, D. C.
Corcoran Gallery of Art
The Freer Gallery of Art

The National Gallery of Art
Williamsburg, Va.
  Colonial town restored
Wilmington, Del.
  Du Pont Winterthur Museum

Worcester, Mass.
  Worcester Art Museum
Yonkers, N. Y.
  The Philipse Manor House

Photographs illustrating the fine and decorative arts are available for purchase from the following sources:

American art

The Metropolitan Museum of Art, New York.
The Philadelphia Museum of Art, Philadelphia.
The Museum of Fine Arts, Boston.

English art

The British Museum, London, England.
The South Kensington Museum, London, England.

French art

J. E. Bulloz, 21 rue Bonaparte, Paris, France.

H. Roger-Vollet, 6 rue de Seine, Paris, France.

Italian art

Alinari Brothers, Via Nazionale, 8, Florence, Italy.

Modern art

The Museum of Modern Art, New York.

Spanish art

Instituto Amatller de Arte Hispanico, Paseo de Gracia 41, Barcelona, Spain.
Moreno, Plaza de las Cortes, Madrid, Spain.

Student's tempera paint and brushes may be obtained from any local art supply store. Color charts may be obtained from Munsell Color Company, Baltimore, Maryland. (See Chapter XXIV before ordering.)

General Bibliography

ARONSON, J., *The Encyclopedia of Furniture.* Crown Publishers, New York, 1938. Text and excellent illustrations in an inexpensive book.

CLIFFORD, C. R., *Period Furnishings.* Fifth edition, Hall Publishing Co., New York, 1950. A comprehensive survey of the historical styles of decoration with drawings and photographs. Excellent for reference and tracing.

FAURE, E., *History of Art,* Vols. 1–5: *Ancient Art; Medieval Art; Renaissance Art; Modern Art; The Spirit of the Forms* (tr. Pach). Harper and Bros., New York, 1921–1930. Well written and illustrated.

FLETCHER, SIR B., *History of Architecture on the Comparative Method.* Charles Scribner's Sons, New York, 14th edition, 1948. A complete history of the styles of architecture, illustrated with drawings and photographs. A standard work.

GARDNER, H., *Art Through the Ages.* Harcourt, Brace and Co., New York, third edition, 1948. An excellent illustrated survey of architecture, painting, sculpture, and the minor arts from prehistoric to modern times.

GIEDION, S., *Space, Time, and Architecture*. Revised edition. Harvard University Press, 1947. An excellent history of architectural construction and the basic principles of contemporary design.

HAMLIN, T. F., *Architecture through the Ages*. G. P. Putnam's Sons, New York, 1940. Excellent architectural history.

HUNTER, G. L., *Decorative Furniture*. J. B. Lippincott Co., Philadelphia, 1927. Out of print. Illustrated text.

JONES, O., *Grammar of Ornament*. London, 1911. Collection of color plates of ornament from prehistoric times to the 19th century.

MEYER, F. S., *A Handbook of Ornament*. Architectural Book Publishing Co., New York. Fourth American edition. Line drawings with descriptive text. Valuable for tracing.

RACINET, A., *L'Ornement Polychrome*, 2 Vols. Fermin-Didot et Cie., Paris, 1885–1887. The finest single book on color ornament.

REINACH, S., *Apollo*. Charles Scribner's Sons, New York, 1924. A standard book on the history of art. Illustrated.

ROBB, D. M., AND GARRISON, J. J., *Art in the Western World*. Harper and Bros., New York, 1935. A good treatment of the art of the Occident, including architecture, painting, and sculpture.

SPELTZ, A., *L'Ornement Polychrome dans Tous les Styles Historiques*. K. F. Koehlers Antiquarium, Leipzig, 1915. Color plates of historic ornament. 3 portfolios.

SPELTZ, A., *Styles of Ornament*. Grosset and Dunlap, New York, 1935. Brief text with chronological arrangement of drawings.

WILENSKI, R. H., *A Miniature History of Art*. Oxford University Press, New York, 1930. Illustrated brief survey of painting and sculpture.

Also, current publications of the Museum of Modern Art, New York. Illustrated books based on the various exhibitions of the museum and covering in general many phases of modern art.

NOTE: On page 813, arranged to correspond with the materials covered in the text, will be found questions and problems in design.

CONTENTS

Introduction 3

PART ONE. PERIOD DECORATION AND FURNITURE

CHAPTER   I. *The Styles of Antiquity* 17
CHAPTER   II. *The Styles of the Middle Ages* . . . . - 69
CHAPTER III. *The Italian Renaissance* 104
CHAPTER IV. *The Hispanic Periods* 137
CHAPTER   V. *The French Periods* 177
CHAPTER VI. *The English Periods* 233
CHAPTER VII. *The American Periods* 282
CHAPTER VIII. *Miscellaneous Styles and Arts* 340

PART TWO. CONTEMPORARY ARCHITECTURE, INTERIOR DESIGN, AND FURNITURE

CHAPTER IX. *Contemporary Architecture and Interior Design* . . . 383
CHAPTER   X. *Contemporary Furniture* 413

PART THREE. DECORATIVE MATERIALS AND ACCESSORIES

CHAPTER   XI. *Decorative Textiles* 431
CHAPTER XII. *Draperies, Slipcovers, and Upholstery* 485
CHAPTER XIII. *Floor Coverings* 513
CHAPTER XIV. *Wallpapers* 541
CHAPTER XV. *Pictures* 558
CHAPTER XVI. *Paints and Painting* 623
CHAPTER XVII. *Ceramics and Glassware* 636
CHAPTER XVIII. *Metals and Hardware* 666
CHAPTER XIX. *Lighting and Lighting Fixtures* 679
CHAPTER XX. *Wall Treatments and Backgrounds* 696
CHAPTER XXI. *Interior Trim and Woodwork* 715

PART FOUR. SELECTION, ARRANGEMENT, AND HARMONY

CHAPTER XXII. *Standards of Taste and Design* 749
CHAPTER XXIII. *Wall Composition* 758
CHAPTER XXIV. *Furniture Arrangement* 775
CHAPTER XXV. *Color and Color Schemes* 788

Glossary of Decorative Art Terms 811
Index i

ELEMENTS OF INTERIOR DESIGN AND DECORATION

INTRODUCTION

B efore proceeding upon a specific study of the art of interior decoration, it will be advantageous to investigate the part that this art plays in life, to analyze its influence upon the individual and the possibility of its contributing to the general happiness of mankind. It will also be advisable to have a mental perspective of the art as a whole, and finally to learn the common terms that must be used in its study.

There are three necessities for human existence: food, clothing, and protection against the elements of nature. To fulfill the last requirement, civilized man constructs an artificial enclosure, called a house, to protect him from variations of temperature, climate, and weather, and to give him the privacy and conveniences required for family life. Aboriginal man was satisfied with a cave dwelling; but long before history began, there is evidence that some form of artificial shelter or enclosure was constructed that fulfilled the necessities of the primitive human being. As civilization slowly improved, simple features that contributed to physical comforts and conveniences were added, and still later, elements were introduced that had visual appeal. The final development in the treatment of the house occurred when elements were introduced that had intellectual or psychological appeal.

The art of interior decoration was unconsciously conceived when the first element of comfort and convenience was introduced in a dwelling. In the highly developed civilization of today, however, the interpretation of the term "interior decoration" implies that it is an art pertaining to the interior design of houses, contributing to the physical, visual, and intellectual comforts and joys of mankind; and it is self-evident that the work of an interior designer must in all cases fulfill these three requirements.

The dictionaries have been very meager in their definitions of the term interior decoration. Many of them state that "a decorator is one who decorates"; others state that a decorator is "an ornamental painter, scene painter, wood grainer" or "a tradesman who paints and papers houses." During a recent legal proceeding, a certain decorator was asked by a judge to explain her services. Her calm reply electrified the courtroom, when she said, "To create beauty"; and no three words could have been a better answer.

One of America's leading decorators once defined the term "interior decorator" as follows: "One who by training and experience is qualified to plan, design, and execute structural interiors and their furnishings, and to supervise the various arts and crafts essential to their completion."

The American Institute of Decorators has given the following definition: "An interior decorator is one who through training and professional experience is skilled in the solution of problems related to the design and execution of interiors of buildings or other structures and their furnishing, and qualified to supervise the arts and crafts employed in the production and installation of decorative and practical details necessary to consummate a planned result."

Of late years the term "interior designer" has often been substituted for "interior decorator" and perhaps the former is more comprehensive in meaning, considering the added duties and obligations that are now undertaken by those who are called upon to plan, furnish, and equip the interior of buildings.

The study of interior decoration. The study of interior decoration may be compared to the study of a foreign language. There is a "vocabulary" and a "grammar" to learn before one can adequately express oneself. The vocabulary consists of a thorough knowledge of the materials of decoration, whether they be colors, textures, or shapes, of wood, cloth, metal, masonry, or other products. One must develop a connoisseurship of quality and form in these individual materials or manufactured objects and a thorough understanding of their physical and structural possibilities and limitations. The grammar consists of empirical principles and formulas for composing, arranging, assembling, or designing the various materials of decoration to produce a unified composition and a desired efficient, esthetic, and psychological effect.

In addition to this knowledge of the vocabulary and grammar of decorating, the artist-decorator must, by his observation and training, comprehend the trends of style and fashion; instinctively appreciate the best standards of taste; and have the creative mental qualities that generate imagination and individuality in his work.

To accomplish such ends implies a certain maturity of judgment, a constant study of the arts, and a never-ceasing desire to increase one's general education. It is hardly conceivable that an embryo author could acquire a good literary style without studying the literature of the past; nor could a hospital intern hope to develop up-to-date surgical ability without a most careful investigation of the records of successes and failures of generations of his predecessors. With like reasoning, it must be admitted that an artist should study the art of the past to learn what has already been tried and to use past experience as a foundation upon which to build and create. An understanding of past efforts does not necessarily imply duplication or imitation in future work; but the basic principles that are unchanging and that have existed since the beginning of time are best learned by studying the work of predecessors. For that reason a study of so-called "period art" is essential to the decorator no matter how "modern" he may desire to be. The historic styles of decoration should be studied not so much for their forms as for the principles of *pure design* * which they may inculcate and to learn the possibilities and limitations of materials and structure.

The roots of the decorative arts are all based on the parent stem of architecture, and as each architectural style has inherited some of the principles or characteristics of its predecessors, it becomes essential for the student of decoration to comprehend the original forces of the architectural expressions. Forms, originating in most cases for structural requirements, often were transformed into decorative elements. Exterior features were transferred to the interior, and in the case of the classic styles form the inspiration of all decoration in Europe from the 15th century to the 20th century.

Sculpture, painting, textiles, wallpapers, furniture, metalwork, and ceramics are merely the natural offspring of architectural evolution and design. It therefore becomes essential in the opening chapters of this book to give a brief outline of the basic architectural styles.

The influence of structure in interior decoration. Many of the most important forms used in interior decoration originated in elementary structures, and although an extensive knowledge of structural principles is not necessary to a decorator, it is advisable for him to study the origin of the most important forms in order to have a logical understanding of their use and to become accustomed to the simple terms associated with them.

Roof forms. The simplest type of house is a single room, a boxlike enclosure formed by walls rising from a platform and covered at the top by a roof. The walls, situated some distance apart, must be spanned by a structural feature which will support the roofing material. There are three types of support for roofs and ceilings: the beam, the arch, and the truss.

The *beam* or *lintel* is a long piece of wood, stone, steel, or other material that must rest on two supports. The beam should be strong enough to span between the two supporting points without sagging, and if the roof

* The glossary, page 811, contains definitions of terms used in interior decoration and related fields. For the convenience of the reader, many such terms are italicized when first mentioned in the text.

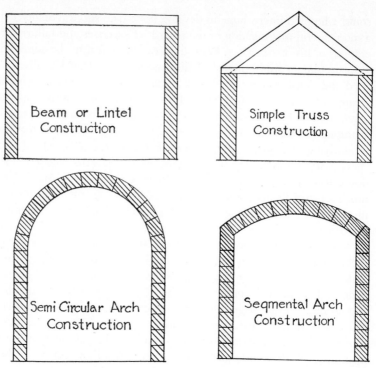

Sectional drawings showing the three types of roof or ceiling construction: beam, truss, and arch.

is heavy, a sufficient number of beams must be introduced so that only a small part of the roof is supported by each beam. The visible portion of the beams and the underside of the roofing material then become the ceiling of the room, or the structural elements may be covered with plaster or some other material which in turn is called the ceiling.

The *arched* roof may be made in stone, brick, cement, or other masonry, and supports itself by its shape and by the laws of gravity. Each side of an arch rises from the top of a side wall in a curve and meets the curve from the other wall in the center. The curve may be semicircular, in which case the roof is called a *barrel vault;* it may be a smaller portion of a circle known as a *segmental arch;* or it may assume some other type of curved form.

The *truss* is used when the supports or walls are placed so far apart that a beam of sufficient length or strength is not obtainable to span the whole distance. In this case a triangle is made with three beams. Two beams are placed on a slant and meet in the middle. They are tied together at their lower ends by means of a long, slender beam known as a *tie-beam,* upon which no weight rests. The tie-beam is in tension only. The triangular

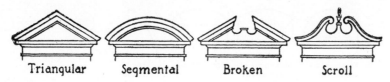

| Triangular | Segmental | Broken | Scroll |

COMPARATIVE FORMS OF PEDIMENTS.

truss form of roof support was first adopted for small structures by early Greek builders, and when the roofing material was added, it followed the slanting lines of the trusses and served to shed the rainwater. The large Greek temples used a slanting roof that was supported by interior stone supports instead of wooden trusses.

Pediment forms. In Grecian architecture the slanting exterior ends of slanted roof buildings were ornamented with moldings and sculpture. These features are today known as *pediments.* In subsequent art periods, variations in pediments were introduced, and some of the forms became purely ornamental. Triangular, segmental, *broken,* and *scroll* pediments are the most common types.

The origin of the column. It is not necessary that a roof should be entirely supported by a wall. Isolated supports may be introduced and placed at intervals. The earliest simple type of isolated support was the round wooden post or tree trunk. Later, isolated supports were made in stone for greater permanence. In the early civilizations of Egypt and Greece much thought was given to the study of the proportions, moldings, lines, curves, and ornamentation of the stone post. A post of this type is called a *column.* When applied to a wall as a decorative feature and made flat rather than round in plan, the column is called a *pilaster.* The moldings and ornament placed at its top are known as the *capital,* and a block and additional moldings placed at the bottom are called the *base.*

Classification of curves. Curved lines are of three different types, and may generally be classified into mechanical, mathematical, and free forms.

The mechanical curve is that made by means of a compass and consists of any part or all of a circle. The half circle which is often used as the form of an arch is called a semicircular curve. One that is less than a half circle is called a segmental curve. The spring-point of a curve is the point where a curve starts. In a semicircular arched opening, the sides are usually straight up to a certain point where the arch commences. A line connecting these two points on opposite sides of the arch is called the *spring-line.* The mechanical curves were used in Roman design.

The mathematical curves are those taken from the conic sections known as the ellipse, parabola, and hyperbola, and such curves as the spiral and helix. In all of these the degree of curvature varies in the length of the curve. The ellipse is roughly an egg-shaped enclosure, the circumference of which may also be drawn mechanically. The half ellipse or semi-ellipse

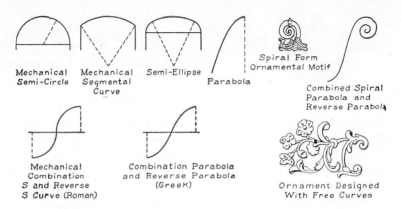

Mechanical Semi-Circle
Mechanical Segmental Curve
Semi-Ellipse
Parabola
Spiral Form Ornamental Motif
Combined Spiral Parabola and Reverse Parabola

Mechanical Combination S and Reverse S Curve (Roman)
Combination Parabola and Reverse Parabola (Greek)
Ornament Designed With Free Curves

EXAMPLES OF MECHANICAL, MATHEMATICAL, AND FREE CURVES.

is often used for an arch or ornamental form. The parabola and hyperbola are somewhat similar to each other in appearance. They start with a rather sharp coil and gradually straighten out as they progress, approaching a straight line but never actually becoming one. The spiral is frequently seen in ornament. These curves are extremely graceful in appearance and were used in Greek design.

The free curve is one drawn by an artist's freehand sweep, and cannot be classified in the mechanical or mathematical grouping. It was used for ornamental forms in the styles of art known as the *Rococo,* particularly during the 18th century in Italy, Spain, France, and England.

Many curved forms used in decoration are combinations of these types. A mechanical S-curve may be produced by two segmental curves meeting at a point of tangency. Each part may have a different radius, so that one half has a sharper degree of curvature than the other half. Parabolic curves may be carried to a certain point and then changed to a straight line. Other combinations are also possible, but compound curves should always meet at a point of tangency and never appear broken at their intersection.

Arch forms. There are many different types of arch forms used in architecture and decoration. Most of them are associated with particular styles of art and they will be taken up under the various chapters on the periods. It is advisable, however, to learn the names of the commonest types, which are shown in the illustration on page 9. Structural arches are used for doors, windows, *niches,* and other wall openings, and ornamental arches are used in furniture and decorative design generally.

The period styles. Since the beginning of civilization, each race—and later each nation or subdivision thereof—has produced a type of art that has suited its requirements and has at the same time expressed its characteristics. This makes it possible through careful study of the arts of peoples to learn their customs and habits and even to know their thoughts.

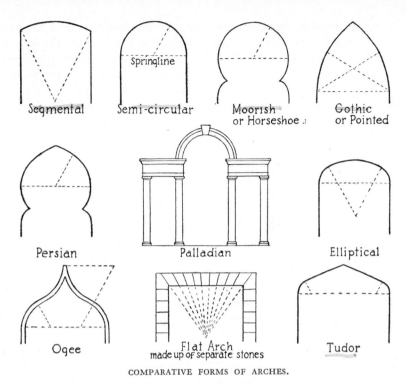

COMPARATIVE FORMS OF ARCHES.

The term "period style" refers to the generally recognizable trends or characteristics of a fine or utilitarian art produced by one such group during a specific time.

In the periods of antiquity the styles were produced with little conscious effort but by logical and natural methods. Because certain materials were available and certain possible forms or objects were necessary for human existence, the artists and craftsmen fulfilled human requirements to the best of their ability. As civilization progressed—and particularly after the Middle Ages—art became more self-conscious, and the craftsmen, for the sake of novelty, commenced to create styles that often were artificial in their inspiration.

The architectural styles of Western culture, Egyptian, Greek, Roman, Gothic, and Modern, are basic, and their character is primarily differentiated by structural differences, and only secondarily by detail, surface ornamentation, and decoration. Structural changes were due to new materials or increased knowledge of engineering principles. All other styles are revivals, adaptations, or imitations of these basic styles, produced at subsequent times, in new locations and under local influences, by artists who claimed that a cultural inheritance permitted their use. The technique of these imitators was often excellent, their productions of great beauty, and their imagination sometimes contributed to the development of the style, but in many cases, and particularly during the 19th century, the style revivals indicated an absence of creative ability and an hiatus in art progress.

Each period style has been created by certain external influences, and, as these influences have changed, the styles have slowly evolved into new forms. The external influences that have produced every style of art are these:

1. Local available materials
2. Local climatic conditions
3. General geographical conditions
4. Social and economic conditions of the people
5. Religion of the people
6. Trade and commercial opportunities
7. Historical and political events
8. Scientific inventions and discoveries

There has been a similarity in the development of all art periods. Simple forms, that fulfill structural functions only, are first seen. The second step is seen in the gradual enrichment of the functional forms with a certain amount of ornament intended to enrich the structure only. At this point the style is usually considered at its point of most characteristic development. The structural forms finally reach their pinnacle of perfection, and novelty can only be introduced by increasing the surface enrichment or by using structural forms for ornamental purposes. This is the beginning of the decline of the style. When the ornamentation eventually submerges the vigorous appearance of the structure or the structure itself assumes shapes that are unsuitable to the material from which it is built, the decadence of the style is established. The style falls because of the impossibility of further development, and is replaced by the initial forms of a new art. In studying the historical styles it will be noticed that each overlaps and influences the subsequent one, so that there can be no exact line of demarcation and any given dates must be only approximate.

Methods of dividing the art styles. The customary method of dividing the styles of art is according to their chronological sequence. This is the method that is pursued in this book. It is further explained in Chapter I.

One may also classify the art styles in the following ways:

1. *Character of structure.* The basic art styles can be subdivided according to the structural methods used to support the roofs in ceilings of buildings. The Egyptian style used only the stone wall, column, or isolated support and the lintel. The Greeks used these same elements but added the wooden truss. The Romans substituted the stone arch for the truss. The builders of the Middle Ages eventually eliminated the wall, using only the isolated support, and modern architects have developed a new style with

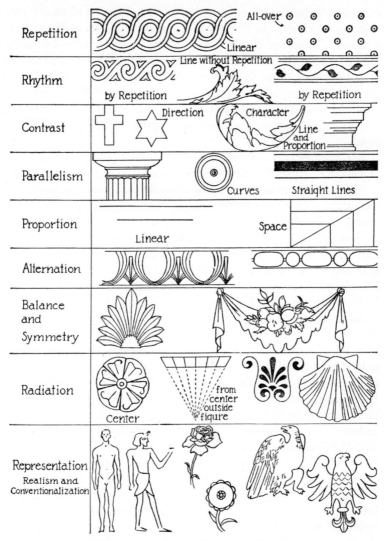

Repetition

Rhythm

Contrast

Parallelism

Proportion

Alternation

Balance
and
Symmetry

Radiation

Representation
Realism and
Conventionalization

COMPOSITION AND CHARACTER OF PATTERNS.

steel and reinforced concrete. While structure relates primarily to architectural forms, the method and detail of enrichment is always related to the structure and therefore the decorative and architectural styles are correlated.

2. *Character of line.* Every solid that is in nature or is made by man must have form, and the form is produced by some sort of line or lines. The lines are produced by the silhouette of the object, by changes or breaks on its visible surface, or by the shadows created by such breaks. Such lines

may be straight, curved, or irregular, or a combination of these types. An object in which straight lines predominate is sometimes spoken of as being rectilinear, severe, or classic. Compositions in which curved or irregular lines dominate are often referred to as curvilinear, Rococo, or romantic.

3. *Direction of line.* In some arts, the productions show a dominant line direction. Horizontal lines produced by breaks, moldings, and shadows are characteristic of the classical styles of Greece and Rome. Vertical lines produced by the same means are characteristic of the styles of the Middle Ages.

4. *Character of ornament.* Ornament is produced by treating a portion of a surface in a manner that creates a contrast with the surface itself. The contrast may be in color, texture, or height, or a combination of any of these three. Color contrast is found in patterns created by paint, *inlay, marquetry,* embroidery, etc. Textural contrasts produce self-tone patterns that are less visible than color contrasts, but such enrichment is often seen in textiles, metals, and woodwork. Ornament produced by height contrast is of two types. If the pattern is below the surface of the field upon which it is placed, as though it were cut out by means of a knife, it is known as *incised* ornamentation. If the ornament projects from the field, it is known as *relief* ornament. The relative height of the ornament is sometimes indicated by using the words *high relief* and *low relief.*

5. *Classification of ornament.* All ornament may be classified according to its character and inspiration. The artist may endeavor to copy the forms of nature closely. This type of ornament is called *naturalistic* or *realistic.* If the artist only inspires himself from nature, and attempts to reproduce these forms only so far as the limitation of his material permits, or if he endeavors to simplify or idealize the form, it is then called *conventional* or *idealistic.* To illustrate the two types mentioned, a painter with reasonable care can copy a flower to almost photographic exactitude in shape, lighting, and color. Such a painting would be realistic. The sculptor, however, in carving the same flower in stone would have difficulty in introducing all the details because of the difference in the texture of the stone and that of the flower. He would be forced to simplify the form of the flower. This simplification or changing of the form to suit the material is known as "conventionalization," and the flower would be a conventional type of ornament. Conventionalization may also be produced by color or by the elimination of all natural appearance. A drawing of a black leaf would be a conventional form because there is no such thing in nature, and a black silhouette of a horse would be conventional because no effort would be made to show detail.

Much ornament is not derived from natural forms at all. It may be an imaginary conception or a geometrical composition. Such ornament is known as abstract.

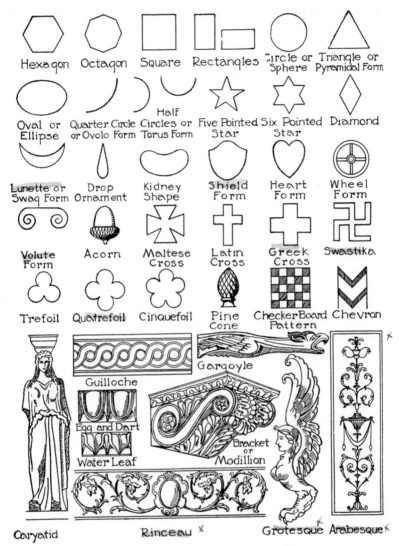

Hexagon Octagon Square Rectangles Circle or Sphere Triangle or Pyramidal Form

Oval or Ellipse Quarter Circle or Ovolo Form Half Circles or Torus Form Five Pointed Star Six Pointed Star Diamond

Lunette or Swag Form Drop Ornament Kidney Shape Shield Form Heart Form Wheel Form

Volute Form Acorn Maltese Cross Latin Cross Greek Cross Swastika

Trefoil Quatrefoil Cinquefoil Pine Cone Checker Board Pattern Chevron

Caryatid Guilloche Egg and Dart Water Leaf Gargoyle Bracket or Modillion Rinceau Grotesque Arabesque

ORNAMENTAL FORMS FREQUENTLY USED.

As the conventional and abstract forms of ornamentation show greater imagination and creative ability on the part of the artist than do the realistic and are better suited to various structural and decorative materials, they have been used in all styles of art; and it is generally acknowledged that the greatest periods of decorative art have been those in which the conventionalized forms of ornamentation have dominated.

6. *Character of patterns and design.* A design is a "plan or arrangement of line, form, mass, and space in a pattern to produce an effect pleasing to

the eye." * This means that an orderly arrangement of various motifs is required to produce a pattern.

In surface design, order may be produced in various ways. Patterns may be applied to running bands, stripes, or borders; these are usually called *border* or *running* patterns; they are of a definite width but an indefinite length, and are usually formed by repeating one or more motifs. Such patterns are found on molding ornaments, frames, and other lineal forms. All-over or *diaper* patterns are formed by repeating motifs in two directions, height and width; they are not limited in area and may cover a surface of any size; such patterns are often seen in wallpapers and textiles. A third type of pattern is usually known as a panel pattern. It is nonrepeating, and is meant to cover a fixed area and cannot conveniently be extended in height or width, having definite limits fixed by its motifs and general composition.

Interest and order in design and pattern are also obtained by repetition, rhythm, contrast, parallelism, proportion, alternation, balance, symmetry, radiation, and representation. Examples of these are shown on page 11, and a thorough understanding of the various methods of producing patterns should be obtained.

Common terms for ornamental forms. There are a few ornamental motifs that are so commonly used in design that it is advisable that the student comprehend their meaning before proceeding further with the study. These are shown on page 13, and are self-explanatory.

* From *The Columbia Encyclopedia.* Columbia University Press, New York.

PART ONE

PERIOD DECORATION AND FURNITURE

CHAPTER I

THE STYLES OF ANTIQUITY

Prehistoric Art

Anthropologists have discovered remains of fossil man that are hypothetically stated to be 1,000,000 years old. Other fossils are supposed to have lived 500,000 and 100,000 years ago. These relics have been found in Java, China, Africa, and other locations. Practically nothing is known of the living conditions or developments of these early creatures. It is perhaps not even entirely wise to associate them with the human race. There is only one point of importance to the art student in mentioning them. In fossils belonging to late eras, there is a larger cranial capacity. One may conclude that as the brain enlarged intelligence gradually increased and during each millennium descendants learned from their predecessors. Although this theory is not supported by all scientists, it would appear that the aggregate of all knowledge and experience at any one time benefited future generations.

The term "civilization" implies an organized state of existence. However primitive its character, there must be a sense of reciprocity, justice, and consideration of others in the same group or tribe. Some form of production of objects and materials useful to man's existence is also assumed. There is a long gap between the early prehuman life and the beginnings of civilized man, but there must have been a gradual progress in intelligence. There are abundant records of prehistoric human existence in Europe that date from approximately 25,000 B.C., and there have been other discoveries indicating sequences of development of men who have lived at later periods but long before history commences.

Cro-Magnon man, the first civilized ancestor of the modern European, is supposed to have made his entrance into Europe from Asia or Africa about 25 millenniums ago. The infiltration was slow and probably extended over thousands of years. He was a fine physical type, over six feet

Prehistoric painting of a wild boar, found on the walls of the cave of Altamira, Spain. The action and anatomy of the animal were well understood by the artist and realistically portrayed.

Prehistoric painting of horses in action, on walls of cave at Montignac, Dordogne, France.

high, and may have had white skin. He set up elaborate housekeeping in caves and decorated the walls of his home with sculpture and painting. He had heat, light, and clothing. He developed efficient tools and was an expert technician in cutting and decorating stone and ivory. He had superstitions and some form of religion. The birth of religion probably is closely interwoven with the origins of art. He buried his ancestors with the greatest of care, surrounding their bodies with personal belongings, indicating a belief in the existence of the soul after death. He invented eating utensils such as spoons, knives, and two-pronged forks, which he made from bone and wood. He lived on the wild vegetation of his locality, and hunted the

The Venus of Willendorf. Limestone, 5½ inches high (30,000 B.C.).*

bison, horse, stag, boar, reindeer, mammoth, and other animals that roamed the plains of Europe. He may have been a cannibal. There is no evidence that he domesticated any animals, nor did he cultivate the land. He knew nothing about the making of pottery, or the value of metals, but he modelled both the human figure and animals in stone, ivory, and clay. Evidences of feminine glamor and appeal have been proved by the discovery of shell necklaces and of cosmetics. Trade was carried on by using beads, amulets, pendants, and ivory buttons as a medium of exchange. The existence of needles would indicate that he knew how to sew, and possibly embroider and weave.

The earliest discovered evidences of artistic effort date from about 25,-000 to 10,000 B.C. and show a highly developed achievement.

The Cro-Magnon people, whose records are mainly found in France and Spain, were neither childlike nor savage in their art conceptions. They boldly and accurately depicted in line drawings and paint, on the walls and ceilings of their caves and on their tools and other *artifacts,* human, animal, and plant forms, the drawing of which must have demanded a high mental concentration and much preliminary training. The different classifications of animals are realistically drawn, with thorough understanding of their anatomy and action. The earliest drawings show profiles only, but simple perspective and foreshortening were attempted later and there is some evidence of a conception of composition in grouping. Undecipherable motifs have also been found which may have been the earliest attempts of hieroglyphic inscriptions.

The purpose of these drawings is not yet fully understood. Undoubtedly they had decorative value, but they may also have had religious significance or were intended to bring good luck in hunting. A symbolism would seem proved in an analysis of the clay sculpture of the human form, most of which was limited to the representation of the female. Conventionalization

---

* This figure was found in Austria in 1909. Anthropologists claim it is 30,000 years old. The sculptor was not trying to reproduce the human form; he knew there was little resemblance. The most sacred idols of the savage were rationalized conceptions of the spirit of fruitfulness; by witchcraft and incantations these were implored to contribute to the fecundity of man, beast, and vegetation. Human birth was inexplicable to most primitive civilizations and the period of gestation too long to associate it with natural causes. Self-perpetuation was so indispensable to early man that it probably formed the basis of all primitive worship. Its concept was carried into the early Eastern religions, all of which offered an everlasting life as the greatest and final reward. The arts of Egypt, Greece, and Rome show that the mythologies of these countries were strongly tainted with this fiction. The rites of Isis and Dionysus were devoted to this cause. In protest the early Christians and Mohammedans restricted the representations of the human figure in their cults and religious arts. The arts of the African Negro and American Indian have similar conceptions. In the appraisal of any work of art, the culture of the time and place of its production must establish the standard by which it is judged.

rather than realism was here indicated. The head, hands, and feet were either omitted or only slightly indicated, while the parts related to reproduction were greatly enlarged, possibly as a divine appeal for progeny.

Art as indicated by these discoveries is then millenniums older than history and may be stated to have commenced as man evolved from the animal to the human state. Creative expression in art can therefore be claimed to be instinctive. The origin of the art of interior decoration can be dated from the dawn of human civilization and is an integrated part of human needs. While the discoveries of the early civilizations have to date been found mainly in Europe, it is probable that man also existed and developed at the same time in Asia, Africa, and, possibly, America. History does not begin until a record of events was kept by man in some sort of written form. The earliest readable inscriptions probably do not predate the 37th century B.C.

The Historic Periods

MESOPOTAMIA AND PALESTINE

Just as there are long mysterious lapses in the records of prehistoric civilizations—so the steps that lead from them to historical periods are unknown. The dawn of history about 4000 B.C. finds a highly developed culture in many parts of the Near East, particularly in Iraq on the borders of the Tigris and Euphrates and on the shore of the Persian Gulf, usually considered the locality from which all Western civilization has sprung. It is self-evident that there must have been an evolutionary development. The enormous advances in the cultures of these early historical groups over the prehistoric types could not have been spontaneous.

It was these Near Eastern civilizations that have given us some of the earliest needs of orderly existence. They developed agriculture; the domestication of animals; the principles of trade and coinage; legal government; principles of justice; the potter's wheel; the wagon wheel; the alphabet; paper and ink; the arts of architecture, decoration, sculpture, music, literature, and dancing; the sciences of mathematics and astronomy; and the philosophical standards of monotheism and monogamy.

Authorities differ as to the primogeniture of early civilizations, but it is not a matter of great importance. Perhaps future discoveries of the archeologist will clarify many points. All the countries of the East were constantly trading with each other so that in the exchange of ideas, contemporary civilizations often had similar features. Various authorities claim the Caucasus, Mesopotamia, Persia, and Egypt as the birthplace of Western thought, but a civilization known as Sumerian existed along the deltas of the Euphrates River in Mesopotamia at a very early date—perhaps 6000 B.C. From where the Sumerians came and the causes of their disintegration and diffusion are not known; but their records inscribed in *cuneiform* characters on clay are extensive and have been transcribed. They have left us tales of the creation and those of a deluge that correspond closely to Old Testament descriptions. They have related the class struggles, the inequality of men, the wealth and luxury enjoyed by the strong and intelligent, and the subservience and labor required of the masses and their interminable demand for betterment that invariably ended in economic paralysis. Thus, from the very beginnings of our culture, was established the basic theme of political history.

Although none of the Sumerian buildings has endured, there are descriptions of palaces treated with colored tiles and enriched with semiprecious stones, with interiors treated in exotic woods and inlaid with alabaster, onyx, lapis lazuli, agate, and gold, and decorated with the statues of gods, heroes, and animals. Architecture, beauty, and luxury commence with explosive violence and our complete ignorance of their immediate origins.

The Sumerian civilization was superseded by those of Babylonia and Chaldea that date from as early as 4000 B.C. The buildings of these nations were constructed in sun-dried brick, but often surfaced with delicately carved translucent alabaster and bas-reliefs. The interiors were hung with magnificent tapestries. Arches were first used in these countries both to span openings and for ornamental purposes, probably because the lack of large stones precluded the use of the beam and the column.

In Babylon was the great palace of Nebuchadnezzar with its "hanging gardens" and from here he marched with his hosts to Jerusalem about 585 B.C. to destroy the temple of Solomon. Here was also the Tower of Babel. There is nothing left of Babylon. Its name has become synonymous with splendor, vice, and luxury, and the city passed to its downfall as described in the Bible. Its ruins became a quarry for the construction of Bagdad. Only mounds now indicate its site. The Babylonians were an agricultural, material-minded people who built rambling palaces in sun-dried brick constructed on arch and vault principles. The many rooms of the buildings were brightened with colorful glazed tiles in designs showing the *tree-of-life,* lotus, *rosette, palmette,* winged bulls, genii, and animal motifs. Low-reliefs in color depicted hunting activities and court scenes.

The Assyrians from the north of Mesopotamia dominated the valley from about 700 B.C. The ruins of the Palace of Sargon in Khorsabad near Nineveh give some conception of the magnificence associated with their buildings in which are found some of the early decorative and structural uses of the arch form. The entrance portals were flanked by great towers and with man-headed winged bulls carved in stone, which in turn supported a semicircular arch covered with brilliantly colored tile.* The rooms were lined with alabaster sculptured *dadoes*. Domed forms are shown as motifs in some of the relief decorations, although no actual structures of this type have remained.

The Assyrians were the great military power of the Near East—they were fighters and huntsmen and their incised wall sculptures portray their cruelty. They were great builders, engineers, scientists, musicians, poets, and astronomers. Their wall tablets show the use of chairs, couches, and tables.

While these great nations of the Mesopotamian plains were maintaining a civilization for three thousand years, farther west along the banks of the Mediterranean Sea, the Hebrews were building in an architectural style borrowed from Babylon, Egypt, and Phoenicia. Little is left of their structures, long since obliterated by Romans, Christians, Moslems, and Crusaders.

The Bible gives a description of the great temple of Solomon, built in Jerusalem about 1012 B.C. The author of the Book of Kings seems to have been impressed by the ostentation and great expense involved rather than by any practical or esthetic values. He describes the dimensions of the building, which was not large, although it was surrounded by enormous colonnaded courtyards. The roof beams rested on projecting wall brackets, the windows were narrow. The stone used for the walls was cut at the quarry so that no hammer or axe or any tool of iron would be heard at the place of construction. The temple was apparently three stories high, the floors connected by stairways. The entire interior was lined with cedar. The doors were made of olive-wood carved with ornament. The interior walls were decorated with carved cherubim, palm tree motifs, and open flowers. The floor was made of fir. Walls, doors, trim, and floor were overlaid with gold. Cedar, olive, and fir must have been rare woods in Palestine at the time of Solomon.

EGYPT

The art of ancient Egypt was her most momentous contribution to world culture. It approached such a degree of perfection that all later art progress must halt in wonderment. Here at the very beginning of history is found a vigorous and matured civilization that had developed from prehis-

---

* The earliest arches were the "stepped" form, appearing like inverted stone stairways. The origin of the true arch form built with wedge-shaped stones or bricks is clouded. It is probable that the Babylonians used the principle in the construction of drains as early as 3000 B.C. In the Assyrian Palace of Sargon at Khorsabad, the entrance consisted of arched gateways. This was the first known use of this form for decorative purposes. The Etruscans of northern Italy used the arch for drains, tombs, and gateways about 500 B.C., and the Romans developed the arch and dome, as they are used today, after the Etruscan invasions. This form became the most important structural and decorative feature of Roman architectural design. In such buildings as the Colosseum it saved an immense amount of labor and material in supporting the rows of seats.

toric eras, the details of which are hidden in the mists of antiquity. Here were constructed colossal engineering works and majestic buildings, designed according to the most ingenious and honest esthetic standards. No other people, ancient or modern, has conceived of structures on such a vast scale, so grandiose, so masculine, and yet so sublime.* Egypt developed a native art independent of preceding foreign cultures that satisfied and uniquely reflected the character of its own people. It was one of the greatest, most powerful, and yet most refined cultures in history. Mesopotamia was primitive in comparison, and Greece and Rome never excelled it.

The land of Egypt is a gift of the Nile. It consists geographically of a stretch of territory approximately 30 miles wide and 800 miles long, entirely dependent upon the river for its vegetation and subsistence. Bordered by deserts and the sea, its inaccessibility served as a protection against invading hordes and gave the Egyptian people an unusual opportunity for a continuous and unadulterated racial and cultural development. This isolation, however, contributed to a constant repetition of art forms during the whole period of Egyptian history; and this unchanging character is one of the most pronounced features of Egyptian art.† The Egyptians devoted themselves more than any other people in the world to the preservation of the memory of past actions. Changes in thought, custom, habit, and art were extraordinarily slow in spite of occasional invasions and social upheavals. Egyptian art followed rises and declines. Novelties were introduced but the basic forms were constantly revived and, in comparison to that of other nations, the style is considered immutable.

The climate of the valley of the Nile was peculiarly delightful, the sky serene, and the atmosphere gently tempered, almost without rain; thus nature contributed to the preservation of its monuments. Social conditions permitted the development of a wealthy and highly cultured ruling class and a middle class, both of which were supported by vast numbers of slaves who were either native born or the captured inhabitants of conquered nations. Wealth was concentrated in the hands of the few and labor was excessively cheap; even the artists and craftsmen were often of the slave classes.

Nature had endowed the land with large quantities of hard and durable building stones such as *granite, basalt,* and *diorite.* Limestone, a much softer and more easily cut material, was also available for use in protected places. A limited lumber supply necessitated the use of the palm tree and

* Herodotus the Greek historian, who visited Egypt in the 5th century B.C., stated "that there is no country that possesses so many wonders, nor any that has such a number of works that defy description."

† The Egyptians were the superconservatives of history. With long intervals of peace, and wars principally conducted in foreign lands, their power and success developed a feeling of both security and superiority, which though contributing greatly to their arts, eventually acted as an opiate to their national consciousness and military vigor. A small Roman army was finally sufficient to conquer them.

the papyrus reed where wood was needed for structural purposes. The acacia and sycamore fig-tree were also used to some extent and heavy lumber was occasionally imported from Syria. The leaves and branches of these trees and the wild flowers from the banks of the Nile became the principal inspiration for ornamental design.

Religion played an important part in the life of every inhabitant. The Egyptian believed that life on earth was but temporary and that one's duty, while here, was to prepare for an eternal existence in the hereafter.* It was, therefore, the habit of the upper classes to build resting places or tombs for their bodies after death. This explains the existence of the many pyramids and *mastaba* tombs which were constructed with the idea that they would exist for eternity. The future life was believed to be spiritual in its character, but material objects were needed to sustain the body of the spirit. When an Egyptian of rank was buried, his mummified body was surrounded with household goods, clothing, food, and mummified animals. The discoveries of many of these tombs, such as that of Tut-ankh-Amen in 1922, has given a very complete knowledge of the daily life of the royal families.

The culture of Egypt was so firmly established that, in the few foreign invasions that occurred during a long history, the culture of the conquerors was always completely submerged. Even Alexander in the 4th century B.C. was politically and socially snubbed by the Egyptians, and was forced to found his own city. Alexandria later became one of the greatest of commercial ports, a center of learning, and a luxurious playground for all Mediterranean people, but, in spite of the Greek culture which it represented, the Egyptians refused to accept the foreign influences, and elsewhere continued the philosophy and customs of their ancestors. The palaces at Edfu and Philae, partly built during the Alexandrian Era, retained the style of the Pharaohs in their design.

The Egyptians were mighty navigators and sent their ships to all the ports of the Mediterranean Sea. The early tribes of Greece, the inhabitants of the islands of the Aegean Sea, even the primitive occupants of the Spanish and Italian peninsulas, all felt the influence of the Egyptian traders, and Egyptian motifs and trends are to be seen in their early arts.

The main divisions of Egyptian history. The history of Egypt is derived from the Bible, from Greek and Roman authors, and from a history written in Greek about the year 300 B.C. by Manetho, an Egyptian priest. Leading authorities differ greatly upon many of the early dates, but the generally accepted divisions are as follows:

---

* The Egyptians were the first to claim that the soul was immortal. According to Herodotus, they believed that after a transmigration of three thousand years, it would return to the human body.

1. ANCIENT KINGDOM, Dynasties I-VIII (4500–2445 B.C.).
During this period the capital was at Memphis and the great pyramids of Gizeh were built.
2. MIDDLE KINGDOM, Dynasties IX-XVII (2445–1580 B.C.).
During this period the capital was at Thebes; and in the latter portion of this period Egyptian art history was interrupted by the invasions of the Shepherd Kings, known as the "Hyksos."
3. NEW EMPIRE, Dynasties XVIII-XXV (1580–332 B.C.).
During this period the capital was again at Thebes, and many of the great temples, such as those at Luxor and Karnak, were erected. This was the most prolific period of Egyptian history, known politically as "The Age of Conquest." The reigns of Thotmes I, Hatshepsu, Rameses I, Rameses II, Nefretete, Tut-ankh-Amen, and others.
4. SAITIC AND PERSIAN PERIODS, Dynasties XXVI-XXXI (663–332 B.C.).
Period of decline in art, with constant foreign invasion, barren of important monuments.
5. GRECO-ROMAN PERIOD (332 B.C.-A.D. 640).
   a. Alexander the Great and the Ptolemaic period (332–30 B.C.). Construction of the palaces at Edfu and Philae.
   b. Roman period (30 B.C.-A.D. 395). The age of Caesar, Antony and Cleopatra, and Constantine.
   c. Byzantine or Coptic period (A.D. 395–640). Christianized Egypt.
   d. Arab domination. Egypt becomes Mohammedan.

The Pyramids. The oldest and mightiest extant examples of architecture are the pyramids of Gizeh near Cairo. These were built about 3700 B.C.,* and were the production of experienced designers and engineers. The purpose of the buildings was religious rather than architectural. They were the tombs of the kings of the early dynasties and their form was probably inspired from prehistoric burial mounds. The engineering methods employed in their construction are still the subject of speculation. Much of the granite of which they are built was quarried 700 miles away. It is difficult to conceive of the labor or the toll in human lives required for their erection.

Character of the Egyptian buildings. The extant buildings of ancient Egypt consist of colossal palaces, temples, and tombs. The first builders of the historic period unquestionably inspired themselves from two prehistoric types of structure, one of which was the wall built of clay or sun-dried brick. These were soft materials that necessitated making the lower portion of a wall thicker than the upper portion, resulting in slanting sides. The other type was an enclosure built of a row of vertical tree-trunks that sup-

---

* Some Egyptologists claim that the Pyramids do not predate 2700 B.C.

A view of the Sphinx and Pyramid of Cheops at Gizeh near Cairo, Egypt. Both date from about 3700 B.C. The origin and meaning of the Sphinx has been insoluble. It has thus become a symbol of mystery but has been used as an ornamental form in many later periods of art. The Pyramids, originally tombs, are the oldest extant examples of architecture. They were built in imitation of the permanent natural mound form with an enormous amount of labor and relatively small esthetic result. The Pyramid of Cheops is 480 feet high.

ported wooden beams, which, in turn, were covered with branches and clay.

With the invention of stonecutting tools, the slanting form of the brick walls was imitated in granite. This is a typical example of the perpetuation of tradition in Egyptian design. With the use of granite, the strongest of stones, the walls could have been carried to great heights at the same thickness. Stone pillars or columns were substituted for tree trunks. These stone supports were either round or polygonal, very sturdy in appearance, and were carved to imitate a cluster of papyrus reeds or palm tree trunks that in wooden construction had been tied together for greater strength. This treatment produced an effect of vertical convex ribs, which was the prototype of the flutings or grooves cut in later columns. The branches at the top of the tree were also frequently conventionalized in the stone column, and formed an ornamental feature, bell-shaped in appearance and known as a campaniform capital. Other capitals were inspired from palm branches, from single or clustered lotus buds, and from the curling leaves of the papyrus. Granite was used for the exterior walls of buildings. Because of the primitive nature of the tools that were available, simple forms and few moldings were used in Egyptian architecture and decoration. The tops of walls were usually crowned with a hollow roll molding, concave

Model of the hypostyle hall in the temple at Karnak, Upper Nile, showing the interior columns supporting the lintels that in turn support the roof. Notice the character of the decoration on the columns and the conventionalized papyrus capital.

in shape, sometimes known as a bird's beak or *cavetto*. Limestone, a much softer material, was often used to line the interior walls as it was easier to cut into ornamental patterns.

Rectangular forms and straight lines dominated Egyptian architecture. Massiveness, solidity, and the effect of perpetuity were the principal characteristics expressed. Walls were excessively thick, and supports were proportionately heavy and sturdy. The Egyptians had little knowledge of the principles of arch construction, so that vaulted ceilings and arched doors or window openings were not used. The columns were spanned by heavy stone beams or lintels that were of enormous size and of great weight, and, due to the material, the length of the span was extremely limited and frequent supports were necessary. Lines of lintels were set close together so that stone roof slabs could be in turn placed upon them. In wide rooms, numerous columns had to be placed in the interior to support the short stone beams. These interior columns were arranged in long rows and richly decorated with carving and color. Many of the rooms appeared to be a forest of columns, as the desire for permanence precluded the use of wooden beams which would have spanned greater distances. This system of column and lintel is known as *trabeated construction* and is one of the most characteristic features of Egyptian design. Many of the temples and palaces were of vast size. In spite of the fact that they were considered as temporary abodes, great wealth was lavished upon them and they were

View of the interior of the temple at Karnak, showing part of a row of columns. Notice the massiveness of the columns, the detail of the capitals, the close spacing, and the incised carved ornament shown on the shaft in the foreground.

decorated with luxury and splendor. Over the entrance door was carved a welcoming sentence. Courtyards were treated with colorful decorations and awnings screened the noonday sun.

Character of Egyptian wall decoration and ornament. The exterior walls were often treated with brilliant color applied to incised wall carvings. These decorations were made by first drawing outline sketches on the wall with charcoal. A groove was then chiselled around the outline of each motif. The figure or pattern was slightly modelled, but did not project beyond the face of the wall. It was next covered with a thin layer of plaster, which when still wet was colored a flat tone. The colors used were limited in number, and gradations, showing highlights, shades, or shadows, were not indicated. In the interiors of buildings the walls were often faced with soft limestone slabs that were decorated with colored carvings in low relief.

The subject matter of Egyptian mural decorations included representations of actions in the daily life of the individual, allegorical and religious events, and many other scenes that have given historians an accurate and detailed knowledge of Egyptian civilization. In the great temple of Queen Hatshepsu, the interior natural rock walls were covered with brilliant paintings of her activities and hobbies. Other rooms depict with

Egyptian limestone relief painting (1600 B.C.).

astonishing accuracy the Nile, its boats and barges, the flowers and birds, and the desert, where every kind of wild animal is being hunted. The dancer, the musician, the warrior, the peasant, and the worker are represented. Humor and tragedy are shown accompanied with brief sentences, jokes, and catchwords of the period. The purpose of the murals was to tell a story, to record history, or to show various consecutive phases of some event. Usually the whole area of a wall surface was covered with figures, patterns, or *hieroglyphics** (inscriptions), so that the eye could wander

* Hieroglyphics were originally a form of pictorial writing which later was simplified by the substitution of symbols for the complete forms. Their use was largely limited to inscriptions on stone walls. They were read from right to left. An abridged form known as *hieratic*, cursive in character, was reserved for religious writings. Ordinary correspondence, conducted by the public scribes, was written in *demotic*, a still further abridged form. The transcription of Egyptian inscriptions was not possible until the discovery, in 1799, of the Rosetta Stone on the banks of the Nile. This small monument, which dates from 196 B.C., contains praises of Ptolemy incised in hieroglyphics, demotic, and Greek. It was found by

Egyptian painting on wood, showing a decorative arrangement of hieroglyphics and the conventional method of drawing a human figure.

from point to point and finally comprehend the whole story. No central point of interest was placed in the mural composition, and the decoration was intended to accentuate the wall, rather than hide it.

The human figure was usually shown with the face, legs, and feet in profile, while the shoulders and one eye were drawn as though seen from the front. The principles of perspective drawing were not understood. Depth was indicated by placing one figure above the other. Important persons were drawn at large scale; the unimportance of slaves and enemies was indicated by drawing them small in size. Women were usually drawn smaller than men. Religious symbolism was attached to most of the ornamental motifs. The sun disk or globe and the vulture with outstretched wings were considered symbols of protection. The sacred beetle or scarab symbolized eternal life. The lotus bud and flower, extensively used in architecture, sculpture, and painted ornament, were the symbols of purity, and the serpent was the badge of royalty. Other motifs originating in Egyptian decoration were the *guilloche, palmette, wave pattern,* and *spiral*.

Egyptian sculpture. The art of sculpture in the round was developed to a high degree of perfection. Portraits and allegorical figures such as the sphinx and the falcon were produced in great quantities. Figures were usually modelled in a state of repose, symmetrically balanced, so that the best view could be obtained from the front. Realistic portraits were made of royal personages but the faces of minor officials often resembled the reigning Pharaoh. Much Egyptian sculpture, because of the hardness of the stone from which it was carved, is extremely simple in detail. The surfaces are smooth and a dignified, majestic effect is obtained by simple, vigorous masses. Many of the stone statues were brilliantly colored in flat tones. Male figures were usually shown with red faces and females with light yellow skin. Exquisite and accurate copies of animal and bird life were often modelled both in relief and in the round.

one of Napoleon's soldiers. Champollion, the French Egyptologist, properly transcribed the Egyptian text and thus made possible the reading of an infinite number of inscriptions clarifying many obscure historical records.

Egyptian furniture. Egyptian cabinetmakers and woodworkers developed a high degree of technical ability. The houses of the wealthy were furnished with chairs, stools, tables, and other articles of great beauty, and a Greek historian informs us that "from the earliest dynasty furnishings were of the greatest luxury indicating an extravagant mode of life." Some of the chairs were similar to a modern folding camp-stool, while others had elaboratedly carved legs, backs, and arms. Many of the chairs were very low, which obliged the occupants to sit in a cramped position, but as they had been accustomed to squatting on the floor, this was not considered an inconvenience. The most characteristic feature in the chair and bed designs was the use of dog-leg forms. The hind leg of the dog was represented in the rear of the chair and the foreleg in the front of the chair. The feet were carved paws placed on small blocks of wood so that the ornamental portion would

Bust of Queen Nefretete, Mother-in-law of Tut-ankh-Amen (1360 B.C.), Berlin Museum.

stand above the straw matting which covered the floors. Lion, swan, and duck heads were frequently used to enrich portions of the furniture. Ivory and ebony were used as inlay. Gold ornament in symbolical motifs was also applied to the woodwork. Brightly colored loose cushions covered in cotton, painted leather, and gold and silver fabric were used for comfort. The Egyptian craftsman thoroughly understood his material. Knowing that wood would warp, twist, split, and shrink, he treated his design and construction so as to render these defects as negligible as possible. Wood was used with proper economy. Comfort was considered in shaping both the seat and back of the chair to fit the human form.

Egyptian accessories. From the earliest dates the Egyptian home was furnished with beautiful tableware made of pottery, alabaster, glass, bronze, gold, and silver. Linen, constantly washed, was always marked with the owner's name and was kept in baskets and chests. The Egyptians also possessed personal accessories of great beauty made of gold, enamel, precious gems, and other materials, which show how luxurious was the

The Scribe, an Egyptian limestone statue of 2700 B.C. Louvre, Paris.

life of the upper classes. Direct evidence of the elaborate character of these articles was given when, in the tomb of the mother of Cheops, builder of the Great Pyramid, personal objects were discovered that were fashioned of precious metals and jewels, and finished in the most perfect technique. There were gold vases, gold and enamel-embossed chests, and gold toilet articles enriched with rare stones. A bed and chair of wood were covered with gold plaques. There was also a great wooden framework for draperies to hang over her throne when her soul returned to her body. The exquisite detail in these pieces shows the perfection of Egyptian craftsmanship even at a date previous to the building of the Pyramids.

Egyptian art was fundamentally an honest esthetic expression of the inhabitants of Egypt. The use of material was always consistent with its nature. Ornament was so designed that it was calculated to increase rather than conceal the vigor and purpose of the structure and to heighten its characteristic beauty and texture. Limited as the craftsmen were in variety of materials and tools, and having behind them a traditional conservatism that was unchangeable throughout the centuries, their art productions in every medium were carried to the limit of their possibilities. The Egyptian artists, superbly skillful and imaginative, accomplished the most that they could with the means and knowledge they had; no greater compliment can be paid to any art.

PERSIA AND CRETE

In a rapid survey of the historical periods of art, it is impossible to describe in detail those of the early periods of Crete, Persia, and the Greece of Homer. These countries contributed definite principles that have become the heritage of later styles.

Egyptian chair frame (c. 1500 B.C.), showing method of construction, dog's fore and hind legs supported on blocks.

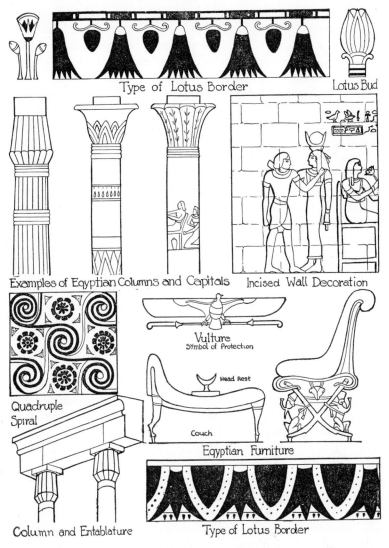

Type of Lotus Border

Lotus Bud

Examples of Egyptian Columns and Capitals

Incised Wall Decoration

Vulture
Symbol of Protection

Head Rest

Couch

Egyptian Furniture

Quadruple Spiral

Column and Entablature

Type of Lotus Border

EXAMPLES OF EGYPTIAN ARCHITECTURE, FURNITURE, AND OTHER DETAILS.

Between 3000 and 1100 B.C. there lived on the islands in the Aegean Sea a pleasure-loving people who were ruled by the famous sea kings of Greek mythology. The art of this group has been called Cretan or Minoan, after the name of Minos, the greatest of the sea kings, who built the Palace at Cnossus with its renowned underground labyrinth where, according to mythology, fourteen of the finest Athenian youths and maidens were annually fed to the great Minotaur. The palace was a large, rambling building, and its interior walls were decorated with brilliantly colored *frescoes* of naturalistic flowers, flying fish, and bullfights and other court activities. Not less beautiful than the frescoes are the fragments of Minoan metal-work and pottery, decorated with geometric patterns, naturalistic designs of fish, dolphins, octopi, interlaced birds, and spiral bands, which have been found in the same rooms.

From 1600 to 1200 b.c. a similar art was produced on the mainland of Asia Minor in the cities of Troy and Tyre, and in Mycenae, in Greece; this is generally termed Mycenaean art. Like the Cretans, the Mycenaeans erected large palaces of wood and decorated the interiors with bas-reliefs and brightly colored frescoes. They also made pottery and metalwork painted with geometrical and conventional designs.

From the arts of Assyria and Egypt, the roving Shepherd Kings of Persia (539–331 b.c.) derived the principles and motifs that they combined in their lavish palaces at Susa and Persepolis. They borrowed the lintel system of construction from the Egyptians and decorated it with the enamelled tile of the Assyrians. The great halls of their palaces were forests of columns crowned with capitals carved to resemble the heads of bulls. Friezes of colored tile, showing archers and animals, covered the walls. Their hunting scenes, winged monsters, griffins, and tree-of-life patterns became a basic part of the designs used by the later Persians (A.D. 226–1736) in weaving the silks and rugs that were eagerly sought by all Europe.

GREECE

The beginnings of civilization in western Europe may be traced to the culture that originated in the Grecian peninsula and adjoining islands as far back as 2000 b.c. The early inhabitants of this part of the Mediterranean were endowed by nature with an unusually logical and observing mentality, a creative instinct, an extraordinary imagination, and a high ambition. They desired to attain perfection in all accomplishments, great or small. This characteristic is evidenced in the great heights they eventually attained in philosophy, literature, and the fine arts.

Originally the Greeks are thought to have been Indo-European nomads who migrated to the Greek peninsula about 2000 b.c. The early classical writers called the indigenous population Pelasgians. Whether their descendants or the Myceneans are the Achaean heroes of whom Homer sings in the *Iliad* is a matter of conjecture, but, at any rate, the pictures of the kings and gods sketched in that epic and the *Odyssey* reveal a civilized people who settled Greece and conquered Troy about the year 1200 b.c. These in turn were overrun by the barbarous Dorians, who invaded and settled the islands of the Aegean Sea, and finally Sparta and Corinth. In Asia Minor, the Ionians, who had migrated before and during the Dorian invasions, built powerful cities and carried on a vast trade with the East. Northern Greece was civilized by the Aeolians. The mingling of these three tribes and the union of their independent city-states under the name of *Hellas* made up the Greece whose history commences about the 6th century B.C. The early period of this civilization, known as Archaic, lasted until the battle of Marathon in 490 B.C. which ended the Persian war. This was followed by slightly less than a century of peace and plenty called the Golden Age. Under the benevolent dictator Pericles, Grecian art and culture rose to a supreme height that has perhaps never been equalled. The Peloponnesian war saw the destruction of Athens by the Spartans in 404 B.C. With the decline of Athens, the Macedonians soon rose to power and finally Phillip and his son Alexander about 323 B.C. conquered nearly the whole of the then known world. Alexander moved his capital to Alexandria, the city he built in Egypt. Greece came under Roman rule in 146 B.C., but its culture and political thought dominated the whole of the Mediterranean until the rise of Christianity.

The climate and geography of the Grecian peninsula were different from those of Egypt. The ragged coastline with bays and inlets bounded a fertile land of sunshine and rain. Tall mountains containing minerals and quarries of rich marble towered above a land abundant and colorful. The ample rainfall and the availability of beautiful soft building stone such as marble greatly influenced the character and detail of Grecian architecture and decoration.

The character of the Greek people. The geographical location and character of the Grecian peninsula served to develop a seafaring race of people which in turn subjected them to foreign and often subversive ideas. The mountainous topography of the land tended to hinder intercommunication between neighboring communities which resulted in misunderstandings, jealousies, and lack of amity. Internecine strife was constant and complete political cohesion was never attained. Independence of thought was a dominant characteristic. The Athenians were the great individualists of antiquity. They were adamant in their desire for freedom to act, speak, and think as they wished. They considered as barbarians all those who lived under despots, accepted rule blindly, or lived without liberty, and these included most of the then known world. They regarded wisdom as the greatest of human attributes, and to attain this, it was essential to be both curious and inquisitive, to doubt and to question all things until they were proved. To know truth and to understand were the Athenians' first passions. Religion, fostered by a romantic landscape, was the worship of Nature, and special gods existed for every event and every place. Man was the measure of all things, hence the legendary deities were the personification of human beings, with like qualities and weaknesses. A mass enthusiasm exacted universal perfection which was considered attainable only by logic, supreme intelligence, and unlimited effort. The useful, good, and beautiful were inexorably bound together, and the collective esthetic conscience evidenced the perpetual conflict between emotional impulse and intellect, in which intellect and self-restraint always rose supreme. Emotional satisfactions attained full scope in festivals, games, religion, and private life. Idealism was maintained in all the best creative efforts. Superlative form, line, rhythm, and symmetry were adored. In the enjoyment of literature, the Greeks were less interested in the contents than in the way the contents were presented. Art was real, a part of the spirit, constantly present, and a valuable commercial asset. As a nation, the Athenians were essentially proud, and convinced, not without reason, that they were superior to all others as warriors, artists, philosophers, mathematicians, and writers. The first duty of the citizen was service to the state, which included its glorification and the promotion of its cultural development. It was such an atmosphere that impregnated their close approach to a cultural zenith that has proved its eternal value.

Qualities of self-discipline and courage dominated the lives of the Doric Spartans for purposes of conquest and material gain. They were a nation of soldiers, which in the end enabled them to dominate Athens for a short period, but they were without philosophers, historians, or artists. All information concerning them is gleaned solely from Athenian writers, and they left nothing of value to posterity except a realization of the futility of force. Athenian idealism and its cultural results have proved to be immortal. It was the dominance of envious traits in the character of the Greeks which prevented political unity and eventually led to their downfall.

The main divisions of Greek art. While the earliest influences of Greek art were of Oriental origin, the later growth reflected a vigorous native ability that resulted in an unusually homogeneous esthetic expression. The consolidation of the independent cities closely paralleled the blending of the independent racial arts that formed the basis of the perfection of the Periclean age.

The dates of the Greek periods are somewhat arbitrary, but the following arrangement will aid in identifying the successive developments.

1. PRIMITIVE PERIOD (2000–1000 B.C.).
   This was the period of the Dorian invasions in 1500 B.C. and their destruction of Cretan and Mycenaean civilization in 1400 B.C. It was succeeded by the Homeric era in the 10th century B.C.—the age of the Olympian gods and goddesses—and later by an age of plunder which terminated in the Trojan War. The dark ages of barbarian invasions followed, with Greek expansion to Asia Minor (1200–1000 B.C.). A period barren of art products save for the Cretan and Mycenaean civilizations.

2. ARCHAIC PERIOD (1000–480 B.C.).
   A period of extensive maritime commerce with Italy and Egypt, and of

Greek colonization on the coasts of the Mediterranean, Aegean, and Black seas. The age of Thales, the philosopher, and Sappho, the poet. The first coinage of money and the first Olympic games. This era was followed by the rise of tyrants and the rise of small city-states. It was marked by an artistic development of crafts—beautiful pottery and coins. In sculpture, it was a period of striving to achieve perfection in rendering the human form, but, though much progress was made, the period closed with an insufficient knowledge of anatomical representation. In architecture, the development of the Doric and Ionic orders was begun.

3. GOLDEN AGE (480–400 B.C.).

During this period the Greeks were victorious in the Persian wars, which were followed by the rise of Athens as a naval power. It was the age of Pericles and the Athenian democracy, of the development of the Greek drama and theater under Aeschylus, Sophocles, Euripides, and Aristophanes. Erection of the Parthenon under the supervision of Phidias, the sculptor, and Ictinus, the architect. Athens was the center of culture and produced the great historians, Herodotus and Thucydides, and the poet, Pindar. This period culminated in the defeat of Athens in 404 B.C., and is considered the greatest period of culture of all times. In sculpture it was a period of perfection and idealization in rendering the human form, and in architecture, of perfect balance and harmony, with the refinement of the Doric and Ionic orders. Socrates, the master of philosophers, died in 399 B.C.

4. FOURTH CENTURY (400–336 B.C.).

This period witnessed the decline of the city-state and the further expansion of Greek civilization. It was the age of Demosthenes, the orator; Hippocrates, the "father of medicine"; Plato and Aristotle, the philosophers; and Praxiteles, the sculptor. In art, realism and sentiment replaced Phidian idealism, with increasing emphasis on technical perfection.

5. ALEXANDRIAN AGE (336–323 B.C.).

A period of expansion of Greek rule and spread of Greek culture through the conquests of Alexander the Great. Invasions of Asia Minor, Egypt, Persia, and India. In art, a period of great realism and monumental effects. Development of the Corinthian order.

6. HELLENISTIC AGE (323–30 B.C.).

The disintegration of Alexander's empire was followed by the Greco-Macedonian rule of the Hellenized world. It was a period of great advance in science and mathematics; but in art it was a period of decline. Realism, sentimentalism, and theatricalism dominated in sculpture. Greece became a Roman province in the 2nd century B.C.

Early Grecian architecture. The prehistoric inhabitants of Greece undoubtedly built their homes of wood cut from the ample forests that covered the hills and valleys of the peninsula. Many authorities believe that at the beginning of the Stone Age the early masons, lacking precedent for their designs, modelled the details of their buildings after the old wooden structures. There is much evidence in the early stone architecture of the Greeks that details and ornament were cut to imitate original wooden features, following the procedure of the early Egyptian builders.

During the Archaic period of Grecian civilization, large limestone and stucco temples were built by the Dorians, both in Greece and in the Greek colonies in Sicily and elsewhere. They were massive in proportion, and their design was dominated by the use of rows of columns on the outside of the buildings. After 500 B.C., an improvement occurred in the general proportions and detail, and greater refinement was evidenced in the character of the sculpture that was used as ornament. The great extant examples of architecture of the early period are the Apollo Temple at Corinth, the Temple of Zeus at Selinus, in Sicily, and several temples at Paestum, in southern Italy.

During the early years of the 5th century B.C., the descendants of the Ionians were also occupied in the construction of magnificent temples in Asia Minor, in some of the Greek islands, and in Greece itself. These were similar in general design to those built by the Dorians, but they differed in proportions and detail. Notable among them was the Temple of Zeus at Olympia, where the religious ceremonies accompanying the Olympic games were held.

The Parthenon. The crowning achievement of Grecian art was the construction of a group of religious and civic structures on the hill known as the Acropolis, in Athens. The buildings were erected under the administration of Pericles during the latter half of the 5th century B.C., as a result of the national enthusiasm that developed after the successful termination of the Persian wars, with the subsequent glory and wealth that came to Athens. At the highest point on the hill was erected the Parthenon, a structure which is generally considered the greatest masterpiece of architecture in the world. Its perfection of line, proportion, and detail, and the beauty of its sculptured enrichment have been the envy and the inspiration of artists in every country and every period.

The Parthenon was designed by Ictinus and Callicrates, the architects, and by Phidias, the sculptor, and was completed in 438 B.C. It was dedicated to the virgin goddess, Athena, whose 40-foot statue, made of gold and ivory with precious stones used for eyes, was in its sacred precincts. The pediments were filled with sculpture and remains of colors have been found on the stonework. Along its exterior wall was the great frieze of Phidias, carved in relief and showing a procession of cavalry, chariots, musicians, maidens, and gods. The building is a rectangular temple surrounded by a covered portico 228 feet long, supported by 46 Doric columns 33 feet high. The interior was also treated with rows of columns that were

Model showing the Parthenon in a restored condition. The order used is the Greek Doric.

covered with gold and color. There probably has never been in history greater thought placed upon the design of any building. It is full of refinements intended to correct optical illusions. Long horizontal features which seem straight are slightly curved so that they will not appear to sag. Vertical features incline slightly inward to counteract the tendency to appear to lean outward. The corner columns are slightly heavier in their proportions than are the others, and are placed closer together to give an appearance of greater strength to the silhouette. The top line of inscriptions on walls was cut in the tallest letters, the lower lines were each reduced in height for the reason that they were nearer to the eye and thus all letters would appear the same size. The Parthenon was considered a perfect and precious jewel not only intended to enshrine a goddess and to hold the treasure of the nation, but to feed the pride and spirit of every Athenian. Its beauty still sparkles through its ruins; its glamor has been maintained for 25 centuries. The architectural principles and forms which reached the acme of perfection in this magnificent work have been used as inspiration and model by civilizations from the Roman period to modern times. The building has been used as a pagan temple, Christian church, and Moslem mosque, and was destroyed in 1687 by a bombardment. It has been restored to some extent in recent years.

Theories of Greek design. Archeologists have often tried to prove that the Parthenon and other Greek temples were designed by the use of geometrical formulas and that the agreeable proportions of pure design are based on mathematics. Conclusions have been arrived at by analysis of existing buildings that there are simple mathematical relationships between parts and proportions, but this is a reversal of reasoning and it is doubtful whether the Greeks predetermined their designs by any such method. The mind through the eye instinctively enjoys assembled forms that have an appearance of unity, interrelationship, and proper structure. Perhaps the visual experience of inherited generations has taught us which goals are most closely approached and may form the basis of our judgment as to the degree of perfection that we consider as beauty in certain types of design. The Greeks seemed to have attained so high a degree of sensitivity to form, line, and proportion that mathematical calculations were unnecessary.

Greek structural principles and materials. The early Greek artists were undoubtedly strongly influenced by Egyptian art. This is seen not only in the continued use of the column and lintel form of construction but also in the resemblance of the early sculptural forms. The Greeks refined the column, made it less a copy of natural forms, made it more graceful, and used more moldings for its enrichment. The Egyptian effort to reproduce the clustered trunks of trees and reeds in the length of their columns was discontinued and concave grooves called *flutings* took their place. The Greeks were the first to use the column as a feature on the outside of a building. A rainy climate necessitated the portico and colonnade. In the temples, the roof extended beyond the main walls of the building a distance of about ten feet. This projection had to be supported, and the column, used for this purpose, automatically dominated the design and appearance of the exterior. Great care was given to its proportions and detail. Greek buildings attain unity and appear as a complete composition, in which every detail is related and plays its part in the whole. The Greeks probably did not fully understand the construction of the arch or dome, and did not use them, but in their smaller buildings they developed the wooden truss instead of the stone beam or lintel for roof construction and ceiling support, which thus eliminated interior columns and permitted walls to be placed a greater distance apart. The slanting rafters of the truss furnished a pitch to the roof for the discharge of rainwater. The roof of the Parthenon was supported by a series of stepped stones that served as a lintel. These had to be partially supported by interior columns. The end trusses on a building were covered with masonry arranged to follow the triangular shape of the truss itself, and in the monumental buildings this area, called a pediment, was decorated with moldings and sculptured ornament. The Greeks also discovered a way to cut stone in a quarry that maintained greater strength in the material. This permitted the use of longer stone lintels when needed, and increased the span between the columns.

Marble and limestone, the materials used for the exteriors and interiors of these buildings, were soft white stones, the surfaces of which took a high polish. They differed greatly in ease of cutting from the granite of Egypt, which explains the use of numerous small moldings in Greek architecture and decoration, and may also be considered an important factor in the development in Greece of the art of sculpture. The ornament on the surface of Greek buildings was carved in relief, rather than being incised, as had been the practice in Egypt. The pattern projected from the face of the stonework, and was effective because of the highlights, shades, and shadows produced by the projection rather than because of the addition of color.

Greek architecture is basically functional, which implies that every feature had a useful and practical purpose. Columns were used solely for support, never for decoration. Little was introduced solely for its decorative effect, and although structural surfaces were enriched, the ornament was never applied to a degree where the appearance of the structure itself became of secondary importance in the design. Walls of the great temples were in solid marble throughout, a material which was of sufficient beauty to serve as the interior decorative finish. The stones were so accurately cut that it was not necessary to use mortar in the joints. Craftsmanship in building was carried to a supreme degree of perfection. The charm of Grecian architecture is in its intellectual rather than emotional appeal. It is a beauty produced by line, form, and proportion, rather than color and surface ornament.

Certain forms originally used for exterior architecture were adapted to the interiors of the buildings. The detail and the proportioning of Greek moldings, the method of their application, and the character of ornament have been especially followed by later designers in nearly all periods of art. It becomes essential, therefore, to study some of the details of architecture as seen in the Parthenon and other buildings on the Acropolis.

The orders of architecture. The Greek buildings were built in one of three styles or *orders of architecture,* known as *Doric, Ionic,* and *Corinthian.* The orders of architecture were probably the interpretation in stone of the prehistoric wooden post-and-beam structure, agreeably proportioned and enriched. As in the Egyptian structures, the wooden post eventually became the cylindrical stone column. To the wooden beam or stone lintel which the column carried were added moldings and ornament, creating the *entablature.* An order consists of a column and an entablature.

The orders differ from one another in proportion and detail. The chief distinguishing feature in each order is the capital of the column. The capital consists of a series of moldings and ornaments placed at the top of the column. The most simple capital is that used with the Doric order, in which the principal features consist of a large square block at the top, called an *abacus,* underneath which is a curved molding known as an *echinus* which springs from the main body of the column. The Ionic

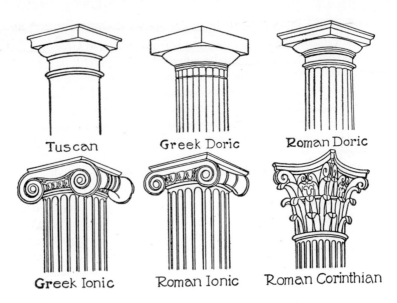

| Tuscan | Greek Doric | Roman Doric |

| Greek Ionic | Roman Ionic | Roman Corinthian |

EXAMPLES OF GREEK AND ROMAN CAPITALS.

capital is characterized by two large *volutes* or spirals, and the Corinthian by two rows of vertical acanthus leaves below four small volutes that are applied to a bell-shaped form resembling the Egyptian campaniform capital. A column has two additional parts. The lower portion of the Ionic and Corinthian column is treated with a series of moldings called the base. No base was used for the Greek Doric column. The central and longest part of a column, called the *shaft,* is frequently treated with vertical concave grooves called flutings, and is tapered slightly at the top. This tapering is known as the *entasis.*

The entablature is also constructed in three main divisions. The lower portion or lintel is called the *architrave,* and is sometimes enriched by the addition of several simple moldings. The central portion, a wide, flat surface, is known as the *frieze,* and is frequently treated with some form of carved enrichment. The upper portion, consisting of a series of moldings, is known as the *cornice.* Portions of the cornice project out over the frieze to protect the carving on the frieze from the weather, and also to create a shadow beneath it that will accent and give a finished effect to the top of the building. The moldings at the top of the cornice usually encase a gutter along the edge of the roof of the building to catch the rainwater that runs down the slope.

In addition to the parts of the order mentioned above, the Greeks frequently placed the column on a high block called the *stylobate,* which the Romans later enlarged and elaborated into the *pedestal.* This pedestal is the origin of the modern interior dado or *wainscot.* The triangular portion

Greek Ionic capital from Sardis, Asia Minor.

at the front and rear of the building, formed by the cornice and the line of the roof, is treated with moldings and sculpture. This feature is known as the pediment. Originating in Greek architecture, it was often used by the Romans and in later styles of architecture, decoration, and furniture design as an ornamental feature. Details of a typical order are shown on page 57.

In the Doric order, the proportions are rather sturdy and heavy, the forms and moldings are simple, and only a small amount of enrichment is used. This order was selected for buildings in which the esthetic expression was to be one of strength and vigor. The Ionic order is lighter in appearance, more elaborate in detail, and was used where dignity was required without the solid strength represented by the Doric. The Corinthian order was still more delicate in appearance, and was selected where the effect of grace, lightness, richness, or gaiety was necessary; it was an outgrowth of the Ionic form, a late development in Greek architecture, and was not frequently used until the Roman period.

The architectural features, all originating structurally, were eventually used by the Romans and others for decorative purposes as well. In the study of interior decoration it is advantageous to learn to identify the architectural orders and to learn their parts by name. The column, pilaster, entablature, architrave, frieze, cornice, pedestal, and pediment have been a constant source of inspiration, since their introduction by the Greeks, for interior wall treatments, the designs of furniture, and other forms of industrial art. It is likewise valuable to know the origin and meaning of these terms.

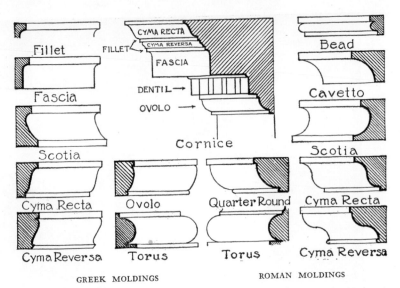

GREEK MOLDINGS   ROMAN MOLDINGS

Typical classical moldings. The Greek moldings are curves produced by the free-hand stroke of the artist. The Roman moldings are produced mechanically by the use of the compass.

Moldings and molding ornaments. The Greeks created the various molding forms that are now used and known by their Latin names. Moldings are the means by which a designer may produce highlight, shade, and shadow upon any surface. They serve to divide the surface into smaller parts and create interest and variety. The Greek moldings were extremely graceful in silhouette and were designed by the freehand stroke of the artist rather than by mechanical means. They resemble portions of the mathematical curves known as the ellipse, parabola, and hyperbola. These curves are complex, the degree of curvature increasing in their length. The Roman moldings were more simple but less beautiful and their silhouettes were made by combining various compass or mechanical curves. Many of the moldings were enriched by ornament that was designed to fit the shape of the molding itself.

The principal moldings were:

1. The *fillet,* a small, flat, plain surface used to separate other moldings.
2. The *fascia,* a wide, straight surface, usually plain, used to contrast with and accentuate smaller moldings.
3. The *ovolo* (egg-like), a convex-curved surface approximating the exterior curve of a quarter-circle. It frequently follows the line of a parabola, and is often enriched with an ornament known as the *egg-and-dart.*
4. The *cavetto,* a concave surface approximating the interior curve of a quarter-circle.

5. The *cyma recta,* an S-shaped, curved surface that starts and ends horizon-tally. It is frequently enriched with a *honeysuckle* motif. This is sometimes called "The Hogarth line of beauty."
6. The *cyma reversa,* an S-shaped, curved surface that starts and ends vertically, frequently enriched with an ornament known as the *waterleaf.*
7. The *torus,* a convex surface approximating the exterior curve of a semicircle. When enriched, it is treated with the guilloche or with overlapping laurel leaves tied with crossed ribbon bands.
8. The *bead,* a small torus molding (semicircle) cut to imitate a string of beads of varying size.
9. The *scotia,* a deep, hollow, concave molding, seldom ornamented, and usu-ally found only on the base of a column.

Greek ornament. In addition to these molding ornaments, the Greeks developed a great number of ornamental forms that were later borrowed by the Romans and, in turn, by the designers of western Europe from the 15th century onward. Although color was often used in connection with Greek ornament, the play of light, shade, and shadow was of greater value in accentuating form and line, the principal elements of beauty that in-trigued and delighted the Greek mind and so vitalized their arts. The Greeks produced no all-over patterns, but were most interested in enrich-ing structural forms in such a way that the structure was accentuated rather than hidden. Although the fundamental forms of Greek ornament were constantly repeated during the whole history of Greek decoration, the variations were so multitudinous and the combinations so complex that exact duplications were practically nonexistent.

Among the ornamental forms borrowed from vegetation were the *acanthus* leaf, lotus bud and flower, palmette, and *anthemion.* From the animal world, the artists represented the complete forms or portions of the bodies of the horse, lion, ox, birds, fish, and other fauna. Mythical and fanciful creations such as the sphinx, griffin, and chimera were also freely used. Ox skulls (bucrania) were combined with ribbons, festoons, and garlands. Of geometrical motifs, the *fret* or *meander* wave or scroll, the rosette, the conventionalized honeysuckle, and the double interlacing scroll or guilloche were the most frequently used. The spiral and the *swastika,* although seen in primitive Greek art, are also associated with the arts of other primitive races, and the use of these forms was discontinued at an early date.

During the Alexandrian period the *rinceau* and the *arabesque* were developed, through a combination of scroll, spiral, vine, and acanthus leaf motifs. The human figure was also extensively used for decorative pur-poses as well as for sculpture, and the *caryatid* or human form crowned with a capital and used as a supporting structural feature was a develop-ment of Grecian architecture.

Types of Honeysuckle Borders

Kylix

Fret Border

Amphora

Acanthus Leaf

Guilloche

Antefix

Honeysuckle Band

Mosaic Pattern

Grecian Figure

Painted Bands from Vases

EXAMPLES OF TYPICAL GRECIAN ORNAMENTS.

Greek sculpture. It is generally accepted that the art of sculpture reached its zenith during the period of Greek civilization. The initiative of the Greeks, inspired by the sculpture of the Trojans, Minoans, and Egyptians, was, in this art, additionally actuated by the fact that in the Greek peninsula, as well as the adjoining islands, and especially the island of Paros, there was available a magnificent white stone that was softer than granite, and harder than alabaster. Marble was a material that had a fine grain and texture and could be cut easily into minute details. The developments in this art were so great that progress was made almost independently of any previous style. The evolution may be broadly subdivided into three parts: the Archaic, Hellenic, and Hellenistic.

The oldest marble statue dates from about 620 B.C. This was more primitive in character than the sculpture produced in Egypt in her earliest history. The Greek advancement was rapid, however, and in two centuries reached its highest point of development. During the Archaic period (620–480 B.C.) sculptural forms were highly conventionalized. Figures were influenced by Egypt, Assyria, Crete, and Ionia. By 550 B.C. the first figure was made in which movement was indicated by the position of the legs, and emotion was expressed in the face by a sort of grimace, now called the Archaic smile. Eyes were modelled with an Oriental slant and the eyeballs bulged in a convex surface. These characteristics continued during the whole of the period.

After Marathon (490 B.C.) a great advance occurred in both relief and free-standing sculpture. Many statues were made commemorating heroic contests. The enthusiasm aroused by the Persian defeat and culminating in the Golden Age of Pericles was reflected in the enrichment of the new temples with sculptural work of the greatest magnificence. During the latter portion of the 5th century, the work of the three greatest sculptors was produced. Phidias, who was responsible for the adornment of Athens and particularly the pediment and friezes of the Parthenon,* dominated the trio, which included Myron and Polyclitus. Polyclitus was the first sculptor to show figures in action, standing on one foot. Myron is particularly famous for his unexcelled statues of athletes in motion in which every muscle is indicated strongly in tension. The style during the Golden Age expressed the Greek adoration of the human body, which approached the majesty and grace attributed to the deities, and delineated physical perfection. Faces were slightly conventionalized and expressed the dignity, strength, and serenity that characterized the people of this period.

After the humiliation of Athens by Sparta (404 B.C.) sculpture increased in emotional representations. Praxiteles and Scopas were the great artists of this period. Their work expressed enthusiasm, pathos, and elegance; there is greater freedom of motion, more realism, and accuracy of detail. Facial expressions indicate a deeper consciousness and intensity of spiritual struggle, hair is modelled more naturally, the head becomes more oval, eyes are deep set, passion and nervousness are apparent. When clothing or draperies are shown, their structure and movement are clearly visible. In the *Victory of Samothrace* in the Louvre, by an unknown sculptor of this period, the figure is represented as standing on the prow of a ship, a windswept tunic covers her body, every fold is indicated, but one is sensitively

---

* Much of this sculpture is now in the British Museum in London. The fragments are known as the *Elgin Marbles*.

conscious of the flesh underneath, of the magnificent grace of the figure, and even of the sea-breeze which it is supposed to be resisting.*

The period of Alexander carries Greek sculpture into a theatricalism that was intended to dazzle the populace and reflect the splendor and grandeur of the regime. The center of culture moved from Athens to Alexandria and the term *Hellenistic* is usually applied to this style, which lasted until Greece became a Roman colony. Realism is expressed to a supreme degree. Anguish, pain, violence, and confusion become the dominant assertions. These are emotions that are not again approached in sculpture until modern times. Portraiture commences as well as the representation of landscapes and rural scenes.

Many of the most poignant examples of Greek sculpture are seen in the funereal monuments and grave stones known as *stelae,* on which the deceased are represented as in life. Husbands and wives are often shown in attitudes expressive of their affection and companionship.

Greek sculpture was often colored, and in many examples fragments of pigmentation remain. Most of the originals of the greatest examples of Greek sculpture have disappeared but the works are known through the contemporary literature. Roman sculptors also made many accurate copies that have been identified.

Greek domestic architecture. Little remains of Greek dwellings, and the records that are obtainable are those of the historians. The houses were small, built around courtyards, and were without windows, the light entering through the doors of the rooms. Undoubtedly the general plan and treatment was similar to the houses uncovered in the ruins of Pompeii, an Italian city of Greek origin.

Greek wall decoration and color. Many of the Greek buildings were covered with painted or glazed color both inside and out. Brick and stone were often covered with a cement stucco that was polished so highly it reflected like a mirror. Scenic decoration, and conventional ornament were used to enrich marble, wood, and plaster. Painted decoration was at first entirely subordinate to the architecture; later it became an independent art. Little remains of Greek painting, but that art never equalled the perfection reached in rendering the human form in marble and bronze.

Furniture. The Greeks used marble, bronze, iron, and wood for the construction of their furniture. These materials were frequently decorated by relief carving and by painting. The ornamental motifs were borrowed from the architectural forms. The legs of chairs and tables often showed the use of *disk-turnings* or animal forms. The feet are frequently dog or lion paws. Chairs had back rails curved in a concave or *klismos* form

* The value placed upon Greek sculpture even in antiquity is well indicated by the fact that records indicate that King Nicomedes offered to pay the entire public debt of the Cnidians providing they would give him their statue of Aphrodite by Praxiteles. His offer was refused.

Basin

Greek Bedstead with Table

Roman Chair

Roman Folding Stool

Greek Chair

Bronze Seat

Roman Lamp

Folding Stool

Roman Marble Table

Roman Tripod

Roman Bed

Pompeian Table

GREEK AND ROMAN FURNITURE.

roughly following the curve of the human back. In some wall paintings chairs are shown with gracefully curved plain legs, the front leg curving forward and the rear leg curving backward.*

Greek minor arts. One of the most interesting and oldest of the Greek minor arts was that of pottery making, and it has been through the decorations of the vases and jars of this craft that one sees some of the earliest applications of the laws of unity and the proportional relationships of pure

* These features were revived in the early 19th century furniture of France, England, and the United States.

GREEK VASE FORMS.

design. The pictorial motifs with which some are adorned have served to inform posterity concerning many of the Greek customs. The purpose of the subject matter was not only ornamental but educational as well. In these vases which were common in all households was found a convenient method to educate the youth. Every possible event in the daily life of the people was represented as well as the legendary history of the deities. The sports such as running, wrestling, and ball games were beautifully indicated as well as the proper methods of ploughing, sowing, harvesting, weaving, baking, and butchering. Boys learned how to use spears, shields, and armor. Religious processions, altar and funerary ceremonies, chariot races, and hunting scenes were beautifully represented, and lovers were instructed in the methods of showing their affection. The human figure, both draped and nude, was usually drawn in profile with full expression and understanding of its structural anatomy, physical power, action, and grace. The pagan mind adored the body as much as the Christian mind adored the soul. There were six principal shapes; the *amphora,* with two handles and a cover, was a large vase for the storage of grain; the *kylix* was a flat-shaped drinking cup; the *hydria* was intended for the storage of water and had three handles used for carrying or pouring; the *oinochoë* was pitcher-like in appearance, with one handle; the *lekythos,* a tall narrow form, was used for storing and pouring oil; and the *krater* was a bowl with a wide top used for mixing.

The Greeks used the potter's wheel, and while the forms were undoubtedly decided upon by the individual worker, the curved silhouettes were always ovoid and generally followed the changing degrees of curvature associated with the mathematical curves. The shapes were primarily functional and practical for the purposes of the vase, and the handles were designed and located for convenience in use, but were also related to the silhouette of the vase itself. The earliest vases, known as Dipylons, were for funerary use and date from 1200 to 700 B.C. These were enriched with horizontal bands painted with primitively drawn flat figures, animals, and symbolic motifs. In the 6th century the background of vases was in reddish *terra cotta,* painted with patterns in a black glaze. On a series of band courses, highlights were sometimes shown with slight tints of white or purple. By 525 B.C., red figures with slightly incised outlines were shown on a soft black background, and the char-

A magnificent Greek krater of the early 5th century B.C.

acter of the drawing resembled that of archaic sculpture. This type was superseded about 500 B.C. by black backgrounds with figures both incised and in slight relief, more naturalistic drawing, and a tendency of showing the third dimension, indicating a greater influence of the painting of the period.

Another art at which the Greeks were supreme was that of making coins, gems, and seals. These were produced with figures, human profiles, animals, and ornaments in low miniature relief, but they were so technically perfect in their modelling that it must have required extraordinary eyesight and a deft and sensitive hand to produce the perfection of their delineation.

The influence of Greece on other civilizations. No nation or race of people in the world's history has had more cultural influence upon later peoples than has ancient Greece. With its glorious history, the ruins of its ancient cities are more splendid than many modern towns. Its architecture, decoration, literature, and sculpture have never been surpassed and have stood as models of perfection for centuries.

The immediate successor to Greek civilization was that of the Roman Empire, whose people, however, never approached the perfection of Greece in any of their art products. Rome copied and adapted many Greek forms and principles, however, and thus preserved much of Greek culture which otherwise would have been lost forever.

The Greek arts are of the intellectual variety. Their beauty is attributed to exquisite proportions and graceful lines. While color and surface ornament are often an integrated part, the emotions aroused by means of these features never exceeded the intellectual appreciation derived from the gracefulness of form inherent in every object of Greek design and craftsmanship. It was this spiritual quality in Greek art that inspired Keats's remark concerning a thing of beauty, "Its loveliness increases; it will never pass into nothingness."

ROME

The character of Roman civilization. The founding of Rome in 753 B.C. is part of the legendary story of Romulus and Remus. The early growth of the city witnessed the struggles and final collaboration of Latins, Sabines, and Etruscans. The Roman insatiable desire for conquest and her consciousness of destiny commence with the final defeat of Carthage in 146 B.C. As Greece had risen supreme after Marathon, Rome, with the destruction of her chief rival, became the supreme power in the Mediterranean and prepared not only to rule the world, but to enjoy the fruits of victory. She continued to spread her control to Greece, Spain, Asia Minor, Africa, Gaul, and Britain. Caesar's conquests made Rome not only the mistress of the older civilizations, but the civilizer of barbarians. The fatal alliance between Antony and Cleopatra brought Egypt into the fold. The period of the Empire, established by Augustus in the 1st century B.C. was the beginning of the Golden Age of Roman culture. For two hundred years the Pax Romana endured, during which period the Roman citizen became the ideal of men. Literature and the arts also first became important, and these were invariably based on Greek prototypes and Greek became the language of the upper classes.

The strongest passion of the Roman people was for political dominance of colonies and for the prospect of draining these of their wealth and manpower to contribute to the luxury and service of the Roman citizens, who collectively were convinced of their own superior governing capacities. During the entire period of her existence, Rome was controlled by a senatorial dictatorship dominated by the patricians. The plebeians could rise from their class, and slaves obtain their liberty, but slave rebellions were cruelly crushed. Rome was never a true democracy. The great blemish on the character of the Roman leaders was their utter disregard for the laws of humanity in gaining their ends. The Romans needlessly burned the cities of the conquered, destroyed whole populations, murdered hostages, broke treaties, provoked unnecessary wars, falsely accused other nations of delinquencies, committed aggression by both propaganda and force, and under the Empire began to persecute those who differed in religion.

In comparison with Greece, philosophy and the arts were of secondary importance. Moral standards permitted the legal acceptance of murder in gladiatorial contests. The Roman gods, appropriated from the Hellenic pantheon, were given Latin names. Religion was allied to the State and used for national advancement. The personal religion of the individual was less important than in Greece. Idealism was subordinated to realism.

The Romans recognized from the first the supremacy of Athenian culture. They borrowed and frequently subverted every Greek concept, principle, or material object that seemed to be useful. Their cultural blood was vitalized by the elixir of Greek thought in all its ramifications. They imported Greek scholars to teach their youth, enslaved Greek craftsmen to educate their artists, and copied Greek art in all its forms. Horace pithily admitted the intellectual conquest in his remark, "Captive Greece has made her captor captive." Lacking the idealistic impulse of the Greeks and steeped in materialism, within two generations the Romans developed a consciousness of might with complete disregard of benevolent qualities.

The world nevertheless owes the Romans a debt for transmitting to the people of western Europe their interpretation of Hellenistic culture. In spite of many deficiencies in character, the Romans were an extremely practical people and excelled as organizers and law-givers; they eventually established justice and order throughout most of the Empire, but for those who refused to accept their government and religion, slavery and mistreatment were carried to extremes.

In the Eastern colonies, the oppression of those who believed in One God eventually reacted upon the national unity. A persistent faith, conscious of its righteousness, finally permeated among the lowly in all parts of the Empire and eventually undermined the pagan philosophy. Christianity was opposed because it taught submission and humility rather than what were considered the manly virtues; it was, however, not the cause but the result of the disintegration of the Roman State. Political selfishness and dishonesty created lack of respect for leadership and destroyed civic pride. The enormous taxes required to support the two armies of soldiers and bureaucrats burdened the masses to a degree where they concluded the Empire was not worth saving. Patriotism was crushed. Meddling with the law of supply and demand caused economic chaos. Exhaustion of natural resources, lowered moral standards, pestilences, and barbarian successes developed a hopelessness that finally wrecked the national initiative. The Roman tendency to self-adulation eventually created an intellectual inbreeding that excluded growth and resulted in a petrifaction of their civilization that could be dissolved only by the barbarian invasions. The year A.D. 476 marks the end of the original Roman Empire and the election of Odoacer the barbarian as the first King of Italy.

Roman architecture. Early Roman art was inspired by both the *Etruscan* and archaic Greek forms. The structures in this style dated mostly from the 5th and 6th centuries B.C. Rome did not develop as a great metropolis until Greece became a Roman colony. Rome then began to accept the heritage of Hellenistic culture. The major portion of the great buildings

The Maison Carrée, Nimes, France. The best preserved Roman temple, built in A.D. *14 and the model of many later structures in Europe and America.*

that were erected in all Roman cities were built as a result of the unusual economic conditions that existed between the 1st century B.C. and the 3rd century A.D. Slave labor served greatly to economize costs of construction, but created indolence and unemployment among the plebeians, who paradoxically enjoyed their leisure and complained of their lack of opportunities to earn a living. In gestures of generosity over a long period, the authorities repeatedly allotted food supplies furnished by the colonies. They established programs of public improvements that temporarily ameliorated labor conditions and had the appearance of enabling the public to share the wealth and luxury, which had been pre-empted by the patricians. An important part of these sops to political unrest was the building of vast structures for public use and entertainment. Among these were the great *basilicas,* or commercial exchanges, that were later to be the model for Christian churches; amphitheaters, such as the Colosseum, for pageants and mortal combats; majestic baths where bathing was secondary to amusement; circuses for chariot races; and religious edifices that have inspired designers for a score of centuries. The great forums built in the center of every city were used for political demonstrations and social gatherings. Exquisite temples and shrines, set in landscaped vistas enriched with statuary, were used for votive purposes, or museums containing Greek sculpture. Elaborate temporary decorations were erected for the great festivals such as the Saturnalia, when class distinctions were suspended, and streets vibrated with revelry.

The residences of the patricians were elaborately planned, with rooms for every purpose and arcaded courtyards containing gushing fountains that centuries later were imitated in ecclesiastical *cloisters* and college quadrangles. Interiors were enriched with marble incrustations, statuettes, floors of colored mosaic, frescoed walls, and expensive furnishings that were the inspiration of Donatello and Raphael. Many of the houses had roof gardens. Terrariums, aquariums, and flower boxes were frequently featured. The details of decoration contributed to the real or suggested tempering of climatic conditions. Cool water was carried by lead pipes to elaborate baths, pools, and drinking taps. Heat was obtained by portable charcoal-burning braziers.

The architecture of a civilization such as Rome produced could not fail to be powerful, magnificent, and ostentatious. Grandeur and boldness were the most characteristic esthetic expressions of the public buildings, sublimity that of the city of Rome itself. Domestic interiors reflected wealth if not always refinement of design and at times had both charm and spiritual mood. The Romans were admittedly cultural upstarts. They believed that all education began with imitation, but that eventually a native stamp would be impressed upon their creative efforts. To administer the heterogeneous population of the Empire, they built with haste and seldom needed or understood subtleties of design in either composition or detail. Bulk, surface enrichment, and rarity of material served them to better advantage in arousing prideful emotions and a sense of security in their untutored subjects. Their art admirably reflected their virtues and faults.

Roman construction and the arch. The Roman builders adopted the principles of Greek construction in using the column, lintel, and truss. In addition, they developed the arch built of radiating wedge-shaped stones, a feature that became an indigenous part of their architecture and greatly affected both external and internal design. From the arch, the Romans evolved the barrel vault or curved ceiling, and the *dome*. This method of spanning the distance between two walls with a fireproof material permitted wider rooms than either the Greeks or Egyptians were able to construct. The span of the dome of the Pantheon is 142 feet and the arched concrete ceiling in the Baths of Caracalla spanned a distance of 80 feet. Arch forms were limited to semicircular and segmental curves. The arch was also used for decorative purposes in doorways, windows, arcades, and niches. Its use served to introduce a variety of line in Roman design that did not exist in earlier styles.

The structural problem in the stone arch lay in the fact that the thrust of its weight gravitated both downward and sideways. A supporting wall had to be of sufficient thickness to resist the side thrust, or the lower parts of the arch itself had to be tied together unprepossessingly by iron rods. It was nearly a thousand years before builders learned the secret of supporting an arched ceiling on slender uprights.

Interior of the Pantheon, in Rome, built by Emperor Hadrian (A.D. *2nd and 3rd centuries). The building is circular in plan and has a domed roof. The interior is treated with the Roman Corinthian order. Notice the arched forms, columns and pilasters, and rectangular niches treated with triangular pediments.*

The use of concrete. Another important structural development in Roman design that completely differentiates it from earlier styles was the use of concrete. This inexpensive and strong material was made by a mixture of small stones, sand, lime, and water that was poured into a wooden form, becoming a solid mass (*monolithic*) when dry. As concrete was considered unpretentious and unsuitable for finished effects, its surface was covered with slabs of marble, alabaster, brick, or stucco, which veneers also served as a protection. Thus Roman walls were less honest esthetically than Greek walls that were built of marble throughout. Concrete was used mainly where downward pressure was the principal force, such as in walls, arches, and domes. There is no evidence that Roman engineers knew of the principles of modern methods of reinforcement of concrete by iron rods, so that the material was never used for beams that were subjected to a bending stress. *Cantilever* beams and projections, so much a part of modern design, were unknown.

Vitruvius and the standard proportions of the Roman orders. The lack of highly trained designers and the necessity for speed in the construction of the various administrative buildings throughout the colonies necessitated a method of facilitating the work of the local builders and stonecutters who lacked esthetic feeling. During the administration of Augustus, an architect named Vitruvius established certain rules for standardizing the Greek orders of architecture. The proportions and details were slightly changed from the originals, and practically all the Roman buildings were afterward designed on Vitruvian principles. In the 15th century, the Italian

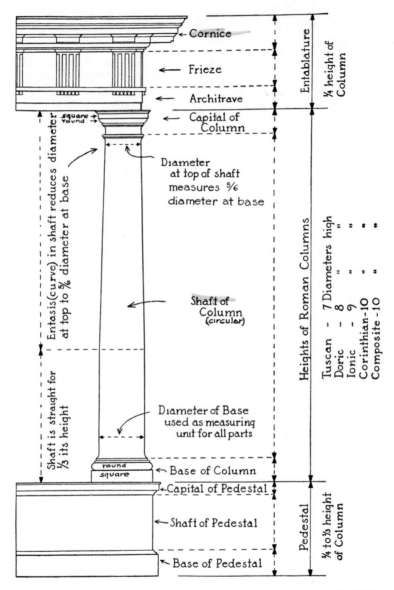

THE ROMAN DORIC ORDER AND ITS PARTS AS STANDARDIZED BY VITRUVIUS.

Roman Corinthian capital, looking upwards. Temple of Mars, Rome. Drawing by D'Espouy.

architects rediscovered these rules, translated the works of Vitruvius, and they form the basis of all the Renaissance styles of western Europe.

The Romans added two orders to the Greek Doric, Ionic, and Corinthian. These were the *Tuscan,* a simplified Doric form which was originally of Etruscan origin and had no flutings on the shaft of the column, and the *Composite,* a combination order, having for the design of its capital the two rows of acanthus leaves of the Corinthian, and the large volutes of the Ionic.

The Doric order was not extensively used by the Romans. They slenderized the proportions of the column, added additional moldings to the capital, and used a base. Occasionally the flutings were omitted.

In the Ionic order, the volutes of the Roman capital are smaller than the Greek, and the ornament on the necking below the volutes is omitted. The Romans also sometimes repeated the volutes on four sides of the capital instead of two.

The Corinthian order, little used by the Greeks until the Hellenistic period, was the most commonly used in Roman buildings. It was always richly treated with ornament. The Roman capital is slightly smaller than the Greek and the character of the acanthus leaves differs.

The Romans introduced the pedestal as a feature of exterior architectural design and later used it as a feature in room interiors. This consisted of a high base upon which the column could stand. It was the Roman development of the Greek stylobate. The height of the pedestal was about one-fourth or one-third the height of the column. It was treated with moldings at the top and a projecting block at the bottom. It became the prototype for the dado and wainscot of later periods of interior design. The Romans introduced the pilaster, which has a square rather than a round shaft, is always attached to the wall, and usually projects from the wall a dimension that is about one-fourth of its width. As the pilaster was a part of the wall, it had little structural value. Its use was primarily decorative and intended to break the wall surface into vertical subdivisions that could be treated as individual panels.

The principles of proportioning the orders based on the rules of Vitruvius were as follows: A measuring unit called a *module* was to be taken for each order; this unit was the *diameter* of the column at the base of the shaft.* By deciding first upon this measurement, the height of the

* In some cases the measuring unit was taken as half the diameter.

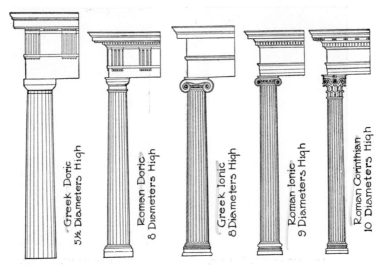

Comparative plate of Greek and Roman orders, showing the entablature heights for each and the increase in delicacy of proportion from the Greek Doric to the Roman Corinthian.

column and entablature became a fixed size, measured in diameters. On this basis the following proportions were fixed:

Column	Height in Diameters
Tuscan	7
Doric	8
Ionic	9
Corinthian	10
Composite	10

The entablature in each case was one-fourth the height of the column. The shaft was one-sixth smaller in diameter at its top than at its base. Standard designs were arranged for column bases and capitals. A fixed number of flutes was designated for the shafts. The form and the sequence of moldings used in the entablature were settled upon. The Greek forms of ornament were used and, in addition, arabesques, rinceaux, *grotesques,* dolphins, griffins, wreaths, ribbons, eagles, masks, swans, lions, and other animal forms were introduced.

The majority of the Roman buildings remaining today were originally monumental structures for public use. The domestic architecture and decoration of the Romans of the first century after Christ can best be studied in the ruins of Pompeii.

Roman sculpture. Sculpture both in bas-relief and free standing figures was first inspired by Etruscan art. Etruria, believed to have been settled by

ARCHAIC GREEK. 600 B.C.   PERICLEAN. 450 B.C.

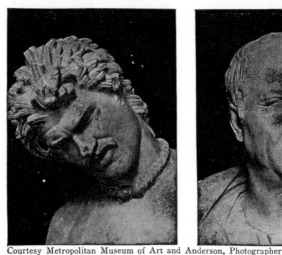 

Courtesy Metropolitan Museum of Art and Anderson, Photographer

HELLENISTIC. 350 B.C.   ROMAN. 50 B.C. (CICERO)

Comparison and development of Greek and Roman sculpture from conventionalization to realism.

immigrants from Asia Minor, became a Roman province in 283 B.C. Its culture had been strongly influenced from an early period by trade with Greece. About 150 B.C. the Romans commenced a methodical pillage of Greek buildings and statues were imported to adorn the villas and gardens of Roman patricians. When a sufficient number of examples were not available, the Greek sculpture was copied by both Roman sculptors and

Greeks who came to Italy for that purpose, and the major portion of Roman examples are of this type. About A.D. 100 during the reign of Trajan, there developed a school of portraiture in which all conventional imitation was eliminated and lifelike representations of Roman leaders were made in which every detail and facial blemish was indicated. This style disappeared with the fall of the Empire in the 5th century and such realism in sculpture did not reappear until the end of the Gothic period.

Roman ornament. Roman ornament was based almost entirely upon the Greek forms, although certain motifs, used more profusely than others, varied slightly in character from the Grecian interpretations. The scroll and leaf patterns were extensively used as both rinceaux and arabesques. The acanthus leaf became slightly more conventionalized, more solid in appearance, and less foliated. Human figures and *amorini* shown both in repose and in action were profusely applied to architectural surfaces, panels, and ornamental accessories. Natural forms, such as the serpent, swan, eagle, lion, and ox, or portions of these animals also were used. Imaginary forms such as sphinxes, griffins, genii, and grotesques formed parts of decorative compositions, and their torsos often protruded from a base of acanthus petals.

Carved stone arabesque found in the Roman Forum. The left edge is obviously the center of the pattern.

Floral and leaf arrangements, composed as wreaths, festoons, and garlands, were also used, and the Greek fret, swastika, honeysuckle, anthemion, spiral, wave pattern, waterleaf, egg-and-dart, bead, and *dentil* continued as characteristic decorative forms for moldings, borders, or panels.

These forms of ornament were used in all mediums. They were cut in stone, cast in bronze, and formed portions of the painted decoration, their character or degree of delicacy slightly changed to suit the material. The Romans also developed the technique of casting stucco or plaster composition into these same patterns and applying the motifs to stucco surfaces. This comparatively inexpensive method of enrichment was studied by the Adam brothers and extensively used by them in English 18th century decoration.

Unable to attain the Greek beauty of line and form, the Romans depended upon the use of ornament to give richness of effect in their buildings. Limestone and stucco did not permit as much delicacy of cutting as marble, so that the Roman relief ornament is usually finished in comparatively coarse detail.

The Roman moldings are coarser than the Greek and lack the refined mathematical curvature; they are profiled as single or compound segments of circles and are given interest by the addition of such ornaments as the egg-and-dart, waterleaf, or acanthus leaf.

Pompeian domestic architecture. The city of Pompeii which was completely covered with ashes by an eruption of Mount Vesuvius in A.D. 79, was a small Greco-Roman town in the southern part of Italy, near Naples. The ruins have been excavated since the year 1753, and at the present time about one-third of the city stands much as it was left twenty centuries ago.

Pompeii was a summer resort for wealthy Romans, intended for amusement, recreation, and pleasure. It had its forum and residential streets, but there were buildings erected for games of chance, cockfights, theatres, baths, restaurants, night clubs, pawnshops, and an amphitheatre for gladiatorial fights.

The exteriors of Pompeian houses lacked the splendor that was dominant in the public architecture of Rome. For the most part, the buildings were plain and finished with cheap stucco. The fronts were built directly on the streets and were frequently flanked with small shops. Because of the hot climate, the rooms were constructed without windows and were lighted solely by doors opening on a central courtyard.

The houses were usually two stories high, having an entrance hall opening on the street and extending back, much like a modern foyer, into the *atrium,* a roofed courtyard. The center of this roof was pierced by an opening that permitted daylight to enter. Directly under the opening was usually located a small pool or basin that caught the rain water and served both as a cooling and decorative feature. The atrium also served as the reception room for guests. It was surrounded by small rooms and by stalls for animals. From the atrium an opening led to the *peristyle* or rear court garden where the private life of the family was centered. Bedrooms, the *triclinium* (dining room), and rooms for the family were grouped around the peristyle. The kitchen and pantry were located near by, and a garden extended beyond the peristyle. Servants lived in separate quarters.

The interior of the house was elaborately decorated. Patterned mosaics in either black and white or colored marbles covered the floor. The ceilings were painted in various geometrical patterns or intertwining floral and leaf patterns, often accented with perched or flying birds. Sometimes gilded timbers or panels were used. Since the wall space was usually unbroken by windows, it was commonly painted in an ordered arrangement of architectural and decorative forms in which a relief effect was produced by a careful rendering of highlights, half-tones, and shadows. Usually the walls were divided into three horizontal sections—the lower section being treated as a pedestal or dado, the high middle section reserved for decorative paintings, and the top painted with a frieze or cornice.

Pompeian wall decoration. The eruption of Vesuvius has preserved for nearly two thousand years wall decorations of the Roman period and has enabled us to study the genius for realism of the Pompeian artists. Practically all rooms were treated with painted architectural decorations, explained perhaps by the fact that painting was a comparatively inexpensive and safe method of adding architectural interest to the interior of dwellings that were subject to frequent earthquake damage.

The main area of the walls was divided vertically into panels by painted columns or pilasters, crowned with entablatures realistically represented in perspective, and the panels thus formed were filled with decorative frescoes. The painted architectural features were often reduced to the most delicate and slender proportions, showing that the painter understood the possibilities of his medium, which was not subject to structural limitations. The panel centers were treated in one of three ways; they were either a plain color framed with painted moldings, or enclosed an arabesque or scenic pattern.

In plain panel areas, the color was generally a yellowish-red or black. The moldings on four sides formed a rectangular frame realistically painted with natural highlight, shade, and shadow effect, with the light indicated as coming from the door of the room. Sometimes a small figure or other motif was placed in the center of the panel or a picture was painted as though hung on the wall, with the frame and the shadow realistically indicated. The panels in the pedestal or dado often imitated marble slabs or a balcony balustrade.

Where conventional arabesque patterns were used, they were sometimes combined with naturalistic climbing ivy or leaf forms that spiralled around the slender columns and continued upward forming part of the ceiling decoration.

By far the most interesting of the Pompeian mural decorations were those showing scenic effects in which the subject matter was drawn from an infinite number of sources. Mythology, allegory, history, landscape, *still life,* humor, city streets, portraiture, and animals were charmingly depicted. Playful nymphs and satyrs were shown in woodland settings. The draperies of a dancing girl would so accurately indicate the movement of her body that one could almost feel the rhythm of the dance. A forest grove would spiritually transport a city-dweller to a verdant retreat. A painted view through an imaginary open window would lead the eye down a shady path by waterfalls or splashing fountains, and serve to enlarge the appearance of the room as well as beguile the occupant. Members of the family were often shown seated in chairs, giving us a record of the

Pompeian painted interior. Notice the use of the dado, the slender proportions of the columns, the painted entablature, the appearance of relief produced by painted shadows, and the painted representations of windows showing distant views, which add to the effect of spaciousness in the room.

wooden furniture, costumes, and hairdresses. Shops, taverns, and other business houses were decorated with subjects appropriate to their activities. The barber, butcher, shoemaker, and fortuneteller had special symbols depicting their talents and wares. Some of the murals give striking proof of the indelicacy of ancient manners.

The drawing and coloring of figures and animals were technically excellent, but the mathematical principles of perspective were not understood, and such representations were inaccurately made. The chief charm in the murals lies in the variety and gaiety of spirit of the subject matter, which is of a character and sufficiently well preserved to arouse the emotions of modern men. The colors were comparatively brilliant, as necessary in rooms having only a dim light. The medium was true fresco, the pigments being applied to and absorbed by the wet plaster; when dried, the surface was waxed and polished for protective purposes. Backgrounds were most commonly in black, white, or red, but other colors were also used.

Mosaics and inscriptions. Because of its permanency, *mosaic* was frequently used for both wall panels and floor decoration. Patterns and pictures were made of small cubes of glass or marble set in cement, often so carefully composed that, viewed from a distance, the finished mosaic re-

A remarkably fine example of a Roman decorative panel in mosaic.

sembled a painting. The panels were usually framed with a geometrical
or floral design. The usual patterns for wall panels show birds and animals
or groupings of masks, heads, garlands, and wreaths. Alert pigeons drink
from a bowl, parrots strut, ducks waddle, and cocks lower their heads in
preparation for the fight. Wit and humor are sometimes expressed in both
subject matter and titles. The field of floor mosaics was generally treated
with a repeating motif, although one of the most magnificent examples
ever made, which covered a floor in a Pompeian villa, shows a battle scene
between Alexander and Darius. The mosaic of a barking dog on a vestibule
floor is combined with the inscription, "Beware of the dog." A justifiable
criticism of the Roman floor mosaics has often been made claiming that
the patterns contrast too strongly with their backgrounds and frequently
appear to project from the floor. The designs often intentionally accentuate
the highlight and shadow values, causing one unwittingly to fear to fall
or stub one's toe. Motifs used in a floor pattern should be flat and unobtrusive, but this principle was apparently considered unimportant to
the Roman mosaic designer who in an unethical approach, imitated the
painter and sculptor as closely as possible. In addition to the titles associated
with mosaics, there are many interesting inscriptions scratched on the walls
of Pompeian buildings. Although these are not directly connected with

The Styles of Antiquity 65

Mosaic from Antioch about A.D. *100 similar to those in Pompeii.*

the decorative arts, they give an excellent insight into the character and daily life of the inhabitants. In one case someone slyly tells his enemy to "go hang yourself." What political oratory is joined with such modern-appearing words as "Elect Marcellinus"? One can easily surmise the associated incidents in reading "Romula trysted here with Stephylus," or when a youth expressed his feelings with "Cestilia, queen of the Pompeians, sweet soul, greetings to you." On a Pompeian wall originated the often quoted jingle, "Fools' names, like their faces, are always seen in public places."

Pompeian furniture. Furniture in the Pompeian rooms was sparse and limited to essentials, an esthetic necessity when walls were so elaborately treated. Each piece was a work of art—made by the hands of an experienced craftsman and intended to be a pride of the owner. Many of the objects were of Greek or Alexandrian origin, showing an early appreciation of antiques. Furniture was made in wood, marble, bronze, iron, and precious metals, enriched with carving or relief ornament, such as arabesques, grotesques, animal features, griffins, and foliage, or inlaid with mosaic, tortoise-shell, ivory, and rare woods. Wooden supports were sometimes treated with disk-turnings resembling a series of unevenly piled platters; metal supports often imitated the wooden ones of this type, resulting in an esthetic falsity. Bronze and marble supports were frequently designed as dog's, lion's, or ram's legs and feet.

The most elaborate rooms were the dining rooms or tricliniums, so called because they contained three couches, each for three people placed on three sides of a central table. The men dined in a reclining position, the women sat on chairs. The couches were covered with tapestries and cushions made in Egypt or Babylon and embroidered in gold and silver thread. The main table was low to accommodate the recumbent guests, and additional small individual tables were used for sumptuous tableware. The table tops were made of richly grained *thuya wood,* a rare wood from Africa. On festive occasions, floors were strewn with flowers or covered with cedar sawdust mixed with saffron and cinnabar.

The bedroom was divided by curtains into three parts, one being a section for the attendant, another for dressing, and another for the sleeping quarters. The bed, made of wood or metal, was the only article of furniture and was stretched with ropes or metal strips supporting a straw or wool mattress covered with silk cushions and costly Oriental textiles. The drawing room or *exedra* was furnished only with tables and chairs.

Alinari

Carved support of a marble table found in Pompeii.

Chairs were made in many types. The design of benches, folding stools, side chairs, armchairs, and thrones usually included the use of Greek curves. Seats and backs were shaped to fit the human body.

The lighting of rooms was extremely inadequate compared to modern standards, but much thought was placed upon the design of lamps, torches, and candelabra. These were made in metal and terra cotta and enriched with low-relief ornament or colored glass. The lamps had only one small wick. The candelabra, holding several lights, were often designed as a column, human figure, or decorated shaft standing on a pedestal or supported by a tripod in the form of animal legs.

Room accessories. Some of the minor crafts were developed to a high point of perfection. This was particularly true of glassware. The Romans created types and finishes that have never been duplicated. The most famous was a fragile opalescent ware known as *murrhine* used to fashion ornamental vases and drinking cups. The *Portland vase,* for which $150,000 has been refused by the owner, is now in the British Museum. It was a blue-black glass upon which were superimposed opaque white figures having the effect of a cameo, a process of manufacturing which is unknown today. Much of the ornamental glassware came from Alexandria where it was first made. Bowls, cups, bottles, and cosmetic containers were made of colored blown glass and by fusing strips of different colors, creating such beautiful finishes that the specimens became collectors' hobbies and vast sums were offered for unusual examples.

Mirrors were of polished bronze or silver, made in small sizes for hand use or to hang on the wall. Large-sized mirrors were set on casters to be easily moved about.

Dining services were made of gold, silver, and a red glazed pottery, Earthenware and terra cotta were used for the production of small household ornaments designed in the form of human, animal, and bird statuettes. In the Museum at Naples can be seen pens and inkstands, kitchen utensils, musical instruments, and toilet articles.

The influence of Pompeian art on later civilizations. When in the middle of the 18th century, Italian, French, and English excavators discovered the ruins of Pompeii, hosts of artists and designers immediately went to Naples to study the domestic arts of the ancient Roman city. The forms and patterns found there were transmitted to Paris and London and strongly influenced the design of the productions in practically every art industry. The influence of the Pompeian decorative details upon other European arts during the 18th century is of major importance. Since the Pompeian artist was mainly called upon to produce the effect of three-dimensional forms of decoration by the use of two dimensions only, he wisely took advantage of his opportunity and permitted fantasy to dominate his imagination. The designer in heavy materials necessarily rejected the use of delicate proportions; but after the discoveries at Pompeii became common knowledge, both the architecture and the decoration of Europe showed a more distinct tendency toward lightness of line, in contrast with the earlier classic forms that had received their interpretation through the eyes of the Italian Renaissance designers.

Bibliography

BREASTED, J. H., *A History of Egypt from the Earliest Times to the Persian Conquest.* Charles Scribner's Sons, New York, 1909. An illustrated history of Egypt.

BUHLMAN, J., *Classic and Renaissance Architecture.* Wm. Helburn, Inc., New York. Reprint. Brief text with scaled drawings. Excellent for tracing.

DURANT, W., *The Story of Civilization.* Simon and Schuster, Inc., New York; 3 vols., *Our Oriental Heritage, The Life of Greece, Caesar and Christ,* 1939 *et seq.* An excellent description of all aspects of these periods.

ESQUIÉ, P., *The Five Orders of Architecture.* Wm. Helburn, Inc., New York. Scaled drawings based on the system of Vignola.

GUSMAN, P., *La Décoration Murale à Pompei.* Éditions Albert Morancé, Paris, 1924. Excellent color reproductions of Pompeian murals.

KROEBER, A. L., *Anthropology.* Harcourt, Brace and Co., 1923, New York. An excellent text thoroughly covering this subject from all points of view.

MAU, A., *Pompeii: Its Life and Art* (tr. Kelsey). The Macmillan Co., New York, 1902. Illustrated text. Standard authority.

RICHTER, G., *Ancient Furniture.* Oxford University Press, New York, 1926. An excellent treatment of furniture, with illustrations.

RICHTER, G., *Handbook of the Classical Collection.* Metropolitan Museum of Art, New York, 1933. Enlarged edition. A brief summary of the development of Greek art as shown in the classical rooms of the Metropolitan Museum of Art.

ZERVOS, C., *L'art en Grèce,* Paris, 1934. Beautiful photographs of Grecian buildings and statuary.

CHAPTER II

THE STYLES OF THE MIDDLE AGES

T he arts of Europe between the 4th and the 15th centuries after Christ, though distantly related to those of modern times, were of great brilliance and interest. The thousand years frequently referred to as the "Dark Ages" produced forms of architecture and decoration that were the fervent expression of the souls of the faithful at a time when political order was at its lowest ebb. Misery existed in all branches of human existence and there was little to live for but the hope of peace and happiness in the hereafter. The masses were fed the incomprehensible, magical, mysterious, and invisible. Such logic that existed was limited to the clerics. Probably no period of art history has been more expressive of the contemporary character of its people.

The Middle Ages were years of magnificent architectural development. Architecture so dominated the minds of the artists and craftsmen of the lesser arts that its forms were copied and applied to the limit of their possibilities. The weaver, wood carver, carpenter, painter, metalworker, book illuminator, and hosts of others borrowed the structural and ornamental forms of buildings and adapted them to their own particular mediums.

Since religion was the dominant interest of Europe, architecture consisted primarily of church construction. Secular and domestic building was given little attention until toward the end of the period. It becomes necessary, therefore, to examine the historical, social, and political events of this period which were responsible for the remarkable impetus in the construction of cathedrals and other ecclesiastical buildings in nearly every city and town of Europe.

The main divisions of the arts of the Middle Ages are:

1. BYZANTINE (330–1453).
   The style developed in Constantinople from the time when it became the capital of the Eastern Roman Empire until its capture by the Turks. The

style is characterized as a fusion between a debased Roman art and Oriental forms. Domed ceilings are typical.

2. EARLY CHRISTIAN (330–800).

The style developed in central Italy and to some extent in other countries bordering the eastern Mediterranean. Churches were built on the basilica plan from stones taken from the ruins of pagan temples. Flat ceilings.

3. ROMANESQUE AND NORMAN (800–1150).

These styles developed in France and other Western countries, respectively. They were characterized by simple, vigorous structural forms with semicircular arched openings used for doors, windows, and ornamental forms. Vaulted ceilings.

4. GOTHIC (1150–1500).

The style originated in France and spread over the whole of western Europe. It was an outgrowth and elaboration of the Romanesque, characterized by the use of the pointed arch, *buttress, tracery,* and large windows, with a corresponding reduction in wall areas. Pointed, arched ceilings supported by ribs carried down to slender clustered column supports. Structure dominated by balancing *thrust* and *counter thrust.* Dominance of the vertical line. Oak used for woodwork and furniture. Furniture designs borrowed from architectural forms.

Introduction of Christianity in the Roman Empire. In the 2nd century of the Christian Era, important events developed in Rome that were eventually to shake the foundations of the Empire. The Roman legions had suffered defeats that weakened the confidence of the people in their existing government. Insurrections, civil wars, and murders of emperors were frequent occurrences. The examples of moral degradation and dishonesty set by the patricians, who endeavored to forget their waning glories in riotous living, were imitated by the middle and lower classes. The pious philosophy of the Christian religion, which had first appealed to the oppressed groups in the Roman provinces of Asia Minor, had been accepted by the lower classes in Rome, whose prayers to the pagan gods had remained unanswered, and who willingly grasped at the simple beliefs and hopes offered by the early Christians.

The teachings of Christ came to the civilized world when they were most needed. The twilight of the power of force and terrorism was to fade before the dawn of the power of humility. The Christians, who were considered the radicals of the period, were in severe conflict with the government of Rome during the first three centuries of our era, and were forced to use the stone quarries of Rome, known as the *catacombs,* as places of refuge, worship, and burial. On the walls of the catacombs still can be seen the sculptured and painted decorations which consist of early Christian symbols and portraits of the early saints and martyrs.

The Roman Empire split into two parts. By the beginning of the 4th century the Christians had become a sufficiently powerful political party to obtain representation in the Roman senate, and the conflict between the Christians and the followers of pagan beliefs was finally brought to a crisis when Constantine the Great came to the throne, in A.D. 323.

Constantine permitted the Christians to worship without molestation, and later he himself adopted Christianity, on gaining a military victory in answer to his prayers to the Christian God. He felt, however, that it was impossible to follow his beliefs in peace within the precincts of Rome, which was still the hotbed of the pagan party. On his visits and conquests in the outlying districts of the Empire he had had ample opportunity to observe the great beauty and the incomparable position of the city of Byzantium, guarded by nature against hostile attack, and accessible to commercial intercourse. Like Alexander the Great, Constantine was not insensible to the ambition to found a city that would glorify and perpetuate his name. He decided to leave the confusion at Rome in the hands of a local governor, while he and his followers removed to the banks of the Bosporus. In the year 330 he changed the name of the provincial city to Constantinople and officially proclaimed it the capital of the Eastern or Byzantine Empire.

The wisdom of Constantine was confirmed by the turmoil that con tinued in Rome during the next century and a half. Rome, repeatedly in vaded by "barbarians" from the North, finally fell in 476; Odoacer, a barbarian from the North, proclaimed himself king of Italy, thereby officially extinguishing the Roman Empire of the West.

During the next five centuries western Europe was in the throes of establishing the racial leaderships which eventually culminated in the nations of today.

The Byzantine Period

Among the followers of Constantine were many leaders of Roman and Greek culture and all types of craftsmen who had been trained in the best classical traditions. As generation succeeded generation, time and distance served to lessen the Roman influence. The new capital became a melting pot for an infinite number of diverse races. Its wealth increased rapidly. The population became lazy, profligate, vicious, and unco-operative, and required a strong-handed leadership that created fear in the hearts of the people and demanded an intense loyalty to the church organization with which the state was synonymous. In spite of these conditions, the Imperial court functioned for over a thousand years and preserved the culture of the ancients while the whole of western Europe was in a state of chaos. The Eastern Church developed doctrinal differences with the Church of

Rome, some of which greatly affected the character of ecclesiastical decoration. The iconoclastic movement of the 8th century forbade the representation in sculpture of all human or animal forms, believing that it savored too much of idolatry and was a violation of the second commandment concerning "graven images." This also eventually culminated in the split between the Roman and Greek Orthodox churches. Roman cultural elements became adulterated with infiltrations from Persia and Arabia. From the fusion of debased Roman art forms with those of the Orient, both affected by Christian doctrine, sprang the culture, splendor, and the magnificent arts of the Byzantine or Eastern Empire.

The brilliance and ostentatiousness of the interiors of Byzantine churches contrast strongly with the severe and simple treatment of the buildings of the corresponding period in western Europe. Each type reflected the intellectual level and respective wealth of the people who built them. While the Eastern Empire was experiencing its most opulent period, France and England were buried in despair and poverty, and lacked the courage or desire to protest until the return of the Crusaders.

Little remains of the domestic architecture of the period. The Byzantine style is primarily important and interesting due to developments in construction methods and the richness of the interior decoration of the first and oldest Christian church, Hagia Sophia in Constantinople. The beauty, magnificence, and color of the interior of this structure overwhelmed the Crusaders, who viewed it with awe and astonishment; the splendor of its ritual was never equalled in the West.

Structural character and pendentives of Hagia Sophia. Constantine the Great in the year 360 built a church on the basilica plan, which after a fire was rebuilt by Theodosius III in 415. The present building was erected by Justinian in 532. It was called at first Hagia Sophia, meaning Divine Wisdom, later St. Sophia. Upon the capture of Constantinople by the Turks in 1453 it became a mosque, and after World War I was made a public museum.

The plan of the church is in the form of a *Greek cross* and it is roofed by a series of domes and half domes, features that since have become characteristic of Near-Eastern Moslem architecture. The intersection of the cross is crowned by a great brick dome 107 feet in diameter, the outward thrust of which is counteracted on two sides by two half-domes of the same diameter leaning against the lower portion and by two enormous buttresses on the other two sides. The Romans were accustomed to building domes on circular structures, but in Hagia Sophia the dome is supported at the square intersection by four heavy piers, one at each corner. This square substructure, intended to support a circular dome, presented a new problem in architectural construction. It was solved by the Byzantine engineers, who by a fantastic feat created an entirely new architectural form

Interior of Hagia Sophia, Istanbul, showing the triangular pendentives support-ing the great central dome.

known as a *pendentive*. A pendentive is a concave triangular stone surface that starts at a point on the corner of a pier, rises and spreads out to the two upper points of the triangle in a concave-curved fanlike shape until it approaches a horizontal and meets the circle of the lowest part of the dome, which the masonry of the pendentive supports. Each pendentive supports one quarter of the dome. Considering the enormous size, weight, and thrust of the dome, this form of support was a miracle in stonecutting. In Hagia Sophia each pendentive rises 60 feet and curves forward 25 feet. This structural principle was later used by the Renaissance architects and is a feature of St. Peter's in Rome.

The interior architectural features of Hagia Sophia. The standard pro-portions of the architectural orders established by Vitruvius had been dis-regarded by the time Hagia Sophia was built. Columns were made in a variety of proportions, the entasis on the shaft was omitted and the capi-tals became crude interpretations of Corinthian forms with clumsily carved acanthus leaves and volutes, or they were carved with a lacelike ornament of Eastern origin. A few of the columns are of green jasper and *porphyry* taken from Roman temples. Moldings and entablatures were omitted. The semicircular arch was used exclusively and extensively for both struc-tural and decorative purposes in windows and openings. Where rows of columns were used as a substitute for the lintel, a semicircular arch sprang

The Styles of the Middle Ages 73

from each column. The ratio between the height of the arch and its width varied greatly.

The wall treatment and mosaics of Hagia Sophia. Due to the ecclesiastical dogma forbidding the use of sculptured forms in decoration, the art of the mosaic worker reached its apex in Hagia Sophia, the interior of which is one of indescribable color. Every inch of wall surface is covered with colored glass mosaic set in a sparkling golden background, or by exotic marble slabs arranged so that the graining shows a pattern arrangement. The small windows admit the slanting sun rays which pierce the atmosphere and produce a mysterious and reverential effect. The purpose of such splendor was to impress the worshipper with the power and magnificence of his Church and State and cause him to forget his own afflictions while contemplating a heaven on earth.

The four pendentives were decorated with representations of the Archangels, and the figure of Christ can still be seen above the *apse*. Other patterns show biblical scenes, saints, historical personages, or symbolic figures such as the peacock, which stood for immortality, the endless knot representing eternity, and the monogram of Christ. The dust and smoke of ages has laid a filmy surface over the lustrous colors, softly blending them into complete harmony. Borders, frames, and band courses were sometimes made in brickwork set diagonally or in herringbone patterns. The acanthus leaf and other small decorative motifs are occasionally shown in incised carvings rather than in relief. The windows are sometimes filled with thin slabs of translucent colored marble through which the sun glows, giving them the effect of stained glass.

Many of the Christian mosaics were covered with stucco after the Turks captured Constantinople, but some of these have recently been uncovered revealing extraordinary examples of the surface decoration of the 8th and 10th centuries.

The minor arts. The inhabitants of the Byzantine Empire were more concerned with abstract questions of theology than with artistic triumphs. Early Church history is filled with the discussions that eventually established the dogmas, doctrines, and tenets of Christian organizations. In Constantinople, the Church and State were one, and the Church drew within its folds the artists and craftsmen as well as the philosophers and leaders. There were practically no secular arts, but within the walls of the monasteries minor arts were lavishly produced. From the 10th to the 12th centuries exquisite religious *cloisonné* and *champlevé enamelware,* ivory carvings, brass utensils, and textiles were made. Many monks spent their lives working on richly illuminated manuscripts. The expenditure of effort and labor was of no consideration so long as it resulted in a perfect object of lasting beauty which would contribute to the glory of the Church.

After the capture of Constantinople, many of the Eastern monks resorted to caves and sheltered rocks in inaccessible places, became hermits, and spent their lives in poverty, inaction, prayer, and meditation. The location of many of the original hermitages are still known; they often commanded magnificent views midst a paradise of beauty. Though little furniture was used, the occupants had their personal altars, kitchen gardens, and rock-cut wells, and for companionship they treasured their dogs and grazed their cattle. Their asceticism was largely mental, as they had the material necessities of life, and their hardships were mitigated by an ardor that produced exhilaration. This was in strong contrast to the monks of the Western Church, the majority of whom felt their duty was to spread the teachings of Christianity and to improve the conditions of the illiterate and downtrodden peasants of Europe by living among them.

The influence of the Byzantine arts. Byzantine art is reflected in the styles of modern Greece, Russia, and other countries where the Greek Orthodox Church has been the dominant religious organization. The influence of Byzantium was also felt in the Gothic arts of France and England, after the return of the Crusaders who had observed the Oriental magnificence and superior civilization of the East.

The Byzantine Empire continued until the year 1453, when Sultan Mohammed II captured and pillaged Constantinople and made it the capital of the Turkish Empire. The fall of Constantinople, its control by the Turks, and the difficulty, thereafter, of trading with the Orient was the greatest contributing factor in the decision of Columbus to find a new route to the East. The capture of Constantinople, therefore, became one of the most important events in the history of the world. It closed the long period of Byzantine culture; the crescent supplanted the cross and Christian churches became Mohammedan mosques.

The Byzantine coins had been stamped with a design of a crescent, symbolizing the shape of the harbor of Constantinople which was known as the Golden Horn. After the fall of Constantinople, the Turks adopted this symbol as their national emblem, and it was frequently used as an ornamental motif in textiles, rugs, and other patterned designs.

Examples of Byzantine architecture and decoration. The Byzantine style extended to the portion of Europe that came under the control of the Eastern Emperors. Examples are found in Greece and Asia Minor. San Vitale was erected in Ravenna in 547, but the most interesting Western example is St. Mark's in Venice, erected in 1071 and known to every tourist. St. Mark's is a Roman Catholic cathedral built in the form of a Greek Cross, roofed with five domes supported on pendentives. The exterior and interior is covered with brilliantly colored mosaics. The building is situated on the great Piazza of San Marco with a background of the deep Venetian sky and the glistening waves of the blue Adriatic. Its domes are crowned in gold and its façade sparkles in the brilliant sunshine. The arches forming its portals support the great horses taken from Nero's triumphal arch.

The Russian churches were the inheritors of the style and show in their general design and detail much that is of Byzantine origin.

The Early Christian Period

The term "Early Christian" refers to the style of art that existed principally in Rome and neighboring towns after the official adoption of the Christian religion by the people of the Roman Empire.

In the year 330 Constantine ordered that the heathen temples in Rome be destroyed and Christian churches be built in their place. In the wave of religious enthusiasm following this command, haste was important, and no stone quarries were more convenient than the ruined temples of the gods of classic mythology. The splendid columns, capitals, moldings, and other stones, many of which had been imported from distant lands, were reassembled to play their parts in the erection of the new churches built in a plan resembling the Christian cross. This type of building was called a basilica. It resembled the Roman building of this form. The astonishing feature of these Early Christian churches was that a reassemblage of architectural fragments originally designed for other buildings should produce such remarkable results.

With the growth of Christian organization came the gradual loss of faith in civic control, law, and order, and the almost complete disintegration of national spirit. It was inevitable that under such conditions the craftsmen should also disregard established traditions of art. Teachers were no longer at hand to instruct in the old way, nor were they even desired. Not many generations were to pass before a new art would be in the making and new traditions established.

The "barbarians" who had overrun and sacked Rome had been sufficiently awed by the merits of Christianity to refrain from invading the precincts of the Christian Church. The Romans, realizing this fact, transferred much of their wealth and many of their most valuable belongings to the religious orders. The Church drew within its gates many of the descendants of the old patrician families, who sought the protection of its robe and veil. Thus was established some of the early wealth of the Roman Church, which was later used to build, decorate, and furnish some of the most elaborate buildings ever constructed.

The character of the Early Christian basilicas. In the rearrangement of the stones and ornamental details taken from Roman buildings for use in the construction of the early basilicas, columns were frequently used without entablatures. Semicircular arched forms were featured in the construction, and, as in the Byzantine style, arches frequently rose directly from the capitals without intervening moldings. The walls of Early Christian churches were straight, rose to a considerable height, were pierced with windows at the top, and supported an elaborate horizontal wood-panelled ceiling. In the decoration of the walls, mosaics, paintings, and marble incrustations produced brilliant and colorful surfaces. The growing wealth of the Church and the elaboration of its ritual gradually contributed to the enrichment of the equipment and furnishings.

Reconstructed buildings in the Early Christian style were not extensively produced in the Roman colonies, because there were few pagan temples to be razed for re-erection. A few examples exist, but the colonies hesitated to destroy their most noble and impressive civic adornments.

Anderson

Fragment of an Early Christian mosaic in St. Paul's, Rome. Notice the portrait-like drawing of the face, the contrasting stone sizes, and the textural quality of the surface.

Examples of Early Christian architecture. The extant remains of the Early Christian style consist of several churches, *baptisteries,* and sepulchral structures. In Rome, St. Paul's Beyond the Walls was built in 386, by Theodosius, and S. Maria Maggiore in 432. In Ravenna, S. Apollinare Nuovo, built by Theodoric the Goth, and S. Apollinare-in-Classe are still standing. In Syria, Early Christian architecture may be found in the Church of the Nativity, Bethlehem, and the Church of the Ascension, Jerusalem.

The Romanesque and Norman Period

The term "Romanesque" is applied to the style of art that arose in Italy and southern France after the time of Charlemagne and continued until it evolved into the forms of the 12th century that are known as Gothic. It progressed slowly until the year 1000. The style was carried by William the Conqueror in 1066 to England where it is known as "Norman." The northern Romanesque differs in character from southern Romanesque because of dissimilarities in climatic conditions and the temperaments of the people.

The activating cause of the Romanesque style was the comparative tranquillity that settled upon Europe after the barbarian invasions, which was followed by a hunger of the masses for peace and security. These essen-

The interior of the Early Christian church of St. Paul's Beyond the Walls (S. Paolo fuori le mura), built in 386 by Theodosius and later rebuilt in 1821. The church was built from the ruins of Roman temples. Notice the use of the semicircular arch springing from the column capitals, the straight walls supporting the wooden ceiling, and the mosaic decoration.

Mural painting in Vatican of 8th century Early Christian basilica showing method of construction, roofing, and clerestory windows.

tials were offered by a leadership that carried a cross as well as a sword, furnished religious salvation, and proposed a practical system of daily life. The response, impelled by loyalty and necessity, resulted in the construction of churches throughout Europe that were to serve not only as places of worship, but as strongholds, schools, libraries, town halls, museums, and centers of social life.

The monks, as amateur architects, were the planners. They taught the enthusiastic natives elementary masonry, carpentry, and ironworking. Untrained as designers, it was logical that the builders used the only models that were at hand. The designs were their own crude conception of Roman architecture adapted to Christian requirements and limited by the materials, craftsmanship, and tools that were

Editions "Tel," Paris, photograph

Interior of the Abbey of Vezelay, France. Late 11th century. Showing semicircular vaulted roof and Byzantine influence in the contrasting voussoirs of the arches. The choir is Gothic.

available in each locality.* The buildings that resulted were massive and strong, simple in surface enrichment, and often forbidding in appearance, but they faultlessly expressed the naïve spirit of a simple people and the vigor of the early church. Romanesque art must be judged with a realization of the intellectual level and general condition of Western society at the time it was produced.

The condition of western Europe from the year 476. After the fall of Rome, the Western colonies were thrown upon their own resources. Intellectual stagnation increased as tribal warfare developed, and countless local leaders endeavored to establish their supremacy. Out of the warring rose Charlemagne (742-814), who conquered and united the barbaric tribes under his rule. He was the great early patron of the arts in western Europe, but as evidence of the utter ignorance into which the people of this period had fallen, it is stated that Charlemagne himself could read, but could not write. Nevertheless, he surrounded himself with the most learned men of the time. The period of Charlemagne was followed by the invasions of the

* The stone carvers of the early Romanesque had only the ax as a cutting tool. The chisel was not used until the end of the period.

Normans in France and Italy, the Crusades, and the establishment of feudalism, an economic and social system binding the serfs to the land, requiring military service in payment for land use, and taxes paid to the suzerain by giving a portion of the agricultural production.

The religious ecstasy of the Middle Ages. Charlemagne fostered the Benedictine Order, which had been founded in 529 at Monte Cassino * in Italy. This order had monopolized and preserved all the records of science, letters, and arts of antiquity through the periods of the invasions of Europe by the Huns, Goths, Visigoths, Vandals, and Saracens. It had undertaken to educate the youth and to control the spiritual and temporal affairs of the masses through the period of confusion. Many other religious orders such as the Carthusians, Knights Templars, Dominicans, and Franciscan Friars were later established, and these assumed the responsibility of peacefully conquering Europe for the Roman popes and establishing some semblance of justice and peace. The monks became the messengers of a new civilization and followed the forest paths into the European wilderness to establish Christianity.

In the 10th century the native population of northern and western Europe dwelt in hovels of mud and straw. For centuries they had been degraded, murdered, dispossessed, and lacked competent leadership. Many believed the superstition that the world would end in the year 1000 and prepared themselves for this event. With the millennium passed without disaster, the surprise and joy of the people developed into a tremendous spiritual reaction, which was to benefit greatly the ecclesiastical organizations. The monks, who were the confidants of the people, needed administration buildings; hospitals; schools; shelters for the weak, poor, and orphaned; and they needed churches in which to congregate the faithful and to demonstrate the benefits of Christian principles. The people grasped at the opportunities that were offered to them, and with gratitude and enthusiasm donated their bodies and souls, their time, energy, and worldly goods to the promotion of a Christian civilization and its external evidences. Church construction was closest to their hearts, and became an urgent necessity.† Thus was the degree of zeal and religious frenzy that

* This monastery standing on a mountain top was used as a fortress by the Germans in World War II. It was unfortunately almost completely destroyed by the necessary American bombardment.

† An abbot who wrote in the 12th century describes the spirit in building one of the great cathedrals as follows: ". . . who has ever before heard of powerful princes of the world, brought up in honor and wealth, and nobles, both men and women, who have bent their proud and haughty necks to the harness of carts, and like beasts of burden, dragged to the abode of Christ, wagons loaded with wines, grains, oil, stone, wood, and all that is necessary for the wants of life or for the construction of the Church? While they draw these burdens—often when 1000 persons and more are attached to the wagons—so great is their difficulty—yet they march in such silence, not a murmur is heard. . . . The priests preside over each wagon exhorting every one to penitence, confession of faults, or a resolution to a better life . . . old people, young people, little children call on the Lord with a suppliant voice . . . with words of glory and praise." Transcribed from *Mont-Saint-Michel and Chartres* by Henry Adams, published by Houghton Mifflin Company, Boston, 1913.

Ruins of Temple of Diana, Nimes, France, 2nd century, considered the proto-type of Romanesque construction. The pile of stones supported by the side arch was necessary to resist the weight and thrust of the main semi-circular vaulted roof.

for five centuries produced the most sublime and awe-inspiring buildings ever created by man.

Structure of Romanesque churches. Some of the early Romanesque churches in Italy were constructed in part from the ruins of ancient Roman buildings, but in western Europe, and particularly southern France, there was an insufficient number of these to fulfill the demand. The stone that was required for the new structures often had to be transported from distant quarries and the character of the arched construction necessitated that such materials be cut into small sizes. The Christians did not have the slave and military labor that had been available to the Romans, but many of the workers contributed their services as a religious obligation. Without this economic system, the majority of the great cathedrals could never have been built.

Many of the Early Christian churches had been destroyed by fire, due to the use of wood in their roof construction. Romanesque builders depended entirely upon the stone arch. The Temple of Diana in Nimes, France, was an example of a 2nd century building which was roofed by a semicircular vault supported on columns, the thrust being counteracted by the weight of an additional small arch placed on either side. This structure is generally accepted as the prototype of all Romanesque and later Gothic churches.

Courtesy William Helburn, Inc.

Interior of Abbaye-aux-Dames, Caen, France, showing the nave and side aisle. The church was erected in the time of William the Conqueror. Notice the round arch exclusively used for the window openings. The roof is arched by the same form. The columns vary in character and proportions.

The basilica plan, perhaps for sentimental reasons, gave way to one in the form of a *Latin cross* by the introduction of the *transept*. The church was usually made to face westward to enable worshippers seated in the *nave* to face eastward toward the altar. The Roman semicircular arched vault was used not only in the construction of the roof, but this arch form was eventually to become the shape of all doors, windows, and other openings, and finally was used for purely ornamental purposes. The semicircular arch form is the most characteristic decorative feature of the Romanesque style.

The nave of the church was separated from the side aisles by a row of heavy columns proportioned without regard to Vitruvian standards, concerning which nothing was known. A semicircular arch rose directly from the capital of each column, and spanned to an adjoining column. This row of arches supported a wall pierced with *clerestory* windows. The arched ceiling was supported by the ribs that crossed the nave both at right angles and diagonally.

Romanesque ornament. For the benefit of an illiterate people, the ornament used to enrich the interiors of Romanesque churches was largely informative or instructional in character. Sculptured panels and column capitals showed scriptural subjects, allegorical scenes indicating the rewards of virtue and the punishment of vice, seasonal occupations, historical events, foliage, and fantastic animals. The sculptured figures were ascetic in character, ill-proportioned, and often intended to terrorize sinners. Capitals of columns showed leaves that are reminiscent of Corinthian classic forms intertwined with Biblical personages. The abstract patterns included the *checkerboard,* the *chevron* or zigzag, rosettes, and embattlements resembling the fret. The technique of the carving was crude and clumsy, and motifs were often conventionalized.

Examples of Romanesque architecture and decoration. The most characteristic examples of Romanesque art are: the Cathedral and Leaning Tower of Pisa, Italy (1172); the Porch of St. Trophime, Arles, France (12th century); portions of Mont St. Michel, France; the Abbaye-aux-

ABOVE LEFT: *Romanesque capital of the educational type. The biblical scene represented is that of Moses breaking the tablets.* ABOVE RIGHT: *Byzantine double capital showing Oriental influence in its lacelike design. In the upper panel is a relief showing Christian symbolism.* LEFT: *Romanesque capital showing leaf type. The modelling of the leaves is crude, but is inspired by the classical acanthus form. This is probably an early 13th century example.*

Hommes (1066) and the Abbaye-aux-Dames (1083), Caen, France; the Abbey (commenced 860) at Vezelay, France; and the Durham (1096–1133) and Peterborough (1117–1190) cathedrals, England.

The Gothic Period

The term "Gothic," meaning "barbarous," is a misnomer as applied to the arts of the Middle Ages. The word was first used by the Italian Vasari (1511–1574), the painter, architect, and biographer, who found his ideals in the arts of Greece and Rome, and applied the term in derision to the arts of western Europe. The term, however, is so generally associated with the architecture and other arts in Europe produced between the 12th and the 16th centuries that it has become a fixture in the language and its implied inferiority has disappeared.

The Gothic style was the florescence of the sturdy Romanesque period and the architectural and esthetic expression of a civilization in which religion and the spiritual side of existence were the most important interests in the life of everyone, and in which a large portion of each individual's wealth and effort was contributed to the glory of the Almighty. The Gothic cathedral, built by the people rather than by the clergy, became the center of town life and filled the requirements of the modern town hall, library, school, museum, and picture gallery. No buildings have ever been constructed that have surpassed the Gothic cathedrals in their effect of exaltation, mystery, awe, and inspiration.

Gothic art in all its branches was conventional and idealistic. The spirit of piety, humility, and asceticism, which was the fundamental teaching of the Church during the Middle Ages, was expressed in architecture, sculpture, painting, and all the minor arts. Starting with vigorous massive construction, the tendency of architectural design was constantly toward height and lightness, until extreme delicacy of structural form and over-ornamentation gradually led to its fall. While the purpose of Romanesque art had been to teach, that of Gothic art was to appeal to the emotional side of a joyless people who were steeped in ignorance and superstition. Through the Church, however, the learning and wisdom of the ancients were preserved through a thousand years of social and political turmoil.

The effect of the Crusades. The seven Crusades that occurred between the years 1096 and 1270 were of great political, economic, and artistic importance. A spontaneous outburst of overpowering sentiment and self-sacrifice, this movement included all classes of people and resulted in a lessening of the social distance between suzerain and serf. Expansion of knowledge occurred, and an impulse was given to trade and commerce. The outfitting of the Crusaders alone demanded an enormous expenditure of money and an introduction to a degree of luxury that many had never known. Elaborate furs, embroideries, gold ornaments, colorful banners, and shining armor were among the splendors introduced. The eastward march brought the Crusaders into contact with the extravagant architecture and wealth of Constantinople; the silk textiles of Damascus, Mosul, and Alexandria; the exquisite glassware of Tyre; and the jewels and pearls of the Byzantine and Mohammedan merchants. These and a vast number of other rich products of art and industry were purchased and sent to the homes of western Europe.

The Crusades did not accomplish any lasting good so far as their original purpose was concerned. They brought, however, a great change in the thought and in the manner of living of the people of Europe that was first noticeable in the Gothic period. They awakened interest at home in the ancient civilizations of Greece, Asia Minor, and the highly developed culture of the Eastern Empire, and they developed a doubt concerning some of the doctrines of the established Roman church, that later formed the roots of the Renaissance.*

The orders of chivalry that had originated in the 8th century were greatly expanded during the Crusades. The knight swore to be the champion of God and woman, to speak the truth, to maintain the right, to protect the distressed, and to practice gallantry, courtesy, and generosity. His military duties however forced him into distant lands for long periods and his wife was not always the recipient of his attentions. Chivalry fostered domestic intercourse, affection, sentiment, a greater respect for women, a refinement of manners in speech and action, and contributed greatly to the development of the home by increasing its privacy, comforts, conveniences, and luxuries. In the absence of the husband, the interests, activities, and responsibilities of the wife were increased. Women were left to take care of themselves and to assume the management of estates. They were generally placed on a higher plane.† Entertainment was furnished by wandering troubadours accompanied by jongleurs, dancers, mummers, and minstrels, who with their *chansons-de-geste* supplied gayer music than the Gregorian chants of the Church. These songs were the origin of all later secular music.

The influence of the Madonna upon art. In the early days of the Christian Church great reverence was given the relics of the Saints. The original cross was claimed to have been found in Jerusalem in 328 by St. Helena, and supposed portions of the shroud of Christ and the tunic of the Virgin were distributed throughout Christendom. *Reliquaries* were made in gold and enamel and inlaid with precious jewels to hold sacred fragments of all kinds. By the 10th century a large commerce had developed in these objects, which sold for enormous prices and often were later proved to be spurious. The sale of relics was forbidden by the Pope in 1198 without effect. The exhibition in church pageants of dismembered corpses was finally ridiculed and people turned from the relics in disgust. The Church authorities, realizing a change in the practice was necessary, began to substitute images of the Virgin for adoration. Christ was considered too sublime, too regal, for this purpose; His divinity placed Him aloof, and He alone could be worshipped, but not even the frailest or most sinful would fear to approach or reverence one whose attributes were in-

* The crusades were not wholly to the credit side of Christianity. In the early years of the 13th century a large group of independent Christians in Albi in southern France who opposed the doctrines and asceticism of the Church of Rome were all put to death by Simon de Montfort who attacked the city with half a million men. A few years later, under the religious hypnosis, occurred the hopeless Children's Crusade, when 90,000 boys and girls left their firesides in Germany and France to drive the Turks from Palestine. These children were nearly all lost by shipwreck or sold as slaves to Mohammedans before they reached their goal. Other disastrous results of the Crusades were the introduction into western Europe of leprosy, influenza, and the bubonic plague.

† During the early Middle Ages, the character of man and woman was much more similar than it is in modern times. Men did not hesitate to show their emotions and women often used vulgar language.

finite humility, love, pity, and forgiveness. The Virgin was human, could be addressed in person, and understood the griefs and passions of a lowly peasant who fully realized that his king and queen also constantly called upon her for help. So Mary, who had long been the patron saint of the Eastern Church, was raised to the position of "Regina Coeli," Queen of Heaven, in the Roman Church, and thereafter her image was carried at the head of every procession, adorned the walls of every hut and castle, and was placed at the masthead of every ship. Her importance began to overshadow the Trinity. Shrines were erected to her. One church in every town was dedicated to *Notre Dame,* and the *Lady-chapel,* the one of greatest beauty in every church, was placed behind the high altar and decorated in the most feminine taste, with softened colors, and was dimly lit to enable the worshiper to commune in silence, feel her presence and sympathy, and address her in person. The earliest development of an esthetic sense and appreciation among the masses of western Europe can be traced to the emotional reactions occurring from constant contact with the representations of Mary and her Infant. The painter, stonecutter, glassworker, and sculptor who worked on her chapel felt that he was in the Virgin's employ and his mistress knew even better than he the quality of his workmanship; and he understood that he would be compensated in the life hereafter on the basis of his efforts and ability. Such ardor could only be the parent of perfection!

The Madonna, as an ideal of artists in every medium, has been used in every art period of the Christian world. Only the style of representing her has changed. The conception of her character has varied from deep compassion and sorrow to one of joyful, healthy motherhood. Her association with theological doctrines has caused a greater financial expenditure by Christians than any single motive except war. Her portrait, attributed to St. Luke, adorns an altar in Rome. The *chef d'oeuvre* of Raphael was painted for the Sistine Chapel. In the Russian *ikons* she is framed in wrought gold studded with precious gems, and the Aztec Indians interpreted her in their own primitive manner to add to the charm and spirit of the Franciscan missions in California.

The characteristics of Gothic church architecture. The transition from the Romanesque to the Gothic occurred during the early part of the 12th century. Gothic art reached its height during the 13th century in France and England when the religious sublimity, enthusiasm, and faith of man combined to conceive the superb cathedrals of the period. The detail of the exteriors of these buildings became the inspiration for the design of contemporary secular buildings, dwellings, and objects used for interior decoration including furniture, wainscots, tapestries, paintings, and other accessories. The affection, care, and effort given to the design, construction, and decoration of these churches covered every inch of their surface.

Notre Dame, Paris, showing west front towers, transept with rose window, flying buttresses at side of nave, and dominance of vertical lines.

Where ornament and pattern were omitted, textural interest was introduced. Adjoining stones were usually of different shapes, sizes, and colors, or chiselled with different surface effects to weather differently and give the effect of a richly woven fabric. The cathedrals of Europe stand today as the supreme creative achievements of Western culture and are only equalled in logic of design by the Parthenon. Yet the names of the men who designed them are in most cases unknown. They were working for a cause greater than their own fame.

The plans are usually in the form of a *Latin cross*. The main body of the building formed the nave, flanked on the sides by low aisles, off which were sometimes built chapels dedicated to saints. Connected with the cathedrals were arcaded cloisters surrounded by the monastic administrative and living quarters. The cross portion of the plan, called the *transept*, furnished additional seating capacity and entrances. At the head of the plan were located the choir and altar, and at the rear of the altar was placed the Lady Chapel with the image of the Madonna. The nave walls were high and, at a point above the low roofs of the adjoining aisles, they were pierced by *clerestory* windows which served to illuminate the central portion of the church. A great stone arched vault covered the length of the nave and at each window a vault of equal height was required, which intersected the nave vault at right angles. This arrangement of intersecting vaults is one of the most characteristic features of Gothic design, and required an almost miraculous solution of structural problems in order to maintain stability. The Gothic designers, however, continually under the urge of the great spiritual movement, hesitated at nothing.

Gothic ecclesiastical architecture was structurally similar to the Romanesque but was elaborated and enriched a hundredfold. The basic structural difference from the earlier style was the fact that the exterior walls of churches served to enclose the building, but were not used to support the arched roof and ceilings, these being sustained on very slender isolated piers, designed as groups of clustered columns with overlapping shafts, and crowned with capitals treated with intertwining foliage forms. This new method of supporting a great arched roof on slender stone piers is the basic principle of Gothic design and was the fundamental cause of the visual details that are usually considered the characteristics of the style.

The use of the isolated supports for the arched roof permitted the introduction of enormous windows, especially in northern France and England where the sun was welcomed. The elimination of the wall precluded the possibility of mosaic and paint for adding color to the interior and created the necessity for colored window-glass decoration, which resulted in the development of the art of the stained-glass worker. The windows, which often were 20 feet wide and 30 feet high, were too large for glass areas without intermediate supports of slender stone subdivisions called *mullions.* The mullion pattern was known as *tracery.* Tracery patterns, originating as a structural requirement, were later adapted as ornamental motifs for furniture and woodwork panels. The early tracery consisted of vertical mullions crowned with simple pointed arches. In the final development of the Gothic style, the arches were *ogive* in type, each side following an "S" curve. This latter form was called *flamboyant,* meaning flamelike, and the term was later used as a designation for the whole late Gothic style.

Above the main entrance portal of the cathedral façades was usually placed a large circular opening called a *rose window,* which was treated with a spokelike design of tracery filled with ruby, violet, and blue glass through which the rays of the afternoon sun would cast a warm and mysterious glow.

The elimination of the supporting wall often placed too great weight upon the piers, a problem that was solved by making the pier thicker in depth by the introduction of a *buttress* on the outside. Where a single buttress was still insufficient in weight, another buttress was built a short distance beyond, which was connected to the pier buttress by an arch. This arrangement was called a *flying buttress.* Buttresses were also given greater weight by crowning them with an ornamental *finial* motif or a *pinnacle.* The buttress, a structural necessity, later became an ornamental feature in furniture design.

Great rivalry developed between each town and village to outdo each other in the beauty, size, and grandeur of its cathedral. This resulted in a trend toward larger and higher buildings. As the construction was by rule of thumb rather than by scientific principles, many of the buildings fell before completion and were rebuilt with stronger supports.

The whole problem of Romanesque and Gothic design was a contest in equilibrium between the weight of the stone arches and the economy of material in the buttresses. It was a matter of equalizing the thrust and counterthrust. This problem differed from the simplicity of Roman design where heavy walls had such inert stability, and were so extravagant of stonework that they could resist the thrust of al-

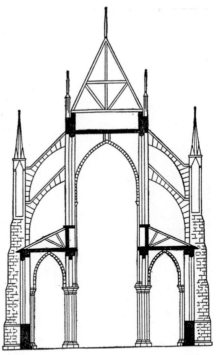

Section of Gothic church showing flying buttresses located to resist thrust of arch over nave. Section of clerestory windows is shown above roof of side aisles.

most any arch that could be placed upon them. Gothic structures were built of small stones and much mortar, which enabled the designers to introduce curved forms with greater ease than could have been accomplished with massive blocks. Marble was not available. There was great necessity for economy in the use of material due to the cost of labor and transportation. There are no monolithic features or concrete used in Gothic design.

The second important feature in Gothic design was the introduction of the pointed arch, which was substituted for the semicircular arch of Romanesque use. The pointed form had been used in ancient times but never to the extent to which it was applied in the Gothic period. The shape probably developed from the necessity for having arches of the same height starting at the same level but of varying spans. The arch across the nave was often 50 feet wide, whereas the arch from pier to pier along the length of the nave averaged 20 feet, yet the design called for near similarity in height. As the height of a semicircular arch is only half its width, similar heights could not be attained from the same spring line. The pointed arch

West front of Chartres Cathedral. The simple south tower (A.D. 1107) is considered one of the most beautiful examples of architecture in the world. The richly spired north tower (A.D. 1506) lacks unity.

fulfilled this requirement, which produced a more harmonious and unified effect in the design, and permitted higher windows for nave illumination. The pointed arch form was first used at Vezelay about 1100 and thereafter became the most important decorative feature in Gothic design.

Gothic ceilings were built by first constructing heavy arched *ribs* composed of a series of wedge-shaped stones connecting directly opposite piers. Other ribs starting from each support ran in a diagonal direction to the adjoining opposite piers. This resulted in an X-shaped pattern of ribs. When this construction was completed, the space between the ribs was filled in with masonry supported by the ribs. As the ribs were visible and projected below the ceiling masonry, the pattern formed by the infinite number of rib intersections produced a gossamer effect. Ribbed construction was one of the most characteristic features of Gothic design.

Gothic design endeavored to accentuate the vertical line, which accounts for the great height of the cathedrals and the use of towers as part of their façades. The verticality was accentuated by the shadows of the buttresses and by the elimination of many of the horizontal moldings and cornices associated with classical design. There may also have been a religious or sentimental feeling that the vertical line symbolized the aspirations of the faithful, and pointed toward their future abode. At least these lines avoided any resemblance to the horizontal accentuation of the pagan temples of antiquity.

Gothic architecture, like Greek, is functional and honest. The main elements were determined by structural requirements and barring sculptured ornament, nothing was introduced that had only visual appeal. It is therefore one of the great styles in art history. The early examples were comparatively simple in detail, vigorous, and masculine. The final development produced fantastic forms of lacelike stonework with intersecting ribs and intertwining tracery that were graceful in character. The warmth, bliss,

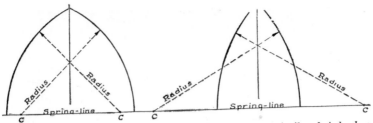

Diagram showing method of designing pointed arches of similar height but varying width.

and exaltation that one feels when in a Gothic cathedral can be only fully experienced when kneeling in its enclosure or contemplating the firmament.

It is essential that the decorator should know and understand the details of the exterior stone structural and ornamental forms, as these eventually became the sole inspiration and basis of design for woodworkers, cabinetmakers, metalworkers, ivory carvers, book illuminators, weavers, enamelers, and all other craftsmen of the period.

Gothic ornament and sculpture. Gothic structural features were often ornamental in themselves but they were also enriched with a great variety of carved forms. At the top of the windows the arched mullions were often treated with *quatrefoils* and *cinquefoils,* resembling four-leafed or five-leafed clovers, forming *cusps* between them. Statues of kings, saints, and other religious personages were extensively used. Less dignified figures such as dwarfs, grinning goblins, devils, monkeys, donkeys, and fabulous animals were introduced in unexpected places to amuse the people. Figures of those who labored on the buildings often were used as decoration. A bust of the architect in a quandary, the mason straining to lift a stone, the carpenter with his raised hammer, or the painter with his symbolic brush and palette would be given due recognition. The finials crowning vertical forms were enriched with *crockets,* cut in the form of projecting buds or leaves. Gutter ends and waterspouts were *gargoyles* carved in fantastic animal forms. Niches were formed with pointed tops to frame the important statuary or projecting *canopies* were placed above free-standing statues. Geometrical forms such as frets, dog teeth, chevrons, zigzags, battlements, and crenelations often formed running ornament. Family crests, monograms, coiling stems with foliage recalling the classical arabesque, and the oak branch and leaf were the most common forms of ornamental motifs. Much of the sculptured representation had a Christian historical or symbolic association, such as St. Peter with his key, St. George and the Dragon, the Creation of Man, Jonah and the Whale, the Wise and Foolish Virgins, and the Last Supper. To the medieval mind nearly everything was symbolic and the ornament of the church was an encyclopedia in stone.

LEFT: *The interior of St. Chapelle, Paris, built by St. Louis, 1242–1247. Note the enormous glass area in the late Gothic construction, with walls reduced to slender, high supports. The pointed arch dominates in both structural and ornamental forms.* RIGHT: *Interior of Notre Dame, Paris, from choir looking toward nave, and clearly showing the ribbed vaulting and rose window of west front.*

Practically all of the sculpture of the Gothic period was designed to fill a particular place in the building. The early human figures had a strong architectural quality, standing stiff and erect, with arms close to elongated bodies, and clothing in minute vertical folds accentuating the perpendicular. The faces of early examples were rather crudely modelled and ascetic in aspect, although portraiture was often intended. The later statues became more realistic in character with larger and more naturalistic folds in the clothing, less rigid bodies, and faces expressing sentiments of meekness and humility. Much of the figure sculpture was painted in natural colorations.

A favorite decorative and religious motif of Romanesque and Gothic designers was the crucifix, a representation of Christ on the cross. From the first appearance of the crucifix, in the 10th century, until the middle of the 13th century, the figure of Christ was always shown with halo, head erect, feet resting on a support, and one nail driven through each foot. In later centuries a more pathetic attitude of the figure was represented, the body sagged, the head bent under the crown of thorns, the eyes were closed, blood streamed from His wound, pain and exhaustion were indicated, and the feet were crossed and nailed with a single nail.

Stained glass. As a result of the reduction in wall areas and the enlargement of windows in Gothic architecture, it was impossible to add mosaic

Examples of French sculpture. LEFT: *16th century figure showing the gradual approach to naturalism in the modelling and in the character of the face and the folds of the robe.* RIGHT: *12th century figure showing architectural emphasis in the accentuation of vertical line in mass and detail, the arms close to the body, and the folds of the garment in parallel lines.*

or painted surface decoration to medieval churches. The mosaic workers therefore turned to window enrichment by introducing colorful patterns and pictures in the glass areas. The early stained glass was of the mosaic type; patterns were produced by small areas of glass held in place by leaden strips that delineated the drawing. These were additionally braced by slender iron bars that served to support the whole window. The glass was not really stained, but was produced by mixing chemicals with the glass while it was being made. Colored window-glass was first made in the 5th century but the earliest extant example is in Germany and dates from the 11th or 12th century. The art of stained glass reached its apogee between the

Medieval book covers. LEFT: *Cover in filigree and cabochon, framing a carved ivory plaque showing the crucifixion as represented in the 12th century. The figure of Christ is erect and His feet are standing firmly on a support. Four nails are used, and His head is surrounded by a halo.* RIGHT: *Cover in enamel, with ivory plaque insert showing the crucifixion as represented from the 14th century onward. The figure of Christ is limp and lifeless, the legs are crossed, pity and pain are expressed, and the head is surrounded by a crown of thorns.*

13th and 14th centuries. The effect of the glass had to be translucent, and variations were made in the thickness and texture of individual pieces of glass as well as in the color. During the 16th century larger pieces of glass were used and enamelling of the glass commenced. Enamel was applied to the glass before being fired. This type of coloring produced areas that were less translucent than the earlier methods and the glass designers commenced to imitate oil-painted pictures, an esthetic error that led to the decline of the art. The finest examples in existence are the 12th century windows in the Cathedrals of Chartres, Canterbury, and York. The Jesse-tree, showing the genealogical descent of Christ from Jesse, the father of David, is one of the most frequently seen patterns. Circles, lozenges, and *trefoil* and quatrefoil all-over patterns were also used. Pictorial subjects were introduced in the 13th century. Colors are usually blue, green, red, and purple, although the Cistercian monks limited the windows in their buildings to *grisaille* effects. The glass patterns were usually related to the stone tracery. The scintillating colored rays of light that entered the buildings contributed greatly to the dignity and impressiveness of the interiors.

Domestic architecture and decoration. The social and political conditions of the Middle Ages permitted little comfort or luxury in domestic living except in the feudal fortress castles of the nobles. The mass of the population lived in log or stone houses roofed with thatch. It was not until the 13th century that the medieval castle began to look less like a fortress and to have a few conveniences and comforts.*

The walls of Constantinople that had stood for one thousand years and had never been entered against the will of the inhabitants were breached in 1453 by a new weapon—an enormous cannon firing stone balls weighing 600 pounds. As a result, the old fortified castles became obsolete and with the increasing power and efficiency of the laws, it was no longer necessary to consider strength before convenience in residential design. Instead of seeking a hilltop or other strong position, people began to choose situations for dwellings that were agreeable or beautiful, where they might be protected from the inclemency of the weather, and where gardens and orchards could be planted advantageously.

In northern Europe the winter was a chill, dark, and damp period. Glass for windows did not become common in dwellings until the 15th century. Before that period the windows had wooden shutters, pierced with small

Late 13th century glass panel in which the leading played an important part in the design. In the later period of Gothic stained glass windows, the leading had a structural purpose, the glass sizes became larger, and painted glass became important.

holes that were filled with mica, waxed cloth, or horn to admit a small amount of light. During the Middle Ages the rooms were heated with braziers or with open fires built on the stone or brick floors in the middle of the room. The smoke filled the room until it made its escape through a door, window, or hole in the roof. Later, the discomfort of this awkward arrangement stirred the Gothic builders to create the fireplace and chimney.

In the houses of the common people, the stone walls were often bare or covered with rough plaster. The interior walls of the castles were sometimes painted in imitation of hung textiles or with mural decorations of historical and religious scenes or legends of chivalry. The paintings were

---

* The fortress Palace of the Popes in Avignon and the fortified monastery of Mont St. Michel are indicative of the degree of amiability and security enjoyed even by the religious orders of the 14th century.

The interior of a 15th century room taken from a French manuscript. Notice the dais upon which is placed the throne where the princess sits with her ladies in waiting. Her guests sit apart, and the tables are supported by temporary trestles. There are no eating utensils. Entertainment is supplied from a small minstrel gallery. A credence is shown at the left.

treated in a flat manner, with few gradations of coloring and no perspective in the drawing. After 1400, tapestries from Arras, France, were extensively used in the princely castles of both France and England to cover walls, to hang over windows and doors, and to enclose beds, or as partitions to subdivide large rooms for greater privacy.

The ceilings of the rooms usually showed the exposed beams or trusses of the roof construction, frequently enriched with colorful painted ornament. On plaster ceilings gold star patterns on a blue or green ground were often painted. When flat-beamed ceilings were used, the ends of the beams were supported by projecting ornamental brackets, variously shaped or carved into figures.

Floors were in stone, brick, or tile, and generally covered with straw or leaves. The first Oriental rugs were imported into England in the 13th century, but were very rare objects for many years.

The great hall. The castles of the nobility of both England and France were built around the *great hall,* principally used for the assemblies of vassals, banquets, trials, and entertainments. The entrance was at one end under a balcony known as the *minstrel gallery.* At the opposite end was a raised platform known as a *dais* that was reserved for the owner and his

From Nash's "Mansions of England," 1849

The great hall at Penshurst, Kent, England, showing the minstrel gallery over the entrance and the fire in the center of the room. The roof is wood truss construction, built in the form of a pointed arch to carry out the style.

family. On the dais stood two thrones or chairs-of-honor, having arms and high backs that terminated in rooflike canopies. A temporary table supported on trestles was brought in at mealtimes; the rest of the dais furniture consisted of a sideboard or *credence,* a chest, and possibly a few stools or benches.

The center of the room was meagerly furnished with benches built or placed against the wall. Sometimes a high post bed surrounded with draperies was placed in the corner of the great hall, although separate bedrooms were eventually introduced.

The plaster walls of the great hall were hung with tapestries or covered with an oak wainscot to a height of about 12 feet. On the upper portion of the walls were hung armor, trophies of the hunt, and colorful flags and standards.

Fireplaces. The great halls at first had a fireplace located in the middle of the room. This was needed for both heating and cooking; but, during the 14th century, the fire was moved from the center of the hall to a side wall, and a projecting hood was built over it to direct the smoke out through either a wall hole or a chimney. The projecting hood was frequently ornamented with architectural forms or with a carved coat-of arms. Chairs or benches and a small rug were frequently placed before the fire. It was at this time that the fireplace and the hearth became the symbols of the home.

Wall panelling. Oak-panelled wainscots were built in both ecclesiastical and domestic interiors to give greater warmth and finish to a room. The panels of the Gothic period were of small dimensions and were usually placed vertically. The panel field was never wider than a single plank of oak. It was sometimes left plain, but was more often decorated with a *linenfold* or parchment pattern, or carved with a design imitating window tracery. Oak branches, leaves, and acorns were occasionally used as decorative motifs for panelled surfaces.

Late Gothic mantel in the château at Blois, France, showing Gothic architectural forms used in a decorative manner.

The framework holding the panels was rectangular, composed of vertical *stiles* and horizontal *rails* with molded edges on only three sides of each panel frame. The top rail and the two stiles of each were usually treated with a simple curved molding; the lower rail was plain and *splayed* (slanted downward). This method of treating a panel frame was due to the woodworker basing his design on that of the stoneworker, who placed a trim molding on three sides of a window with a slanting sill at the bottom to carry off rainwater. A few moldings ran along the top of the wainscot, and the cresting was often treated with a carved tracery design and finial motifs. The average dimension for a Gothic panel was about 9 inches wide by 2 or 3 feet high. The wood was generally waxed.

Furniture. Nearly all furniture of the Gothic period was in natural-finished oak. Occasionally walnut was used. Thrones and seats-of-honor were sometimes gilded. Most of the pieces were heavy in their proportions and dimensions, and rectangular in design. The parts were assembled with wooden *dowels, mortises,* and *tenons,* and with handcut *dovetails.* The ornamental forms consisted almost entirely of small-scale carved architectural motifs such as tracery, pointed arches, rose windows, buttresses, finials, and crockets. Sometimes the face of the stiles and rails of the case furniture were enriched by parallel grooves or reeds running lengthwise; as these features were cut before the piece was assembled, the grooves did not *miter* at the corners. Furniture panels were usually enriched with carved linenfold and tracery motifs or coats-of-arms, and, as in the wainscoting, moldings were placed only on the top and two sides of the panel, the lower stile having a splayed edge.

The *chest* was the most important piece of furniture, because it could be easily transported, a necessary advantage during unsettled political conditions. The chair was a small chest with arms and a high back, and was reserved for the use of important persons. The panel in the back was usually decorated with a carved pattern and often crowned with a wooden canopy. The dominant lines of the design of chairs were straight, the seat was square and covered with a loose cushion for comfort. The cupboard was a chest on legs. The credence or serving table originally derived its name from the Latin word *credere*, meaning "to believe," because food placed upon it was tested by a servant before it was offered to the master of the house, who lived in dread of poison potions.

Gothic beds were gorgeously carved

French Gothic interior showing projecting hooded mantel, oak wainscot with panels decorated with the linenfold motif, high beamed ceiling, tile floor, and large tapestry high on the wall.

and were sheltered with a canopy and curtains hung from the ceiling or supported by corner posts. Sometimes the canopy was made larger than the bed, to enclose a chair within the drawn curtains. A *hutch* or chest containing the family valuables was placed at the foot of the bed where it could be watched by its owners. A lamp hung within the canopy, and a stool or step was placed beside the bed. Beds were covered with mattresses, finely woven linen sheets, and many pillows. Servants or children frequently slept on a low truckle or *trundle bed* that was stored under the large bed and pulled out at night. A few benches and stools were placed in the smaller rooms, and in front of the fireplace was placed a bench with a movable back that could be swung so that the occupants could sit with either their faces or their backs to the fire.

Dining tables were merely planks supported on temporary trestles. Linen tablecloths in evenly spaced folds hung well over each side to hide the supports. Guests sat at one side of the table, the other being left free for service. Individual plates were seldom used, but a large dish was placed in the middle of the table, in which all dipped their fingers. No forks were used, as it was customary to eat with the fingers until about the 16th century. Before dining, everyone washed his hands at the table, that he might give assurance of his cleanliness to the other guests. At the end of the meal, the washing again took place. Forks and table-service knives were not

Oak Chest with Tracery Carving

Late Type of Capital

Early Rose Window

Window showing Stone Tracery

Finial Motif showing Crockets

Linenfold Motif

Clustered Columns

Chair showing linenfold, tracery and buttresses

Credence

GOTHIC FURNITURE AND DECORATIVE AND ARCHITECTURAL DETAILS.

used in England until 1600. Knives were used to cut food from an early date, but they belonged to the individual, were carried in his belt, and were not part of the regular eating equipment furnished to the guest. Use of individual plates did not become common until the 18th century. The earliest plates were made of metal. The word "plate" originally meant "silver," and had no relation to the shape of the dish, but indicated the material from which it was made. The use of crockery for tableware did not occur until the middle of the 16th century. The *trencher* was originally

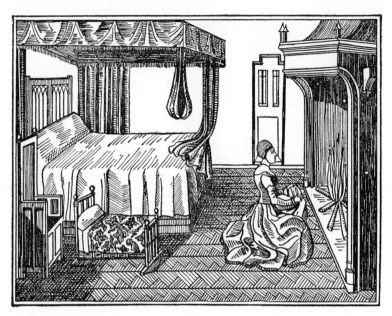

Small Gothic bedroom, taken from an illustration in a 15th century manuscript.

IMPORTANT GOTHIC STRUCTURES

COUNTRY	ECCLESIASTICAL	SECULAR
France	Notre Dame Cathedral, Paris (1163–1214) Chartres Cathedral (1194–1240) Rheims Cathedral (1212–1241) Amiens Cathedral (1220–1288) Notre Dame Cathedral, Rouen (1202–1530) St. Ouen, Rouen (1318–1515) St. Maclou, Rouen (1432–1500) Mont St. Michel (13th–15th c.)	Palais de Justice, Rouen (1499–1508) House of Jacques Cœur, Bourges (1443) Château at Pierrefonds (14th c.) Château at Coucy (1220–1230) Walled city of Carcassonne Walled city of Aigues-Mortes
England	Westminster Abbey (1245–1269) Salisbury Cathedral (1220–1258) Wells Cathedral (1214–1465) York Cathedral (1261–1324) Lincoln Cathedral (1185–1200) Ely Cathedral (1198–1322)	Penshurst Place, Kent (1335) Windsor Castle (1359–1373) Stokesay Castle
Italy	Milan Cathedral (1385–1418) Florence Cathedral (1294–1462) Siena Cathedral (1243–1284)	Palace of the Ca d'Oro, Venice Doges Palace, Venice (1424–1442) Palazzo Vecchio, Florence (1298)
Spain	Seville Cathedral (1401–1520) Burgos Cathedral (1221–1567) Barcelona Cathedral (1298–1329) Toledo Cathedral (1227–1290)	Porta Serraños, Valencia (1482) Casa Consistorial, Barcelona (1369–1378)
Germany	Cologne Cathedral (1270–1322)	Wartburg Castle (1150)

Gothic bedroom in the Château of Langeais, France, 1465.

a slice of bread upon which food was placed. Later, pieces of wood in this shape were used, and the word finally came to mean a plate upon which food is served.

The hardware on doors and Gothic case furniture was in hammered wrought iron and was always placed on the surface of the woodwork. Hinges, locks, and bolts with scroll and foliage designs were used.

Minor arts. One of the greatest of the minor arts of the Gothic period was that of tapestry weaving, carried on during the 15th century principally in the cities of Arras and Tournai. Elaborately ornamented metalwork in the form of military armor, church utensils, and reliquaries were made in France, Spain, and Italy. The city of Limoges became famous for its enamelware from the 12th to the 14th century. Ivory carving reached its greatest period in the Paris productions of the 14th century. Ecclesiastical embroideries of the most magnificent types were made to enrich the elaborate church ritual. The arts of book-illuminating and hand-lettering attained their highest point of development, but were abruptly terminated after the invention of printing in the middle of the 15th century.

Examples of Gothic architecture and decoration. Nearly all the large cities of western Europe contain buildings of the Gothic period. Each country showed slight variations in the development of the style, because of differences in climate and taste, and for other local reasons. The table, which appears on page 101, includes the most important examples of Gothic architecture.

Bibliography

ADAMS, H., *Mont-Saint-Michel and Chartres*. Houghton Mifflin Co., Boston, 1913. Beautifully written text covering history, romance, and art. Few illustrations.

ANTHONY, E. W., *A History of Mosaics*. Porter Sargent, Boston, 1935. Excellent illustrated text tracing the development and use of mosaics from preclassic times through the 20th century.

DURANT, W., *The Story of Civilization*. Vol. IV, The *Age of Faith*. Simon and Schuster, Inc., New York, 1950. An excellent description of all aspects of the Middle Ages.

GARNER AND STRATTON. *Domestic Architecture in England during the Tudor Period*. Wm. Helburn, Inc., New York, 1926. Photographs of exteriors and interiors of late Gothic works.

Gromort, G., *L'Architecture Romane*, 3 Vols. Vincent, Fréal, Paris, 1928–1931. Excellent plates.

Hamilton, J. A., *Byzantine Architecture and Decoration*. B. T. Batsford, Ltd., New York, 1933. A standard book. Well illustrated.

Harvey, J., *Gothic England, 1300–1550*. B. T. Batsford, Ltd., New York, 1947. An excellent architectural history of this period.

Lowrie, W., *Monuments of the Early Church*. The Macmillan Co., New York, 1923. An illustrated handbook of Christian archeology.

Parkinson, J., *Old Cottages, Farm Houses, and Other Half-Timber Buildings in Shropshire, Herefordshire, and Cheshire*. B. T. Batsford, Ltd., London, 1904. Brief text with excellent photographs.

Quenedy, R., *La Normandie*, 5 Vols. F. Contet, Paris, 1927-1931. Plates of exteriors of medieval French domestic architecture.

Viollet-le-duc, E., *Dictionaire Raisonné d'Architecture*. B. Bance, Paris, 1854. Out of print. Standard book on the art and architecture of the Middle Ages. French text. Available in most large art libraries.

CHAPTER III

THE ITALIAN RENAISSANCE

B ecause of an advantageous geographical location, Italy during the Middle Ages became the distributing point for the trade of the Orient with western Europe. On mule, camel, and elephant, the salt, spices, silks, and other luxuries were brought from the East to the shores of the Black Sea, transshipped to Adriatic ports, and thence distributed to Florence, Venice, and other north Italy cities. As a consequence of the Crusades and the voyage of Marco Polo, Italy became the merchandising and banking center of Europe. Buyers from the North and from the West made their annual pilgrimage there in search of supplies.

During the Middle Ages the misery of the masses had been intense, and doubts arose in the minds of certain intellectual leaders concerning religious doctrines as well as the statements of the Church relating to natural phenomena. Later, scientific discoveries were made which conflicted with the claims of the Roman Church and aided in shaking the faith of the people in the established order. The conclusion that the earth was spherical in form and revolved about the sun and the principle of the compass were among these discoveries. An intellectual group known as the "Humanists" was organized, with the purpose of investigating and eliminating some of the superstitions and mysticisms that were current, and of protesting against the authority of the Church in matters of secular importance. By the 15th century the works of Dante, Petrarch, and Boccaccio had had ample opportunity to influence the thought of the people. These three authors had carefully studied the philosophies and political treatises of antiquity. Writing in Italian rather than in Latin, which was the language of the scholars, they contrasted the pagan ideals of the early Greeks and the Romans with current conditions. The fundamental thought of the times seemed to be that the nations of antiquity had been better organized, better controlled, and on the whole happier than those of western Europe during the Middle Ages. The invention of printing in the 15th century aided the spread of the new knowledge. The revival of interest in classical philosophy was aided by the sight of the ruined architectural masterpieces of the Roman Empire that stood at every crossroad to remind the inhabitants of the achievements of their race. The fall of Constantinople in 1453 caused an influx into Italy of many Greek scholars and craftsmen who were steeped in classical knowledge.

The time was also ripe for a reaction against the suppression of the joyous human emotions, which had been brought about by the ascetic attitude of the Middle Ages. As the pleasures of human existence were realized, less was thought of the spiritual side of man. Naturalism and realism were reflected in thought and action. Art returned to earth to represent the joy of living, the beauties of nature, the happiness of youthful faces, the charm of graceful form and movement, and the less ethereal emotions. Lorenzo the Magnificent expressed the kernel of the thought of the period in his stanzas that open with "How fair is Youth, though speeds its day. Let heart be ardent while it may"—a philosophy thoroughly excoriated by Savonarola.

The term "Renaissance" is used as the name of the intellectual protest that resulted in the revival of classical philosophy and art, beginning in Florence about the year 1400. Although the word implies "rebirth," and the forms of art produced during this period were based on classical inspiration, the movement eventually developed into one of extreme esthetic originality. The Renaissance was not the revival of antiquity alone but its union with the Italian people. It could only have been conceived in the land of Augustan memories replete with alluring landscapes, with a turquoise sea, glowing sun, and the olive, grape, cedar, and cypress that served to rationalize a heaven on earth.

The character of Italian society. The Italians of the Renaissance were the inheritors of the Greek ideal of individualism. During the Middle Ages the northern Italians had, in their own opinion, maintained a higher intellectual level than the "barbarians" of northern Europe, and it was perhaps inevitable, though paradoxical, that, in the geographical and administrative heart of the Roman Church, men should first react against the inaccuracies, limitations, and negations of medieval thought. While accepting the Church as an organization, the Italian discarded it as an authority to control his private life, and, as his lack of faith and respect for the civil authorities was quite understandable, he had no alternate but to take the law into his own hands and decide for himself between right and wrong. When emotional restraints were violated, the Church pardoned them by the sale of indulgences, a policy which became a scandal when major crimes could be condoned by the cost of a mass. The State, often tyrannical, despotic, and illegitimate, was usually dominated by an egotistical leader, who had established and maintained his supremacy by violence and the

Machiavellian standard claiming that the end justified the means. Egotism was obviously successful and its processes, adopted by most Italians, produced an excessive individualism, which was the cause of both the greatest faults and most commendable qualities of the race. With blunted morals, the most flagrant crimes were committed, and public standards reached a point where perpetrators were absolved if the motive was revenge and the act accomplished with theatrical courage. These actions, first practiced by the nobility, set a precedent for the whole population, and, as usual, the masses tended to ape the classes.

In the 13th century, Dante had taught that man was master of his own destiny and that he should not be the intellectual slave of either Church or State. Bonds are inherently irksome, and it is a primal law of nature to hold in aversion whatever savors of the obligatory. The movement toward individualism lessened the class distinctions of the Middle Ages. Birth and origin were of little importance unless they were combined with wealth. The intelligent, regardless of class, had an opportunity to rise to power. The Italian came to feel, in truth, that he was a citizen of the most advanced nation of his time; he took pride in being unlike his neighbor and developed a morbid passion for fame. Women became completely emancipated and were recognized to have the minds and courage of men.

In the 14th century, the public felt the need of new ideals and a new authority for personal guidance. Antiquity was an obvious recourse. It was the symbol of past greatness and the highest claim to glory that Italy possessed. Petrarch had climbed the ruins of Roman buildings and recalled the history that passed beneath his feet. The empire of Augustus, prostrate for a thousand years, possessed the popular mind.

Literature was the first of the arts to spread the new doctrines of realistic paganism. Dante had spoken of the reverence due the stones of ancient Rome. Boccaccio had surpassed Ovid and openly violated all the restraints of medievalism in describing feminine pulchritude. Another author referred to laughter as "a radiance of the soul." Petrarch was the first to enjoy the view of a landscape and from a mountain top had looked down on the clouds and urged men to go forth to admire lofty hills, broad seas, roaring torrents, and the stars, and forget their own selves while doing so. The pleasures of contemplating savage scenery had been unknown to the Italians of the 13th century.

The Latin language was easy for the Italians and the memory of pagan Rome aided the development of a national and secular sentiment. The movement, explosive in character and conflicting with established religious standards, spread to all branches of human thought and creative effort. A desire developed to prove that nobility could be found outside the bounds of theology, that omniscience was not limited to cloistered walls, and that the emotions of man could be expressed without dishonor. In the development of this individualism, both public and private morals reached extreme levels. By the side of the greatest corruption were found the most noble of sentiments and the most vicious of human expressions contrasted with those of highest artistic splendor. The stoic philosophies of Cicero and Seneca had as many adherents as the Epicurean devotees of pleasure.

Although disturbing changes occurred in the outlook of the upper-class Italian, the fever for religious crusading had subsided and the fear of foreign invasion lessened. This enabled him to plan his life according to the opportunities offered by a peaceful prospect. It affected the character of his residence. In the house plan, rooms became smaller and were distributed and used for the purposes that they are today. In the activities of daily life the Italian found time to develop the customs and amenities of modern social intercourse. Manners promoted by sincerity and kindliness became polished and conventionalized; the Florentine dialect was adopted as the standard of refined people, and conversation became intellectual, witty, humorous, and gay; dress became elaborate and varied for every occasion; and individual table cutlery was first used. In social gatherings the entertainment consisted of indoor and outdoor sports played by young and old, reading from the classics, or listening to the music of the lute, lyre, and viol. Dilettantism and connoisseurship developed in the arts and crafts. Novelty and originality became essential qualities in any creative effort. Public festivals were celebrated with glamorous pageants and tournaments. Boccaccio in his *Decameron* produced the first "novelle." Palestrina later popularized the motet and madrigal, and the opera was evolved from the fusion of ancient Greek drama, music, song, and the decorative arts. Pantomime and the classical ballet were finally established. The antique revival penetrated into every cultural activity.

An accidental combination of pertinent historical events, geographical locale, economic and political conditions, scientific discoveries, and the protest against excessive ecclesiastical conservatism impregnated the Italian intellect and creative instinct, and caused it to blossom into an artistic force that spread its seeds on the whole of Western civilization.

The condition and attitude of the Church. The Church, with its head in Rome, had, during the Middle Ages, developed tremendous power at a time when faith in political leadership was at its lowest ebb. Coincident with the attainment of this supreme position, the luxury and the morals of some of the clergy were the extreme opposites of those adopted by the founders of the Christian Church. Combined with excessive taxation by ecclesiastical authorities, violent protests developed against the doctrines, the misconduct, and the worldliness of certain church leaders.

The Dominican monk, Savonarola, was burned at the stake in Florence in 1498 in spite of his many efforts to reform the Church from within. Martin Luther, more safely located, issued his 95 theses from faraway

Wittenberg in 1517, and was excommunicated by the Pope in 1520. Nearly the whole of northwest Europe eventually refused to acknowledge the supremacy of Rome, in spite of war and intrigue. Protestantism was the result of independent thinking and feeling in contrast to the maintenance of the medieval traditions of the Roman Church.

To counteract the weakening effect of the spreading Reformation, a movement started by the Jesuits developed within the Roman Church. This was known as the Counter Reformation, and, as will later be seen, had an important influence upon the decorative arts. The Church objected to the freedom and liberty that came from the revival of pagan thought, but the exposure of the evils of church administration contributed to the growth of the protest in art as well as in religion. During the Middle Ages all education and culture had been restricted to the precincts of the Church, and it was natural that the authorities taught only that which would be most advantageous to them. In the arts it was necessary to promote what was related to sacred life, such as religious history and the philosophy of the Church. Secular tendencies were at first regarded with hostility, but the spread of classical thought among the masses became too over-whelming to be crushed by ecclesiastical edict. After the failure to halt the Reformation, the Church became powerless against the renewed interest in the arts of antiquity, and adapted these products of secular mentality to her own use, finally succumbing wholeheartedly and embracing them with open arms.

The patrons of the arts. For a thousand years after the fall of Rome, Italy had been divided into petty sovereignties that were constantly at war with each other. Leaders had risen to power only to be destroyed by other claimants. By the 15th century, the wealth that had been brought to Italy by its trade became concentrated in several distinct groups, which, once the financial control of the country was in their hands, grasped also the political and ecclesiastical control. Each city and town was dominated by one or more leading families. Intermarriage was frequent, but the condition of ethics and morals was such that mutual confidence could not be sufficiently developed to permit alliances that might have eventually aided in the growth of a national consciousness.

In spite of political weakness, great civic pride developed. This was fostered by the controlling families as a matter of pleasure, but also, in part, to hide their own extravagances. Palatial dwellings, with rich furnishings produced by the most able artists and craftsmen, were built to out-shine each other in splendor and magnificence. The villas of Florence and Rome, surrounded by elaborate formal gardens, almost equalled in size and beauty those built for the ancient Roman emperors.

The better known of the Italian Renaissance families were the Medici, Pitti, Strozzi, and Riccardi of Florence; the Sforza and Visconti of Milan;

the Colonna, Este, Borgia, Orsini, and Borghese of Rome; the Vendrimini of Venice; and others in Genoa, Verona, Siena, Ferrara, and Vicenza. Members of these families exerted immense power for both good and evil. Much of their wealth was spent in patronizing the arts and artists, and the rivalry thus developed contributed greatly to the extraordinary achievements of the period.

From the middle of the 15th century, art and the appreciation of art formed the principal subject of conversation of every Italian. John A. Symonds in his book *Renaissance in Italy* states, "It has been granted only to two nations, the Greeks and the Italians, and to the latter only at the time of the Renaissance, to invest every phase and variety of intellectual energy with the form of art. . . . From the Pope upon St. Peter's chair to the clerks in a Florentine countinghouse, every Italian was a judge of art. Art supplied the spiritual oxygen without which the life of the Renaissance must have been atrophied. During that period of prodigious activity the entire nation seemed to be endowed with an instinct for the beautiful, and with the capacity for producing it in every conceivable form."

Many artists and craftsmen were placed on the annual payroll of the great patrons. Studios and workshops were furnished by generous benefactors. Time was not a consideration in the completion of any work of art. This system of remuneration contributed greatly to the quality of the productions and eliminated the economic risk on the part of the artist, whose whole effort, continuous and repeated, could be applied toward the attainment of perfection.

The versatility of the artists. The tremendous popular interest in art, linked with the financial security and the rewards offered for the works of the artists, developed an astounding group of creative craftsmen in all forms of esthetic endeavor. Not the smallest mark of their genius was their wonderful versatility. Many worked in several mediums and expressed themselves with nearly equal effectiveness as architects, painters, sculptors, decorators, musicians, engineers, poets, philosophers, or as craftsmen in the minor arts.

To mention but a few of the immortals—the earliest Renaissance constructions were the Hospital of the Innocents (1421) and the dome of the Cathedral of Florence (1434), designed by the architect, Brunelleschi, a goldsmith by training. In connection with this church is the equally notable Baptistery, an earlier building that contains the bronze doors made by the sculptor and goldsmith, Ghiberti, which Michael Angelo is said to have called the "Gates of Paradise." Giotto and Cimabue seem almost to have invented painting. Fra Angelico, the mystical monk of San Marco in Florence, transferred the sweetness of the art of the illuminator of Christian manuscripts to wall decoration. Leonardo da Vinci, one of the greatest painters who ever lived, wrote a letter to the King of France,

VIGNOLA (1507–1573)   BERNINI (1598–1680)

Courtesy New York Public Library and A. B. Bogart, Photographer

PALLADIO (1518–1580)   MICHAEL ANGELO (1475–1564)

describing his abilities as a constructor of fortresses, and modestly added a postscript stating that he could paint as well as any other man. Botticelli, the painter of "Spring," was one of the earliest to bring life, action, and nature to the art of painting, after the asceticism of the Middle Ages. The della Robbia family, great sculptors, reproduced their swaddled babes and other exquisite figures and patterns in colored terra cotta to enrich the exteriors and interiors of the Florentine buildings. Bramante was the first architect of St. Peter's. Michael Angelo, the profound poet, deeply religious, dignified the human figure and in the ceiling of the Sistine

Chapel painted it as none had done before; modelled the immortal David in marble; and designed the fortifications of Florence and the great dome of St. Peter's. Raphael, the youthful and prolific painter, mural decorator, architect, tapestry designer, and ornamenter of pottery, is most famous for his paintings of the Madonna. Palladio and Vignola rediscovered the standardized proportions of the Roman architectural orders established by Vitruvius, and left a written record of them for future designers. Benvenuto Cellini, the autobiographer, wastrel, and sculptor of the Perseus in the Loggia of the Lanzi in Florence, was one of the greatest of goldsmiths. Donatello, the sculptor, when youthful, thin, and poor, slaved with pickaxe and shovel to unearth the buried treasures of antiquity in Rome, and was seized with paroxysms of joy when he discovered a column, a capital, a statue, or even a few old stones.

Subdivisions of the Italian Renaissance period. The Italian art periods are usually given the names of the centuries in which they occur, and the Italian names are used in referring to them. As in all art periods, there is much overlapping of styles, which explains the apparent conflict in the dates given herewith.

1. QUATTROCENTO (1400–1500).
The transitional period between the Gothic arts and the classical revival, characterized by the use of architectural forms, ornament, and detail of both styles in decoration, furniture, and other arts.

2. CINQUECENTO (High Period, 1500–1600).
The first half of this century is considered the high period of the Italian Renaissance, and the word *Cinquecento,* as the name of an art style, is usually applied only to the work produced during those years. Classical forms used, with beauty of line and mass more important than surface enrichment. The period of activity of most of the greatest artists.

3. BAROQUE (1506–1630), HIGH BAROQUE (1630–1670), and ROCOCO (1650–1750).
The Jesuit style that commenced with the construction of large churches, followed by the overdecoration of both ecclesiastical and secular buildings. Use of concave and convex walls and cornices, spiral columns, and movement and assymmetry in design. Florid and meaningless ornament. Optical illusion and false use of materials for effect. Boisterous and theatrical types of design. First operatic performances. Beginning of the decline of native Italian creative ability.

4. FOREIGN INFLUENCE (1650–1815).
The French and English styles in the decorative arts were reproduced by the Italians, who lacked the initiative for further development along native lines. This influence was started during the Rococo period and extended through the Napoleonic period.

Examples of Renaissance design. LEFT: *Characteristic pilaster capital. The design is based on the Corinthian form, but the details are entirely novel in conception.* RIGHT: *Arabesque wood carving. The design is symmetrical in mass, but variations in detail are introduced to produce interest.*

The palace. The use of gunpowder by the armies of Europe was greatly increased during the 15th century. By 1450 the medieval fortified castle with its moat, drawbridge, and portcullis was of little value for defensive purposes, and as the forts were removed to more strategic outlying districts, the towns themselves burst the bounds of their ancient walls, and the construction of the more luxurious city dwelling and suburban villa commenced. The feudal system had never obtained a firm foothold in Italy. Destiny, therefore, permitted the Italians to be the earliest designers of a type of domestic architecture in which comfort, convenience, and beauty were the important considerations, rather than safety, strength, and protection. The beginning of the modern art of interior design is coincident with that of domestic architecture.

The exteriors of the palaces built during the 15th century showed evidence of the Gothic influence in design, and retained some of the vigorous characteristics of the old fortified castles; but, as the century progressed, the use of the architectural forms of classical antiquity greatly increased, and these were applied to the decorative treatment of the important rooms of the interior. Pedestal, column, pilaster, entablature, pediment, and panel were employed for both structural and ornamental purposes, and these features aided in producing rooms of great formality, dignity, and magnificence. Column capitals, on the whole, followed classical lines, but novelties and variations were introduced. Door and window openings were treated with architrave moldings as trim. In the more elaborate examples, open-

112 ELEMENTS OF INTERIOR DESIGN AND DECORATION

ings were frequently flanked with pilasters supporting triangular, segmental, or semicircular pediments. To supplement the architectural forms, painted frescoes, elaborate embroideries, velvets, or tapestries were used on the walls. The subject matter for the mural decorations consisted of scenes of antique ruins, distant garden views, scenes from classical history and mythology, religious and astronomical subjects, and portrayals of memorable events in the owner's family history.

In the latter years of the 15th century, the Italians discovered the mathematical principles of linear perspective. This discovery greatly benefitted painters and artists in other mediums. Even woodworkers endeavored to show their abilities by producing *intarsia* (inlay) pictorial panels representing buildings and other objects drawn with proper foreshortening. Designers hit upon the ingenious device of giving a larger aspect to a room by lining its walls with wainscots treated with intarsia showing accurate perspective views of cabinets with open doors and shelves containing armor, vases, musical instruments, bird cages, books, etc. Architectural features were also introduced by using contrasting colored woods to produce the effect of natural highlights and shadows on the moldings.

During the Cinquecento and later, elaborate use was made of colored marble slabs for wall treatments and architectural trim. Wall panel effects were produced by the use of borders or stripes in one color, with contrasting fields. Columns and pilasters with gilt-bronze capitals were added for further enrichment. Moldings and relief ornament were either carved or made of gilded stucco. Cast plaster heraldic devices, flower and leaf forms, amorini (cherubs), and grotesques eventually increased in size and number. Wood-panelled walls left in a natural finish or decorated with paint were a late development.

Examples of Renaissance interiors may be seen in the Palazzo Vecchio in Florence, the Farnese Palace in Rome, the Villa d'Este in Tivoli, and in many other palaces throughout northern Italy. The majority of rooms in these palaces are of a degree of richness in decoration that is far beyond the requirements of the present day.

The villa. During the early Renaissance many smaller palaces and country villas were built by wealthy merchants. These were decorated in a more modest fashion than the homes of the nobility. The academic architectural forms were used reservedly or were omitted in such interiors, and the thick stone walls were pierced by doors and windows having deep reveals without trim. The openings were treated either with a flat lintel or had a segmental or semicircular arch. The *Florentine arch,* usually used in arcades, was semicircular, and consisted of an architrave molding springing from a classical column. The coarse sand plaster used on the walls was accentuated by an irregular surface produced by the plasterer's trowel, giving an interest and richness in tone and texture. Walls were sometimes painted

Alinari

Painted arabesque ornament of the 15th century in the Palazzo Vecchio in Florence. The design is inspired from classical art.

Alinari

Room in the Palazzo Davanzati, Florence, Italy, showing early Renaissance details and furniture.

to imitate hung textiles; not only the pattern of the fabric, but the folds, nails, highlights, and shadows, as well, were reproduced. The rooms of these smaller dwellings were large in comparison with those of a modern home.

Ceilings. Ceilings were high, and the general scale of details was correspondingly heavy. They were often elaborately treated in either wood or plaster or a combination of the two. The wood ceilings consisted of enormous walnut, oak, cedar, or cypress beams, spaced several feet apart, spanning the width of the room. The large beams in turn supported smaller beams, spaced one or two feet apart, running in the opposite direction, and supporting the floor above. The beams were striped with paint in vivid colors, and an occasional *cartouche, medallion,* or coat-of-arms was introduced in the center. Wood-panelled and *coffered* ceilings also were used in which both the wood and the panel were decorated with painted arabesques, conventional ornament, or scenic patterns. The plaster ceilings were usually flat and appeared to be supported at the wall with *coved* arches springing from brackets resembling pilaster capitals. Vaulted ceilings were also sometimes made in the form of a low segmental arch.

Floors. Tile, brick, and marble were the materials most suitable for floors in a warm climate, and all were extensively used. The accessibility and supply of colorful marbles made them popular for flooring. Checkerboard and scroll patterns in black, white, gray, and color were made. Floors were also made of a crushed colored marble mixed with cement, known as *terrazzo*. Tiles were usually 6- or 8-inch squares or hexagons, and were both plain and patterned. Brick floors were usually laid following a herringbone design. Plank floors of oak and walnut were used, as well, in the early period, and after 1600 elaborate *parquetry* patterns in rarer, colored woods came into use. When floor coverings were used, they consisted of small Oriental rugs placed where most needed.

Fireplaces and mantels. The hooded fireplace was used in rooms of the late Gothic period in Italy, and with the introduction of Renaissance forms, the same general arrangement for carrying out the smoke was used; the detail of enrichment, however, gradually assumed a classic architectural character, and the projection of the hood was reduced to a minimum.

When the fireplace opening was countersunk in the wall, the opening was trimmed on three sides with a flat architrave molding. The *bolection molding,* used as a trim, was also very typical. This latter form consisted of a heavy torus molding grouped with smaller moldings projecting several inches from the wall. In the more elaborate fireplace treatments, the architrave form of trim was crowned with a carved frieze and projecting cornice moldings, forming a mantelshelf. Dwarf columns, pilasters, caryatids, and acanthus leaf *brackets* were also used as side supporting motifs to support the entablature or cornice. Ornament consisted of carv-

Interior of the late Gothic period in the Palazzo Davanzati, Florence, Italy, showing painted wall decoration and Gothic fireplace with early Renaissance furniture.

Cell of Savonarola in the Museum of St. Mark, Florence, showing the simplicity of treatment characteristic of the early Renaissance.

ings, marble inlay, and paint, showing arabesques and rinceaux, classical figures, heraldic forms, portrait busts, or grouped foliage patterns.

Built-in features. The niche, a recessed wall space, was borrowed from classical architecture and adopted by the Renaissance interior designers for both ornamental and useful purposes. The ornamental niche, both with and without flanking pilasters, usually contained a statue in bronze, marble, or glazed or painted terra cotta. The useful niche was used as a storage space, and sometimes contained shelves or a washbasin. It often had two wooden doors or shutters that were plain, painted, or treated with a simple pattern. The niche heads were flat, segmental, or semicircular.

Early Renaissance interior showing typical beamed ceiling, rough plaster walls with Gothic niches and herringbone-tile floor and hooded fireplace.

An ornamental feature that was frequently built into the wall was the glazed terra-cotta *plaque* or panel. The della Robbia family of sculptors became particularly famous for the production of these panels, which were valuable as decorations and for color interest, where plain plaster walls existed.* The plaques were modelled in high relief, and consisted of cherubs, human figures, and wreaths and garlands of fruit, vegetables, and leaves. The coloring of the background was principally in light blue, with white used for relief ornament and figures.† Small portions of the pattern were sometimes colored in yellow, green, or purple.

The Baroque style. The term "Baroque" is a word that originated in France in the 17th century to describe what was then considered a bizarre type of Italian architecture and decoration. The limiting dates of the style are debatable, but its earliest evidences were seen in St. Peter's in Rome (1506); it reached its height in Italy about 1650 and then evolved into the Rococo, a style which had its roots in Italy, but its most extensive development in France. Italy later borrowed the French forms and the Rococo terminated as a result of the Pompeian discoveries in 1755. Esthetically the development of the Baroque was a revolt against the frigidity and lack of spirit in the Vitruvian formulas as interpreted by Vignola and Palladio. Freedom in design was needed to express the ebullient qualities of the 17th

* See Chapter XVI.
† The most notable of these products were the swaddled *bambini* which decorate the spandrels of the Hospital of the Innocents in Florence, copies of which are sold to nearly every tourist.

The Nave of St. Peter's, Rome, looking toward the baldachino centered under the dome above the crossing. The baldachino is 100 feet high and covers the High Altar built over the alleged tomb of St. Peter. The interior over-all length of the church is 600 feet. The nave is 84 feet wide.

century rather than to surround them with an antique framework. The Counter Reformationists, headed by the Jesuits, recognized their opportunity, harnessed the movement to suit their requirements, and through a boisterous art endeavored to restore the religious wanderers to the fold and to confound the skeptics.

The Baroque was discontinued in Rome after 1670 but was adopted by the Spaniards, Portuguese, Mexicans, and Germans, in whose countries it approached a theatricalism that was never equalled in Italy. A Protestantism that adored simplicity prevented its absorption by England. France under Louis XIV remodelled it to suit his needs, and out of it grew a French Rococo that reached a zenith in originality.

St. Peter's. The early Baroque style was seen at its best in St. Peter's Cathedral in Rome (1506–1626), which was built on such a colossal scale that it is almost impossible visually to gauge its dimensions. St. Peter's is 710 feet long, and covers 227,000 square feet. Its dome is 450 feet high; the nave is 84 feet wide, roofed by a great barrel vault 150 feet high, and the supporting Corinthian pilasters are 84 feet from base to capital. The colonnade of its forecourt encloses an area that has contained 250,000 persons. Over a period of 120 years many famous architects and artists were employed in building it. Among them were Bramante, Raphael, Michael

Angelo, and Bernini, the latter being the greatest of the High Baroque. The statues of the saints in its niches are 16 feet in height and the cherubs are 7 feet. The interior is a vast surface of arches, columns, pilasters, and other classical architectural features in colored marbles, frescoes, mosaics, sculpture, grilles, candelabra, paintings, intarsia, organ pipes, and gilded plaster ornament. Alabaster altars and chapels are loaded with the gold, rock-crystal, and enamel accessories of the Catholic ritual.

St. Peter's magnificent throne occupies the western apse. Emotions become ecstatic as one looks at the High Altar, crowned by the great *baldachino* of Bernini that is placed under the center of the dome and over the traditional grave of the Saint.* The baldachino is 100 feet high, supported by gigantic spiral columns and enriched with a wild extravagance of detail. The upward vista from this point includes in its perspective the great pendentives that support the *drum,* and reaches to the top of Michael Angelo's dome, a point 350 feet above the marble floor. Its soaring effect is intensified by dramatic lighting. The rays of the sun infiltrate through the upper windows, penetrate the mist and drifting smoke from the burning incense, and produce a celestial effect. The Cathedral is one of the most awe-inspiring works of man.

The High Baroque. Although St. Peter's was never afterwards surpassed in its scale or dimensions, it was used as an inspirational model for hundreds of churches built throughout Christendom, and the richness of its interior decoration formed the basis for the High Baroque that occurred in Italy between 1630 and 1670. This was a style that discarded bulk and large scale but increased surface enrichment and color brilliance, a type of decoration that made a stronger emotional impression upon the masses.

The High Baroque used curved forms instead of straight for structural as well as ornamental purposes. Walls were often planned with undulating curves and the orders of architecture were often ornaments as well as structural elements. Columns were sometimes twisted into spirals and shamelessly supported nothing. Entablatures and moldings followed bulging shapes, or were warped into three-dimensional curves. Scroll and serpentine pediments were broken in two, and each half faced in the wrong direction. Angels, cherubs, and genii, in strange positions and realistic coloring, seemed to be flying through the air or emerging from clouds. An extensive use was made of *peintures-vivantes,* high reliefs of religious groups, modelled and colored in lifelike reality, framed in fanciful architectural detail, and lit by natural and artificial means that brought them to the verge of animation. Elaborate gilt ornament often smothered struc-

---

* It is believed that Peter suffered martyrdom under Nero in A.D. 67. Tradition says that he was crucified with his head downward on the Vatican Hill. In Matthew 16:13–20 it is stated he was given the keys to heaven. This established him as the head and first Pope of the Roman Church. The keys to heaven have always been used in the decorative arts to symbolize St. Peter.

Characteristic early 18th century Italian interior showing a strong French Baroque and Rococo influence.

tural forms under its mass. Honesty of material was disregarded; theatricalism and scenic effect were the first requirements, and if plaster or tin could substitute for marble or gold, the artistic conscience did not suffer.

The Baroque church decoration spread to palace and villa and merged with garden design. Balconies, belvederes, fountains, terraces, and flower beds showed an outburst of florid effects. Artists and craftsmen in every medium produced furnishings and household accessories that were in accord with the architectural movement and the public demand for esthetic turbulency. In palace decoration the walls were frequently covered with rich brocades, brocatelles, velvets, and damasks, and hung with paintings or huge mirrors in gilt frames. Elaborate frescoes simulating architectural features were also introduced. Stucco ornament replaced the carved wood and marble of the classic Cinquecento. Ceilings were at times loaded down with plaster cherubs flying here and there supporting heavily fringed stucco draperies in full color. Walls were sometimes japanned or lacquered; wainscots were of ivory, of marble, or of painted imitation marble. Mother-of-pearl, silver, and tortoise-shell inlay were used in doors, panelling, and furniture.

Furniture. In the early Renaissance, furniture was sparingly used, and what existed was consistent with the large dimensions of the rooms. By the middle of the Quattrocento a more general demand for greater richness and comfort in the movable furnishings of the house was prevalent, and as great thought was placed upon entertaining and social intercourse, the general design and arrangement of the furniture was made with these activities in view.

A great deal of the furniture was monumental in character, and its logical position was against the wall, forming a dominant note in the wall composition, with such subordinate motifs as chairs, decorative wall plaques, portrait busts on brackets, heavily framed paintings, or panels of relief sculpture.

There were certain characteristics of Italian furniture that carried through the whole period of native design from 1400 to 1700. The principal one was the use of walnut as a cabinet wood. The fertile soil and temperate climate of Italy were particularly suitable to this tree, which often grew to a height of 75 feet. Walnut planks with beautiful grain and rich brown color could be had over three feet wide, and these were made into table tops or panel fields. While various other woods were used by the country cabinetmakers, almost 90 per cent of the furniture of these centuries was made of walnut.

The earliest Renaissance cabinetmakers followed the principles of their Gothic predecessors in applying architectural forms to the ornament and decoration of their furniture. The change required only the substitution of classic orders, acanthus leaf, *grotesque,* and arabesque for pointed arch, tracery, and linenfold. The straight Gothic structural lines produced by stile and rail were maintained. Italian Gothic furniture frequently had painted panels showing historical or religious groups, events, and sequences, and the charm of this type of enrichment caused it to persist well into the 15th century. *Gesso* ornament, made of chalk and white lead cast in a mould, was also used to make relief patterns that were to be gilded or *polychromed,* and where repetition of motif was admissible, the advantages of this material were obvious.

Certain types of furniture decoration were local in origin. In the vicinity of Lombardy, small ivory inlay patterns were set in the woodwork. This ornamentation was known as *certosina.* Venice produced much furniture that was covered with intricate scroll and arabesque patterns, made by inlaying different colored woods—an enrichment known as intarsia. From the beginning of the Cinquecento, Roman furniture was enriched both by carved relief patterns and painted decorations consisting of cartouches, rinceaux, arabesques, grotesques, gadroons, dolphins, and other forms borrowed from antiquity. The ornament on Florentine furniture was frequently touched up with dull gold, which gave it added sparkle and interest and caused it to harmonize well with all other colors used in a room.

In spite of characteristics featured in particular localities, the same forms

Florentine Table

Dante Chair

Savonarola Chair

Sqabello→

←Candelabrum

Cassone

Armchair Cassapanca

SIXTEENTH-CENTURY ITALIAN FURNITURE.

were almost immediately copied in other parts of Italy. By the middle of the Cinquecento, gesso and painted decoration were less applied to furniture, and the Roman method of carving the ornament became popular. At the same time, curved structural forms began to be introduced with the Baroque influence in architecture. Ornament increased in quantity and capriciousness. Venice became particularly noted for the extravagant forms that were later partly influenced by foreign models.

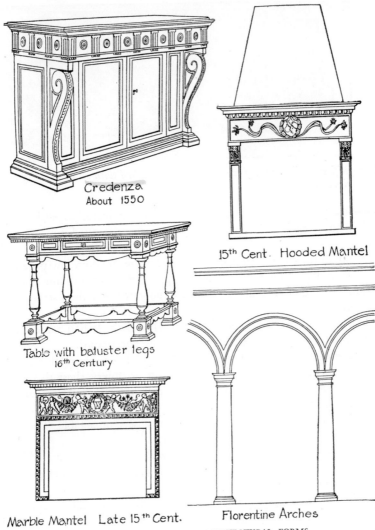

Credenza
About 1550

15th Cent. Hooded Mantel

Table with baluster legs
16th Century

Marble Mantel Late 15th Cent.　　Florentine Arches

ITALIAN FURNITURE AND ARCHITECTURAL FORMS.

The panels on the early furniture were small and rectangular in shape, although the dimensions were often larger than those of the Gothic period. The early panels were sunk below the stiles and rails and were bordered on four sides with simple moldings. Sometimes narrow stripes of color-contrasting woods formed part of the panel framework, and borders in checkerboard effects were also seen. When decorated, the early panels were painted with scenes or arabesques. Intarsia and carving enriched the later panels. During the Rococo period, the panels were made in irregular shapes, and the field often projected beyond the stile, producing the raised or

A magnificent 16th century walnut cassone enriched with an elaborately carved rinceau motif.

bolection panel. Semiprecious stones and other materials such as lapis lazuli, onyx, amber, ivory, and *crystal* were also used for inlay purposes.

Many of the larger pieces of Italian furniture stood on low pedestals or projecting steps, to give them added dignity. Beds, chests, and heavy *case furniture* were often built up from the floor without the use of legs for support.

Italian furniture, as a general rule, is called by its Italian name. The important pieces are described in the following paragraphs.

The *cassone* was a chest or box of any kind, from the small jewel casket to the enormous and immovable wedding or dowry chest that was the most important piece of furniture in the Italian room. The cassone was also used as travelling baggage. The lid was hinged at the top, and when the piece was closed, it could be used as a seat or a table. The cassone served the purposes of the modern closet.

The *cassapanca* was a large cassone with a back and arms added to it to form a settee or sofa. This was particularly a Florentine production. Loose cushions were used for comfort.

The *credenza* was a cabinet-sideboard with doors and drawers intended for the storage of linen, dishes, and silverware. It was made in various sizes. The small type was known as a credenzetta. The crendenza often had an ornamental wooden back rising from its shelf.

The *sgabello* was a light wooden chair used for dining and other purposes. The early types had three legs, small octagonal seats, and stiff backs. The later examples show two trestles or *splat* supports, and when carving was introduced, both the trestles and backs were elaborately treated. The sgabello was also made without a back, forming a low bench.

The *sedia* was a chair, of which there were several varieties, all lacking comfort, if judged by modern standards. The armchair was rectangular in its main lines, with square, straight legs. The legs were connected with stretchers, which were sometimes placed so as to rest on the floor. A characteristic feature was the upward extension of the rear legs to form the back uprights, which were terminated with a finial motif intended to represent an acanthus leaf bracket. The arm support was usually turned in a *baluster* form. Upholstery of back and seat consisted of velvet, damask, or ornamental leather, trimmed with silk fringe. The smaller side chair was built on the same general lines as the armchair, but often was made entirely of wood and enriched with simple turnings. Seats were made of rush, wood, or textile. Ornamental nailheads were used with leather upholstery. Other chairs were of the folding or X-shaped type, of which there were three varieties. The "Savonarola" type was composed of interlacing curved slats and usually had a carved wooden back and arms. The "Dante" or "Dantesque" type had heavy curved arms and legs, and usually had a cloth back and seat. The "monastery" type was smaller and was built of interlacing straight splats. Folding chairs were also made of wrought iron with brass trimmings and cushion seats.

The *letto,* or bed, was often a massive structure with panelled headboard and footboard, the whole surrounded by cassoni standing solidly on the floor without legs. Other beds were of the four-poster variety, with *tester* above. All were treated with richly carved, painted, or intarsia ornament and draperies.

Tables were made in all sizes. Large rectangular *refectory* tables often had tops made of single planks of walnut. The supports were elaborately carved trestles, dwarf Doric columns, or turned baluster forms. Both plain and carved *stretchers* were used. Small tables often had hexagonal and octagonal tops, and were supported by carved central pedestals. The edges of the table tops were usually treated with ornamented moldings.

Drop-lid writing cabinets, double-deck storage cabinets, wardrobes, framed pictures and mirrors, pedestal supports for statues and ornaments, clothes racks, bookcases, firescreens, and hanging shelves completed the list of furniture types used in the Italian interior before the 18th century.

During the High Baroque and the latter years of the 17th century, the same lavishness displayed in interior architecture was also to be found in furniture design and construction. Cassones were eliminated, but variations of the credenza remained. Raised panels were used on enormous cabinets. All furniture was large and heavy. Nailheads were arranged in patterns on leather- and fabric-covered chairs. Furniture inlay offered lavish decorative possibilities, with the introduction of pietra dura, lapis lazuli, onyx, ivory, mosaic, rock crystal, marble, and other semiprecious stones. Decorative painting was also frequently resorted to for the enrichment of furniture, particularly on panels and on the headboards of beds. Furniture woods were often of an inferior grade, and the painted surfaces and decorations helped conceal the inferior construction.

Polychromed stucco relief panel of the Virgin and Child, sculptured by Benedetto da Maiano in the 15th century. It is framed with the characteristic architectural frame of the period. Total height, about 50 inches.

Minor arts and accessories. The love of beauty so penetrated the Italian mind that the most insignificant article of household use was designed with care and thought. As a result, most of the decorative accessories used in the rooms were of extraordinary charm, and maintained the standard of excellence set by the productions of the greater artists, many of whom had spent their apprenticeships in the metal, jewelry, and glass ateliers, or as designers of pottery or textiles.

The fine arts of painting and sculpture during the Italian Renaissance need no emphasis here. The smaller easel paintings of the masters and their pupils were in constant demand as room decorations, and were usually given places of honor on the walls. Pedestals, wall brackets, niches, and architectural treatments were designed for pieces of sculpture. Picture frames were handcarved, and frequently took the form of architectural compositions, with pedestals, pilasters, entabulatures, and pediments. Small relief panels, similarly framed, often showing the Madonna and Child, were carved in marble, cast in plaster, and made in glazed or painted terra cotta.

Among the most important accessories in the Italian rooms of the 16th century were the large enamelled earthenware plates which were known as *majolica* ware. Their principal value was as ornament. Their manufacture was centered in the towns of Deruta, Faenza, and Urbino. They were painted by minor artists, although Raphael is known to have been employed in this manner in his youth. The range of colors was limited, because of the difficulty of obtaining pigments that would not fade in the kiln. The decoration was either in arabesque or pictorial form, covering both rim and center. Scenes of classical history and mythology were often shown. The drawing was generally naïve in character. Pitchers, vases, pharmacy pots, and other useful articles were also made in this ware.*

The Italians developed extraordinary ability as workers in both precious and base metals. Cellini's greatest ability was as a goldsmith, though his genius was also exceptional as jeweler, sculptor, and author.

* See Chapter XVI.

Sixteenth-century majolica plate made in Urbino, showing one type of scenic pattern in which the difference in the height between rim and center is disregarded.

Alinari

While such men as Sansovino, Maiano, Donatello, Ghiberti, and Verrocchio are best known for their figure sculpture, they did not hesitate to model, for bronze reproduction, decorative relief panels, lanterns, candelabra, inkstands, andirons, door hardware, knockers, and other articles of architectural and household use. Sculptors such as Il Riccio and Vittoria devoted themselves to small objects, and the production of bronze statuettes by the *cire-perdue* process, in imitation of large classical originals, was a flourishing art that enriched mantel, shelf, and table.

Venice was the center of the ornamental glass and table glassware industry, and from medieval times her painted products had been exported to other European countries. Small wall mirrors, substituted for polished metal, were introduced during the 15th century. So costly and valued were the early mirrors that they were usually covered with a wooden door or panel, and great attention was paid to their frames. In the 16th century, mirrors increased in size and the convex mirror was made. Rock crystal carving, the enamelling of metal panels, and the carving of *cameo* and *intaglio* medallions were also extensively carried on in Italy.

Italian textiles used for draperies and upholstery were usually of silk. Velvets and damasks were the most common weaves during the early Renaissance; brocades and brocatelles, during the late period. Patterns were large. Dress velvets made in Genoa were used for loose cushions and for the upholstery of the smaller pieces of furniture. Flemish and Italian handmade tapestries were used as wall hangings in the larger homes. Lacemaking became an important industry in northern Italy, and the materials

Seventeenth-century bronze statue of a centaur, modelled after the antique and cast by the cire perdue process. About 12 inches in height; used as an accessory.

were largely used for both clothing and interior decoration. Oriental rugs were frequently used for table covers as well as for floor coverings.

Color schemes. The Italians had a sophisticated understanding of the use of color for interior work. The large scale of many of the rooms permitted strong tones in *primary colors* to be used, although discretion was maintained in the distribution. When plain, neutral-colored plaster was used for a wall, draperies and accessories could afford to be in brilliant reds, blues, yellows, purples, and greens. In the later Renaissance, colors were softened. When brocades and damasks were used for wall treatments, the size of the room was taken into consideration in the selection of the colors. Strong tones were still used in the larger rooms, but delicate shades were selected for the smaller ones.

The decline and its causes. The decline of the Renaissance style in Italy dates from 1650, and coincides with the transfer of the political, financial, and cultural control of Europe to France under Louis XIV and later to England under Queen Anne. The vast funds collected through the exorbitant taxes levied by Louis, and spent in enriching his palaces, attracted the artistic talent of the world to Paris, where the rewards were high. The Italian trade with the Orient lessened as the discovery of America occupied the attention of Europe. The decline in the wealth of Italy and the establishment of superior French and English prestige in Europe were the final blows to the creative spirit of the Italians. The magnificent and novel productions of the Parisian ateliers began to set the standards of industrial art for the whole of Europe. Italian artists were forced to meet the demand for foreign designs. In imitating the products of other nations, they produced many crudities, although an effort was made to copy the general character of the originals. The products of this period in Italy clearly show a far less capable conception of good form than was maintained by the designers of the originals, and yet the productions were not lacking in a charm and quaintness of their own.

The Rococo (1650–1750). The style known as the Rococo in Italy started well before the High Baroque had exhausted itself, and to some extent may

LEFT: *Italian Louis XV interior from a palace in Turin, showing the voluptuous character of carving required of the French workmen imported to do the work.* BELOW: *Eighteenth century Italian interior.*

Courtesy L. Alavoine and Company; Samuel H. Gottsho, Photographer

Italian 18th century room showing plaster Rococo wall panelling and ceiling.

be considered merely a further development. Although its first manifestations were seen in Italy, the transfer of the economic and artistic leadership of Europe from Italy to France was in progress and the real development of the style occurred in the latter country. The Italians looked across the Alps for their inspiration. The name of the style was taken from the initial letters of both the Italian and French words for rock and cockleshell. These were features borrowed from nature that eventually were commonly imitated in architectural stonework and ornament. Decorative designers in search of novelty also seized upon book engravings of the period that were beginning to show fantastic leaf and scroll ornaments never intended to be produced in relief. These motifs began to be applied to walls and furniture in wood carving and plaster, and metalwork. The most able Italian designers who went to France at the invitation of Louis XIV carried the ideas with them and the Rococo style developed in France even more rapidly than it did in Italy. Although its roots began before the end of the 17th century, it did not reach its culmination in France until the middle of the 18th century. During this period there was a constant interchange of both ideas and workers between France and Italy. Restraint in the use and structure of ornament was eventually completely discarded. The French interpretation of the style returned to Italy, where it received still further development in the exaggerations of curved lines and forms, although the scale was smaller than during the Baroque period.

Italian rococo art, as compared to the contemporary French art of the period, was coarse, and at times approached artistic vulgarity. Ornament was badly designed and was applied without regard to suitability. Proportions were usually awkward in comparison to the French originals. Much gilding was used. The Italian creative imagination tended toward theatrical effects. In the matter of furniture design, the Italians also turned extensively to England, and the William and Mary, and Queen Anne styles were freely copied. Lacquer was employed for furniture decoration, and in the desire for cheap lacquered effects, colored engravings were cut out,

Courtesy Taft Museum, Cincinnati

ABOVE LEFT: *Group of Italian 18th century furnishings, mainly Louis XV influence.*

ABOVE RIGHT: *Venetian chair of about 1735 showing extremely florid French Rococo character.*

LEFT: *Venetian secretary-desk made about 1720 showing English Queen Anne design influence. The lacquer was often simulated by the application of painted and highly varnished paper veneers.*

glued to furniture surfaces, and covered with a heavy coating of varnish. The Chinese influence was also introduced in design forms as well as in finish. The work of the Englishmen William Kent and Chippendale fired the Italian imagination. The Italians often confused and combined the styles of 18th century France and England.

The social life in Italy of the 18th century borrowed the superficiality of the French. Dignity was cast aside, as artists, scholars, cavaliers, ecclesiastics, and ballet dancers hobnobbed with dukes and princes. The great

Head Board of
Venetian Bed

Venetian Chair

Venetian Sofa

VENETIAN 18TH CENTURY FURNITURE.

families of the early Renaissance were extinct. The finances of the petty
kingdoms of Italy were at a low ebb. Venice and the Papacy alone maintained their power and prestige. The frivolity and gaiety of the 18th century were largely centered in the ancient city of the Doges. As the elite of
Venice squandered their time and resources in pleasure and vanity, trade
and industry were at a standstill and the end was inevitable.

Italian rococo decoration and furniture is often labelled "Venetian,"
because of the orgy of decoration in that city during the 18th century. Furniture in imitation of the French styles was made and used in many north
Italian cities, and is sometimes designated as Italian-Louis XIV, Italian-
Louis XV, or Italian-Louis XVI. Much of the furniture made for the less
important houses during the 18th century was simple in design, yet gay,
colorful, and romantic in effect, and very adaptable to homes of today.

The classic revival in Italy. Toward the end of the 18th century and in the early years of the 19th, the Italian people felt the influence, in spite of their comparative poverty, of the excavation of antique cities going on in their midst. All Europe was engaged in the search of Roman and Pompeian ruins. It would have been strange, indeed, if Italy had not shared in this enthusiasm. The continued adherence of the Italian aristocracy to French modes and manners further centered their attention on the use of French decoration, which in turn had been inspired

Group of Italian 18th- and early 19th-century furnishings, mainly Directoire and Empire influences.

by the discoveries of Pompeii and Herculaneum. The Italians, however, accused the French of being too correct in the use of the antique style, and they felt that the Adam leadership in England produced a style that was too cold and bloodless for southern temperaments. Interior designers in Italy, inspired by their natural exuberance and love of florid decoration, continued to draw upon their imaginations for innovations and variations of the northern styles. Toward the end of the century, greater delicacy and refinement were seen.

Marquetry patterns and marble intarsia or inlay were extensively used for furniture enrichment, and this type of ornament enabled the craftsmen to produce some of the loveliest contributions to 18th century art. Painted

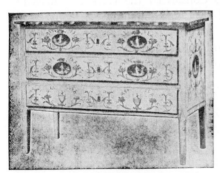

furniture continued to be much in favor, and many of Italy's most talented decorative painters, such as Cipriani, Pergolesi, Zucchi, and Piranesi, produced in their delightful paintings an art of unrivalled charm. Both the English and the French, by offers of greater compensation, induced Italian painters who had studied the antique details to leave Italy and pursue their activities away from home. Other countries also benefited by Italian talents.

Painted chest of drawers. Late 18th century, showing Pompeian pattern influence.

The Empire style in Italy. With the exception of France, nowhere else was the Empire style as originally and successfully expressed as in Italy. Napoleon was master of Italy for ten months in 1796. His sister, Pauline, married into the princely house of Borghese and further stimulated the devotion to the arts of France. Napoleon himself became Emperor of Italy in 1805, made his stepson Viceroy of Naples, and later called his infant son the King of Rome. Many of the old Italian palaces were redecorated in the French Empire style and were enriched with furniture and accessories made in Parisian workshops.

Leaders in the Arts of Italy

The following list contains the names of the most well-known leaders in the Italian arts, together with the dates when they flourished and a statement of the work for which they were noted:

Alberti, Leone Battista (1404–1472). Early Renaissance architect, scholar, and author.

Angelico, Fra (1387–1455). Poetical and mystical painter of religious subjects.

Bernini, Giovanni Lorenzo (1598–1680). A Neapolitan under Spanish influence. The leading architect of the Baroque period. Sculptor and painter. Designer of the *baldachino* in St. Peter's.

Boccaccio, Giovanni (1313–1375). Novelist of pagan ideals, author of the *Decameron*.

Botticelli, Sandro (1444–1510). Poetical painter of classical mythology and allegorical subjects.

Bramante, Donato d'Agnolo (1444–1514). Painter and architect of St. Peter's in Rome.

Brunelleschi, Filippo (1377–1446). Considered the earliest Renaissance architect. Designed the dome of the Cathedral and the Hospital of the Innocents in Florence.

Caravaggio, Michelangelo (1569–1609). First Italian realist painter.

Cellini, Benvenuto (1500–1571). Goldsmith and sculptor.

Cimabue, Giovanni (1240?–1302?). Florentine painter called the father of modern painting. Designed mosaics and frescoes.

Da Vinci, Leonardo (1452–1519). Great Florentine painter, sculptor, architect, scientist, engineer, writer, and musician. One of the most imaginative and inventive of men.

Dante Alighieri (1265–1321). Poet and father of vernacular literature, author of *Divina Commedia*.

Della Robbia Family: Luca, Andrea, Giovanni, Girolamo (1400–1566). Sculptors and originators of Della Robbia *faïence*.

Donatello (1386–1466). Florentine sculptor of the naturalistic school. Great student of the antique.

Ghiberti, Lorenzo (1378–1455). Sculptor famous for his bronze doors in the Baptistery of Florence.

Giorgione da Castelfranco (1478–1510). First Renaissance painter among the Venetians.

Giotto di Bondone (1266?–1337?). Florentine primitive painter, sculptor, and architect.

Masaccio, Tommaso Guidi (1401–1428). First Florentine painter of naturalism.

Michael Angelo Buonarroti (1475–1564). Painter, sculptor, architect, and poet. Called the father of the Baroque.

Palladio, Andrea (1518–1580). Architect and excavator of Roman ruins. Author of book on antique architecture. Designer of villas.

Petrarch, Francesco (1304–1374). Scholar, humanist, and author.

Pinturicchio, Bernardino (1454–1513). Decorative painter.

Raphael Sanzio (1483–1520). Painter and architect.

Sansovino, Jacopo (1486–1570). Venetian architect and sculptor of the 16th century.

Savonarola, Girolamo (1452–1498). Italian monk and reformer who was burned at the stake.

Tintoretto, Il (1518–1594). Venetian painter renowned for his grandiose effects achieved by the play of light and shadow. Real name Jacopo Robusti.

Titian (1477–1576). Venetian painter of the sensuous spirit of the Renaissance. Real name Tiziano Vecellio.

Veronese, Paolo (1528–1588). Painter of the luxurious Venetian life, renowned for his silvery tones.

Vignola, Giacomo Barocchio (1507–1573). Italian architect who wrote the *Treatise on the Five Orders,* and revived the standardized proportions of Vitruvius.

Bibliography

Brunelli, *Ville del Brenta.* Milan, c. 1936. Italian text and illustrations of Italian 18th century villas.

Burckhardt, J., *Civilization of the Renaissance in Italy.* Oxford University Press. Reprint, 1944. One of the finest books on this subject.

Durant, W., *The Renaissance.* Simon and Schuster, New York, 1953. A comprehensive history.

Hunter, G. L., *Italian Furniture and Interiors,* 2 Vols. Wm. Helburn, Inc., New York, 1917. Illustrated text.

LETAROUILLY, P., *Edifices de Rome Moderne,* 4 Vols. Reprint of original edition. John Tiranti and Co., London, 1928. Collection of measured drawings of Italian Renaissance buildings.

LOWELL, G., *Smaller Italian Villas and Farm Houses.* Architectural Book Publishing Co., New York, 1929. Text with photographs.

MARAZZONI, G., *Il Mobile Veneziano Del'700.* Casa Editrice d'Arte Bestetti e Tumminelli, Milan, 1927. Italian text with excellent photographs of Venetian furniture.

MIDANA, A., *L'Arte del Legno in Piemonte nel Sei e nel Settecento.* Casa Editrice "Itala Ars," Torino. Brief Italian text with excellent photographs.

ODOM, W. M., *A History of Italian Furniture.* Doubleday and Co., Garden City, N. Y., 1918. Excellent illustrated text.

ROSENBURG, L. C., *The Davanzati Palace, Florence, Italy.* Architectural Book Publishing Co., New York, 1922. Brief text with measured drawings of the restored 14th century palace.

SCHOTTMULLER, F., *Furniture and Interior Decoration of the Italian Renaissance.* Brentano's, New York, 1921. An introductory text with fine collection of photographs.

SYMONDS, J. A., *The Renaissance in Italy: The Fine Arts.* Smith, Elder and Co., London, 1899. A beautifully written text on the lives and works of the Italian artists. A standard book.

THOMAS, W. G., and FALLON, J. T., *Northern Italian Details.* The American Architect, New York, 1916. Text with measured drawings and photographs.

TINTI, M., *Il Mobilio Fiorentino.* Casa Editrice d'Arte Bestetti e Tumminelli, Milan, 1929. Italian text with photographs.

CHAPTER IV

THE HISPANIC PERIODS

T he civilizations of the Iberian Peninsula are unique among the countries of modern Europe. They have linked the cultures of the Near East and the Western world and enjoyed the riches of both. On their soil was placed that spectacular drama of Moor and Christian fanatic that lasted nearly a thousand years, and ended in a blending of characteristics of the two races that has produced the modern Spaniard and Portuguese.

Racial origins and early history. Nearly all the great nations of antiquity made settlements in the Peninsula. The original inhabitants were the Iberians, who at some time were fused with a Celtic stock. The Basques in the Pyrenees are supposed to be the most direct descendants of these groups and are probably nearer to the aboriginal Europeans than any other people. Settlements were made by Phoenicians, Greeks, Carthaginians, Berbers, and Romans, the latter calling the area Hispania. Each of these peoples have left their marks and the Romans have left impressive architectural ruins. When the barbarians struck at the heart of the Roman Empire, the most distant Roman legions were recalled to the banks of the Tiber for the last stand against the invading hordes, and Hispania was one of the first localities to suffer the loss of Roman military protection. In the first decades of the 5th century the Visigoths, a Teutonic people who had become partly Christianized, crossed the Pyrenees, occupied the Roman settlements, and, unmolested, commenced the construction of churches and dwellings.

The Visigoths traded with Constantinople and their art was strongly under Byzantine as well as other Near Eastern influences. There are examples of Visigothic architecture remaining in Spain, the most renowned being those in Toledo. The other evidences of Visigothic culture are largely those of the goldsmith's art, as proven by the discovery in the last century of a buried treasure, consisting, among other objects, of golden crowns set with pearls and semiprecious stones. In the realm of thought and letters, the Visigoth Saint Isidore of Seville distinguished himself by compiling an encyclopedia which was to become an authoritive book of learning in the Middle Ages. Of importance, too, was a codification of laws known as the *Fueros Juzgos*. In the main, however, Visigothic civilization was of insufficient potency to leave a permanent impress or to modify subsequent influences.

In the early years of the 8th century, the Moors, of Saracenic origin, who were then at the height of their vigor and glory, crossed the Straits of Gibraltar and found a weak and disorganized group of feudal states having only the Christian faith in common. The frenzied zeal of the Mohammedan, his reverence for the Koran, and his faith in Allah developed a psychology that made the destruction of adherents to rival creeds both a duty and a pleasure.*

The battles at the Guadalete River and Jerez de la Frontera (A.D. 711) were followed by the fall of Granada, Cordova, Valencia, Seville, and other southern cities. After temporary setbacks at Covadonga in 718, the victorious Arabs marched northward, bent only on spreading their faith and crushing the growing power of Christianity. In the year 732, they crossed the Pyrenees and were met by the Franks, under Charles Martel, the grandfather of Charlemagne, near the city of Tours. There, one of the decisive battles of world history was fought, a battle that released western Europe from the political and religious yoke of the Koran. The Moors retreated across the Pyrenees. From their strongholds in southern Spain, they waged for five centuries a bitter struggle against the slowly but inexorably advancing Christian armies, aided, at the beginning, by Charlemagne.† In the 13th century the Moorish holdings were reduced to the Kingdom of Granada. The early exploits and encounters of the Christians and the "infidels" form the subject matter of the "Chansons de Roland" and of the legends, romance, and minstrelsy so poetically related in the epic of El Cid.

In the first days of the year 1492 the city of Granada surrendered to the united armies of the unscrupulous King Ferdinand of Aragon and his able but bigoted wife, Queen Isabella of Castile. The Moorish King Boabdil was forced to take refuge in North Africa. The eight-century-old process of the Reconquest was brought to its conclusion. The inhabitants were given the choice of conversion to Christianity or emigration. Much disorder occurred, and it was not until 1609 that the final expulsion of the

---

* There was not as much difference between Mohammedan and Christian philosophy as is supposed. The Mohammedan culture at this period far outshone the Christian. Mohammed the prophet of Islam, who was born in Mecca and died in 632, considered himself the last of the prophets and successor to Jesus. Upon his death his followers, in an explosive enthusiasm combined with a martial ardor, developed an urge to spread his teachings throughout the world.

† Charlemagne, however, was considered an intruder, and his rear guard was ambushed and destroyed by the Basques in 778 at Roncesvalles in the Pyrenees. It was in this battle that Roland and Oliver were slain.

Moors took place. The union of the Kingdoms of Aragon and Castile was effected by 1506 and, joined by the less powerful states, formed the nucleus of the present Spanish nation.*

During the period of the Spanish invasion, the Moors were at the height of their civilization. The leaders were said to be models of integrity and justice, and to be tolerant in their treatment of the conquered. Philosophers and creative artists, the Moors established schools and universities and, in collaboration with the Jews, who were the leaders of commerce and industry, dominated the cultural life of the peninsula for 800 years. When Spain finally threw off the yoke of the Mohammedans, she found imperishable traces of the Orient in her blood, her customs, her arts, and her intellect.

Period of discovery and conquest. In the latter years of the 15th century, Castile and Portugal launched forth on careers of discovery and exploration. The voyage of Columbus that legend says was made possible by Isabella's pawning her jewels astounded the world and aroused the interest of Europe in the Western Hemisphere. The discovery was an event which developed untold enthusiasm and a sense of national unity and ambition in the Spanish people. Pinzon, de Cordova, Magellan, Balboa, de Soto, de Leon, and Coronado set sail for unknown shores and aided in establishing an empire upon which the sun never set. Vasco da Gama, for Portugal, rounded the Cape of Good Hope to India and brought untold wealth to his nation. Cabral discovered Brazil. The Portuguese, by an astounding expansion of their shipping, obtained their Indian, African, Chinese, and Brazilian colonies, and discovered the Azores. Portugal became one of the great empires of the world. Within the next century the Spanish conquistadores, Cortez and Pizarro, conquered Mexico and Peru, and for a century, Spanish galleons returned to Cadiz loaded with quantities of silver and gold. The ships that sailed under the Portuguese banner returned to Lisbon with the spices, silks, porcelains, and other products of both the East and the West. These events were later to influence greatly the arts of their respective countries.

Political supremacy and decline. In 1518 Charles I of Spain succeeded to a throne worth governing. This was the age of Spanish glory, and as the Holy Roman emperor Charles V, he united Flanders, Austria, and Germany under a single sovereignty. Charles was succeeded in 1555 by his son, Philip II, a zealous Catholic, who was determined to promote the power of Rome and to destroy the nations that had established heretical teachings. Holland, groaning under Spanish control, and Elizabethan England in-

* Portugal was at intervals under the Crown of Spain but this arrangement was never acceptable to her people. She finally regained her independence and her former empire in 1665, but her people are of the same racial and cultural origins as those of Spain; her language is easily understood by the Spaniard and differs less than Catalan and Basque from the best Castilian. Portugal faces the ocean, turns her back on Spain, and waits for the world to discover her.

curred special antagonism. In 1588 Philip, supported by the Pope, amassed the "Invincible Armada" that jubilantly set sail to invade the English shores and crush the nation that was beginning to threaten him with serious conflict in the Western Hemisphere. The English fleet, under the leadership of Lord High Admiral Howard of Effingham, aided by the weather, completely routed the Spaniards in one of the world's decisive naval battles that permitted the growth of Protestantism and the English and Dutch colonial development. Spain never fully recovered from this overwhelming defeat.

During the latter part of the 15th century the Inquisition had been instituted. While this policy helped to maintain the power of the Church, it crushed liberty of thought, eliminated initiative, prevented reforms, and hindered the creative imagination that was essential for the growth of the arts. The military splendor of Spain vanished at Rocroy where the Grand Condé of France at twenty-one defeated a reputedly invincible infantry in 1643. The Dutch struggles, ending in 1648, wasted Spain's energies, and with the loss of her naval and military prestige, she relinquished her temporary position as the leading political and maritime nation of Europe.

Under Philip IV and his son Charles II (1621–1700) the Spanish domains were still the largest held by any European monarch, but wars continually bled the public treasury despite the influx of gold from across the seas. Lack of administrative skill, high taxation, and the maintenance of a vast pleasure-loving court led to a disastrous state of affairs. While immense wealth was concentrated in a landowning and office-holding aristocracy, fiscal conditions could neither keep alive a prosperous middle class nor could they ameliorate the abject poverty of the peasant. Corruption in colonial administration was widespread, and the decline that started in the 17th century continued until the war with the United States in 1898 bereft Spain of all her colonial glory.

Character of the people. Spain is a mountainous, arid country where pigment-soaked skies and landscapes alternate with snowy peaks that reflect the Southern sun. The topography has tended to develop isolated groups of people having different interests and customs. Politically the nation was for centuries a collection of small states unified only by the fact that one king ruled them all, and this unity was created by religious rather than political or economic methods. Spain has always been a land of unrest; emotional qualities dominate the will power of her inhabitants, and they prefer to postpone inconvenient but necessary tasks to a future time. An excessive devotion of the Spaniard to his family and friends has led to political immorality. The people are honest, simple, genial, stoical, individualist, romantic, tenacious of their traditions, and true to their own instincts. They are gay in manner, but have a capacity for violence in action, and submit willingly to pain and suffering. Chivalry lasted longer in

Spain than elsewhere in Europe, and the Spaniards flatter their vanity and accentuate their romantic qualities by the often heard remark concerning their language, "English for commerce, French for diplomacy, Italian for song, but Spanish is the language of love." There is a love of leisure and a racial lack of energy. Earning a living is less important than the joy of living, and the Spaniard would deny his needs rather than increase his efforts for greater material benefits.* Spain has drained her manhood by centuries of warfare, the Inquisition, and emigration in settling half the Western Hemisphere. This has led to matriarchal tendencies in political and social life. Women are generally considered superior to men and nature has dealt the feminine sex a generous largess in pulchritude. The Berber social organization was entirely matriarchal and in Spanish countries it is still the custom to add a mother's name or initial to a father's surname. In spite of a languorous appearance, the women are robust and alert and the traveller is impressed with the beauty of both aristocrat and peasant.

The philosophy of the Spanish nation was largely established by Cervantes, who in his *Don Quixote,* the world's greatest novel, ridiculed the social, ecclesiastical, and intellectual conditions of the Middle Ages and called for individualism and realism in thought. The Reformation never obtained a foothold in a land that was too occupied with the extermination of heretics to worry about an internecine religious strife; but the Council of Trent was proposed, and strongly backed, by Spanish cardinals and bishops.

It was natural that the emotional qualities that characterized the people of the Iberian Peninsula should culminate in the pyrotechnics of art that were produced in the 17th and early 18th centuries. Today there is universal pride in the cultural glories of bygone centuries. There are places in Europe more beautiful than Spain, there are people who have accomplished more in politics, art, and industry, but there is an inimitable charm that permeates the whole atmosphere of the Peninsula and re-echoes in the breeding and gallantry that are dominant in the character of every inhabitant.

The subdivisions of the Spanish and Portuguese periods. Because of the widely divergent influences affecting Spanish art, there is less cohesion and

* Spain is the only remaining western European country that still retains the remnants of feudalism in its agricultural and industrial organization. Wealth is poorly distributed and solid peasant fortunes are rare. The lassitude and submissiveness of the working classes is not intrinsic but is due to primitive economic standards, lack of peasant land ownership, and the tardiness of the authorities in modernizing irrigation, transportation, and agricultural methods and equipment, and there has been little accomplishment in broadening educational opportunities or training the masses in republican political procedures. The Spanish are the most rabid individualists of any Europeans and their emotional qualities have interfered with their political ability to lose gracefully, with a result that there is no other European country where so many separatist movements exist. Some form of absolutism has been an essential policy in all Spanish governments, even though such is contrary to the wishes of the majority.

less consecutive development of style in the arts of Spain than in other European countries.

The general divisions of the post-Visigothic periods are as follows:

1. a. HISPANO-MAURESQUE OR HISPANO-MOORISH. (8th to 15th centuries)
   The art of Mohammedan Spain, seen particularly in Andalusia and as far north as Toledo.

   b. MUDEJAR (OR MORISCO ART). (13th to 17th centuries)
   The work of the Christianized Moor or the traditional continuance of Moorish art in Christian territory; either purely Moorish or a mingling of Moorish and Christian art.

   c. MOZARABIC.
   Art of the Christians living in the Mohammedan territories of Spain, and the influence of this art in other sections of the country.

2. ROMANESQUE AND GOTHIC. (12th to early 16th centuries)
   Though under French, Italian, Flemish, and German influences, Spanish art of these periods shows manifestations of an individualistic character.

3. PLATERESCO. (End of 15th to middle of 16th century)
   Usually considered the most beautiful of the Spanish styles. Derives its name from *platero*, meaning silversmith. Refers to the minutely scaled ornament in imitation of silversmiths' work used for embellishment of architecture and the minor arts of both the late Gothic and Renaissance periods. The terms *Isabellina* in Spain and *Manuelino* in Portugal are often applied to the Gothic phase. The abundance of precious metals from America did not occur until after 1500 and minutely scaled ornament had been a Moorish specialty. During this period there was also a Flemish influence in art and manners.

4. RENAISSANCE AND DESORNAMENTADO. (16th to middle of 17th century) The unornamented style. A reaction from the Plateresco. The arts developed under the influence of the Italian Renaissance. The leading exponent was Juan de Herrera, who built the enormous Escorial (1559–1584). The omission of ornamental detail caused the style to be known as the *Desornamentado*.

5. CHURRIGUERESCO OR BAROQUE-ROCOCO. (Early 17th to mid-18th century)
   The reaction from the Herrera style. Exuberance in form and ornament, splendor in color. The Churrigueresco marks an extravagant epoch in Spain as well as in her American possessions. The Baroque persisted at the side of the Rococo. During this period Portugal was being largely infiltrated with ideas from the East.

6. FOREIGN INFLUENCES. (1700–1815).
   The rise of power and increase in wealth of France and England enabled these countries to set new artistic standards that were copied by the Spanish artists and craftsmen. Portugal's trade with the East also added Indian and Chinese influences in her arts.

General character of the art of the Peninsula. In awarding opportunities for the development of a consistent national style of art, destiny did not deal so kindly with the Spanish and Portuguese people as with other European nations. The repeated military, ecclesiastical, and intellectual invasions by conflicting races and groups with opposing customs and philosophies prevented a continuous esthetic evolution. The mountainous character of the Peninsula hindered transportation and the rapid exchange of ideas, so that a similarity of art forms in all parts of the country was not possible. Artists and craftsmen worked independently. Time, however, aided by nature, produced an emotional people, effervescent in temperament and given to fanciful dreams, who in spite of their handicaps created virile art expressions. Spain's supremacy as a world power was of such short duration, and her sovereigns, surrounded by intrigue, were so uncertain of their political position that patronage of the arts was not established on as firm a basis as occurred in Italy and France. In Spain, the decorative arts were never promoted as a national industry as in France. The Spanish kings, however, supported the arts for their own benefit, and the Prado Museum is filled with contributions from the royal collections, none of which were developed by confiscation from other countries as a result of war.

The climate tended to perpetuate the use of materials that were most suitable to southern temperatures, and the Moorish elements that best fulfilled those requirements will probably persist as long as the Spanish sun continues to shine. The arts of the Peninsula were never dainty; they have always been distinctly masculine and frequently brutal. Their most chaste period was seen in the art of the Christianized Moor; the most exuberant and far-reaching was that of the 17th century, when restraint was cast to the winds and the warmth of the Arabian blood combined with a Christian religious fanaticism was visible in the most daring and sumptuous effects in both architecture and decoration. Spanish and Portuguese art were the opposite of the Greek conception, inasmuch as the examples emphasize the dominance of the emotional rather than the intellectual qualities in the nature of the people. In every medium of expression the artists have been more under foreign influence than those of other nations of Europe.* The

* The most indigenous art development in Spain has been that of the classic dance, a ritualistic expression closest to the heart of the masses. The Spaniards have always been impressed with rhythmic sound, an inheritance from their North African ancestors. The native dances are directly descended from Egyptian, Greek, and Roman prototypes, and the literature of the Caesars frequently mentions entertainments by the dancers brought from Hispania. Spanish dancing is unique in that it requires complete co-ordination and simultaneous movement of the arms, torso, and feet, combined with facial expressions that run the gamut of passions. The grace and emotional excitement that enter into the chacona, fandango, malagueña, bolero, and seguidilla are unequalled in the dance styles of other races, and the accompanying rhythm of the castanets alternately expresses anger, cajolery, revery, and romance. The flamenco dancing practised by the gypsies carries with it an unsurpassed frenzy and fire, and although impudent, is never vulgar. Of recent years, the art has been influenced by modern elements borrowed from the former Spanish colonies in America.

Moors, Italians, French, and English have each in their turn been the inspiration of production, and both India and China have strongly influenced the Portuguese. Spain and Portugal have, however, produced great personalities, and such men as Lull, Cervantes, Camoens, Velasquez, El Greco, Herrera, Murillo, Churriguero, Goya, and Picasso have in their own mediums and in their own times been unique and unsurpassed. Lesser known craftsmen in ceramics, precious and base metalwork, ivory carving, and other materials have also shown a technical ability and artistic understanding of a supremely high order.

The Hall of Justice in the Alhambra, showing stalactite detail on arches, tile wainscot, and flooring, and yesería ornamentation above arches.

Moorish architecture and decoration. Although the Moor was the hereditary enemy of the Spaniard, he left to Spanish culture far more than he took from it. The cities and villages of Andalusia are filled with the evidences of his occupation. The most marked characteristic of the important Moorish buildings is the sharp contrast between a plain exterior and an exquisitely ornate interior. This was a development in permanent form of the nomad's tent, the interior of which was richly hung with hand-woven decorative textiles. The Moors were from the beginning exquisite planners and craftsmen. Castles, palaces, mosques, bazaars, hospitals, and caravansaries enriched every settlement. The Great Mosque in Cordova (A.D. 876) was the glory of Western Islam until it became a Christian Church in 1238.* This building was built in part from the ruins of Roman structures and the interior is rich in jasper and porphyry columns and colored marbles; its arches retain the semicircular Roman form and its floors are treated with sparkling mosaics in glass and gold.

The Alhambra in Granada (1309–1354), made famous to Americans by Washington Irving, was the Sultan's pleasure palace from which Boabdil was driven by Ferdinand. It was the last of the palaces constructed by the Moors and remains today the supreme pearl of Moorish architecture and

* The mosque at Cordova still stands and is the largest religious edifice in the world.

Hall of Ambassadors in the Alcazar, Seville, showing the tile dado, yesería ornament, horseshoe arches, and vistas.

decoration. It is a fragile structure that stands on an eminence overlooking the city, and in spite of its adobe brick construction, has defied centuries of neglect, yet it eloquently expresses the magical and dreamlike qualities that are associated with the tales from the *Thousand and One Nights*. The building is planned around numerous arcaded courtyards and the interior walls are covered with fantastic and minutely colored ornamental details that are subordinated to the effect of the whole. The architecture is agreeably blended with gardens, fountains, and reflecting pools, and one seldom loses the sound of splashing waters or the perfume of jasmine and orange. Its enclosing walls retain the desired Oriental seclusion while arched openings create vistas that overlook the distant snowy peaks. The interior is a perfect expression of the times in which it was built, and reflects the luxurious life of ease maintained by its occupants. In the private apartments of the Sultan and his favorite wife is a gallery for the use of blinded musicians. Elaborate baths contained taps from which spouted cold, hot, and perfumed water. The building is unrivalled elsewhere in Mohammedan countries and proves that the Moors were supreme in decorative talent as well as structural design. The majority of the rooms are treated with tiled wainscoting in colorful geometric patterns to a height of about four feet, above which there is a wall surface covered with plaster all-over ornament of minute scale, delicately tinted in various colors, a type of work known as *yesería*. Near the ceiling the walls are treated with a frieze usually en-

Entrance hall in Moorish house, Andalusia.

riched by decorative cursive inscriptions stating that "There is no God but Allah." These are placed on a groundwork of an elaborate abstract pattern. In some cases the friezes contain a running geometrical motif of intersecting polygons, stars, and crosses.

The Alcazar in Seville, another important monument, dates from the middle of the 14th century. It has suffered from the ravages of time and is in a state of partial ruin. The portions that are extant, and many other smaller buildings of the same date, show in their interiors a type of decoration that is similar to that used in the Alhambra.

The villas of the Moors were usually located on sloping ground. Structurally they were simple, with plain exterior walls, and few windows. They were built around a landscaped *patio* off which the rooms were placed. Elaborate arrangements were made for reception rooms, master's quarters, and baths, and an isolated section with a private garden was walled for the use of the women and children. The Moor was adept at formal gardening and used this art to its fullest extent as a contribution to the enjoyment of life. His gardens, closely related to the composition of the house, were terraced and trellised with winding pathways lined with black cedars, tamarisks, myrtle, and orange trees. Alleys of trimmed hedges and rosaries of scented thorn were located for surprise vistas showing pavilions or extensive landscapes. Short flights of low brick steps connected the various levels, each of which was treated differently. Circular and semicircular landings enclosed with balustrades were paved with pebbles arranged in mosaic patterns. Fountains, troughs, and squirting jets of water played their cooling streams in all directions.

These dwellings contained little furniture—benches were often built-in and attached to the wall. Cushions and straw mattresses were placed on the floor, a custom that carried over from nomad times. Rugs were

Yesería ornament showing stalactite arches and Arabic script. Alhambra.

used in profusion on floors, benches, and as wall hangings. Leather and wood chests were used for the storage of clothes. Pottery, bronze, and copper were the materials for cooking and eating utensils. Elaborate embroideries, laces, and loom-made textiles added color and pattern interests. Bottles, flasks, and perfume containers were made of an iridescent glassware of great beauty.

An important structural feature in Moorish architecture was the *horseshoe arch,* the origin of which has not definitely been traced. This form is sometimes called a Moorish arch. The horseshoe form is seen in Visigothic ruins, but it is possible that the Moors introduced it independently, and that both races inherited it from early Syrian architecture. The curve of the arch forms approximately three-fourths of a circle and springs directly from a column capital. The arch is often enclosed in a rectangular frame showing inscriptions from the Koran and other ornamental motifs.

Two other arch types were also occasionally used in Moorish buildings. These were the pointed form, and the *multifoil* or scalloped arch, the latter being somewhat similar to the Gothic cusped arch.

Columns were slender, with straight shafts. Capitals were frequently square and covered with minutely carved scrolls, crescent-shaped forms, and other highly conventionalized motifs. A form of ornament known as *stalactite work* was also used; this consisted of several rows of minute niches, the upper rows projecting over the lower ones, bringing the square capital down to the round shaft by easy gradations.

The interior walls were treated with plain plaster, colored tiles treated with a geometrical pattern, brickwork, colored plaster ornament in relief, and ornamented leather, or a combination of these materials. Woodwork was limited to the doors and ceiling. The floors were in tile, brick, or stone, and were covered with rugs of both tapestry and pile weave in Mohammedan patterns. Heavy earthenware pottery was arranged in definite compositions on shelves and walls. Colors used for tilework, plaster ornament, painted woodwork, and in the rich wool textiles were the brilliant primary hues inherited from nomadic forbears.

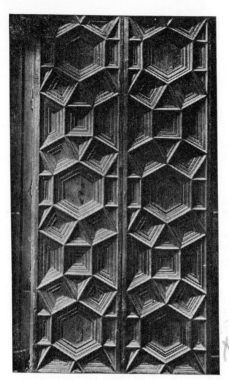

Moorish ornament. The rules of the Koran forbade the copying of natural forms. Therefore, the Moors, who were excellent mathematicians, resorted to geometry for pattern inspiration, and they developed an extraordinary originality in the design of surface ornament. The most intricate arrangements of interlacing straight and curved lines were devised. Squares and rectangles were usually avoided, but stars, crescents, crosses, hexagons, octagons, and many other forms were used.*

Geometrical ornament was particularly adapted to wood, plaster, tile, and textile designs, and was accentuated by gorgeous coloring in red, blue, green, white, silver, and gold. The pine cone and the cockleshell, re-

Geometrical panelling used for window shutter, 16th century.

garded as good luck symbols, were extensively used as decorative motifs, and the latter was carried over into Christian art as the symbol of Santiago. The yesería and painted all-over patterns produced by the Moor were invariably at a minuscule scale, a characteristic of design in which he seemed to be a specialist.

To the Moor also is attributed the development of the arabesque, a designation that was later misapplied to similar forms of classical ornament. This pattern consists of a stem rising from a root, from which branch conventionalized flowers, fruits, leaves, and abstract shapes that overlap and interlace. The conception of the arabesque was probably originally taken from the Assyrian tree-of-life pattern.

Moorish tile work and ceramics. While the Moors did not introduce the manufacture of pottery in the Spanish peninsula, they greatly expanded the use of this material for decorative and practical purposes, and added ceramic refinements such as the lead and tin glazes as well as the luster technique.

* There were two Mohammedan sects, the Sunni, who were the more orthodox and completely excluded living forms from their ornament, and the Shi'a, who were more tolerant of their use. In the 14th century a Sunni traveller visiting Granada was shocked by the evidence of lowered morals as indicated by the pictorial representation of human figures, animals, and flowers.

The floors of rooms were frequently covered with small quarry or baked clay tiles of a dull red color. Color accents were often introduced by insertions of glazed tiles in contrasting tones. Black and white checker effects were popular. Brick floors were usually laid in square or herringbone patterns.

Tile was also used for dadoes carried up the walls to a height of three or four feet. These were invariably in polychrome effects and in geometrical patterns. A band course at the top of the wainscot, consisting of a repeating conventionalized pine-tree motif, varied the pattern of the field. Door and window facings, window jambs and seats, risers of steps, linings of niches, fountains, and washbasins were also made of this material. After the subjection of the Moors, human and animal figures and Christian symbols were more commonly represented in the tile patterns.

Taylor and Dull, Photographers

Hispano-Mauresque copper luster plaque, made about 1500.

In addition to the production of the architectural and ornamental wall tiles, vast quantities of heavy earthenware plates, jugs, ewers, vases, and pitchers were made. Hispano-Mauresque ware often miscalled *majolica*, was made in many small southern Spanish towns. The major portion of these useful pieces, however, came from Malaga, Valencia, and Seville. Patterns were both stamped and painted on the ware, and consisted of geometrical and abstract forms, coats-of-arms, figures, and conventionalized floral forms, covered with an enamel glaze or luster. Pitchers and vases were scattered profusely on shelves, and plates of all sizes were hung on the walls in circles, curves, and other arrangements often producing a dazzling appearance. These products were considered of such high quality that in 1455 the Venetian Senate decreed that "the majolica of Valencia should be admitted duty-free (to Venice) for such is their quality that local kilns cannot compete with them."

Moorish woodwork. The Moorish carpenter was far more skilled than his northern fellow-worker. He applied his ability particularly to the design and construction of ceilings and doors, which were the only visible wooden portions of the Moorish house.

There were two kinds of wooden ceilings. One was the exposed structural beam type that consisted of heavy wooden girders spaced some distance apart, in turn supporting closely spaced smaller beams running at

The Hispanic Periods 149

Tile niche in dining room of house in Barcelona, 16th century.

right angles to the girders. Both the beams and the girders were painted with ornamental motifs. This was a simple structural arrangement seen in all countries. The other type of ceiling was of Mohammedan origin, and was therefore more local in character and more unique in design; it consisted of shallow wooden panels arranged in complicated geometrical shapes. Stars, hexagons, and irregular forms were produced by the use of series of moldings forming the framework of the panels which often occupied greater space than the field of the panel itself. Doors were subdivided into a multitude of small panels of irregular geometrical shapes.

Moorish woodwork was known as *artesonado* and was made from local cedar, a soft wood of fine grain, somewhat resembling red pine. In dwellings, the wood-panelled ceilings and doors were usually left in natural finish; in public buildings, gilding or color was sometimes used.

The ornamental niche in Moorish interiors. A special decorative feature that was popular in the Moorish house was the wall niche. Recessed for a distance of about 18 inches, it started at the top of the wainscot, and normally carried two hinged doors similar to modern window shutters. Sometimes the doors were pierced with silhouettes or painted with bright patterns on both sides. The rear and sides of the niches were treated with colored tiles or painted in brilliant colors, forming a strong point of contrast with the neutral plaster walls. The niches were furnished with shelving which supported useful and ornamental accessories.

The Mudéjar and Mozarabic periods. Perhaps the most interesting periods of Spanish decoration were the transitional styles produced by the fusion of the arts of the Moor with the Gothic forms and later with the arts of 16th century Italy.

There was much that was beautiful in the Moorish decorative materials and patterns, and those that were suitable and free from Mohammedan religious significance continued to be used by Christian builders. As Renaissance features were gradually popularized and transposed from church to secular construction, they were used simultaneously with the Moorish elements. The forms and proportions of classical architecture and ornamental detail, however, were not well understood by Moorish craftsmen, and this lack of knowledge often produced awkward results. The finer designs were unquestionably produced by Italian designers and workmen, or by Spaniards and Moors working under Italian masters. Much of the work in these fused styles was seen in accessory production such as pottery, textiles, furniture, and metalwork.

The tile floor and low dado maintained their popularity. Polychrome ornament in geometrical patterns persisted in spite of the introduction of painted figures. Plain plaster walls were often enriched by heavy silk textiles or tapestries hung in loose folds. Tile panels showing heraldic devices were frequently inserted in the wall near the ceiling, and the extensive ornamental use of majolica plates and ewers continued for a long time to count as an important feature in the color interest of the rooms. Windows were small, as a rule, with deep reveals, and the glass, if any, was leaded in either circular or rectangular forms. Heavy wooden interior shutters, with pierced holes or *spindled* panels, for ventilation, were common. Segmental, semicircular and horseshoe forms were employed for arched openings. The *Persiana* or *Venetian blind* was also used. Where *colonnades* were used the column capitals often consisted of brackets extending outward on both sides to support a lintel.

The ceilings and doors continued to be treated with elaborately designed wood panels, as they had been in the Moorish rooms. Fireplaces began to assume the early Italian Renaissance character, with projecting hoods, and with lower portions treated in a classical architectural manner. Framed paintings hung on the wall were more common than mural decoration and pottery continued to be extensively used for both practical and ornamental purposes.

The Hispanic Romanesque and Gothic styles. These arts were chiefly introduced into Spain by the Cistercian monks of Cluny. Churches with sculptured portals and their adjacent cloisters, famous for their carved columns and capitals, rose along the roads that were used by the pilgrims to visit Santiago de Compostela, shrine of the national patron saint, in northwestern Spain. Throughout other sections of Christian Spain, ecclesiastical edifices, domed or roofed, attest to the art and originality of Romanesque architects and artists.

Although the Gothic cathedrals of Burgos, Toledo, Leon, Salamanca, and Seville are of a later date than those in France,[*] they give evidence of

* Alfonso the Wise (1221–1284), who reigned during the construction of most of the

Eighteenth century Ecce Homo, showing agonized expression that is typical of many Spanish representations of this subject.

the splendor and power of the movement. The Cathedral of Seville, the second largest church in Christendom, was probably designed by a German, but the others are distinctly of French origin. The "Giralda" tower, a part of the Seville cathedral, was originally the *minaret* of the mosque that formerly stood in the same location. The tower is considered one of the most beautiful structures of its type ever erected. The romance of the period is exemplified by the legend current in Burgos that the ornaments in its cathedral were worked by the hands of angels. The shrine of Toledo, impressive by its location on the crest of a rocky hill, appears to point a pathway to paradise.

These and other cathedrals with their almost incredible wealth of altarpieces, sculptured alabaster, polychromed woodwork, gilded wrought iron grills, and marble tombs are treasure houses of unforgettable inspiration. The Spanish Gothic churches usually have smaller fenestration than those in northern climates, a necessity for tempering the glare of the southern sun. The large wall areas produce a marked austerity, and there is an extensive amount of surface ornament due to Moorish influence. Geometrical patterns and the horseshoe arch are often used. The somberness of the interiors accentuates the brilliance of the color on the walls and pavements produced by the diagonal rays of the sun through the stained glass windows. In the darker corners there is an impressive use of candlelight.

The religious sculpture of the Spanish Gothic churches deserves special mention. It was generally more realistic than contemporary work in the northern countries. Greater emotion is shown in figure work and this is particularly in evidence in many of the representations of the crucifix in which a starved Christ is frequently seen in the most excruciating pain and

great Gothic cathedrals, contributed greatly to their support. He advanced education and was quite conscious of his abilities and judgment. He is perhaps best remembered by his remark that he could have suggested improvements in the Universe had the Creator consulted him. He also passed a law that permitted an impoverished father to sell his son, and allowed a starving father, if in a besieged city, to eat his children.

gruesome aspect. The Spanish religious painters had a similar conception of reality and in the fiestas and religious processions, images of the most repulsive character were often exhibited.

The Middle Ages were a great period of castle-building. There are probably a larger number of extant fortified castles in Spain than in any other European country. These were mostly built on precipitous heights and were not only of formidable defensive strength, but in their residential sections, elaborately treated in Gothic detail. It was not without reason that the phrase "castles in Spain" became synonymous in both the French and English languages for an impossible achievement, and one of the most important Spanish provinces, Castile, was so named because of the number and splendor of the castles which it contained.

Gothic furniture. The peninsular furniture of the 14th and 15th centuries was similar to the contemporary types in northern Europe. Detail was taken from Christian Gothic architectural elements but many pieces show Mudéjar influence in the use of geometrical inlay. Heavy proportions were the rule, the pieces were well joined and were often braced with wrought iron.

The chest with a hinged lid was the most common piece and was used in nearly every room; it served for storage for the elaborate clothes used at banquets, fiestas, jousting tournaments, and bullfights, and could also be used as a seat, table, writing desk, or couch. It was made in all sizes and in many different woods, and was often covered with embossed leather, decorated with metal ornaments, and furnished with complicated locks.

Contemporary paintings and inventories clearly indicate the few types of furniture that were used at this time. Chairs of honor, benches, stools, folding seats, simple desks, canopied beds, occasional sideboards, and cabinets with drawers were seen. Loose planks set on trestles were used for tables and these were generally covered with an Oriental rug. Much of the Gothic furniture was painted in bright colors and gold.

Italian influences. At the end of the 15th century, it was only natural that Spain, with its close ecclesiastical association with Rome, should come under the vitalizing influence of the Italian Renaissance. Spain had great political influence in the Italian States, and Spanish officials who visited Italy returned to their homes dazzled by the evidences of Italy's culture, luxury, and beauty. The accretions of Naples and Sicily to the Spanish crown also increased the maritime influence of Spain in the Mediterranean, and revitalized her commercial relations with Italy. Influences were shuttled back and forth between the two countries.

Even before this period, Italian intellectual influence had strongly penetrated Spain, and, finding there a groundwork similar in many respects to its own, it persisted until well into the 17th century, through the exchange of artists and writers. Spain, however, did not have the advantages of Italy in the variety and number of Roman buildings to use as reference. She could not, to the same extent, delve into the grottoes of the Forum for source information. The Renaissance details of architecture and decoration were obtained second hand, and the local artist and designer lacked the opportunities to study classical composition and proportions, or the models for sculptural motifs. Broadly speaking, the Renaissance in Spain, in the majority of instances, must be considered a provincial interpretation of Italian forms with added local variations that produced its native character and created its unquestioned charm.

The Plateresco. This term, taken from the Spanish word for silversmith, *platero,* originated in the 16th century. It referred to the influence upon the architects and designers made by the beauty and fine detail of the products of the craftsmen in precious metals during the late Gothic and early Renaissance periods. The term was not exact in its application, however, because the glut of gold and silver did not occur until after America had been discovered. The excess of small-scale ornament covering wide surfaces was more likely a carry-over from Moorish decoration, as this race had always been lovers of the microscopic in pattern design. Spanish authorities use the word *Isabellina* and the Portuguese the word *Manuelino* as names for the Gothic phase of minutely scaled ornamental superabundance and apply *Plateresco* to the Renaissance examples.

The Plateresco was primarily a style exemplified in exterior architectural treatments, patios, formal rooms in churches and public buildings, and for furniture and accessory design; it was not extensively used as a style for the interior walls of dwellings,* but domestic interiors of this period began to reflect the greater richness of detail, increase in types of furniture and improvements in comfort and conveniences that were seen in contemporary Italian rooms. Walls usually consisted of plain or painted plaster or they were hung with leather or textile coverings. Plaster figures in relief and ornamental motifs in color and gold leaf were placed in important locations. In the main public room the master's prerogatives were maintained by an *estrado* or raised platform placed at one end, which was furnished with two elaborate seats of honor, a table, and cabinet. The walls surrounding the platform were enriched with tapestries, Oriental rugs, and other hangings. The rest of the room contained a formal arrangement of seats, tables, and cabinets. Chairs and benches were covered with velvet cushions enriched with fringes and *appliqué* ornamentation. Sideboards, cabinets, desks, and tables were at first treated with silver, ivory, and ebony inlay and eventually with elaborate carved detail. Family coats-

---

* During this period many houses were built only one story high. This was due to a legal imposition that required the second story of every house to be at the disposal of the King. As royalty travelled with hundreds of courtiers and guests, local inhabitants were often greatly inconvenienced.

Room in the reputed House of El Greco, Toledo, showing tile dado, plaster wall, wooden ceiling, yesería frieze, and mantel with Renaissance detail.

Kitchen in reputed House of El Greco, Toledo, showing tile dado and pottery.

Room in modern Spanish house furnished with 16th- and 17th-century furniture.

of-arms, *cartouches,* amorini clasping garlands, the scallop-shell of Santiago, and the eagle of San Juan played prominent roles in the decorative motifs. Columns, pilasters, pedestals, cornices, and pediments of classical architecture became integral parts of furniture design. Paintings by famous masters of subjects not always consistent with Christian thought were hung on the walls. Majolica ware; small mirrors with elaborately carved and gilded frames; religious statuary in gold, silver, and ivory; and iron and brass braziers that exuded a perfumed smoke completed the decorative detail of the formal rooms. The braziers were often designed as circular tables and their location formed a center for conversational groups.

The Desornamentado. The unornamented and austere character of the architecture and decoration designed by Juan de Herrera, a pupil of Michael Angelo, under Philip II, for the vast, gray Escorial (1559–1584) precluded the general application of this style for domestic use. Architecturally the style was one of classical purity, effective by its grandeur, but the interiors were too esthetically frigid to permit their application in the homes of the middle classes who had inherited a love of color and ornament. The style was so correct in its use of Vitruvian forms that there was no opportunity to inject in it evidences of Spanish imagination, spirit, and temperament. The Escorial appears as a lonesome pile in a desolate wilderness and resolutely reflects the orders given to the architect by Philip. "Above all do not forget what I have told you—simplicity of form, severity in the whole, nobility without arrogance, majesty without ostentation." The bareness of the building is partly due to the fact that granite was used in its construction.

For a time the Herrera influence was extremely strong. Many other buildings were designed which are impressive but they are all melancholy, monotonous, and morbid in appearance. One of the finest was the Alcazar in Toledo, unhappily destroyed in

The office of Philip II in the Escorial, typical of the Desornamentado style.

the revolution of 1936; it was in this building that a stairway was introduced that was on such a grand scale that Philip when mounting it, stated that it made him *feel* like an emperor.*

Many Italian works of art were imported during this period and Spanish artists went to Italy to study.

The Churrigueresco. The architecture and decoration of the Peninsula came into its own in the century between 1650 and 1750. During this period was produced a style that was not only unique, and incapable of being created by other races, but one that was steeped in a riotous enrichment that seemed to express the volatile Spanish character in its most passionate moments. With the death of Herrera in 1597 a reaction against the severity of the Desornamentado quickly developed. This style had always been limited to Court structures and ecclesiastical buildings and it had never been fully suitable to domestic use. The substitute movement was one which revived the use of excessive ornamentation. Due to the necessity of reasserting the vigor of the Roman church after the Reformation movement, the Jesuits promoted the new style because of its emotional effect on the masses, whose intellect had not permitted them to appreciate the classical proportions and lack of detail of the Desornamentado. The new architectural conceptions were promoted by José Churriguero (1665–1725) and his family of architects, whose surname was later used to designate the style.

The Churrigueresco was primarily a style of surface decoration, rather than one of structural changes. Its most characteristic features were applied to exterior entrance doorways and to the interior decoration of churches and palaces. In a considerably subdued form it reached the homes of the people, although it was seen in the furniture and accessories rather than

* It is perhaps interesting here to note that the Spaniards about 1500 were the designers of the first interior neweled and hand-railed stairway built in an open square stair well with straight runs meeting at a landing halfway up. The earliest example was at Holy Cross Hospital in Toledo, which was destroyed in 1936. This stairway was later to be the model for the English Tudor period stairways. Medieval castles had contained concealed steps and the Italian buildings had straight stairways placed between two walls.

Interior and detail of Sacristy of La Cartuja, Granada (1727), characteristic of the Churrigueresco style.

in the decorative treatment of the walls. The movement attained great popularity, spread throughout the Peninsula, and eventually crossed the Atlantic to Latin America, where, fused with indigenous elements, it intoxicated the colonials and Christianized Indians with combinations of color, ornament, sculpture, and twisted architectural forms that stagger description. The new style differed from the Plateresco in the scale of its detail; natural objects used for the ornamental motifs were in bold relief and frequently were heroic in size. In the design of public buildings the rules of Vitruvius were entirely discarded and the orders became elements of applied decoration without structural meaning. Columns and pilasters had spiral and baluster-form shafts, or lost their identity by heavy *rustication*. Entablatures and moldings bulged upward or outward or were tortured into writhing masses. Broken and scroll pediments were misplaced in the design and ended in squirming volutes; Doric capitals sprouted Corinthian acanthus leaves; brackets were nonsupporting, and pyramidal forms stood on their apexes. Stucco decoration was modelled to imitate rock formations, waterfalls, and drapery swags. Nude figures cringed under heavy loads; cherubim and seraphim emerged from plaster clouds, and religious symbols were in important locations; optical illusions bewildered their observers; and transparent alabaster carvings glowed with the light from dozens of candles. Silver, tortoise-shell, and ivory inlay enriched the remaining wall surfaces. Fantasmagory and anarchy ruled everywhere in detail, although a mass balance and compositional approach to symmetry was usually attempted.

The style was anathema to the purist, and has been attacked by countless critics, but its force and splendor have kept it close to the hearts of its adherents. The peasants adored it and even in the poorest districts money poured into the church coffers for the construction of religious edifices that would satisfy their pride and fervency. The great examples of the Churrigueresco are the church at Loyola, the birthplace of St. Ignatius, the Provincial Hospital in Madrid, the interior of the Sacristy of La Cartuja in Granada, and the Transparente in the Toledo cathedral, the latter the supreme theatrical combination of sculpture, painting, and architecture with optical illusions and dazzling illumination of religious figures and scenes.*

The style was found to be particularly suitable in the design of the retables, altars, and screens of the cathedrals, where colored

Moreno, Photographer

The Transparente in the Toledo Cathedral.

stucco ornamentation vied with the gold ritual accessories. Its most important example in residential work is the Palace of the Marques de Dos Aguas at Valencia (built 1744). In the minor dwellings the style was expressed by elaborate fresco wall decorations showing floral and tropical growth combined with distorted architectural forms in plaster, gilded stucco cartouches, heraldic motifs, and exaggerated door and window trim. Many rooms were finished in plain sand-finish plaster and left a natural color, which served to accentuate the brilliancy of the drapery and cushion materials. Small wall niches were sometimes introduced, an idea inherited from Moorish interiors; these were lined with patterned tiles or painted in bright colors. They usually contained shelves for pottery and sometimes a water tank and washbasin. Parquetry and inlaid floor patterns became popular and beamed or frescoed ceilings completed the interior.

The Churrigueresco continued at full pace until the accession of Philip V, grandson of Louis XIV, to whom it seemed uncouth. This sophisticated Frenchman preferred that the more dignified character of Versailles should serve as a model for royal use and his palace at Aranjuez faintly re-

* The Transparente is perhaps the most extreme example of Western iconography. The modest intellect is perhaps awed in viewing it, but the mature art student is only impressed if he retains his sense of humor.

flected the grandeur of his ancestor's masterpiece. From this period the Churrigueresco commenced to fade in its native land, but for a long time it was to continue to express its capriciousness in the lands across the sea.

Portuguese historical influences upon the arts. In the development of Portuguese culture, there were many influences differing from those of Spain that contribute to unique characteristics. An indigenous quality was also developed by the national pride that resented Spanish leadership. Portugal had freed herself of Moorish control long before Spain, as a result of the victory of Ourique (1140), and first gained independence from the Spanish at the battle of Aljubarrota (1385). This victory was memorialized by the erection of the Monastery of Santa Maria of Victory, completed in 1433, on the spot where the battle occurred. The building stands today as the most beautiful example of Gothic art in Portugal. The Manuelino style which followed was brought to its apotheosis during the reign of Dom Manuel I (1495–1521) and roughly corresponded in point of time and character to the Spanish Plateresco. The Portuguese style, however, was more hybrid in origin, and included reminiscences of Roman structure, Gothic arches, Arabian and East Indian architectural features, and marine ornaments that were chosen because they seemed to symbolize the destiny of the country. Among these were rope, cockleshells, sails, prows of vessels, pennants, sea plants, and armillary spheres.

Portugal fell once more under the control of Spain at the accession of Philip II, who was the legitimate grandson of Dom Manuel, and during his reign was greatly influenced by the brilliancy of the contemporary Spanish intellect.

Since the Gothic period, the Portuguese have produced great works of literature and exquisite examples of the minor arts. The blue enamelled ware known as *azulejos* was often used to line interior walls and substituted for the tapestries used in the northern countries. Transparent porcelains of great beauty are still made at Vista Alegre. The ironwork at Coimbra, and the embroideries of Madeira are world renowned. A unique feature of Portuguese interiors has been the use of cork. Since the Middle Ages, sheets of this material have been used as wall linings, as it has insulating qualities. Cork also has been used for cabinet construction in the making of doors, benches, and tables.

Spanish furniture of the 16th and 17th centuries. The Italians of the Renaissance introduced luxury of living to the Spaniard. Practically all Spanish furniture from 1500 to 1650 was of Italian inspiration. Local conditions affected the designs, which were often of hybrid origin and awkward appearance. Little was produced that was entirely indigenous. The fact that some of the finest furniture was created for the church affected the character of ornament, which included such symbols as the Pope's miter, the Keys to Heaven, and the Instruments of the Passion.

Varqueno

Spiral Shaft

Table with Trestle Support

Nailhead Patterns

Leather Upholstered Chair

Chair

Wood Panelled Door

Shell Motif

Geometrical Tile Pattern

Torch Stand

Window Grille

Moorish Arch Form

SPANISH FURNITURE AND ARCHITECTURAL DETAILS.

The woods most commonly used for furniture construction were walnut, chestnut, cedar, oak, pine, pear, box, and orange, with ebony, ivory, and tortoise shell used for inlay purposes. There was also a tendency at this time among Spanish cabinetmakers to cover inferior workmanship with paint; hence, from an early date, polychrome effects were more common in Spain than in other European countries. The Spaniards were the first Europeans to use mahogany (about 1550) as a cabinet wood. This wood, which had been discovered in the West Indies, because of the enor-

Seventeenth century Spanish chairs.

mous size of the trees was first employed in the construction of the Spanish galleons. When these ships were wrecked or became superannuated, the wood was salvaged for smaller structures and furniture.

In constructing furniture, the Spaniard often paid more attention to strength than to design. As a result, unnecessarily heavy proportions may frequently be seen. In many pieces of furniture the separate parts were joined by nails that were left visible, although joinery was well understood.

The character of the carving in Spanish furniture varied greatly. On the best Renaissance pieces the work was probably done by Italian woodcarvers and it shows an accurate interpretation of classical motifs, but in the smaller towns and country districts carved enrichment was designed in naturalistic and conventional patterns unrelated to traditional classic forms. Much of it seems to have been created as the carver proceeded in his work. There was no set standard, and the carving was lacking in unity of composition. One of the most frequent methods of surface enrichment was by chiselling a series of short grooves in a wavy line along a rail or chair leg, a form that seems unsuitable to the shape of the surface upon which it was placed. Panel areas often consisted of square, diamond-shaped, or circular rosettes distributed on the surface as an all-over pattern.

Moldings and turnings lacked the smoothness of line and the refined curves of the Italian workmanship. Short *clavated* turnings * were common in furniture supports; these lacked the graceful lines seen in the

* These are sometimes known as spool or disk turnings.

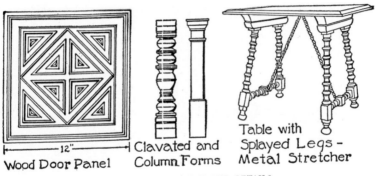

Wood Door Panel ├──12"──┤ Clavated and Column Forms Table with Splayed Legs – Metal Stretcher

SPANISH FURNITURE AND DETAILS.

Italian baluster forms. The use of the splayed or slanting leg was typical. Nailheads of both iron and brass were large and elaborate, and were constantly used, not only to secure upholstery materials, but by themselves as the decoration of plain surfaces. Metal ornaments, for use as furniture enrichment, were made of both iron and silver in the form of rosettes, scallop shells, and stars, and in pierced sheet patterns.

Wrought iron was extensively used as a material for the production of many types of household equipment. Chairs, beds, chests, washbasins, candlestands, tables, and other objects were frequently made entirely in this material, and it was often used in combination with wood; chairbacks and table-leg bracings were also made in graceful curves, with hammered ornament.

Of the individual pieces of furniture, the chest or *arca* continued to be the most common and, as in Italy, was made in all sizes. The ornament consisted of wooden and ivory inlays, metal mounts, carving, and color. Many were covered with leather or velvet.

Chairs of the Dante type were made, although the upper portion was often larger than the support, creating a top-heavy appearance. Italian Renaissance chairs of rectangular design were also copied. These have both velvet and tooled or embossed leather seats and backs. Sometimes a double row of ornamental nails was used to attach the leather to the wood frame. Wooden seats with loose cushions for comfort were used, and rush seats were very common even in the most elaborate homes. Through the 17th century Spanish ladies often used floor cushions for seats both at home and while attending Mass; they also carried at all times cosmetic boxes of great beauty. In Barcelona, a form of *ladder-back* chair was made, in which the topmost slat was greatly enlarged and elaborately carved. Chair legs were braced by stretchers ornamented with simple rosettes and short or long chiselled grooves.

Tables were unusually characteristic; the tops frequently had a long overhang, with plain, square-cut edges. Table supports were of two types,

The Hispanic Periods 163

LEFT: *Spanish 17th century papelera and table.* RIGHT: *17th century Spanish vargueño.*

the four-legged and the trestle. Legs represented straight or spiral classical columns or balusters. The trestle supports were much simpler than those found in Italy; they were usually pierced and silhouetted in a series of contrasting curves often taking the approximate shape of a lyre. Both table legs and trestles were often splayed and braced by a diagonal wooden or curved iron piece which started at the center point of the underside of the table top and ended at the stretcher connecting the end legs, near the floor. Many of the tables were collapsible. Beds were made both with and without corner posts. Spiral posts with valances and ornaments were frequently used. Headboards were sometimes separate from the bed, and were either elaborately painted, designed as an architectural pediment, or carved with a pattern of intricate scrolls. Beds were usually draped with silk damask enriched by fringes and tassels.

The vargueño. The Spaniards developed only one piece of furniture more extensively than the Italians, and that was the writing-cabinet known as the *vargueño*. No Spanish interior was complete without one of these pieces. The origin of the name is uncertain; some authorities claim the piece came originally from Flanders, others that it was first made in the small town of Bargas near Toledo. It was introduced during the Plateresco period, and the earliest examples were simple unadorned boxes, with a hinged lid at both the top and the front, which were furnished with strong locks. Handles were always placed at each end, so that the vargueño could be quickly transported. The interior was subdivided into many drawers and compartments, some with secret sections, and the front of each subdivision was elaborately decorated with geometrical or other inlaid patterns made of ivory, mother-of-pearl, and wood, or with miniature classical architectural motifs. The body was always separate from its supports, and the latter varied greatly in design—simple trestles, turned legs braced by wrought iron forms, and elaborate tables with column and arch supports. Pulls were provided to support the lid when it was used as a writing surface. The vargueño was usually made of walnut but in the early years of the 17th century, mahogany was sometimes used. In the later examples the front of the drop-lid became highly decorated with inlay or with lacelike pierced metal mounts, gilded and applied to small squares of velvet that were distributed in a pattern over the woodwork. The locks, corner braces, key-holes, bolts, and handles were both numerous and decorative and were often supplemented with ornamental nailheads arranged in patterns such as swags, circles, and geometric shapes. A smaller chest of compartments without a drop lid was known as the *papelera*.

Portuguese furniture of the 16th and 17th centuries. All of the types of furniture used in Spain were seen in Portugal; in fact many novelties introduced in Portugal were copied by the Spaniards. The Portuguese exaggerated the size of the turnings that were used for chair and table supports and for the headboards of beds. Spiral and bulbous shapes were also more common. The most important difference, however, was seen in the East Indian and, later, the Chinese influence in Portuguese furniture, which was the result of a monopolistic commerce conducted with these countries. It is claimed that furniture caning and the *cabriole* leg were first used in Europe by the Portuguese, who brought them from China.

The Indo-Portuguese furniture manufactured in Goa,* on the Malabar coast of west India, was made in teak, ebony, and amboyna with ivory inlay or veneer. The Hindu craftsmen often endeavored to copy Western designs. Pierced metal patterns, nailheads, and carving form the ornamental detail. Lacquered furniture was also brought from the Far East, and Oriental woven and printed textiles were first imported into western Europe by the Portuguese traders.

During the Manuelino period (1495–1521), in such places as Batalha and Tomar, the East Indian influence was very strong and expressed itself in an extravagantly rich detail that seemed to be inspired by crustacean and tropical vegetation forms that were the first Far Eastern influence on Western art.

French and English influences of the 18th century. The development of France as a dominant political power in Europe and the intermarriage of the French and Spanish royal families contributed greatly to the influence that French cultural life had upon that of Spain. After the power of Louis

* Goa was the principal center of activity of St. Francis Xavier, one of the greatest missionaries, and the first to bring Christianity to the Far East. He died in 1552 and is buried there.

Spanish 18th century mahogany table of English Georgian influence.

XIV had been established, the French political, social, and artistic influences were seen in architecture and decoration, and by the middle of the 18th century, nearly all important new buildings in Spain were based on French prototypes. In the early years of the 18th century, the rising power of England under Queen Anne also impressed both the Spaniards and the Portuguese. The glittering luxury and brilliance of English social life was beginning to triumph, and the styles prevalent in England were borrowed by the designers, who themselves seemed to be incapable of creative imagination. As this trend was contemporary with the social developments in the Latin American colonies, it was natural that there, too, evidences of it were seen. These foreign influences in Portugal created the style locally known as "Pombalino" named after the Marquez de Pombal, who re-built the city of Lisbon along French lines after it had been destroyed by the great tidal wave of 1755.

The 18th century interior. By 1725 the nobility and the upper classes of both Spain and Portugal began to decorate and furnish rooms in the French manner. Rooms became smaller and furniture was reduced in scale. By the middle of the 18th century, the curved line dominated the shapes of the wooden wall-panels and the design of all furniture. Lacquered panels were brought from the Orient and inserted in both wall and cabinet panelling. The Spanish craftsmen, in copying the French forms, usually lost some of the refinement of the proportions and detail of the originals and did not cater to feminine demands to the same degree as did the French. The charm of the designs lay in the suggestion of barbaric richness and exaggeration of form, color, and ornament, and productions were heavier in appearance than the French. There was a general tendency to finish furniture in white lacquer and gold or in pastel tints. Mirrors played a prominent part in interior design and were inserted in the wall panels or placed in elaborately carved frames and hung on the wall. Many new types of fur-

Vernacci, Photographer

Spanish 18th century carved bench.

Moreno, Photographer

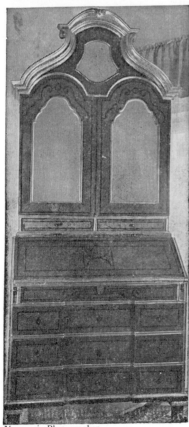

Vernacci, Photographer

ABOVE: *Eighteenth century room in Royal Palace, Madrid, showing an extravagant adaptation of French Rococo detail.* LEFT: *Spanish 18th century secretary desk showing English Queen Anne influence.*

Spanish 18th century porcelain plate showing French chinoiserie influence.

niture were introduced, such as card tables, consoles, varieties of sofas and settees, clocks, and commodes. Comfortable upholstery was introduced. The Spaniards remained loyal to the use of leather, and often applied this to French furniture framework.

From the beginning of the 18th century the English also shipped a great deal of furniture to both Spain and Portugal. The style of Queen Anne became popular and was extensively copied by local craftsmen. The chair backs, however, were usually much higher than in the English examples. Later in the century the Chippendale forms were adopted. England made special furniture for export, and many of the English pieces were finished in red lacquer, to appeal to the Latin tastes. With this finish, cheaper woods could be used in construction, with the result that both tables and chairs often required the use of stretchers. Many of the chairs had caned seats and backs. In much of the furniture made in Spain, both English and French elements were combined in the same piece.

The Mediterranean regions, Valencia, Catalonia, and the Balearic Islands, came strongly under Venetian influence. This accounts for the fine lacquered furniture, at first imported and later copied locally, found in these regions. Chairs, console and corner tables, and handsome secretary-cabinets were generally lacquered in red, yellow, green, and sometimes in blue. The surface decoration, consisting of *chinoiseries* or stylized 18th century motifs, was applied in different shades of gold, reinforced with black lines. The preferred type of chair was a splat back with cabriole legs based on modified Queen Anne models. The earlier secretary-cabinets were often crowned with elaborately curved and ornamented pediments, but in the later examples a more classic type of pediment was used. Another Venetian influence was seen in the copious employment of mirrors, with or without lighting fixtures, hung against the brilliant red or yellow damask wall coverings.

Toward the end of the century, both interiors and furniture began to be influenced by the Adam brothers of England who had studied the ruins of Pompeii and other cities of antiquity. Antique classical, rather than Renaissance forms, also came through French designers who were creating the Neo-classical style called Louis XVI. The straight line was sub-

stituted for the curved or
Rococo forms, the cabriole
leg was eliminated, and all
the sentimental elements of
design associated with Louis
and Marie Antoinette be-
came fashionable. The English Hepplewhite and Sheraton furniture in satinwood
and painted finishes were
also much in demand.* Silk
woven textiles for draperies
and upholstery followed the
French patterns and the East
Indian cotton prints were
extensively used in both
Spain and Portugal.

The period of Napoleon
also had its influence upon
Spanish decoration. Joseph
Bonaparte, the brother of
Napoleon, was a justifiably
unpopular and inefficient
King of Spain for four years

Courtesy The Art Institute of Chicago

A Portuguese 18th century wall treatment showing French influence with Oriental lacquered walls alternating with mirror panels.

until 1813, but it was long enough to introduce the French Empire style of
decoration into some of the royal palaces. With the fall of Napoleon, however, the industrial age began to affect the arts of Europe. The English 19th
century Victorian period, which bore a similarity to the Louis-Philippe and
Napoleon III styles in France, was adopted wholeheartedly by the Spanish
upper classes.† While these changes were occurring, the masses continued
to retain their old ways of living.

In designating the Spanish and Portuguese styles that developed
through external influences it is customary to use the foreign names as an
appendage to the native designation; for example, Spanish-Louis XV,
Spanish-Queen Anne, and Spanish-Empire.

Spanish textiles and leathers. In spite of a Mohammedan ruling against
the use of silk, the Moors produced silk textiles of great beauty. The patterns, usually arranged in bands, were mainly of the geometrical type,
often combined with Arabic inscriptions. Highly conventionalized floral
and animal patterns were also used. Colors were brilliant. Embroideries

---

* These forms should be studied in the chapters on French and English furniture.

† The romantic love match between Eugenie, the daughter of a Spanish nobleman, and
Napoleon III played its part in reviving the French styles that were of eclectic origin.

Spanish
Commode
Louis XVI Inf l.

Spanish Chair Louis XVI Infl.

Spanish Chair
Queen Anne Infl.

Spanish Door 18th Cent.
Louis XV Infl.

EXAMPLES OF 18TH CENTURY SPANISH FURNITURE.

were made in silver and gold thread. During the Renaissance, the textiles used for draperies, cushions, and upholstery were either imported from Italy, or velvets, damasks, and brocades were woven in Spain in Italian designs. Walls in the royal palaces and mansions of the nobles were often hung with tapestries from Flanders. In the 18th century, Portuguese cotton prints were also in favor. Many ecclesiastical chasubles, dalmatics, and other church vestments were made in rich embroidered patterns; these however were not used for household decoration at the time.

The Moors in Cordova produced superb examples of decorated leather called *guadamacileria*. The sumptuous horse-trappings of a 10th century Caliph have been well described by eyewitnesses. An edict in 1502 by Queen Isabella forbade the sale of leather passing as Cordova leather but made elsewhere. The material was used for wall and floor coverings and for cushions. The finish was in several colors, including gold and silver, and enrichment was added by tooling and *embossing*. Tooled, punched, and quilted leather of a very fine black and deep chocolate finish was used in the 16th and 17th centuries for chair seats and backs. Portuguese leather upholstered chairs are unmatched in their decorative beauty; mythological or other figural subjects were introduced amidst rich Baroque scrollwork, and the beauty of the leather was further enhanced by bold brass nailheads, which fastened the material to the wooden frames. With the expulsion of the Moors in the first part of the 17th century, the leathercraft began a decline in Spain, while it prospered in Italy, France, and the Netherlands where it had been established some years previously. Leather was a particularly warm material for lining walls, and a demand developed for the

Cordovan product in the northern countries of Europe, where colder winters required greater interior protection. Exquisite examples of rooms lined in this material still exist. A room in a Roman palace still retains its turquoise leather. One of the rooms in the Governor's Palace in Williamsburg, Virginia, has walls covered with a beautiful example of embossed and painted leather. Many of the rooms in the châteaux built in France in the early 16th century were also treated with this material.

Courtesy Catalonian Museum of Art

Spanish 18th century decorative tile wall panel.

Tile and metalwork. No description of the decorative arts of Spain would be complete without mention of the remarkable metalwork produced by Spanish craftsmen from the time of the earliest civilized settlements. Spain has always been rich in the production of silver, gold, lead, iron, and tin. The supply of precious metals in Spain was greatly augmented after the conquest of Mexico and Peru in the early 16th century.

Exquisite objects for church and household were made in gold and silver, ornamented by *repoussé* and embossing. The silversmith used *filigree* ornament, of fine twisted wires; *damascening,* consisting of gold inlay; precious stone insets; and *enamel,* to enhance the hammered and cast forms.

The Spanish steelworker became famous for his armor and, from the time of the Roman settlements, for the production of Toledo blades and daggers. The ironworker produced sparkling grilles, gates, hardware, lighting fixtures, screens, metal furniture, and accessories in wrought material in which the pattern and interest were obtained by bending, hammering, twisting, and repoussé work.

The use of tile as a decorative feature was carried over into the 18th century work. Porcelain rooms in the Royal Palace in Madrid (1765) and the palace at Aranjuez (1760), both completed by Charles III, are remarkable for the use of this material. Charles had imported the craftsmen and moulds from the factory at Capo-di-Monte near Naples, and installed them at the factory of Buen-Retiro in the park of his palace in Madrid, where figurines, vases, and other ornamental forms were produced in designs based upon both Oriental and Western motifs. These were used in profusion as plaques and appliqué ornaments on the walls of the rooms, and groups of figures were supported on Rococo brackets, and combined with

Chapel of the Rosary in Santo Domingo Puebla, Mexico, showing the elabo-rate Churrigueresco decoration that is typical of many Latin American churches.

elaborate gilded and polychromed plaster ornamentation, designed in sensuous curves and floral detail. Contemporary scenes showing the daily activities of all classes were also painted on tile and used as dado and wall panels. The Portuguese produced similar tiles known as "azulejos" that added great brilliancy to their rooms.

Influences in Latin America. From the discovery of Columbus to the early years of the 19th century, practically the whole of Central America and South America and a large portion of the West Indies were under Spanish or Portuguese control. The work of the early conquistadores had been com-pleted by the middle of the 16th century and almost immediately the settlers, led by their leaders and by the Franciscan and Dominican padres, began to construct religious and administrative edifices of considerable size. These predate, by about sixty years, the first primitive white settle-ments in New England and Virginia, and, by nearly two hundred years, buildings of equal importance. It was natural that the amateur architects who designed the first buildings were lacking in a knowledge of design principles and the craftsmen whom they employed were mainly the Indian natives. The designs on the whole were dictated by structural require-ments. It is remarkable to contemplate the size and splendor of some of these early buildings, in which Moorish, Gothic, Plateresco, Aztec, and Mayan details and patterns were naïvely and unintentionally mixed. In the middle years of the 17th century trained designers began to arrive in the colonies. Most of them had already become imbued with the spirit of the Churrigueresco, and as this style seemed particularly ap-preciated by the white pioneers and Christianized natives, it was these exuberant types of design that were used for nearly all the important structures erected from Rio de Janeiro to Havana and from Santiago de Chile to the borders of Texas and up the coast of California. These countries were filled with buildings that in many cases are more fantastic in appearance than those in Europe. In the countries on the Pacific coast there was also some Chinese influence due to the trade with the Orient. The enormous mineral wealth of Mexico and Peru combined with the religious fanaticism of the natives permitted the interiors of many churches to be freely covered with gold. Indians spent their whole lives on the wood carvings. The gleam and glitter of the prodigiously ornate treatments combined with the

Detail of Churrigueresco decoration in the church at Tepoztlan, Mexico.

most brilliant colors and gold are often bewildering in their effects.*

The residences of these countries were more simple in construction and detail. The majority of dwellings built with adobe brick followed the Spanish patio plan, and the interior decoration and furnishings reflected the style changes in Spain and Portugal. During the 18th century French and English furniture was both imported and reproduced in such local woods as mahogany, embuya, pine, jacaranda (rosewood), larch, and other hardwoods. The most frequently copied styles were those of Queen Anne and Louis XV. There was a general tendency in the furniture reproductions to create heavy proportions, which caused the pieces to lack the grace of the originals. Both carving and inlay enriched the surfaces of the woodwork. The Latin love for brilliant color dominated the chromatic treatment of rooms and both walls and textiles were often far more intense in color than those in Northern countries.

An additional craft that was carried to the New World was that of pottery making. Potters from Talavera, Spain, emigrated to the Mexican city of Puebla where they reproduced the wares of the homeland, and also introduced Chinese forms and modes of decoration copied from the

* Among the most notable examples in this style erected between 1560 and 1780 are the churches at Tlaxcala, Taxco, San Caystanc, Tepoztlan, and Oaxaca in Mexico; at Lima, Cuzco, and Arequipa in Peru; at Quito in Ecuador; at Bahia in Brazil; and at Popayan in Colombia.

porcelain vases brought from the Orient to the Pacific port of Acapulco These are still important decorative accessories in Mexican homes.

The 19th century saw the use of many of the Victorian forms of furnishing with a final tendency toward the eclecticism that was seen throughout Europe and North America. The difficulties of transportation that handicapped many of the Latin American countries caused a drag in their culture that was finally eliminated with the invention of the airplane. Since World War I there has been an enormous development of economic resources and an advantageous increase in foreign travel. The people of these countries have inherited the personal charm and cordiality of their European ancestors, and they offer a true friendship to those who reciprocate. Today there is great study and appreciation of modern movements in architecture, decoration, and the industrial arts, and all countries have developed designers of the first rank.

Leaders in the Hispanic Arts

The following list contains the names of the most well-known leaders in the Hispanic arts, together with the dates when they flourished and a statement of the work for which they were noted:

Aranda, Buenaventura, Count of. Art patron and founder of Alcora ceramic factory (1727).

Arfe, or Arphe (15th and 16th centuries). Family of famous German silversmiths whose work influenced the Plateresco architectural ornament.

Calderón de la Barca, Pedro (1600–1681). The greatest of the Spanish dramatic poets. Contemporary of Shakespeare.

Camoens, or Camões, Luiz Vaz de (c. 1524–1579). Portuguese poet, author of The Lusiads, one of the great poems of the world.

Cervantes Saavedra, Miguel de (1547–1616). Author of Don Quixote, the world's greatest novel, which was important in forming the thought of the Spanish Renaissance.

Churriguera, José (1665–1725). Most outstanding member of a family of architects, who were mainly responsible for the Baroque and Rococo styles in Spain, which were later known as the Churrigueresco. Powerful influence in Latin America.

Egas, Enrique de (d. 1534). Plateresco architect; designed Holy Cross Hospital in Toledo (destroyed).

Goya Y Lucientes, Francisco de (1764–1828). Aragonese realistic artist, tapestry designer. Portrayed scathing and macabre scenes of Spanish life.

Greco, El (Domenikos Theotocopoulos) (1541–1614). Greek artist,

Titian's pupil, who worked in Spain and imbued his paintings with the spirit of Spanish mysticism.

Guas, Juan and Enrique (15th century). Plateresco architects, perhaps of French origin.

Hernandez, Gregorio (1566–1636). Baroque sculptor of northern Spain, noted for polychrome statues.

Herrera, Juan de. Architect of the Escorial (1575–1584). Protagonist of the Desornamentado style. Pupil of Michael Angelo.

Juvara, Felipe (18th century). Architect, pupil of Bernini. Worked in Turin; was called to Spain to design the Royal Palace.

Lull, Ramon (c. 1236–1315). Catalan philosopher and missionary who tried to convert the Moslems to Christianity.

Martinez, Antonio (18th century). Silversmith; work influenced by Pompeian discoveries.

Murillo, Bartolome Estaban (1618–1682). Deeply religious painter of madonnas and Andalusian beggar-boys.

Palomino y Velasco, Acisclo Antonio (1653–1726). Painter and author.

Picasso, Pablo (1881–). Modern exploratory painter and sculptor, founder of Cubism and Post-impressionism. Worked chiefly in France. His style, technique, and general approach to art have been subject to constant changes.

Ribera, José (or Juseppe) de (1591–1652). Valencian painter; worked in Naples for Spanish Viceroys.

Rodrigue, Ventura (1717–1785). Architect, became leading exponent of Neo-classic style.

Rovira, Hipolito. Churrigueresco architect; designed Palace of the Marquis de Dos Aguas at Valencia (1740–45).

Sarcillo, Francisco (1707–1748). Sculptor. Most of his productions were in terra cotta.

Siloe, Diego de (c. 1495–1563). Early Renaissance architect; designed the Cathedral at Granada and the "golden staircase" of Burgos Cathedral.

Valdevira, Pedro (d. 1565). The cathedral of Jaen, the style of which had an important influence in Latin America, was begun under him.

Vandergoten, Jacobo (d. 1725). Brussels tapestry maker called to Madrid by Philip V. Directed the Royal manufactory of tapestries and rugs.

Velasquez de Silva, Diego (1599–1660). Of Andalusian and Portuguese ancestry. Court painter of Philip IV. Noted for portraits of royal family and their buffoons. One of the greatest painters of all times.

Villapando, Francisco Corral de (d. 1561). Architect; designed silver choir screen of Cathedral of Toledo.

Zurbaran, Francisco (1598–1664). Baroque painter.

Xavier, Saint Francis (1506–1562). Basque Jesuit missionary to India and the Far East. Aided in developing trade with these countries.

Bibliography

BEVAN, BERNARD, *History of Spanish Architecture.* Charles Scribner's Sons, New York, 1939. An excellent short history, well illustrated.

Burlington Magazine, Monograph II, "Spanish Art." B. T. Batsford, Ltd., London, 1927. Excellent text with photographs and colored plates.

BURR, GRACE H., *Hispanic Furniture.* The Hispanic Society of America, 1941. Excellently prepared guide to the Spanish collections of this society. Text and illustrations.

BYNE, A., AND M. S., *Decorated Wooden Ceilings in Spain.* Hispanic Society of America, New York, 1920. Collection of photographs and measured drawings with descriptive text.

BYNE, A. AND M. S., *Spanish Architecture of the Sixteenth Century.* G. P. Putnam's Sons, New York, 1917. An illustrated survey of the Plateresco and Herrera styles.

BYNE, A. AND M. S., *Spanish Interiors and Furniture,* 2 Vols. Wm. Helburn, Inc., 1921–1922. Brief text with fine collection of photographs.

BYNE, M. S., *Popular Weaving and Embroidery in Spain.* Wm. Helburn, Inc., New York, 1924. Illustrated text.

CONTRERAS, J. DE, *Historia del Arte Hispanico,* 4 Vols. Salvat Editores, S. A., Barcelona, 1934. The standard history covering all branches of Spanish art, copiously illustrated. Reprint, 1945.

DOMÉMECH, R., AND BUENO, L. P., *Meubles Antiquos Españoles.* Wm. Helburn, Inc., New York. Folio of photographs.

ELLIS, H., *The Soul of Spain.* Houghton Mifflin Co., New York. A beautifully written description of Spain and her people.

MACK, G., AND GIBSON, T., *Architectural Details of Northern and Central Spain.* Wm. Helburn, Inc., New York, 1930. Measured drawings and photographs.

MACK, G., AND GIBSON, T., *Architectural Details of Southern Spain.* Wm. Helburn, Inc., New York, 1928. Measured drawings and photographs.

MADARIAGA, SALVADOR DE, *Spain.* Creative Age Press, New York, 1943. Excellent political and cultural history from earliest times through the civil war.

MAYER, A. L., *Architecture and Applied Arts in Old Spain.* Brentano's, New York, 1921. Brief text with fine photographs.

PRENTICE, A. N., *Renaissance Architecture and Ornament in Spain.* B. T. Batsford, Ltd., London, 1893. Text and measured drawings.

SALADIN, H., *L'Alhambra de Granade,* Paris, 1920. Brief Spanish text and photographs.

CHAPTER V

THE FRENCH PERIODS

D uring the early years of the 15th century, Saint Joan of Arc, by what appeared to a simple peasant people to be supernatural means, aroused the national consciousness of France by expelling the last of the English and ending the Hundred Years' War. The years immediately following the victory of Joan witnessed a consolidating of political and nationalistic gains and an organizing for foreign conquest. This period was coincident with the decline of Gothic art. Medieval mysticism and spiritual man were fading before the onset of a more worldly and realistic philosophy. The flamboyant poems in stone of the Middle Ages had reached their zenith and a new esthetic interpretation was needed to reflect the vigor, ideals, and ambitions of the emancipated nation.

The Italian influence. From the period of Charles VIII (1483–1498), the eyes of the French kings had looked with both jealousy and envy across the Alps. Primarily interested in political gains, they also had the opportunity to contrast their own fortress-like castles with the splendor, comfort, and luxury that surrounded the Italian nobility. The questionable military victories of Charles and his successor, Louis XII, were followed by an invitation to Italian craftsmen to visit France. This movement culminated under Francis I, who induced both Leonardo da Vinci, in 1516, and Cellini, in 1537, to work at the French court. Vignola, the architect, Primaticcio, the mural decorator, Andrea del Sarto, and others followed.

To the reign of Francis I (1515–1547) is ascribed the true beginning of the Renaissance arts in France. Certainly Francis, more than his immediate predecessors, was responsible for the direct encouragement of both art and literature. Francis had been unsuccessful in his military ventures, and in 1525 had been defeated by Charles V in Italy and held prisoner in Pavia. There he had had ample opportunity to observe the fruits of the great Cinquecento, and after his release, his greatest ambition was to make his

The exterior stairway at the Château of Blois, built by Francis I.

reign notable for the glories of art rather than for military or political successes.

Francis' domestic interests lay primarily in the province of Touraine, some 150 miles southwest of Paris. He developed the social life of the nobility in this region and built many delightful châteaux along the Loire River.

Francis was followed by Henry II (1547–1559), who married the Italian, Catherine de' Medici, a woman of cruel but forceful character, who completely controlled him and their three sons, each of whom succeeded to the throne. She was instrumental in giving additional impetus to the Italian arts in France. She surrounded herself with Italian courtiers, who aided in introducing at the French court the amenities of Florentine social existence. Catherine died in 1588 after an active life as the central figure of the religious wars. Tradition ascribes to her the instigation of the Massacre of St. Bartholomew's (1572), which occurred during the reign of her son, Charles IX.

Spanish and Flemish influence. Henry IV (1589–1610), the successor of Henry III, was born in Navarre, a small kingdom in the Pyrenees. Originally a Protestant, he turned Catholic to gain the crown of France, stating that "Paris is worth a mass," and married Marie de' Medici, of Florence. Henry was an enemy of fanaticism, a friend of the people, and thought that groups of conflicting beliefs could live in amity. He was active in the final settlement of the religious difficulties of the people, and by the Edict of Nantes (1598) created a religious tolerance that brought peace to the country, permitted untrammelled activity, and encouraged the development of the industrial arts. As a result of the edict, many Protestant artists and craftsmen, who had been persecuted under the Spanish control of the Low Countries, emigrated to France. By this means, the Flemish interpretation of the Spanish crafts was popularized in France.

Henry IV was succeeded by his son, Louis XIII, when Louis was nine years old. His mother, Marie de' Medici, continued to rule as regent. She was a woman without principles, who lavished the resources of her crown upon nobles, and leagued herself in various ways with Spain. Louis XIII himself was a feeble ruler. He eventually banished his mother, but there was little peace in France until Cardinal Richelieu, spiritual adviser to the court, became the virtual ruler of France from 1622 to 1642.

The king, according to Richelieu, was "the first man in Europe, but the second in his own kingdom." Richelieu wore alternately the helmet of generalissimo of the French army and the cardinal's hat. He was a statesman of extraordinary genius. He was also a great patron of art and literature; he it was who established the French Academy—those Forty Immortals. Richelieu left his mark on French history and culture.

With a Spanish wife, Louis was hostile to the Hapsburgs of both Austria and Spain. Spanish and Flemish influence, however, continued in the arts, which began to show elegance, grandeur, and heaviness.

During the reign of Louis XIII, the influence of both Italy and Spain gradually lessened, and during his final years, the way was paved for the magnificent development of the first truly native French artistic triumphs under his successor.

France established as the cultural center of Europe. A few months after the death of Richelieu, Louis XIII died, leaving his son Louis XIV—a child of five—to reign for 72 years (1643–1715), first under the restraint of Mazarin, and later as absolute monarch. Louis XIV attained complete cohesion of the conflicting political parties in France, and established the French settlements in the Mississippi and St. Lawrence river valleys in America. The development of trade with the Western Hemisphere contributed greatly to Louis' wealth and power, and played an important part in the advancement of the decorative arts. Under the unbroken influence of a long reign, all the arts flourished to an extraordinary degree. *Le Roy Soleil,* lover of pomp and splendor, ruled with a magnificence and state unknown since the days of the Roman Empire. French taste became the standard of excellence, and the French court the social and artistic arbiter of Europe. Louis was the most regal of kings, and his reign one of the most extravagant of modern times. The resources of the realm were so taxed by foreign wars, by the building of his palace and gardens at Versailles, and by his extravagant entertainments that the seeds of the French Revolution may be traced to these events. In his daily life he established elaborate forms of etiquette and surrounded himself with nobles who sought advancement through his favor. Architecture, decoration, and art in general were an essential part of his system to create work and emphasize the glory of King and State. Festivals, plays, ballets, banquets, and dazzling fireworks were the costly amusements of his vast entourage. Poets, artists, and scholars were richly patronized. It was the age of Molière, Racine, and Corneille, the great French dramatists; of Lulli, the musician; and of La Fontaine, the fabulist. His whole reign seemed crowned with a halo of splendor and fascination which made French fashions, literature, language, and arts the envy of Europe.

At the height of his career Louis made his greatest error in the revocation of the Edict of Nantes (1685), which denied freedom of worship to the Huguenots, many of them talented craftsmen, and was followed by terrible persecutions. As a result, thousands of Frenchmen were forced to emigrate to Holland, Switzerland, England, and America.

When Louis died he left France burdened with debt, its resources exhausted, its credit gone, its ships and foreign trade subservient to England, and its people impoverished. The mobs rejoiced and cheered in unison "Vive le Roi," but Louis had left as a heritage the ultimate of all the arts. He had taught the people the art of living.

Louis XV (1715–1774) was a great-grandson of Louis XIV. He was five years old when he inherited the crown. A regent was appointed until he was thirteen, after which he assumed control of the realm. During the Regency, a reaction of frivolity and pleasure set in against the austerity which Louis XIV had imposed upon the court of Versailles in his declining years when he was under the religious and moral influence of Madame de Maintenon. But underneath this gaiety, the economic state of France was chaotic. To replenish the emptied coffers of the French treasury, the regent undertook unwise financial risks. A period of feverish speculation and inflation resulted, followed by a disastrous panic. The economic importance of this finanical fiasco was its tempering of the social order, so that rank and dignity by birth gave place to a new society, whose standard was wealth, elegance, and refinement of manner.

When Louis XV attained his majority and reigned with absolute authority, he continued the mad round of pleasure that the courtiers had instigated under the regent, and indulged himself with unlimited luxury and entertainment. Although for a while economic conditions improved, the country was overburdened with taxation to keep up the extravagances of the court and of the king's favorites, Pompadour and Du Barry. The reign ended in that lurid deathbed prophecy of the king: "After me, the deluge."

The France inherited by the physically and mentally immature Louis XVI was a nation stripped of its American colonies, without prestige in the eyes of other European nations, and torn by political and religious strife within. The condition of affairs had been both aggravated and made public by the writings of Rousseau and Voltaire. France needed stronger hands than those of Louis XVI and his impulsive Austrian wife, Marie Antoinette. Together, lacking sympathy with a licentious court, they stood childlike on the edge of a volcano. Court scandals developed and, while revolution smouldered, the queen played dairymaid in her improvised hamlet at Versailles, and picnicked amidst ribbons and laces, satins and curls.

This was the period that preceded and precipitated the destruction of the Bastille, the execution of the king, and the other events which marked the reign of terror of a bloodthirsty and bitter mob. The battle of Valmy in 1792, in which a French nonprofessional army defeated the highly trained Prussian troops, ended the effort to restore the king to the throne and established the control of the state by the people rather than by the aristocracy. Liberty, equality, and fraternity were proclaimed.

Social effects of the Revolution. The Revolution was followed by the Directorate (1795–1799), a period of slow reorganization and of little constructive effort along esthetic lines. The fortunes of the nobility, dispersed during the Revolution, gradually fell into the hands of a new group, many of whose members had little acquaintance with the credentials of culture.

Napoleon was proclaimed Consul after his campaigns in Austria and Egypt, and in 1804 became Emperor of France. He appointed his brothers kings of Holland, Westphalia, Naples, and Spain. As Emperor his career was brief, but of great importance to France and to the rest of the Western world. He improved public buildings, and he gave France the basis of contemporary French law, in the "Code Napoléon."

Socially and economically, the Napoleonic period created a new distribution of wealth and honors. The royal aristocrats had been destroyed or had emigrated to foreign countries, and in their place was established a new nobility, created by the favoritism of Napoleon and by the obligations he incurred. The *nouveaux-riches* had neither the suavity, the culture, nor the sophistication of the *ancien régime,* yet they desired to surround themselves with the luxuries and the evidences of wealth proper to their position, without recalling too vividly the prerevolutionary forms. Thus a new art period known as "Empire" was created, which, like other periods of French decoration, spread throughout Europe and influenced established local styles until about 1830.

The subdivisions of the French periods. The French art periods are often called after the names of the reigning monarchs, but as the changes in the art forms do not exactly correspond to the lifetimes of the rulers, it is preferable to use the nomenclature given herewith.

1. EARLY RENAISSANCE (1484–1547). Reigns of Charles VIII, Louis XII, and Francis I.
   Transitional period. Mixture of Gothic structural forms with Italian Renaissance architectural detail and ornament.
2. MIDDLE RENAISSANCE (1547–1589). Reigns of Henry II, Francis II, Charles

IX, and Henry III. Gradual elimination of Gothic forms, with greater use of Italian ornament and Renaissance architectural detail, with local variations. Catherine de Medici dominates the kingdom.

3. LATE RENAISSANCE (1589–1643). Reigns of Henry IV and Louis XIII. Continuation of Italian Renaissance influence mixed with Dutch and Flemish influence. Enlargement of wall panelling. More formal effects. Edict of Nantes issued 1598.

4. BAROQUE STYLE (1643–1700). Reign of Louis XIV, 1643–1715. Golden age. The first of the purely native styles. Splendor and magnificence. The use of classic architectural orders. Rectangular wooden wall panelling. Enormous rooms, large-scale furniture. Richly carved ornamentation and strong color contrasts. Curves formed by the compass. Edict of Nantes revoked 1685.

5. REGENCY STYLE (1700–1730). Regency 1715–1723. Beginnings of economy in architecture and decoration. Large scale of rooms continues, but free curved forms are introduced. Transitional style.

6. ROCOCO STYLE (1730–1760). Reign of Louis XV, 1723–1774. Further economies in decorative art production. Smaller scale rooms and furniture. Effeminacy and sentimentality introduced. Artificialities, pastorals, and conventionalizations. Accentuation of free curved forms and delicate color schemes. Elimination of classic orders. Introduction of Oriental influence.

7. NEO-CLASSIC STYLE (1760–1789). Reign of Louis XVI, 1774–1789. Further economies in production. Return to naturalism and simplicity in decorative forms. Straight lines and compass curves. Revival of classic architectural orders. Pompeian, Greek, and English Adam influence dominant.

8. REVOLUTION AND DIRECTOIRE (1789–1804). Temporary stagnation. Effort to eliminate previous forms of art. Introduction of military motifs. Transitional style.

9. EMPIRE STYLE (1804–1820). Napoleon 1804–1815. Symbols of Napoleon's victories. Egyptian motifs, allegorical symbols of Roman and Grecian architecture, decoration, and furniture.

10. RESTORATION STYLES (1830–1870). Reigns of Louis XVIII, Charles X, Louis-Philippe, and Napoleon III. Revivals of late 18th century furniture and industrial art forms, cheapened by machine manufacturing. General decline of good taste.

French initiative in the arts. France is distinctly a spiritual as well as geographical and political entity. From time immemorial distinguished persons of divergent origin have flocked to her protective confines, have contributed to her racial and cultural development, and have become as loyal to her as her native sons. She has welcomed with open arms the thinkers and creative artists of every race and has benefited greatly by this elixir.* The attraction has existed because the soul of France has been

* Charlemagne, Mazarin, Napoleon, Chopin, Zola, Mme. Curie, Stravinsky, Picasso, and Le Corbusier, as well as many of royal blood, were of alien origin.

nourished for centuries by the existence of a completely free intellectual atmosphere. Although France has both profited and suffered from the results of this policy, this freedom has saturated her people with a lust for life and a restless energy and has impelled her continually onward. The motto of Paris, *Fluctuat nec mergitur* (She rocks but never founders), has characterized the spirit of the country as a whole. The modern philosophy of her people commences with Rabelais, the first of her Renaissance scholars who preached the joy of living, tolerance, and the candid acknowledgment of human instincts that the Middle Ages had preferred to screen; Montaigne, who followed him, taught the futility of fanaticism and the value of skepticism; and finally Descartes, the analyst of doubt, became the forefather of democracy and the intellectual ancestor of Franklin, Washington, and Jefferson.

In spite of the diverse origin of her people, and varied geographical and climatic conditions, France has been a closely knit country with citizens proud of their birthright. The essence of French thought has been derived from roots buried in Paris. From this city have come the imagination and explorative efforts in the arts that have ranged from magnificence to absurdity, but which have been necessary elements in the French intellectual development.* The truth-delving qualities of the French mind, the insistence upon quality in industrial and artistic production, the traditions of individualism and desire for novelty have made Paris the arbiter of elegance for over four hundred years. For the major portion of this period, France has been the most advanced outpost of European civilization and all the countries of western Europe, and their progeny in the Americas, have turned to her for artistic nourishment.

Psychological and economic influences. There are two fundamental characteristics of the French mind that have contributed greatly to the charm and originality of French art. These are the love of romance and the love of order. Each of these conflicting qualities has tempered the other, and each has in turn dominated.

The kings of France promoted the art industries partly through their natural desire for luxury and beauty, and partly because such support advanced the economic condition of the country. Extravagances of this type might have been endured had it not been for the added weight of the unsuccessful military ventures attempted by the French kings, the too liberal policy of distribution from the treasury to favorites, and the diversion of government funds to the pockets of petty officials. All French art until the 19th century was essentially monarchical and palatial in character, and the history of French decoration must be traced by a study of the royal resi-

---

* Since the Middle Ages, the literature of every century has proclaimed the allure of Paris, but each generation has nostalgically asserted that "Paris is not what it used to be." The Parisians paradoxically remark, *"Plus ça change, plus c'est la même chose,"* but the road to Paris has always been one of hope and expectation.

Fireplace from the château at Blois, in the Francis I style, showing early Renaissance forms and the salamander.

dences, many of which were designed in a manner that is more elaborate than today's democratic conditions would warrant.

It was not until the 18th century was well started that the financial status of the French nobility forced them to build and decorate their homes along comparatively simple lines and to search for materials and mediums of expression that have become reasonably adaptable to the living conditions of today. It is essential, however, for a proper understanding of French art, to study the development of the Renaissance influences from the beginning.

Interiors of the Renaissance period (1484–1643). Buildings and interiors during the reign of Louis XII were more truly Gothic than Renaissance. In only occasional instances were Italian features seen, and although the importation of Italian artists and craftsmen began during this period, substantial evidences of the new style were not seen until Francis I ascended the throne in 1515. The social life of Francis demanded the construction of numerous small châteaux in Touraine, the exteriors of which strongly recall the medieval fortress in miniature, with the embattlements, towers, and *machicolated* galleries becoming mere ornaments, since gunpowder had made their practical use obsolete.*

The rooms of this period were large, dark in appearance, and often had plaster walls treated with painted patterns or with Cordovan leather, or hung with Arras tapestries. Gothic wood panelling also continued to be used. Floors were in colored or decorated tile. Ceilings revealed structural beams of comparatively small size, placed close together, and ornamented with colorful stripes, armorial devices, and cartouche forms. The mantel was the most important decorative feature in the room, and projected from the wall as in the Gothic period. The overmantel was frequently supported by columns or pilasters the designs of which were inspired by classic detail but not always by classic proportions. The Francis I rooms at Fontainebleau show walls treated with both orders and panelling which follow closely the Italian Renaissance version of the Vitruvian forms. Ornamental motifs borrowed from Italy, such as the arabesque and the candelabra

---

* Examples of these châteaux are seen at Blois, Chambord, Azay-le-Rideau, Chaumont, Chenonceaux, and Fontainebleau, and in a portion of the Louvre in Paris.

Room of the Henri II period in the château at Blois. The Gothic form of panelling is still used, although Renaissance architectural forms and arabesques are introduced.

form, were combined in wood and stone with Gothic pointed arches, finial motifs, and decorated buttresses. The letter "F" in monogram form, and the salamander, selected as a symbol by Francis because of its fabled ability to withstand fire, were everywhere used as ornamental motifs.

Under Henry II and his three sons, the decorative use of Gothic elements dwindled. Rooms were treated in much the same general manner as in the preceding period. There occurred, however, a better understanding of the true classical proportions in the use of the orders. In many rooms the walls continued to be covered with wood panelling of small Gothic proportions, but the field of the panels was often carved or painted with Renaissance arabesque forms. Ceilings were still beamed, but the coffered panel was also introduced. In some rooms of this period have been found fragments of *domino wallpaper,* in marbled effects, probably imported from Italy. Henry adopted the crescent as a symbol and an ingenious monogram of the letters "H" and "D," the latter being the initial of Diane de Poitiers. Both motifs were frequently carved in the woodwork of this period.

The 16th century in France developed a small group of artists whose versatility was only second to that of the Italians. Among them were Pierre Lescot, Jean Goujon, Jacques du Cerceau, and Philibert Delorme.

During the Henry IV and Louis XIII periods, France commenced to be more self-conscious in her art expression. The Gothic forms of design were by this time completely eliminated, and attempts were made to create interiors that were less foreign in feeling. Royal patronage and protection of the artists became an established policy. The rooms of the palaces became more dignified and formal. The architectural orders commenced to be used more frequently as an important feature of decoration. Wall panels in wood were greatly enlarged, and were seen in a diversity of shapes. The moldings used to form the panels were heavy, and the fields of the panels began to be painted and carved with large baroque patterns borrowed from Italian, Spanish, and Flemish sources. Painted wall decorations were used for overmantel areas and in wall panels that reached from floor to ceiling. Floors were in marble squares or parquet wood patterns. Ceilings continued to be beamed or in coffered panels.

Furniture during the Renaissance periods. The rooms of the early Renaissance châteaux were sparingly furnished. The furniture was massively built, and the structural forms of the Gothic period continued in use, although the ornamental forms of the Italian Renaissance were gradually applied. Both oak and walnut were used as cabinet woods. As a result of the fact that a large number of Italian cabinetmakers were in France, and that many of the pieces made by these men were entirely Italian in character, French design characteristics were not in evidence much before the middle of the 16th century. The important chairs maintained the aspect of thrones and were built up from small chest underbodies. Stools and benches, the X-shaped chair, and the *escabelle,* similar to the Italian sgabello, were used. The *caquetoire* or small conversational chair standing on four legs was first used in the middle of the 16th century. The credence and an Italian form of double cabinet known as the *armoire,* enriched with an excess of miniature classical architectural motifs, became typically French pieces. Panels were beautifully carved with graceful figures, arabesques, and grotesques. *Gadrooning* was common as an ornamental motif. Small rectangular insets of jasper, onyx, and other semiprecious stones were sometimes added to the designs. Both carved trestle supports and column legs were used for heavy tables, some of which had extension tops. The bed was massive, with four heavily carved posts supporting a cornice from which hung velvets or tapestries. Hugues Sambin and Jacques du Cerceau were the leading designers of furniture during the latter years of the 16th century.

Under Henry IV and Louis XIII the Flemish influence was more strongly seen in furniture than in decoration. Walnut and oak continued to be used, but ebony also became popular as a furniture wood. In case-furniture, made in the north of France by less expert craftsmen, panels were of the pyramidal type with either three or four sides. *Bun feet* or *Flemish feet* with scrolls were used, and supports consisted of slender classic column forms or spiral turnings. Flat stretchers arranged in the shape of a letter "X" with a vase form or turned finial placed at the inter-

Louis XIII Cabinet

Salamander Motif

Louis XIII Cabinet
Flemish Influence

Henri II Caquetoire

Henri II Cabinet

Francis I Chair
Henri II Wood Panel

FRENCH RENAISSANCE FURNITURE AND DETAILS.

section were introduced to brace table and cabinet legs. In the better grade of furniture, ornaments were carved or inlaid in woods of contrasting colors, in tortoise shell, semiprecious stones, and gilded bronze. Upholstery consisted of elaborately embossed Cordovan leather, velvet, damask, and needlework, often trimmed with fringes.

Louis XIV and the Palace of Versailles. Early in the reign of Louis XIV, the King had as Minister of Finance a man named Nicolas Fouquet

Reproduction of old engraving of the Palace and Gardens of Versailles.

who had built (1655–61) for himself on the outskirts of Paris a château that was known as Vaux-le-Vicomte.* One day Fouquet invited the King and his Court to visit him. What greeted Louis' eyes was a structure and gardens the splendor of which he had never seen before. It surpassed in novelty any of the royal palaces. It was incredible. The King, intolerant of rivalry, suspected irregularities in the royal accounts, discovered them, jailed Fouquet for life, and decided to build a palace that would never be excelled in size or beauty. Thus was conceived Versailles, which up to that moment had been but a small hunting lodge erected by Louis XIII. This building, which was planned to house 10,000 persons comprising the immense retinue and guests of the King, was the supreme architectural and decorative achievement of his reign. Charles Lebrun, the painter, a man of inexhaustible ingenuity, was appointed art director of the realm. Louis LeVau, the architect, commenced the building in 1668, but Jules Hardouin-Mansart, a follower of Vignola, continued it after 1679. Bernini, the great Italian Baroque architect, was also consulted. Decorators, sculptors, painters, industrial designers, and master craftsmen were collected from far and wide to plan and embellish the new building. The greatest French artists in all mediums were placed on the royal payroll, among them Antoine Coysevox, Lefèvre, Boulle, Marot, Berain, and Lepautre. The palace became a city in itself. It was the first complex dwelling that was planned in contact with nature. The great park and gardens planned by Le Nôtre have been the prototype of all town-planning since their inception. The plan consisted of vast parterres of "green carpets," flowers, lakes, canals, fountains, interminable radiating avenues, vistas, and arbored

* This château had been designed by LeVau and decorated by Lebrun. It is still in existence.

walks; its canals were filled with gondolas and luxury craft, and provision was made for every sort of activity—sports, hunting, fishing, festivals, and love-making. The most important public room in the palace was the great *Galérie des Glaces* or Hall of Mirrors, designed by Mansart and decorated by Lebrun. This room is 240 feet long, 34 feet wide, and 43 feet high. Its walls are lined with Corinthian pilasters of green marble which alternately separate arched windows and arched mirrors. The ceiling, which springs from a richly treated entablature, is a semicircular plaster vaulted arch painted by Lebrun.*

In addition to the Palace at Versailles, Louis built many small châteaux. Bernini designed the great colonnade at the east end of the Louvre. Louis purchased the Gobelins tapestry looms in 1662, appointed Lebrun director and chief designer and later purchased the Beauvais looms. The Gobelins factory not only made tapestries but embroideries, furniture, mosaics, bronzes, and goldsmiths' work for the royal palaces and for presentation purposes. In 1666 the French Academy in Rome was founded. The Savonnerie rug factory was eventually combined with the Gobelins factory; the potteries at Rouen and St. Cloud were given royal encouragement as were many other art industries. The French National School of Fine Arts and the Paris Conservatory of Music were organized; stately government buildings were erected; libraries were founded; halls of science, astronomy, botany, and zoology were established. The arts and sciences were welcome and useful allies in aiding the King to make the Court of France the most magnificent in Europe.

Interiors of the Baroque period. The public rooms in the Palace of Versailles, which are all of great size, were designed for entertaining vast assemblages in the most regal manner. This purpose created the key to the whole style, and explains why it is called the French Baroque. Great formality of design and pompousness, produced by large-scale detail and extravagance of workmanship and material, were the most characteristic decorative features. In the salons, the permanent elements of the large rooms, such as walls, ceilings, doors, and windows, were the important features of decoration. Movable objects and furniture were regarded as secondary motifs. As a result, most of the furniture was placed against the walls, leaving the center of the room clear. The walls and ceilings were treated as one magnificent composition of decorative paintings, carvings, tapestries, panelling, and mirrors.

An architectural arrangement in which the orders were used in true classical proportions formed the basis of the wall design. Columns, pilasters, and entablatures were enriched with gilded metal and carved ornaments. In the more formal public rooms, stone and colored marble were

*Here King William of Prussia was proclaimed German Emperor in 1871 and the Germans in 1919 were obliged to sign the Treaty of Versailles.

Extraordinary bedroom of Louis XIV in the palace at Versailles. The supreme example of royal magnificence, vigor, and splendor typified by large-scale orders and detail, strong color contrasts, and gilt ornament.

used for both the orders and walls. In the private apartments wood panelling was more generally used. The pilasters rose either from the floor or stood on a pedestal which formed a low dado around the room, and the wall area between them was enriched with one or more large panels of great height, extending from the dado to the underside of the architrave. Wide panels alternated with narrow ones. An *attic* was often placed above the entablature, and above the attic the ceiling was curved downward in a quarter circle called a *cove* to meet the woodwork of the wall.

The panels were sometimes painted with portraits and historical or mythological scenes. Large plate glass mirrors, considered the height of luxury and extravagance at that time, were also used as panel enrichment. The wood panels were in oak, framed with large moldings ornamented with finely detailed carving. The panel shapes were rectangular, although at the tops the moldings would sometimes follow a semicircular or segmental curve. Circular frames above the panels enclosed portraits or flower paintings. Carved ornamental forms enriched the panel field at the top and bottom, and a conventional medallion or naturalistic drop motif was often placed in the center. Wooden walls were usually painted, although some were of waxed oak left in a natural finish. It was customary to gild the moldings and carved ornament to contrast with a background painted in an off-white tone. This produced an exceedingly regal effect and became a standard method of decorating the woodwork. The French word *boiserie* is generally used to designate the carved wood panelling of all the French 18th century periods.

Door and window trim was architecturally treated with a heavy molding, crowned with a cornice. Overdoors were frequently enriched with wooden sculpture in high relief showing cherubs surrounded by foliage, or portraits framed in the woodwork. Mantels of enormous size were invariably in colored marble, sumptuously carved with ornament, the shelves slightly shaped, with molded edges. Overmantels were in mirror or painted panels framed in an architectural treatment.

Floors were oak parquet patterns or black and white marble squares. The floor coverings were usually Savonnerie pile rugs in colors and patterns that harmonized with the architecture and carved ornament. Coves were elaborately enriched by plaster panels and painted ornament, and the central portion of ceilings was painted with celestial scenes. Crystal or carved wood chandeliers hung in the center of the room, but additional light was given by *torchères,* wall brackets, and elaborate candlestands. The character of the ornamental motifs alternated between the abstract and the realistic; flower and leaf forms, masks, grotesques, and religious symbols were used in the carving. The king's monogram, two intertwining "L's" in script form, was often placed in a cartouche located over a door or window or in the center of a panel. The king's symbol, a sun with spreading rays, was also frequently used. Accessories consisted of busts, hanging mirrors, Oriental pottery, terra-cotta urns, statues in bronze or marble, paintings, and portraits, and an extensive use of wall tapestries of the Gobelins and Beauvais looms. The large scale and great richness of the interiors of the Louis XIV period make them inappropriate for modern use.

Furniture of the Baroque period. With the ushering in of the Baroque influence, the design of furniture and accessories assumed a richness of character equal to the room treatments. The furniture industry in France was very well organized as early as the 16th century. Individual pieces were usually made only upon order until the period of Louis XV. The earliest furniture makers were known as *huchiers-menuisiers* or hutch-carpenters. These were later divided into *menuisiers d'assemblage,* makers of solid wooden furniture, and *menuisiers de placage et de marquetrie,* makers of veneers and marquetry. About the middle of the 18th century, the term *ébéniste* (cabinetmaker) became common, although ebony as a cabinet wood had lost its popularity, and the title *maître-ébéniste* (master cabinetmaker) was given to those who had served their apprenticeship, passed the required tests, and received a royal license to practice their trade. Records have been retained of most of these names, and as the makers usually branded their products with their initials or surname, the origin and ap-

Showing Ormolu Mounts and
Tortoise Shell and Pewter Marquetry
Boulle Cabinet

Walnut Stool
Showing Flemish
Influence

Chair
About 1675

Ornament for
Panel Corner

Carved Wood
Panel

Wood Carving
Detail of Chapel Door, Versailles

**Mantelpiece,
Versailles**

BAROQUE FURNITURE DETAILS.

proximate dates of manufacture of most of the finest of the old French pieces can be accurately identified. A special guild of cabinetmakers and apprentices was organized by Lebrun, who appointed André-Charles Boulle *maître-ébéniste* to the king. The cabinetmakers were given quarters in the Louvre, and were directed to create more magnificent, more beautiful, and more novel furniture than had ever before been produced. Boulle had the ability to execute such an order, and his influence upon subsequent French cabinetmakers and upon the cabinet productions of other

European countries was phenomenal. Boulle established the tradition of French cabinetmaking that was carried on by his sons, by his pupil Charles Cressent, who became particularly famous for his priceless chased metalwork, and, later, by Jacques and Philippe Caffieri.

The large rooms of the period, to maintain a consistent effect, called for heaviness of proportions and structure in the furnishings. Rectangular forms dominated in furniture design, with compass curves used where required. The typical furniture legs were heavy, square, and tapered, braced by square-sectioned, diagonal stretchers. Wood-carving was popular, and many pieces were gilded. Two new types of furniture enrichment were developed by Boulle. *Ormolu* (gilded bronze) motifs and moldings were used as applied ornaments, which, in addition, served to brace the structure of the furniture; and panels were decorated with what is today known as *boulle work*, which consists of marquetry patterns made from sheets of tortoise shell and German silver, brass, or pewter. Boulle work was very typical of Baroque furniture, but its use was discontinued in the later French periods. The use of ormolu, however, was characteristic of all the styles that followed; the only change being in the modelling, scale, and subject matter of the motifs which were altered to correspond to the patterns of each style.

Ebony, oak, walnut, chestnut, and sycamore, as well as rarer woods, were used for wooden framework. Tabletops were of marble. Comfortable upholstered and cushioned chairs and sofas were made, the upholstery materials consisting of tapestry, needlepoint, leather, cane, and heavy silk textiles such as damasks and plain or brocaded velvets. Upholstery trimmings were elaborate hand-woven fringes or gold or silver nailheads. The textiles used for draperies were the same as those used for the upholstery. Patterns were large and the colors of the figures contrasted strongly in tone with the backgrounds. Chromatic values were comparatively brilliant, a necessary feature in the large rooms.

Toward the end of the reign of Louis XIV and during the Regency, when the curvilinear period of design was beginning, the cabriole leg was first used. This was a curved form of support conventionalizing an animal leg, with knee and ankle usually terminating in the form of a goat's hoof. Curvilinear forms were also used for chair and table stretchers.

Interiors of the Regency period. The art style designated by the term Regency does not coincide with the political period of the same name, but the word is used as a convenient method of describing the transitional forms which were seen as early as the closing years of the 17th century. In brief, this style maintains the scale and richness of the Louis XIV treatments, yet it begins to show some of the gracefulness and curvilinear elements that qualify the style named for his successor. This transitional form applied both to the wall panelling and the furniture. The Regency overlapped and blended with the two styles from which it drew its forms, so that a clear division was imperceptible. The style (1700–1730) was a bridge between the classic severity of that of the Sun-King and the romanticism that developed during the reign of his great-grandson, Louis XV. The change in art forms was slow, but the demand for austerity, grandeur, and formality lessened with the political misfortunes of the closing years of the reign of the great Louis. The temper of the king must have been softened greatly in his old age, if we are to judge by his statement to Mansart that he wished to see playing children instead of classical heroes used as subjects of decoration. By the early years of the 18th century the decorative arts had become popularized. Nobles as well as the wealthy bourgeoisie vied with each other in the purchase of art products and in procuring the services of artists. Even the farmers began to feel the return of prosperity and required stylized furniture for their cupboards, dressers, and wardrobes. Every one began to take pride in his home furnishings. The beginnings of much greater economy, however, were noticeable in the construction of smaller dwellings, with rooms suitable for more simple living and a more intimate type of entertaining than had been in vogue before. The demand for a reaction from the severity of existing social formalities was reflected in the value placed upon small pleasures, which was, in turn, reflected in the decoration of rooms in a more playful, fanciful spirit. The change was perhaps first reflected in the work of the painters. The style of Watteau, who began to dominate the arts after the death of Lebrun in 1690, was a complete reversal of the overpowering impressiveness of the work of the former art director, and Watteau was able to reflect the change in the thought of the times. Smilingly, but with a melancholy soul, he painted imaginary paradises and *fêtes galantes* showing the aristocracy charmingly and delicately playing at the game of love. His masterpiece in the Louvre "Embarkation for Cythera" expresses the hopeful escape from the social formalities of the period to an island, the epithet of Aphrodite where love-making was prolonged eternally.

Interiors of the Rococo period. The style commonly known as Louis XV is pre-eminently one of interior decorative rather than of architectural application; the term *Rococo,* to which it alone has claim, originates in a combination of the two French words *rocaille,* originally referring to rockeries, artificial grottoes, and rustic treatments, and *coquille,* meaning cockleshell. Both of these motifs had been represented in the pottery designs of Palissy in the 16th century, but they were revived and simplified by the designers of the 18th century, and applied to the industrial arts. Meissonier, an Italian who came to Paris in 1723, is generally credited as being the early influence in the development of the style. He produced a book of engraved designs using the shell motif in deft and engaging compositions that caught the fancy of the French craftsmen, who began to adapt his designs to woodwork and cabinetmaking. The whole concept of Louis XV art was the reverse of that of Louis XIV, in which everything had been sacrificed for splendor. In the Rococo style, human comforts were paramount and practical changes occurred; the rooms were reduced in size and many were added for special purposes. There were definite public and private subdivisions of the house; reception rooms for winter and summer use; drawing rooms; small private libraries; boudoirs; and sitting, dressing, writing, conversation, coffee, play, music, and powder rooms—in fact, every type that is used today excepting the bath. There were, also, *cabinets particuliers* or secret rooms, for private rendezvous, that were entered through the back of wardrobes or through sliding panels in the wainscoting; the private dining room planned for Louis in the Petit Trianon contained a table that could be lowered through the floor to the pantry beneath for resetting between courses—an arrangement that enabled the king and his guests to carry on a conversation that could not be heard by the servants. Inventions were made for the improvement of heating,

Courtesy Alavoine, Paris

French provincial bedroom of about 1765, showing recessed bed and Rococo frame for niche.

Courtesy Alavoine, Paris

French provincial library, showing Rococo doors treated with wire grilles for built-out bookcases.

which, also, caused a change in the design of the clothing that was worn.

The Rococo style in its spatial development was wholly of French nativity although its germs had come from Italy. Its florescence was as untrammeled by foreign influence as had been the Gothic, and it was one of those immaculate conceptions of the imagination that art history has occasionally witnessed. It was fathered by nothing and vanished in a vacuum when the Vesuvian dusts were swept from Pompeii, yet it was imitated throughout nearly the whole of Europe. Whereas the purpose of the art of the Baroque had been to glorify the King, the art of the Rococo was for everyone, and particularly for pretty women—to please them, to accentuate their physical attractions, and to establish their supremacy and power. With the greater participation of women in politics, in literature, and in active life, French art became effeminate, sensuous, and pagan, yet light, graceful, and fantastic; its purpose was not the expression of a heavy dignity, but to please its beholder by an emotional and often voluptuous appeal.

During the Regency, the germs of rococo forms had already appeared and were blended with the great traditions formulated by Lebrun. With the reduction in scale of the decorative forms to suit smaller rooms, there also occurred a progressive change in the character of linear and mass composition. The straight lines and the compass curves of the Louis XIV period gradually gave way to freehand and often riotous curves, which were eventually used at every opportunity. The orders, inconsistent and inharmonious with the new forms, were completely eliminated in interior architecture. The eye was to be distracted and amused by continuous but irregular flowing motion produced by abstract detail that resembled nothing more than constantly changing froth, flames, or splashing water.

The later rococo rooms were extraordinarily charming, precious, and almost doll-like in their artistic concept. Small in their dimensions, they were consistent to the most minute detail and their decorative treatment bespoke cordiality, warmth, comfort, and convenience to a supreme degree. In such an atmosphere their occupants, dressed in luscious silks, could not refrain from the most genteel amenities, which foredoomed them to mutual flattery and amorous conversation. In the boudoirs the ladies of the court would receive their friends and admirers seated *en deshabille* on their *chaises-longues* while perfuming, rouging, or placing a beauty spot on their cheek, but modesty decreed that they should at least conceal their bare feet with an embroidered coverlet. France is still flooded with small châteaux and country houses created during this period. Many of the rooms in the Palace of Versailles were redecorated in an elaborate interpretation of the new style, but the most interesting were those built in the minor residences. Foyers and entrance halls were usually treated in panel designs of marble or *Caen stone,* but in the living quarters the walls were covered with wood panelling. The dado was used less frequently and it was usually lower than in the previous style. The orders of architecture were always omitted, the wall being finished at the top with a simple architrave molding—never a complete entablature—and rising from this molding was a decorated plaster cove that eliminated the angle between wall and ceiling. There was a constant effort to avoid straight intersections where possible and the corners of the rooms were often curved in plan.

The panel moldings were much reduced in size and at the top and bottom of the panels they were curved, in a form resembling a woman's upper lip, or were in irregular free curves gracefully combined in a continuous line. The corners of the panels were often broken or softened by the addition of a covering ornament. There was also a tendency toward assymmetry in panel shapes in which the top and bottom molding would form an irregular curve reaching its apex or ornamental motif at the corner rather than the center of the panel. Panel shapes were always vertical in their proportions. Anything approaching a square was usually avoided, and variety was introduced by alternating wide panels with narrow ones, the latter being formed by very small moldings. There was an attempt to panel opposite walls in a similar manner. In the royal palaces the moldings and panel fields were treated with gilded carved ornament; but, in the smaller dwellings, the moldings were plain and painted a color similar to, or contrasting with, the panel surface. As a substitute for the earlier more expensive carved ornamentation, the panel centers were often enriched with a painted scenic decoration or floral composition in delicate colors by Watteau, Boucher, Fragonard, Pillement, or one of their imitators. These decorative artists were strongly influenced by the life that fluttered around them. Their work was sensual, but purified by a grace and winsome beauty that exhilarated and quickened the heartbeat. In some rooms the oak woodwork was merely polished with wax, but in the majority, the background woodwork was painted either rose, turquoise, straw, mustard, putty, or pale green. During this period, textiles were sometimes stretched in the panel centers as a substitute for the painted decoration; these were either painted or moiré silks, or printed cottons, and their use confirmed the tendencies toward economy in the production of decorative effects. Painted and decorated mirrors also were much used for their glamorous reflections of flickering candlelights, exquisite costumes, and feminine pulchritude.

The king's favorite, Madame de Pompadour (1721–1764), a woman of great culture and refinement, was intensely interested in the decorative arts, and spent both time and money in furthering them. She contributed large sums for the excavations in Herculaneum and Pompeii. She also obtained royal patronage for the ceramics manufactory at Sèvres, where exquisitely delicate pieces were produced, and where new chemicals were discovered to produce the rose, king's blue, and gold for which the ware became famous. Pompadour was also interested financially in an Oriental trading company, and succeeded in popularizing Oriental importations.*

* The Compagnie des Indes in which Pompadour was interested was the French equivalent to the British East India Company. It was responsible for the enormous importations of silks, pottery, porcelain, wallpaper, and other varieties of eastern products. Ships sailed to China as well as India, and the French established factories in these countries that manufactured products that would appeal to the home markets. The Company started operation in 1664. It was particularly prosperous around 1750. Clive defeated the French in India in 1761 and the Company was disbanded in 1769.

Detail of painted chinoiserie panel.

Artists, seeking her favor, contributed to the vogue; and not only were Oriental patterns reproduced in various mediums, but several decorative artists developed an extraordinary degree of originality in creating designs based on Chinese motifs for use in wall panels, screens, fans, and wall paintings. Among these artists were Pillement and Christophe Huet, who produced the most fantastic arrangements of mandarins, pagodas, parasols, monkeys, ladders, and foliage. A host of imitators added to the popularity of the movement, the designs being known as chinoiseries and *singeries,* according to their use of Chinese or of monkey motifs. Another inspiration for painted panel designs was obtained from Turkish sources, and decorations *à la turque* represented beauties of the harem, men in turban or fez, pashas, dervishes, odalisques, and other Mohammedan types, intertwined with delicate arabesques.

The ornamental motifs in all mediums often reflected the purpose of the room or the interests of its occupants. Pastoral scenes and objects, such as the shepherdess' hat, basket, and crook, were extremely popular; music was often symbolized by the bagpipe, violin, flageolet, horn, and tambourine; hunting, fishing, science, and literature were represented; bouquets and garlands of roses, daisies, narcissi, eglantine, and sweet briar were arranged with sprays and tendrils. The attributes of love, such as Cupid with his bow, quiver, and arrows, the blazing torch, and pairs of burning hearts, were frequently introduced toward the end of the period. The conventionalized cockleshell was one of the most common motifs used for the enrichment of both furniture and wall panelling; it usually formed a crowning or central feature in the design and was accompanied by sprigs of leaves.

The demand for decorated wall panels in the Chinese manner extended to the middle classes, and was supplied through the importation of Chinese

Room in Paris apartment using Rococo panelling and furniture.

hand-painted wallpapers, which could be had for less than French artists demanded for their work. Wallpaper, which had first been made in France by Jean Papillon in the latter years of the 17th century, was thus popularized. *Flock paper* imitating velvets and damasks was imported from England and was much in demand in the smaller residences.

Mantels were made in marble, with sweeping curved shelves and fire openings. The overmantel, known as a *trumeau,* combined woodwork, mirror, and painting, and a large mirror above a console was placed on the wall directly opposite the mantel to increase the illumination by an infinite number of reflections of the candlelight. Elaborate cast-iron firebacks, gilded bronze lighting fixtures, and andirons in rococo forms were used. Textile patterns were reduced in scale and consisted of scrolls, ribbons, flowers, and shells in a flowing or all-over pattern that would harmonize with the curved lines of the panels and furniture. Brocades, damasks, taffetas, satins, moirés, and other fine silk weaves were used for draperies and other decorative purposes. Printed cottons were introduced in the *toiles-de-Jouy* made by Oberkampf, who designed pictorial groups in large repeats in red, blue, green, and eggplant, and printed them on a white ground.* Window treatments were sumptuous, with full curtains and valances. Colors were light in value, and soft, neutral hues were used.

Floors were in rectangular parquet patterns or in elaborate marquetry arrangements made in contrasting woods. The public rooms had floors in

* See Chapter X.

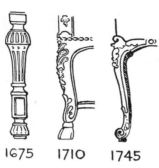

1675   1710   1745

Typical French Baroque, Regency, and Rococo chair supports.

marble squares. Floor coverings were made at the Aubusson and Savonnerie looms in Rococo patterns and delicate colors.

The height of the Rococo style was reached about 1760, and the use of the exuberant forms lessened thereafter, as the public tired of the artificiality and super-sophistication of the period. The exquisite taste of Madame de Pompadour was a dominant influence in the movement toward greater restraint. At least fifteen years before the death of Louis XV, the character of the interiors as well as the detail of furniture and accessories began to assume the classical forms usually called "Louis XVI."

Furniture of the Rococo period. The cabinetmakers of the Rococo or Louis XV period developed so many new types of furniture that they left few possibilities to their successors and they reached the limits of perfection in technique and comfort. Rococo furniture was designed to fit human dimensions and not intended for pomp or pageantry. While some examples were of overpowering splendor, most of them were small and unpretentious. The infallible characteristic was the use of the curvilinear form at all times and particularly the cabriole leg with a scroll foot instead of the goat's hoof. The straight line was diligently avoided, the framework of the furniture was designed to eliminate the appearance of joints; legs appeared to flow into the upper framework in an unbroken line and the principle of continuity was maintained wherever possible. The ornament was designed for a particular location and its relationship to the whole design; it was never overwhelming, and always served its purpose of enriching the structure without competing with it. Turned forms were never used except in country-made pieces. The furniture was always described as having "an agreeable contour," perhaps unconsciously following the lines of the feminine form. Much of the case furniture had bulging fronts known as *bombé* or *serpentine*. The cabinetmakers performed structural miracles in adapting wood, a straight-grained product of nature, to curved yet adequately strong assemblages. The cabriole support, when well designed, appeared to have all the muscular qualities of the leg of a vigorous animal. The enrichment consisted of carving, marquetry, paint and lacquer or *ormolu mounts,* or a combination of these. The woods that were used were infinite in variety and were drawn from both domestic and exotic sources. Walnut, oak, wild cherry, beech, and elm were the most common, but many pieces were made in whole or in part of the fruit woods, apricot, pear, and plum, or the imported almond, palm, mahogany,

Bergère

Console Table

Side Chair

Marble Mantel

Wood Panel

Chair Leg
Showing Cabriole Form

Commode with • Painting showing 'Singerie'
Ormolu Mounts • and 'Chinoiserie' Motifs   Wood Panel

ROCOCO FURNITURE AND DETAILS.

rosewood, olive, ebony, sandalwood, or satinwood. Marquetry designs
were made in tulipwood, kingwood, violetwood, yew, amaranth, palisander, and lignum-vitae. Black whalebone was used for narrow strips.

Although some painted furniture had been made in earlier periods, this
finish became common toward the middle of the 17th century. The colors
were always pale and neutral and moldings frequently were accentuated by contrasting hues. Gilding was occasionally applied.

Chinese lacquer, which had been imitated in the 17th century, was in-

Painted room showing transition between Rococo and Neo-classic styles about 1760. The fine scale of detail and low ceiling are typical.

troduced as a furniture finish by four brothers named Martin who discovered its secret process and maintained it as a monopoly. They founded their Royal Manufactory in 1748. The early products of the Martins maintained the curvilinear forms which were lacquered with copies of Oriental patterns finished in black and gold. Later they introduced polychromed effects using Western motifs. Their lacquer was known as *Vernis-Martin,* which term was later used to designate their furniture. Their success was phenomenal and the ownership of one of their productions was considered expressive of the height of refinement and luxury.

The Martins applied their secret finish to every conceivable kind of object, such as snuffboxes, fans, *spinets, sedan chairs,* coaches, and every type of furniture. Many of their competitors, confronted with the vogue for the Oriental, sent panels, drawer fronts, and other parts of furniture to China to be lacquered. When these portions were returned to France they were inserted in the locally made framework. The real Chinese lacquer was of better quality than that made by the Martins, and was often applied to *coromandel* wood.

Ormolu mounts continued as furniture enrichment, but the patterns changed to reflect the reduced scale of the furniture and to correspond to the subject matter and style of the period. Jean Jacques Caffieri and Gouthière were the great *ciseleurs* and their metalwork for clocks, lighting fixtures, shelf ornaments, and furniture was equal to jewelry in chiselling and finish; edges were sharp, undercuts were deep, and modelling was of the highest quality.

Many pieces of furniture were enriched with marquetry but the curved surfaces of the panels made this type of enrichment difficult to produce with the inferior adhesives then available. The marquetry patterns included squares, lozenge shapes, herringbone, and floral or figural representations.

Many tables and nearly all the consoles, commodes, and low case-furniture had colored marble tops that harmonized with the room color. Library tables and desks usually had a Morocco leather or velvet top. The interior of dresser drawers was often lined with a textile or wallpaper. Ordinary dining tables, which were usually round, were not decoratively designed as they were entirely covered with linen when in use and with an ornamental cover between meals. Trestle tables on temporary supports were used for dining when numerous guests attended.

The leading cabinetmakers of the period were Jean François Oeben and Georges Jacob, whose principal customer was Pompadour. Among other *maître-ébénistes* were René Dubois, Michel Cresson, Jean Baptiste Boulard, Mathieu Criaerd, and Adrien Fleury.

The principal textiles used for upholstery were brocades, damasks, velours, lampas, Aubusson tapestry, needlepoint, colored leathers, and cotton and linen prints. The patterns definitely avoided straight lines. Stripes were in waves and all-over patterns were used to harmonize with the curved forms of the furniture. *Toile-de-Jouy* prints made by Oberkampf were also extremely popular. Less costly chairs had seats in caning, rush, and straw.

At the end of this chapter is a list of the types of furniture which were produced during the Rococo period. As there is no exact equivalent in English for many pieces, the French name is given with a description of the piece or its nearest name in English. In a few cases names of pieces that were made in other than the Rococo period have been included. These have been noted.

Interiors of the Neo-classic period. When Louis XVI came to the throne, the nobility were exhausted financially and fatigued by a half century of superficial pleasures. The protests of the mobs had already begun to rumble and to demand vehemently a cessation of the public policies. Both prudence and boredom with their life called for a change in the outward living conditions of the aristocrats, and a definite trend toward simplicity was the art reaction of this movement. For several years the designers of Paris had been divided by insoluble problems of esthetic legalities concerning the use of the straight and curved line. One group supported their stand on the claim that the straight line does not exist in nature—even the ocean's horizon being a curve; while the other group argued that excessively curved forms violate every sound structural principle. The actual root of the argument was the natural desire for variety and change. The curved forms had been universally used for upwards of sixty years, and changes in fashion are irrepressible.

The Neo-classic interiors retained all the charm and intimacy of the previous period, while discarding the rococo curves. Changes were in the forms and details. Architectural orders were revived, the free curve gave way to the semicircle, segment, and ellipse, and all panels were rectangular. Carving and ornament, delicate in scale, were used less profusely and the motifs were borrowed either from natural flowers, sentimental alle-

Neo-classic room in the palace at Fontainebleau. The rectangular panels are characteristic; the moldings and ornament are gilded; the general informality of arrangement is typical.

gories, or classical leaf and scroll patterns that were inspired by the Pompeian discoveries of 1755. Piranesi the Italian painter and engraver had flooded Paris with his drawings of Roman monuments, vases, candelabra, and bas-reliefs, and this contributed greatly to the popular revival of interest in antiquity.

The majority of the rooms in châteaux were treated with wood panelling and there was usually an attempt to design each as a symmetrical composition. This was often accomplished by placing a large panel as a central feature with subordinate flanking panels, or a false door was introduced to balance a real door; or, if an opening was located inconveniently in the composition, a secret door to cover it was placed in the panelling. Opposite walls were similarly treated and architecturally balanced if possible. Real bookcases were often imitated by book-backs placed on false shelves, and overmantel mirrors were balanced with mirrors placed over a console table on the opposite wall.

The walls usually had low dadoes. In high rooms the panelling was crowned with a complete entablature, while low rooms had merely a cornice or a small cove at the top. The orders were smaller than those used in the Louis XIV period. Panel moldings were sometimes painted a color contrasting with the field, or a narrow paint stripe would be added near the edge of the panel to accentuate the frame. Panel centers were often left undecorated, but in the more elaborate rooms they were painted or enriched by stucco relief patterns showing arabesques combined with classical figures and naturalistic flowers, arranged in garlands and drop ornaments. In Marie Antoinette's bedroom in Fontainebleau, the background treatment of the wood panels is silver leaf rubbed with dull gold,

Wall panelling showing chinoiserie paintings in Neo-classic room (1760). A semicircular arch form is superimposed over a Rococo mantel. The cornice is reduced to a few small moldings.

Unusual example of a provincial Neo-classic room from Dijon, France. Characterized by fine-scale classical architectural detail, with rectangular panels and semicircular curves. The panel fields are hung with brocade. The overdoor is a plaster cast showing an allegorical grouping of amorini.

Courtesy Jansen, Paris

Neo-classic room in Paris apartment, showing painted silk panels with mirror borders. Rococo mantel with overmantel mirror.

and on this sparkling surface are painted classical arabesques. Classical and Sèvres vase forms holding bouquets of garden flowers often formed a part of the painted decoration. Colors tended toward pale tints. The French were extremely adept at combining conventional and realistic motifs.

The tendency toward economy in the smaller houses was evidenced in the use of stretched textiles and wallpaper for panel centers. There were also many rooms in which wood panelling was omitted; the walls of these were merely painted or covered with wallpaper or textiles. Réveillon, the paper manufacturer, combined with Oberkampf to produce similar designs in wallpaper and printed cotton. Scenic papers also began to be made for formal rooms. Overmantel and overdoor decorations often consisted of grisaille paintings. These were highly realistic monotones imitating bas-relief sculptured panels, in which the painter considered the actual direction of the light that entered the room in planning highlights and shadows. The subject matter was usually cupids or classical figures. In entrance halls plaster walls were often painted to imitate marble panelling.

Mantels were comparatively low and almost invariably made in marble. The designs were simple with classical moldings and detail. The fireplace openings were rectangular and the mantelshelf was straight. The overmantel usually consisted of a trumeau composed of a framed mirror combined with a superimposed painting or some other decoration. Doors and windows had elaborate trims; in salons and in the public rooms of the house they were treated with a complete entablature and an overdoor decoration. Ceilings were usually left plain, but sometimes they were painted in sky and cloud effects. Floors were usually in oak parquet patterns and were covered with Aubusson, Savonnerie, or Oriental rugs.

The ornamental forms and motifs used in all branches of the decorative arts during the Neo-classic period consisted of garlands, festoons, swags, and wreaths composed of natural roses, daisies, and chrysanthemums, commonly tied by a ribbon bowknot with floating ends; Pompeian arabesques and rinceaux; Greek ornaments such as the honeysuckle, fret, and guilloche; sentimental objects such as cherubs

View of Petit Trianon, Versailles. Designed by Gabriel. Built 1762–1768.

and cupid's bow and darts; scenes from La Fontaine's fables; and pastoral motifs such as shepherd figures, farm tools, wheat sheaves, and beribboned hats. Pillement continued to produce his delightful chinoiseries, and the classical influence was seen in the use of both nude and draped mythological figures, sphinxes, vases, and masks. Drop ornaments composed of musical instruments, hunting paraphernalia, and other objects of symbolism were often used. Montgolfier had invented the first successful balloon in 1783 and it made such an impression upon the French people that pictures, textiles, and wallpapers showing patterns related to this subject became extremely popular for decorative use.

The outstanding decorative artists of the period were: Houdon, the realistic sculptor, who made portrait busts of the aristocracy, artists, and philosophers, and who later came to America and modelled the early Federal statesmen; Clodion, famous for his decorative terra-cotta nymphs and satyrs; Saint Memin, known for his crayon portraits; and Hubert Robert, noted for his paintings and panel decorations of imaginary Roman ruins and landscapes. Fragonard lived until the turn of the century, and the influence of Boucher continued in the work of his pupils.

The Petit Trianon. The most important and interesting structure that characterized the Neo-classic style is the small château or garden pavilion designed by Gabriel for the park at Versailles. This building was commenced in 1762 at the suggestion of Pompadour. As her death occurred in 1764, it was occupied upon its completion in 1768 by the Countess du Barry. History however has associated the building with the activities of Marie Antoinette. The Trianon at the time it was built represented a complete novelty and a reaction from the rococo forms that preceded it. Its design was perhaps inspired by similar residences erected by the architects Adam and Chambers in England. Both without and within it is almost wholly of classical inspiration. In only one or two places does the interior panelling indicate a form reminiscent of the Rococo, and the ornamental details are the classical acanthus, rosette, guilloche, garland, and wreath. All the rooms are rectangular; there are no rounded corners, the ceilings

Marie Antoinette's bedroom in the Petit Trianon at Versailles. The walls are painted an off-white, the textiles are yellow damask. Contrasts are subdued, scale is small, and comparative simplicity of effect is developed.

are flat, complete entablatures are generally used with the customary classical molding ornaments, panels are rectangular, and compass curves are used. Gilding and lacquering of surfaces are avoided and most of the rooms are painted an off-white.

Near the Trianon was built the picturesque "hamlet" for Marie Antoinette, a group of Normandy half-timber thatched cottages located on the bank of an artificial lake. These consisted of a small manor house, mill, dairy, keeper's house, and farmhouse, all of which were furnished in a provincial manner. These buildings, which are still in existence, were planned by Hubert Robert in 1782 to permit the Queen and her ladies to indulge in an idyllic life, a desire that had developed after reading Rousseau's *Le Devin du Village.*

Furniture of the Neo-classic period. This period, short as it was, saw a reaction in furniture design. The same pieces of furniture that had been developed in the preceding period continued to be made, proportions remained light and delicate; but, the free curve gave way to the mechanical curve, the dominant line of design was straight, and the silhouette became rectangular. A short transitional period occurred during which elements of both styles were seen in the same piece.

The furniture supports are the distinguishing feature of the style. During the transitional period, the cabriole leg began to straighten out with less curvature between the knee and the ankle. The scroll foot disappeared.

Rosettes

Console Table

Side Chair

Urn Motif

Commode

Arabesque

Detail of Chair Leg

Over-door Motif—Medallion, garland, ribbon

Arm Chair

NEO-CLASSIC FURNITURE AND DETAILS.

By 1770 the legs of all pieces of furniture were straight and tapered, either round or square in section, and the surface was usually enriched with vertical or spiral flutings. The leg was almost invariably crowned at the top by a square block, on which was carved a rosette set in a small sinkage. Cabinet-pieces and case furniture were rectangular from both front and side views, and were enriched with either wood or metal moldings forming rectangular panels that sometimes had their corners broken around a rosette. Tables of all kinds had straight-edged tops. Chair seat-frames had

Arm Chair   Side Chair   Commode

Bouillotte

Sofa or Canapé

Console

Bergère   Bow and Quiver Motif   Bed Upholstered in Toile de Jouy

NEO-CLASSIC FURNITURE.

sides that were either straight or elliptical, and chair backs were usually rectangular or oval. Some beds were made with headboards of equal height. The four-poster returned to popularity and the canopied and alcoved beds of the previous period continued to be used. Many small tables and much of the case furniture were topped with colored marble. Writing tables and desks usually had tooled leather covers.

The woods for both construction and veneer were the same as in the previous period. Mahogany was used more extensively as greater appreciation developed for grained effects, and ebony again became popular.

Painted furniture also became more common, but Oriental lacquer lessened in use. Furniture ornamentation consisted of simple carving, marquetry, ormolu mounts, and painted decoration. The ornamental motifs were naturalistic roses, garlands, festoons, ribbon bowknots with flying ends, bouquets, Cupid's bows and darts, lyre forms, acanthus leaves, rinceaux, and arabesques. Architectural details such as colonnettes and miniature pilasters were frequently employed for both structure and decoration, but the Louis XVI style borrowed from the antique only what was compatible with comfort. Sèvres porcelain and English Wedgwood plaques showing classical figures and urns were often applied to furniture in small cameo-like decoration.

About 1780 many books were issued on Greek, Etruscan, and Egyptian art and architecture, with a result that artists in all mediums began to use motifs drawn from these sources. Sphinxes, winged vultures, sarcophagi, hawks, jackals, palm, lotus, fret, guilloche, and *acroteria* began to appear. The contemporary critics complained that everything from snuffboxes and costumes to furniture and architecture was *à la grecque*. The leading *ébénistes* of the period were Riesener, who had been Oeben's pupil; Carlin, who was the earliest proponent of the classical revival; Beneman; Jacob; and Weisweiler.

Upholstery materials were Aubusson tapestries, needlepoint, tooled leather, plain-striped and moiré silks, brocades, damasks, taffetas, and printed cottons. All colors were in light tones. Caning and rush were also used for the seats and backs of chairs and sofas.

Accessories in 18th century rooms. The accessories used in French rooms during the 18th century were numerous, always of the highest quality and extremely important in their contribution to the character of the decoration. Mantelshelves usually had an ormolu clock or a terra-cotta or marble bust in the center, with vases, perfume burners, or porcelain figurine groups at each side. Sometimes crystal *lustres* or brass candlesticks formed part of the shelf composition. Brass fireplace accessories stood on the floor at the side of the hearth. High rooms were lighted by hanging Bohemian crystal chandeliers; sconces or *appliques* and table lamps also frequently added to the illumination. Wall accessories consisted of ormolu hanging clocks, decorative wooden barometers and thermometers, and small rectangular or oval framed mirrors. Many pictures were used; these included period oil paintings, water colors, pastels, engravings, and ink and *sanguine drawings*. French and Oriental glass paintings and small hand-painted wallpaper panels were also frequently seen. Other accessories were Roman and Pompeian bronze statues, and small objects of Chinese, Japanese, and East Indian origin. There were also no end of examples of St. Cloud, Sèvres, and Dresden ceramics. Leather, enamel, porcelain, silver, and gold cases were studded with precious jewels. Books with tooled

Circular Directoire room with painted panelling, and marbelized pilasters and dado. Such motifs as the four seasons, lamp of knowledge, and distaff are represented.

leather bindings were placed on shelves and tables, and vases were filled with flowers that harmonized in color with the hues of the room.

Popularization of the decorative arts. During, and following, the last quarter of the 18th century, interest in the subject of home decoration spread much more generally to the middle classes, whereas it had previously been limited to the aristocracy. This was in part due to the cheapening of production by mechanical methods and the introduction of many products that could be used as substitutes for costly ones. Typical of these were wallpapers used to replace the hand-painted panel, and hand-blocked linens and cottons introduced as substitutes for silk damasks and brocades. The French people had always been instinctively conscious of art and beauty in all of their manifestations, and the royal promotion and support of the art industries was observed by the bourgeois society. The simplification of living, and the reaction from the extravagances of the past, tended toward the production of rooms whose costs were within the economic limits of a greater proportion of the population. The beauty and originality of the styles that were produced at that time have persistently permeated the cultures of other countries to the present day.

The Revolution and the Directoire periods (1789–1804). The years of the Revolution were destructive rather than constructive so far as the decorative arts were concerned. During the Directoire period were produced the transitional forms of art that filled the gap between the periods of Louis XVI and Napoleon. Elements of both styles were seen, although the short political duration of the "Directorate" did not permit the construction of many examples of either architecture or decoration.

Directoire fireplace, wall treatment, and furniture.

During the Reign of Terror and the events that followed, many of the craftsmen were ill-supported; lacking clients, they entered other fields, and with the disorganization of the apprentice system, much of the exquisite tradition of French art of the 18th century was lost. Craftsmen who were able to continue work endeavored to maintain their sense of tradition and good proportion, and searched for art forms and details of ornament that were not associated with the old aristocracy. During the Directoire period, the delicacy of the forms and some of the refinement of detail of the Louis XVI period were continued, but new ornamental motifs were introduced. Both wood-carvers and painters inspired themselves from military objects such as spears, drums, trumpets, stars, and the Phrygian or Liberty cap of the revolutionary armies. Since Pompeii and Egypt had nothing to do with the French kings, the use of architectural forms and ornament drawn from these sources continued. Motifs were also introduced to reflect the growing power of the agricultural classes such as the plough, flail, scythe, and sheaves of wheat.

Panelled rooms continued to be produced but the details were much simplified. Very little carving was used and painted decoration continued to be influenced by classical forms, although rustic scenes and figures sometimes formed the subject matter. The plain painted wall and striped wallpaper became popular. Walls were also decorated with draped and plaited textiles hung from below a draped wall valance that extended around the room. Printed cottons showing revolutionary subject matter continued to be used for draperies and upholstery.

The furniture of the Directoire began to show structural forms that were borrowed from ancient Greece. These included the use of Greek curves wherever possible, such as the slight backward roll at the top of a chair back, the klismos chair back, and the outward curve given sofa arms. On many chairs the front legs curved forward and the rear legs backward,

Directoire chair showing star and Greek motifs in its design.

while on case furniture a slight outward flair occurred in the short supports. Straight turned legs that had previously been seen only in Provincial furniture began to be used by the Parisian cabinetmakers. Another structural and ornamental form of support was the Egyptian or Grecian head used at the top of a square leg that was tapered and slightly reduced in section at the bottom and ended with two human feet. Headboards of beds and tops of cabinets often were crested with a low-pitched pedimented form, or the uprights of headboards were given a slight curve outward at the top. Bent wrought iron and bronze furniture, with tripod supports designed in the Greek manner, became popular.

Color schemes showed a tendency to use stronger hues and tonal contrasts than in the earlier styles, and one of the most popular was based on the colors of the new Republican flag—large white areas accented with small areas or lines of scarlet and bright blue for trimmings, edgings, and small moldings.

The Empire style. The Empire style was so designated because of its association with Napoleon, who was proclaimed Emperor of the French in 1804. The importance of this style is due to the immense political, economic, and social changes that occurred as a result of Napoleon's victories. Every European artist and craftsman, during the first quarter of the 19th century, came under the hypnotic spell of the movement, and the results were diffused over the whole of Europe and the Americas. The promotion and growth of the style were sudden and arbitrary, and were completely out of proportion to the short career of Napoleon himself. The Empire period was the first in art history in which an attempt was made to impose a decorative style upon a people by artificial methods rather than to permit it to develop by natural evolution. The movement was contemporary with the beginnings of factory and mass production, and with the growing importance and self-consciousness of labor. The style commenced when there was still vitality in French art tradition and the hand-craftsman maintained pride in his product; it ended when steam power could manufacture an inferior object at one-tenth the cost of the hand product—resulting in an economic appeal that was more potent than the artistic.* The Empire was the last of the French styles to produce what is today known as the real "antique."

Napoleon's coronation was the first act, after the storming of the Bastille, in the return of the French people to a monarchial form of government and social organization. A new aristocracy, the *nouveaux-riches,* trained in military tactics and get-rich-quick abilities rather than social amenities, had had little opportunity to develop a true connoisseurship of the arts. The emperor, however, with history in mind, recognized the value of promoting a public appreciation of the arts and the satisfaction of his ego required visual evidence of his imperial glory. He was determined to invest his court with every form of external expression that would reflect and magnify his grandeur and power.

Jacques Louis David, who had been one of the signers of the death warrant of Louis XVI, was appointed court painter and art director of France and strove to emulate his famous predecessor Lebrun. Although handicapped by the self-conceits of Napoleon, David became the man of the hour in art, politics, and society. He had founded the classical school of painting during the Revolution and had received widespread acclaim. David was acquainted with the *Classical Antiquities of Athens,* written by the Englishmen Stuart and Revett and published in 1762, a book which enabled the world for the first time to see depicted the glories of Athenian architecture. His first great picture was "Blind Belisarius Asking Alms," and was followed by "The Oath of the Horatii," "Brutus," "The Coronation of Napoleon in Notre Dame," "The Rape of the Sabines," "Madame Recamier," and "Death of Socrates," the last in the Metropolitan Museum of Art, New York City. His influence upon the intellectual life of the period was enormous. Proud, cold, austere, he was at first a believer in Spartan simplicity; but with the rise in power of Bonaparte he turned to the splendors of Greece and Rome for inspiration consistent with the Emperor's desire for majestic grandeur.

The new society despised the immediate past and desired an art expression that represented it alone. What could be more appropriate for an Emperor who had conquered nearly the whole of Europe than a revival of the paraphernalia and pomp of Alexander and Caesar? Alexander had conquered Egypt, Caesar had crossed the Rubicon, but not the Rhine or the Danube; the Little Corporal had crossed all three, and had conducted a spectacular campaign in Egypt when he was only twenty-nine years of age. The artists and designers, in an urge to co-operate with David's plans, and having convinced themselves that antiquity had reached the pinnacle of perfection in art, informed the public that every creative idea from

---

* This predicament was even more true of England, where industrialization had progressed further than in France, a predominantly agricultural country.

the time of Pericles and Rameses to Constantine was logical and perfect. Thus was the style conceived!

The style reached its height about the time that Bonaparte returned from Elba. Waterloo in 1815 did not entirely crush the movement, which continued with diminishing vitality until about 1830. Its demise was due as much to the changed economic conditions, which resulted from the growth of the industrial revolution and machine production, as it was to the elimination of Napoleon's influence. An effort was made to revive its external forms during the reign of Louis Napoleon and Eugenie from 1852 to 1870.

The Empire style spread to Austria as a result of Napoleon's marriage to Princess Marie Louise, and it later was popularized in both Germany and Austria as the Biedermeier style. The Bernadottes introduced it into Sweden; Pauline Borghese, Napoleon's sister, brought it to Italy; Joseph Bonaparte promoted the style in Spain; its influence was strongly felt in England during the Regency period; and its earmarks were plainly visible in the homes of North America, South America, and Central America.

Interiors of the Empire period. Napoleon upon his accession appointed Percier and Fontaine as government architects. These two men, who made many studies of classical ruins, became official interpreters and leaders of the new style in architecture and decoration. They designed every detail of the interiors of their buildings including furniture, textiles, hardware, ornament, wallpaper, and utilitarian objects. The spirit behind their designs was to maintain dignity and masculinity and to avoid the slightest effect of frivolity or gaiety. Rooms were often square in plan, though many of them had semicircular or segmental ends imitating those in ancient Roman palaces. The partners redecorated rooms in the Louvre, Versailles, Compiegne, Fontainebleau, and other châteaux; one of their best known works was Malmaison near Paris, the residence of Josephine, the first wife of Napoleon, who occupied it during Napoleon's campaigns and after her divorce.

Nearly all Empire rooms had architectural features of Pompeian inspiration. These consisted of columns or pilasters spaced at intervals around the room, or forming part of door and window treatments, or arranged with an arched form to constitute an overmantel decoration. Door and window arches were either semicircular or segmental. The majority of rooms had cornices and many were crowned with a complete entablature. There was often an oversize painted frieze that contrasted with the color of the wall and was enriched with spaced vases, medallions, or classical figures that were connected by rinceaux, or garlands made of husks or of laurel leaves. Occasionally delicate Pompeian arabesques were introduced to enrich vertical panels. Doors either had square panels with center rosettes or rectangular panels that contained a diamond-shaped

*Original Empire room and furniture in a house in Paris. The only moderni-
zation has been in the introduction of electric lighting.*

interior panel. Windows were hung with two or three sets of complicated
draperies with elaborate valances, fringes, tassels, jabots, and swags. The
textiles were silk, wool, and cotton, and all three fibers were frequently
combined in the same set of draperies.

The walls of Empire rooms were often in plain painted plaster,
decorated with painted classical motifs and finished in a semigloss polish.
Marbleized effects were also common. Wood panelling and wallpapers
were also used, but the most novel wall treatments were those hung with
stretched, shirred, or loosely draped textiles; these occupied the whole area
from the underside of the cornice to the top of the dado or baseboard.
When the textiles were draped they were caught up at intervals and held
with tassels and gold-headed nails. Josephine's bedroom at Malmaison was
circular and represented the interior of a Roman emperor's military tent;
its walls were draped in red silk that appeared to be supported at intervals
by tent posts; the ceiling was also in draped cloth that was partly enriched
with gold appliqué ornaments.

Marble mantels were severely classical in detail, with plain straight
shelves. In palace rooms, they were often richly carved under the shelf
and were supported at the sides by caryatides or dwarf columns. In the
small houses, the carving was often omitted, the side supports were simple
pilasters, and interest was maintained by the color and graining of the
marble. In the latter type, moldings were reduced to a minimum. The
mantelshelf was usually furnished with an ormolu clock, designed with
Grecian standing figures and covered with a glass dome. The side shelf-

Military tent bedroom built by Percier and Fontaine for Empress Josephine's use in Malmaison. The panels are draped in red silk. The bed drapery is lined with ermine.

ornaments varied from Grecian or Egyptian caryatides holding multi-branched candelabra, or reproductions of classical vases filled with arti-ficial flowers.

Floors were often left bare and were built with black and white marble squares or wooden parquet patterns; when covered, both Aubusson and Oriental rugs were used.

Accessories were nearly always classical or Egyptian in character, or represented adjuncts of the Napoleonic regime. Many framed engravings and relief-silhouettes of Napoleon's family and officers were used as in-dications of loyalty. These were combined with busts and statues, Greek vases, sphinxes, Pompeian bronze table lamps, and other objects. Wall sconces, torches, and hanging chandeliers were usually of bronze in de-signs adapted from Roman prototypes.

Furniture of the Empire period. Under the Directorate, cabinetmakers eagerly endeavored to prove their loyalty to the republic, and attempted to eliminate patterns and designs that recalled the old regime. They found difficulty, however, in creating an artistic revolution that was as sudden and complete as were the cataclysmic changes in politics, philosophy, and social life. Furniture design retained the delightful lines and proportions of the monarchy, but economic conditions forced a cheapening of con-struction, a lowering of quality in materials, and the using of less carved ornament.

Room in house in Paris using authentic Empire furniture and grisaille scenic wallpaper.

The Directoire ornamental forms merged into those of the Empire, but a change occurred in the structural proportions of furniture. The leading cabinetmakers, Jacob, Jacob-Desmalter, Lignereux, Rascalon, and Burette, were imbued with the cult of antiquity, but they were confronted with the necessity of producing types of furniture that did not exist in the ancient periods. It was necessary to invent nearly everything, and to maintain the spirit of the antique by applying its ornamental detail rather than to make exact copies. Percier and Fontaine were in sympathy with the compromise, but they insisted that furniture at least should look as though it had been made for Caesar. The designers therefore turned their backs on all the intimacy and gracefulness of the 18th century and began to work on a grand, severe, and masculine scale, whether or not it was comfortable and convenient. The basic forms of the furniture were simple, with definite and severe outlines; rather heavy in proportion, with sharp corners; and often were monolithic in appearance. Moldings and panels practically disappeared, and the doors, sides, and lids of case furniture were one solid piece of veneer in which the graining and polish were the sole element of beauty. The heavy Tuscan and Doric orders were used in a simplified form for both structural and ornamental detail. The capitals and bases were in metal, and the shafts usually stood on a heavy block. Both square-sectioned and straight turned legs were used. The baluster form was never seen. Rigid symmetry was always attempted in the general composition. Carving was largely eliminated and ormolu mounts in classical detail were used promiscuously for hardware and ornament. While such ciseleurs as Odiot, Ravrio, and Thomire maintained the tradi-

Table Support

Band Ornament

Console Table

Swan Motif

Tripod Table

Armchair

Directoire Chair

Ormolu Ornament

Armchair

Classical Figure
used in metalwork
and painting

Sofa

Cornucopia

EMPIRE FURNITURE AND DETAILS.

tions of Gouthière, much of the metalwork was cheaply cast, untouched by the chisel, unsuitably designed, inaccurate in scale, and poorly distributed. The furniture was often smothered with metal ornament which tended to hide the graining of the veneers.

Few new types of furniture were introduced. Nearly all tables were round or octagonal with marble tops, and many were supported by a central pedestal leg, which rested on a triangular block. Tripod tables with metal and wooden supports were made in imitation of those found in Pompeii. Empire beds were usually designed to be placed sideways against the wall, and were called boat-beds; the rear posts were higher than the front ones and were crowned with a vase form; the board connecting the head and foot piece was sometimes shaped in a segmental curve. Klismos, round-about, rolled, and Greek-curve chair backs and sofa arms were common. The front legs of chairs were usually straight, the rear legs slightly curved. In some cases both front and rear legs were curved forward or backward respectively. Spring seats were used for upholstery. There was an infinite variety of chair designs. Consoles were made with either rectangular or half-moon tops and the lower portion was often backed by a mirror. The standing floor mirror or *pier glass* that pivoted horizontally, known as a *psyche,* was often seen in Empire rooms. The piano superseded the harpsichord about 1800.

Directoire bronze clock showing use of Egyptian motifs after Napoleon's return from Egypt (1799). These continued to be used in the Empire period.

The most popular wood for furniture was mahogany, but elm, yew, maple, and lemon were also used. Woods for veneers were imported from Africa, the West Indies, and the East Indies, such as thuya, amboyna, amaranth, palisander, and rosewood. Marquetry and fluting were completely avoided, but ebony, silver, and other metals were sometimes used for inlay. Gilding was often applied. Much of the furniture was made with inferior materials.

Empire ornament. Ornamental forms were almost entirely drawn from antique or military sources and the same ones were used in every medium of design—stone, wood, metal, plaster, textiles, and wallpaper. The sphinx with upraised wings, winged lions and disks, vultures, cobras, obelisks, and hieroglyphics were taken from Egypt. Some of the more common classical motifs that were revived were the fret, rinceau, arabesque, guilloche; and honeysuckle; anthemion, antefix, amphora, and krater vase forms; Roman lamps and torches; Winged Victories; caryatides; dancing girls; sacrificial scenes; heads of Bacchus, Hermes, and Apollo; rams' and horses' heads, and masks of wild beasts. The griffin and chimera were used for both ornaments and for structural supports of tables and consoles, as well as for arms of chairs. Swans were seen in astonishing quantities. Cornucopias, laurel wreaths, fasces, Neptune's trident, casques, cuirasses, swords, lances, and military musical instruments were some of the motifs of symbolical origin.

Empire textiles and wallpapers. The invention by Jacquard in 1801 of the first mechanical loom to weave multicolored patterns eliminated the more costly hand-woven textiles of the royal periods. The weaves that were mainly produced were lampas, damask, and velvet. The patterns were usually of the spot variety formed by victory wreaths, rosettes, palm branches, laurel sprigs, torches, fasces, the initial "N," and the bee, the last selected by Napoleon as an emblem because of its traditional symbolism. The rose and the swan were symbols of Josephine, and Empire patterns frequently show the rose surrounded by bees sipping its honey. Textile colors were of the darker tones but chromatically more brilliant than those used in the preceding periods. Patterns contrasted strongly with backgrounds. Deep browns, violets, olive and emerald greens, and clarets were the most popular colors. Gold thread was often used in the weaving. The toiles-de-Jouy continued to be made by Oberkampf, the patterns being changed to please the new regime.

During the Empire period, wallpaper greatly increased in use; the greatly lowered costs had been due to the invention of the cylinder printing process. The all-over patterns were similar to those used in textiles, and flock papers imitating velvets and damasks were much in vogue. Patterns were also made to give the effect of plaited and draped textiles. Some designs showed repetitions of vignetted groups of Empire costumed figures in garden settings. Stripes and marbleized papers were also used. Panels reproducing the bas-relief sculpture of the Parthenon frieze were made for overdoor and overwindow enrichment. Narrow border strips with the wave, guilloche, egg and dart, and waterleaf were also used at the tops of walls, above the dado cap, and around door and window trim. Some of the greatest of the scenic papers were made during this period by Dufour, Jacquemart, and others. These usually represented classical groups of figures, scenes that glorified Napoleonic events, or other contemporary subject matter.*

The French provincial styles. In studying the interior decoration in the provinces of France it is often difficult to draw a line between the provincial and peasant types. Whereas the term "provincial" usually refers to rooms that were more or less designed according to the styles of Paris,

* It is generally acknowledged that the finest scenic paper ever made was the set issued in 1816 by Dufour known as "Cupid and Psyche." Other equally famous sets printed before 1815 were "Bonaparte Crowned," "The Battle of Austerlitz," "The King of Rome in the Gardens at Malmaison," and "The Monuments of Paris."

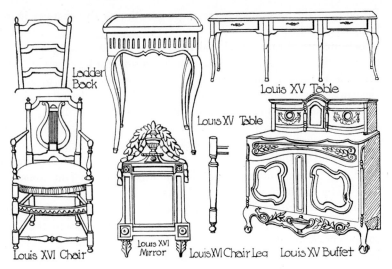

FRENCH PROVINCIAL FURNITURE.

there were many peasant rooms the decorations of which were more naïve in their appearance, but were still taken from the same source. Expert craftsmanship is only possible when groups of connoisseurs and amateurs exist who will appreciate and pay for this grade of workmanship. For centuries throughout France there has been a liberal patronage of the arts in all classes. It is a common sight today to see two laborers in one of the Regional museums discussing the relative merits of a painting. Arts and artists have a broader public appreciation and recognition in France than in any other country. This is exemplified by the fact that many streets of Paris have been named after France's greatest men of art,* as well as statesmen, military heroes, and others.

From the Louis XV period onward, many farmers' and fishermen's homes contained furniture that was beautifully designed, expertly made, and enriched with carved ornament. In addition to these there are the distinct peasant types, unrelated to the Parisian styles, most of which are in the eastern and southern parts of the country. The provincial styles near the borders were partly influenced by adjoining countries. Thus the styles near the Pyrenees were influenced by Spain; in the northeast, by Flanders and Germany; and in Provence,† by Italy. Normandy and

* Among those who have been so honored are Fragonard, Boucher, Pigalle, Garnier, Toulouse-Lautrec, Gustave Doré, Lebrun, Mansart, Boulle, Houdon, Champollion, Oberkampf, Rabelais, Massenet, Ingres, Gounod, and many others, to say nothing of such foreigners as Rembrandt, Rubens, Raphael, Ibsen, Goethe, Cervantes, Velasquez, and Michael Angelo.

† The Provençal style should not be confused with the term "provincial." Provence, one of the old county subdivisions of southern France, was settled and named by the Romans. It adjoins Italy; many of its inhabitants are of Italian blood; and it has a culture, language, and literature that differ considerably from those in other parts of France.

Brittany on the west coast were more sensitive to the changes in royal fashions and aped the Parisians.

Seventeenth-century provincial styles. The provinces were slow in outgrowing the Gothic style. The Renaissance forms that had been introduced between Francis I and Louis XIV were largely limited to the royal châteaux. In the latter years of the 17th century, the lesser nobility and well-to-do merchants of the provincial districts were still living in rooms having walls hung with imported textiles, leather, or tapestries, or with oak wainscots designed in small Gothic panelling. The ceiling beams were exposed and the floors were in tile or wide oak planks. The mantels had projecting hoods, and were detailed in mixed Gothic and Renaissance detail. The furniture was based upon Italian forms.

Eighteenth-century provincial styles. The Louis XIV style was little imitated beyond the royal palaces, due to its costliness and the lack of competent craftsmen to produce it, but it served as an agent of propaganda in engaging the attention of the public in matters of home furnishings. By the middle of the 18th century the interest in the new styles of decoration and furniture was widespread, and the demand for stylized furnishings in turn caused an increase in the number of provincial designers and craftsmen of all degrees of competency. By 1750 the rococo style was adopted wholeheartedly by the provinces. Its comfort, scale, warmth, gaiety, and novelty had a universal appeal and its popularity continued well into the 19th century. With few exceptions, the inhabitants of the provinces were more conservative and slower of thought than those of Paris; they remained truer to the royal regime during the Revolution and persisted in the use of the decorative style popularized by the Bourbons. The provincial style of France is dominantly that of Louis XV. As a result it is difficult to judge the age of this type of furniture by its design. The Louis XVI and Empire forms were never manufactured to the same extent.

In general all provincial work was simplified and less costly to produce than the Parisian models. Economy was ever the watchword. Rooms were often completely lined with wood panelling, but frequently only one wall was so treated, the other walls being either painted or covered with textile or wallpaper, or stencilled to imitate a wallpaper pattern. The panel moldings were simple and the curved forms at the tops and bottoms of the frame varied between having graceful and vigorous lines to those that seemed to be uncertain in their direction and ending. The woodwork was generally painted in the delicate colors of the period and the moldings were often accented by a contrasting color. There was less carved ornament in the provincial panelling, and such as existed was concentrated in important locations in the design. Some of the panelling was enriched with painted decoration, which usually consisted of landscape subject matter, and every room had a mantel and trumeau above. Mirrors were often set into the woodwork and large mirror areas were usually assembled in small rectangles. Bookshelves were built-in and sleeping rooms contained alcoves for the beds. The rooms were often small, but of the utmost charm.

The selection of textiles depended upon the wealth of the owner. Silks and printed cottons were used for panel areas, draperies, and upholstery, and the toiles-de-Jouy were in great demand over a period of two generations. Full credit must be given to the nimble fingers of the French peasants and housewives, whose persistence and energy with the needle, bobbin, and shuttle produced some of the most delightful, colorful, and original textiles ever made. These contributed profusely to the decoration of the country rooms of this and subsequent periods as well as to the regional costumes. Embroidery of all kinds, including *gros-point* and *petit-point* needlework was used for draperies, bedcovers, and upholstery of both formal and informal rooms and added to the gaiety of the provincial interior. Hand-painted and stencilled linens were also made. The wallpaper consisted of all-over floral and flock patterns and at the turn of the century scenic types became popular.

The Louis XV types of provincial furniture were reproduced in local woods such as cherry, elm, apple, oak, beech, walnut, and ash. Mahogany and ebony were occasionally used. All pieces were simplified in design, with less carving and ormolu. While the provincial nobility sometimes purchased their furniture in Paris and Versailles, the smaller landowners supported the local craftsmen. There was less style consistency in the furniture of the country rooms. Through reasons of economy, owners were less willing to discard old pieces unless they had become completely dilapidated. Even the Louis XIII types continued to be used in the same rooms as those of Louis XV and XVI.

Local varieties and types of furniture were developed. Among these were the *ménagère* and *vaisselier,* both of which were low cabinets upon which were open shelves with racks and guard-rails for the storage and display of china and dining-table accessories. The *panetière* was intended to store bread and cakes. The dough-mixing table was often an elaborately designed box furnished with a lid that could be used as a table. Practically every room had its armoire or wardrobe; this piece was usually the important dowry present of every bride, necessitated by the fact that closets were not an integrated part of French residential architecture. As the armoire was often of large dimensions it became the dominating feature in every room in which it was used; it was usually made in oak and the doors were always elaborately panelled and carved, hung with large hinges and hardware elaborated by escutcheons of sheet brass treated with a pierced pattern.

In the simpler types of homes, benches, settees, and chairs were made with straight turned legs and with wooden or rush seats upon which were placed cushions covered in silk or a homespun material. The peasants often had beds that were enclosed in closets that had doors or shutters pierced for ventilation; while these must have been unsanitary, they were at least warm at a time when heating was still of a primitive character.

The decorative accessories of a provincial home were naturally of a less luxurious sort than were found in the royal palaces. Much local pottery painted in gay colors was used and those who could afford it purchased the beautiful examples from Rouen, St. Cloud, and other French and German potteries. Pewter was the common substitute for silver. The ships that landed at Bordeaux and Lorient brought from the Far East useful and decorative objects made of porcelain, wood, paper, and glass, and such as were not destined for Paris were eagerly purchased by the provincials.

Leaders in the French Decorative Arts

ARCHITECTS, DESIGNERS, AND CRAFTSMEN

Bérain, Jean (1638–1710). Designer at the court of Louis XIV. Designed much of the ornament, notably engraved arabesques and cartouche forms.

Boucher, François (1703–1770). Decorative painter under Louis XV.

Cerceau, Jacques du. Sixteenth-century architect and furniture designer under Henry IV.

Clodion (1738–1814). Sculptor of amorous nymphs and satyrs in terra cotta. Real name Claude Michel.

Coysevox, Antoine (1640–1720). Sculptor under Louis XIV.

David, Jacques Louis (1748–1825). Revolutionary and Empire painter. Director of art under Napoleon.

Delorme, Philibert (1515–1570). Court architect under Francis I, Henry II, and Charles IX.

Fontaine, Pierre-François-Léonard (1762–1853). Architect and designer, whose association with Percier made them the leaders of the Empire style.

Fragonard, Jean-Honoré (1732–1806). Decorative painter.

Gabriel, Jacques-Ange (1698–1782). Architect of the Petit Trianon and Place de la Concorde under Louis XV.

Goujon, Jean (1510–1566). Sixteenth-century architect and sculptor who worked on the Louvre.

Gouthière, Pierre (1740–1806). Ciseleur and metal sculptor, who made ormolu mounts, ornaments, and lighting fixtures.

Houdon, Jean-Antoine (1741–1828). Sculptor, notable for portrait busts.

Huet, Christophe (d. 1759). Decorative painter at the court of Louis XV.

Huet, Jean-Baptiste (1745–1811). Designer of toiles-de-Jouy for Oberkampf and wallpaper for Reveillon.

Jacquard, Joseph-Marie (1752–1834). Inventor of the Jacquard attachment for producing colored woven patterns in machine-made textiles.

Jacquemart and Benard. Wallpaper manufacturers, successors to Reveillon, 1791–1840.

LaSalle, Philippe de (1720–1803). Designer and manufacturer of textiles, and inventor of devices for weaving, under Louis XVI. Most famous for his lampases and realistic floral patterns.

Lebrun, Charles (1619–1690). Director of fine arts under Louis XIV.

Lenôtre, André (1613–1700). Architect famous for his garden designs at Versailles and Vaux-le-vicomte.

Lepautre, Jean (1618–1682). Royal architect under Louis XIV.

Lescot, Pierre (1510–1578). Sixteenth-century architect under Henry II; worked on the Louvre.

Mansart, Jules Hardouin (1646–1708). Royal architect of Louis XIV. Most notable works: Dome of the Invalides and Palace of Versailles.

Marot, Daniel (1661–1720?). Designer of ornament, panelling, and furniture under Louis XIV. After the revocation of the Edict of Nantes, he emigrated to Holland and established the French Baroque style there; later, he introduced it in England.

Oberkampf, Christophe-Philippe (1738–1815). Creator of toile-de-Jouy and founder of Jouy manufactory.

Palissy, Bernard (1510–1589). Early potter, inventor of enamelled pottery.

Papillon, Jean (1661–1723). Wallpaper designer and maker.

Percier, Charles (1764–1838). Architect and designer who, with Fontaine, established the Empire style in France.

Pillement, Jean (1727–1808). Decorative painter, noted for his chinoiseries.

Ravrio, Antoine André. Brilliant *ciseleur* in the Empire period.

Reveillon, J. B. Wallpaper designer and maker from 1752 to 1789.

Robert, Hubert (1733–1808). Painter and decorator under Louis XV and Louis XVI. Noted for his landscapes and paintings of Roman ruins.

Sambin, Hugues. Architect and furniture designer under Catherine de' Medici.

Thomire, Pierre Philippe. Brilliant *ciseleur* in the Empire period.

Watteau, Antoine (1684–1721). Decorative painter under Louis XIV and XV.

For a complete list of the French cabinetmakers of the 18th century readers are referred to Salverte, François, *Les Ebénistes du XVIIIe Siècle,* Paris, 1929. The most important ones are listed below.

The year of appointment as Maître-Ebéniste is given following the letters M. E. Dates in parentheses give years of birth and death.

Beneman, Guillaume. M. E. 1785. Most important craftsman before revolution. Worked for Marie Antoinette at St. Cloud. Also produced some of Percier's designs.

Boulard, Jean Baptiste (1725–1789). M. E. 1754. Both ébéniste and sculptor. His most important work was a magnificent bed for Louis XVI at Fontainebleau.

Boulle, André Charles (1642–1732). In 1672 appointed head cabinetmaker to Louis XIV.

Boulle, André Charles, Jr. and Charles Joseph, sons of above. M. E. 1745.

Burette, Charles Marin. Flourished toward the end of the Empire period.

Caffieri, Jacques (1678–1755), and son, Philippe (1714–1774). Cabinetmakers and sculptors under Louis XIV and XV.

Canabas, Joseph (1712–1797). M. E. 1766. Particularly noted for mechanical contrivances, such as folding tables, for armies or to be carried aboard ships.

Carlin, Martin. M. E. 1766. Made charming, delicate furniture during Louis XVI period, using rosewood and Sèvres porcelain.

Cochois, Jean-Baptiste. M. E. 1770. Inventor of dual purpose and changeabout furniture, such as a chiffonière which became a night table.

Cressent (d. 1749). M. E. 1715. Ebéniste to Duc d'Orleans.

Cressent, Charles (1685–1768). Pupil of Boulle, famous for ormolu work.

Cresson, Michel (b. 1709). M. E. 1740.

Criard (or Criaerd), Mathieu. M. E. 1747.

Cucci, Domenico. Cabinetmaker under Louis XIV.

Delanois, Louis (1731–1792). M. E. 1761. Protegé of Mme. Du Barry, and did much of the furniture for Versailles.

Dubois, René. M. E. 1755. Cabinetmaker to Louis XV and Louis XVI.

Evalde, Maurice. M. E. 1765. Originally German. Worked for Marie Antoinette. Famous piece was a jewel cabinet he made for her.

Fleury, Adrien. Worked between 1740 and 1775.

Gambard. M. E. 1779. In the services of the Court at Versailles between 1771 and 1779.

Gaudreau, Antoine Robert (1680–1751). Worked for the Court from 1726, on the Tuileries, and on the Bibliothèque Nationale.

Guillemart, Francois (d. 1724). M. E. 1706. Active under Louis XIV and the Regency. Built two commodes for the King's room at Marly.

Huffelé, Lambert (d. 1766). M. E. 1745. A collaborator of André Charles Boulle, the son of the famous ébéniste of Louis XIV.

Jacob, Georges. M. E. 1784. One of the most famous cabinetmakers of France, active during Louis XVI, Directoire, and Empire periods.

Jacob-Desmalter, François Honoré (1770–1841?). The son of Georges Jacob, very active as a cabinetmaker, in business with his older brother during the Empire period. Made furniture for Percier and Fontaine.

Joubert, Gilles (1689–1775). M. E. 1749? Renowned for small furniture, such as tables and secretaries, ornamented with wood inlay. Date of appointment as maître-ébéniste not definitely established. Employed at Court from 1748.

Lelarge, Jean Baptiste. M. E. 1786. There were three members of the same family with the same name. This one worked at Fontainebleau, and made *bergères* and *fauteuils*.

Leleu, Francois (1729–1807). M. E. 1764. Famous for marquetry. Worked under Oeben, on Versailles. Also worked for Mme. Du Barry.

Levasseur, Etienne (1721–1798). M. E. 1767. Made furniture for the Petit Trianon. Very celebrated.

Lignereux, Martin Eloy (1750–1809). Associated with Jacob-Desmalter about 1798 in the furniture business, chiefly during the Louis XVI period. Previously had directed the design, making, and sale of various decorative accessories. Firm believed to have been discontinued in 1800.

Macret, Pierre (1727–1796). M. E. 1758. Made furniture for Versailles.

Martin brothers. Cabinetmakers during the reign of Louis XV. The four brothers introduced Chinese lacquer as a finish on French furniture. The finish and the furniture so treated are called Vernis Martin.

Montigny, Philippe Claude (1734–1800). M. E. 1766. Repaired much of Boulle's furniture. That furniture which he made was inspired by the work of Boulle, but he copied his predecessor with taste.

Oeben, Jean Francois (d. 1765). M. E. 1754. Worked for Mme. Pompadour. Trained Riesener. Louis XV period.

Rascalon, Barthelemy (b. circa 1745). M. E. 1781?.

Riesener, Jean Henri (1734–1806). M. E. 1768. Worked for Marie Antoinette. First worked under Oeben, and became his successor.

Roentgen, David (1743–1807). M. E. 1780. Of German origin. Worked for Marie Antoinette.

Weisweiler, Adam. M. E. 1778. Louis XVI ébéniste.

Glossary of French Furniture Terms

Acajou. Mahogany.

Ajouré. A design in ceramics, metal, wood, or other material, in which a design has been produced by piercing holes.

Applique. An applied motif, a wall bracket or sconce.

Armoire. Clothes wardrobe. (Gothic and later.)

Banquette. Bench.

Bergère. All upholstered armchair.

Bibelot. Small art object for personal use or as decoration.

Bibliothèque. Bookcase.

Bobêche. Candle socket.

Bombé. A swelling curve; when the curve is applied to the front of a piece of furniture, it swells outward toward the center, at which point it recedes again.

Bonheur-du-jour. Small desk with cabinet top.

Bonnetière. Hat cabinet.

Bouillotte. Small table with gallery edge. Also a foot-warmer. (Louis XVI.)

Boiserie. Carved woodwork.

Bronze-doré. Gilded bronze.

Buffet. Sideboard or cupboard. (Gothic and later.)

Bureau. Desk.

Bureau-à-cylindre. Roll-top desk.

Bureau-à-pente. Folding slant-lid desk.

Cabinet-sécretaire. Desk with cabinet above.

Cabinet-vitrine. Cabinet with glass doors.

Cabriolet. Any chair with a concave back.

Cachepot. Pot of china or porcelain used as container.

Canapé. Sofa.

Canapé-à-corbeille. Kidney-shaped sofa.

Caquetoire or caqueteuse. Conversation chair. (Early Renaissance.)

Chaise. Side chair.

Chaise-à-capucine. Low slipper chair.

Chaise-brisée. Chaise-longue in two parts (with foot rest).

Chaise-longue. Literally "long chair," or chair for reclining.

Chandelier. Hanging lighting fixture.

Chêne. Oak.

Chenets. Andirons.

Chevet. Bedside.

Chiffonier. Chest of drawers.

Chinoiserie. Decorative motif in the Chinese manner.

Ciseleur. A craftsman who ornaments bronze and other metals by chiselling. A chiseller.

Coffre. Chest.

Coiffeuse. Dressing table.

Confortable. Name used for the first all-upholstered chair.

Commode. Low chest of drawers.

Compotier. Container for stewed fruit, jellies, jams, etc.

Confidante. Three seats attached as a single unit.

Console. Wall table.

Console-desserte. Serving table.

Crédence. Sideboard.

Cremaillere. Swinging crane. Hearth.

Demilune. Semicircular.

Desserte. Serving table or sideboard.

Dos-à-dos. Chair with two attached seats arranged so that they face in opposite directions.

Duchesse. Chaise-longue in one piece.

Duchesse-brisée. Chaise-longue with separate foot-piece.

Ecran. Screen.

Ecran-à-cheval. Frame with sliding panel used as fire screen.

Encoignure. Corner cabinet or table.

Encrier. Inkwell.

Entresol. A mezzanine floor.

Escabelle. Chair supported on trestles. (Early Renaissance.)

Etagère. Hanging or standing open shelves.

Etui. Container or box.

Eventail. Fan.

Faïence. Terra cotta.

Fauteuil. Upholstered armchair with open arms.

Garde-robe. Wardrobe.

Garniture. Any motif used for enrichment.

Girandole. Wall sconce for candles, often mirrored.

Guéridon. Small ornamental stand or pedestal.

Huche. Hutch or chest.

Jardinière. Plant container.

Laqué. Lacquered.

Lambrequin. Valance board for draperies.

Lavabo. Table and washstand.

Lit. Bed.

Lit-à-la-Francaise. Bed placed sidewards against wall, with canopy.

Lit-à-la-Polonaise. Bed with pointed crown canopy.

Lit-à-travers. Bed placed sideways against wall, without canopy.

Lit canapé. Sofa bed.

Lit d'ange. Bed with small canopy.

Lit duchesse. Bed with large canopy.

Lustre. Table light or wall sconce in crystal.

Manchette. Padded arm cushion.

Marquise. Small sofa.

Menagère. Dresser with open shelves for crockery.

Meridienne. Sofa with one arm higher than the other. (Empire.)

Miroir. Mirror.

Noyer. Walnut.

Objet d'art. Any small art object.

Ormoulu. Gilded bronze. Ormolu.

Panier. Basket or scrap basket.

Panetière. Bread box.

Petite-commode. Small table with three drawers.

Placage. Veneering.

Poudreuse. Powder or toilet table.

Psyche. Cheval glass. (Empire.)

Rafraîchissoir. Refrigerator.

Rez-de-chaussée. Ground floor.

Rognon. Kidney-shaped.

Scrutoire. Slope-top desk, which has a lid that opens to form a horizontal writing surface.

Sécretaire. Desk.

Sécretaire-à-abattant. Drop-lid desk.

Semainier. Tall bedroom chest with seven drawers.

Singerie. Decorative motif using the monkey as subject matter.

Table-à-écran. Table with sliding screen.

Table-à-jeu. Game table.

Table-à-l'anglaise. Dining room extension table. (Louis XVI and later.)

Table-à-l'architect. Table with hinged top.

Table-de-chevet. Night table.

Table-jardinière. Table with top pierced for plant containers.

Tabouret. Stool.

Tambour. Literally a drum. Drum-shaped.

Terre-cuite. Terra cotta.

Tôle. Painted sheet metal or tin.

Tric-trac table. Backgammon table.

Tricoteuse. Small sewing table.

Trumeau. Overmantel or overdoor panelling, usually with mirror with superimposed picture.

Vaisselier. Dining room cabinet and shelves.

Verrier. Glassware cabinet.

Vis-à-vis. Two seats facing in opposite directions, attached in the center.

Vitrine. Curio cabinet with glass front. (Louis XVI.)

Bibliography

ALGOUD, H., *Le Mobilier Provençal.* Paris, 1923. Photographs of Provençal interiors and furniture.

ARNOTT, J., AND WILSON, H., *The Petit Trianon.* B. T. Batsford, Ltd., London, 1908. Reprint by the Architectural Book Publishing Co., New York, 1914. Series of measured drawings and photographs of the entire building, supplemented with a historical account.

COLAT, L. *Le Mobilier Basque.* Paris. Photographs of Basque interiors and furniture.

CONTET, F., *Anciens Châteaux de France,* 22 Vols. F. Contet, Paris. Excellent portfolios of plates, covering the various styles of architecture.

CONTET, F., *Intérieurs Directoire et Empire.* F. Contet, Paris, 1932. Color plates of designs reproduced from the original works of the artists of these periods.

CONTET, F., *Le Style Empire,* 5 Vols. F. Contet, Paris, 1925. Portfolio of very fine plates.

CONTET, F., *Les Vieux Hôtels de Paris.* F. Contet, Paris, 1908–1934. Twenty-one volumes of plates, showing both interiors and exteriors of old French architecture. A standard work.

CRAM, R. A., *Farm Houses, Manor Houses, Minor Châteaux, and Small Churches from the Eleventh to the Sixteenth Centuries in Normandy, Brittany, and Other Parts of France.* Architectural Book Publishing Co., New York, 1917. Good collection of photographs.

FRENCH, L. JR., AND EBERLEIN, H. D., *The Smaller Houses and Gardens of Versailles, from 1680 to 1815.* Pencil Points Press, Inc., New York, 1926. Brief text with excellent illustrations.

GÉLIS-DIDOT, P., AND LAFFILLÉE, H., *La Peinture Décorative en France,* 2 Vols. Ancienne Maison, Morel, Paris, 1888–1890. French text with beautiful color plates.

GELIT, P., *Le Mobilier Alsacien.* Paris, 1925. Photographs of Alsacian interiors and furniture.

GOODWIN, P. L., AND MILLIKEN, H. O., *French Provincial Architecture.* Charles Scribner's Sons, New York, 1924. Excellent text and photographs of exteriors, gardens, and interiors.

GROMORT, G., *Choix d'Elements Empruntés a l'Architecure Classique.* Aug. Vincent, Paris, 1904. Plates of measured drawings.

GUERBER, A., *A Short History of France.* W. W. Norton and Co., New York, 1946. Well-written outline of the development of French culture.

HAVARD, HENRI. *Dictionnaire de l'Ameublement.* Paris, 1891. A book of source material on French furniture.

HINCKLEY, F. LEWIS, *A Directory of Antique Furniture.* Crown Publishers, New York, 1953. Excellent comparative photographs.

HOURTICQ, L., *Art in France.* Charles Scribner's Sons, New York, 1917. Illustrated general history of French art.

KEIM, A., *Le Beau Meuble en France.* Paris, c. 1934. Excellent history of French furniture. French text.

KIMBALL, F., *Creation of the Rococo.* Philadelphia Museum of Art, 1943. Standard text on this subject.

LONGNON, H., AND HUARD, F. W., *French Provincial Furniture.* J. B. Lippincott Co., Philadelphia, 1927. Excellent illustrated text.

RICCI, S. DE, *Louis XIV and Regency Furniture and Decoration.* Wm. Helburn, Inc., New York, 1929. Excellent photographs with brief text.

RICCI, S. DE, *Louis XVI Furniture.* W. Heinemann, Ltd., London, 1913. Introductory text to an excellent collection of photographs.

SALVERTE, FRANÇOIS, *Les Ebénistes du XVIII Siecle.* Paris, 1927. A book of source material concerning the French cabinetmakers of the 18th century.

STRANGE, T. A., *French Interiors, Furniture, Decoration during the 17th and 18th Centuries.* Charles Scribner's Sons, New York. Reprint. Line drawings and photographs with descriptive text.

WARD, W. H., *A History of French Renaissance Architecture,* 2 Vols. B. T. Batsford, Ltd., London, 1926. An excellent illustrated history.

Also numerous French publications available in America through William Helburn, Inc., New York.

CHAPTER VI

THE ENGLISH PERIODS

T he British people, product of the fusion of the Celts, Angles, Saxons, Jutes, Danes, and Normans, have been to modern history what the Roman nation was to antiquity. The most important British contribution to civilization has been her colonization of distant lands and, with rare exception, the establishment therein of justice to minorities, of order, of industry, and of progress.

British history commences with Caesar, who invaded the island. The Romans established camps that later became cities and have left some well-built roads and baths. Upon the fall of the Empire in the 5th century, the Teutonic invaders settled in the western and northern sections, became Christians, and established kingdoms that endured until the time of Harold in the 11th century.

The religious ecstasy of France during the Middle Ages crossed the Channel in 1066 with William the Conqueror, and was recorded in art by the construction of the romantic Norman and Gothic cathedrals at Durham, York, Lincoln, Salisbury, Canterbury, Wells, and elsewhere. For 500 years the English kings were loyal to the See of Rome. The growing dissatisfaction with the Pope's administration of English affairs, the visit of Erasmus, the Dutch humanist, to the English Court in 1498, and finally the refusal to the king of a divorce from Catherine of Aragon, culminated in Henry VIII's throwing off the papal authority and separating the Church of England from the Papal See.

From the beginning, owing to her isolated position, Great Britain had necessarily developed a seafaring race. The activities of Spain and Portugal in the New World during the 15th century were observed with envious glances, and the bleak coast of Labrador had been the sole reward of the efforts of John and Sebastian Cabot. The rising power of Spain under Ferdinand and the political and cultural ambitions of Francis I provoked Henry VIII to action. The unsurpassable splendor exhibited in the tournament on the "Field of the Cloth of Gold," contributed to the belated but growing desire on the part of the English nobility to surround themselves with some of the refinements and luxuries of Italy, which were then being adopted by her neighbor nations. English navigation and commerce began to expand, the seeds of the British Empire were sown, and with the increase in wealth, Henry strove to enrich court life. Holbein, the German painter, John of Padua, the Italian architect, and other artists and craftsmen were invited to work in England at a time when the English knew of no style but the Gothic. The Renaissance forms at first bewildered the English and they did not become popular until about one hundred years after they were used in Italy, where they had already become a past style.

Elizabeth's reign (1558–1603) has been called the Golden Age of England and compared with Greece under Pericles. After the defeat of the Spanish Armada in 1588, which gave England control of the seas, her attention turned to economic development. Elizabeth regarded with amusement the looting of Spanish treasure ships by Drake, and constantly encouraged English trade with foreign countries. The increase in the wealth of the middle class permitted the development of country estates and the building of manorial houses. Textile manufacturing was stimulated by the influx of weavers and tradesmen from the Netherlands, who fled from the persecutions of the Spanish Inquisition. Sir Walter Raleigh attempted to settle Virginia. The inborn love of liberty and independence of thought of the English people, first evidenced by the demand for the Magna Carta in 1215, gave birth during Elizabeth's reign to the Puritan and Pilgrim movements, which were later to have such an important influence upon the development of the American colonies. The theater became the favorite form of amusement, under the auspices of Ben Jonson and Shakespeare. All England bloomed under a regime of peace, increased wealth, and the influence of Renaissance ideas.

After the death of Elizabeth, political disorder occurred during the reigns of her successors, James I and Charles I. Van Dyck, the Flemish painter, went to England to paint portraits of the court nobility. Inigo Jones introduced the Palladian style of architecture. The East India Company was organized. Charles I was tried and executed in 1649. The English civil war was a period of great destruction of both ecclesiastical and private property, and was followed by the Protectorate under Cromwell. To the Puritans art had been associated with corruption, immorality, and inefficiency, and a ban was placed on everything that had any appeal to the senses.

In 1660 the monarchy was restored, and Charles II was called to the throne. Charles was sympathetic with his cousin, Louis XIV of France; in his reaction to the repressed and subdued spirit that had prevailed during the Puritan Protectorate, he endeavored to imitate the lavishness and extravagances of the French court. The Great Fire, which destroyed a large part of London, occurred in his reign, and this disaster gave impetus to the construction of new homes, public buildings, and churches. Sir Christopher Wren, the architect, became the leading influence in the artistic life of the period and was called upon to design St. Paul's Cathedral in London and to redesign Hampton Court Palace, the home of the English king. Sir Christopher was strongly influenced by Palladio, the Italian architect, and by French architects. Many French and Flemish craftsmen, among them Daniel Marot, came to England upon the revocation of the Edict of Nantes, and Charles supported several art industries, including the tapestry factory at Mortlake outside of London. It is said that 40,000 French weavers entered England at this time.

The corruptions of Charles' reign created a reaction after his death. James II succeeded to the throne, but was ousted because he attempted to restore the Roman Catholic Church as state church. James' daughter, Mary, and her husband, William, Prince of Orange, a Stadtholder of Holland, were invited to rule as joint sovereigns. Prosperity, economy, and simplicity characterized their reign. The reigns of Queen Anne and George I (1702–1727) witnessed a further expansion of the empire. England, by the Treaty of Utrecht with France, obtained Nova Scotia, Newfoundland, Hudson Bay, and the West Indies. Trade with India, the Far East, Virginia, and New England increased. Wealth poured into the nation. New ways of thinking, new modes of life helped to develop social intercourse. The nobility settled down to enjoy comfort and culture. While the men followed the hounds or drank their flip and ale, women consumed tea, played cards, and plied their needles.

The reigns of George II and George III (1727–1810) continued along the same lines of social development as those of their immediate predecessors. In spite of the loss of the American colonies, great industrial changes were wrought in manufacturing by the inventions of machinery. In 1764 the spinning jenny was invented by Arkwright, the steam engine by Watt in 1769, cylinder printing for textile manufacturing in 1783, and the power loom in 1785. The excavations at Pompeii strongly influenced the arts.

England's ships carried English products to all shores, and returned with holds filled with the luxuries and necessities produced in foreign lands. The 18th century was a period of cultural, as well as industrial, growth. The Society of the Dilettanti was organized in 1733 with the idea of promoting the arts, and it influenced greatly the development of public taste in architecture and decoration. In literature the 18th century produced such men as Johnson, Pope, Fielding, Richardson, Defoe, Swift, and Goldsmith; in science, Newton and Halley; in statesmanship it brought forth such men as Burke and Walpole; in religion and philosophy, Locke and Wesley; in history, Edward Gibbon.

In 1810 George IV became regent, because of the illness of George III. Napoleon's ten years of threats and actions were brought to a close at Waterloo by Wellington. Once more England and Europe had an opportunity for the development of peacetime pursuits. With the aid of the new mechanical inventions, old industries began to produce on a much larger scale. Home production with one's own tools gave way to large-scale production in the factory. Population began to increase and concentrate in the cities. Manufacturing began to compete with agriculture. The greatly increased wealth became concentrated in the hands of the newly rich, who dazzled the world with their display. The post-Napoleonic era witnessed a reaction in the manners and customs of society, from the self-discipline imposed during the uncertainty of war years to liberty and license carried to extremes that were not counteracted until the youthful Victoria inherited the crown.

The effort of the Greeks to throw off the yoke of Turkey had a strong sentimental appeal for the English people. Keats, Shelley, and Byron romanticized the classic spirit in their poetry; and with the additional influence of the standards of taste of the French Empire, classic—and particularly Greek—forms in the decorative arts were revived.

Queen Victoria came to the throne in 1837. The industrial age continued to expand to unimagined proportions. Wealth came from quantity rather than quality production. The craftsmanship of the handworker in industry was submerged by the economic advantage of machine work. The appreciation on the part of the public for beauty in line, form, texture, and color vanished as though it had never existed.

Character of the British people. The insular position of Great Britain has contributed greatly to an unusual homogeneity of race and a mutual understanding of the classes. A peerage has been acceptable because it has been a recompense for public service and because its members have justified their existence by fully realizing the meaning of *noblesse oblige*. Leaders have considered honor more important than personal gain, and the country has been ruled by law rather than by autocratic methods. Reforms in public policies have been slowly made, but they have been made by peaceful means. The English have learned to argue rather than to battle and to choose a middle way of compromise and concession by the use of the logic of experience rather than theory alone. The Britisher has been a lover of liberty and individualism and, throughout most of his history, has felt that the best government is the least government, a theory that has been seriously questioned as governments have assumed the responsibilities of social welfare. The basic economic policy until World War I was to retain the privilege of manufacturing into saleable products the raw materials furnished by the colonies and dominions. This policy was highly successful for two hundred years, but under modern war conditions, resulted

in food shortages and the eventual establishment in the dominions themselves of the means of manufacturing at the expense of the homeland.
Great memories, persistent traditions, and courageous loyalties have rhythmically echoed in the heart of every son of Albion and these have served
to build the pluck, tenacity, and pride of the nation.

The verdure of the rolling, luscious countryside is nourished by the
mists that roll in from the adjacent seas, and has contributed to the love
of outdoor life. Rural activities have built the physical vigor of the nation
and have contributed to a social existence that has strongly influenced the
charm and character of English country architecture and decoration. Interest in sports has taught the Englishman to lose with equanimity and
helped to form a characteristic that is at the base of its democracy. Art has
never been a national industry as in France. Thoughts of Empire and commerce have been uppermost, but the aristocracy has assumed the responsibility of an art patronage. The decorative arts have evolved conservatively
because the Britisher has loved the past and has been content to live in a
home mellowed by vines and ivy. Except in literature and gardening, the
arts of England have been freely borrowed, although isolation, security
from invasion, moist climate, and ample resources have in times of peace
aided in the development of nationalistic art expressions. The placidity of
the British character never prevented a richness of expression in the decorative arts, but at no time did the English reach the degree of prodigality
that typified the Rococo excesses of the continental nations.

The subdivisions of the English periods, 1500–1900. The English Renaissance periods of decorative arts are by some authorities divided according to the popular woods used for furniture-making. The Age of Oak
lasted from about 1500 to 1680; the Age of Walnut, from 1680 to 1710; the
Age of Mahogany, from 1710 to 1770; and the Age of Satinwood, from
1770 to 1820. The usual historical divisions are as follows:

1. Early Renaissance (1500–1660. The Age of Oak).
   a. Tudor (1500–1558).
   (Reigns of Henry VII, Henry VIII, Edward VI, and Mary.)
   Transitional period. Gothic forms dominated; gradual introduction of
   Italian Renaissance forms.
   b. Elizabethan (1558–1603).
   Transitional period. Additional Renaissance features introduced.
   c. Jacobean (1603–1649).
   (Reigns of James I and Charles I.)
   Transitional period. Few remaining Gothic elements. Flemish influence
   Strapwork carving. Renaissance forms used. Inigo Jones.
   d. Cromwellian (1649–1660).
   Religious wars. Period of industrial and artistic stagnation.

2. MIDDLE RENAISSANCE (1660–1750).

    e. Restoration, Stuart, or Carolean period (1660–1689).
(Reigns of Charles II and James II.)
Flemish and French Baroque influence. Greater formalism in design. Rooms treated with large wooden panelling. Influence of Wren and Gibbons, with accurate conception of Renaissance architecture. Elaborate carving and rich textiles used in furniture.

    f. William and Mary (1689–1702).
Interiors same as in previous period. Changes principally in furniture. Little carving. Enrichment by wood graining and marquetry. The Age of Walnut.

    g. Queen Anne (1702–1714).
Interiors slightly simplified. Wallpaper became popular. Curvilinear influence in furniture. Walnut and mahogany used. Oriental influence in design and finish. Continuation of Wren's and Gibbons' influences.

    h. Early Georgian (1714–1750).
(George I and portion of George II's reign.)
Architectural interiors in pine and walnut. Tendency toward heaviness of proportion and detail. Furniture made exclusively of mahogany. Early Chippendale work. Curvilinear furniture designs. Swan and Kent influence.

3. LATE RENAISSANCE (1750–1830).

    i. Middle Georgian (1750–1770).
(Portions of George II's and George III's reigns.)
Reaction toward lighter proportions in interior design and furniture. Chippendale period. The Age of Mahogany (1710–1765).

    j. Late Georgian (1770–1810).
(End of George III's reign.)
Adam leadership in the arts. Pompeian and Greek influence. Chippendale, Hepplewhite, and Sheraton. The Age of Satinwood.

    k. Regency (1810–1820, style continued until 1837).
Period of severe Neo-classicism. Influence of Sir John Saone and French Empire. Decline of handcrafts.

    l. Victorian (1830–1901).
Growth of industrialism and quantity production. Eclecticism.

Interiors of the Early Renaissance periods (1500–1660). English domestic interior decoration commences with the charming *half-timber,* brick, and stone dwellings erected during the 16th century. The feudal castle was less necessary in England than on the Continent, and was of little protective value after the cannon superseded the bows of the yeomanry and nullified the value of the moat and drawbridge. The castle gave way to the rambling country house, situated in the center of exquisite gar-

Oak Tudor room from Somersetshire, England. Built about 1490. Notice the molded beam ceiling, the Tudor arched fireplace, the small wall panels, and the Gothic influence in the windows.

dens and velvety lawns beautified by the alternating sunshine and mist of the English climate. The transition from the habits and customs of the Gothic period was slow, however, and the great hall persisted well into the Tudor period. Many of the houses were built in irregular shapes, around quaint quadrangular courtyards.

The general character of all early English decoration was vigorous, masculine, sombre, and austere. The rooms were spacious and dignified in appearance, and many of them were extremely long and narrow, or planned in the shape of the letters "L," "E," and "H." Variations in floor levels frequently occurred, and adjoining rooms or wings were connected by several steps. The bay window built up from the ground and the *oriel,* an upper story projecting window supported externally on a large bracket or *corbel,* were typical and persistent features, and were at times so large that either one formed almost an extra room by itself. The windows were designed in the manner of those in the Gothic church, although the glass was usually limited to small rectangular or diamond-shaped panes separated by narrow strips of lead. Color was confined to small patterns showing coats-of-arms, although even the plain squares of glass had various unintended color tints. The window openings were subdivided with stone or wooden mullions, joined at the top in a flat pointed form known as a

Room in a half-timber house of the Elizabethan period. The vertical posts form the skeleton structure and become a part of the interior decoration.

Tudor arch. The same type of arch was also extensively used for the heads of doors, for fireplace openings, and for other decorative features. The interior walls of brick and stone houses were sometimes in rough-finished plaster, covered with a wainscot treated with small oak panels in Gothic detail and proportions. The panels were not always superimposed; they varied in dimensions, and their arrangement sometimes lacked symmetry. The field of the panel was sometimes plain, but was frequently enriched by a linenfold carving or diamond-shaped motif. The wood was usually left in its natural finish or rubbed with oil and beeswax. In half-timber houses, the heavy posts of the structure, placed about two feet apart, with an occasional one in a slanting position for extra bracing, were exposed on both the exterior and the interior. These posts, being visible, became an unintentional feature of the interior decoration.

From the Tudor period onward, interior treatments included the architectural orders borrowed from the Italian Renaissance, although not in correct classical proportions. Pilasters, columns, and entablatures were combined with small wood panels, two or more vertical rows of panels being placed between each pilaster. In low rooms the wall panels sometimes rose from the baseboard at the floor to the few moldings forming a cornice at the ceiling. In high rooms an oak dado or pedestal motif about three feet high was used from the floor, and the wall panelling started from the molding at the top of the dado, and was crowned by an entablature, the whole wainscot being about 10 or 12 feet high. In the Jacobean period the panels were slightly enlarged, and geometrical forms, broken

Oak Jacobean room from Bromley-by-Bow, England. Built in 1606. Notice the slight enlargement of the panel sizes, the introduction of classical architectural forms, and the pargework ceiling.

corners, hexagons, arches, and other irregular shapes were introduced. The flooring in the ground floor of these early houses was usually of flagstone or slate. The upper floors had irregular or random-width oak planks of the size of the log from which they were cut.

Ceiling beams were exposed, and the beams varied in size, but were always heavy, with moldings at the corners and patterns of oak leaves, stems, and acorns occasionally carved on their sides. In narrow rooms the ceilings were flat or slightly slanted upward to a point in the middle. In wide rooms elaborate triangular wooden truss forms were used, composed of many small beams fitted together to support a steeply pitched ceiling. In great public rooms the *hammer-beam truss* was used for roof support. This consisted of enormous wooden Tudor arch forms supported on large wooden brackets projecting from the wall, the whole being elaborately carved.

Decorative plaster work became an important feature in ceiling treatment during the latter part of the 16th century. The rough beams were covered with a flat plaster ceiling, and the plasterers endeavored to imitate the wooden beams by means of applied plaster moldings, as both the moldings and the carved ornament of the wood could be more economically produced in plaster. The plasterers, however, were not limited to the straight-line forms of the beams, and soon developed elaborate all-over patterns of curved and geometrical interlacing forms, enriched with cast plaster ornament in relief, showing *Tudor roses,* scroll motifs, portraits,

The English Periods 241

cartouches, and *fleurs-de-lis*. Color was sometimes applied to these plaster patterns, producing a very rich effect. This type of ceiling treatment is known as *pargework* or *pargetry*.

Because of the dampness of the English climate, fireplaces and mantels played a more important part in the decoration of English houses than in those on the Continent. During the 16th and first half of the 17th century, the stone fireplace opening was usually in the form of a Tudor arch, but the woodwork at the side and that of the overmantel consisted of academic architectural features and of richly carved forms of classically inspired ornament.

The stairhall in the early house was made a special feature, the climate precluding the use of an exterior stairway. Of immense size, the staircase was built with elaborately carved newel posts, rich balustrading, and the side walls were treated with small oak panels and leaded glass windows similar to those of the main rooms.

The rooms of the early period were sparsely furnished. Accessories were few, according to modern standards. Arras tapestries, helpful in keeping the rooms warm in temperature and color effect, frequently decorated the walls and at times were used as partitions for dividing large rooms into smaller parts. Armor and trophies of the chase were fastened to the walls, and portraits were hung over the fireplace and in other important positions.

During the reigns of Henry VIII and Elizabeth, England established her naval supremacy, and English ships travelled to distant shores with little molestation. The Far East and India were not neglected, and many Oriental objects of household adornment were brought to enrich the homes of the king and nobility. Chinese pottery, porcelains, paintings, Turkish rugs, and East Indian hand-painted cottons were most in demand. The East Indian painted cotton fabrics, known as *palampores,* were frequently decorated with a pattern of religious significance, known as the "tree-of-life." This type of pattern, consisting of interlacing branches and foliage with peacocks and various birds, became immensely popular in England and was reproduced in paint and crewel embroidery, and was later manufactured by the hand-block process. Variations of this pattern eventually became the most frequently used designs in English weaving.

Lighting fixtures, as a rule, were in wrought iron or brass. Silver, *pewter,* and heavy earthenware platters and drinking cups stood on the shelves of dressers and cupboards.

Furniture of the Early Renaissance. The sources of inspiration in the design of the furniture of the Early Renaissance in England were the same as those in France. Both types were a fusion of Gothic and Italian Renaissance forms, differing, however, in the wood that was used and in the character and design quality of ornamental detail. The English, less closely associated with Italy both geographically and intellectually, were slower to adopt the Italian forms, and in the early stages did not understand the correct proportions of classical architecture as a basis of furniture design. In England the use of oak, the great wood of the Gothic period, persisted well through the 17th century, whereas in France walnut, a fine-grained wood, was substituted during the early years of the 16th century, and permitted the development of more minutely carved ornament and smaller moldings.

During the Tudor and Elizabethan periods, English social life was boisterous in its manners and customs. These characteristics are reflected in the strength of the furniture, which was made for service, rather than for comfort. The principal pieces used were chests, cupboards, wardrobes, desk-boxes, dressers for tableware, settles, chairs, stools, tables, beds, and cradles. All pieces were heavily constructed and massive in appearance. The structural forms were rectangular, continuing the Gothic tradition, the various parts being held together by wooden dowels and pins, and by the mortise-and-tenon or dovetail joint.

The structure of the case and cabinet furniture was similar to that of the wainscots. The stiles and rails, however, were often enriched by simple surface grooving, by a narrow strip of inlay in contrasting wood or checker effect, or by a crudely carved pattern in low relief, inspired by the classical rinceau, arabesque, or guilloche. The field of the panel was usually carved with a linenfold or a coat-of-arms; and as the Italian influence increased, the panels were enriched by a carved or inlaid arabesque pattern or medallion, or by a dwarf arch—the latter type being called an *arcaded panel.* During the Jacobean period the panels became larger, were treated with moldings on four sides, often had plain fields, and sometimes were shaped as diamonds, crosses, hexagons, double rectangles, and other geometrical forms.

Furniture supports during the Elizabethan period were often of the *bulbous form,* resembling a large melon and occupying all but the extreme top and bottom of the support or leg. The melon portion was usually carved at the top with a gadroon and at the bottom with an acanthus leaf. The top of the support crudely imitated a Doric or Ionic capital. During the Jacobean period, the bulbous form of support gradually gave place to dwarf columns of straight or spiral shape or to the twisted rope form.

The characteristic chairs of the Elizabethan period were those known as turned and *wainscot chairs.* The former, extremely heavy in proportions, had a triangular wooden seat with arms, back, and legs entirely composed of short, thick turnings; the latter had a nearly rectangular wooden seat with turned or column legs, arms that were slightly shaped, and a solid, high wooden back enriched by low relief carving or inlay. During the Jacobean period, chairs were improved in comfort by the addition of up-

1697 1605
Table Legs

Elizabethan Cupboard

Jacobean Chair

Strapwork Carving

Stool

1500
Linenfold
Panels

1510

Jacobean
Wainscot Chair

Bun Feet

Arcaded Panels

Elizabethan Table

1656-1612
Chair Legs

Slant-top
Desk

CHARACTERISTIC DETAILS OF EARLY ENGLISH FURNITURE AND ORNAMENT.

holstered seats and backs nailed to a rectangular framework. For smaller country dwellings, chairs of lighter weight, such as the *Yorkshire* and *Derbyshire* types, were also made.

The beds used in the homes of the nobility were of great size. They were designed with four carved corner posts, often enriched by a bulbous ornament and an architectural capital that supported a wooden tester, modelled as a simplified entablature. Long velvet hangings were drawn at night for warmth and privacy.

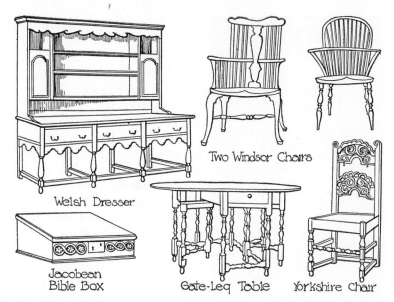

Welsh Dresser

Two Windsor Chairs

Jacobean Bible Box

Gate-Leg Table

Yorkshire Chair

EXAMPLES OF 17TH- AND EARLY 18TH-CENTURY PROVINCIAL FURNITURE.

Although temporary trestle tables continued to be used during the 16th century, the permanent table was also a feature of the furnishings. Large refectory tables were built with solid oak tops, some of which were of the extension type. These were used for the elaborate banquets and turbulent entertainments that took place during the holidays, after the hunt, or on special occasions when the boar's head, yule log, holly, and mistletoe were featured. Drop-leaf and gate-leg tables were used in the smaller houses.

In addition to the simple inlay work and crude low relief and *strapwork* carving, furniture was sometimes enriched by an ornament known as the *split-spindle*.* This consisted of a short, turned piece of wood, often ebony, that was split into two parts, and applied to the surface of the stiles of an oak cabinet or chest. Drawer-pulls and knobs at the top of chair backs were sometimes carved in a caricature of a human head; this type of finial ornamentation was known as *romayne work*. Carved Italian grotesques, face profiles, and the upper part of the human body, rising from a group of scrolls and leaves, were also used for furniture enrichment.

Introduction of Palladian influence. Inigo Jones (1573–1652), the architect, was primarily responsible for introducing the Renaissance into England. Many Renaissance architectural details and ornaments had been applied to English buildings before he entered upon the scene, but Jones' personality and his long studies in Italy of the works of Palladio made him a dominant figure in the English arts. His first designs were for the Court

* Both of these features originated about 1565 in Flanders and are common to German, Dutch, and Flemish architecture, interior woodwork, and furniture.

Courtesy Victoria and Albert Museum, London

Detail of Jacobean pilaster in the Bromley room, showing character of the strapwork carving.

Masques and theater scenery in which the new style could be displayed without too much expense, but after 1640 he was able to apply his knowledge to the design of real structures. His most outstanding work was the great Banqueting House in Whitehall, London, the first English building where the classical architectural proportions as interpreted during the Italian Renaissance were used in the correct manner.

Interiors from the Restoration through the Middle Georgian periods (1660–1770). As a result of the accession of of Charles II, of the Great Fire of London in 1666, of changes in social living, and of the desire to imitate the king in his introduction of French luxury, many dwellings, both large and small, were built, reconstructed, or redecorated. Jones was followed by Sir Christopher Wren (1632–1723), who had visited Versailles while the palace was under construction, and had made a careful analysis of French design. In the face of such a classical architectural onslaught, all Gothic and Tudor forms completely disappeared from English decoration.

Under the Restoration, the walls of the majority of rooms continued to be treated with wood panelling, although the panels themselves were enlarged to run the full height of the room from the dado cap molding to the wooden cornice, after the manner of the new designs introduced at Versailles for Louis XIV. A small panel was also placed between the dado cap and the baseboard. The panels were rectangular, framed with a heavy *bolection molding* which permitted the field of the panel to project slightly beyond the stile. The wood, oak or walnut, was usually left in a natural waxed finish, although rich effects were sometimes produced by painting the woodwork to imitate marble. Where cheaper woods, such as fir and *deal* (pine), were used for the panelling, the wood was frequently grained to imitate walnut and olive-wood. Moldings and ornament were sometimes gilded. Where wood panelling was not employed, the plaster walls were covered with stretched velvet or damask.

Door openings were formally treated with an architectural trim and complete entablature, including architrave, frieze, and pedimented cornice.

Restoration room showing the classical influence, with large bolection panelling, a tendency toward heaviness in detail, and carving of the Grinling Gibbons type. From Clifford's Inn, London, about 1686.

Occasionally both door and window openings were framed in a heavy projecting bolection molding in marble or wood. Carved ornament on the moldings and cornice was customary in the more sumptuous interiors.

An innovation of the first years of the 18th century was the introduction of the built-in arched niche, which formed an important feature of the architectural composition of the room. The niche was usually decorated at the top with a large shell motif, and was lined with shelves for holding china and other ornaments. Many of these niches were framed—like door and window openings—and crowned with triangular or broken pediments.

During the latter years of the 17th and the early years of the 18th century, the work of Grinling Gibbons, the wood carver, became popular in the enrichment of rooms of the period, and the character of his designs and modelling was adopted by artisans working in other materials, as well. Textile-weavers, stone cutters, and decorative painters began to copy his designs. Gibbons was an unknown craftsman discovered in 1671 by John Evelyn, the diarist, who wrote, ". . . of this young artist . . . I acquainted the King and begg'd that he would give me leave to bring him and his worke to White-hall, for that I would adventure my reputation with his Majesty that he had never seene anything approach it. . . ." A few days later Evelyn wrote, "This day din'd with me Mr. Surveyor Dr. Christopher Wren, and Mr. Pepys, two extraordinary and knowing persons. . . . I carried them to see the piece of carving I had recommended to the King."

Mirror frame in carved limewood made by Grinling Gibbons. The total height is 5 feet 10 inches.

Thus we have the record of the start of Gibbons' success. After this introduction, Wren, who was employed in remodelling Hampton Court Palace, and other architects employed Gibbons extensively to ornament the woodwork of many buildings. Gibbons became particularly famous for his wood carvings of garlands, *swags,* and drop ornaments composed of natural objects realistically portrayed in high relief, minute detail, and with deep undercuts. The ornament was carved in fine-grained woods such as lime, box, and pine; it was then gilded, and nailed to the wood-panelled walls, and was generally used as an overmantel decoration or as a frame for portraits. The motifs reproduced included fruit, vegetables, game, fish, leaves, flowers, and other objects. The character of Gibbons' ornament continued to be used in English interiors long after his death in 1720. He had many imitators, and his designs practically dominated the ornament in English decoration for over fifty years. Gibbons, although believed to have been born in the Netherlands, was one of the most important characters in the history of the English decorative arts.

Ceilings in the smaller rooms were left plain. In the ceilings of more elaborate rooms, ornamental plaster moldings formed a border; the center portion received a painted decoration. The complex plaster motifs imitated the realistic detail of Gibbons' work. Italians, Frenchmen, and Hollanders were largely employed in both the modelling and painting.

Oriental pottery continued to be popular as a decorative accessory in the rooms of the Restoration. English and French tapestries hung in important panels. The floor was in parquet patterns in which oak, ebony, and other colored woods were used. Oriental rugs covered the floor. Painted landscapes, hunting scenes, and mirrors were framed and placed on the walls; and the making of stump embroidery for wall hangings, and of needlepoint for upholstery materials, occupied the ladies of the household.

In the early years of the 18th century, the fireplace trim changed from the simple bolection molding to a complete classical architectural treatment, with dwarf columns, architrave, frieze, and a projecting cornice forming a mantelshelf. Marble was extensively used as a mantel material,

Early Georgian knotty pine room from Hatton Garden, built about 1735. The design continues the use of the academic architectural forms, with a tendency toward heaviness of detail. The bolection molding has given place to a simpler form.

Early Georgian room of about 1740, treated with an English wallpaper in the Chinese style, with borders. The overmantel in plaster ornament is unusually interesting.

Georgian room designed by Abraham Swan about 1750 for house in London. The heavy bolection panel molding has given way to the smaller molding with countersunk panel.

and different-colored marbles were frequently employed in the design of the same mantel. The carved ornament was, as a rule, done in a white statuary marble, and its character was the bold, vigorous relief of Gibbons' inspiration. A warm, orange-colored Sienna marble and a dark green or Verde marble were used for the plain areas. The moldings and general proportions of these mantels were heavy.

Knotty pine, left in its natural color, began to be used for the wall panels, and wallpaper, as a cheap substitute for textiles, was introduced on plaster walls that had not been wainscoted. The first wallpapers were what are known as flock papers, made to imitate Italian cut-velvets, and were introduced into England as early as 1634. Marble papers and papers imitating tapestry were also used, and, by the end of the 18th century, were replaced by pictorial and scenic papers of Chinese origin.

About the middle of the 18th century a romantic movement resulted in a revival of Gothic structures.* Horace Walpole's Strawberry Hill home was the most notable example, filled as it was with fan ribbed vaulting and tracery patterns and details of medieval tombs. The movement was extended later to garden design, which included sham Gothic ruins and later Turkish, Chinese, Moorish, and other exotic pagodas, colonnades, pavilions, sheltered seats, and *gazebos*.

Furniture of the Restoration period (1660–1689). The change in living conditions after the return of the monarchy in 1660 was reflected in the

---

* Interest in Gothic design continued for a hundred years, was carried to the United States, and was in constant conflict with the classic influence of the Adam brothers and the later Greek revival of the early 19th century.

character of the furniture as well as in the interior treatment of the rooms. The tendency toward extravagance became widespread. John Evelyn wrote in 1673, concerning a visit to the home of an English countess, "She carried us up into her new dressing room . . . where was a bed, two glasses, silver jars, and vases, cabinets and other so rich furniture as I had seldom seen; at this excess of superfluity were we now arrived, and that not only at Court, but almost universally, even to wantonness and profusion."

Under Charles II, furniture was strongly influenced by both France and Flanders. The popularity, on the Continent, of walnut as a wood for cabinet use created a demand for this wood in England, where the tree had been a rarity. Intense cultivation of this wood developed from the middle of the 16th century, but it was not until the middle of the 17th that an English supply was available. Because of its novelty, therefore, its frequent use for furniture dates from the Restoration. As it was particularly subject to worm-decay, its use was discontinued when mahogany became available, at the beginning of the 18th century. Walnut, however, did not displace oak entirely.

Furniture design under Charles began to show greater consideration for the comfort of the individual, as well as increased richness of form and ornament. The low relief carving of the earlier type continued to be used. The spiral turnings for legs and stretchers became much more frequent, and the most characteristic feature was the Flemish S- and C-curve, sometimes known as the *Flemish scroll*. Legs and stretchers, arm uprights, backs, aprons, and crestings were created with Flemish scroll arrangements.

The design of chairs underwent the most definite change. In addition to the use of the scroll, chairs were made with caning and covered by loose cushions. Elaborate upholstery textiles and leather, both plain and patterned, with heavy handmade silk fringes, were also used. The textile industry was greatly enlarged and perfected in England by the Huguenot immigrants after the revocation of the Edict of Nantes. Textile colors became particularly brilliant. Woodwork was gilded to some extent. The backs of large chairs were slanted for comfort. The wing-back was introduced, and was first called a "sleeping-chair." Stools and benches were also important pieces of furniture during Charles' reign, and they were made quite as elaborate as chairs. Romayne work continued to be used as an ornamental feature of wooden chairs and other pieces of furniture.

Round tables were first introduced during the Restoration, no doubt because they afforded greater opportunity for conviviality. Smaller tables were also seen, and both marquetry and Japanese lacquer ornament were applied, although this type of enrichment did not reach its maturity until the latter part of the 17th century. Bookcases and gaming tables also began to be used at this time.

Firescreens were made in wood and painted to represent life-sized human beings dressed in the costumes of the day; these are called *fireside figures*. Lighting fixtures were made of iron, brass, and silver, and in large rooms, crystal chandeliers were hung from the center of the ceiling.

Furniture of the William and Mary period (1689–1702). When William the Hollander came to England as king, he authorized Wren to remodel and refurnish Hampton Court Palace. William had little knowledge of English traditional art, although Flemish influence had already begun to be felt in English furniture design when he arrived. William's tastes were simple, and were reflected in a tendency toward more delicate lines and proportions, with less carving than during the reign of Charles. The extravagances of Charles' reign also undoubtedly had much to do with the reaction toward more simple forms of furniture. Three changes in furniture decoration took place: (1) Thin wood veneers were applied to flat surfaces, permitting the grain of the wood its full glory of effect in panels and *cross-banding*. (2) Various forms of marquetry and of Japanese and Chinese lacquer work became more common. (3) The most important change, however, was the almost exclusive use of walnut as a furniture wood. The period of William and Mary is most characteristically known in English cabinetmaking history as the "Age of Walnut."

The Flemish scroll form gradually disappeared as a decorative motif. The legs of chairs and tables returned to the straight form. Some were square and tapered, after the French fashion of Louis XIV. Most of them were turned with large mushroom, bell, and inverted-cup turnings. Flat-shaped stretchers were usually used, and feet were made to imitate spherical or flattened balls—usually called bun feet. The *spiral leg* and *trumpet leg* were also seen in a variety of patterns. The marquetry used at this time frequently took the form of elaborate floral patterns. Colored woods and natural and stained ivory veneers added to the richness of effect. One type of marquetry design, representing minute rambling foliage, is known as *seaweed marquetry*.

Many new types of cabinets, clocks, writing desks, dressing tables, and bureau mirrors were introduced in William's reign, but the most important novelty was the *highboy*. This very characteristic piece consisted of a chest of four or five drawers supported by a table. The top of the chest was finished with a group of moldings recalling the classic entablature. The frieze of the entablature was usually in segmental form, and hid a secret drawer. The table support obtained its interest from an elaborately shaped *apron,* the curves of which carried down to the turned legs.

The furniture of the William and Mary period was usually highly polished. A few pieces, which were probably designed by Frenchmen, show carved ornamentations gilded to imitate the ormolu mounts of the French furniture of the period.

Daniel Marot, an engraver and designer, who in his youth had studied and worked under Mansart in France, had been obliged to flee that country after the revocation of the Edict of Nantes. He went to Holland and entered the service of Prince William III, of Orange, who had begun building his palace at Het Loo in Gelderland from French plans. Marot is known to have taken charge of this work in 1692, and designed the interiors and gardens, and also patterned some of the contemporary Delft pottery. About 1695, he moved to England and is known to have been employed in the design of Hampton Court, although his actual work is obscure and he was never mentioned by Wren. He is believed to have returned to Holland about 1697. His early training and reputation as an interior designer, however, probably strongly influenced his English contemporaries, and aided in the popularization of French and Dutch details of design.

Furniture upholstery materials continued to be made on the English looms set up by the French emigrants. Velvets, brocatelles, brocades, damasks, crewel embroideries, and needlepoint were used. The latter years of the 17th century saw the introduction of chintz as a decorative material for window and bed draperies.

Furniture of the Queen Anne and George I periods (1702–1727). The early years of the 18th century ushered in the reign of Queen Anne, and her name has become associated with a style of furniture in the development of which she was neither interested nor influential. Many of her courtiers, her statesmen, and even the poorer people of England were beginning to take a very conscious interest in the comfort and appearance of their homes, and many of them were becoming collectors of various sorts. It has been said, relative to the importations of chinaware at this time, that everyone was "a judge of teapots and dragons." Chinaware covered every available shelf in many rooms, and was sometimes even hung on the walls.

Changes in the wall treatment of the rooms during the Queen Anne period were inconsequential. The style, which overlapped the reign of George I, was primarily one of furniture evolution. The products of the joiner and cabinetmaker were of great purity and beauty, and once again showed, in turn, a complete reaction from the previous period of William and Mary. The principal characteristics were seen in the introduction of the curved line as a dominating motif in furniture design; in the first use of mahogany as a cabinet wood; in the introduction of Chinese forms in the structure of the furniture; and in the great development of the use of lacquer as a finishing material.

The curvilinear principle was most typically seen in the design of chairs, and its introduction was contemporaneous with similar forms in French furniture. The backs of chairs were given a curved top similar to a bent form, and were made slightly concave at shoulder height. A splat was in-

Charles II Chair

Trumpet Spiral Bell Composite
Turning
William and Mary Supports

Wm. and Mary Marquetry Table

Wm. and Mary Walnut Highboy

Queen Anne Lacquered Corner Cabinet

Lion Mask Cabriole Leg

Two Queen Anne Mirrors

Claw and Ball Cabriole with Shell Motif

1708   1715   1735

Queen Anne Chairs   Early Georgian Chair

CHARACTERISTIC EXAMPLES OF RESTORATION, WILLIAM AND MARY, QUEEN
ANNE, AND EARLY GEORGIAN FURNITURE.

troduced in the center of the back which ran from the seat to the crest. The splat first obtained its interest only from its curved *silhouette* and beauty of grain. The frame of the seat of the chair was curved on the sides and front, and the legs were designed in a cabriole fashion, having a conventionalized knee-and-ankle form, and coming down to a pad or *club-foot.* The cabriole form was undoubtedly inspired by Oriental designs, although it was much simplified in detail. The framework of the back of the chair near the top was frequently treated with one or two small breaks in the general sweep of the curve. These breaks are distinctly Chinese in origin. In armchairs, the arms also followed irregular curved forms.

The first change in the development of the Queen Anne chair was in the piercing of the splat with simple curved cutouts. The next was the addition of a small amount of carving, usually an acanthus leaf, on the shoulder of the splat, and the addition of a *scallop-shell* motif on the knee of the cabriole leg. From this point the carving increased, and the splat of the back began to be pierced to a greater extent, forming a much more complicated design. The shell motif was then used in other portions of the chair, particularly in the front center of the seat frame and at the top of the back. At the same time, the clubfoot disappeared, and the *claw-and-ball foot* was introduced. This is supposed to have been taken from the Chinese symbol showing the dragon's claw clasping the "pearl of wisdom," and the English probably obtained the idea from the Dutch. Stretchers between chair legs were discontinued after 1708.

The elements of design used in the chair were applied to other types of furniture. Settees or sofas designed with two, three, and four chairbacks were introduced. Coffee, chocolate, and tea drinking became popular; and *tilt-top, pie-crust,* and *gallery-top* tables for serving purposes were made in great numbers. China cabinets for side walls and corners were made to display the collections of imported ware. Highboys were treated with a broken or scroll pediment at the top, and were made in natural mahogany finish or treated with Chinese or Japanese lacquer. The use of marquetry as an enrichment for furniture was gradually discontinued as walnut became unfashionable. Wall and table mirrors had frames in veneered woods; the lines of these were broken at the top with the same curves used in the chair backs. Cross-banding, although used to some extent during the preceding period, became more common during the reign of Queen Anne; it is a term used in veneering frames and panel borders, to indicate that the grain of the wood used in the veneer is at all places at right angles to the strip forming the frame or panel border itself. The glass for mirrors was usually made in two pieces, since there was a revenue tax on mirrors over a certain size. The edges of the glass were *bevelled*. Case furniture, such as cabinets, bookcases, and secretary desks, had double doors with single panels that were designed with broken curves at the top.

The furniture designs known as Queen Anne greatly overlapped the Early Georgian period. There is no exact line of demarcation. Many of the features introduced at the turn of the century were used until 1735. The Early Georgian may be considered as the flowering of the more simple Queen Anne forms. There was evident a general tendency toward greater heaviness of structure, but the subtle curves, the natural beauty of the graining, the almost exclusive use of mahogany after 1733, and the irresistible charm of the increased carving contribute to the general opinion that the years between 1720 and 1750 produced some of the greatest examples of furniture ever made.

About 1725 occurred the "lion mask" period, in which this motif was placed on the knee of cabriole legs, or frequently used as a central motif on the apron of tables, consoles and other pieces of furniture. At the same time, the claw foot gave way to the lion's paw grasping the ball. Variations were seen in the use of satyr and human mask motifs as furniture feet. The Oriental element in furniture structure and finish became less common about 1725, and lacquer-work disappeared; Chippendale later revived Chinese forms during a short period.

Unquestionably, the influence of the architects, Sir Christopher Wren, Batty Langley, and Abraham Swan, had much to do with the introduction of classical architectural elements in furniture design. This tendency necessitated the gradual elimination of the curved line in structural and panel forms. Columns, fluted pilasters, and entablatures were once again used, with the broken or scroll pediment, in the center of which was usually placed a bust or other ornament. Mirror frames made of mahogany were frequently of architectural design, with pilasters at the side rising from pedestal moldings at the base, and crowned with a pediment; the carving on these frames was frequently gilded. At this time gilded gesso ornament was also applied in arabesque and scroll patterns to furniture frames and panels.

The claw-and-ball, lion's paw, duck, cloven hoof, grotesque mask, and scroll feet continued in use with the cabriole form of leg until about 1766. Low-built case furniture, such as bureaus and writing desks, was usually supported on *bracket feet* of varying forms and degrees of enrichment.

The splat-back chair also continued in popularity, although after 1725 the splat itself was elaborated to an extreme degree by means of piercing and carving. The tops of chair-backs assumed what is known as the *yoke* form, and variations of the acanthus leaf and other types of foliage were substituted for the shell motif of the earlier part of the century. Wing armchairs and other forms of upholstered seats, stools, benches, and sofas became much more popular. Commodes, wardrobes, chests with drawers, wall tables, sideboards, dressing tables, and consoles were seen in most homes.

William Kent, architect and furniture designer, had an important influence upon English furniture between 1725 and 1750. His designs attained great popularity, although all of them showed considerable heaviness of effect. Most of them were architectural in inspiration, although a heavy cabriole leg form was generally employed. He designed many table supports for boxlike lacquered cabinets that were in great demand at the height of the craze for Oriental importations.

Queen Anne

Yoke Back

Comparison of early 18th century English chair backs. The yoke back indicates the beginning of the Georgian style.

The use of mahogany for cabinetmaking was of gradual growth. It was probably used in isolated cases in the late 17th century. In 1720 there was placed upon it a high import duty that was not removed until 1733. After that year its use grew to such an extent that all native woods were eliminated for cabinetmaking, except in the provincial districts. Mahogany was imported from Santo Domingo, Cuba, and Honduras. The importations from Santo Domingo were considered the finest, and were of a dark, rich red color. Mahogany trees grew to a very large size, and the wide boards that were available eliminated the necessity for veneered surfaces, which were particularly unsuitable for dining tables. The wood was free from worm attack, to which walnut was particularly subject; and, as it was also stronger than walnut, certain structural portions of furniture, such as the legs, could be made in more slender proportions. Although the graining was, perhaps, less interesting than that of walnut, mahogany could be carved for enrichment with greater ease. The popularity and advantages of this new wood were also among the causes of the decline in the use of marquetry.

English Windsor chairs. During the first quarter of the 18th century, a provincial type of chair was produced which later became known as the "Windsor." The origin of the design is unknown, but the type is supposed first to have been made by wheelwrights. The chair was based on the same principle as the Queen Anne form. The back splat, however, was not so gracefully silhouetted, and often showed a small wheel in the center. Additional spindles flanked the splat; these are thought to have been wheelspokes. Some of the Windsor chairs had straight turned legs set at a slight splay, and others had typical cabriole legs. The seat was solid wood scooped to a slightly concave shape. Farm and orchard woods were commonly used in the manufacture of these chairs, and many mahogany examples were also made. In the majority of Windsor chairs, several different woods were combined.

Chippendale furniture. In the year 1754, the first edition of a book * named *The Gentleman and Cabinet-Maker's Director* was published by Thomas Chippendale, a furniture maker, who, having learned his craft from his father, also named Thomas Chippendale, had inherited a London

* A later edition was published in 1759 and an enlarged edition in 1762.

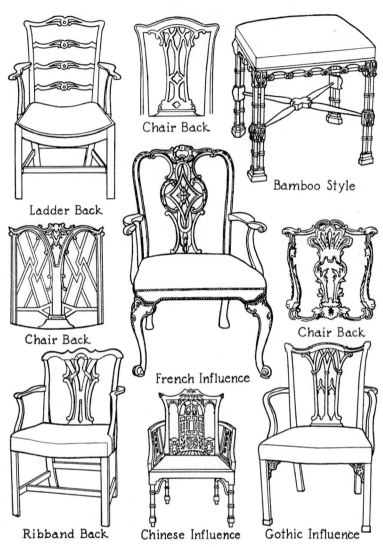

Chair Back

Bamboo Style

Ladder Back

Chair Back

Chair Back

French Influence

Ribband Back

Chinese Influence

Gothic Influence

EXAMPLES OF CHIPPENDALE FURNITURE.

cabinetmaking shop. The elder Chippendale had arrived from Worcester in 1727. Chippendale reached a higher pinnacle of fame than any other English cabinetmaker, and he is undoubtedly credited with accomplishing much more than he actually did, although his production must have been large for those days as he had three shops in St. Martin's Lane. He was elected a member of the Society of Arts in 1760.* His book, which would

* This was obvious proof of his position in the arts at this time, as others who were elected about the same period were Robert Adam; Boswell, the biographer; Benjamin Franklin; David Garrick, the actor; Gibbon, the historian; Samuel Johnson; Pitt; and Walpole.

Panelled and painted room attributed to Chippendale, but showing a strong French influence in the panel shapes.

today be called a trade catalogue, no doubt contributed greatly to the publicity given his work and name, and to the popularity of the styles of furniture shown therein. What Chippendale really did, however, was to capitalize upon the trend of the times. He took the furniture styles that were prevalent, refined them to a certain degree, selected the finest woods, constructed his forms in a most perfect and solid manner, and, with a highly developed sense of salesmanship, unusual for his day, sold his products to the nobility and leading connoisseurs of cabinetmaking. The designs for his furniture were taken from many sources. Classic, French, Louis XV, Chinese, and Gothic forms and ornament were combined in most extraordinary harmony and unity. He worked almost exclusively in mahogany, although after 1765 he made a few pieces in satin, rose, and other exotic woods, and there are in existence a few painted, gilded, lacquered, and japanned pieces attributed to him.

The publication of his book brought hosts of imitators, and the local cabinetmakers in every town in England were enabled to follow the fashions of London. Plagiarism was rampant, but Chippendale had invited it by giving instructions in the *Director* on the best methods of making his furniture. It has, therefore, become almost impossible definitely to identify furniture as having been made in the Chippendale shop, and the name "Chippendale" has been freely applied to the style in which he worked, although he did not originate it. Leading authorities on English furniture attribute specific pieces to Chippendale only providing the original bills of sale are in existence, and these are pitifully few.

Commode

Brass Keyholes

Candle Stand

Brass Drawer Pulls

Pie-Crust Tip-Top Table

Gilded Mirror

Frets

Secretary Bookcase

EXAMPLES OF CHIPPENDALE FURNITURE.

The Chippendale designs are seen at their best in chairs, although all types of furniture were made, from insignificant washstands to magnificent bookcases, desks, chair-back sofas, clocks, organ cases, four-poster beds, pie-crust and gallery-top tables, sofas, benches, consoles, mirrors, and dining and serving tables. Motifs in such great variety were used for ornamentation that it is difficult to classify them.

In the earlier work of Chippendale, the chair, stool, and chair-back sofa showed a great similarity to the Early Georgian development of the Queen

Anne type. The cabriole leg with carved foot and the elaborated splat back with a yoke form at the top were characteristic. He undoubtedly made much furniture before his *Director* was published, and, although no proof exists, he probably also used the claw-and-ball foot in many pieces. In the later work of Chippendale, the straight leg, known as the *Marlborough* form, was used, and intricate backs imitating Gothic tracery were introduced; Chinese latticework, bamboo forms, ribbon, and Rococo motifs borrowed from Louis XV furniture, and ladder slats designed in graceful curved lines were also used. Greek and Chinese foliage, fretwork, flutings, paterae, husks, and cartouches were the principal ornaments. In his earlier work, in which the cabriole form of support was frequently used, the scroll foot, similar to the French Rococo form is often seen, although a great

Chippendale type carved and gilded mirror frame showing French Rococo and Chinese influences. Total height, 6 feet 9 inches.

variety of foot designs were produced. No claw-and-ball foot is shown in the *Director,* and, while Chippendale may have used the feature before his book was published, it is probable that other contemporary cabinetmakers were responsible for the continued use of this typically Queen Anne detail. When Chippendale began to use the straight leg for his chairs, he added stretchers for greater strength. Chippendale designs ranged from the extreme rococo to classical severity. There are many designs in the *Director* that are so fantastic in conception that it is hardly possible that they were ever manufactured, and they were probably introduced for purposes of prestige. Undoubtedly he made many simple pieces to fulfill the needs of a less wealthy clientele but these were not publicized.

Furniture designs in the Chinese manner have been given the specific name of "Chinese Chippendale." While these influences are visible in many pieces, they are of unusual interest in the mirror frames, where French rococo forms were combined with Chinese figures. The frames were generally gilded and served to show the astonishing ability of Chippendale as a master of curved line; the most fantastic forms and irregular shapes were composed to produce an extraordinarily unified whole. Wall

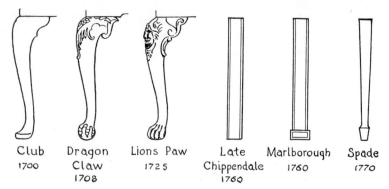

Club	Dragon	Lions Paw	Late	Marlborough	Spade
1700	Claw	1725	Chippendale	1760	1770
	1708		1760		

The development of the 18th century English chair leg giving approximate date of the introduction of the various forms.

mirrors and overmantel designs were the usual types in which this decoration was prevalent. During the last years of Chippendale, his workshop was given over to making, in co-operation with the Adam brothers, furniture in which the more restrained classic forms predominated, and straight lines took the place of the Early Georgian types. Furniture made under the Adam influence is considered his best. This began about 1758 and the style lasted a full quarter century. The florid style, however, overlapped the classic to a great degree, and no exact date may be given as to when the change occurred. In general, most examples of Chippendale's type of work tend to heaviness of structure and proportion, which accounts for their durability.

The designs of Chippendale were copied extensively in both Scotland and Ireland. The Scotch craftsmen were proficient in their reproductions. The Irish, however, were more playful in their interpretation of Chippendale's work. Both the proportions and the ornament of "Irish Chippendale" furniture were less sophisticated than in the original examples.

Chippendale had a son, also named Thomas, who carried on the cabinetmaking business until his death, in 1822. The firm was of less importance, however, after the death of the father, in 1779. With grandfather, father, and son all of the same name, the Chippendale influence covered a period of nearly a century of English cabinetmaking. The use of mahogany lasted from about 1710 to 1770; this period has been called the "Age of Mahogany." There is much furniture in existence today that bears Chippendale's name; but very little that bears his credentials, and most of the pieces called Chippendale are not shown in the *Director*.

The publication of art books. Chippendale had not been the first to issue a book of furniture designs. William Jones had published one in 1739, Copeland, in 1746, and other books covering the subjects of interior woodwork, mantels, cornices, and moldings had been published by

Langley and Swan; but Chippendale's book had brought him such success that many cabinetmakers immediately followed suit. In 1762 Ince and Mayhew published *The Universal System of Household Furniture,* showing designs remarkably like those of Chippendale, that were described on the title page as "Designs in the most elegant taste." In 1765 Manwaring published *The Cabinet and Chair Maker's Real Friend and Companion,* the designs of which showed rococo forms carried to excess. Illustrations of iron garden furniture were also shown in this work for the first time. Robert and James Adam published three volumes on classical architecture in 1773. This was largely of the Pompeian type.

French influences. The influence of France was seen in English furniture during the whole of the 18th century, and as French furniture tended to more delicate proportions during the first quarter of the century, similar characteristics became popular in England. The later work of Chippendale shows distinct signs of this trend, but it was left to other cabinetmakers to carry lightness of line to its final perfection.

Toward the end of the 18th century many English cabinetmakers openly copied French furniture of both Louis XV and Louis XVI types. This was particularly true of Hepplewhite and his imitators. The difference between the English work and the French (as in all cases where copies are made) was that proportions were not so carefully analyzed, with a resultant clumsiness of effect when placed side by side with an original French piece. Even an expert, however, is sometimes deceived in the identification of such pieces.

Hepplewhite furniture. George Hepplewhite, who made furniture in London as early as 1760, was the leader of the reaction toward delicacy of line and proportion in home furnishings. He frequently co-operated with the Adam brothers, producing furniture that they had designed. He died in 1786, but his business was carried along for a few years by his wife, Alice, who in 1788 published his posthumous work, *The Cabinetmakers' and Upholsterers' Guide.* Hepplewhite is credited with two features of English furniture design: the popularizing of satinwood after 1765; and the use of painted motifs as a means of surface enrichment. The last quarter of the 18th century and first quarter of the 19th are sometimes called the "Age of Satinwood."

Hepplewhite's furniture was, in most cases, weak in its construction. This was partially because of the slender proportions of the design, and partially because many of the pieces were veneered on soft wood carcases. What the furniture lost in strength, however, it made up most substantially by its extreme grace and elegance, its beauty of color and enrichment, and its exceptional charm and loveliness. There are no authenticated examples of furniture made by Hepplewhite in existence.

The chair was the most typical example of Hepplewhite's designs, and

Sheraton Arm Chair

Two Hepplewhite Shield Back Chairs

Sheraton
Pediment for Bookcase

Sheraton Mirror

Hepplewhite Mirror

Sheraton
Satinwood Dresser
Painted Decoration by Angelica Kauffmann

Hepplewhite Sideboard

EXAMPLES OF HEPPLEWHITE AND SHERATON FURNITURE.

the forms and ornament used in that piece were seen in nearly all other pieces. Both mahogany and satinwood were used. The legs were always straight and slender, were either round or square, tapered toward the foot, and sometimes ended in what is known as a spade, thimble, or sabot form. Five different types of backs were used: shield, camel, oval, heart, and wheel. Carved ornament was sparsely applied, and consisted of wheat blossoms, oval paterae forms, ribbons, fluting, *reeding,* vases, and festoons. Painted decorations showed the three-ostrich-feather crest of the Prince of

Wales, natural flowers, and classical figures in the style of Angelica Kauffmann, the painter. Marquetry was frequently seen in tulip, sycamore, yew, holly, pear, ebony, rose, cherry, and kingwood.

The top rail of the shield chair-back was in the form of a serpentine curve. This curve was frequently seen in other types of furniture. The shelf of Hepplewhite sideboards, table, and console tops were usually made in this form. The testers of four-poster beds had a similar shape, and pediments and aprons on case furniture followed the same line.

Contemporaries of Hepplewhite were Gillow and Shearer. Shearer designed many pieces of furniture that fulfilled two purposes, such as chairs that opened into ladders, cabinets that were folding beds, and a firescreen that contained a writing table.

Sheraton furniture. Thomas Sheraton, the third great name connected with English furniture design, ranks with Chippendale and Hepplewhite. Born about 1751, he was self-educated, became a preacher and a scholar, wrote religious tracts, studied mathematics, and tried his hand at almost everything. He arrived in London from Stockton-on-Tees in Durham about 1790, published *The Cabinet-Maker and Upholsterer's Drawing Book* in 1791, and unquestionably designed much furniture that was made by other cabinetmakers. Leading authorities claim that he made no furniture himself after he arrived in London. After the publication of his book, however, his influence was enormous, and although he borrowed design forms from everywhere and everybody, he has been given credit for creating a furniture style. Many of his designs were of unusual originality and showed great inventive genius.

Sheraton designed furniture to be made in the same woods as had Hepplewhite; but the straight line dominated to a greater extent than in the designs of his predecessor. The serpentine form was replaced by segmental curves or surfaces that were connected by straight lines or flat areas. He worked in conjunction with the Adam brothers, Wedgwood, the potter, Angelica Kauffmann, the painter, and others. He was the first to use *porcelain* plaques for furniture ornamentation.

The Sheraton chair legs were the same as those of Hepplewhite. The chair backs, however, were rectangular in shape. The rear legs of the chair usually continued upward to form the side braces of the back. A horizontal rail was placed near the seat, between the two back uprights, and an ornamental rail was placed at the top. The space between the rails was filled with one or more ornamental splats, the center one often having the form of an elongated vase. Many of Sheraton's designs were for very small pieces of furniture suitable to the dressing room and boudoir. Dining-room furniture was also his specialty. His book showed designs for twin beds and for Pembroke (drop-leaf) tables. Sheraton also seemed to be interested in designing folding furniture for double purposes and

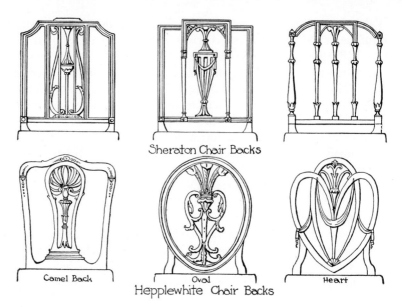

Sheraton Chair Backs

Camel Back | Oval | Heart
Hepplewhite Chair Backs

COMPARISON OF SHERATON AND HEPPLEWHITE CHAIR BACKS.

cabinets with secret compartments. He paid great attention to the design of the complicated mechanical contrivances that served to operate secret locks.

As 140 cabinetmakers in England and America subscribed to the various editions of Sheraton's book, it is no wonder that his style became popular. The Sheraton designs for chair-backs have probably been imitated more than any others by modern manufacturers.

The latter portion of the Sheraton period was influenced by the French Directoire and Early Empire, in which the delicate curves of Greek design were introduced into English furniture.

Interiors of the Adam or Neo-classic period (1762–1794). The last half of the 18th century was signalized by investigation of everything concerning classical antiquity and its possible adaptation to contemporary use. The fashion for imitating the Italians, French, and Dutch had spent itself. The discoveries of the ruins of Pompeii and Herculaneum interested not only the rich, who travelled to Rome, Pompeii, and Athens, but the enterprising artists and architects who had been busy in the excavations. Stuart and Revett's *Antiquities of Athens* was published in 1762, and drawings of the temples in Paestum were made in 1768. This book eventually was to completely change the architecture and decorative arts of Europe and America by a return to Greek classicism after two centuries of Italian Renaissance influence. Classic forms became a standard of design, not to be copied exactly, but to be applied with such limitations of economy or

Bedford Lemere, Photographer

ABOVE: *Room from Landsdowne House, London, now in the Metropolitan Museum of Art, New York City. Designed by Adam, it shows the characteristic plaster niche, inspired by Roman interiors, and the profuse use of composition ornament in panels and ceiling.* BELOW: *Room in Chandos House, London, showing plaster panel moldings and fine-scale classical architectural motifs.*

technique as modern conditions would permit. In fact, the English were ahead of the French in adopting the classic inspiration; and when the movement reached its climax, the aristocrat, merchant, and tradesman, from the design of their dwellings to the smallest article of household furnishing, demanded and obtained classic precedent.

The leaders during this period were Sir William Chambers, Robert and James Adam, and Sir John Saone, architects; and Henry Holland, decorator. These men were creditably followed by a host of lesser artists Since many books on the subject of contemporary art were published, the styles of this period spread rapidly, not only over the whole of the British Isles, but to the American colonies, as well.

An interesting feature of this period of British decoration is the fact that in it for the first time a conscious effort was made to obtain complete unity of effect in every form, ornament, or object used in a single room. Robert Adam, who was the dominant figure in the artistic life of England for two decades, after having designed the walls and ceiling of a room, proceeded to design practically every article of equipment, including furniture, floor coverings, lighting fixtures, textiles, silver, pottery, and metalwork.

The general character of the rooms of the last quarter of the 18th century, and particularly of those attributed to the Adam brothers, showed great formality of design. The Adams themselves had made excavations and measured the ruins of Diocletian's Palace in Spalato, Dalmatia, the results of which they published in 1763; they had become strongly imbued with the true classic spirit in contrast to the Italian Renaissance interpretation of antique forms. Both the exterior and interior of each Adam building reflected this enthusiasm. As royal architects, the Adams had many commissions of unusual importance which required monumental treatment with an extensive use of the orders. In only a few instances were columns or pilasters entirely omitted from an interior wall treatment, and in these cases an architectural effect was obtained by means of an entablature, arch forms, domes, and panels ornamented with classical motifs. The semicircular arched wall niche, a very common Adam feature of design, was used to frame a plaster cast or marble reproduction of an antique statue or urn. Many of the Adam rooms had semicircular, segmental, or octagonal end walls treated with architectural orders. This was copied from old Roman prototypes.

Although Chambers and the Adam brothers were the great minds in the arts till nearly the end of the 18th century, their followers, designing less monumental work, produced many delightful smaller buildings and interiors.

The exclusive use of wood panelling for rooms was discontinued after the middle of the 18th century. Plaster walls took the place of it. In the occasional examples of wood walls, the panelling was much simplified, with small *ogee* moldings separating the stile from the panel; and the wood itself was painted. The plaster walls were sometimes left white or painted a pale color. Sunk plaster panels or panel effects, produced by applied plaster moldings, were commonly introduced. But as such moldings were pure decoration and had nothing to do with the structure of the wall finish, the panels could be separated from each other much further than in the case of wood panels, and an entirely different effect was obtained from that in a wood-panelled treatment.

Marbling and graining of both plaster and wood were frequently resorted to. Plaster panels were also occasionally enriched by the introduction of a delicate arabesque in plaster relief. This was particularly typical of the work of the Adam brothers, who had become enamored of gesso ornament during their studies in Italy. The plaster relief ornament was usually left white to contrast with the colored background.

The architectural orders that were used were those which followed the more slender proportions of the Pompeian types. The majority of the rooms had complete entablatures with delicate moldings. The moldings and friezes were enriched by painting or plaster ornament inspired by Greek or Pompeian detail. The vase form, fret, and honeysuckle were particularly used.

The mantels designed by the Adams were very beautiful and eventually came to be the inspiration of many mantels used in the American Colonial rooms. The architectural mantel consisted of an entablature with a wide projecting cornice forming a shelf, which was supported at each side by a decorative feature. This type had been used during the early 18th century. The Adams continued the principles of this design but slenderized the proportions of the details. The frieze under the projecting shelf was often in two different colored marbles, and a center panel was carved with delicate classical figures. Sometimes the frieze was treated with a series of vertical flutings. The supports at the side were pilasters or columns with the Greek Ionic or Pompeian Corinthian capitals. The caryatid was also used. Wood, usually pine, was often used; the ornament consisting of classical vase forms combined with garlands, *paterae,* or delicate rinceaux made in either gesso or cast lead. The woodwork was usually painted but sometimes it was left in its natural color.

Ceilings were always in plaster. In small houses, the ceilings were plain and flat; but in the more pretentious rooms a great deal of cast plaster ornament was arranged in straight moldings and arabesque forms. The general effect was one of delicacy and refinement in contrast to the heavy ornamental forms of the Restoration period. In palatial rooms the ceilings were painted by well-known artists.

Robert Adam published a book of furniture designs which were im-

Adam mantel from Portland Place, London, showing overmantel treatment of classical medallion surrounded with composition ornament and applied plaster moldings.

provements upon designs originated by the Italian, Piranesi, and first published in a book that the latter had dedicated to Adam. Many of Adam's designs for furniture were influenced by his architectural training. A good many designs were for very large pieces that were in scale with the palatial rooms Adam had created for his clients. When Adam commenced to co-operate with Chippendale, Hepplewhite, and other cabinet-

makers, smaller pieces were produced. Because of this joint working-
out of the problems of furniture design and style, it is very difficult to
designate the original creators of
much of the furniture of the last
quarter of the 18th century. Certain
definite ornaments that have been
commonly attributed to the Adam
brothers were used in pieces made
by others. Robert and James Adam
were never cabinetmakers themselves, with the result that pieces in
which co-operation is evident are
called by the terms "Adam-Chip-
pendale" or "Adam-Hepplewhite."
Sheraton, too, was greatly influenced
by the Adam style, and he may
have designed furniture influenced
by the Adam motifs and designs.

Adam paterae motifs.

The most characteristic ornaments popularized by Adam were the
Grecian honeysuckle and fret, the fluted frieze or apron, the patera and
rosette, the husk, and the several forms of urns. Husks were arranged in
swags or drop ornaments and were frequently tied with ribbons.

Robert Adam was not a chair designer. He was particularly noted for
his designs for sideboards, side tables, settees, cabinets, and bookcases. He is
credited with having developed the English sideboard as it is known today.
The original sideboard table flanked by two separate pedestals was eventually made in one piece and raised on tapered legs. This occurred about
1775, and the earliest known example is of Adam design.

Bossi, an Italian who worked under Adam, developed the stone intarsia
or colored patterns inlaid in marble by means of other colored cement.
This material was used for table and console tops in the more elaborate
examples of furniture.

The influence of Adam in the English decorative arts is nearly equalled
by his influence upon American Colonial architecture. The best of the
post-Colonial structures in the United States were based upon Adam taste
and principles.

The Adam brothers' influence upon other artists. The Adam period is
particularly noted for the influence that Robert and James Adam had upon
artists and designers of decorative accessories. The most pronounced effect
was on the furniture designers, Chippendale, Hepplewhite, and Sheraton.
Josiah Wedgwood made lovely jasper porcelain plaques, medallions, vases,

Corner of Door Trim   Mantel   Paterae

Frieze Ornament   Vase Motif

Sconce   Architectural Wall and Doorway   Pedestal and Urn

EXAMPLES OF ADAM ARCHITECTURAL DETAILS AND ORNAMENT.

and tableware that were designed by John Flaxman and other competent sculptors to harmonize with the lovely Adam interiors. The work of the Italian painters Pergolesi, Zucchi, and particularly of Angelica Kauffmann, who was of Swiss origin, covered the walls, the overdoors, overmantels, and furniture of this period with the most delightful groupings of mythological figures, Italian landscapes, and paintings of the ruined temples of Greece and Rome.

Classical figures played an important part in the designs of all types of craftsmen. Marble-worker and plasterer, wood carver, textile designer, and painter turned to classical mythology, and represented Mercury, Achilles, Cupid and Psyche, and the Muses.

The typical marble mantel that was characteristic of the Restoration period continued to be used during the whole of the 18th century. During the latter third of the century, however, moldings were made smaller, and the character of the carving followed the trend toward delicacy of detail.

On wooden mantels, composition and lead ornament was applied to the frieze under the shelf. Doors and windows were

Regency room showing painted plaster wall.

architecturally treated with slender pilasters and narrow entablatures.

Lighting fixtures consisted of crystal chandeliers and of delicate bronze and silver lanterns, *sconces,* torchères, and candelabra.

The increase in the use of accessories. During the 18th and early 19th centuries the use of decorative accessories greatly increased. After the collection and exhibition of Oriental and domestic china became the rage, Delft ware was imported from Holland and Meissen ware from Germany, and the productions of the English Lowestoft, Chelsea, Derby, and Wedgwood factories were pushed to their highest point of perfection. Pictures consisted not only of portraits and figure paintings by Gainsborough, Romney, Reynolds, Lawrence, and Raeburn, but of landscapes and sporting subjects, as well. Processes of pictorial reproduction were introduced, and the use of *engravings, aquatints,* and *mezzotints* became common. The works of Hogarth, Morland, Constable, Sartorious, Alken, and Wolstenholme were particularly in demand. Other accessories included mirrors of a great variety of designs, clocks, statues, and busts in both marble and bronze.

Minor interiors of the late 18th century. In the simpler country houses of the late 18th century, furniture was comparatively scarce, considering the great amount that was used in the homes of the wealthy. Records show that the country parlors were furnished with a table, a tall clock, a looking glass, and a few chairs. Upholstered chairs were far from common. On the mantelshelf stood two candlesticks and a pair of snuffers. Box beds, with

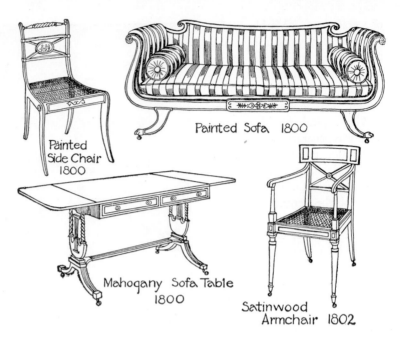

Painted Side Chair 1800

Painted Sofa 1800

Mahogany Sofa Table 1800

Satinwood Armchair 1802

EXAMPLES OF EARLY 19TH CENTURY FURNITURE.

sliding doors to keep out the air at night, were the custom. All cooking was done on turnspits that were operated by dogs trained for that purpose. The dining rooms had tables, chairs, and sideboard tables, with pedestals surmounted by vases used as water coolers or knife-holders.

The Regency period (1810–1820). With the Regency period, English furniture design commenced its decline. Originality and quality lessened. Great masterpieces in this art had been produced during the second half of the 18th century, but by 1810 the creative genius of the English cabinet-maker atrophied. Imagination became exhausted. The French Empire style, glorifying Napoleon, had become antipathetic to the British, but its splendor and its source could not fail to have their appeal. After all, Trafalgar and Waterloo had maintained the English prestige. The public, however, was fast losing its taste and becoming insensible to simple beauty. Imitation of former periods began, as the national initiative became concentrated on commercial enterprise.

Lacking better inspiration, the cabinetmakers embraced the classical forms with undivided enthusiasm. The honeysuckle, the klismos chair-back, the Greek curves, the cornucopia, and other features of antiquity were not only adopted, but exaggerated to a point of ultraclassical affectation. Egyptian motifs were introduced. The forms became clumsy, almost vulgar. Ornament seemed at times to submerge the structure or to be completely unrelated to it. Supports appeared unstructural and construction was cheapened.

During the Regency period, under the influence of Sir John Saone, the forms of Greek antiquity influenced the designers to a greater extent than did those of Pompeii. A reaction occurred from the extensive use of the plaster ornament of the Adam period. Wall surfaces were mainly in plaster, painted in rather strong dark colors, such as browns and deep reds. The heavier Greek Doric and

Design for octagonal tent room. Taken from George Smith's "Cabinet Makers Guide" (1825).

Ionic orders were used. Ornament was largely limited to a conservative use of the honeysuckle and fret. Less careful study was given to the proportions of rooms and to the architecture within. Simplicity and severity became the keynote, although dignity and charm were maintained. Marble busts of classical heroes and philosophers ornamented the rooms, often standing on short portions of column shafts.

The Victorian period (1837–1901).* The forms of the Regency style continued until the time of Victoria, who ascended the throne when still a young girl. Her strait-laced early education was reflected in her later official acts, and her punctilious life served as an example for her people. Her interest in art was negligible, reflecting the dormant spirit of the times concerning this subject. Fashion demanded novelty, however, and furniture producers, in their mental stagnation, turned to all periods of the past for inspiration. This movement lacked intelligence, carelessly avoided both the spirit and the accuracy of detail of the original, and to a large extent intermingled the most incongruous styles and motifs.

After 1830, Greek, Turkish, Gothic, Venetian, Florentine, and Egyptian motifs were used indiscriminately as inspiration for furniture designs. The French Louis XV style, however, was probably the strongest influence, and in most cases clumsy proportions and fantastic gingerbread ornaments were used to reproduce it. Occasionally, inexpensive pressed metal ornaments were gilded and applied to the furniture. Mother-of-pearl inlay was sometimes used on table tops in naïve floral patterns. The popular woods were black walnut, mahogany, ebony, and rosewood. Fruit, flowers, leaves, and nosegays were among the motifs used for carving. *Papier maché* furniture was introduced.

* See also American Victorian period, page 325.

The entire output of the Victorian period, however, is not to be condemned. Occasional pieces of great beauty were produced, and several efforts were made with variable success to break away from the pall of esthetic stagnation. Charles Eastlake, Jr. made an unsuccessful and unfortunate effort about 1865. His interiors were based upon Gothic detail, with varnished oak, glazed tiles, touches of black lacquer, and little thought of color harmony. John Ruskin and William Morris led the revolt toward the end of the century. To Morris is accredited the doubtful glory of inventing the Morris chair.

The most creditable industrial art development during the Victorian period took place in the production of chintzes. Textile designers carried on the traditions of the best periods of earlier work, but with direct appeal to the flower garden, the field, the brookside, and the meadow for their design sources. These natural forms were reproduced in bright colors, and did much to redeem the otherwise drab character of the period.

Leaders in the Arts of England
ARCHITECTS, PAINTERS, DECORATORS, AND CRAFTSMEN

Adam brothers: Robert (1728–1792); James (1730–1794). Designers in the Neo-classic style. Known for architecture, interior architecture, and furniture.

Bromwich. Wallpaper manufacturer under George II.

Chambers, Sir William (1726–1796). First treasurer of the Royal Academy. Author of *Treatise on the Decorative Part of Civil Architecture*. Adhered to Palladian tradition during the Greek revival. Shares honors with Chippendale in adapting Chinese forms to furniture, after travelling in the Orient.

Cipriani, Giovanni Battista (1727–1785). Italian decorative painter during the Adam period.

Columbani, Placido (18th century). Italian architectural designer of the school of the Adams and of Pergolesi.

Constable, John (1776–1837). Landscape painter.

Eastlake, Charles L., Jr. Architect and furniture designer. Advocate of Gothic revival. Wrote *Hints on Household Taste* in 1868.

Flaxman, John (1755–1826). Sculptor and draughtsman.

Gainsborough, Thomas (1727–1788). Portrait painter of English nobility.

Gibbons, Grinling (1648–1720). Wood carver and sculptor.

Gibbs, James (1682–1754). Architect and furniture designer. Published architectural designs in book form. Follower of Wren. Designed St. Mary la Strand, London. Most famous work is Radcliffe College,

Oxford. Also designed interior architectural features, such as mantels.

Halfpenny, William (18th century). Architect, influential in popularizing the Chinese taste in architecture and decoration.

Hogarth, William (1697–1764). Satirical painter of middle-class life.

Holland, Henry (1740–1806). Decorator and architect.

Jones, Inigo (1573–1652). Architect who introduced the Palladian style of architecture into England.

Kauffmann, Angelica (1741–1807). Swiss decorative painter of furniture and interiors, who worked in England. Wife of Zucchi.

Kent, William (1685–1748). Collaborated with his patron the Earl of Burlington in the design of Chiswick House, Chiswick, known as the Palladian Villa. Painter and landscape gardener, architect and furniture designer.

Langley, Batty (Early 18th century). Architect and designer.

Lawrence, Sir Thomas (1769–1830). English portrait painter.

Pergolesi, Michael Angelo (Late 18th century). Decorative painter, architect and furniture designer.

Piranesi, Giovanni Battista (1720–1778). Italian engraver whose engravings of ancient Roman monuments were imported into England and there influenced the designs of the architects.

Raeburn, Sir Henry (1756–1823). Scottish portrait painter.

Reynolds, Sir Joshua (1723–1792). Portrait painter of the English court.

Romney, George (1734–1802). Historical and portrait painter.

Saone, Sir John (1750–1837). Regency architect.

Swan, Abraham (Early 18th century). Cabinetmaker known for his mantels, door and window trim, and staircases.

Turner, Joseph Mallard William (1775–1851). Landscape painter.

Wedgwood, Josiah (1730–1795). Staffordshire potter who established the Wedgwood works.

Wren, Sir Christopher (1632–1723). Inventor and astronomer. Architect after 1666; designed St. Paul's Cathedral in London.

Zucchi, Antonio Pietro (1726–1795). Venetian painter who did decorative paintings for interiors.

Pre-Raphaelite Brotherhood (Second half of the 19th century): Burne-Jones, Sir Edward; Hunt, William Holman; Morris, William; Rossetti, Dante Gabriel; Ruskin, John. This group revolted against the mechanization and eclecticism in the arts of the Victorian era and the decline in craftsmanship. They started a movement back to Italian primitives, to nature, and to hand production in the crafts.

CABINETMAKERS

Bradshaw, George and William. Active 1736–1750, in the mid-Georgian period, cabinetmakers and upholsterers.

Chippendale, Thomas I (Early 18th century). Cabinetmaker and father of Thomas II. Went to London from Worcester in 1727. Some authorities claim that this Chippendale's Christian name was "John."

Chippendale, Thomas II (1718–1779). Cabinetmaker and furniture designer. Published *Gentleman and Cabinet-Maker's Director* in 1754. Native of Otley in Yorkshire. Was under influence of Adam brothers from 1770–1779.

Chippendale, Thomas III (1749–1822). Son of Thomas II. Carried on his father's business with Thomas Haig, but became bankrupt in 1804. Worked mostly in the Regency style.

Cobb, John (d. 1778). Partner of William Vile, from 1750 to 1765. From 1766 on, worked alone.

Gillow, Richard and Robert (Active 1740–1811). Made furniture in Lancaster and London. Shipped much to the British colonies in the West Indies.

Goodison, Benjamin. Supplied furniture to Royalty between 1727–1767.

Grendey, Giles (1693–1780). Georgian cabinetmaker who exported furniture on a considerable scale. Simple, domestic type, much of it japanned.

Haig, Thomas (Active c. 1771–1796). Taken into partnership with Chippendale's son after the father's death, until 1796.

Hallett, William (1707–1781). Popular cabinetmaker under George II.

Hepplewhite, George (d. 1786). His *Cabinet-Maker's and Upholsterer's Drawing Book* was published in 1788. Produced satinwood and inlaid furniture in the classical style. No authentic pieces of his remain.

Hope, Thomas (1770–1831). Designer of furniture in English Regency style.

Ince, William (Active 1758–1810). Partner of Mayhew, with whom he published *Universal System of Household Furniture* (1759–1763). Follower of Chippendale.

Johnson, Thomas (Active 1755). Carver of girandoles, etc. of eccentric and fanciful design.

Langlois, Peter (Active c. 1763–1770). Probably an immigrant Frenchman who worked in a metal technique based on that of André Charles Boulle, using brass and tortoise shell.

Linnell, John and William (Active 1720–1763). John (d. 1796) was a carver and cabinetmaker. William was a carver and upholsterer. Worked in rococo, Chinese, and classical styles.

Lock, Matthias (Active 1740–1769). Early rococo designer. Disciple of Chippendale, and later, of the Adams.

Manwaring, Robert (Active 1765). Known only through his publications of *Carpenter's Complete Guide to the Whole System of Gothic Railing* and *The Cabinet and Chair-Maker's Real Friend and Companion,*

1765. His designs have originality, though the perspective is bad and the engraving is crude.

Mayhew, Thomas (Active 1758–1810). Cabinetmaker, partner of William Ince.

Seddon, George (1727–1801). Active about 1760–1775. Cabinetmaker, furniture designer, and upholsterer. From 1793 to 1800 firm was known as Seddon Sons and Shackleton, Seddon having taken his sons, George and Thomas, into partnership in 1785 and 1788, and his son-in-law, Thomas Shackleton, in 1793. Made much satinwood furniture.

Shackleton, Thomas. George Seddon's son-in-law and partner, 1793–1800.

Shearer, Thomas (Active c. 1788). Did 29 plates in the *Cabinet-Maker's London Book of Prices* (1788), which were reissued in the same year under his name as *Designs for Household Furniture*. Designs are almost entirely limited to case furniture. Associated with Hepplewhite.

Sheraton, Thomas (1751–1806). Published *Cabinet-Maker's and Upholsterer's Drawing Book* (1791–1794). Probably only a furniture designer. No authenticated pieces of his are in existence.

Vile, William (d. 1767). Partner of John Cobb from about 1750. Responsible for the finest rococo furniture made for the crown in the early years of George III's reign.

Bibliography

BLOMFIELD, SIR R. T., *A History of Renaissance Architecture in England,* 2 Vols. G. Bell and Sons, London, 1897. Illustrated text.

BOLTON, A. T., *The Architecture of Robert and James Adam,* 2 Vols. Charles Scribner's Sons, New York, 1922. Text with line drawings and photographs.

BRACKETT, OLIVER, *English Furniture Illustrated.* The Macmillan Company, New York, 1950. Revised by H. Clifford Smith, Keeper of Woodwork, Victoria and Albert Museum. Authoritative text and illustrations.

CESCINSKY, H., *English and American Furniture.* Grand Rapids, 1929. A handbook of English and American furniture of the 17th and 18th centuries, profusely illustrated.

CESCINSKY, H., *English Furniture of the Eighteenth Century,* 3 Vols. George Routledge and Sons, Ltd., London, 1911–1912. Illustrated text.

CESCINSKY, H., *English Furniture from Gothic to Sheraton.* Grand Rapids, 1929. Excellent text, profusely illustrated.

CESCINSKY, H., AND GRIBBLE, E. R., *Early English Furniture and Woodwork,* 2 Vols. G. Routledge and Sons, London, 1922. A thorough study of furniture and woodwork, with illustrations including diagrams and plans.

DULTON, R., *The English Interior, 1500–1900.* B. T. Batsford, Ltd., New York. Excellent handbook with colored illustrations.

EDWARDS, RALPH, *Georgian Cabinet Makers.* Country Life, Limited, London, 1944.

A list of the leading known Georgian cabinetmakers with a description of their work by an official of the Victoria and Albert Museum.

ELLWOOD, G. M., *English Furniture and Decoration, 1680 to 1800.* B. T. Batsford, London, 1922. Brief introduction to good collection of furniture, interiors, and architectural details.

HINCKLEY, F. LEWIS, *A Directory of Antique Furniture.* Crown Publishers, New York, 1953. Excellent comparative photographs.

JOURDAIN, M., *English Decoration and Furniture of the Early Renaissance.* B. T. Batsford, Ltd., London, 1924. Illustrated text.

JOURDAIN, M., *English Decoration and Furniture of the Later XVIIIth Century.* Charles Scribner's Sons, New York, 1922. Text illustrated with photographs and line drawings.

JOURDAIN, M., *English Interiors in Smaller Houses from the Restoration to the Regency, 1660–1830.* B. T. Batsford, Ltd., London, 1923. Text illustrated with photographs and line drawings.

JOURDAIN, M., *Regency Furniture, 1795–1820.* Country Life, Ltd., London, 1934. Excellent illustrated text.

LATHAM, C., *In English Homes,* 3 Vols. Charles Scribner's Sons, New York, 1904–1909. Fine collection of photographs taken by author.

LENYGON, F., *Decoration in England from 1660 to 1770.* Charles Scribner's Sons, New York, 1927. Text and photographic illustrations.

LENYGON, F., *Furniture in England from 1660 to 1760.* B. T. Batsford, Ltd., London, 1914. Text and photographic illustrations.

LLOYD, N., *A History of the English House from Primitive Times to the Victorian Period.* William Helburn, Inc., New York, 1931. Text with photographs and drawings.

MACQUOID, P., *A History of English Furniture,* 4 Vols.: *The Age of Oak; The Age of Walnut; The Age of Mahogany; The Age of Satin Wood.* G. P. Putnam's Sons, New York, 1905. Illustrated text. A standard authority.

MACQUOID, P., AND EDWARDS, R., *The Dictionary of English Furniture from the Middle Ages to the Late Georgian Period,* 3 Vols. Charles Scribner's Sons, New York, 1927. Text illustrated with photographs and line drawings.

PILCHER, DONALD, *The Regency Style.* B. T. Batsford, Ltd., New York, 1948. Good description of architecture and description.

RAMSEY, S. C., *Small Houses of the Late Georgian Period, 1750–1820,* Vol. I, *Exteriors.* Vol. II, *Interiors.* Technical Journals, Ltd., London, 1919. Text and photographic illustrations.

RAMSEY, S. C., AND HARVEY, J. P. M., *Small Houses of the Late Georgian Period, 1750–1820,* Vol. II, *Details and Interiors.* The Architectural Press, London, 1923. Text and photographic illustrations.

STRANGE, T. A., *English Furniture, Woodwork, Decoration, Etc., during the 18th Century.* Charles Scribner's Sons, New York. Reprint. Excellent drawings of furniture, details, etc., with descriptive text.

STRATTON, A. J., *The English Interior.* B. T. Batsford, Ltd., London, 1920. Excellent illustrated text covering English homes from Tudor times to the 19th century.

SYMONDS, R. W., *English Furniture from Charles II to George II.* International Studio, Inc., New York, 1929. Text illustrated with photographs and line drawings.

TIPPING, H. A., *English Homes*, 8 Vols.: *Period I, Norman and Plantagenet; Period II, Early Tudor; Period III, Late Tudor and Early Stuart; Period IV, Late Stuart; Period V, Early Georgian; Period VI, Late Georgian.* Charles Scribner's Sons, New York, 1921. Text copiously illustrated with photographs.

WENHAM, E., *The Collector's Guide to Furniture Design.* Collector's Press, Inc., New York, 1928. Fine collection of photographs with descriptive text, covering English and American furniture and accessories.

CHAPTER VII

THE AMERICAN PERIODS

Perhaps the most important influence in the development of the industrial arts in the United States has been the racial origin of the inhabitants. It has been estimated that over 50 per cent of the present population of the United States is descended from the English settlers of Virginia and New England who landed before 1800. Small settlements of Dutch in the Hudson River Valley, of French in South Carolina and Louisiana, of Germans in Pennsylvania, of Swedes in Delaware, and of Spaniards in Florida and the West have affected their respective localities, but have had negligible bearing upon the thought of the country as a whole. The English language and the virility of the English blood have submerged or absorbed the characteristics and customs of the other settlers, and have impregnated the expanse of the continent with their cultural imprint.

The 19th century witnessed Irish, German, Italian, Russian, and Balkan immigrations. These people have affected economic and industrial conditions, but as yet have had little influence upon cultural and esthetic developments.

The original lists of emigrants from England to New England and Virginia describe them as "persons of quality, emigrants, religious exiles, political rebels, serving men sold for a term of years, apprentices, children stolen, maidens pressed, and others." Unquestionably these early arrivals were a mixed lot, but among the early grantees in Virginia were younger sons of the English nobility who had been acquainted with the luxury and culture of their time in England. The Plymouth settlers, on the other hand, with the exception of a few outstanding leaders, were largely members of the yeomanry of England who wished to escape from the unhappy political conditions under James I and Charles I, or who, like the Pilgrims and Puritans, had protested against what they considered religious abuse. In spite of the insupportable oppression at home, the early emigrants must have been endowed with extraordinary courage and vigor to have been willing to risk their lives travelling in the small sailing vessels of the period across an uncharted ocean to an unknown land.

Settled by those who emigrated to achieve freedom of thought and action, the United States has become the haven of the political, religious, and economic oppressed of Europe and has fathered their industrial and intellectual capacities. The poorest and least educated have risen through energy and ambition to controlling positions. A democratic republic has been sufficient to solve most differences of opinion, and natural competition has developed a powerful and dynamic race that leads the world toward the spiritual and material goals of humanity.

Differences between North and South. The differences in the character of the geography and condition of the soil in Virginia and New England tended from the start to develop contrasting interests and variations in the customs and culture of the two sections.

The South had the advantage of several navigable rivers that penetrated an exceptionally fertile farming district. Plantations of thousands of acres could be worked with slave labor; and tobacco, rice, and indigo were easily exported. The owners, who had obtained their land by royal grant, lived like lords—followed the hunt, kept blooded horses, and visited the adjoining plantations in their coaches-and-six. They built elaborate dwellings, furnished them richly with imported luxuries, dispensed a generous southern hospitality, and occupied themselves with social and political life.

The North, settled largely by religious enthusiasts, developed the small town, in which the independent church was the center of thought and influence. Only small sections of farm land could be cleared of the rocks and stones that had been in New England since the glacial period. No great estates were developed, and the Northerner was at first satisfied with simple living conditions. Early industry consisted of fur trading, cod and other fishing, and shipbuilding.

Nationalistic developments. From 1666 to 1720 there occurred little emigration from England, largely because of the cessation of political and religious strife. This period proved a breathing space for the colonies and gave them an opportunity to co-ordinate their efforts, establish their traditions, develop native industry and commerce, and strengthen their cultural foundations and racial characteristics.

By the first years of the 18th century the economic condition of the country was such that it began to attract a new emigration from England and Scotland. Among the new immigrants were expert craftsmen, carpenters, and cabinetmakers. The early struggle to conquer the eastern wilderness and the Indian had been successfully completed, and the population settled down to enjoy the fruits of victory, represented in part by the construction of more luxurious home surroundings.

During the middle years of the 18th century the colonies continued to grow in wealth and to develop a realization of their self-sufficiency. This sense of nationalism was nurtured by the unreasonable taxation of George III, combined with the frequent injustices of royal governors. Unheeded protests culminated in the Revolution, during the course of which there was little opportunity for peacetime pursuits.

The post-Revolutionary period was undoubtedly influenced culturally by Franklin, Washington, Jefferson, and Hamilton. Both Franklin and Jefferson became ministers to France, and made as deep an impression upon the court of France as the court made upon them. These four men were not only patriots and statesmen, but may also be considered among the first gentlemen in America, if one includes among the characteristics of a gentleman an affection for, and understanding of, the arts. The importance of the arts as a contribution to a full life was realized by them and by others, and their astute connoisseurship undoubtedly contributed to a more careful study and analysis of European productions by American designers, and fostered a greater demand and appreciation on the part of the upper-class public for more sophisticated home surroundings.

Early 19th century cultural influences. The years from 1790 to 1810 produced the finest examples of post-Colonial interior and exterior architecture. The tendency to look to the ancient Roman democracy for inspiration in all important branches of human activity was seen, politically, in the choice of such words as "capitol" and "senate," in the organization of the United States government, and in the selection of a Latin motto. The Society of the Cincinnati, organized in 1783 by the officers of the Continental Army, recalled and perpetuated the virtue and simplicity of an ancient Roman hero. Architecture, decoration, furniture design, and the other industrial arts turned to Greece and Rome for ideas, and as the population spread westward many of the new settlements were given names of classic origin.

Americans warmly sympathized with France during her struggle toward democracy. The purchase of Louisiana in 1803 made many Frenchmen citizens of the United States. The art of the French Empire was strongly influencing English production. Therefore it is not surprising that for a while French styles were followed in the United States. The forms of French art did not displace prevailing English forms, but were frequently fused with them.

Industrial expansion and artistic stagnation. The early 19th century in the United States witnessed the same industrial expansion that swept England, France, and other European countries. The initiative of the American people was evidenced in Whitney's invention of the cotton gin, Fulton's first steamboat, Cooper's first locomotive, and Morse's telegraph, all of them machines that were completely to revolutionize social and economic conditions. While these industrial developments were progressing, the new nation was pushing its frontier further westward, mining wealth, settling new lands, and building new cities. In these new settlements the struggle for existence was too great to permit thought of cultural or artistic development, although at the earliest opportunity schools and colleges were established.

The spiritual side of life during the middle of the century was stimulated by prominent evangelists and by the literary productions of Irving, Cooper, Poe, Hawthorne, Whittier, Emerson, and Longfellow. Music saw the development of the American folk song and the negro spiritual; but architecture, painting, sculpture, and the industrial arts were stagnant. The voices of such cultural giants and individualists as Horatio Greenough, Walt Whitman, Herman Melville, John Fiske, and Louis Sullivan were little more than whispers during the last half of the 19th century, and the truths that they uttered were not fully recognized until long after they had passed away. Problems of secession and slavery occupied the minds of the people during the middle of the century, culminating in the unfortunate war between the North and the South.

During the latter half of the 19th century, the economic advances were so notable and the "laissez faire" philosophy so successful, in a land that abounded in such natural resources, that there was little inclination on the part of the old inhabitants to alleviate the difficulties of the newer immigrants. Material prosperity and scientific discoveries solved few of the fundamental problems of the existence of the masses. The rich considered the accumulation of money as an end in itself and there was an absence of a leisure class that could have established an art patronage. Women controlled both education and religion during a good portion of the 19th century and dictated the standards of art and culture. A masculine interest in the cultural branches of thought seemed to denote effeminacy.

Revival of art appreciation. The Centennial Exposition held in Philadelphia in 1876 was the first definite step toward an artistic awakening in a period of half a century. This exhibit contributed much to an esthetic revival, which came at a time when industrialists who had profited from the natural resources of a virgin land were beginning to establish the great American fortunes, and to have sufficient funds to fulfill a natural desire for ostentation. Thus, in the last two decades of the century many of the newly-rich built homes in New York, Chicago, Newport, and elsewhere, were designed to imitate Old World palaces and châteaux, and furnished with antiques and reproductions of various periods.

The subdivisions of the American periods. It is more specific to delineate the American periods, though the styles produced before the 19th century are often linked together under the general heading, Colonial. The subdivisions are as follows:

1. EARLY AMERICAN (1608–1720 in Virginia; 1620–1720 in New England). Characterized by unpretentious wooden architecture and interiors, with little thought of design. Local materials used. Furniture in crude copies of Jacobean, Carolean, and William and Mary types.
2. GEORGIAN PERIOD (1720–1790).
   Increase in sophistication. Gradual introduction of Georgian architectural forms and furniture in more accurate copies of English Queen Anne, Early Georgian and Chippendale, Hepplewhite, and Sheraton forms.
3. POST-COLONIAL OR FEDERAL PERIOD (1790–1820).
   Influence of the Adam brothers. Hepplewhite and Sheraton influence continued.
4. GREEK REVIVAL PERIOD (1820–1860).
   "Temple" style of architecture. English Regency and French Empire influence in furniture design.
5. VICTORIAN PERIOD (1840–1880). Industrial developments submerged interest in the arts. Eclecticism dominated architectural and decorative designs. Romanesque, Gothic, and Mansart influence in architecture. Belter, Louis XV, and Eastlake influence in furniture.
6. ECLECTIC PERIOD (1870–1925). Architectural influence of the French National School of Fine Arts. Residential architecture influenced by Colonial, English, French, Italian, Spanish, and other historic styles, with corresponding interiors and furnishings. The end of this period witnessed the beginning of the reaction against style revivals and the acceptance of functionalism as a style directive.
7. CONTEMPORARY STYLE (1925 to present day). Buildings, interiors, furnishings, and industrial arts designed to fulfill modern requirements with the possibilities and limitations of new materials dominating as style directives.

Early American architecture. The principal difference in the development of the decorative arts in the United States and in those of European countries is that the early expression in America was that of an unsophisticated pioneer people whose demand was for satisfaction of the primary necessities of life; appearance was a nonessential, and beauty only an accidental result. The earliest productions were structural and functional in their forms; good proportions and charm of detail were gradual developments. European industrial art, on the contrary, originated in nearly every case in a conscious effort to produce luxurious surroundings for royalty or rich patrons of the arts in which visual appeal had as important a part as utility; these forms were finally imitated and cheapened for the middle classes and eventually influenced the peasant productions.

American architecture and decoration began as a distinctly provincial style in a country where the inhabitants were possessed of a humble refinement but had few of the earmarks of sophisticated culture. There was

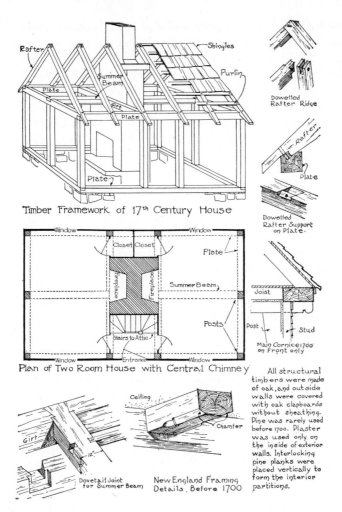

Timber Framework of 17th Century House

Window — Window

Closet Closet

Plate

Fireplace Fireplace

Summer Beam

Posts

Stairs to Attic

Window Entrance Window

Plan of Two Room House with Central Chimney

Dowelled Rafter Ridge

Rafter

Plate

Dowelled Rafter Support on Plate.

Joist

Post

Stud

Main Cornice 1700 on Front only

Ceiling

Chamfer

Girt

12″

Dovetail Joint for Summer Beam

New England Framing Details, Before 1700

All structural timbers were made of oak, and outside walls were covered with oak clapboards without sheathing. Pine was rarely used before 1700. Plaster was used only on the inside of exterior walls. Interlocking pine planks were placed vertically to form the interior partitions.

Plan, framing, and joining details of an Early American house showing twin fireplaces and location of structural posts, beams, and plates that were visible characteristics of the interior.

practically no thought of decoration in the earliest homes and at least at first the Early American style was the result of the effort of the first settlers to protect themselves from the weather, from the marauding beasts of the forest and from the intermittent attacks by Indians. It was not until the early settlers felt a comparative security in regards to these dangers that they were free to devote conscious effort in the direction of comfort and beauty.

Written records by Captain John Smith and others would indicate that those who first stepped ashore from England to become permanent settlers in America built huts or wigwams of clay, mud, bark, and limbs of trees, roofing their flimsy structures with thatch; but this type of dwelling need hardly be considered in a history of the decorative arts. It is even doubtful that the log-cabin type of structure was early adopted by English inhabitants. Probably the Swedes, who had come from a land of small wooden homes, and who settled in Delaware in 1638, were responsible for introducing the method of laying the trunks of trees on top of one another to form a wall, interlocking them at the ends with those of the adjoining wall, and filling the cracks with clay to make them weather-tight.

Practically all houses in both New England and Virginia were built entirely of wood during the 17th century. Oyster-shells, the early material for making lime, were difficult to obtain and made a plaster of poor quality. Other materials for making mortar were not found in abundance until around 1680. Stone houses were attempted without mortar, but were found to be too damp. A few houses were built of domestic bricks. Bricks were not imported into America, except possibly in a few cases as ship's-ballast on boats sailing from Holland to New Amsterdam. When plaster became more abundant but was still expensive, only the inside of the exterior walls of the house were sealed with it; the interior partition walls remained in wood planking. Three plastered walls and one wooden wall became a characteristic feature of the interior treatment of the rooms in the two-room house.

New England was extremely slow in developing an appreciation of architectural design or in adopting any of the academic forms of classical architecture for either the exterior or the interior of the house. While nearly all houses from the earliest period had wooden plank interior walls, it was not until the first years of the 18th century that rectangular panels became common, and some years later the design of trim began generally to be based upon classical architectural forms.

Houses in Massachusetts, Pennsylvania, and Virginia and other southern states were built of brick as early as 1670, and a few of these showed the first evidences of the use of classical trim in the interiors, or, as in the William Penn House in Philadelphia, of a definite frame to a mantel.

Colonial house plans. The development of the plan of the domestic dwelling in America follows an evolution that both reflects the growth of the country and gives increasing formality to room decoration. Variations occur in each locality but definite trends are seen. The earliest 17th century houses consisted of one all-purpose room with a large fireplace that served for both cooking and heating. This was followed by the two-room house with a central chimney located in the partition dividing the rooms and having a fireplace opening toward each side. The front door was centered in the middle of the long side of the house, and opened on a small entrance hallway which enclosed a steep stairway to the attic. The four-room house

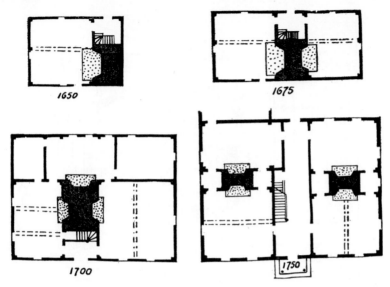

The development of the plan of the Early American house. After 1725 many more complex plans were introduced.

with a single central chimney was then attempted, but this required a diagonally placed mantel in the corner of each room and was found to be impractical. Two chimneys were then used, each one serving two rooms, and finally the central hallway running the full depth of the house was introduced. The "salt-box" type was characteristic of New England; this consisted of rooms added to the rear of the two-room house, while the rear part of the roof continued downward in the back to cover the extension. The southern houses usually had extension wings at each side added to increase their size. Virginia and the Carolinas were far in advance of the North in elaborateness of planning. In the South the first third of the 18th century saw many interesting arrangements intended for formal entertaining as well as comfortable living. Entrance halls and elaborate stairway designs became particularly important features. After the Revolution, the complexity of the plans increased. The Oval Room of the White House, planned in 1792, which was considered a great novelty and copied in many other localities, shows this advancement.

The Early American interior and the visibility of structural forms. The early settlers found oak and pine forests had to be cleared in order to obtain land for farming purposes. With an enormous supply of waste lumber, it was natural that the earliest houses were built of these woods.

The houses were constructed by the braced framing system. This was an adaptation of the English half-timber or whole-timber house, which had been in existence since Saxon days. A skeleton frame of heavy posts, *gird-*

Sketch of a typical Early American interior of about 1675, with fireplace wall treated with vertical pine planking, gun-stock corner post, summer beam, and visible structural form.

ers, and beams was assembled and interlocked by mortise, tenon, dowel and dovetail. The oak members forming the skeleton were larger than structurally necessary. The spaces between the posts were filled with wattle. Oak planks were used generally to cover both the inside and outside walls until about 1700. Pine was used thereafter.

The planks on the inside of the room were placed vertically, forming what is known as a *palisade* wall. On the outside they were placed horizontally, the upper one overlapping the one below, forming a *clapboard* wall. The planks, cut from first-growth trees, were of great width, sometimes exceeding three feet each, and they were used as they came from the log, in varying dimensions. To compensate for shrinkage of the vertical planks, and to make the wall as weather-tight as possible, a tongue was cut along the edge of each plank to fit into a groove on the adjoining plank. Simple ornamental moldings of varying shapes were also added along the joints. The wall thus had both an outside and an inside layer of planks for better weatherproofing, but the structural posts and beams always protruded on the inside. The exposure of the structural forms became a characteristic part of the room decoration. A very noticeable element in nearly all of these rooms was the large beam that spanned the width of the ceiling of the room near its center, one end of which was supported on the stone chimney, the other end resting on a post in the wall. This beam was known as the *summer beam*. All the woodwork was left in a natural finish; as pine

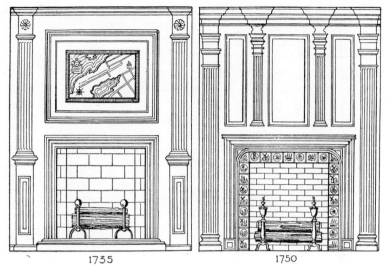

1735   1750

Two 18th century Colonial mantel treatments showing the early use of academic architectural features.

became red with age, the walls were warm in color and dark in appearance.

The earliest two-room frame houses had a central stone chimney with a single flue serving a fireplace in each room. One room was used as a combination kitchen, dining, and living room; the other was used as a bedroom for the whole family. The entrance hall was placed in the center of the house, and it often contained a steep ladder or stairway to the attic. The space at the side of the masonry of the fireplaces, between the two rooms, was usually turned into closets or cupboards. The attic was floored over, and the floorboards formed the ceiling of the first-story rooms.

The rooms were low-ceilinged, being seldom over seven feet high. The windows were at first of the casement type. Glass, oiled paper, or isinglass filled the panes, which were either rectangular or diamond-shaped, and were separated by either lead or wooden sash bars, forms borrowed from Jacobean architecture. Many windows had no glass at all, but were furnished with blinds. It is doubtful whether double-hung sliding sashes were used until after 1700.

The flooring of the first story was at first just earth. Stone was used, in some cases, but pine, oak, and chestnut planks of varying widths were soon adopted.

Design influences after 1700. It was not until the opening of the 18th century that the English trend in classical architectural forms, as introduced by Inigo Jones and Sir Christopher Wren, began to be reflected in America. Considerations of form and line only gradually developed importance. The styles of England were transmitted to the colonies partly

Connecticut interior of about 1735, showing early use of pine panelling as a substitute for vertical plank walls, an architecturally designed fireplace treatment, panelled summer beam, and cross-stiles in lower wall panels.

through immigration, partly through the importation of books on building and architecture, and partly by royal governors, who insisted on having for their residences houses that conformed to the dignity of their position.

The printing press was immensely influential in spreading the details of classical architecture among the general run of carpenters and builders. The English version of Palladio's work was particularly in demand, but the works of James Gibbs, Abraham Swan, Batty Langley, and William Halfpenny were eagerly purchased, and they had a very direct bearing upon the development of decoration as well as on that of architecture. The diffusion of these book designs tended to develop similarity in style in all parts of the colonies, and left little to the originality of the designer.

Furniture of the Early American period (1608–1720). Design and the development of furniture in the United States were influenced by the same elements that affected decoration. During the 17th century, the craftsmen who built the houses in many cases also produced the necessary interior equipment. The general divisions of the styles are, therefore, the same as those of architecture and interior decoration.

The major portion of American furniture followed English prototypes, and, broadly speaking, may be considered an English provincial style, since the same degree of crudity in both detail and proportion is seen that invariably occurs where furniture is imitated in a locality far removed from its original place of design and manufacture. Style changes were made slowly in the colonies, and new forms became popular several years after they had been introduced in England. In addition to the English types, styles of Holland, Germany, and France influenced the furniture craft where inhabitants from those countries had settled.

The early homes were but sparsely furnished; only the essentials were made or purchased. The whole of the 17th century reflects the design and character of Jacobean and Restoration forms.

The chest, cupboard, and desk-box, the turned and wainscot chair, the stool and settle, the trestle table, a few smaller tables, and such space-saving types as the table-chair and the gate-leg and drop-leaf table were used in the combination kitchen, living, and dining room. Four-poster beds, trundle beds, and wooden cradles formed the principal furnishings for the sleeping rooms, with additional chests for storage purposes. Clocks and mirrors were rare. Comfort was introduced by the use of loose cushions for chairs and stools, and the materials used for covering were usually imported silks, needlepoint, and embroidery. The housewife was too busy to weave textiles that could be used only for ornament or comfort. Textiles for clothing were more important.

Differences between Early American and Jacobean furniture. Although some of the early furniture was brought from England—especially the chests, which were used as travellers' trunks are today—the limited capacity of the early ships prevented quantity importation. Local carpenters and joiners were therefore called upon to produce the necessities, and it was natural that they should copy the existing imported models to the best of their ability, or that they should reproduce from memory the furniture they had known in England.

Certain local limitations characterized the productions of the period. Tools and facilities for fine cabinetmaking were less complete than in England. The American variety of oak and walnut was lighter grained than the English, and it was frequently found to be more convenient to use such native woods as pine, beech, ash, cherry, maple, elm, cedar, and cypress. Several different woods were frequently used in the same piece of furniture. The general tendency of furniture enrichment was toward simplification of both moldings and ornament. The American reproductions were often smaller than the English originals, to fit better the smaller rooms and lower ceilings in the colonial houses. Although the rectangular construction of the furniture of Jacobean England was maintained, the execution and enrichment were of a more primitive character.

Ornamental forms used with Early American furniture. The ornamentation consisted of turnings, strapwork patterns, applied split spindles, round or oval wooden handles, carving, and painting. The carved motifs were usually a crude imitation in low relief of English prototypes. Frequently they consisted of jackknife incisions in patterns unrelated to traditional forms, obviously representing the playful fantasy of some farmer's

Oak Chest of Drawers
Showing Split Spindles

Wainscot Chair

Ladder
Back Rocker 1740

1740

1650

Butterfly Table 1725

Hadley Chest 1680

Cupboard 1650

EARLY AMERICAN FURNITURE.

son or apprentice joiner who chose this method of passing the long winter evenings. The Tudor rose, the tulip, the sunflower, the acanthus, and the arcaded panel were frequently seen as carved motifs.

Character of individual early pieces. The chest, used as a container or seat, was by far the most important piece of furniture in the home, and was made in a variety of forms. The lid at the top was hinged, the sides were panelled, and occasionally it had one or more drawers at the bottom. As chests were heightened, the tops were used for the display of small objects of metal or pottery, and the hinged top then became impractical. The chest eventually evolved into the chest of drawers or bureau as it is known today. A special type, known as a *Connecticut chest,* stood on four short legs, had two rows of double drawers below the chest proper, and was decorated with large split spindles painted black to imitate ebony. The handles of the drawers were wooden ovals, usually placed diagonally. The *Hadley chest,* also of Connecticut origin but misnamed for a Massachusetts town, was similar, but it generally had only one drawer and was decorated with a very crude incised ornamentation. One type of small chest was known as a desk-box; this had a flat or slanting pine top, while the sides of the box were in carved oak. It held writing materials and a few books, among them the family Bible. The desk-box was finally placed on legs, evolving into the early type of slant-lid desk.

The chest was eventually placed on higher legs and became the cupboard, very similar in form to the English Elizabethan or Jacobean cupboard. There were many variations such as court, press, and livery cupboards, and all were used for the storage of food, clothing, linen, and other articles. The cupboard was made in two sections and was the most decorative piece of furniture in the room. It was usually panelled and richly carved or ornamented.

The tables of the period had turned legs; the tops were frequently of pine and had wide overhangs. Molded stretchers connected the legs. Drawers were sometimes placed in the apron under the top. Occasionally the apron was cut into a curved silhouette.

The drop-leaf tables were designed with many different types of contrivances, such as gate-legs, swinging arms, butterfly wings, and pulls, for supporting the hinged flap.

Chairs of the 17th century were built on straight lines. The oak wainscot chair, reserved as the seat of honor, was more simply ornamented than its English prototype, and had a panelled back, curved arms, and turned legs. The *Carver chair* had straight turned legs, the rear legs continuing upward to form the back uprights, between which were placed vertical and horizontal turned spindles. Stretchers strengthened the leg construction. *Slat-back chairs* were of similar design, but they had wide horizontal ladder rails between the back uprights. The tops of the legs and back uprights in both the Carver and slat-back types were usually terminated in a turned finial motif or a mushroom form. The seats were made of rush or of plain wood boards.

Most of the early chairs showed heavy proportions, but as the century progressed, the individual parts became lighter. Upholstered chairs with spiral turnings were introduced in the latter half of the 17th century, and these considered both comfort and design to a greater extent than had the slat- and spindle-back chairs. The upholstery material was either leather or

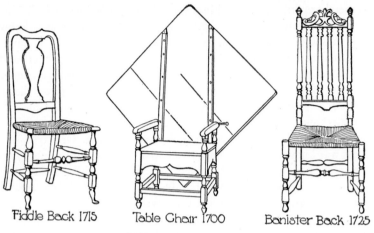

Fiddle Back 1715   Table Chair 1700   Banister Back 1725

EARLY AMERICAN CHAIRS.

turkey-work, a crude homemade material which vaguely imitated an Oriental rug weave and pile pattern, and was made by drawing wool yarn through a coarsely woven fabric backing.

Stools and long benches, called *forms,* fashioned in a manner similar to the chairs, were used with loose cushions.

Toward the end of the century the influence of the Restoration period in England was noticed in the introduction of the Flemish scroll forms of ornament. The S- and C-curves were seen in the carved cresting of the chairbacks or in the stretchers. The back upright sometimes consisted of split spindles or flat bars, called *banisters,* giving their name to the *banister-back* chair. The *Spanish foot* was also introduced during this period. Seats were made of caning.

At the turn of the century, trained cabinetmakers began to make furniture. The walnut forms of the William and Mary style appeared, with their bell turnings, shaped aprons, flat stretchers, and bun feet. Highboys known as tallboys, lowboys called dressing tables, and chests-on-chests were introduced in simplified designs. As a rule, the tops of these pieces were crowned by a simple molding rather than by a complete entablature, as in the English versions. Veneering and cross-banding in walnut and butternut were first used as furniture enrichment during this period. The elaborate marquetry patterns seen in England were not adopted in America. Trade with the West Indies was conducted from the American seaports on a large scale from an early date and mahogany, as a cabinetmaking wood, was probably first used in America about 1700, which predated its general use in England. On the whole, furniture began to be designed in more sophisticated forms in response to a demand for greater comfort and beauty in home furnishings.

Mid-18th century bedroom in the Isaac Royall House, Medford, Massachusetts.

Interiors of Georgian manor houses (1720–1780). As more formal dwellings of stone, brick, and wood replaced the early structures, the interiors were laid out with larger rooms and higher ceilings; and the columns, pilasters, entablatures, and cornices, which were first applied to the exterior only, were brought to the interior. At first the carpenters, who were untrained as designers, merely applied classic architectural details to the trim of doors, windows, and mantels, having little consideration for the composition of the walls or for organization of the spaces that were to be filled. Even the motifs were but rudely copied, and proper scale and proportion were neglected. Moldings were either too large or too small for their purpose. Cornices and entablatures were frequently too massive in their relationship to the height or size of the room for which they were intended. Balance in the arrangement of the architectural treatment of walls was considered seriously only in the largest houses. Unsymmetrically treated walls were common in farmhouses and in town houses of lesser importance. Mantels were placed in corners or at one end of the room, and doors and windows were used wherever necessary. In the same room, panels varied considerably in size and shape.

The North saw few of the academic forms in architecture used until after 1725 and these were mainly employed in the design of entrance porches; the South, however, was slightly more advanced. The earliest examples were those at Graeme Park, near Philadelphia, built in 1721, and at Westover, in Virginia, built about 1726. Both of these houses have wood-

*Salon from the Samuel Powel House, Philadelphia, 1769, showing one panelled
wall and the other three walls covered with hand-painted Chinese wallpaper. In this room the increased refinement of design is clearly indicated.*

panelled rooms, the panels of which rise the full height of the room from
a low dado to the underside of the entablature. Some of the doors were
framed with architrave moldings and treated with triangular pediments.
Overmantels were also elaborately crowned with well-designed pediments,
and the trim of doors and windows was frequently broken by "ears."
Arches were used for openings or to give an interesting form to a built-in
cabinet or niche.

In general character the rooms varied considerably between the severe
straight-line forms which dominated the designs of Palladio and the irregular curved forms evident in the scroll pediments of Louis XV origin that
were introduced through the French influence in Wren's designs.

Contrary to popular belief, no authentic proof exists that any building in
the colonies was ever directly designed by Wren. There exists, however, a
letter written in England in 1724 by the Reverend Hugh Jones to the effect
that Wren "modelled" the original building of William and Mary College
in Williamsburg, Virginia. The Wren and other English influences in
church and residential building developed through the local builders' application of published designs.

Pilasters and columns were extensively adopted, at first in crude proportions, but by 1760, in the traditional classic proportions. Doric and Ionic capitals were seen more frequently than Corinthian, possibly because the latter were more difficult to carve. As a general rule, pilasters were used to flank the mantel, accentuating its importance; but in a few rooms, as in the drawing room from Marmion, Virginia, now in the Metropolitan Museum, pilasters were spaced around the room, dividing the walls into vertical panels. In this room the complete order was painted to imitate marble, while the panels were painted with urn and ormolu forms, landscapes, and other decorations that were obviously copied by some itinerant painter from the illustrations of a book on French 18th century art. These paintings reflect an insufficient understanding of scale relationship to the architectural features.

Until about 1765 the popular type of panel molding was one formed by a narrow quarter-round on the stile; the panel itself was bevelled outward and raised so that the field of the panel was flush with the stile.* Occasionally, fireplace openings were trimmed with a large projecting bolection molding. This was borrowed from the bolection panelling introduced in England just after the Restoration period. Where the bolection molding was used, the shelf was usually omitted. Marble was frequently imported for mantel facings. Details of Colonial plank and panel moldings are shown on page 710.

From the middle of the 18th century a few rooms were finished with plain painted plaster walls between dado and cornice, although mantels continued to be treated architecturally, and the structural posts at the corners of the rooms were covered with pilasters. The painting of woodwork did not become common until about 1735, after which time many hues were used—gray-blue, pearl, cream, brown, red, mustard, and white being the most popular. Marbling and graining were also occasionally seen. Wallpapers were first imported about 1737, and from that year onward scenic and all-over patterns were used in both large and small houses.

Interiors of small Georgian houses (1720–1780). There are not many towns that can surpass the loveliness and fascination of the few remaining untouched southern and New England colonial settlements. Although at first only the most important citizens in each locality were able to build houses with a definite architectural character, the smaller landowners and wealthier farmers soon endeavored to introduce the classical academic forms in some or all of the rooms of their houses. With less experienced local workmen, the architrave trim, pilaster, cornice, and panelled walls of the mansions were copied, and in many instances, designs of extraordinary merit were created. In the majority of cases, the very lack of understanding of balance, composition, and scale became an asset. Odd forms and ideas

* See Chapter XX.

were carried out, producing a picturesque result that was simple, charming, and expressive of the culture of the period. The colonial gentleman of the mid-18th century desired and obtained home surroundings that expressed a considerable degree of culture and refinement.

In the smaller farmhouses, where wood panelling was not employed for wall decoration, the plaster walls were whitewashed, painted, or papered. Stencilling was sometimes resorted to as a decoration for both floors and walls, and many interesting old patterns still remain intact. Mural decoration was also resorted to as a means of enrichment. These paintings usually showed landscape effects; they were probably done by passing journeymen, who painted fences, barns, houses, furniture, portraits, or murals—the last two obviously showing the lack of technical ability on the part of the artist, and a resulting naïveté of interpretation that was consistent with corresponding architectural detail.

Georgian furniture (1720–1790). The new immigration of the early 18th century brought many craftsmen from England who had made the furnishing for the luxurious dwellings that were built in the Renaissance style. The developments in social living, in tea and coffee drinking, and in parlor games of chance had necessitated the introduction of many new forms of furniture, and the colonies were eager to adopt the rapidly changing manners and customs of the mother country. Style consciousness appeared in the early years of the 18th century, and people bought furniture for its design merits as well as for its use.

The cabriole leg with club foot, popularly known as the *bandy,* was followed by the claw-and-ball form. Curved lines began to dominate in the design of many pieces. The Queen Anne splat-back chair, called the *fiddleback* in America, was introduced. China cabinets to hold the precious collections of imported earthenware and porcelain were made as separate pieces of furniture and usually had triangular or scroll pediments. Oriental lacquer and Japan finishes were introduced, and imitations of these were made in ordinary paint. *Japanning* and *decalcomania* became fads with young ladies.

Desks and secretaries with slant lids and cabinet tops were popular and richly treated. Sofas, daybeds, and couches with upholstered coverings or loose cushions were introduced. The tilt-top, pie-crust table was adopted. Consoles, pier tables, knee-hole desks and tables, and *roundabout chairs* were much in vogue. Framed mirrors with bevelled glass, in both vertical and horizontal designs, were imported and copied. Tall case-clocks replaced wall clocks. For the first time, furniture was turned out in sets or in matched pieces for the same room. Spurred by the interest of the English people in the work of their individual cabinetmakers—largely a result of the publication of the books of Chippendale, Manwaring, and others—the Colonials, if they could afford to, hastened to follow the fashion of the

Sheraton Armchair

Hepplewhite Sideboard

Goddard Type Desk
showing block front

Mirror 1775

Philadelphia Highboy

Chippendale Sofa

Chippendale Chair

LATE COLONIAL AND EARLY FEDERAL FURNITURE.

times. English books on architecture, interior decoration, and furniture design had a large sale in America. From 1750 onward, the furniture of the popular cabinetmakers of England was both imported and reproduced. The reproductions were at times accurate, but they more frequently varied from the original in both detail and proportion. Soon, individual cabinetmakers in the colonies became prominent for their remarkable ability to reproduce the Queen Anne, Early Georgian, Chippendale, and later types of English furniture. Examples of their early work showed the cabriole leg with club, claw-and-ball, and lion's-paw foot. Just before the Revolution, the Marlborough form of heavy, straight, grooved leg with a small block foot was introduced. Highboys, lowboys, chests-on-chests, and bureaus were made for bedroom use. To give some idea of the type and number of household objects used in the residences during the Colonial period, the following advertisement is quoted from the New York *Gazette* of March 31, 1769:

"JOHN TAYLOR *Upholsterer* and *House-Broker* from *London;* BEGS leave to inform the gentlemen and ladies, and the public in general of the city of New-York, &c. that he has taken a large commodious house, situate on Cowfoot-hill in the city of New-York, aforesaid; where he intends carrying on the above branches in the most neat, elegant and newest taste possible. As the asserting the different prices of workmanship, is a thing frequently made use of to prejudice the too credulous part of mankind in favour of the advertiser, and is a means of their being exposed to impositions, which they at one time or other dearly experience, when too late to remedy; He therefore takes this method of informing them, that whoever shall be pleased to honour him with their favours, may depend on being served with any of the under described articles, with the greatest punctuality, and finished according to the above inserted manner, at the most reasonable rates, viz. Four post, bureau, table, tent, field and turnup bedsteads, with silk and worsted damask, morine, harateen, China, printed cotton or check furnitures; festoon, Venetian, and drapery window curtains, easy chairs, sophas, tent and camp equipages; floor and bed side carpets, feather beds, blankets, quilts and counterpains, sconce, chimney, pier and dressing glasses in mahogany, carved and gilt frames; card, dining, tea, dressing, and night tables; mahogany and other chairs, fire-irons, brass fenders, shovels, pokers and tongs, copper-tea-kettles, sauce-pans, and all manner of chamber, parlour and kitchen furniture too tedious to be mentioned. He likewise proposes where conveniency may suit the party, to take in exchange for work executed, any manner of old household furniture, as he intends furnishing houses with the above articles second hand as well as new.

"N.B. Plantations, estates, negroes, all manner of merchandize and household furniture bought and sold at public vendue.

"FUNERALS decently performed."

A group of craftsmen who worked in these styles were located in Philadelphia, and formed what is known today as the Philadelphia school of cabinetmakers; their productions are broadly classified as "Philadelphia furniture." They were particularly famous for their mahogany chairs, highboys, lowboys, and other pieces in the early Georgian and Chippendale styles. Among these men were Thomas Affleck, John Folwell, Benjamin Randolph, William Savery, and Thomas Tufft. Many of their productions

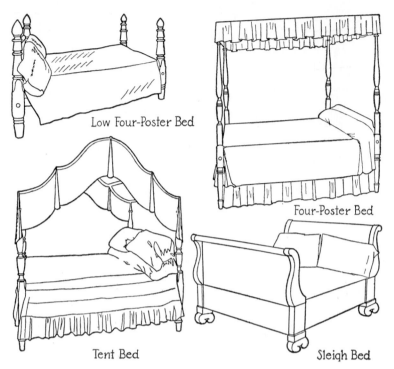

Low Four-Poster Bed

Four-Poster Bed

Tent Bed

Sleigh Bed

VARIOUS TYPES OF COLONIAL AND FEDERAL BEDS.

between 1742 and 1796 are considered among the finest examples of colonial craftsmanship, although they made many simple and inexpensive pieces, such as maple rush-seat chairs with slat, splat, or fiddle backs. Their successors continued to follow English fashions and produced Hepplewhite and Sheraton types of furniture in mahogany and satinwood. A great deal of this furniture is still owned by leading Pennsylvania families and many pieces still contain the labels of the makers. The few existing labels on Savery productions state that he is a joiner who makes and sells chests of drawers (highboys), coffins, and chairs.

About 1760 in Newport, Rhode Island, John Goddard, a cabinetmaker, and his relative, John Townsend, produced remarkable desks, cabinets, and chests of drawers of the *block-front* type. This form consisted of dividing the fronts of these pieces into three vertical panels, the two outside panels convex, the central one concave. A shell motif was placed at the top of each panel. In the majority of the Goddard pieces, the bracket foot was used.

In both the Philadelphia and Newport types, the rococo influence in design predominated. The curved line was seen in the legs and in steep scroll pediments. A certain amount of rich carving of French origin was

Fan Back 1770   Comb Back 1770   Loop Back 1770

AMERICAN WINDSOR CHAIRS.

also applied to small surfaces. Door panels were shaped in either rectangular or irregular Louis XV curves. The majority of pieces were made in well-selected Santo Domingo mahogany, while for others maple, cherry, and Virginia walnut were used.

The Windsor chair. The Windsor chair, modelled after its English prototype, became popular in America during the 18th century. It was probably not actually made in America until about 1725. The first official record dates from 1745 and the chairs were not made in quantity before 1750. Windsor settees appeared about 1766. By 1760 the Windsor form had completely superseded the inexpensive rush-seat chairs for common use.

The Windsor chair, although produced in great quantity and at low cost, reached a position of great dignity. Practically every house had one or more for both interior and garden use. George Washington had many at Mount Vernon. There is a record of 24 "ovel" back Windsors having been sold to Washington in 1796 by Gilbert and Robert Gaw of Philadelphia for use at Mount Vernon. This type of chair, which had a great number of variations, was also particularly in demand for public institutions and taverns. They were also used in dining rooms. Philadelphia was the earliest and principal place of manufacture, although great numbers were also produced in New York and Wilmington. In fact the Windsor chair was first known as a "Philadelphia chair."

The American Windsor had quite different characteristics from those of the chair produced in England. Its wooden seat was slightly shaped for comfort. Its legs and stretchers were composed of rather slender turnings, and the legs were set at a distinct slant or splay, the upper ends piercing the seat toward the middle instead of at the four corners, with a wooden wedge holding them in place. The backs were the most distinctive feature, and appeared in a great variety of forms. Hoop or sack, fan, brace, comb, and low backs were typical. The frame of the back was frequently bent and held in place by slender spindles starting from the rear of the seat. Windsors were also made to imitate bamboo. The English cabriole leg form and the pierced, ornamental, central back splat were very rare in American-made Windsors. Several different woods were used in the same piece, and the chairs were painted in black, and bright reds, greens, grays, and all other colors. White was not used. A few are recorded as having been stained or painted a mahogany color. The Windsor design continued to be manufactured throughout the 18th century. Rockers were made as early as 1745, although these probably had rush seats and were called "nurse chairs." The rocking chair was indigenous to America, and was first made by adding the curved supports to ordinary chairs. The Windsor type was the most common, but almost every other type of chair was used. The term *Boston-rocker* was applied to all. Although this type may have been made first in Boston, it was eventually manufactured in every state in the Union. Many were exported to Europe and South America and their popularity extended to the early years of the 20th century.

Country-made furniture. Travelling joiners and cabinetmakers were responsible for much country-made furniture. Kitchen and dining room dressers with open shelves, cupboards, corner cabinets, china cabinets, stools, chests, candlestands, and tables were made in local woods, such as pine, hickory, walnut, butternut, maple, ash, apple, cherry, and pear. The construction and detail of these pieces was of the crudest type, the styling of the simplest, and the finish usually paint. The most logical forms usually dominated the design, and it is often impossible to date them accurately, as the ornamental detail lacks relationship to traditional style development.

Pennsylvania German crafts. An interesting isolated development in peasant art was seen in that of the German and Swiss Mennonites,* who settled in eastern Pennsylvania near the cities of Germantown, York, and Lancaster. These impoverished refugees began to come from the Palatinate shortly after 1683 at the invitation of William Penn, who offered them peace, freedom of worship, choice of leaders, and a fertile land, all of which had been denied them as a result of the Thirty Years War in their homeland. The immigration continued until the outbreak of the American Revolution and consisted of almost every type of artisan. These simple peasants were industrious and ambitious and only too anxious to establish a new life for themselves and their descendants. The fact that they were settling in a land that was predominantly inhabited by the English has caused

---

* The Mennonites spoke German and called themselves "Deutsch"; their English neighbors anglicized the word and erroneously called them "Pennsylvania Dutch," a familiar designation that has persisted to the present day.

Kitchen from Millbach, Lebanon County, Pennsylvania, 1752, showing characteristic Pennsylvania German furniture and details.

them to the present day to be interdependent and isolated in their social, agricultural, and industrial activities. They have maintained their customs, language, religion, and arts by having little contact with their neighbors, and they have considered marriage with one outside their church a sinful union. They refuse to take oaths or bear arms and are not interested in politics. They dislike all forms of modernization, including bathrooms and electricity. Until the middle of the 19th century all that they used was produced by their own people, and in spite of their Quaker neighbors (who had no use for art or beauty), they never lost their love for color or sense of humor. Their productions were both ornamental as well as utilitarian. Simple lines and functional forms dominated the designs of their houses, furniture, and household accessories; symbolic ornament, gay colors, and sentiment were features of their patterns for textiles, paintings, and pottery. Their houses and barns in general resembled Colonial types and were often built in local stone. The wooden buildings were usually painted red. Symbolic *hex signs,* supposed to protect the inmates from the activities of witches, are painted on many of the exteriors to the present day.

The furniture was well made, of pine, cherry and other local woods, and was either painted or left in natural finish. Many of their chairs and seats resembled the Windsor forms. Brides' chests, hanging wall-cabinets, and wardrobes were usually enriched with naïve painted motifs in bright colors. Other furniture types were spice-boxes, work boxes, saw-buck tables, and dough-tables. The most usual motifs in the patterns were tulips, peacocks, eagles, rosettes, hearts, farmyard birds, deer, trees-of-life, leaves, and hex signs. The plaster walls of the rooms were usually white-washed, but folk pictures and elaborate birth, baptismal, and wedding certificates, called *frac-tur paintings,* were framed and hung as decorations. These latter consisted of elaborately painted scrolls and wreaths com-bined with birds and other mo-tifs with text material in Ger-man script. Wall panelling was usually frowned upon as being evidence of too great wealth, but overmantels were often treated in this manner. Pottery, tinware, and toys were ingen-iously designed and decorated with characteristic patterns. Many of their productions had both the maker's name and date of manufacture painted or carved on some part of the surface. Textiles were made from home-grown flax, and the linen was embroidered in nee-dlework and adorned with ap-

Taylor and Dull, Photographers

Pennsylvania German painted oak and poplar dower chest.

Pennsylvania German "Fractur" record of birth and baptism, dated 1801.

pliqué motifs. Kitchen and dining utensils were made in iron, copper, and wood, and were often hung on the walls of the kitchens as decoration.

The Dutch settlers in New York, Long Island, New Jersey, and the Hudson River Valley made painted peasant-type furniture at an earlier date than that made in Pennsylvania by the Germans, but very few exam-ples are extant.

Colonial mirrors. Looking glasses, as they were called, were not com-mon in America until the end of the 17th century. From 1700 onward, they closely followed the English patterns. The Queen Anne vertical wall and dresser mirrors were the first types used. These had plain walnut frames, often cross-banded or lacquered, with the characteristic broken curves at the top of the frame. The glass was usually bevelled, following the outline of the frame, and was divided into two panels. The upper panel often had an etched floral pattern. A single piece of glass was used after 1750. The frame frequently had an elaborately silhouetted cresting at top and bottom.

The Georgian post-Revolutionary type showed a rather heavily ornamented frame of architectural forms starting from a simple pedestal; the sides consisted of fluted pilasters, and the upper portion showed a scroll pediment, with a vase or eagle sometimes placed between the scrolls. The moldings were enriched with gilded carving. This type is known as the "Constitution" mirror.

Rococo and Chinese mirror forms were also popular, particularly in shapes suitable to be placed over mantels and sideboards. The irregular curved scrolls and leaves forming the sumptuously carved frames were usually gilded or painted white. The glass was frequently divided into two or three parts, and certain varieties showed pictures, painted decorations, or portraits of famous men as part of the design. These types were often the product of craftsmen who had imaginative skill and a great degree of understanding of traditional design. Occasionally, candle brackets were attached.

Simple Adam and Hepplewhite mirror types in rectangular, oval, and shield-shaped frames, with the customary paterae, classical figures, husk garlands, drops, and arabesque forms, were also made in either carved wood or composition material. These were hung on walls or made for table and bureau tops, and often stood upon small boxes of drawers.

The *girandole,* dating from 1760, but popular only after the Revolution, was originally a lighting fixture, as it was always made with candle-bracket holders. The mirror portion was round, and had either a concave or a convex surface. The frame was heavy, richly carved or ornamented, and was usually crowned with an eagle, and gilded. This type of mirror was prominently placed in the family parlor or dining room.

The Sheraton-type mirror was architectural in design and of slender proportions. Its frame consisted of a colonette upright at each side, crowned with a simple entablature that was frequently ornamented with a row of acorns. A small glass panel at the top was painted with a conventional pattern, a patriotic motif, or a scene. The wood was usually gilded. This type was not used until after 1800.

Clocks. The history of clockmaking in America is of considerable interest. During the 17th century, all clocks were imported from Europe. These were invariably of the wall clock type, consisting of an uncovered, decorated face made to set on a wall bracket or to hang on a nail, with the weights below. This type eventually became unpopular, and the face was later inserted in a tall case to form the grandfather type.

The first clocks made in America were probably produced in Boston and Philadelphia about 1700, and by 1712 Ebenezer Parmele in Guilford, Connecticut, was hiring apprentices to make clocks. Tall case-clocks came into use in the early years of the 18th century, and, so far as is known, the

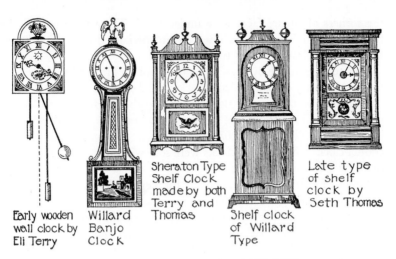

Early wooden wall clock by Eli Terry

Willard Banjo Clock

Sheraton Type Shelf Clock made by both Terry and Thomas

Shelf clock of Willard Type

Late type of shelf clock by Seth Thomas

DESIGNS FOR CLOCKS AND CLOCK CASES.

first made in America was by Bagnell in Boston in 1722. At this time the works were either in wood or brass, the case was in mahogany or maple, and the design followed the general form of the Queen Anne style.

Boston maintained the leadership in clockmaking during the first three-quarters of the 18th century largely because of Simon Willard and his brothers and sons. Benjamin Willard, the older brother, established a factory in Grafton, Massachusetts, about 1765. He probably made only tall case-clocks. Simon lived most of his life in Roxbury, near Boston. He made both wall clocks and tall-case clocks, but about 1800 he produced the banjo clock, which won immediate popularity. Willard retired from business in 1839, although his firm was continued a few years by his son, Simon, Junior. Simon Willard did not make his own cases. The wheels were always of brass, and the lower glass panels of his banjo clocks were rarely painted, and were left plain to show the swinging pendulum. The lower panels of the banjo clocks of other makers of the period were usually decorated with naval battle scenes, ships, flags, eagles, or landscapes. Aaron Willard was Simon's younger brother. After first working in Roxbury, he started a business in Boston in 1790. He made all kinds of clocks, and retired a wealthy man about 1823. His banjo clocks usually showed a painted picture in the lower panel.

Daniel Burnap was a clockmaker between 1780 and 1800 at Andover, Massachusetts, and later at Hartford and East Windsor, Connecticut. Very little is known about him, except that Eli Terry worked in his shop. His tall case-clocks had brass works, and often had moon-phase and calendar attachments. The dials of his clocks were frequently of etched metal, and the corners of square faces were undecorated. There were several clock-makers in Hingham, Massachusetts, who specialized in making "Grand-father" and "Grandmother" types.

Not to be outdone by Massachusetts, Thomas Harland started a clock-making industry in Connecticut. Harland had come to America from England in 1773 on the famous Boston Tea Party ship. He went to Norwich, Connecticut, and became the foremost clockmaker of his day, conducting a shop until he died in 1807. He advertised "Spring, musical, plain, and church clocks." Most of his clocks were sold without cases, the cases being made by local cabinetmakers.

One of Harland's apprentices was Eli Terry, who, with Seth Thomas, became the leading clockmaker in America. These two were responsible for establishing clockmaking on a large commercial footing. Terry made his first tall clock in 1792. In 1793 he moved to Watertown, Connecticut, where he made clocks with both brass and wooden works. This shop was continued until 1810, when Terry sold out to Seth Thomas and Silas Hoadley and transferred his operations to Plymouth Hollow.

Terry became particularly noted for his shelf clock, first made in 1814, and designed with the delicate proportions popularized by Sheraton. The clock case consisted of an architectural composition with pediment and base, slender columns at the side about 21 inches long, and a simple molding and scroll pediment at the top. The lower glass panel covering the weights and pendulum was usually decorated with an eagle or other ornament. A similar type of shelf clock was made by Seth Thomas about 1830, but the proportions were heavier and the clock lacked the grace and delicacy of the earlier Terry clock. Thomas, however, enlarged the clock-making industry to an enormous extent.

Miscellaneous accessories. The accessories used in 17th century American rooms were largely limited to necessary utensils: pewter cups, basins, ewers, tankards, and platters, occasional clocks, damask or needlework tablecovers, printed East Indian cottons, loose cushions, turkey carpets, spinning wheels, wrought iron and brass fireplace accessories, a lantern or two, candlesticks, copper kitchenware, pestles and mortars, and a warming-pan. Pictures and maps were sometimes hung on the walls. Inventories describe, also, window curtains, and valances in linen and silk—the latter probably imported. Very early wills list firearms, pikes, halberds, armor, and similar articles. Earthenware and china were also often mentioned. How many of these articles were imported is not known. The colors of textiles are described as red, blue, green, and yellow. Obviously, the early householders were fond of gaiety in their homes, and they attained it to the best of their abilities. The more well-to-do had an ample supply of jewelry, silverware, and books, and a few lived in an almost manorial manner.

After 1700 the decorative accessories increased in number and improved greatly in design. Many of them were still imported, but gradually the colonists themselves began to make certain types. Tall clocks and wall and mantel clocks were added as both useful and ornamental pieces of furnishing. Window draperies, made of imported textiles, were hung with valances, swags, and jabots with elaborate fringes and tie-backs. Velvets, damasks, taffetas, and other silks were brought to America in great quantity from France, Italy, Spain, Portugal, and England. Leather and haircloth were also used for upholstery purposes. Wallpaper from China, France, and England was used in many houses. Floor coverings were imported from the Orient. The smaller homes had loom carpets made of rags, and braided and embroidered rugs. Oriental china, both useful and ornamental, was popular in all homes from very early times. English Staffordshire, Wedgwood, Worcester, Chelsea, and Derby wares were largely imported from a date just previous to the Revolution. Delft tiles frequently were used to trim fireplace openings after 1750. Stiegel started his glassmaking in Pennsylvania in 1765. The Sandwich glass factory was opened in 1825. The wares of both of these factories were popular in Colonial or Federal rooms.

One of the most interesting developments in late 18th and early 19th century decoration in New England came as a result of the expansion of American shipping. The harbors of Salem, Boston, Newport, and other towns were swarming with ships of all sizes as early as the middle of the 17th century, and many of these sailed to the Orient. After the Revolution, trade with the Far East developed to great proportions, and the artistic and useful products of China, Japan, and India were brought to this country. These included furniture, silk, glass paintings, fine porcelains, Canton china, hand-painted wallpapers, embroideries, and other wares that became a part of the decoration of the American house.

The use of portraits in room decoration dates from a very early period. Until after the Revolution, these were painted, as a rule, by unknown artists. A group of American portrait painters developed during the Federal period, however, among whom were Gilbert Stuart, John Trumbull, and the Peales. Several French artists also came to America; among them were Saint-Memin, who worked mainly in Baltimore, and made crayon portraits, etchings, engravings, and silhouettes of great beauty between 1796 and 1810, and Houdon, the French sculptor, who modelled some of the early statesmen. Many interesting oil and water-color folk paintings were made in the 18th and early 19th centuries by unknown painters who, with their immature ability, produced work that was highly sympathetic in character and quality to the informal interiors of the period.

Engravings were first made in America in 1729. Maps and plans were the earliest subjects, but representations of places, people, and events were soon drawn. These formed the pictorial enrichment of the Colonial in-

Living room of John Ash House, Charleston, South Carolina, built in 1800, showing the tendency toward the delicate detail that was typical of the period.

terior. Foreign engravings, mezzotints, and other prints were popular during all periods.

The story of the art of the silversmith in America equals the history of architecture, decoration, or furniture. The artistic standard set by these craftsmen even from a very early date was astonishing, and deserves a special study. It is perhaps sufficient to say here that Paul Revere's real gift to the American people was in metalwork, and not in his more frequently mentioned patriotic deeds.

Crystal, mirror, silver, gilded wood, *turnings,* wrought iron, tin, and pewter were used for making chandeliers, whale-oil lamps, and other types of lighting fixtures.

In the early 19th century European manufacturers made many products for the American markets. Printed cottons, chintzes, toiles-de-Jouy, pottery and porcelain, bronze ornaments, clocks, and statues were produced showing figures of Washington, Franklin, and other American heroes. The Staffordshire potters reproduced, by transfer prints, American scenes and historical events on platters, teapots, and other earthenware pieces. All of these items served to introduce much variety and color in the decorative treatment of Colonial homes.

Interiors of the Post-Colonial and Federal period (1790–1820). The Revolution temporarily halted the arts but building quickly revived. The English influence, inbred in the race, was persistent, but the Declaration of Independence was to assert itself in the arts as well as in politics. This period witnessed the first appearance in the United States of professional architects and designers. The influence of both Jefferson and Washington in promoting a classical style for federal buildings was very strong. These men had felt that the new republic should be represented by the architectural forms of democratic Greece and republican Rome. Jefferson, who had been strongly impressed by the Palladian style adopted by Wren and Chambers, the English architects, had visited, while Ambassador to France, the Maison Carré in Nimes, an ancient Roman building; the Richmond Capitol, which Jefferson designed in 1789, was inspired by this building. Monticello was completed in 1809. The plans for the White House were made by Hoban of South Carolina in 1792. Charles Bulfinch of Boston and Samuel McIntire of Salem favored Adam classicism. John McComb of New York was undoubtedly influenced by the French Neoclassical style. Thornton, who designed the Capitol in Washington, had strong leanings toward Greek architecture and ornament. All of these men, however, were imaginative in their conceptions and added an American interpretation to these classic forms.

Perhaps the most important development was the consciousness of designers that a basic principle of design recognizes that each material has its own possibilities and limitations and that forms produced in one material should not and need not imitate those in another. The available books on architecture showed classical orders intended to be produced in stone. The Americans were using woodwork for both exterior as well as interior detail because it was available in large quantity, was cheap, and was easily worked. A trend developed to produce classical detail in slender proportions. Wooden columns were attenuated, moldings became relatively smaller, and ornament followed the Adam-Pompeian delicate detail and motifs. Rooms had higher ceilings in the more elaborate homes that were

Courtesy Museum of the City of New York

Courtesy Metropolitan Museum of Art

ABOVE: *Formal drawing room from a New York City residence built in the early years of the 19th century. The dignity, simplicity, and refinement of design evident here were typical of this period.* BELOW: *Room from Haverhill, Massachusetts, built about 1818, treated with a late 18th century wallpaper. The upholstered chair and the bed and window draperies show an English chintz patterned with American patriotic figures.*

built as the stride of the new nation began to be asserted. Less wood panelling lined the walls, but the dado and cornice continued in use. Many rooms had only the fireplace wall covered by woodwork, the other walls, being plaster, covered with either paint, imported silk textiles, or wallpaper. Greater formality and symmetry were introduced. Corinthian and Ionic columns were often part of the wall treatments. Scenic papers were imported from China, England, and France. Elaborately detailed trim was used for doors, windows, mantels, and arches. Pediments often crowned the doorways. Slender columns and pilasters were often enriched by a small-scale fluting or reeding. Moldings were treated with beads, pearls, and variations of dentil forms. Both semicircular and elliptical trimmed arches separated adjoining rooms. Charmingly detailed china cupboards aided in forming interesting balanced wall compositions. Dining rooms often had a wide, shallow, trimmed niche to hold the sideboard. Many mantels were made in white and colored marbles, following designs from the current books that showed Adam forms and ornament; small panels were centered under the shelf, and were carved in relief with classical figures, urns, medallions, swags, and garlands. Both carving and composition ornament were used for the wooden mantels. Ceilings were often treated with elaborate plaster relief patterns in Adam designs. Restraint and refinement in all trim was required for consistency with the more delicate proportions of the Sheraton and Hepplewhite furniture. Much unusual planning developed in residential design. Greater prominence was given to some of the stairways. Circular, oval, and octagonal rooms were introduced in both country and city residences.

Federal furniture (1790–1820). The Revolution to a certain extent halted the development of furniture craftsmanship in America, just at the moment when rapid style changes were occurring in England. Chippendale, Hepplewhite, the Adam brothers, and Sheraton were all influencing English taste, and it was not until peace had been restored for several years, that the changes in foreign fashion were reflected in the United States.

The Adam influence in America was seen more in interior architectural treatment than in furnishings, but the post-war furniture strongly reflected the designs of Hepplewhite and, more particularly, of Sheraton. The Hepplewhite sideboard, with its serpentine front, became popular. Chests of drawers and chests-on-chests were made with straight, segmental, and serpentine fronts. Fine veneering and inlay were seen. Proportions became light and delicate. Secretaries, tambour desks, dressing tables, and china cabinets were made with beautiful designs and finishes. Delicate scroll pediments enriched bookcases, cabinets, and desks. Tables were made in every shape and for every purpose. The popular woods were mahogany, satinwood, cherry, rosewood, maple, apple, and pear. Tall clocks, shelf clocks, and architecturally framed mirrors were used as accessories. Much

Courtesy Museum of Fine Arts, Boston

Courtesy Museum of Fine Arts, Boston

ABOVE: *Room from a house in Hanover, New Hampshire, about 1800. The Adam inspiration is evident in the architectural forms. The use of scenic wallpaper is especially interesting.* BELOW: *Room by Samuel McIntire, designed about 1801, in a house at Peabody, Massachusetts. Notice the Adam influence in the architectural forms.*

of the furniture after the Revolution and before 1820 was the product of trained English craftsmen, who had come to America for just this purpose. As a result, the American product is often indistinguishable from the English by design comparison, but can be identified by the woods that were used. Pieces made in the smaller towns by Americans have a tendency to be a little clumsy in their lines and proportions as compared with the English originals.

The French Revolution brought an influx of aristocrats, who carried with them what belongings they had been able to salvage. The influence of these French furniture importations was noticeable, particularly in the southern states.

The opening years of the 19th century saw a definite trend toward the furniture forms of the French Empire, interpreted by American cabinetmakers in a rather heavy and, at times, ostentatious manner. Simplification in detail and ornament usually occurred, although the construction of the furniture was equal to the European models. When ormolu mounts were used they were often of pressed and gilded wrought iron instead of cast brass.

Samuel McIntire. Salem, Massachusetts, became the capital of the state for a few years after 1774. While the British occupied Boston, it was the most important port on the Atlantic coast, and was the home of the fastest sailing ships on the ocean. Its four-masters sailed to India and China and returned with luxurious cargoes that enriched the homes of New England. Wealth flowed into Salem until the period of the War of 1812.

Samuel McIntire, the most famous citizen and craftsman-architect of Salem, was born in 1757 and was a man of considerable parts, according to the inscription on his tombstone, which reads, "He was distinguished for genius in Architecture, Sculpture, and Musick: Modest and Sweet manners rendered him pleasing: Industry and Integrity reputable: He professed the Religion of Jesus on his entrance on manly life; and proved its excellence by virtuous Principles and Unblemished Conduct." In addition, he was a carpenter, who built gates, fences, and doghouses; he designed and produced interior woodwork and furniture. He sang and taught instrumental music and he was a great inspiration in the arts for those who followed him. In 1792 he submitted designs for the proposed Capitol in Washington, which, however, were not accepted. He designed many of the dwellings in Salem and particularly the brick houses on Chestnut Street, which street is thought by many to be, in the springtime, the most beautiful city street in the United States. He was a master of proportions, detail, and texture. He admired the work of Bulfinch and owned many of the contemporary English books on classical architectural design.

McIntire's designs for interior woodwork were greatly influenced by the Adams of England. He was particularly noted for his beautifully pro-

*Salon in the Pingree House, Salem, Massachusetts, designed by Samuel Mc-
Intire in 1804. The woodwork is limited to the mantel, trim, and dado.*

portioned and carved mantels, cornices, dadoes, window and door trim,
and curved stairways. The fireplace walls of his rooms were usually entirely
covered with panelling. On the other three walls, plaster was used above a
dado. He was also famous for his ornamental wood carving, which was
sometimes reproduced in a composition material. The motifs used were
baskets of fruit, horns of plenty, sprays of grapes, festoons, rosettes, eagles,
urns, cherubs, female figures, musical trophies, and pastoral groups. He
modelled a bust of Voltaire, a profile relief of Washington, and many of the
ships-heads for the clippers that sailed from the port. He designed and
made fine furniture and obviously worked from the books of both Hepplewhite and Sheraton. When he died in 1811, his son Samuel Field McIntire
carried on his business for a few years but died "of intemperance" in 1819.

Duncan Phyfe. Duncan Phyfe (1768–1854) is popularly considered the
outstanding American cabinetmaker of the early 19th century. There is no
doubt as to his remarkable ability; whether he is to be considered superior,
however, to some of his predecessors or even to some of his contemporaries
is open to question. He came to America from Scotland as a young man,
in 1784. After learning the trade of cabinetmaking in Albany, New York,
he removed to New York City about 1790 and opened a shop of his own.
His success was almost instantaneous, and although he died a disappointed
man in 1854 at the age of 86, he left a distinct mark upon the industrial
arts of America. His finest work was produced between 1795 and 1818,
during which years he closely followed the Sheraton designs. His best
furniture was made in mahogany and satinwood and showed proportions

Cornucopia Leg Sofa

Lyre Back Side Chair

Sewing Table

Console
Showing flared legs

Arm Chair

Tall Case Clock

Sheraton Type Sofa

FURNITURE MADE BY DUNCAN PHYFE.

of the most graceful sort, with exquisite delicacy of line and detail. The Grecian curve in chair backs and legs, and the pedestal support for tables with concave flared legs were the principal forms that were used. Turning was also employed. Carved ornament of the most refined variety was executed with extraordinary craftsmanship. He used reeding a great deal on his frames for chairs and sofas, the legs of which often ended in conventionalized animal feet. The lyre form was frequently used for chair backs, sofa arms, and sometimes for table supports. The cornucopia leg was also

Courtesy Parke-Bernet Galleries, Inc.

American Empire sideboard attributed to Duncan Phyfe, made about 1815.

used. Other motifs were swags, tassels, rosettes, vase forms, bowknots, and the thunderbolt. In his later work he used maple, rosewood, and black walnut, as well as mahogany. Metal feet, roller casters, and metal surface ornaments were also occasionally employed. Toward 1830 his productions showed French Empire and English Regency influences that are often referred to as "American Empire" pieces. Carved ornament followed Grecian forms and furniture was additionally enriched with cast or wrought brass mountings. Around 1840, competition with the manufacturers of machine-made furniture caused him to produce massive, clumsy pieces that he knew to be ugly, and in which the only agreeable feature was the graining and color of the woodwork. It is said that he referred to this furniture as "butcher furniture" and much of it was made when his shop was under the direction of his son.

The American Eagle period. The wave of patriotism that developed at the time of the War of 1812 caused an increase in popularity of the use of the bald eagle as a national emblem. The Continental Congress had decreed the use of the symbol in 1782, and it had been the symbol of power used by ancient nations. American designers adopted it as a pattern motif in every medium. It was used to crown the pediment of entrance doorways, it was painted on windowpanes, and it was used as a finial motif on vertical features of every type in architecture and decoration. American cabinetmakers commercialized the form and it was introduced as a support for chairs, tables, and consoles, and became part of the designs for wall sconces and candelabra. Mirrors, picture frames, and clocks were crowned with the motif and it formed the basis of glass and chinaware patterns. Every conceivable manner of drawing, painting, and carving the American eagle was utilized.

Patriotism was further expressed by painted decorations and decalcomania pictures showing the naval engagements of the War of 1812. The fight between the U. S. F. *Constitution* and the H. M. S. *Guerriere* was a particularly popular scene. Most of these scenes were placed on the upper panel of the Sheraton mirrors or on the lower portion of shelf clocks.

Hitchcock chairs. During the early 19th century a "fancy chair," based on Sheraton Empire forms, was manufactured in Connecticut and widely sold among New England farmers and owners of small homes. In 1818 its originator, Lambert Hitchcock, established a factory of chair parts in Barkhamsted, Connecticut, sending them to the South for assembly. By 1823 he was assembling them himself at his factory in Hitchcocksville, Connecticut, marking them "L. Hitchcock, Hitchcocksville, Conn. Warranted." In 1832 his business failed, but before long he was busy again. During this period, the chairs bore the marking "Hitchcock, Alford and Co. Warranted." In 1841 he established a new factory in Unionville, Connecticut, where a large production occurred. The chairs made in this factory were signed "Lambert Hitchcock." He died in 1852. His product was made in slender proportions, partly by hand and partly by machine, and was usually painted black. The legs were turned, the seat was painted rush, and the back was usually designed with horizontal rails and vertical slats. The top rail was widened, gently curved, and was stencilled, or decorated with a gilt

From "Early American Decoration," by Brazer   ©

An original stencilled chair labeled "L. Hitchcock, Hitchcocksville, Conn. Warranted." Made about 1827.

decalcomania pattern. Motifs included the horn of plenty, drinking birds, eagles, leaves, flowers, and fruits. The pattern has been imitated by other New England chair factories to the present day.

Shaker furniture. The Shakers were a communal religious sect that believed in frugality, industry, integrity, and celibacy. They produced some of the most honest and forthright furniture made in the United States during the latter part of the 18th and the early 19th century. They were active in New England, New York State, and Kentucky. Quality of workmanship was a part of their religion, the standards for which were set by the community at Mt. Lebanon, New York, the "mother house." The furniture was plain, free from carved ornament, moldings, or veneers. Though sturdy, it was, as a rule, delicate in its proportions. The cabinetmakers were spiritually dedicated to their tasks and every piece was made with great technical care.

Nineteenth century Shaker table.

The Shaker belief in the utility of every household object produced a type of furniture which bears out the modern precept that form should follow function and that true beauty rests on the suitability of an article to its purpose. The furniture was made of pine, cherry, maple, and other local woods that were lightly stained or given a thin, clear wash of red, blue, or yellow. Almost all of the furniture was made for the use of the community, and not for the "world's people." Some of it was sold to outsiders in later years. The rooms of Shaker houses were marked by the predominance of built-in cupboards, chests, and drawers, each designed for a specific storage purpose. Cleanliness and orderliness were dominating requirements of the group. All furniture was carefully joined by mortise, dowel, or dovetail. Built-in pieces and dining tables were large because their use was shared by many persons. By contrast, free-standing pieces, such as chairs, were rather light in scale, as the Shakers had nothing in their houses which could not easily be moved for cleaning. Straight chairs resembled early American ladder-backs, with seats of woven splints or brightly colored hand-woven tapes in herringbone, chevron, striped, and checked designs. Certain chairs recall the American Windsor type. Beds, usually painted green, had low head- and foot-boards, and wooden casters

Nineteenth century Shaker rocker.

for easy rolling. Highboys, chests, washstands, slant-top desks, sewing cabinets, blanket chests, stools, benches, and swivel chairs were also made.
Other interesting Shaker products were their handmade tools for carpen-
tering, agriculture, and household duties.

Shaker furniture, because of its simple, clean lines, and functional qualities, may be successfully combined with contemporary pieces in modern
interiors as well as used in informal Colonial rooms.

The Greek Revival (1820–1860). The second quarter of the 19th century
witnessed a stylistic revival of complex origins. The early statesmen had
urged the use of Greek and Roman types of architecture as being most
suitable for federal buildings and this thought penetrated the minds of
the residential designers. The French Empire forms and Sir John Saone,
the master of Regency design in England, also had their influence. Books
covering the architecture, decoration, and furnishings of these foreign
styles began to flood the United States. Sympathy for the Greeks in their
war of independence (1821–27) had a powerful appeal for the public.*
Byron became the literary god of the day and the secret passion of every
romantic young woman. The expansion of the country and its mounting
wealth and immigration developed an urgent need for new dwellings from
the Atlantic to the Middle West. Magazines began to discuss architecture
and the arts, showing an increasing interest in these subjects. Americans
began to make the "Grand Tour" of Europe. Eastern cities were given
Greek names, such as Athens, Troy, Ypsilanti, Sparta, Ithaca, and Syra-
cuse. The English Renaissance forms of Wren and the Pompeian types of
Adam had become old-fashioned. They were Colonial. In the natural
human demand for change, what could be more worthy than the per-
fections of Greek art? The "Temple" style of architecture, with its pedimented portico, based on the Parthenon, was being used for public buildings and churches; why not apply it to residential construction? † Style
interest surged toward Hellenic forms. The Greek orders began everywhere to be used for both exterior and interior design. Consistency called
for Greek detail and ornament in interior trim. Doors and windows were
crowned with pseudo-Greek pediments, often simple triangular panels
without moldings; friezes were enriched with *triglyphs,* rosettes, or classical figures. The anthemion, acanthus leaf, honeysuckle, and fret became
the basis of all ornament. The Greek moldings of changing curvature were

* Horatio Greenough at this time made a colossal statue of Washington, his nude body
draped to represent a Greek god. The Father of his country is shown surrendering the
sword, the symbol of War and Victory, and directing the Nation to the God of Peace. This
statue is now in the Smithsonian Institution.
† American cities from Maine to Georgia and as far west as Michigan and Missouri are
replete with examples of this style, such as the Subtreasury and the residences on Washington
Square in New York City; Lee's Mansion in Arlington, Virginia, the Custom House in
Boston, Massachusetts; the university buildings in Lexington, Virginia, and in Amherst,
Massachusetts; the Ohio State Capitol; and many houses in Natchez, Mississippi; Athens,
Georgia; Harrodsburg, Kentucky; and Charleston, South Carolina.

*Victorian room in Richmond, Virginia, showing pressed brass window cornices
and mixed French and Greek revival details in furnishings.*

everywhere in evidence in both stone and wood construction. The drawings rooms or parlors in the houses of this period were usually separated
from the dining room by Greek Ionic or Corinthian columns that formed
an important decorative feature and were intended to frame the sliding
doors between the rooms. Ceilings were high and walls were usually
painted a plain color or covered with a wallpaper. Window draperies were
often treated with pressed brass valances. Furniture was designed in the
heavy "American Empire" style with frequent use of the Greek curves
and metal ornaments. Chair and table legs were often capped with plain
or ornamental cast-metal feet and usually had swivel casters.

The Greek Revival was a borrowed style but the adaptations produced
by the American designers had charm and dignity sufficient to give it a
native character. As the designs of the period were American first and
Greek afterward, a continuous national stylistic expression might have
evolved. The decline was due largely to the Civil War and the economic
changes of the reconstruction period. The entrance of the millionaire upon
the American scene, the adulation of wealth and materialism, and the sudden love of display were the death of art. The country grew more rapidly
than the supply of connoisseurs, artists, and designers. Fortunes were made
overnight and the gods were those who were lucky. Ostentation and effect,
regardless of the materials and methods of attainment, became more important than character, logic, and refinement of line, form, and color. The
result of this philosophy was seen in the last half of the century, which was

characterized by boldly conceived eclectic efforts that were based on the principle that if beauty must come from a past style, why should one be limited to the Greek? The 20th century was to question this esthetic theory.

The Victorian trends in architecture and decoration (1840–1880). The term "Victorian" as applied to the mid-19th century decorative arts in America is only partially correct. With a public mainly interested in industry, art was quite secondary. The promising seeds that were sown during the Greek Revival apparently were considered inadequate to reflect the wealth and power of the rapidly growing nation. No great stylistic leaders appeared and the few voices that expressed themselves were disregarded.

From "Charleston: Photographic Studies," by F. S. Lincoln. Copyright F. S. Lincoln.

Detail of doorway and cornice, Steele House, Charleston, South Carolina, built about 1815, showing early evidence of Greek revival.

Novelty was demanded, but connoisseurship was lacking. Ideas could be borrowed more rapidly than conceived, and logic and a native expression seemed unnecessary. England was the most obvious source of inspiration, although the eternal leadership of France could not be ignored. Designers also searched fields that were more distant in both time and place. The Victorian period witnessed a rapid succession of confused style revivals, all of which overlapped, were nonreflective of their times, and were impurely and inconsistently applied.

The Greek Revival overlapped a Gothic revival. This had been inspired by the building of the Houses of Parliament in London, by Ruskin's, Morris', and the later Eastlake's books, and by Pugin and Viollet-le-duc, the French Gothicists.* The result in the decorative arts was an absurd use of wooden pointed arches, vaults, and windows; clustered columns; jigsaw ornament; and stained glass. These details were accompanied by furniture and accessories in naïve Gothic detail. Engravings and lithographs showed religious, sentimental, or depressing subject matter. However, this style, logically suited to church design, produced excellent applications of Gothic architecture in Trinity Church and Saint Patrick's

---

* The protests of these men were studied more attentively in the first quarter of the 20th century when "functionalism" became a much discussed esthetic principle.

Greek revival doorway to Victorian parlor, Stanton Hall, Natchez, Mississippi, showing overlapping of the two styles.

Cathedral in New York City. About 1850 Louis Napoleon had revived the style of Mansart in adding new wings to the Louvre, and Garnier later built the Paris Opera House. Napoleon's Spanish wife, Eugenie, with a sparkling personality and clothes of extraordinary chic, entranced the Western world with her cultural dictates. American builders, with a woeful lack of data, were hardly competent to interpret Mansart. Their attempts produced some fantastic architectural abortions that have been designated the "General Grant" style. Houses were given steep mansarded roofs, pierced with dormers. Façades were enriched with incorrectly proportioned classical orders. Ostentation was expressed by cupolas, porte-corchères, and large bay windows, all of which affected the interiors. Lawns were covered with hydrangeas. Castiron dogs and stags startled approaching visitors. Cities were crowded with houses having high-stooped brownstone fronts and a standard plan with a front and rear room completely devoid of esthetic consideration. Ceilings were high, halls were narrow, and interior rooms were without windows or lighted by the most meager of shafts. The jerry-built house was on its way.

The next influence in American design was that of H. H. Richardson, the architect who built Trinity Church in Boston, Massachusetts. A man of extraordinary genius, he revolted against both the Gothic and Mansart revivals and turned to the primitive forms of the round-arched Romanesque. He employed John LaFarge the muralist to decorate the most colorful and famous church in America, finished in 1877. Richardson's influence was enormous. The style he worked in was logical in stone, but thousands of imitators produced the Romanesque wooden house to which the appellation "Queen Anne cottage" has been misapplied. Supposedly picturesque, romantic, and rambling, this type of residence had high gabled roofs, corner towers, and balconies and was covered by shingles applied in patterns. The interiors were badly planned, and rooms were often irregular in shape, with circular bay windows. Ornament was almost entirely produced by the turning-lathe. Machine-made detail accomplished its worst. Balusters, spindles, wooden grilles, and dwarf columns were used in profusion. The

Parlor in Theodore Roosevelt House, New York City—about 1860.

use of golden oak was the cachet of respectability. Panelled wainscots, false beamed ceilings, parquet floors, heavy wooden trim, and massive moldings in this wood were introduced in all important rooms. The contemporary architectural and decorative publications show a very mixed effort for room adornment. Wall composition and orderly furniture arrangement were apparently disregarded. Antique furniture was little in demand and unity of style was not contemplated at all. An excessive use of unrelated patterned surfaces on walls, floors, and upholstery often occurred. Walls were covered with wallpaper of poor design, painted stencil patterns, or real or *papier-mâché* imitation Spanish leather. Furniture and accessories of hybrid styles cluttered the rooms to a disturbing degree. The Oriental rug became popular and was often covered with a lion, tiger, or bear skin, with a head having a snarling mouth. Marble slab mantels with arched fireplace openings were often used; the ornament was crudely made with an incised and gilded line. Bright colored bricks and tiles were also used for mantel facings. Overmantels were treated with numerous shelves and vertical subdivisions. A high decorative frieze was carried around the room. Portieres were often made of glass beads, shells, or short lengths of bamboo. Windows were swathed with heavy draperies, swags, valances, and jabots, enriched with heavy fringes. The Turkish divan became the most important decorative feature in every interior.

Victorian furniture and the beginnings of machine production. As previously mentioned, by the beginning of the third decade of the 19th century the American people were dominated by industrial and geographical expansion, and science and invention, being highly profitable, occupied the imaginations of the most talented. Even those artists who had already made names for themselves had turned to industry for a living. Robert Fulton, the portrait painter, perfected the steamboat in 1806. Samuel F. B. Morse, the painter and professor of fine arts, perfected the telegraph instrument in 1844.

However, during this period, furniture had to be manufactured and sold. Many manufacturers endeavored with poor success to make the machine do what the hand had done before. Style books on furniture design continued to be produced and published in both England and America showing clumsy interpretations of the French Empire forms, of classic frets and honeysuckles, and of Egyptian motifs. For want of better inspiration, many designers harked back to the Gothic period, which had, in part, been popularized by the writings of Sir Walter Scott and Victor Hugo. Beginning about the middle of the century, the most fantastic interpretations of the rococo forms of Louis XV furniture were made in black walnut, rosewood, and imitation ebony. Few cabinetmakers had sufficient design knowledge to retain the charm of the structural curved forms of the original models. The movement continued well into the last quarter of the century. This was the result of blindly following Paris fashions, which had tended toward a revival of Louis XV work after the short restoration of the monarchy under Louis Philippe in 1830, and the popularity of French fashions under Louis Napoleon.

One of the most important developments was the introduction of all-upholstered furniture as a result of the invention of the coiled metal spring. Single seats, built-in sofas, circular seats, dos-à-dos, vis-à-vis, three-seated "confidantes," "comfortables," and a host of other cushioned types became popular as the public lost their sense of dignity and demanded Oriental ease in both public and private rooms. Upholstered furniture was made with elaborate cord, fringe, *galloon,* button, and tassel trimmings, harmonizing with the elaborate draperies of the period. Popular upholstery fabrics were bright red and green plush and black horsehair. The furniture of this period was, on the whole, unpleasant in appearance. Jigsaw ornament, which was easy to make with the new machines operated by steam, became common. Furniture legs were usually turned, because this form was inexpensive to produce. The English Eastlake influence was seen in the shallow grooves following straight and curved lines, accentuated by gilding that was applied as ornament to the wood frames.

The Victorian period produced the *whatnot,* the *hassock* and *ottoman,* the Turkish divan, nests of tables, gas lights, papier-mâché furniture, mother-of-pearl inlay, *blackamoor* statues, parlor-gem pianos, tidies, *antimacassars,* needlework mottos, shell and bead curtains, sentimental steel engravings, chromolithographs, and charcoal portraits. The machine production of wallpaper and rugs tended to reduce the scale and length of pattern repeats. The use of these objects continued well into the last quarter of the century.

The most complimentary statement that can be made concerning the American Victorian period is that it exactly expressed the lack of taste of the people. Interested in almost everything but art, they obtained no art. Art, beauty, and the spirit were

Carved rosewood chairs by John Belter, made about 1855.

doomed under the assaults of materialism and industry. This period is a perfect example of how the cultural level of a people is reflected in their art forms and how no art can be produced without a public which has an understanding and need for it.

Belter furniture. One of the leading furniture makers of the Victorian era was John Henry Belter, who made chairs, sofas, and case-pieces in fanciful but durable designs, displaying vitality, spirit, and master craftsmanship. (Most of the forms were vaguely based on Louis XV designs, the revival of which was extremely popular.) Belter was a native of Germany, who in 1844 established a shop in New York City, and in 1856 applied for a patent on his method of making furniture. Though some pieces were of stained oak, black walnut, or "blackwood" (hardwood painted to look like ebony), the finest ones were of richly figured tropical rosewood, built up of several layers of thin veneer glued together, each layer laid at right angles to the next, then steamed and pressed in a special matrix designed to mould them into the desired curved surfaces. He was therefore one of the earliest cabinetmakers to use laminated products. The surfaces were pierced with elaborate lacelike openwork designs and then carved with fruit, flower, and foliage forms. Some pieces are carved, without piercing; others are plain but shaped in a serpentine curve to give them interest. Another feature of Belter's work was the application of extra pieces of solid wood to the veneers for ornament in high relief. Drawers of case pieces show precise joinery and are lined with plain or bird's-eye maple. The frames of chair and sofa backs, instead of being upholstered, were often covered with rosewood veneer. Belter's designs were in great demand among the wealthy residents of New York and of other cities farther afield during the 1840's and 1850's. Evidence of the volume of his business is given by the fact that, in 1858, he owned a factory said to have employed forty apprentices. From 1860, Belter's furniture declined in popularity due to the increase in cheap mass-production goods and the disappearance of the rich market that had existed before the Civil War. After his death in 1863, Belter's partners continued production until the post-war financial depression brought about the final collapse in 1867.

Victorian accessories. During the mid-19th century period John Rogers (1829–1904) produced small statues, in bronze or a putty-colored composition material, the use of which became popular as parlor ornaments. The subject matter was usually sentimental or historical. Civil War heroes, personages, and groups of figures taken from the popular literature of the day were represented. Characteristic titles were "One More Shot," "The Wounded Scout," and "Rip Van Winkle."

The Currier and Ives colored lithographs were also produced during this period. Currier established his business in 1835 in New York, taking Ives in as a partner in 1857. An enormous range of subject matter was covered in these prints, which wholesaled at anywhere from six cents apiece to a little over a dollar. Popular subjects were disasters, important news events, various sentimental subjects, scenes of family life and all types of sporting events. The pictures were not meant for drawing-room use. They were hung on the walls of less ostentatious homes, schoolrooms, nurseries, stores, offices, steamboats, taverns, and hotels. The original drawings were produced by several artists, the quality of whose work varied greatly. While both the Rogers groups and the Currier and Ives productions can hardly be called works of art, they were representative of the taste of the times.

Another popular and inexpensive accessory found in almost every small home in America between 1770 and 1845 was the portrait silhouette. Itinerant artists peddled their skill from door to door, or held forth at country fairs. The usual method used was to reduce the shadow of the subject's profile by means of a lens, then trace or cut the image from paper. In some cases the profile was sketched by the artist and elaborately painted with very fine detail. They were of white paper mounted on a ground of black silk, velvet, or paper, or of black paper mounted on a white ground. So popular were silhouettes all over the country that many people with an urge to travel turned to this means of livelihood, sure of a welcome and a night's lodging wherever they went, selling their services for a few cents. By the 1850's, however, the popularity of silhouettes had been killed by the introduction of the *daguerreotype* process of photography. Sensing the coming change, many silhouette artists opened photographic studios. Daguerreotyping was discovered by Louis Daguerre in France in 1839. The chemical process involved the coating of a copper or glass plate with silver, sensitized with a solution of iodine. On exposure of the treated plate to light, an image was produced that was afterward fixed in the plate by the application of other chemicals. The image in a daguerreotype is rather faint, and must be viewed at an angle to be clearly seen. Between 1848 and 1860 these photographs were produced in great quantities and a collection was to be found in every Victorian parlor.

Daguerreotype cases with covers represent the first use of plastics in America. They were moulded of gutta-percha, the sap or gum from a Malayan tree, mixed with a combination of wood, flour, and other bonding ingredients, in a variety of styles. Historical, patriotic, and sentimental themes; political and fraternal emblems; baroque and rococo forms; as well as Christmas, Easter, and Valentine designs were used as patterns. Characteristic subjects were the Capture of André, the Coming of Saint Nicholas, Jenny Lind, and the Shield and Stars. These patterns were produced on the covers in relief by means of a die. Daguerreotypes and their cases are now collectors' items; but, they are also often used as accessories in the modern interpretations of Victorian rooms.

Influence of the Philadelphia Exposition of 1876. Mention has already been made of the influence of the Centennial Exposition held in Philadelphia in 1876. This exhibit undoubtedly contributed to a greater appreciation of the relative importance of art in daily life. No standards of design were set, but the art-consciousness of the nation was given a definite start again, after more than a generation of lethargy. The improvement of economic conditions after the Civil War reconstruction period, the development of natural resources, and the general industrial and agricultural expansion, combined with the building of the railroads, had helped to create a more widespread wealth. Wealth brought leisure, and leisure gave impetus to a demand for art and culture. A natural urge developed among those who had acquired wealth to surround themselves with furnishings that reflected their growing culture.

Improvement in art education. The Metropolitan Museum of Art in New York City was founded in 1870. Several books were issued on home decoration, and new monthly and weekly publications on art subjects were initiated. A movement was started urging wealthy men to leave endowments for the support of art schools and societies. One New York art monthly stated in 1885, "It is time the importance of this branch of education [architecture] was brought to the notice of our rich men, that they may do something to promote this practical and useful division of knowledge. The schools are few where the architect and decorative arts student can even learn the rudiments of his art, much less the historic and scientific parts."

The gradual improvement in comfort, speed, and safety in ocean-going vessels, which was coincident with the growth of the leisure class, increased the popularity of pleasure travel to Europe; and the visits of thousands of

Americans to the well-established museums of France, England, Germany, and other countries undoubtedly contributed greatly to the growing art consciousness.

Paris, leader of style and fashion, and center of the art production of the continent, with an annual salon and many well-known art ateliers, had a particular appeal for the new American connoisseurs. American architectural students in considerable numbers attended L'Ecole des Beaux Arts in Paris, and upon their return were called upon to design reproductions of French châteaux * to house the newly rich. The fortunes made from the railroads, from the steel and oil industries, and from the gold, silver, and copper mines paid for them. As a result, New York became the center of the art world of America, and during the decade from 1870 to 1880 many important art schools and organizations were founded there.

Eclecticism of the end of the 19th century. During the last two decades of the 19th century, many Parisian decorators, finding a ready market for their *antiques* and reproductions of the Louis styles, opened branch shops in the United States. These shops promoted the use of reproductions of 18th century French styles in the pseudo-French châteaux that the rich were building.

In the smaller residences in New York, little intelligent thought was given to creating an original or appropriate decorative style for interiors. The art periodicals of this period showed source material from Italy, Spain, Germany, China, Japan, India, and Turkey, and all were frequently used in the same rooms. Lack of consistency and harmony was prevalent. Sentimentalism was rampant in pictures and in accessories, and eclecticism was more important than originality.

Many of the attempts to improve home surroundings by transposing the arts of other countries were haphazard and illogical. A generation was to pass before intelligent results were seen in adapting foreign styles to local conditions; and even then, both the artists and the public little realized the anemic and unimaginative quality of an artistic effort that was imitative without being creative. The movement was not, however, entirely without merit. Many magnificent importations and accurate reproductions of Italian, Spanish, French, and English rooms were assembled. The movement served as a stepping-stone, was educational, and showed the results of the art expression of other peoples and other times, even though, for a long period, an analysis was not made of the basic principles that produced these outward forms, nor was their suitability of adaptation considered. Clients arbitrarily chose to have a Tudor Mansion, a Normandy farmhouse, a Georgian manor house, an Italian villa, a medieval castle, or any one of dozens of other styles and types, so long as they were accurately reproduced, effective, comfortable, furnished in antique or correctly re-

* "Biltmore" in Asheville, N. C. is the most prominent extant example of this period.

*The belfry and a view of the interior of San Carlos Mission, Carmel, California,
showing catenary arched vault.*

produced furniture of the style of the house, and equipped with modern
plumbing and mechanical conveniences. This trend continued during the
entire first quarter of the 20th century.

The Spanish missions in North America. One of the most interesting
developments of Spanish Colonial culture was its northward expansion
across the Rio Grande between 1690 and 1836. The Franciscans and Dominicans penetrated this Western wilderness to bring the aborigines within
the realms of the King of Kings and the King of Spain. From Texas into
California, as far north as San Francisco, the Padres erected chapels, hos-
pices, and administrative buildings in adobe brick and stone. Those that
have withstood the ravages of time are among the most charming and
romantic architectural groups in the United States. Outstanding are the
Alamo, in the Spanish-Mexican style, and San José, with traces of the
Gothic, both in San Antonio, and the California missions known as San
Luis Rey, San Juan Capistrano, Santa Barbara, and San Carlos Borromeo
del Rio Carmelo. The latter were founded by Fra Junipero Serra, a man
of extraordinary character, who, in a labor of love, and under great hardships, gained the confidence and affection of the natives and induced them
to act as willing vassals in bringing peace and plenty to the land. Considering Serra and his successors' limited technical knowledge, meagre tools,
and pagan craftsmen, the architectural and decorative results were astonishing in their stability and spiritual expression. The pedimented façades,
colorful tile-roofed towers, graceful belfries, and cloistered patios pictur-
esquely nestle in the hills and look down upon the blue waves of the
Pacific.

The principal decorative effort was concentrated in the chapels. The
interiors of these are enriched with painted imitations of archaic appearing
classical columns, pilasters, and cornice moldings. The roofs and ceilings
are usually supported by exposed beams. In a few cases barrel vaults and
catenary arches were attempted. Walls and altars were hung with religious

paintings, embroidered cloths, and Christian symbols imported from Spain and Mexico. Other decorations consisted of painted patterns that were inspired by Moorish-Gothic, Plateresco, or exuberant Churrigueresco forms. Occasionally the artisans interpolated motifs of Aztec origin, not realizing the inconsistency of these with Christian iconography. In spite of the crudeness of technique, the general effect was one of sincerity and warmth.

Such original furniture as remains shows little relationship to Spanish detail. The Padres contented themselves with primitive living and the simplest of conveniences. Sturdily built, rectangular, and heavily proportioned chairs, chests, tables, and wardrobes were made in native woods, assembled and joined with mortise, tenon, and dowel. This furniture has formed the basis for modern productions of questionable merit that are known as "Spanish Mission."

Prominent Architects and Craftsmen in America from the 17th to the 20th Centuries

ARCHITECTS

Benjamin, Asher (1773–1845). Architect, and author of architectural handbooks.

Bulfinch, Charles (1763–1844). Designed the Maine statehouse and put Thornton's plan for the capitol at Washington into execution.

Hoban, James (1762–1831). Built the statehouse at Charleston, South Carolina.

Jefferson, Thomas (1743–1826). U. S. President, and father of the classic revival in the United States. Designed Monticello and the University of Virginia.

Kearsley, Dr. John (Active during the first half of the 18th century). Supervised the construction of Christ Church and the statehouse in Boston.

Latrobe, Benjamin Henry (1764–1820). Designed the Bank of the United States (1819–1826).

L'Enfant, Pierre Charles (Arrived in America at the end of the 18th century). Planned the city of Washington, D.C.

McComb, John (1763–1853). Designed the New York City Hall in association with Joseph Mangin, a French engineer.

McIntire, Samuel (1757–1811). Colonial architect, master carpenter, and wood carver, who designed many of the houses built in Salem (1782–1811) in the classical tradition.

Richardson, Henry H. (1838–1886). Architect; leader in Romanesque revival in architecture.

Sullivan, Louis H. (1856–1924). Architect; early promoter of functional design in architectural structures.

Thornton, Dr. William (Arrived in U. S. in 1793). Designed the first capitol at Washington.

Wright, Frank Lloyd (1869–1959). Architect, author, follower of Louis Sullivan in promoting functional and organic design in architecture and the industrial arts.

CABINETMAKERS

Affleck, Thomas (Active 1763–1795). Leading figure in the Philadelphia-Chippendale school.

Belter, John Henry (1800?–1865). New York City. Rosewood and carved laminated forms.

Folwell, John (Active last quarter of the 18th century). Philadelphia-Chippendale school. Made the furniture for the Continental Congress. Called the Chippendale of America.

Goddard, John (b. 1723. Active third quarter of the 18th century). Cabinetmaker of Newport, Rhode Island, who worked in the Chippendale style. Renowned for his use of the block front.

Lannuier, H. L. (Active 1805–1820). Frenchman who produced Directoire type furniture in New York City.

Miller, G. New Yorker who made furniture following that of the Englishman Hope (active 1820–1830). Greek Revival.

Phyfe, Duncan (Produced 1795–1847). New York cabinetmaker and furniture designer of late 18th century English and Empire styles.

Randolph, Benjamin (Active last half of the 18th century to 1790). A leader in the Philadelphia-Chippendale school.

Savery, William (1722?–1787). Prominent in the Philadelphia-Chippendale school. Particularly noted for highboys.

CLOCK MANUFACTURERS

Burnap, Daniel (Active 1780–1800). Early clockmaker known for engraved faces.

Harland, Thomas (1735–1805). Came to America in 1773. Organizer of the clockmaking industry in Norwich, Conn.

Hoadley, Silas (1786–1870). Clockmaker and partner of Eli Terry.

Rittenhouse, David (1732–1796). Philadelphia clockmaker.

Terry, Eli (18th, early 19th, century). Apprentice of Burnap, and later partner of Hoadley.

Thomas, Seth (1785–1859). Active in Thomaston, Connecticut, and founder of Seth Thomas clock factory.

Willard Family: Simon, Benjamin, Aaron, and Ephraim (Active 1743–1848). Famous family of Massachusetts clockmakers. Simon is credited with introducing the banjo clock in America from England.

PAINTERS AND ARTISTS

Audubon, John J. (1785–1851). Ornithologist and painter. Made illustrations for *Birds of America*.

Copley, John Singleton (1737–1815). Portrait painter and member of Royal Academy in 1779.

Fulton, Robert (1765–1815). Artist as well as inventor.

Greenough, Horatio (1805–1852). Sculptor who first remarked that the design should be based on the function of the object and the possibilities of the material from which it is made.

Morse, Samuel F. B. (1791–1872). Painter and lecturer on fine arts as well as inventor of the wireless telegraph.

Peale Family: Charles Wilson (1741–1827); his brother, James (1749–1831); and Charles Wilson's son, Rembrandt (1778–1860). Celebrated family of Colonial portrait painters.

Saint-Gaudens, Augustus (1848–1907). Sculptor.

Saint Memin, Charles B. J. F. de (1770–1852). Artist and engraver, a native of Dijon, France, who, a refugee from the French Revolution, came to the United States about 1796. Made portraits of famous Americans between 1796 and 1810.

Stuart, Gilbert (1755–1828). Portrait painter, famous for his portraits of George Washington.

West, Benjamin (1738–1820). Painter of historical and mythological subjects.

Whistler, James Abbott McNeill (1834–1903). Painter and etcher.

POTTERS, PEWTERERS, AND GLASSMAKERS

Boardman, Thomas D. (1784–1873). Hartford pewterer.

Danforth, Samuel (Active early 19th century). Hartford pewterer.

Fenton, Christopher (1806–1860). Manufacturer of Bennington pottery ware.

Hubener, George
Leedy, John
Mesz, Johannes
} Pennsylvania potters who designed slip and sgraffito ware.

Greatbach, Daniel (Active 1839–1860). Designer of Bennington pottery.

Spinner, David (Active 1800–1811). Pennsylvania German potter.

Stiegel, Heinrich Wilhelm (1729–1785). Iron-founder and manufacturer of fine glass in pre-Revolutionary days; founder of the factory at Mannheim, Pennsylvania.

Coney, John (1655–1722). Boston silversmith and engraver.

Dummer, Jeremiah (1645–1718). Massachusetts silversmith.

Hull, John (1624–1683). Worked in Boston.

Kierstead, Cornelius (Active during the 17th century). A Dutch silversmith who worked in New York and New Haven and was renowned for his tankard designs.

Le Roux Family (Active during the last half of the 17th century). Family of Huguenot silversmiths who worked in New York.

Revere, Paul (1735–1818). Boston silversmith and copperplate engraver, caricaturist, and bell-founder.

Sanderson, Robert (Active 1638–1693). Boston silversmith.

Winslow, Edward (1669–1753). Boston silversmith.

Van Dyck, Peter (Active during the 17th century). Dutch silversmith in New York.

Bibliography

American Folk Art. The Museum of Modern Art, New York, 1935. A survey of the crafts of the common man in America.

American Index of Design—Pennsylvania German. Metropolitan Museum of Art, New York, 1943. Excellent text and illustrations.

BENNETT, G. F., *Early Architecture of Delaware.* Historical Press, Inc., Wilmington, 1932. Photographs and measured drawings of exteriors and interiors, with a brief text.

BRAZER, E. S., *Early American Decoration.* Pond-Ekberg Co., Springfield, Mass., 1940. A treatise on the technique of early American decoration.

COFFIN, L. A., JR., AND HOLDEN, A. C., *Brick Architecture of the Colonial Period in Maryland and Virginia.* Architectural Book Publishing Co., New York, 1919. Photographs and measured drawings with brief text.

CHRISTENSEN, E. O., *The Index of American Design.* The Macmillan Company, New York, 1950. Full-color illustrations from water-color originals, and descriptive text, covering popular arts and crafts.

DREPPERD, CARL W., *First Reader for Antique Collectors.* Doubleday and Co., Garden City, N. Y., 1945.

DREPPERD, CARL W., *Primer of American Antiques.* Doubleday and Co., Garden City, N. Y., 1946. The two books above on American antiques are excellent with much material not found elsewhere. Text and illustration.

DYER, W. A., *Early American Craftsmen.* D. Appleton-Century Co., New York, 1915. Illustrated text.

EBERLEIN, H. D., AND HUBBARD, C. V. D., *Colonial Interiors, Federal and Greek Revival,* 3d series. Wm. Helburn, Inc., New York, 1938. Text and plates.

FRENCH, L., JR., *Colonial Interiors.* New York, Wm. Helburn, Inc., 1923. Photographs and measured drawings of interiors.

Great Georgian Houses of America, 2 Vols. Drawn and compiled by the Architects' Emergency Committee, New York, 1933 and 1937. Excellent collection of photographs and architectural drawings.

HAMLIN, TALBOT, *Greek Revival Architecture in America.* Oxford University Press, New York, 1943. Text and plates.

HIPKISS, E. J., *18th Century American Arts.* The Karolik Collection. Harvard University Press, 1941. Furniture, silver, needlework, paintings, etc.

HORNOR, W. M., JR., *Blue Book—Philadelphia Furniture, William Penn to George Washington.* Philadelphia Craftsmen of 1935, Philadelphia, 1935. Text for collectors illustrated with authentic examples of furniture. A standard authority.

JOHNSTON, E. B., *The Early Architecture of North Carolina.* University of North Carolina Press, Chapel Hill, N. C., 1941. Text and plates.

KELLEY, J. F., *Early Connecticut Architecture.* William Helburn, New York. 2 Vols., 1923, 1931. Excellent measured drawings of exterior and interior work.

KELLEY, J. F., *The Early Domestic Architecture of Connecticut.* Yale University Press, New Haven, 1924. Text illustrated with photographs and measured drawings.

KETTELL, R. H., *Early American Rooms.* Southworth-Anthoensen Press. Portland, Maine, 1936. Excellent survey of American interior design. Colored illustrations.

KETTELL, R. H., *The Pine Furniture of Early New England.* Doubleday, Doran and Co., Garden City, N. Y., 1929. Illustrated text.

KIMBALL, F., *Domestic Architecture of the American Colonies and of the Early Republic.* Charles Scribner's Sons, New York, 1922. A good study of the background of Colonial architecture. A standard authority.

KIMBALL, F., *Mr. Samuel McIntire, etc.* Southworth-Anthoensen Press. Portland, Maine, 1940. An authoritative study of his work.

LICHTER, F., *Folk Art of Rural Pennsylvania.* Charles Scribner's Sons, New York, 1946. Well-prepared presentation of German settlers.

LITTLE, F., *Early American Textiles.* D. Appleton-Century Co., New York, 1931. Excellent illustrated text. A survey of textile manufacturers from the first settlements through the early 19th century.

LOCKWOOD, L. V., *Colonial Furniture in America,* 2 Vols. Charles Scribner's Sons, New York, 1913. Excellent photographs of American Colonial furniture. A standard authority.

LYON, I. W., *The Colonial Furniture of New England.* Houghton Mifflin Co., Boston, 1925. A standard book for reference on this subject.

McCLELLAND, N., *Duncan Phyfe and English Regency.* Wm. H. Scott, New York, 1939. Text and plates.

McCLELLAND, N., *Furnishing the Colonial and Federal House.* J. B. Lippincott Co., Philadelphia, 1936. An illustrated text on the complete furnishings of a home of this period.

MILLER, E. G., JR., *American Antique Furniture,* 2 Vols. The Lord Baltimore Press, Baltimore, Md., 1937. Complete text and illustrations.

NEVIN AND COMMAGER, *A Short History of the United States.* Modern Library, New York, 1945. Excellent brief outline of American history.

NEWCOMB, R., *Old Kentucky Architecture, Colonial, Federal, and Greek Revival.* Wm. Helburn, Inc., New York, 1943. Text and plates.

NUTTING, W., *Furniture Treasury,* 3 Vols. Old America Co., Framingham, 1928. Five thousand illustrations with descriptive text.

RICCUITI, W. I., *New Orleans and Its Environs.* Wm. Helburn, Inc., New York, 1938. Plates and measured drawings.

SALE, E. T., *Colonial Interiors.* William Helburn, Inc., New York, 1930. Photographs of authentic Colonial interiors.

STOTZ, C. M., *The Early Architecture of Western Pennsylvania.* William Helburn, Inc., New York, 1936. Plates, text, and maps.

TALLMADGE, T. E., *The Story of Architecture in America.* W. W. Norton and Co., New York, 1927. An interesting illustrated history of American architecture written for the layman.

CHAPTER VIII

MISCELLANEOUS STYLES AND ARTS

In addition to the great historical styles of art of western and southern
Europe, there have been many other countries and races who have
expressed themselves in terms of decorative arts that are equal in intrinsic
merit to the Western and vary only in their relative importance. All of
them are of interest to the decorator and connoisseur. In some cases these
styles are the creative effort of great civilizations that have frequently influenced Western design, or whose productions have been valued and
used in both former and modern types of Western interiors. In other cases,
they are examples of the arts of sections of Europe, which, with less initiative and imagination in the decorative arts, have freely borrowed the styles
of Italy, France, and England and have interpreted these arts under local
conditions and influences to form variations of great interest. In addition,
there are the art expressions of simple or primitive people all over the
world who under indigenous philosophies have produced limited but
exceedingly interesting arts that are unrelated to those of Western culture.
Some of these isolated arts were merely the result of a natural desire on the
part of people with simple esthetic standards to surround themselves with
visual and spiritual joys; others had a deeper significance or were the result of religious impulses. Selections from these distant styles and arts, if
used with discretion, may serve to contribute interest and individuality to
the decoration of any room.

The character of these productions varies greatly in degree of refinement, depending upon the intellectual level of the people who produced
them. Several require a life study for full appreciation and understanding,
and only the merest outline of their development can be given in a text of
this character. The student is referred to the bibliography for further information. Broadly, they can be classified into five main divisions, as follows:

Oriental Arts of China and Islam
Renaissance Arts of the Germanic Nations
Peasant Arts of Europe
Indian Arts of the Americas
African Negro Sculpture

Oriental Arts of China and Islam

Marco Polo returned from his overland trip to Cathay in the 13th century and created Asia for the European mind. Since then the West has been eager not only to import Eastern products but her designers and artists have fed their imagination upon Oriental art forms.

All Eastern art, regardless of time or locality, has been entwined with religious impulses and deeply concerned with human philosophy. The mentality of the artists has been saturated with poetry and mysticism. Zest and imagination have been combined with a passion for excellence. The principles of pure design have been fully understood. Artists have vigilantly suited the spirit of their designs to the material in which they were working, and have expressed the substance of the material in the final outcome. Both intellectual and emotional appeal have been used, and in every medium there has been intrinsic beauty in expressive contours, subtle colors, and surface ornamentation. Effects have ranged from dignity and grandeur to those of delicacy and fragility. Realism, conventionalization, rhythm, and contrast have played their essential parts. Motion and repose have been expressed at will. The hilarious, grotesque, and erotic have not been neglected. The indestructible vitality of the Oriental arts has been proved by their tenacity through repeated periods of discouragement and chaos.

The Oriental styles may be subdivided into those of the Far East, of which that of China is by far the dominant, and those of the Near East, which are mainly those of the Islamic countries, Persia, India, Turkey, and Moorish Spain. The Far Eastern arts were in the main indigenous from prehistoric times. Some of the Near Eastern arts are as old, but in their early periods there were Babylonian, Egyptian, and Hellenistic influences, and the Mongol invasions of the 13th century caused all to feel the magic touch of China.

Although the rarest products of these styles are in museums, there are many available objects of beauty, both old and new, that can be used to contribute great charm to the rooms of any style in countries that were unconceived when many of the objects were produced.

Chinese arts. Chinese civilization commences with a Stone Age that lasted from approximately 5000 B.C. until the Shang Dynasty, which started about the year 1766 B.C. This dynasty is considered the first of the historical

Courtesy Worcester Art Museum

Chinese pottery horse. A.D. *500.*

periods, and was followed by a series of dynasties known as the Ch'in, Han, Wei, Sui, Tang, Sung, and Yuan, the latter ending in A.D. 1368. During the dynasties of these thirty centuries, there were produced remarkable examples of bronze work, pottery, jewels, sacrificial vessels, articles of personal adornment, candelabra, harness for horses, ceremonial and religious objects, statuettes of humans and animals, and many other works of art of an astounding degree of technique and beauty. Until about A.D. 500, a large portion of Chinese art was intended for ritual and funerary purposes. Ancestor worship was responsible for the practice of painting the interior of tombs to enable the deceased to enjoy his resting place; his body was surrounded with pottery and bronze food containers, and other objects necessary for use in the hereafter. In spite of their great interest, these periods are mainly of importance to the archaeologist, curator, and collector,* and are, therefore, outside the scope of this text.

Chinese art has been a native product, but in its long history it has occasionally been affected by the arts of border nations such as Scythia, Persia, and India; and China has suffered the invasions of the Mongols and the Tartars. In each case, however, the culture of the conquering nations has been submerged and assimilated in that of the conquered. Many dynasties started with brilliance and ended under the leadership of a descendant of the founder, who, with apathy and a false sense of security, often permitted himself to be ruined by an unscrupulous woman. Religion as such has perhaps played a less important part in Chinese art than in that of other nations, although art has prospered under Buddhism to a greater extent than under Confucianism or Taoism. The Chinese have been a superstitious and fearful people; much of their art has been created for the purpose of ceremonial appeals for the rotation of the seasons, the intimidation of evil spirits, or for special benefits, and an immense symbolism has been developed for these and other purposes.

The two long and important dynasties which concern the decorator are the Ming (1368–1644), noted for its architecture and pottery, and the

---

* There have been an enormous number of human and animal figurines recently found in very early tombs. Many are available at reasonable valuations. The quaint and gaily modelled equestrian figures of these periods are especially popular.

Ch'ing or Manchu (1644–1912), noted for its porcelains of great beauty.* China, as other Far Eastern nations, has never developed an important style of architecture. The most interesting structures are temples and palaces, which usually have been of one-story wooden construction. The most important of these are in Peiping and include the Sacrificial Hall of the Ming Dynasty, the Forbidden City, and the Summer Palace built by Empress Tz'u Hsi in the 19th century. The *pagodas* are merely towers that enclose idols. None that remains is of great size or antiquity. Their esthetic appeal is mainly in the color and patterns that are the chief features of their interior decoration. The exterior interest lies in the curving roofs covered with earthenware or stoneware tiles and their carved rafter ends and brackets. In some cases exterior walls are built of colored or patterned porcelain slabs. The interior planning of dwellings is interesting and partitions are often built of flimsy materials. The construction of the buildings is skeletal, with posts and beams of *nanmu*,† an aromatic lumber that turns a deep rich brown. The woodwork is often treated in colorful designs in which mandarin red predominates. As the Chinese seldom mix their pigments, strong colors are characteristic. Windows are often covered with intricate latticework and surfaced with paper, an arrangement that casts interesting shadows by day or by night. Railings also are designed in complicated lattice patterns. Split bamboo screens and shades are also frequently used for window coverings. In important rooms, ceilings are painted with patterns. The Chinese are excellent wood-carvers and apply much of this effort to enrich door frames with elaborate relief and pierced ornament.

The majority of Chinese dwelling houses have interior courts, which are necessary to the owner for purposes of tranquility and contemplation.

* The Chinese Periods are given herewith:

Patriarchal Period	3000–2205 B.C.	Sui	A.D. 589
Hsia Dynasty	2205–1766 B.C.	T'ang	618
Shang Dynasty	1766–1122 B.C.	5 small dynasties	908
Chou Dynasty	1122– 255 B.C.	Sung	960
Ch'in Dynasty	255– 206 B.C.	Yuan	1280
Han Dynasty	206– 220 A.D.	Ming	1368
San Tai, or, Three States	220– 280 A.D.	T'a Ch'ing (Manchu)	1644–1912
Wei	220–265	divided as follows:	
Shu Han	221–265	K'ang Hsi	1662
Wu	222–280	Yung Cheng	1723
Lu-Chao, or, Six Dynasties	265– 589 A.D.	Ch'ien Lung	1736
		Chia Ch'ing	1796
Chin	265–420 ⎫	Tao Kuang	1821
Sung	420–479 ⎪	Hsien Feng	1851
Chi	479–502 ⎬ Southern	T'ung Chih	1862
Liang	502–557 ⎪	Kuang Hsu	1875
Ch'en	557–589 ⎭	Hsuan T'ung	1909
		Republican	1912
Northern Wei	386–535 ⎫		
Eastern Wei	534–543 ⎪		
Western Wei	535–557 ⎬ Northern		
Northern Ch'i	550–589 ⎪		
Northern Chou	557–589 ⎭		

† This is the Chinese name for Persian cedar.

Courtesy Orra Lott

Suite of rooms in modern house in Peiping.

These courts are planted with weeping willows, quivering ginkgos, thuyas, cypresses, bamboo, and flowering shrubs, and further beautified with potted flowers. Each house is surrounded by a garden in which foliage, moss, rocks, water, and architectural features are of equal interest; trees and shrubs cast their shade on paths, pools, and canals; steppingstones, mosaic paths, footbridges, pavilions, archways, and walls pierced with *moon gates* or vase-shaped openings create subdivisions that contribute the surprise elements of the design. Flowers and rock gardens with dwarf growths are arranged for perfect seasonal blooming; the lotus, sacred to the Buddhist faith, grows in profusion and is the first of the spring flowers, followed by magnolias, peonies, azaleas, lilies, chrysanthemums, and many others, all of which have symbolic meanings. The gardens are often lit by colorful lanterns hanging from archways, beams, and posts.

The houses of the small landowners, farmers, and peasants are of the most simple sort and do not contain the features that are customarily associated with Chinese architecture. They are built of stone or wood with simple roof lines and in appearance do not vary greatly from the small houses of southern Europe.

Rooms are sparingly furnished, but each piece of furniture or decoration is an object of quality. During the Ming period, cabinets, chairs, tables, multifold screens, and many smaller pieces were made in blackwood, coromandel, and rosewood or were lacquered in gold or silver combined with red. Bamboo was used for summer furniture and camphorwood for wardrobes and other containers. During the K'ang Hsi reign of the Ch'ing dynasty, richly carved objects were covered with an overelaborate gold lacquer and inlaid with mother-of-pearl. During the 17th and 18th centuries when Europe demanded unlimited supplies of lacquered work, there was a decline in the quality of the Chinese technique, which was aggravated by the competition due to the discovery in Europe of the secret formulas. Lacquer was also used as a plastic material in making such small objects as cups, saucers, scent jars, and in-

Eighteenth century Chinese vermilion lacquered altar table with two jade table screens with floral patterns in semiprecious minerals, supported on teakwood stands.

Chinese carved teakwood chair decorated with bats and cloud motifs and painted landscape panels.

cense burners. The majority of lacquered products that are available today are of 19th century workmanship.

Wall surfaces, textiles, porcelains, and other mediums were often enriched with motifs and patterns in which symbolism played an important part. The peach, tortoise, and pine indicated longevity; the pomegranate, fecundity. Other frequently used decorative motifs were birds, cloud designs, and an infinite number of trees, flowers, and leaves, which were applied particularly to the porcelains, textiles, and wallpapers and rendered naturalistically in the most graceful patterns and colors on a very light tinted background. The swastika and other geometrical forms were also used. When scenic patterns were introduced they were generally

drawn in a parallel perspective. Officials had their symbolic identifications embroidered on their robes. The five-clawed dragon was reserved for the Emperor and the four-clawed dragon for the rest of the Imperial family; the phoenix was considered the symbol of the Empress. The most important functionaries were identified by the white crane and unicorn, the second in rank by the golden pheasant and lion, and the third grade by the peacock and panther, with other animals for officials of less importance. Segmental curves and rectangular forms were vigorously avoided; angles and corners were generally rounded. Both realistic and conventional forms were used, but the latter never lose the essence of vigor, life, and action. There is much humor and grotesqueness in Chinese motifs. Gnomes, birds, and animals often are shown in intentionally comic actions and faces are indicated with droll expressions.

Ch'ien Lung imperial white jade teacup, 2¾ inches high.

The Chinese have been extraordinary carvers in semiprecious stones. Massive stone sculpture is mostly of an early date, but jade,* coral, and ivory sculpture, ornaments, and charms carved with an unbelievably painstaking technique are still being made in a style that has changed little with the centuries. Jade, the symbol of vitality and authority, is a material that has a peculiarly sensuous quality that satisfies the touch; its surface feels like that of the flesh of an infant. The Chinese have realized the possibilities of an art that combines the senses of touch and sight, and in the use of jade have captured it to a greater extent than other people. Objects made of jade were used extensively in ceremonials. A jade carving of a cicada (a type of grasshopper), the symbol of everlasting life, was usually placed in the mouth of a deceased person. Much ivory carving was done in the Manchu period, and this art is carried on to the present day; particularly in carving such figures as that of Kuan-yin, the Goddess of Mercy, and the eight Immortals of Buddhism. Many of these carvings are large considering the limitations of the material, and there is necessarily a slight curve to the figures due to the natural form of the elephant's tusk. They show a minuteness of workmanship that could only be attempted by one for whom time is not precious. In the neighborhood of Peiping, thick lac-

* The term "jade" was first used in 1683. Jade includes jadeite and nephrite. The former is translucent and varies in color from cream to green; the latter, not always translucent, is a hard, fine-grained material that is found in green, red, yellow, white, and other colors.

Nineteenth century ivory tusk statuette of swaying maiden.

quer surfaces were also used as a medium for carved enrichment, and carved lacquered boxes have been found in graves that date from 500 b.c.

The Chinese have almost from the beginning of their culture been great painters. The greatest periods in this art were those immediately preceding the Ming dynasty, but as the painters have been great traditionalists, copying has always been considered honorable and many of the works of the old masters have been reproduced in later periods. The Chinese painters until recent years were always amateurs; ladies and gentlemen and even statesmen considered painting one of the necessary accomplishments for the person of rank and culture. The offer of monetary compensation for the product of one's leisure time was considered an affront.

The Chinese claim to have invented paper in a.d. 105, but it is more probable that this material was first made by the Egyptians long before the Christian Era. Rags, however, were not used as a content until about 1300. As printing was invented by the Chinese in the 8th century, the earliest wallpaper probably dates from that period. Chinese paintings were made on both silk and paper and usually consisted of long scroll forms which had to be unrolled from right to left to grasp their significance. The scroll paintings were composed with rhythmically related voids and motifs that require the eye to move vertically as well as horizontally in viewing them. They are to be enjoyed in the same manner as a musical symphony because of the time element that is required to appreciate them. Many of these ancient scrolls have been cut into smaller units forming more convenient shapes for framing and hanging. Fan painting was also an important art. Ink was more frequently used as a medium than color and the artists were dexterous in the production of various shades of this material; when colors were added, they were limited to the pale tinting of the ink drawings.

The subject matter of paintings varied to a remarkable degree. Many authorities believe that the greatest periods in Chinese painting occurred during the Tang (618–907) and Sung Dynasties (960–1280). During the latter period, peaceful and imaginative scenes included fairies, beautiful women, flowers, and birds. In the Yuan or Mongol period that followed

Chinese landscape scroll painting on silk. Ming dynasty.

(1280–1368) remarkable paintings were also produced; these were black and white landscapes often showing horses, pools, birds, flowers, and moons. During the Ming period, garden and household activities were represented in rich colors, and portraiture was developed. Tempera painting on paper and on glass and mirror painting were extensively practiced. Brush-stroke *calligraphy* played an important part in all paintings upon which titles and descriptive matter were indicated with remarkable skill. Large calligraphic scrolls and carvings quoting the philosophy of Chinese sages are often used as decorative features in the rooms of present-day dwellings.

Cloisonné enamel work was also produced but it is probable that this art was learned from Byzantine sources after the Western invasion of the Mongols. This type of work is still being done, and the same ancient methods are used in its manufacture. Other arts, which reached perfection, were those of textiles, rugs, porcelains, and wallpaper, descriptions of which are given elsewhere in this text.

In nearly every great decorative style in Europe, objects of Chinese origin were used from the 16th century onwards. Due to the intrinsic beauty and perfection of most pieces, examples of Chinese art possess the fortunate quality of being friendly with other styles, and, if intelligently used, are as much at home with contemporary decoration as they were with the historic periods. There is still an ample supply available for decorative uses.

During the 20th century, China has begun to feel the effects of western industrialization, and the political and economic situation has been so disturbed that a definite hiatus has occurred in the development of the arts. Architecture and decoration have strongly shown the influence of American structural methods and materials, and the industrial arts are being increasingly commercialized. Reproduction of antique examples has continued with lowering of standards, technique, and structural qualities. The arts of China will revive as they always have, but the 20th century must be considered as one of those periods when the energy and creative forces of

Chia Ch'ing coromandel lacquered screen, 9 feet 4 inches high, painted with landscape.

the people have, by necessity, been concentrated upon other than art production.

Islamic arts. The arts of the Mohammedan countries are generally classified in one group and known as *Islamic*. Several of these nations maintained a high degree of civilization long before their adoption of the Koran. They cover an enormous geographical area and contain people of the most diverse origins, but their culture has been knit by a powerful religious unity that has surpassed that of Christian peoples.

Mohammedanism dates from the Flight of its founder, an Arab, from Mecca in A.D. 622. His claim of being the Prophet of the One God, Allah, was accepted with ecstasy by the masses of the Near East. The Arabians immediately determined to conquer the world and offer the blessings of their faith to a demoralized Christianity. The Koran illumined vast visions, and the Arabs almost accomplished their ambitions within a period of a century. Zeal brought them to a sudden and terrible success. Within twenty years they had subdued Syria, Mesopotamia, Egypt, North Africa, Persia, and Afghanistan. Spain fell in 713, northern India in the 10th century, and Constantinople in 1453. The Mongols from eastern Asia under Ghengis Khan, and later, under Tamerlane, invaded Persia in the 13th century, but accepted the superior civilization and religion of the conquered people; they broke the Turkish power in Asia Minor, and in the 16th century established the Mogul dynasty and Iranian * culture in India.

* "Iran" is the native name for Greater Persia; "Persia" is the Latinized name of one province.

Courtesy Arthur A. Pope

Sixteenth century tile decoration from the Great Mosque at Ispahan.

The Christian Copts of Egypt turned Moslem and under the Mamelukes resisted both the Mongols and Crusaders. In A.D. 732 Charles Martel saved Europe from the Koran by his defeat of the Saracens at Poitiers, France, and Ferdinand finally expelled the Moors from Spain in 1492. The last aggressive effort of the Moslems resulted in the defeat of the Turks at Vienna in 1683. Thus ended the expansion of Islam.

Following each military conquest between the 7th and 14th centuries, great cities were built that became seats of learning, science, and art, many of them preserving the records of antiquity while western Europe was a disorganized entity. Mecca was the center of the Faith; Kufa and Basra were the seats of Arabian theology. Damascus boasted of her poetry, science, industry, and lax morals. Bagdad, built on the ruins of ancient Babylon, was one of the proudest cities in the world. The mere mention of Tabriz, Ispahan, Mosul, Samarkand, and Herat recalls the entrancing descriptions and events related in the "Thousand and One Nights." Delhi, Agra, and Lahore, in India, and Cordova, Seville, and Granada, in Spain, were centers of luxury and splendor whose beauties still remain.

The Mohammedans were great architects and greater decorators. Although their designers and craftsmen were drawn from foreign and conquered lands, Islamic structures retain a unity of style that resulted from a single religious belief. There is less originality of constructive design than of surface decoration.

The greatest examples of Islamic architecture are mosques, palaces, citadels, bazaars, and mausoleums. The mosques of Cairo are outstanding in their richness of detail. The great mosque of Cordova is the largest religious edifice in the world. The Alhambra in Granada and the Alcazar in Seville are evidences of the brilliance of the Moorish occupation. Moorish elements of decoration continued to be used by the Christians of the Renaissance, and the combination of details drawn from both sources formed the basis of later Spanish design.* The Jews in Spain employed Moorish designers and workmen to build their synagogues, and adopted the Moslem style for this type of building. Upon the expulsion of the Jews from Spain in 1610 the style was transported to other countries, and Moorish forms are generally used for the design of synagogues to the present day. The bazaars in Teheran, Ispahan, and Bagdad show magnificent blending of colored patterns.

The jewelled Peacock Throne of Shah Jehan in Delhi.

The Indian structures of white marble glisten in the sunshine and brilliantly reflect the colors of nature; the palace at Delhi built by Shah Jehan contained his Peacock Throne of gold and jewels; the mosque of Jumma Musjid is considered one of the most splendid buildings in the world; the Taj Mahal in Agra, the tomb of Jehan and his wife, has a bulbous dome and pointed arches, and is accepted as the pearl of Indian architecture.

The Egyptians in the 10th century were the first to use the geometrical patterns that were later to become a characteristic feature of Islamic art. The Copts used the pointed arch, the Moors preferred the horseshoe form, and the Persians, the pointed horseshoe and ogival, applying the latter form to their bulbous domes. Columns were slender and crowned with capitals that vaguely resembled the Corinthian shape but were covered with minute leaves of lacelike detail. Scrolls were developed from stems and pseudo-acanthus and palmette leaves, and from these emerged the arabesque. Walls were often given interest by alternating red and white stone courses producing horizontal stripes, a system that was also used in the *voussoirs* of arches. Stalactite forms were occasionally used for brackets

* See Chapter IV.

Lacquered door from Royal Palace in Ispahan, 1587.

Courtesy Asia Institute

or a decoration on the underside of domes. Plain and patterned tiles and small-scaled plaster relief ornament became the most usual method for surfacing wainscots and interior walls. Stained glass was used for windows. There was usually a noticeable absence of pictures and sculpture. The prayer niche or *mihrab* was a feature of every mosque.

The patterns used in all branches of Islamic art have a wide range of origin and subject matter and there is a tendency to use similar motifs regardless of medium. In wall decorations, textiles, rugs, ceramics, metalwork, and painting, patterns change only by the limitations of their various techniques. The Mohammedans were divided into two sects, the Sunni, represented by the Turks, Moors, and Arabs, and the Shi'as, represented by the Persians and East Indians. The former interdicted the representation of living motifs in art, on the assumption that they recalled pagan idolatry, and their designers therefore developed geometrical patterns; although violations of this ruling occurred, they were frowned upon by the orthodox. The more liberal Shi'a doctrines account for the floral, animal, and human subject matter used in their designs. Generally all patterns were relatively small in scale, and much conventionalization was used. Emphasis was always placed on the decorative quality rather than the representational. Early works of art show the use of debased forms of acanthus, lotus, palmette, and scrolls undoubtedly inspired by early Asiatic and classical models.

In the development of geometrical patterns, the most complicated interlacements of straight lines occur. Squares, rectangles, hexagons, octagons, stars, and an infinite variety of irregular and overlapping forms are seen. In ceramic and textile design, rosettes, pearls, dots, hatchings, diamonds, circles, stars, vase-forms, and many other motifs were employed. Diaper patterns were often subdivided into panels formed by lines or bands arranged in an ogival, circular, or scalloped manner.

In Shi'a productions, real and imaginary animals play a prominent part; the ibex was a royal symbol, and the lion represented power. Equestrian subjects were common. Human beings, birds, leaves, flowers, ivies, and trees were often beautifully combined in patterns or arabesques. Pine cones were considered a symbol of good luck. After the Mongol invasion, patterns often showed the use of Chinese motifs such as clouds, butterflies, rose and peony blossoms, and plants growing out of rocks.

The Persians, in particular, worshipped beauty as did the ancient Greeks, and lavished care and affection upon everything they created. They produced great works of art in the minor fields, and from the 15th century onward set a standard for the other parts of Islam. Their artists were frequently anonymous, and seldom signed their names; the result, only, was what mattered. They excelled in the arts of illuminating manuscripts and miniature painting. Many of these productions must be considered among the masterpieces of painting in the world. An infinite range of subject matter was used, including court and amorous scenes, folklore, historical and biblical events, landscapes, animal fights, houris of the Mohammedan paradise, and portraiture. The pictures are story-telling devices; the eye roams until the whole event is digested, and one easily imagines sequences that are not delineated. The compositions show breadth of conception, perfect balance, mastery of detail and color, and with a high horizon line, usually appear as a bird's-eye view. Perspective was used but shadows were generally omitted. The artists showed skill in eliminating unnecessary features, and often conventionalized for the

East Indian carved ivory elephant, set with gold and precious stones, 8 inches long.

Courtesy Asia Institute

Manuscript miniature, "The Pleasure Party." Mogul, 1625.

sake of simplicity. The majority of the paintings were titled or described in Kufic or cursive calligraphy, an art that was as important as that of painting itself. The Persians were masters at many other arts; their gardens intoxicate the visitor by combinations of fragrance and natural beauty, and their literature will be remembered eternally by the "Rubai-

TOP LEFT: *Persian 16th century painted stucco and tile work.* TOP RIGHT: *Persian calligraphic tile.* LEFT: *Fourteenth century bronze candlestick damascened with gold and silver.* ABOVE: *Manuscript miniature, "The Flight of Yusuf." Persian, 15th century.*

yat." The achievements of the Persians in textile and rug weaving and in ceramics are described elsewhere in this text.

Extraordinary examples of stone, stucco, and wood-carving were produced in every Mohammedan country. Ivory, bone, and mother-of-pearl were used for decorative plaques, jewel containers, caskets, mosaics, and furniture inlay. Door panelling was often enriched with ivory appliques. Metals were used for chests, lamps, candlesticks, ornaments, furniture, and jewelry, and were worked by casting, hammering, or embossing and filigree. In Damascus a method was introduced of inlaying patterns of gold or silver wires in base metals, by the process known as damascening.

Renaissance Arts of the Germanic Nations

Dutch and Flemish arts. The importance to America of the industrial arts of the Low Countries during the early years of the Renaissance is the result of the close trade and social relationships of these countries with England.

The section of Europe in the 16th century that was the approximate equivalent of Holland and Belgium today, was known as Flanders, and was under the rule of Charles I of Spain, who was also Emperor Charles V of Austria, Germany, and parts of Italy. It was natural, therefore, that the cultural influences of Spain should to some extent have dominated in Flanders and Germany, in spite of the fact that from the early years of the Renaissance the inhabitants had protested against both the political and religious demands of Charles and his son and successor, Philip.

It was also impossible that some of the splendor and magnificence of the Cinquecento of Italy should not drift northward through Germany and directly affect the arts of the Lowlands. England supported Flanders in her efforts to throw off the Spanish yoke. Through the Elizabethan days and on through the close of the Marlborough campaigns, continual help and sympathy were extended to Holland. The Dutch Republic was established in 1577, at which time Holland was a dominant power upon the high seas. The common desire to crush the Pope's power and to spread the teachings of the Reformation gave an added impetus to the co-operation of England and Holland and eventually culminated, in 1689, in the English invitation to the Dutch Stadtholder, William of Orange, who had married the English Princess Mary, to become King of England.

The 16th century style of decoration in Flanders was essentially a Spanish provincial type. Its principal characteristics were seen in the furniture designs. The furniture of the period was made in both oak and walnut. It was primitive, heavy, massive in detail, and frequently clumsy in appearance. A vase-shaped, turned leg was much used. In the smaller houses much of the furniture was of the built-in type, and became a part

A 17th century Dutch interior showing plaster and tiled walls alternating with panelling. The ceiling consists of exposed heavy beams.

Seventeenth century Dutch room, showing Spanish Plateresque influence in the mantel design and wall panelling. The tiled fireplace, the vase-shaped furniture legs, and the use of the Oriental rug as a table cover are typical.

Dutch Kas

Marquetry Design
17th Century

Flemish Chair

DUTCH AND FLEMISH 17TH CENTURY FURNITURE.

of the architecture of the room. Furniture panels were framed in heavy moldings, panel fields were often pyramidal, and much heavy carving of the type used during the Italian Renaissance was introduced. Ornamented leather and rich velvets were used for upholstery materials.

From the middle of the 16th century until the end of the 17th century, furniture was architectural in character. Columns, pilasters, entablatures, pedestals, and other forms of classical design were used in unusual arrangements and proportions. Of particular importance were the enormous chests, cabinets, and wardrobes which were placed in nearly every room. Walnut was almost exclusively used in place of oak. The spiral leg for tables and chairs was introduced, usually braced with flat stretchers. The so-called "Flemish scroll" was first used about the middle of the 17th century. This form was sometimes known as "ear-shaped carving" because of its resemblance to the human ear. The ball foot became common for case furniture. Toward the end of the 17th century marquetry was introduced, in combination with selected woods used for veneering. Marble inlay patterns were often used for table tops.

The trade of the Dutch vessels with the Far East was responsible for the introduction of Chinese lacquer as a furniture finish and of Oriental porcelain as an important decorative accessory in the furnishing of rooms. Oriental rugs were used both for floors and as table covers. The original appearance of many of the 17th century Dutch interiors is shown in the paintings of Jan Steen, Teniers, Rembrandt, Dou, Vermeer, and others.

The Oriental influence eventually gave a great impetus to the development of Dutch pottery-making at the Delft and other furnaces. Ornamental plaques and platters often formed an important part of the decorative accessories and were either hung on the walls or stood on plate-racks or moldings carried around the walls of the room. Small painted tiles showing biblical scenes, peasant activities, ships, and other motifs were often used for fireplace enrichment or for the construction of large free-standing stoves.

In 1685 Daniel Marot, the Baroque designer, was driven from France by the revocation of the Edict of Nantes. He fled to Holland, where his ability was instantly recognized, and his stay is evidenced by the introduction of many French forms in Dutch art. Charles II of England, who had been a refugee in Holland, took the Franco-Dutch style to England upon his restoration to the throne, and this style continued in England when the Dutch William was called to the throne.

From 1700 onward the decorative arts of Flanders followed French leadership and sequence of style, although usually exaggerating the designs of the originals. Great luxury in living prevailed in both Antwerp and Amsterdam.

German, Austrian, and Scandinavian decoration. The Teutonic nations of Europe, although supreme in the musical arts, have never shown the same degree of creative initiative in the production of the plastic and decorative arts as have the nations of Latin origin. The political, economic, and religious confusion that for centuries was the lot of the central and north European countries precluded the development of an indigenous art tradition, and an art patronage of sufficient vigor to nurture native talent. It was not until the early years of the 20th century that these countries began to take the initiative in various forms of industrial art.

During the Middle Ages the great ecclesiastical structures were built largely on French patterns, and the early Renaissance witnessed a migration of Italian architects and craftsmen who designed the palaces for the nobility, the town halls for the cities, and the dwellings for the wealthy burghers.

During the 18th century, the French esthetic dominance of Europe not only spread across the Rhine, but reached the Scandinavian peninsula and the Baltic shores. Baroque and particularly rococo forms of art, both exotic to northern temperaments, seemed in their sumptuous fantasy an agreeable contrast to a people who had become accustomed to a rigorous medieval severity in their home surroundings. French designers who journeyed to foreign lands, perhaps less expert than those who remained at home, furnished their clients with exaggerated rococo forms in wood, paint, and plaster, often resembling confectioners' work.

Interior architectural composition frequently lacked formal symmetry

Eighteenth century room from a castle in Bavaria, showing gilt stucco decoration on a silver background, typical of the German interpretation of French work.

and proper scale. Impurity in style was often seen in the details, and the architectural orders were improperly used or surfeited with an excess of ornamentation. In spite of these deficiencies in design, the picturesque quality of many interiors imparted an undeniable charm and was gay and rich in effect.

Pseudo-French boiseries alternated with painted decorations, plaster relief ornament, and stretched textile wall coverings. Color schemes ranged from the regal gold or silver and white to bizarre and voluptuous combinations of strong primary hues. Mural decoration showing scenes of Norse mythology or Germanic legends often enriched the walls of important rooms.

The furniture of the 18th century was characterized by the same influences as the interior architecture. The romantic curvilinear forms of the Louis XV period dominated all design. At times, and according to the particular craftsmen who produced them, the furniture productions had all the dignity, subtle charm, and sophistication of the best of the French work, while other capricious examples distinctly showed their hybrid origin in successive swellings and contractions, lack of structural quality, and inappropriate selection and distribution of ornament. The enormous palace of Schönbrun near Vienna, what remains of the "Residenz" built in Munich for the Kings of Bavaria, and the delightful group of playful buildings at Nymphenburg contain hundreds of rooms that are characteristic of the influence of the French decorative art of the 18th century upon the Teutonic designers.

In the northern countries the close of the 18th century and the early years of the 19th century were influenced by the classic trend of the styles of both France and England. In Germany the Greek revival became strongly intrenched, but the results were often heavy in appearance and unsatisfactory in detail. The Bernadotte family helped to maintain the art influence of Napoleon in Sweden for some years after it had lost its vigor in France.

Biedermeier is a name given to a style of furniture that was produced in Austria and Germany during the first half of the 19th century. Because of its quaintness of character, its comparative cheapness, and its harmony with other styles, it has been used in the United States in recent years. The design influences of the style were from the two apparently incongruous sources, French Empire, and German painted peasant work. The results were usually based on one source alone, but in many examples a mixture of the two was seen.

The name *Biedermeier* was borrowed from an imaginary character, originating in cartoons published in a humorous magazine. The character was represented as a rather stout country gentleman called "Papa Biedermeier," who was well satisfied with himself, and was opinionated about certain subjects concerning which he had little knowledge, among them the fine and industrial arts.

The furniture that was produced varied considerably as to quality of design and structure. As this was an imitative style, the proportions were often sturdy, rectangular, and awkward in appearance. Many small, delicate pieces were produced, however, in the design of which grace was sought by the introduction of curved forms; but the curves were clumsy, often childish, and frequently unstructural. Case furniture, such as secretary desks, wardrobes, and cabinets, was architectural in character, with classical columns and pilasters of rather heavy proportions, simple classical moldings, arches, and triangular crestings simulating pediments. Little carving was used for ornament, but surface enrichment was produced with simple marquetry patterns and borders, with pressed brass ornaments of Greek inspiration, and particularly with painted forms in gilt, black,

BIEDERMEIER FURNITURE.

and color. The painted motifs consisted of floral, animal, and human forms, and objects such as wreaths, urns, and baskets. A few classical and Chinese patterns were also used occasionally. The painted ornament was often playful and humorous in character.

The woods used for the furniture were usually the products of farm and orchard, such as maple, elm, apple, pear, cherry, and birch. Mahogany, however, was also employed, and the cabinetmaker fully appreciated the beauty of the natural color and graining of this wood for panel use. Un-

Typical Bavarian peasant interior. The sgabello type chair is frequently seen in Germany, and the enclosed bedstead is common to all peasant interiors.

fortunately the separate wooden parts of individual pieces of furniture were sometimes ineffectually joined, and glue many times took the place of the more substantial dowel or tenon.

Peasant Arts of Europe

The term "peasant art" applies to decorative homemade objects of daily usage, designed and executed in rural communities, in the conception of which local traditions and race played a governing part. The peasant styles were those produced by the simple folk of each country whose natural love of color and beauty, often combined with traditional symbolism and superstition, enabled them to create gaily decorated rooms and to make and beautify many useful and interesting articles of home furnishings. Fishermen, shepherds, mountaineers, and farmers in all countries had their special patterns, designs, and forms for everything that they used. They knew little and cared less about the fashions of the metropolis. They made what they needed with their own hands and employed knife, chisel, hammer, paintbrush, and needle to produce their material necessities in a manner that would also contribute to their spiritual joys.

The most interesting varieties of peasant arts have been produced by the natives of central Europe, from the Balkan States northward through Czechoslovakia, Austria, Switzerland, Germany, and Scandinavia. None of these countries has produced original court styles, such as those seen in Italy, France, and England; their peasant crafts have been their natural

ABOVE: *An old Normandy peasant bedroom with furniture of various styles.*
BELOW: *A corner of a Normandy peasant house, with a Gothic door and wall treatment, the usual ménagère in the Louis XV style, and a Louis XIII chair.*

contribution to the industrial arts, the higher spheres of esthetic expression having been left to foreign talent. The more distant a nation was from the centers of production of the great period styles of arts, the less discernible was the influence of a sophisticated neighbor. The closer to the soil the craftsman happened to be, the more indigenous was his art expression.

Peasant arts and crafts were, of course, produced in Italy, France, England, and Spain; but, so far as household furnishing and decoration were concerned, they were so strongly influenced by the royal fashions about them that the forms strongly overlapped and it is often difficult to differ-

Carved Wood Panel

Chair Back

Carved and Painted Mirror

Painted Wooden Clock

Chair Back Painted

Chair Back

Wall Clock →

Table

Sqabello

Bed Alcove   Corner Shelf   Pottery

TYPES OF PEASANT FURNITURE AND ACCESSORIES.

entiate between the peasant and the provincial arts of these countries.

The introduction of easy means of transportation and communication and of cheap printing has practically throttled European peasant productions. Machine manufacturing, quantity production, and commercialization have taken the place of the hand-producing system of the country craftsman, working for himself or his neighbors and placing great care, love, and affection upon his product in his effort to carry out the unchanging traditions of his people.

The peasant art productions of all countries were, for the most part, crude. Painted patterns and naïve carving were the most usual forms of enrichment. Colors were vivid and primary; forms, gross and clumsy. But these defects were redeemed by the sincerity and conscientiousness of the craftsman and by his love for the craft.

Among the fascinating objects produced by the peasants and their industrious wives were regional costumes, embroideries, tiles, pottery, laces, textiles, toys, clocks, rugs, kitchen utensils, pewter tableware, tin and wooden moulds, jewelry, brass and iron articles, musical instruments, and ornamental harnesses.

The furniture made by the peasants was of the simplest variety. Chairs, stools, tables, free-standing and enclosed beds, chests, wardrobes, cupboards, plate shelves, dressers, and various food containers were the usual pieces.

In the peasant productions most of the patterns were geometric, particularly those of embroideries and wood-carvings. Abstract design quite naturally showed regional stylizations; but it is amazing to find that the simple mind of the peasant had so few avenues open to his creative vision that the concept was often of such a childish nature as to make its localization difficult.

Human figures and floral and animal forms quite naturally captivated the fancy of the peasant artist, who made lavish use of these subjects. The interpretation was usually exceedingly elementary and devoid of academic taint. Religious, legendary, and social influences often played a great part in the determination of patterns and forms; special articles and costumes were usually made for the celebration of holy days, for patriotic commemorations, and for special events. In the design of these, associated patterns and symbols were introduced.

The interest of the public in peasant or folk art has greatly increased during recent years, at a time when production has nearly ceased. In the decoration of traditional but informal rooms today, the use of the peasant-made articles of Europe adds much to the color and gaiety of effect.

Indian Arts of the Americas

The American Indian arts. "Pre-Columbian" is a term used to designate the arts produced by the indigenous inhabitants of both North America and South America before the arrival of the white man. Anthropologists believe that the Indians arrived perhaps twenty thousand years ago from Asia, via the Bering Straits. The principal migration was down the West Coast and the major final settlements were established from Mexico to northern Chile, although stragglers moved eastward and established the Indian races of the Northern Hemisphere. Many of the living individuals of these races retain physical characteristics that confirm an Asiatic origin, and archeologists claim occasional resemblances between early Indian and Asiatic art forms. The original settlers brought with them a knowledge of stone-chipping, basketry, and fire-making, but there is ample evidence that agriculture and the crafts of weaving and pottery were not developed until long after their arrival. Although an archaic culture existed for thousands of years, their recorded history probably dates only from the beginnings of the Christian Era. The final geographical distribution of the various groups was over such an immense territory that it is doubtful that any cultural contact occurred between them, and such isolation accounts for the different character of the esthetic expressions. There were minor parallelisms, but these were probably due to similarities of native requirements, soil, and climate, and the western groups in due time produced a civilization that cannot be lightly considered. Each developed a primitive culture that over a period of several centuries rose to a magnificent apex and finally declined, probably due to overconfidence in their own security, and the envy of neighboring tribes. Both the Peruvian and Mexican nations, who were conquered in the early years of the 16th century respectively by Pizarro and Cortez, were already on the decline when the Spaniards arrived, and although the conquistadores are accused of cruelties in the extermination of these civilizations, final judgment must be tempered by a consideration of the times, the conditions of the period, the customs of the natives, and the Christian fanaticism with which all Europeans were saturated.

The important examples of the arts of these ancient groups are contained in museums, but there are still available both old and recent productions of these people. The textile patterns and pottery of Indian origin are of great interest and valuable for decorative use. It must also not be forgotten that these ancient American civilizations have left modern man much that is valued. Among such items are maize, potatoes, tomatoes, pumpkins, cotton, quinine, cocaine, rubber, chicle, and such animals as the llama, alpaca, guinea pig, and turkey.

Central American Indian arts. The greatest and perhaps earliest Indian civilization was that of the Mayas, whose center of activity was in southern Mexico. It is estimated that their historical records date from the birth of Christ, and perhaps reached a zenith between A.D. 300 and 600. The Mayas developed hieroglyphic inscriptions as an element of surface design and measured time by an accurate knowledge of astronomy. They developed methods of irrigating their fields, which brought them great wealth and a well-organized social existence under an aristocracy who lived in the greatest splendor. Evidences of their culture are seen in the remains of the great temples and pyramids which were built under the incentive of religious fanaticism. The interiors of these buildings were decorated with both wall sculpture and mural paintings. The patterns were well composed all-over treatments, often in geometric conventionalization, in which the dominant lines were an interplay of rectangular forms and exact 45 degree diagonals. Many of their sculptural and painted patterns were obviously inspired by their textiles in which were indicated both brocade and lace techniques. In figure drawing the Mayas had a greater knowledge of the principles of perspective than did the ancient Egyptians or Assyrians. They produced minor arts in clay, precious and base metals, and semiprecious stones. They were excellent potters, making figures, dishes, bowls, and other containers which were enriched by painting, hand modelling, engraving, and stamping. Gold, silver, and copper; jadeite, turquoise, and other stones were worked into ornaments of fantastic shapes and colors. The decorative motifs used were hieroglyphics, geometrical patterns, grotesque figures, supernatural beings, and the birds and animals of the local jungles, such as monkeys and jaguars. The winged serpent or rattlesnake seemed to be the most sacred of living creatures, and a symbol of divinity; it was usually represented in a highly conventionalized, almost unrecognizable interpretation, and often clothed or enriched with human attributes and ornaments.

Courtesy American Museum of Natural History

Mayan carving dating from about A.D. *700 from Yaxchillan, Chiapas, Mexico.*

Courtesy Heye Foundation

Mexican Indian turquoise mosaic shield.

The Mayan supremacy ended shortly before the discovery of America. The cause of its decline has not been clarified, but its civilization was in-

Toltec Temple of Quetzalcoatl, Teltihuacan, Mexico, showing sculptured surface ornament.

Mayan laughing face from Vera Cruz, Mexico.

Mural painting from Chichen Itza, Yucatan.

herited and developed by other Indian tribes who were of contemporary or later date. Among these were the Zapotecs in the State of Oaxaca. In the city of Mitla, which was the burial ground of the kings of this tribe, are ruins of great stone and concrete temples and tombs, the exteriors of which were covered with plaster, painted red, and decorated with frescoes done in

Zapotec funerary urns.

red and black patterns on a white base, showing religious ceremonies. Sculptured figures in relief show personages and gods dressed in elaborate capes, girdles, aprons, skirts, and headdresses. Extraordinary gold jewelry has been found in the graves of Monte Alban.

The Totonacans, a tribe related to the Zapotecs, who lived near the city of Vera Cruz, produced extraordinary clay-modelled heads with slanting eyes and countenances often indicating unrestrained mirth, an expression not yet explained.

The Toltecs, who were contemporary with the Zapotecs, flourished in Yucatan and Oaxaca from A.D. 600 to 1100 and what remained of their culture is described in the writings of the Spanish conquerors. The great city and Citadel at San Juan Teltihuacan near Mexico City is the principal architectural ruin of this group. This city contains the remains of great pyramids, brightly colored temples, and richly ornamented stairways. The architecture was enriched by representations of feathered serpents, shells, butterflies, and large sculptured figures. Remarkable painted pottery vases, figurines, and heads have been found, and a special type of ware that resembles cloisonné enamel was also made. Clay dolls with movable limbs were produced and figures of the various gods were represented in fantastic personifications.

In the vicinity of Costa Rica and Panama have been found interesting types of gold work. These have been both of the plain and hollow-cast varieties and are both solid and plated on copper sheets. The process that was used in plating is not known. Many ornaments are of pure-gold sheets beaten into repoussé designs. The motifs are human forms, frogs, lizards, turtles, crocodiles, jungle animals, and birds with outspread wings that were used for amulets.

When Cortez entered the highlands of southern Mexico, he found the Aztecs, who had developed a culture that was at its height. This is the only one of the ancient Indian civilizations with which contact was made at its supreme point, and concerning which knowledge has been obtained

Aztec water motifs.

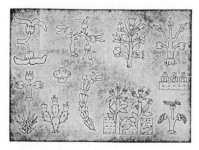

Aztec floral motifs.

directly rather than through archeological research. The Aztecs had inherited the civilization of the Toltecs and built (probably about A.D. 1325) their island capital in Tenochtitlan, now Mexico City. Cortez was overwhelmed by the grandeur that he saw, but this did not prevent him from destroying the ancient city and building the new city of Mexico over its ruins. Only in recent years have excavations been made that have brought to light extraordinary evidences of a rich architecture, ceremonial objects, and ancient relics of the former inhabitants. Aztec culture was completely dominated by religious fear, fanaticism, and sadism. Human sacrifices by a bloodthirsty people were constantly required to guarantee favorable crops and political events. These horrible ceremonies have probably never been equalled in world history.* Wars with neighboring nations were undertaken to obtain adult and child victims for these perpetual sacrifices, and thousands were often sacrificed during a single ceremony that lasted for several days.

The Aztecs had a well-organized government headed by a king who left his throne to his most able son. Their literature, inscribed on paper and deerskin, and illustrated in brilliant colors, has been translated. They were extraordinary workers in many of the arts and crafts as well as the more important art of architecture. Their pottery was usually made in an orange-colored clay decorated with black painted figures of both realistic and conventionalized forms. Clay figurines were made from moulds and were not as fine as the earlier hand-modelled figures produced by other races. Jadeite carving was extensively practised, and, considering the primitive tools and the patience required for this work, the results were astounding. In the production of heads and masks, human features were often exaggerated to a point where they must be considered far from

* Written records describe those in which a single victim was considered a god, was feted, given every honor, adorned with the richest of garments, given the freedom of the city, and married to the most beautiful maidens. He was expected to go willingly to the altar, uplifted by a supreme religious ecstasy. The slightest hesitancy was considered an omen of the greatest misfortune. On the day of the sacrifice he was stripped of his garments and mounted the steps of a pyramid, where priests cut his heart out, and offered it to the god he had impersonated.

beautiful by modern standards. Jewelry was made in gold and mosaic decorations, consisting of turquoise, probably obtained by trade with the peoples north of the Rio Grande. Red jasper, jet, and shells of various colors were also used in mosaic work. The Aztecs also excelled in feather work; gay headdresses and cloaks were patterned with pluckings from macaws, parrots, hummingbirds, black vultures, and harpy-eagles.

The Spanish conquerors, followed by their priests, ended the growth of the Aztec culture and dominance, taught the Indians such Christianity as they could absorb, and introduced the arts of their homeland.

South American Indian arts. Contemporary, but entirely independent, of the Central American Indian civilizations was that of the Empire known as the Incas, which extended from Peru to Chile and included parts of Ecuador and Bolivia. Cul-

Courtesy American Museum of Natural History

Early Inca pottery jar.

turally related branches existed in Colombia and as far north as Panama.

When Pizarro arrived in 1532, he found a very ancient civilization with its capital at Cuzco, a city in the Andes that is 11,000 feet above sea level, where a well-organized government controlled a territory of enormous extent on the Pacific coast. Unity was maintained by well-established laws, a common religion of sun-worship, and an extraordinary system of roads, canals, bridges, and aqueducts. Human sacrifice was not as extensive as in Mexico, but warriors shrank the severed heads of conquered enemies and carried them as proof of valor. When an Inca leader died, his wives and servants struggled for the honor of being buried with him, and his riches were placed in his tomb.* The intellectual level of the people was less high than that of the northern races; they knew little of astronomy, although time was measured by the shadow of towers. They had no written language, yet they were superior to the northerners in agriculture and weaving, and equalled them in many of the other crafts. Surgery was

* The Spanish conquerors often tortured the inhabitants to force them to indicate the location of these tombs, and much of the ancient treasure was brought to Spain where it was melted for its metal value.

ABOVE: *Inca pottery bowl from Peru.* LEFT: *Inca feather headdress made about 1500 in Peru.*

Courtesy American Museum of Natural History

practiced, amputations successfully made, and evidences are clear that they knew the principles of skull trephining.

In their buildings, the Incas used stones of immense size that were cut to the most accurate fit. One of these stones is 38 feet long, 18 feet high, and 6 feet thick. They were brought from quarries 30 miles distant and it is presumed that to place them, such stones were raised on inclined platforms by means of levers and rollers in a manner that resembled Egyptian methods. The architecture of the Incas was impressive by its size rather than by the extensive surface enrichment that is evident in the Mexican work.

Although the potter's wheel was unknown, the Incas reached a high degree in beauty of outline of container forms, and decorated their ware with painted ornamental designs that run riot in conventionalization. Basket weaving was developed in both coarse and extremely fine weaves to a high degree of proficiency. Personal ornaments were made with beads, stone, bone, shell, seeds, and berries. Beads were of gold, silver, emerald, lapis lazuli, amethyst, turquoise, agate, and quartz. Bands of both solid and plated gold were worked into bracelets and finger-rings, and copper, lead, and bronze ornaments were made by casting and hammering. Iron was unknown. Textiles for clothing, tapestries, and blankets were colorfully woven with finely twisted yarns and fast dyes in cotton, alpaca, and vicuña wool. Patterns were composed of highly conventionalized representations of the human figure, condor, puma, and fish, all of which seemed to have a sacred significance. Many mythological figures were shown in both surface patterns and free sculptural forms that fancifully combined human, animal, fish, and bird features. Feather weaving was also developed to a high degree.

North American Indian arts. The Indians of North America never developed a culture that equalled that of the original inhabitants of Central America and South America. There are ample evidences throughout the United States of prehistoric cave dwellings, and there have been many artifacts and cave paintings discovered, proving an archaic period. The Indians who, during the last ten centuries, inhabited the confines of the present United States were broadly divided into two main types. The nomads were warlike tribes who lived in temporary shelters, migrated from valley to valley according to their agricultural needs, and developed only the most meagre of crafts. Those whose arts are of more interest were the pueblo groups who were permanently settled, constructed large community dwellings of stone and adobe brick, established a comparatively peaceful organization, developed utilitarian crafts, and harvested their crops and stored them for use in times of shortages. The latter, who were probably the ancestors of the Hopis, Zunis, and Navajos, were mainly located and pursued their lives unmolested in the States of Arizona and New Mexico from A.D. 1000 until the coming of the Spaniards in 1540. Their descendants have carried on their arts to the present day, although many of these have become commercialized for the tourist trade.

The pueblos * consisted of a group of hundreds of living and storage rooms, which were set against each other, usually surrounding courtyards or patios where official and religious ceremonies were held. In these courts altars and stone seats are still intact today. The individual living areas usually consisted of one room, in which all the activities of the family were carried on. A very small door opening was covered with a blanket or rushwoven screen and no windows existed. Fireplaces were built in the middle of the room, and stone grain-grinders adjoined one of the walls. The floor was earthen, but cloth and rush mats were used for sitting and sleeping purposes. Existing ruins show no other evidences of room decorations or furniture.

These Indians produced patterned textiles, ornamental pottery, baskets, personal ornaments, tools, and hunting implements on which much intelligent thought was placed in developing a suitable enrichment. The materials were silver, stone, gypsum, wood, clay, shell, horn, bone, grass, yucca,

* This word is taken from the Spanish word for *town,* but it is also applied to the houses and to the people themselves.

Four Ages

Hogan (Home)

Clouds (Prosperity)

Deer Track (Game)

Water

Sun Rays (Constancy)

Rainbow (Prosperity)

Rain (Crops)

Large Mountain (Abundance)

Rain Comes

Thunder Bird (Happiness)

Snake (Defiance)

Gila Monster (Desert)

Swastika (Good Luck)

Bear Track (Good Omen)

Day and Night (Time)

Clouds

Seed

Star (Guidance)

Butterfly (Beauty)

Lightning

Mountain Range

Bird (Carefree)

Rain (Prosperity)

Arrow (Protection)

Moon

Conventional Bird Motifs

SYMBOLIC MOTIFS TAKEN FROM NAVAJO AND PUEBLO INDIAN POTTERY AND TEXTILES.

cotton, wool, feathers, and hides. Personal ornaments consisted of beads, pendants, necklaces, bracelets, and finger-rings and earrings made of shells, turquoise, and other colored stones. Turquoise was considered a good-luck stone, and a defense from evil and misfortune. Many types of baskets and mats were made of willow, reeds, and yucca, woven in plain, basket, or twill weave. Well-made baked clay products such as bowls, cups, pitchers, and bottles were made from a very early period; these were usually enriched with a painted decoration in white, black, and red. Paints were made from various minerals mixed with clay, and some were used that give the effect of a burnished or luster ware.

The most interesting of these Indian patterns are seen in their textiles and pottery. The motifs probably had a symbolic meaning, and they were as a rule of geometric conventionalizations. As the religion of the Indians consisted mainly in a worship of the forces of Nature, symbols such as sun-rays, lightning, clouds, rain, and thunder were frequently employed. The swastika, chevron, steps, rectangle, triangle, disc, ring, fret, dentil, zigzag and coil were also used for borders or all-over patterns. There are also many irregular and abstract forms that were probably the product of the imagination of the individual craftsman. Diagonal and rectangular hatching were resorted to in pottery decoration and herringbone effects in woven products. The human figure, deer, foxes, bears, bush, and plant forms are represented in both naturalistic and highly conventionalized interpretations. There was no mass production and no two objects were ever made alike.

The Indians of the Northwest coast produced an ingenious primitive art that included wooden statues closely resembling the work of other prehistoric races. When the Russians arrived at the end of the 18th century, the Indians were given better tools, and during the 19th century their arts were greatly elaborated. The Nootkas of Vancouver, the Haidas of British Columbia, and the Tlinkits of Alaska have been among those who have advantageously used the timber of the giant red cedars that grew in their territory. They have constructed wooden plank dwellings, the walls and partitions of which are decorated with colorful large-scale symbolic motifs. Having no nails, the structural portions and planks are joined with cedar-root cords. Totem poles are still used to identify the inhabitants of each house; these, and the canoes that they made by hollowing enormous tree trunks, are covered with painted relief carvings showing family crests and legends. The women of these tribes show supreme craftsmanship in basketry. Working with infinite patience they produce the finest of grass weaves, using slips of minuscule diameters to create patterns of geometrical, animal, and marine motifs. Many of the tribes are noted for painted wooden chests, boxes, bowls, and rattles, and the most northern tribes make blankets of mountain-goat hair, which they embroider with shells.

Arizona Pueblo Indian baskets.

New Mexico Pueblo Indian pottery.

All tribes carve fantastic wooden masks for religious and pageantry uses, modelling them into symbolic, humorous, and terrifying facial expressions.

The Eskimos live in widely separated settlements near the Arctic Circle from Alaska to Greenland, in the most unpleasant climate in the world. There is neither vegetation nor natural resources. These people depend entirely on wild life for sustenance. They are healthy and eat much raw meat and fish. They live in skin tents in summer and in underground shacks made of driftwood and earth in winter. They have invented the blubber lamp for heating and cooking. In spite of the dearth of materials and tools, they are endowed with extraordinary inventiveness in making utilitarian objects. Clothing is made from animal skins. Hunting equipment is made from driftwood and walrus tusks. The handles of tools are often carved or engraved with animal motifs. They have contributed the dog sled and the kayak to civilization. Living drab lives, they provoke humor and amusement by carving grotesque masks.

In the arts of all these northern Indians, there are individual group characteristics. The craftsmen of each remain loyal to the character of the productions and the ornamental motifs used in the art interpretations of their own group. The encroachments of civilization in recent years have greatly modified their native productions and art expressions.

African Negro Sculpture

An art expression that has been given considerable study during recent years is that of the sculpture of the primitive races that inhabit the Central West Coast of Africa. These arts have been a native product with little adulteration from European sources. Their provenance has been mainly from the Belgian Congo, although important finds have been made in the Gold Coast, southern Nigeria, French Guiana, and Sierra Leone. Dahomey and Benin, from an early period, were perhaps influenced by European trade.

Public interest has been due in part to the resemblance of these objects to those found in Europe of the Aurignacian and Solutrian periods,* as well as the primitive Greek and Etruscan statuary of the second millennium B.C. Archeologists have been intrigued with the African arts because of the probability of a similarity of impulse in their production, which, if understood, would help to clarify the thought that created the earliest arts of Western civilizations.

African sculpture is to some extent a paradoxical art. The aboriginal Negro adorns his body

Gouro mask from Ivory Coast and carved figure of antelope from French Sudan.

with ornaments but wears little clothing. Rhythm and the dance are important factors in his life and he lives in close contact with jungle animals, yet these influences have not affected his art. Animals are seldom represented and most of the sculpture shows the static human body. Figurines show no idealism of form, materialistic purpose, nor appreciation of beauty according to white race standards; perfection of modelling or eroticism have never interested the artist; his art has been purely spiritual, an expression of vital religious beliefs, and an effort to maintain the memory and influences of his deceased ancestors. The Negro has concentrated on the all-absorbing necessity of placating the spirits and controlling destiny by creating distorted images of his deities or good-luck fetishes that are intended to promote a perpetuation of his race. His arts have been closely associated with biological needs; the majority of sculptural figures are those of the female. In the creation of his artistic forms, his esthetic efforts, imagination, and mental processes have been similar to those of a child. Emotions rule the actions of the native African. Seemingly unmotivated causes suddenly change his feelings from gaiety to tears, or from love to hate, and he does not reason logically or with foresight. The immediate present is his only concern; to him an intellectual past and future is of little importance. This attitude has been the cause of the

* These are names of prehistoric cultural periods that existed about thirty thousand years B.C.

lack of cultural traditions, or artistic evolution.

In modelling the human figure, the dominance of the head is usually noticeable and the facial features are often exaggerated. In some examples, facial elements are suppressed to the most simple detail and mere indications of modelling are shown by angular, blocklike, or plane arrangements. The restraint and technical ability displayed produce a most forceful effect. The portions of the human body related to fertility and reproduction are often exaggerated, as in the prehistoric Willendorf figure (see page 19), and probably for the same reasons. The Negro, without the use of logic, unconsciously arrives at a depth of artistic principles that is nearly the equal of that of the generally accepted superior races.

Negro art has strongly interested modern Western painters and sculptors because of the avoidance in its production of the Greek ideals upon which classic art has always been produced; but modern artists, though working on the assumed principles of Negro thought, have been too saturated with their own traditions. Without the native impulses, the results have been largely abortive. There exists therefore a continued demand for original African examples, which are of great interest to the connoisseur.

Courtesy American Museum of Natural History

The majority of figures of Negro sculpture are in native woods, ranging in height from 9 to 24 inches. Many examples are colored or stained black. None of the wooden examples is probably over a century old, due to the activities of the white ant, the destructiveness of which has prevented a continuous tradition in art forms. As a result, great variations in detail and patterns occur, as each sculptor has produced according to his own standards, with little knowledge of previous works. Other Negro crafts of considerable ingenuity are those of palm-fibre textiles and household utensils.

Colonial governments have prohibited the exportation of the productions of the African hinterland, and there are few opportunities to obtain sculptures that show evidence of the emotional intensity that was essential in creating objects for the religio-magical rituals. There has been a disintegration of native talent and present production is of inferior quality and made for the tourist trade.

Bibliography

ACKERMAN, PHYLLIS, *Guide to the Exhibition of Persian Art, 1940.* The Iranian Institute, New York City. A well illustrated descriptive guide to the remarkable exhibit held in New York in 1940.

ADAM, L., *Primitive Art.* Penguin Books, Harmondsworth, Middlesex, England. Revised 1949. A short but excellent illustrated text on all primitive art types.

BENNET, WENDEL C., *Ancient Art of the Andes.* Museum of Modern Art, New York, 1954.

BOSSERT, H. T., *Peasant Art in Europe.* Berlin, 1926. Foreign text illustrated with photographs and color prints.

CARTER, DAGNY, *Four Thousand Years of China's Art.* Ronald Press Co., New York, 1948. An excellent short but well illustrated historical outline of the various arts of China from the earliest days.

DIMAND, M. J., *A Handbook of Muhammadan Art.* Hartsdale House, New York, 1947. An excellent outline by the Curator of Near Eastern Art of the Metropolitan Museum of Art.

DOUGLAS AND D'HARNONCOURT, *Indian Art of the United States.* The Museum of Modern Art, New York, 1941. Well illustrated in color and black and white with excellent descriptive captions.

DREXLER, ARTHUR, *Architecture of Japan.* Museum of Modern Art, New York, 1955.

ERIXON, S., *Möbler Och Heminredning I Svenska Bygder, Vol. 1181.* Stockholm, 1926. Photographs of Swedish furniture with Swedish text.

FRY, ROGER, *Last Lectures.* Macmillan Co., New York, 1939. Lectures on primitive arts by the Professor of Fine Arts of Cambridge University, one of the greatest authorities on this subject. Beautifully illustrated.

HOLME, C., *Peasant Art in Austria and Hungary.* The Studio, Ltd., New York, 1911. Text and illustrations on Austrian, Hungarian, and Roumanian art.

INVERARITY, ROBERT BRUCE, *Art of the Northwest Coast Indians.* University of California Press, Berkeley, 1950.

JONGE, C. H. DE, AND VOGELSANG, W., *Hollendische Möbel und Raumkunst von 1650–1780.* Martinus Nishoff, S-Gravenhage, 1922. Photographs with introductory text in German.

KATES, C. N., *Chinese Household Furniture.* Harper and Bros., New York, 1948. One of the few publications in English on this subject.

LINTON, RALPH, AND WINGATE, PAUL, in collaboration with René d'Harnoncourt, *Arts of the South Seas.* Museum of Modern Art, New York, 1946. Color illustrations and maps.

MEAD, CHARLES W., *Old Civilizations of Inca Land.* American Museum of Natural History Handbook Series, No. 11, New York, 1924.

Metropolitan Museum of Art, *American Index of Design–Pennsylvania German.* New York, 1943. Excellent illustrations and text.

MEYER, J., *Fordits Kunst: Norges Bygder.* (Norwegian Peasant Art, Oslo, 1934. Standard book on this subject.

POPE, A. U., *Introduction to Persian Art.* Charles Scribner's Sons, New York, 1930. Excellent text.

REUGHER, O., *Indische Palaste und Wohnhauser*. Berlin, 1925. Excellent German text on East Indian architecture.

SCHMITZ, H., *Deutsche Möbel des Barock und Rokoko*. Verlag von Julius Hoffmann, Stuttgart, 1923. German text with excellent photographs showing German adaptations of Italian and French 17th and 18th century furniture.

SCHMITZ, H., *Deutsche Möbel des Klassizimus*. Verlag von Julius Hoffmann, Stuttgart. German text with fine plates.

SCHMITZ, H., *Vor Hundert Jahren: Festraume und Wohnzimmer des Deutschen Klassizismus und Biedermeier*. Verlag fur Kunstwissenschaft, Berlin, 1920. Interiors of the late 18th century and early 19th century in two volumes; the first of text and photographs and the second of excellent color plates.

SINGLETON, E., *Dutch and Flemish Furniture*. McClure, Phillips and Co., New York, 1907. Illustrated text.

SIRÉN, O., *Gardens of China*. Ronald Press, New York, 1949. Beautifully illustrated authoritative book.

SPINDEN, HERBERT, J., *Ancient Civilizations of Mexico and Central America*. American Museum of Natural History Handbook Series, No. 3, New York, 1922.

SWEENEY, JAMES JOHNSON, Editor. *African Negro Art*. Museum of Modern Art. New York, 1935.

ZWEIG, M., *Zweites Rokoko*. Kunstnerlag, Anton Schroll and Co., Vienna, 1924. German text with fine collection of early 19th century German furniture.

Also, publications of the Museum of Modern Art, New York. Books and pamphlets on contemporary fine and industrial arts are frequently published by this organization. Those interested should write for the latest catalogue.

PART TWO

CONTEMPORARY ARCHITECTURE, INTERIOR DESIGN, AND FURNITURE

CHAPTER IX

CONTEMPORARY ARCHITECTURE AND INTERIOR DESIGN

<hr>

The Industrial Revolution and its manifestations were the greatest forces in the development of 20th century art. It is, therefore, necessary to start a study of the 20th century with a description of conditions and events that first took shape during the 18th century.

The schism between the architect and the engineer that characterized much work at the end of the 18th and during most of the 19th centuries was the principal part of an over-all split between art and science. The times were rich in scientific development; engineering inventiveness was evident in terms of new materials and bold uses of old materials. As the scientist uncovered new horizons, the artist hid in the cloak of romanticism; as the engineer triumphed, the defeated architect found comfort in styles of the past.

The use and the refinement of iron and the further refinement of iron into steel were essential concerns of the engineer. These developments helped solve the functional needs of enclosed space, first for industrial use, and later for commercial use. These new needs and materials also created new space forms.

The architect refused to cope with the new problems created by the Industrial Revolution. Nevertheless, the engineer, supplying both structure and material, became profoundly involved with these problems. The architecture of the present century owes its roots to the engineer who, through new building technology, created new enclosed space for industry. Only when the architect faced up to the problems of the Industrial Revolution did architecture begin to grow. As it began to replace mere building the architecture of the present century was born.

In terms of the arts, the Industrial Revolution was the change from hand-crafted products made in the home for local consumption to machine-fashioned products made in the factory for national and international consumption. The change was gradual. It started in France prior to the Revolution and continued through the actual industrialization of Germany in the early decades of the present century. The initial impact of industry was seen as early as 1750, at which time power-driven machines had influenced society, politics, industry, trade, and transportation, particularly in England. The tremendous growth of population and the movement of people to find work in centrally located factories stimulated both the growth of existing cities and the beginnings of new ones.

The revolution in textile manufacture. This first occurred in France where Jacquard and Vaucanson employed water power to run machines that wove elaborately patterned fabrics. By the beginning of the 19th century there were more than ten thousand Jacquard Looms in France. In 1797 Oberkampf introduced cylinder printing at Jouy, claiming that one machine could do the work of 40 block printers. The English invented the flying shuttle (John Kay in 1733), the spinning jenny (James Hargreaves in 1770), the water-operated roller spinning frame (Richard Arkwright in 1769-1775), and the spinning mule (Samuel Crompton in 1779). The power loom developed by Edmund Cartwright in 1785 resulted in the growth of the cotton industry and the demand for raw cotton. Whitney's cotton gin of 1793 soon made the United States the major supplier of raw cotton to the industrialized world.

The most important invention was, however, the steam engine of James Watt (1769) which permitted a rotary as well as the up and down movements of the piston, thereby facilitating the process of weaving. This permitted the expansion of the textile industry, as the more laborious utilization of water power was no longer necessary.

The change to coal and the revolution in iron. This event resulted from the inventions of the Abraham Darbys and of Henry Cort, which permitted the use of coal instead of charcoal in blast furnaces and forges. Their effects were even more far-reaching. Although France was rich in woodland and could produce an abundance of charcoal, very little coal was mined. Quite the opposite situation existed in England, so the inventions of the Darbys and Cort permitted England to take production leadership away from France. (This change in the iron industry was parallel to the invention of the steam engine in the textile industry.) Iron was first used in the construction of machinery. Then shortly after the casting of iron rails was begun, the first cast iron bridge, over the Severn, was erected in 1779. The Theatre-Francais in Paris was roofed in iron (1786), and by 1800 the rage for iron construction was widespread.

The Romantic revivals. These revivals, which occurred during the late 18th and the 19th centuries, are presented as part of the specific material of Chapters IV through VIII of this book. However, they are noted here so that the romantic escapes of the architect can be measured along with the objective contributions of the engineer—at least until 1875. Naturally there is a time lag between the occurrence of specific revivals in Europe and their appearance in the United States. The classical revival ended the 18th and began the 19th century. The Roman revival, as illustrated by the Neo-classic in France and the work of the Adam brothers in England, preceded the Greek revival; the Gothic revival, which at first overlapped the Greek revival, was followed by the Renaissance revival. A kind of chaos sometimes referred to as "The Battle of the Styles" resulted when rival stylism shared the forefront of contemporary attention.

The development of new structural systems. These grew out of the need for larger spaces in factories. As cast and wrought iron were improved in quality and appearance, a new architecture of iron, wood, and glass emerged. At first, cast iron columns were used with timber girders and beams. Outer walls of masonry (hence called bearing walls) carried part of the roof weight and enclosed this framework. Later, girders made of iron were introduced, and by means of these new structural members, greater spans between cast iron columns became possible. Free standing columns supporting iron girders and timber roofs created the typical flexible factory interiors of the mid-century.

Industrial expositions. Ever larger column-free spaces were needed to house these exhibits of machine-made products, paintings, and sculpture, which were popular attractions during this period. The smaller iron-framed factory, which was achieved through the use of iron arches, ribs, trusses, girders, beams and columns, was the beginning of the growth of these huge structures. Building forms were designed about a linear framework of iron. Once the actual structural frame became self-sustaining, the covering of this frame lost structural significance and nonstructural materials such as glass, which is able to carry only its own weight, were used for exterior surfacing. Greenhouse construction, developed early in the 19th century, is a fine example of the iron cage with a nonstructural glass skin.

The Crystal Palace at the London exposition of 1851 was a daring demonstration of the tremendous spaces that the iron frame could span. Its floor area was four times that of St. Peter's in Rome. Joseph Paxton, the builder, achieved this great showcase of industrialization through the remarkably simple application of the best-known structural principles to the best-known materials. He placed the glass skin in wood frames, rested the frames on arches and girders of iron which were bolted together, and carried the girders on iron columns. As each section was the same as the others, his building could have been of any length, depending upon the number of times he repeated the original structure. Amusingly, he stopped the building at 1851 feet—the year of its construction! All the parts were made in factories and were assembled at the building site. The Crystal

An interior view of the Crystal Palace showing the remarkable freedom of space and intensity of natural light that the modular iron frame and glass panels produced.

Palace may therefore be considered an early example of prefabrication. Once the parts had been made, the erection of the entire building took less than six months. This modular design was based upon the use of the largest pane of glass (four feet square) then manufactured. Both prefabrication and modular design were to become of great importance in 20th century architecture.

Other steel structures. Other needs for large span construction appeared during the 19th century. The new structural frame of iron created enclosures for markets, railroad stations, department stores, libraries and other new building types. Large-span iron structures were used for the exhibition halls of the 1855, 1867, 1878, and 1889 Paris Expositions. Henri Labrouste (1801–1875) developed the first library buildings using iron, and his plan concepts are still used today. The Saint Genevieve Library (1850) and the National Library in Paris (1869) were built with iron frames. The National Library used unusually large areas of glass. The famous tower that Gustave Eiffel erected as the center of the Paris Exposition of 1889 was the monumental symbol of the great creative engineering of the 19th century. In present times the Eiffel Tower has become the romantic symbol of Paris.

The design philosophy of the machine-made product. The social revolutions that were concurrent with the Industrial Revolution created the initial purpose for the machine-made product: to turn out, inexpensively, by the yard what had been made by hand, expensively, by the inch. The growth of a middle class created new demands for symbols of success. These symbols were the materials of aristocracy. The machine, therefore, attempted to copy in large quantities the hand-produced decorative arts of the upper classes. As the number of status seekers grew, the machine was able to satisfy the growing demand for status symbols. These copies were most apparent in the designs of wallpaper, textiles, metalwork, glassware, ceramics, floor coverings, and in the joinery and carving of furniture and cabinetwork. By 1830 there was little demand for hand-crafted products, and machine-made imitations, which were inferior, flooded the market. The closer a machine-made product resembled a hand-made product, the better it was considered; and this criterion of evaluation carried into the first half of the present century.

The problems and the products of industrialization. These contributed to the social protests of the times. God made the country; man made the city. The country is good and the city is evil. Some moralists varied this cry: hand-work is good and machine-work is evil. In fact, the Industrial Revolution was making a poor social mark. It created technological unemployment, long working hours, child labor, and poor urban living conditions. The moralists argued for the denial of industry and the return to hand-crafts as the only way to correct the evils of the machine. Aside from the social objections to the effects of the machine, there were esthetic objections to the designs that the machine produced. These protests, social on one hand and esthetic on the other, proved to be catalytic in the development of a new design philosophy: the making of new designs that were expressive of the materials the machine had created, and that were expressive of the machine itself.

Reactions to the Industrial Revolution. Once the social and esthetic values of the Renaissance revival were overthrown, the manufacturing facility of the machine changed the Western World. Society tempered the machine only when moral and esthetic criticisms were clearly voiced. Sermons were preached against the soullessness of the machine, and the moralists offered the righteousness of early Gothic design as the conscience of the times.

The Arts and Crafts Movement in England. This movement, which burst forth about 1860, advocated the hand fabrication of products as opposed to machine fabrication. The leader of the new school was the pre-Raphaelite poet, William Morris (1834–1896). By the 1860's Morris was preaching a return to the inspirational values of the late Middle Ages. He founded the firm of Morris, Marshall and Faulkner, whose work then concentrated on church decoration, stained glass, textiles, carving, wall hangings, and furniture. Morris commissioned Philip Webb to design his own residence, "Red House." This famous building was a far cry from the mannered revivals of the period.

The writers John Ruskin and Horace Walpole were in accord with Morris. Ruskin, the great arbiter of taste, urged in his book, *The Seven Lamps of Architecture* (1849) a return to honest craftsmanship, particularly the honest craftsmanship of the Gothic period. The styles of the past afforded escape from the realities of the new times. This was attested by A.W.N. Pugin in England and Viollet-le-Duc in France. In England the reversion to the styles of the past was completed early in the 19th century; the area of conflict concerned itself only with which actual style should be used. The Gothic style of the Houses of Parliament in London (1836) designed by Pugin, proved that Gothic was the momentary winner.

In the judgment of today, Morris' contributions were most significant because he insisted that art and design be part of the normal life and because he established a movement of great idealism and honesty. That he was identified with the Neo-Gothic group is of no importance; the fact that he questioned how the machine was used is his contribution. His actual answer to the question is not important, but because Morris prepared the way for further new investigations, he enters the realm of history.

Art Nouveau. While the Arts and Crafts Movement against the machine was primarily motivated by morality, the causes of *Art Nouveau* were primarily esthetic. Art Nouveau was a conscious attempt to produce a new style that owed nothing to the past; it went no further than the invention of a new kind of ornament. It was a style of art for art's sake. The design premise was the adaptation of the asymmetrical flowing lines of plant forms. The movement, undoubtedly influenced by the drawings of the British artists Mackmurdo and Beardsley, started in Belgium in the 1880's. The Town House (1893) in Brussels, designed by Victor Horta, is the most celebrated, if not the best work of this period. Floral forms in iron are the essence of the interior ornamentation. Rail designs, floor patterns, window divisions and column ornamentations use this same decorative source. Henri Van De Velde was the spokesman of the period. His writings speak of function and structural clarity as part of the movement, but there are no architectural evidences of Art Nouveau being other than a superficial system of ornamentation.

Furniture, fabrics, and even stained glass in the style of Art Nouveau

This foyer by Victor Horta is a remarkable example of linear floral ornamentation, the hallmark of Art Nouveau.

were the great success of the Paris Exposition of 1900, and its popularity spread throughout Europe and the United States. The French architect, Hector Giumard, used Art Nouveau forms in his most delightful works, the Paris Metro (subway) entrances. Even the great engineering masterpiece, the Eiffel Tower, uses iron ornamentation derived from Art Nouveau. In Germany the movement was known as *Jugendstil,* and in Italy it was called *Floreale.* As it had been in Paris, the movement was the hit of the Turin Exposition of 1902.

The two great architects of Art Nouveau were the nonconformists Charles Rennie Mackintosh (1862–1928) and Antoni Gaudi (1852–1926). Mackintosh designed buildings of remarkable originality, his greatest work being the School of Art (1898) in Glasgow. The interior ornamentation combines slender verticals with panels decorated with curves, flowers, and mermaid-like forms. Gaudi's superiority lies in the great force in his work. His style was wild, vehement, and at the same time capricious. Working in stone as well as iron, his warped surfaces flow like molten lava. Gaudi also created surfaces of great complexity, using unbelievable original mosaics. His most celebrated work is the Church of the Sacred Family in Barcelona (1903) and his most delightful work is the Guell Park (1900) also in Barcelona.

At best Art Nouveau was a protest movement that attempted to find a freer outlook for design. It was most popular as a system of interior architectural ornamentation. Its historic importance is in the fact that it was the first style that was not influenced by the styles of the past, and although it broke from the period styles, it soon became a period style itself. Like all other design fads, it quickly faded into oblivion.

Iron construction in the United States. During the Classical revival, as the European engineer concentrated on the development of larger column-free enclosed spaces, the American engineer became involved with the creation of a new building type, possible only through the use of iron. As land in the centers of cities became built up, the amount of available land became more expensive. As business boomed, space could no longer expand horizontally, because additional land was both expensive and scarce. Therefore the only logical expansion of space was vertical. The multistoried building was the solution. This concept, when projected, brought forth the greatest building contribution of the 19th century—the uniquely American skyscraper.

An American, James Bogardus (1800–1874), invented the system of construction that made the skyscraper structurally feasible. English factories used iron columns and girders for interior structure, but still used masonry bearing walls for exterior enclosure. Bogardus, who built multi-storied structures using the same principle, was the first to substitute iron columns for masonry outer walls. The iron skeleton was completed and was used for commercial architecture in dense urban areas from 1859 to 1880. Bogardus even imagined that the iron skeleton (the framewok of horizontal floors and vertical walls) might radically change residential design.

His most famous design was for the publishing house of Harper and Brothers (1854). This cast iron facade, detailed in the style of the Renaissance (Bogardus was aware of the plight of architectural taste), is astounding for its abundance of glass. The combination of a skeletal structure of iron and glass in-fill is ideal for controlling temperature and permitting good light and ventilation.

Bogardus' unbuilt project for the New York World's Fair of 1853 proves his unusual understanding of the skeleton frame. It anticipates both the American skyscraper (vertical, multistoried space) and the European exposition hall (horizontal and vertical, one story space). The central tower was three hundred feet high (thirty present-day stories), and the amphitheater was twelve hundred feet in diameter (from Forty-Second Street to Forty-Eighth Street in present day New York). Bogardus started the movement, and after him there followed a great age of iron building throughout the United States by anonymous designers. Unlike Bogardus, these designers were not familiar with the historic styles and so they developed in New York, Philadelphia, Chicago, and particularly St. Louis, unbelievably modern buildings of iron and glass that were devoid of historic ornamentation.

The same post Civil War period that witnessed the anonymous iron and glass buildings also saw the influence on mannered American architecture of the Second Empire of France and the High Victorian Gothic of England.

Henry Hobson Richardson. This second great American architect (the first being the classicist, Latrobe), was also the second American architect to study at the École des Beaux Arts. (Richard Hunt was the first.) Richardson united the architect and the engineer. He did so much so, in fact, that the modern American architects call Richardson their father and the American traditionalists refer to him as the great Romanesque revivalist.

After the completion of his training in Paris and following the popular grand tour of European art and architecture, Richardson (1838–1886) returned to Boston. He had been deeply impressed with the French Romanesque and had perceived that these massive surfaces of brick and stone with their rounded arches formed a great emotional identity with his own age. His first major work was Trinity Church (1870) in Boston. This great building on Copley Square, designed for the famous clergyman Philips Brooks, immediately established Richardson's reputation as an architect who was not a revivalist in the imitative sense, but was rather a creative artist inspired by the emotive qualities of the Romanesque. His best-known works are railroad stations for the Boston and Albany Line and the Marshall Field Warehouse (1887) in Chicago. The hallmarks of Richardson's work were clear: blocks of simple, massive, arcaded masonry. He made great contributions to the development of residential architecture. His houses in Boston and New York (Richardson maintained offices in Brookline and in Brooklyn) demonstrated looser, freer, more informal planning. Casually rambling masses with freely organized fenestration and wide sprawling verandas were employed in residential designs. He believed in the continuity of masonry textures, using little or no detail. Richardson had little interest in technological advancements; there are no new structural systems or new materials to be seen in his work. He was, nevertheless, the first American to attempt to find an architectural expression of his times through the use of simple masonry forms. In a sense, his

Richardson's feeling for the French Romanesque is seen in the stone forms used in this late 19th century room.

work is a continuation in the United States of the English country architecture the Arts and Crafts Movement had inspired. Richardson's specific interest in the Romanesque also influenced the design of miniature Romanesque castles that soon became the residential rage in both the city and the country throughout the Northeast and the Midwest. In the city, for example, the brownstone house was built. Further evidence of this kind of thinking was also to be found in European work done just prior to World War I.

The first American School of Architecture, Massachusetts Institute of Technology, was opened in 1865. Nonetheless, the properly schooled young architect was required to study at the École in Paris and round out his education with a tour of the great buildings of Europe's past. After the European experiences of both Hunt and Richardson, a background similar to theirs became the only acceptable entree to the architectural profession;

all young men interested in this field turned their eyes to Paris. The teachings of L'École Des Beaux Arts were manifest in eclecticism—the use of many and diverse historic styles. The returning young American architect was equally at home with the styles of France, England, and Italy and even with ancient classicism. As previously noted, the actual superimposition of these styles upon the architectural needs of the 19th century created the deathblow to the architect. However, the dichotomy of the 19th century continued. The romantic architect was involved with eclectic escapes, and the objective engineer was concerned with new structural systems and building forms. Only Richardson and a few other architects were able to bridge the work of both. During his lifetime, engineering made such astonishing contributions to building that by 1893 the architect and the engineer were in head-on battle. At the Columbian Exposition of that year in Chicago eclecticism finally won the great victory and further development of modern architecture in this country was for the most part held back until the 1940's.

Louis Sullivan. Sullivan possessed the engineering inventiveness of Bogardus, the architectural expressiveness of Richardson and the intellectual art-consciousness of the Art Nouveau. In fact, the culmination of architecture in the 19th century was reached through four totally American phenomena: the Otis elevator safety device, the multistoried iron frame, the great Chicago Fire—and Louis Sullivan. In 1853 Elisha Otis of New York invented the first safety device that could control the then popular hoisting platform. He designed the first passenger elevator in 1859. Further development of commercial vertical structures followed. Evidences of this development have been discussed along with Bogardus and the commercial structures that followed. The real importance of the Bogardus School was the development of the multistory iron frame.

Whether or not Mrs. O'Leary and her cow were real, the great Chicago fire in 1871 left the Loop (the intensive commercial area of downtown Chicago bounded by an elevated railroad loop) nothing but rubble. The steel-framed structure then was ready to provide the solution for exorbitant land costs. The elevator made vertical movement feasible, and the experiments of architect-engineers like William LeBaron Jenney gave rise to the great American architectural contribution, the skyscraper. The great fire had already provided the site. The Chicago School grew: first as architecture of interior iron frame with masonry bearing walls, and later of complete, vertically soaring iron frames.

Sullivan's education was spotty. He started at M.I.T. and then went to the École in Paris. He travelled in Europe and then, still dissatisfied, returned to the United States hoping to apprentice himself to an architect whose work earned his enthusiasm. When Louis Sullivan reached Chicago, where his family had originally settled, architects were still split between archeology and science, particularly European influences versus American resourcefulness.

In 1881 the architectural firm of Adler and Sullivan was formed and until 1890 Sullivan designed pseudo-Richardsonesque buildings in Chicago. At this time he was not yet involved with the glass and steel skyscraper. His first great skyscraper was the Wainwright Building in St. Louis (1890–1891). At the same time he designed the Carson Pirie Scott Building and the Gage Building in Chicago and the Bayard Building in New York. Although Sullivan is credited with the credo of early 20th century architecture (form follows function), and his buildings are inventive in their use of the steel frame and huge expanses of glass, his work is best characterized by the application of nonperiod naturalistic ornamentation, which was clearly influenced by the Art Nouveau designs he had seen in Europe. The robust Chicago School lost out, however, in the designs for the Columbian Exposition of 1893 (Chicago). That World's Fair, the "White City," was designed in the style of the Venetian Renaissance and, although Sullivan designed the provocative transportation building, the great work of the Chicago School ended. Later followed the building of skyscrapers clothed in the historic styles of the past. Eclecticism came forth to dominate all architecture in the United States. Adler and Sullivan separated in 1895, and Louis Sullivan was a forgotten man by 1900.

Frank Lloyd Wright. Although his work was not recognized in this country until 1935, a young architect who had worked in the office of Adler and Sullivan carried the traditions of the Arts and Crafts Movement, along with those of Richardson and Sullivan to their greatest height. This was, of course, the great American architectural genius, Frank Lloyd Wright (1869–1959).

After studying engineering at the University of Wisconsin, Wright settled in Chicago and joined Adler and Sullivan at the time that the Chicago Auditorium was being designed. Wright, evidently a favorite of Sullivan's, was soon put in charge of all the residential architecture that the office produced. As a matter of fact by 1893, when Wright set up his own office, he had been given credit in his own name for several houses. From this time until 1910 Wright developed his now famous Prairie Houses. Usually cruciform or windmill-like in plan, they concentrated the mechanical plants and fireplaces in the center of the house and permitted each of the four wings to have three exterior walls. Frequently two of the four wings intersected the other sides at higher levels, so that the forms interpenetrated each other. Spaces within each wing could flow into each other and the spatial continuity from one wing into another was also exploited. Long, low overhanging roofs gave accent to the flat land upon which the houses were built. Horizontal fenestration and projecting balconies stressed the strong parallelism with the ground. Wright used basic mate-

Designed by Frank Lloyd Wright   Photo by Stoller

This is one of the earliest examples of a "modern" interior in the United States, showing Mr. Wright's living room in his home at Taliesin, Wisconsin (1925). The structural elements form their own decorative effect. Light, space, view, and ventilation were given first importance in the design. Furniture is primarily utilitarian. (Reproduced from the August, 1946 issue of FORTUNE *magazine by special permission of the editors.)*

rials: wood, masonry and glass; he did not use reinforced concrete and steel until the 1930's.

The most important house of the Prairie period is the Robie House completed in Chicago in 1909. Built of brick, wood, and glass, this house develops the concept of open-planning within, as well as a visual continuity between inside and outside. Wright was certainly the most creative American architect to date, and when his work appeared in Europe in 1910, his influence upon European architects was seen immediately.

In 1911 he designed for his mother the first of his Taliesin houses. By building it on a softly rounded hilltop instead of the flat land around Chicago, he achieved more variety in levels and roof lines, thus proclaiming more strongly his premise that a house must grow out of the land. At Taliesin, Wright handled walls, roof overhangs, and terraces so masterfully that complete visual continuity from inside to outside was frequently achieved.

Wright was invited to Japan to design a hotel in Tokyo, so he lived

Courtesy the Museum of Modern Art, New York

Wright's bold concrete forms cantilevered over a waterfall make a masterpiece of architectural placement.

there from 1915 to 1922. He received world-wide acclaim when his Imperial Hotel in Tokyo, built on floating foundations, withstood the earthquake of 1923. After returning to the United States, Wright continued designing houses in the southwest. Nevertheless, his work in this country was not fully recognized until the American Institute of Architects finally awarded him its Gold Medal in the mid-thirties. His most famous house, "Falling Water," was built in 1937. Cantilevered over a waterfall, this house carries out the principles of the old Prairie Houses, but goes beyond through the daring use of reinforced concrete. Although he was nearly 70 years of age when "Falling Water" was completed, Wright continued to design many houses and even built two great buildings in the nonresidential field—The Johnson Wax Tower in Racine, Wisconsin in 1950 and the spiral Guggenheim Museum in New York City, which was completed in the year of his death, 1959.

In residential architecture Frank Lloyd Wright will always be identified with (1) the positioning of his houses within a natural terrain, (2) the development of a house from inside outward, (3) the use of an original vocabulary of design without regard for traditional forms, (4) the use of primary materials and bold structural cantilevers, and finally (5) with a dedication and intensity that permitted him to create his houses in a cultural environment that was violently hostile to his ideas.

European architecture after 1900. The development of steel through the 19th century has already been discussed. However, the use of concrete as a building material was known long before iron. Concrete, or the mixture of cement, crushed stone, sand and water, has great compressive value.* It is an excellent material for bases of buildings—for foundation walls and footings. However concrete has little tensile value.† Steel works the other way. It is excellent in tension but not as good as concrete in compression. Imagine a lighting fixture hung from a ceiling by a shaft of concrete or a heavy piece of sculpture on a thin pin of steel attached to the floor.

Auguste Perret (1873–   ). A French architect was the first to combine steel and concrete to make a material that is equally good in both tension and compression. Reinforced concrete has another great advantage. Since the concrete is poured in a fluid state, it takes the shape of the forms into which it is poured. Therefore, great design freedom became possible with the use of concrete. Easily bent reinforcing bars are used to reinforce concrete. Auguste Perret's apartments at 25 Bis Rue Franklin (1903) employed a skeleton of reinforced concrete for the first time. It is important to note that Perret's work with reinforced concrete gave the architect still another new structural material and, as in the case of steel, new ideas and new architectural forms became possible.

After the death of Art Nouveau there were still many European architects who attempted to free design from eclecticism. Perhaps the first was Professor Otto Wagner (1841–1918) of Vienna who wrote in his textbook *Modern Architecture* that new principles and materials must lead to new forms and that the artist must create what the public ought to like, not what it does like. Wagner, who worked in complete isolation, was a proponent of freedom to design rather than to imitate. Two students of Wagner's, Adolf Loos (1870–1933) and Josef Hoffman (1873–   ) continued to fight for freedom of design. Hoffman's Stoclet House (1914) is particularly interesting because it is one of the first buildings that was influenced by a new esthetic movement in Holland. Hoffman's design was a cube of white stucco with straight black lines edging all of the flat surfaces or planes. The young Dutch group, known as De Stijl, claimed that as pure

---

* A compressive material is one that can carry great weights or forces on top of it and can withstand great forces pushing up at it. It is, in a sense, capable of being squeezed.

Diagrammatically compression can be shown o . O is being pushed down by force A and pushed up by force B at the same time.

† A material of tensile value is one that can withstand one force that pulls up and another force that pulls down simultaneously. It is capable of withstanding opposite pulls.

Diagrammatically tension can be shown o . O is being pulled up by force A and pulled down by force B. Therefore, tension and compression are opposites.

representation of the spirit, art will express itself in a purified—that is abstract—esthetic form. The backbone of the De Stijl movement was clarity and order. In painting, all forms were simplified into rectangles outlined in black and only the primary colors plus white and grey were used. Piet Mondrian was the great painter of this school. In sculpture all forms were simplified into flat rectangular planes and the sculptures were combinations of these flat planes (sometimes called constructivism). Malevitsch was the most successful of De Stijl sculptors. At this time the work of Frank Lloyd Wright was being published in Europe, and the similarity between the interpenetrating planes and hovering roofs of his houses and the constructivism movement were immediately realized. The abstract principles of composition and form that Wright had developed in his architecture were identical with the objective, intellectual conclusions reached by the De Stijl group!

In Germany, Peter Behrens (1868–1940) became concerned with industrial architecture and the expressive forces concealed in new materials. The titans of modern architecture—Gropius, Le Corbusier, and Van Der Rohe apprenticed in Behren's studio. In Holland, H. P. Berlage (1856–1934) worked for the unity of the flat surface. He was a great admirer of Frank Lloyd Wright. Primarily of brick, his work exemplified honesty in architecture. J. J. P. Oud (1890–   ), like Berlage, built houses of brick. Oud added humanism to early 20th century architecture. He was concerned with scale and proportion in order to make people comfortable in his spaces as well as to create simple, refined architecture. And so the revolt started by William Morris in the mid-19th century reached architectural fruition in the early 20th century in both Europe and the United States. All development was abruptly terminated with the outbreak of the first World War.

The contribution of Walter Gropius to the development of modern architecture. The fact that Germany was the last European country to industrialize has already been mentioned. Perhaps its unification late in the 19th century and its lack of strong nationalistic traditions explain why this new country was able to face up realistically to the conflicts between art and the machine. The *Deutsche Werkbund* of 1907 conscientiously sought to find a synthesis of "machine style" and the Arts and Crafts Movement started by Morris. In essence this was the first attempt to effect real co-operation between the artist and the craftsman; art and industry. Walter Gropius (1883–   ) was one of the youngest *Werkbund* leaders. As early as 1910 Gropius had helped Peter Behrens (he worked in Behrens' studio) draft a "memorandum on the industrial prefabrication of houses on a unified artistic basis." Gropius' efforts toward the exploitation of the new lightness which was made possible as a result of modern building construction were manifest in early industrial architecture that bespoke

The interior of this Bauhaus faculty house by Gropius indicates the cold intellectuality of the early International Style.

the intellectuality of the De Stijl movement in Holland and the romanticism of the then recently published work of Frank Lloyd Wright.

After World War I Gropius consolidated the Art Academy and the Arts and Crafts School in Weimar, creating a consulting center for industry and the trades which he called the Bauhaus. Each student at the Bauhaus was trained by two teachers—an artist and a craftsman. The purpose of this school was to unify art and technology and, for the first time, under the Bauhaus system artists united creative imagination with a practical knowledge of craftsmanship. Thus a new sense of functional design was realized. In 1925 the Bauhaus moved from Weimar to the buildings in Dessau designed by Gropius. By this time a new generation of teachers had been trained, each of whom was at once a creative artist, craftsman and industrial designer.* From this environment are derived many familiar adjuncts of contemporary life: steel furniture, modern textiles, lamps, dishes, and modern typography and layout. The spirit of functional design was carried even into the fine arts and applied to architecture, and to city and regional planning. The Bauhaus faculty included besides Gropius, the painters Klee, Kandinski, Albers, and Feininger; the artist-typographers Bayer and Schawinsky, the textile designer Anni Albers; the architect and furniture designer Marcel Breuer, and the revolutionary scenic designer Oscar Schlemmer. During the twenties the Bauhaus was the international center of the crafts, architecture, painting, sculpture, and

* The industrial designer became necessary as a result of new design problems created by industrialization.

A restful room designed by Mr. Gropius for his own home in Massachusetts. Its quality is its extreme simplicity with pattern interest produced in a constantly changing landscape.

music. The Bauhaus, in retrospect, was the most important school since Louis XIV had codified art in the Institut De France and Napoleon I had united art and science in the Polytechnique. As far as education in design is concerned, Gropius established the ideas that are still prevalent in the provocative schools of architecture and design in the United States today.

Since the Bauhaus principles could not flourish under totalitarianism, Gropius went to England before the growth of Nazi Germany and came to the United States in the late 1930's. He assumed the chairmanship of the Department of Architecture at Harvard University and established an architectural practice in New England. Most American designers of consequence have either studied with Gropius himself or with a Gropius-trained teacher. In the simple directness of traditional New England architecture Gropius found a sympathy with the forthrightness of the Bauhaus ideals, and a vital American architecture based upon forms in stone, wood, and glass resulted. Soon after World War II Gropius founded The Architects Collaborative—a group of young architects and designers dedicated to the American traditions that are implicit to the concepts of the Bauhaus. Although now eighty, Walter Gropius is not only one of the most celebrated and honored architects and teachers of the century but still one of the most virile practitioners in the design field.

Le Corbusier. Charles Edouard Jeanneret (1887–   ) was born in Switzerland. Like many Europeans, however, he studied and travelled extensively and no particular country nor culture can claim exclusive rights

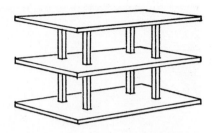

Diagram showing principle of cantilever floor construction. The floors are carried by interior supports instead of exterior walls. The walls when built are mere screens without structural function.

to his development. Le Corbusier travelled in Italy, Greece, Egypt, and North Africa; and worked with Behrens in Germany and Perret in France. He is, however, considered a French architect. Le Corbusier is both a painter and an architect of a new generation of artists who ignored the traditional Beaux Arts training. He established several devices which are characteristic. For example he conceived a skeleton structure of floors and roof supported by a few isolated steel columns located well within the walls of the building. As the weight of the ceiling rested on the columns this permitted the free placement of both interior and exterior walls.

Le Corbusier preferred a beauty of simplicity and good proportions as against surface enrichment, and his designs were based on functional principles and geometric forms. The final hallmark of Le Corbusier is the use of the flat roof as a roof garden. A great house that embodies the development of Le Corbusier's residential architecture is the Savoye Villa at Poissy, France (1929–1931). Here is a three story house, the upper two stories of which are raised on free standing columns (*pilotis* or stilts). The regularity of the structure on the lower floor is contrasted with the free-flowing nonstructural walls. Space flows easily through the house; above it and below it. An interior ramp and stair lead to the middle floor, which reflects the rectangularity of the structural system—here again Le Corbusier ties together the interior and exterior spaces. The living areas open upon a walled terrace with a large horizontal window (from outdoor terrace to free outdoor space). The terrace is open to the sky. An exterior ramp connects to the roof garden where again free screens protect the user from wind and sun. Here we find the Le Corbusier credo and the beginnings of the sculptural influences upon modern architecture. Although influenced by De Stijl as well as by the pioneering modern painters and the Constructivists, Le Corbusier has added a plastic poetry to the intellectual rationalization of the Bauhaus. Nevertheless, Le Corbusier has been fascinated by prefabrication. He is the author of the phrase "A house is a machine to live in." He again demonstrated a structure floating on stilts and the play of the interior and exterior spaces with his celebrated Swiss Pavilion (1932) in Cite Université Paris. As always Le Corbusier contrasts the modular regularity of the concrete structure with the free plasticity of the nonstructural stone wall.

A remarkable juxtaposition of interior and exterior space raised on stilts. The Villa at Poissy, France designed by Le Corbusier.

Most of Le Corbusier's early work was done with his cousin Pierre Jenneret. Le Corbusier resembles Beethoven and Picasso in that he is an artist who is constantly striving to surpass his previous expressions. Although the painter-sculptor qualities are always evident in his work, he can never be called self-imitative. Recently he has again in his latest works in France and in India proved that his is an unending, driving creativity. Although his sketches were used for the basic design of the United Nations complex, the first American example of Le Corbusier's work is Carpenter Hall (1962), at Harvard University.

Le Corbusier has been extremely influential in the development of South American architecture as well as that of many European countries. He was invited to Rio de Janeiro in 1936 and prepared sketches for the Ministry of Education and Public Health. Oscar Niemeyer, chairman of the committee of architects was profoundly influenced by Le Corbusier and carried out the design of the building in the spirit of these sketches. This building became the most influential modern structure completed in South America since 1940. Every young South American architect in a sense therefore was directly influenced by Le Corbusier's architecture. Niemeyer's great work is the total design of all of the buildings for Brazil's new capital, Brazilia, according to the site plan designed by Costa.

Ludwig Mies van der Rohe. Born in Aachen, Germany in 1886, Van der Rohe had a quite informal early training. After four years with Peter Behrens and working in other architectural offices, he set up a private practice in 1912. He became director of the Bauhaus after Gropius and

A brilliant example of Niemeyer's lyric use of reinforced concrete is seen in his Palace of the Dawn at Brazilia.

then came to the United States in 1937 to become director of architecture at Armour Institute (now called Illinois Institute of Technology). Mies van der Rohe is the rationalist of modern architecture. His work, primarily using steel, is easily understood and teachable. His great design principle is "less is more." Mies' structures are clear, modular, and understated.

The most important building of Van der Rohe's European period was the Tugendhat House in Brno, Czechoslovakia (1930). This flat-roofed structure had a free lower floor resting on regularly spaced chrome-plated columns. A 100-foot-long glass wall opened to a commanding view. A curved wooden screen and a free-standing slab of marble suggested separations between the living room, dining room, and study. Spaces were subtly subdivided by furniture arrangement and floor coverings.

The most striking house designed by Van der Rohe in the United States is the Farnsworth House in Plano, Illinois (1950). Eight welded steel columns support the roof as well as the floor, which floats above the ground. All exterior walls are glass, from floor to ceiling. A "core" of heating plant, fireplace, kitchen, and bathroom create the only separation in this completely open plan. Van der Rohe's influence upon American architects has been tremendous. His scientifically simple designs have most successfully caught the spirit of American technology. He is best known

Mies van der Rohe uses a marble plane and a curved screen of wood as minimal suggestions of space separation.

for the Lake Shore apartments in Chicago and Seagram Building in New York.

20th century architecture in the United States. At the turn of the century, Chicago's creativity declined, but new contributions began to come from California. In the San Francisco Bay region an informal architecture using natural materials developed. The climate permitted minimal distinction between indoors and out-of-doors and large areas of glass gave notice to the superb views of almost every site. The works of John Galen Howard, Bernard Maybeck, and the Brothers Greene offered the best contemporary regionalism of this country and fathered the current California school of Richard Neutra and William Wilson Wurster. Few, if any, other American contributions to the development of modern architecture were made. Aside from the work of Wright and of the Viennese, Richard Neutra, who worked in Chicago with Wright and then went to California in 1924, there was no significant work in the 1920's. The depression hit the building industry in the thirties with particular severity, and World War II ended what little had been done during that decade. Actually the post-war growth of modern architecture in the United States was anticipated in the late 1930's when Gropius, Breuer and Van der Rohe came to the United States, not only to teach but also to build.

A relaxed, informal interior by Rudolph. The influence of the International Style transplanted to the United States.

The flowering of American architecture took place after World War II. The work of the late forties and fifties can be divided into five groups: the followers of Frank Lloyd Wright who studied with him at Taliesin; the Harvard architects who studied with Gropius and Breuer and were also influenced by Le Corbusier; the Van der Rohe disciples at the Illinois Institute of Technology; the California school led by Neutra and Wurster; and the few determined individualists who were not part of any school. Wright and Van der Rohe produced followers who tended to imitate the styles of their masters. Since Gropius taught an ideology rather than a style, a more varied architecture can be found in the work of his students. This is also true of the architecture of the California school.

The houses that Walter Gropius and Marcel Breuer designed in New England just before World War II were the most important influences upon American residential architecture since the work of Wright and the early Californians. The German international style was comfortably translated into traditional clapboard and stone. The austerity of the architecture and of the Massachusetts landscape were remarkably compatible. Hugh Stubbins and Carl Koch were early American followers of Gropius and Breuer. Their houses continued the use of flat roofs, vertical boarding (usually painted white), and masonry fireplace walls. However, a kind of warmth appears in their work; the more American gabled roof and a less precise architectural geometry are features of their buildings. Houses by Eliot Noyes are similar in spirit. Edward L. Barnes' houses may be considered the transition between the intellectual justification demanded by

Photograph by Stoller

A most successful integration of indoors and outdoors can be found in John-
son's all glass house. The furniture was designed by Van der Rohe.

the international style and a freer more emotional approach justifiable in
the true Gropius sense, since he concerns himself with the creation of
spaces that are beautiful rather than merely functional. The leader of the
youngest Harvard group is Paul Rudolph whose earlier works are a series
of delightfully original houses in and around Sarasota, Florida. His more
current work demonstrates a philosophy of form for form's sake. In the
twenty-five years of the Gropius school in this country the architecture has
changed from rigid translation of the international style to a freer examination of visual delight.

As change is characteristic of the evolution of the Gropius school, refinement is true of the development of the Mies school. The chaste, one-
room house, all glass and steel, built by Philip Johnson for himself in New
Canaan, Connecticut, is the best residential example of Mies' influence. A
brick cylinder housing the fireplace and bath is the only closed element in
this completely open house.

Early modern European architecture as well as the vigorous Chicago
school combine in the work of Richard Neutra in California. William Wilson Wurster, California born and educated (he studied with John G.
Howard at the University of California), has created an architecture of
wood and glass that is more informal than Neutra's work. The low rambling asymmetric houses of redwood boards and batten and glass are characteristic of his work. Today William Wurster is also Dean of the School
of Architecture at the University of California.

Designed by Richard J. Neutra   Photo by Shulman

A combination study and sitting room in a house in California, economically and compactly designed and taking full advantage of nearby landscaping. Local materials were used in a logical manner for both structural and decorative effect.

Japanese architecture has had a unique influence upon west-coast work in this country. An openness of plan is achieved through the use of sliding and removable partitions, th. care in the detailing of the wood, and a simplicity in handling of interior spaces and furnishings. Wide overhanging eaves are characteristic, and perhaps most important is the intimate relation of house to grounds and landscaping. These considerations have affected the work of many California architects and through them also the work of other domestic architects throughout the country.

Another vigorous regional architecture not unlike the California school has grown in the northwest. The Italian-born Pietro Belluschi is the leading architect in this region.

Architects such as Eero Saarinen and Edward Durrel Stone do not represent specific schools. While they were certainly influenced by the European masters, most of their buildings are uniquely personal. Saarinen was born in Scandinavia and was brought to this country when his father, a great architect, took charge of Cranbrook Academy in Michigan. Saarinen completed his formal education at Yale. His best-known projects are the General Motors Research Center, the Massachusetts Institute of

A complete integration of painting, sculpture, and lighting in this house by Edward Stone.

Technology chapel, and the Trans-World Airways terminal at Idlewild Airport in New York. He did some interesting houses with the designer Charles Eames. His death in 1961 abruptly ended the career of one of the most gifted younger architects.

Even less influenced by other modernists is Edward Stone. American born and educated, he began to build modern houses in the 1930's. He reached his full growth in the fifties when he designed the American Embassy in New Delhi, India and the American Pavilion at the Brussels World's Fair. Both buildings were enriched by the hallmark of Stone's work, the pre-cast perforated concrete grille.

The architect today. This chapter has so far concerned itself with the development of contemporary residential architecture. Certainly, credit must be given to the great architectural firms, such as Skidmore, Owings and Merrill; Harrison and Abramovitz, and other large-scale industrial and architectural firms. Today's architecture is primarily concentrating on town and city planning. However, this is not a new realm for the architect. As we have noted, Sir Christopher Wren redesigned much of London after the great fire of 1666 and L'Enfant designed our federal capital. The direction of the architect is away from the design of the individual building, and toward the design of complexes of buildings. The design of many square blocks of buildings in the city and the total design of new cities have again become the realm of today's architect.

Contemporary Interior Planning and Backgrounds.* With high construction costs, lack of domestic help, and increasing complications in living, every room should be as flexible as possible. The problem becomes one of space distribution. The term *fluid plan* has been applied to arrangements that permit more than a single purpose for one room. In detail, such arrangements may include the following features: sliding, folding, and transparent partitions; side openings between adjoining rooms; the omission of doors; the introduction of niches, alcoves, or wings for secondary uses; the elimination of corridors; screened outdoor rooms; and glass walls that open to adjoining terraces or permit a full view of the near or distant landscape.

Fluid planning often necessitates irregularity in room shapes, which in turn produces problems in furniture arrangement. Much furniture is now part of the wall construction. Symmetrical compositions and groupings are usually difficult to attain, and lack of symmetry has become characteristic of contemporary interiors. The interpenetration of rooms and planning for double or triple use often permits variations of wall materials or treatments in the same room. Brick, stone, concrete block, wood, plastic, tile, glass, mirrors, and synthetic wall materials have the advantage of permanency and low upkeep, and are acceptable for interior walls if logical reasons exist for their use. The use of natural materials is also common, and nature itself is often introduced into contemporary interiors; the rock of a hillside setting has been used for one wall of a room; gardens and pools often intrude into living rooms or terraces; flowers and foliage are healthful and decorative.

For simplicity of effect and saving of floor space, bookcases, desks, chests, cabinets, and other types of storage items are often built into the walls and are furnished with sliding doors made of the same material as the wall. Standing cabinets and wardrobes are also sometimes used as partitions to separate a room into two or more parts for different uses. There is a great variety of materials suitable for wall treatments; exotic plywoods, veneers, plastic wallboards, metal sheets, and natural surfacing products are possible. Some of these are suitable for structural purposes, while others must be applied to an existing surface. These sheet materials are

* See also Chapter XIX on wall treatments.

furnished in plain colors, grained, marbleized, or imitative of other finishes; others require paint or wallpaper. Many of the synthetic sheets are waterproof and fireproof, and some may be bent around curved surfaces. Plywood, veneers, and synthetic sheets are used in full widths applied either vertically or horizontally. Materials such as cork and leather may also be used.

Fireplaces are considered primarily from the functional rather than the decorative point of view, although the romantic aspect of the hearth has not been entirely neglected, even though modern heating systems have made its use unimportant. Fireplace openings are usually countersunk in masonry walls and are purely functional and well proportioned for proper drafts. Some fireplaces project into the room with open sides for lateral as well as frontal distribution of the heat. There has also been a return to the very practical medieval types with a hearth located on the floor apart from the wall with a superimposed metal hood that radiates the heat in all directions.

Wood remains one of the most satisfactory of flooring materials, but floors are also made of cement, tile, brick, terrazzo, and slate. Plastic floors made of magnesium oxide are also excellent and are furnished in many colors. Linoleum, rubber, asphalt, vinyl, and vinyl asbestos tiles are durable and resilient.

Miscellaneous features: * There have been many technical inventions during recent years that have contributed much to the conveniences, comforts, and economies of contemporary living. The equipment for most of these is not directly associated with the appearance of a room, but portions must often remain visible.

Among the new developments is *radiant heating,* which is a method of imbedding heating pipes or coils in floors, walls or ceilings. This system eliminates the radiator and hot-air register. It is most advantageously used with hot-water heat. *Solar heating* has been much attempted, but this requires that a house have large areas of glass facing a southern direction, and eaves, or exterior shades, proportioned to the local angle of the sun.

Systems for conditioning, humidifying, and filtering the air if combined with temperature control have many advantages and are readily available. Individual air conditioners installed in windows serve to cool the air of a single room. Both water and air are used in systems that warm in winter and cool in summer.

The soundproofing of rooms has been attained, in part, by reducing sounds at their source, and by introducing thick or insulated partitions, walls, and floors. Plywood walls also have been found advantageous for

* For more complete information on accessories, textiles, draperies, upholstery, floor coverings, and lighting used in contemporary rooms, see the respective chapters on these subjects.

this purpose. There are also soft plasters, which are sound-absorbing, that may be used on surfaces not subject to constant wear. Perforated panels of synthetic substances may also be applied to walls and ceilings for this purpose; these have an interesting texture and may be painted any color.

Bibliography

BURCHARD, J. AND BUSH-BROWN, A., *The Architecture of America: A Social and Cultural Study*. Little Brown & Co., Boston, 1961. A comprehensive study of the evolution of American architecture. Excellent.

GIEDION, S., *Space, Time and Architecture*. Harvard University Press, 1947. The definitive study of the growth of contemporary design, particularly architecture.

GIEDION, S., *Walter Gropius, Work and Teamwork*. Reinhold Publishing Co., New York, 1954. A well-illustrated account of his life and work.

GROPIUS, W., GROPIUS, I. AND BAYER, H., *Bauhaus 1919–1928*. Charles T. Branford Co., Boston, 1959. The complete history and philosophy of the Bauhaus copiously illustrated with designs by masters and students.

GUTHEIM, F., *On Architecture*. Duell, Sloan & Pearce, Inc., New York, 1941. Frank Lloyd Wright, selected writings.

HITCHCOCK, H. R., *Built in USA*. Museum of Modern Art, New York, 1945. Summary of modern buildings erected in the U.S. from 1923 until 1945.

HITCHCOCK, H. R., *Built in USA: Post-War Architecture*. Museum of Modern Art, New York, 1953. Illustrations of the best modern buildings in the U.S. erected since 1945. Text.

JOEDICKE, JURGEN, *A History of Modern Architecture*. Frederick A. Praeger, New York, 1959. Excellent survey.

KIDDER-SMITH, G. E., *The New Architecture of Europe*. World Publishing Co., Inc., Cleveland, 1961. Illustrated guide book of modern buildings in sixteen countries with appraisals.

LE CORBUSIER, *Creation Is a Patient Search*. Frederick A. Praeger, New York, 1960. The consummate artistry of the great master. A wide selection of his drawings augment a vast variety of photographs. Autobiographical.

LE CORBUSIER, *Towards a New Architecture*. John Rodker, London, 1931. Text fully illustrated with photographs and line drawings.

MOCK, E., *Built in USA: Since 1932*. Museum of Modern Art, New York, 1944. Text and illustrations of modern architecture, both public and residential.

PETERS, J., *Masters of Modern Architecture*. George Braziller, Inc., New York, 1958. Excellent illustrations, with building descriptions, brief writings and biographical sketches of the masters.

PEVSNER, N., *An Outline of European Architecture*. Penguin, Baltimore, 1961. Excellent coverage from the 6th century to the present.

PEVSNER, N., *Pioneers of Modern Design* (Pioneers of the Modern Movement).

Museum of Modern Art, New York, 1949. A study of the period from 19th century engineering to Walter Gropius.

RICHARDS, J. M., *An Introduction to Modern Architecture*. Penguin, Baltimore, 1959. Inexpensive, irreplaceable. The one book all should have.

ROTH, A., *The New Architecture*. Les Editions D'Architecture, Erlenbach-Zurich, Switzerland, 1946. Modern architecture exemplified by twenty buildings from various countries, each fully illustrated and described. (In English, French, and German.)

SELZ, *Art Nouveau*. Museum of Modern Art, New York, 1959. Complete coverage of that period with illustrations.

SULLIVAN, L., *Kindergarten Chats*. Wittenborn, Shultz, Inc., New York, 1947. A mixture of autobiographical and architectural philosophy from this great American architect.

YORKE, F. R. S., *The Modern House*. The Architectural Press, London, 1935. European and American houses from World War I through the mid-thirties.

Masters of World Architecture. George Braziller, Inc., New York, 1960. A series of books covering the life and works of the great architects of the world, including among others, Le Corbusier, Alvar Aalto, Oscar Neimeyer, Louis Sullivan and Eric Mendelsohn by such well-known authorities as A. Bush-Brown, A. Drexler, F. Gutheim, and J. M. Fitch.

CHAPTER X

CONTEMPORARY FURNITURE

<hr>

Historically, furniture has developed in the footsteps of architecture. The climates that have nourished the growth of 20th century architecture are the same that have created the furniture of today. Reference to Chapter IX will clarify the impact of the Industrial Revolution, with its machine and machine-made products, upon contemporary design. To avoid duplication of information, this chapter will concentrate on the contributions of specific furniture designers rather than the historic situations that led to the design in our times.

Thonet, the first furniture designer to creatively employ systems of mass production. Michael Thonet, of Belgian descent, was born in Germany in 1796. In 1840 he invented the process of bentwood furniture production. He designed chairs of which all parts were beechwood softened by steam and then bent into continuous structural shapes. Thonet also developed systems of bending many layers of veneer that were shaped in molds by heat. His furniture was shown at the World's Fair in London in 1851, and won the highest awards. All contemporary furniture of bentwood or plywood has been developed from the early manufacturing techniques that were invented by Michael Thonet. After his death in 1871, the Thonet family continued to manufacture furniture, and by 1891, 7 million bentwood chairs of Michael Thonet's 1850 design had been produced. The components of these chairs, which were joined by simple metal screws, were shipped unassembled. This technique of shipment has become particularly important today. By 1921 the concern owned twenty-one factories and employed more than twelve thousand people. At this time they started the mass production of tubular steel furniture and manufactured chairs designed by Breuer, Van der Rohe, and Le Corbusier. This vast organization, now called Thonet Industries, has manufactured significant furniture of bentwood, plywood, steel, and aluminum. The Thonet name

Three early Thonet chairs that were produced between 1860 and 1876. The chairs use frames of bent beechwood. The armless Vienna cafe chair has been one of the most popular chairs in Europe and the United States.

has been associated with the growth of contemporary furniture since the early 19th century. In the past few years the assemblage of original Thonet furniture has enabled the modernist to join the ranks of "antique collectors."

The design reformation in England. By 1850 the flood of inferior machine-made products created an indelible effect still evident even on work designed today. Although William Morris is recognized as the first voice against the abuse of the machine, the earliest reformers really were Henry Cole, Owen Jones, and Richard Redgrave. Cole was a propagandist; Jones a decorator; and Redgrave, at best, a genre painter. This group, collectively in favor of good

The famous Morris chair was made of heavy solid wood sections. The simplicity of construction and the honesty of concept have made this easy chair the symbol of Arts and Crafts furniture.

machine-produced design, failed because it could not produce an approach to the visual aspects of machine-made design. Nevertheless there were no other groups in Europe at that time capable of directing industry. Cole will therefore be remembered as the pathfinder for William Morris and the Arts and Crafts Movement. Morris and his followers would not rank as designers of great importance if his group had not been composed of basically great talents. Unlike Cole, Morris was surrounded by creative people who easily transcended the questionable moralistic values of the Arts and Crafts Movement. The movement suggested new design values and attempted to concentrate on honest workmanship and fair expression of materials. Had this search for honesty not led Morris back to the Middle Ages, his individual importance in the development of contemporary design would not be questioned.

Certainly the most interesting designer in the Morris coterie was Philip Webb, the architect and furniture designer. Webb designed "Red House" for Morris. This comfortable country house not only freed architecture from the pomposities of pseudo-romanticism, but also enabled Webb to design tasteful astylar interiors and furniture (ornamented and decorated by Morris and the pre-Raphaelite Brotherhood). Though his disciples kept alive the traditions of honest workmanship, Gimson, the Barnsleys, Heal and Voysey could not affect the development of 19th century design. European furniture designers became involved with the design philosophy of Art Nouveau.

An English walnut chair designed and made by Ernest Gimson. Although similar in scale and silhouette to 18th century English chairs, this side chair is devoid of historic detail and ornamentation.

The followers of William Morris. Ernest Gimson (1864–1919) was trained as an architect. In 1884 he met Morris and, following in Morris' footsteps, exchanged the drawing board for the work bench. Like Morris he took as his credo "art is doing, not designing." No drawing board designer can gain the technical knowledge of material and construction possessed by the working craftsman. Gimson modified this by stating that the designer must be a complete master of his craft. He made friends with two other young architects, the brothers Sidney and Ernest Barnsley, and the three were given the chance to show their furniture at Morris' Arts and Crafts Exhibition Society in 1890. Their furniture was generally modest in scale and devoid of historical ornamentation. They used oversized members which gave their early furniture a clumsy or provincial quality. At times they overstressed joinery by displaying too many dovetails. They tended to use several different woods in the same piece and the fussiness of banding diagonal strips of ebony and kingwood was at times ostentatious.

The architect Charles F. Annesley Voysey, a remarkable visionary, was easily fifty years ahead of his times, and designed houses with long low horizontal lines and gay colors. He also designed the furniture for his houses. This work is particularly significant since Voysey attempted to apply arts and crafts thinking to machine-made furniture. Voysey's work indicated "an urgent desire to live and work in the present and to make decorative art once more full of life and vigor." Van de Velde later acknowledged his debt to Voysey. "It was," he said, "as if Spring had come all of a sudden." Sir Ambrose Heal, at the turn of the century, successfully produced commercially manufactured contemporary furniture. It was more than fifty years from the time that Morris protested against the machine before his followers understood that his values were applic-

LEFT: *a pearwood side table by the French architect, Hector Giumard (1908), demonstrates the curvilinear floral forms of Art Nouveau.* RIGHT: *Mackintosh's perpendicular period is well represented by this oak arm chair (1900). The unusually high back is typical of his work.*

able to machine-made furniture. Heal's machine-made furniture was simple, clean and carefully detailed. The natural beauty and color of unstained wood and the simple furniture forms were not only expressive of honest materials and craftsmanship, but were also expressive of the machine.

Art Nouveau. Van de Velde and Mackintosh. "Morris chases ugliness out of man's heart," said Henri Van de Velde, "I, out of his intellect." The basic difference between Art Nouveau and the Arts and Crafts Movement was the intellectual as opposed to the emotional approach to machine production. Van de Velde saw the machine as an insult to logic and reason just as Morris saw machine ugliness as offensive to mankind. Henri van de Velde was born in Antwerp, Belgium in 1863. He studied painting and became involved with the impressionist movement in France. Then his interests changed from fine arts to applied arts and by 1890 he was familiar with the products of the craft revival in England. Van de Velde became the spokesman for the Art Nouveau movement and, in his *Les Formules,* set the intellectual bases for the new art. He analyzed ornament and found that *line* was the common feature in both nature and styles of the past. He spoke of the dynamic quality of *line* and believed that *line* determined and completed *form. Line* developed *form* and did not merely ornament it. It was here that Van de Velde was misunderstood and the movement grew on the premise that line as it appeared in nature should be the basis for ornamentation. The curvilinear swing subsequently associated with Art Nouveau was seen in chair legs and chair backs and in the division of glass. The flowing line, popularly called "The Belgian Curve" (the flat segment of an ellipse), was used for wall openings, furniture supports and furniture forms.

By 1900 and the great Paris Exposition, the parabola took the place of the ellipse, and woodwork, mirror frames, and furniture were parabolically formed and linearly ornamented with parabolic shapes. Maxim's Restaurant in Paris, 1900, particularly exploited this theme. Although the movement was popular in France, Austria, Germany, and Italy, Belgium remained the source for new ornamental ideas and Van de Velde still naïvely believed that Art Nouveau was the intellectual answer to the machine.

The Scottish architect, Charles Rennie Mackintosh, had designed many buildings that were remarkable because they showed no evidence of period styles. When it came to furniture and decoration, Mackintosh superimposed Art Nouveau ornamentation on the "Morris tradition." "Mackintosh took the wriggling tendrils of those water lily roots and with his stern hands drew them tight and held them perpendicular." This restless perpendicularity became the hallmark of Mackintosh's furniture and decoration.

The new furniture—Rietveld. As the Art Nouveau rage waned, the moralistic principles of William Morris cleared the air once again. He had moved people and set them to thinking. The Deutsche Werkbund included industry and architecture. New furniture came from architects instead of decorative artists, since new visual premises were the starting points for new design. It became necessary to forget everything that had been done in the past and start all over again. The Dutch Neo-plasticists were the first to clarify "the new vision" in the historic periodical *De Stijl*. Here Rietveld (like Malewitsch, the constructivist sculptor and Mondrian, the painter) stated that the framework of furniture must be made of simple

FACING PAGE, UPPER LEFT: *Like the constructivist sculptors, Gerrit Rietveld built this chair (1917) using articulated planes of painted wood.* UPPER RIGHT AND CENTER: *Three chairs that show the development of Marcel Breuer's work during the 1920's. The wood chair (1924) follows the work of the constructivists. The chrome-plated steel tube chair (1925) led to the design of the cantilevered steel tube chair (1928).* LOWER: *The Van der Rohe steel tube chair (1926) anticipated the famous "Barcelona" chair (1929). Designed for the German exposition at Barcelona, this chair is now manufactured by Knoll Associates, Inc. The chair of chrome-plated steel bars and quilted leather has strongly influenced other design during the past five years.*

All pictures courtesy the Museum of Modern Art, New York

square elements that are screwed together. The individuality of the elements of the furniture must be stressed, resulting in complete articulation of all parts. Furniture was exploded into a series of vertical and horizontal planes, visually weightless in space. This manifesto was to start new painting, sculpture, architecture, music, and literature as well as furniture. The new vision of Rietveld joins the honest expression of Morris to create the design of our times.

The nineteen twenties. Breuer and Aalto. Marcel Breuer studied at the Bauhaus, and as a designer-craftsman became the first master of its furniture workshop. His early furniture of wood reflects the new vision of Rietveld's works: clarity of structural form and precarious visual balance. Breuer analyzed form in terms of line and, in a sense, referred back to the bentwood linear forms of Michael Thonet's chairs. Instead of wood, Breuer then began working with tubular steel and in 1925 invented the first continuous tubular steel frame. A loose canvas seat and back completed the design. In this first steel tube frame Breuer enlarged the design palette so that furniture could defy gravity visually, could be of linear form, and could easily become a machine expression. By 1929 Thonet Industries were mass producing Breuer designed tubular steel chairs. Tubular steel furniture reached its height when the resiliency of the material was realized. The architects Stam, Van der Rohe, Le Corbusier as well as Breuer became involved with the cantilevered tubular steel frame which rested on two rather than four legs as part of the continuous tubular frame. At this time Breuer developed the chair shapes that spread throughout the western world. Throughout the thirties these simple chairs were mass produced in Europe and the United States.

The Finnish Architect Alvar Aalto continued the work of Breuer and Van der Rohe. He exploited the resilient qualities of wood, particularly Scandinavian white birch. The Nordics were certainly familiar with molded skis, made of many veneers of wood curved under steam or heat. Actually Aalto's point of departure was a chair of tubular steel frame with a molded plywood seat and back (1932). The use of molded wood was not new; American designers had worked with this material for half a century, and the Dutch designer Rietveld had also used curved sections of plywood. Aalto realized the cantilever potential of this material and he was able to design chairs that paralleled the tubular steel chairs of Germany. Aalto used the indigenous white birch as the working material. The qualities of the wood are firmness and hard surface combined with unusual pliability. Birch is relatively knot-free and can reach immense glueing strength. The color of the wood is rather bland—pale yellow as compared with the stronger reddish tan of American birch. Aalto founded his own manufacturing plant, Artek Ltd., in 1936 and his furniture was distributed throughout Europe and the United States. Artek-Pascoe, in

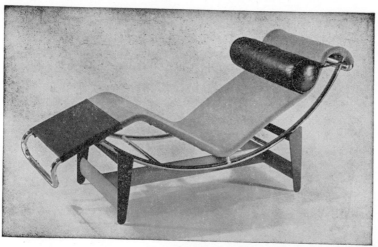

Le Corbusier's designs in steel tube add to the work of Breuer and Van der Rohe. Both pieces were manufactured by Thonet Industries. The lounge chair (1927) and the arm chair (1929) are adjustable.

New York distributed Aalto's furniture before 1940. This Scandinavian furniture was the second European collection of modern furniture to enjoy tremendous popularity (Thonet Industries were firmly entrenched in this country in the 1920's). The Swedish Mathsson and the Danish Klint also pioneered in the development of molded wood furniture.

The conclusion of an era. Industrialization started the problem. William Morris, indirectly, gave conscience to the machine. The followers of Morris escaped into hand-craftsmanship and were able to make peace with their times only when they designed and modified hand-crafted chairs that could be manufactured by the machine. The design tradition of essentially hand-made furniture modified for the machine is responsible for much of today's contemporary furniture, which has grown from these

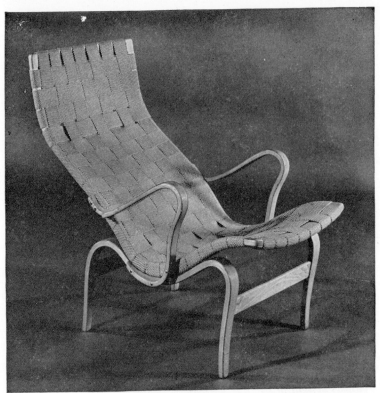

Both pictures courtesy the Museum
of Modern Art, New York

LEFT: *A molded and bent birch
plywood chair (c. 1934) designed by Alvar Aalto. The
seat-back form offers resiliency
within the stabile frame.*
ABOVE: *A Bruno Mathsson design (1940) of laminated bent
birch plywood, using fiber
webbing. The complex bending of the plywood offers additional structural strength.*

roots. This was the first approach to modern design. On the other hand Morris's plea for honesty of material and honesty of construction when applied to the machine (as well as the hand) became the second approach to design. This became most important when designers threw away the crutch of the past and investigated form afresh. The clarity of design that was the result of space–time and new concepts of light, when combined with Morris's values of material and construction, established the backbone of inventive design. Here, too, lies the essence of great traditional design—an esthetic feeling of the time expressed honestly through materials and systems of construction that were unique to the time. Morris's contribution was universal; the particular materials and the particular method of construction identified the particular time. The third approach, new materials for the sake of new materials, used with little understanding of their potential expression, was to create the stumbling block of the thirties.

A delightful chair design by Bonet, Hurchan, and Ferrari-Hardoy (1938) utilizes a metal rod frame and a sling of leather. The American market has been flooded with inferior copies of this ingenious construction.

The nineteen-thirties. Aalto, Mathsson, and Klint continued their work in Scandinavia, and Breuer designed a group of molded plywood furniture for Isokon in England. Much of Breuer's tubular steel furniture was copied in Europe and the United States. There was little additional significant furniture designed before World War II. Instead, French and English designers became involved with arbitrary, low, freely formed furniture that became known as "modernistic." Light and bleached woods were combined with clear glass, plastic, and gleaming metal. Cabinet forms were stepped and zigged, and the kidney shape became popular. New materials and new methods of manufacture were used to create this pseudo-modern style. The selected forms were expressive of the restlessness of the period rather than the materials that were employed.

The period after World War II. American, Scandinavian and Italian contributions. Although the furniture of Aalto and Mathsson had been imported since the late 1930's, there was little modern furniture manufactured in the United States. A remarkably high level of industrialization had been reached however and many metals had been improved and refined. Plywood was extensively used and plastics were both developed and produced. This environment of high industrialization using both new and man-improved materials was to become the first American contribution to today's furniture. The center of Scandinavian furniture design moved to Copenhagen. This change of location from Helsinki and Stock-

The last group of furniture designed by Eero Saarinen (1960). Plastic pedestals are cast to form bases for chairs and tables. The pedestals fuse to form chairs with the plastic seat-back shells. A particularly original group designed by one of America's great architects and furniture designers.

holm was largely due to the high standards of the Copenhagen Cabinet-makers' Guild, the respect for Professor Kaare Klint and the particular work of the teacher-designers Hans Wegener and Finn Juhl. The honesty of wood construction and the introduction of sculpture-like forms are important Scandinavian contributions. The Italian designers added combinations of many materials in the same piece of furniture. They also made designers aware of the textural values of materials, both visual and tactile. Here, then, was the scene at the end of World War II: the Scandinavian integrity of design, the Italian richness of materials, and the American development of materials and mechanization.

Saarinen, Eames, Wegener, and Juhl—the post-war designers. Eero Saarinen, son of the famous architect, was born in Finland in 1910. He studied architecture at Yale and then went to work with his father at Cranbrook Academy. In 1941 Saarinen won first prize with Charles Eames in the Functional Furniture Competition of the Museum of Modern Art. The winning chairs were made of plywood shells fitted with foam rubber and then upholstered. The legs were attached to the shell by means of electro-welded rubber connections. Saarinen subsequently designed four

LEFT: *The first great post World War II chair was designed by architect Charles Eames for the Herman Miller Collection. It was one of a group made of molded plywood seats and backs attached to frames of metal rods or molded plywood. The connections use pads of solid rubber.* BELOW: *One of a group of chairs designed by Eames in 1960. The same aluminum pedestal can be adapted for all seating and table forms. The furniture can be used in the home and the office; indoors and out-of-doors. This pedestal-based universal design concept is characteristic of the furniture of this decade.*

Courtesy the Museum of
Modern Art, New York

Courtesy Herman Miller, Inc.

groups of furniture. Included in the first was a lounge chair using an exposed molded plywood frame and an upholstered molded contour shell. The final group that Saarinen designed was dining furniture resting on a cast plastic pedestal. Saarinen felt that solid wood furniture was of the past and only concerned himself with man-made and man-improved materials. His architecture established structural principles that were always evident in his furniture. Eero Saarinen's untimely death in 1961 ended a personal design growth that might have gone beyond the tubular steel and molded plywood furniture of Breuer and Aalto.

Charles Eames was born in 1907 in St. Louis. After completing his architectural education, he joined the Saarinens at Cranbrook. During World War II he designed molded plywood splints for the armed forces. In 1946 the Museum of Modern Art exhibited Eames' first group of molded plywood and metal furniture. These chairs were commercially produced and are among the most significant chairs that have been designed during this century. Eames has also worked in plastics, aluminum, and steel. He is the universal designer, and has designed toys, wedding cakes, moving pictures as well as buildings and furniture. Like Saarinen, he has produced a limited collection of furniture and also, like Saarinen, every piece that he has designed has proven significant in our times.

Danish Hans Wegener is a trained furniture craftsman and has a special feeling for wood. He often makes full-size models of his designs himself, and his chairs are never put into production until they are tested in his own home. Wegener is the true craftsman: he selects the material and then makes a design for the specific wood. Wegener is symbolic of the high level of integrity and refinement found in Danish contemporary furniture. In a sense he is of the tradition of Morris and Heal. Finn Juhl is the other great Danish designer. His furniture is more cosmopolitan than Wegener's and generally it is highly sculptured. Juhl works the wood to the limit of its yielding capacity and the richly modelled curves are carried to their elastic limit.

The nineteen-fifties. During this period the Barcelona chair of Van der Rohe went back into production and its influence was immediately apparent. The metal frame of stainless or chrome-plated steel won in popularity over the molded wood frames that were derived from the work of Aalto. Toward the end of the decade the four-legged chair gave way to the three-legged chair and finally the single-legged or pedestal chair became the expression of current taste. The pedestal was certainly not new. However, pedestal tables and chairs certainly eased the problems of table seating and continued the esthetic feeling of precarious balance. The furniture designer became concerned with the use of one structural base that could support all furniture types. The sofa, the dining table, the lounge chair could all be supported by the same structural system. George Nelson, Florence Knoll, Ward Bennett, and others joined with Saarinen and Eames in the development of groups of furniture that were all supported by a uniform structural form, usually a pedestal and usually of metal. The chairs were generally upholstered in plastic or leather and the upholstery was quilted or tufted (again a Van der Rohe influence). Jens Risom designed simple wood furniture in the Scandinavian tradition and Edward Wormley and Paul McCobb worked in the solid wood traditions of William Morris and Ambrose Heal.

The tremendous square footage of office space that was built during the 1950's created a new need for office furniture. The designers and manufacturers of residential furniture attempted to universalize furniture so that the same designs could be used in residences and offices. This approach caused the anonymous room, which, save for accessories, could be a living room or an executive office. Awareness of the over-uniformity

The sophisticated forms of this solid wood frame are typical of Finn Juhl's refined designs.

Hans Wegener's oak, teak, and cane armchair (1949) is a fine example of the designer's understanding of solid wood. This is one of the first post World War II Danish designs that were imported to the United States by Georg Jensen.

Jens Risom designed this solid wood chair in 1949. The foam rubber seat and back and the zippered upholstery fabrics are easily removable for maintenance and change.

that identically structured furniture (equally comfortable in the home and the office) creates should result in a re-evaluation of oversimplification for production and for use. Good contemporary furniture will continue so long as the designer controls the machine. If industrialization once again intimidates good design, let us hope that there will be a future William Morris to "chase ugliness out of man's heart" by steering an intermediate course between functionalism and fantasy.

Bibliography

Aronson, Joseph, *The Encyclopedia of Furniture*. Crown Publishers, New York, 1938. All encompassing source that needs additional pictures.

Bayer, H., Gropius, I., Gropius, W., *Bauhaus: 1919–1928*. Charles T. Branford Co., Boston, 1959. A thorough documentation by the founders of the Bauhaus.

Breiner and Kocker, *Architecture and Furniture*. Museum of Modern Art, New York, 1938. Valuable source until 1938.

Fabro, Mario D., *Furniture for Modern Interiors*. Reinhold Publishing Co., New York, 1954. Drawings & details of creative modern furniture.

Giedion, S., *Mechanization Takes Command*. Oxford University Press, New York, 1948. The second book by one of our foremost art historians.

Gloag, John, *English Furniture*. Adam & Black, London, 1952. A competent summary of the growth of furniture in England.

Joel, David, *The Adventure of British Furniture*. Ernest Benn, Ltd., London, 1953. Excellent 19th century coverage, overstressing the British contribution.

Karlsen, A. and Tiedemann, A., *Made in Denmark*. Jul. Gjellerup, Copenhagen, 1960. A summary of all Danish arts and crafts. Good pictures.

Kaufmann, Edgar, Jr., *What is Modern Interior Design?* Museum of Modern Art, New York, 1953. Competently prepared and illustrated book.

Lenning, Henry F., *The Art Nouveau*. Martinus Nijhoff, The Hague, Netherlands, 1951. Successful specific study of the subject.

Margon, Lester, *World Furniture Treasures*. Reinhold Publishing Co., New York, 1954. Valuable pictorial survey of contemporary furniture.

Noyes, Eliot F., *Organic Design in Home Furnishing*. Museum of Modern Art, New York, 1941. A report of the historic furniture competition.

Pevsner, Nikolaus, *Pioneers of Modern Design*. Museum of Modern Art, New York, 1941. The best history of 19th century art and architecture.

Architects' Yearbook, Vol. 4, 1949 and Vol. 6, 1955. Elek Books Ltd., London. Specific information in a yearly publication.

New Furniture: Edited by Gerd Hatje, Vol. 1, 1952, Vol. 2, 1953, Vol. 3, 1955, Vol. 4, 1958. George Wittenborn, Inc., New York; Vol. 5, 1960, Vol. 6, 1962, Frederick A. Praeger, Inc., New York. An encyclopedic effort that presents good world-wide furniture.

PART THREE

DECORATIVE MATERIALS

AND ACCESSORIES

CHAPTER XI

DECORATIVE TEXTILES

I t is hardly necessary to state that textiles are among the most important materials of decoration, and that a thorough acquaintance with them is an essential part of the decorator's equipment. A study of textiles and their use must be approached from many angles, as their suitable selection in decorative work may depend upon all or any of the following characteristic features: fiber, weave, color, pattern, cost, and durability, and their relationship to the general decorative scheme.

The Basic Fibers

Textiles are woven fabrics made of yarns that are spun from fibers obtained from various natural or synthetic sources. The fabric is manufactured on a power or hand loom by means of interlacing two sets of yarns at right angles to each other. Textiles may also be produced by knitting, a process of interlocking rows of loops; or they may be made to adhere to each other by pressing, and formed into a cloth such as felt, but the latter method does not produce a true textile.

In the weaving of decorative textiles there are natural fibers and several synthetic types. Textiles may be woven by using one fiber only or by mixing two or more. In combining fibers, the mixture may be in the twisted yarn itself, or it may be in the weaving by interlacing yarns of different fibers.

The important fibers are as follows:

Cotton. The most important vegetable fiber, cotton, is taken from the bolls of the cotton plant, which grows prolifically in warm climates. The fiber varies in length from two-thirds of an inch to over two inches. The finest variety is the Egyptian, although the American medium-length fiber is produced in greatest quantity; cotton is also produced in Brazil, Peru, Persia, Mexico, Russia, and several other countries. India and China rank next to the United States in quantity production. There are many different grades that depend upon the natural color, length, softness, and crimpiness of the fiber. There are over two hundred kinds of cloth that can be made from cotton. The spun thread is usually dull and limp, though it can be given a glossy appearance by *mercerizing*. Examined under a strong microscope, the thread reveals that it is spirally twisted, and when tightly spun has greater strength than wool. Cotton reflects heat to a greater extent than wool or silk but less than linen or rayon. It suffers little from laundering, and stands boiling water and mild cleaning alkalies without serious detriment. Continuous exposure to sunlight causes it to disintegrate. Cotton is particularly used for draperies, upholstery, and slip-covers.

Linen. The oldest known fabrics (used in prehistoric times and unearthed in the early Egyptian tombs) were made of flax, a vegetable fiber that is now grown in most parts of Europe, in the northern portions of the United States, and in Argentina. The American flax plant, however, is used only for the growing of seed for the manufacture of linseed oil and other products. Flax fibers are very long, averaging about 18 inches, so that little spinning is necessary to make the yarn. The yarn is usually of a grayish color, and has a silky luster. It can be bleached without too great damage, but is not easily dyed; patterns are therefore usually printed or embroidered. Linen cloth is crisp and cool to the touch and reflects heat more readily than cotton; it is particularly used for sheeting and for table wear. Linen and synthetic fibers often are combined in the making of textiles to give them a lustrous appearance.

Silk. The most beautiful of all fibers and one of the oldest is silk, which is considered the "gold standard" of textile fibers. Tradition ascribes its origin as a material for weaving to China about 1725 B.C. The secret of its source and manufacture was carefully guarded for many centuries. Silken textiles were brought from Persia to Greece in 325 B.C., and were known to the Roman Emperor Tiberius, at which time they were worth their weight in gold, but it was not until the 6th century that the Emperor Justinian learned the secrets of sericulture.* During the early Middle Ages the caravans from the Far East brought from Byzantium, Persia, and Asia Minor some of the wondrous textiles made of this material, and from the 9th century silk production rapidly spread to Africa, Sicily, Italy, Spain, Portugal, and France. There have been many unsuccessful attempts to grow silk in America.

The grayish worms that produce the white cocoons must be fed from the leaves of the mulberry tree and handled with great care. When the

---

* Sericulture is a technical term used to define the processes required in silk production. It includes the growing of the mulberry tree, the rearing of the silkworm, the creation of the cocoon and the manufacturing of the yarn. The word originated from "Seres," the Latin name for the Chinese.

cocoons are matured, they are first placed in boiling water to remove the gummy surface, after which the filament is unreeled. An average length filament from each cocoon is about 600 yards, but many have a much greater length. The filament is extremely fine, but strong for its diameter; many spinnings are required to make a yarn the size of a human hair. It requires about 2,500 cocoons to make one yard of silk fabric.

There are many different grades of silk. The best cultured silk yarn, made of the longest filaments, is called organzine or *thrown-silk*. Other types made of shorter or broken strands have less luster and are known as tram, spun-silk, and bourette. Tussah is a wild silk made from the cocoons of worms that feed on oak or other trees; it has a rough quality, is light brown in color, cannot be bleached white, and is used for weaving the rougher textiles such as pongee, shiki, and shantung.

Silk is a very strong fiber; it is only surpassed in this respect by nylon. After the fiber has been degummed, it has a soft, beautiful luster. Silk textiles are sometimes weighted with metallic salts, but since this causes them to be brittle and less durable, the custom is now less practiced than heretofore. Strong light tends to discolor silk fabrics and disintegrate the fiber. Silk has a natural affinity for dyes but it is deteriorated by bleaching and most cleaning acids.

Wool. Wool is one of the oldest and most important fibers for weaving, and comes from the fleece of animals. The Spanish sheep known as the *merino* is the ancestor of nearly all wool-growing sheep in the world, but wool is also sheared from camels, goats, alpaca, and llama. Vicuña, the rarest and most valuable of all wools, is taken from a South American wild camel. Cat, cow, and horsehair are also used in textile production. The greatest quantity of high grade textile wools now come from Australia, although these fibers are of shorter length than the English wools. The best wools for floor coverings come from the Far East and Near East. Wool shorn from the sides and back of animals is superior to that taken from the other parts of the hide, and the hair from live animals known as "fleece-wool" is better than the "pulled-wool" that is taken from slaughtered stock. The length of wool fiber varies from 1 to 18 inches depending upon the animal, the climatic conditions, and the length of time it has grown before shearing. Wool fiber is springy, resilient, soft, kinky, and extremely durable. Woolen goods are often given special names like mohair, made from the angora goat, cashmere, alpaca, etc., depending upon the animal or place from which the wool is obtained. Worsteds are made from long fibers and are often woven in patterns. Woolens are woven from short fibers. The natural color of wool ranges from light brown to black and most wools can be readily dyed. Wool yarns are often mixed with cotton, rayon, and other fibers in textile production. A great number of decorative textiles are woven from wool, such as tapestries, blankets, draperies, and rugs, and due to the lasting qualities, woolen textiles are especially valuable for upholstery uses.

Synthetic fibers and yarns. Textiles woven from synthetic yarns were first produced by Chardonnet, a pupil of Pasteur in Paris in 1889. The fabrics were at first called artificial silk, but in 1924 the designation *rayon* was adopted by common agreement. It was not until 1930 that large-scale commercial production commenced, and since that year many varieties and improvements have been introduced and the use of such textiles in both the clothing and decorative art fields has increased to vast proportions. For many purposes, these materials have proved to be superior to those woven with natural fibers.

The chemical compounds that are used in making these yarns include cellulose, acetate, cuprammonium, viscose, casein, copper sulfate, aluminum, and others. Vinyl plastic is also used for coatings. The yarns are produced by pressing a liquid through a spinneret or disk pierced with small holes. The emerging streams come in contact with the air or an acid bath that gives them cohesiveness and tensile strength. The yarns are therefore a continuous filament and differ from those made by twisting short lengths of cotton, wool and linen. In weaving, synthetic yarns are often interwoven with natural ones. Both dull and lustrous surface appearances may be produced in a textile by using either simple or spun filaments. The textiles are easily dyed or printed, the majority are mothproof and mildewproof, and dry quickly. Several are resistant to creasage and shrinkage, have excellent draping qualities, and clean easily.

In fabricating for upholstery and draperies, they should be sewn with a nylon thread. As each type of synthetic textile differs in its characteristics, it is advisable, before purchasing, to check with the distributor its suitability for a particular purpose. Chemists continue to research for newer and superior products in this field, and the improvements are often so rapid that a review of trade publications is necessary to keep abreast of developments.

While the term *rayon* continues to be used to designate certain types, the variety of source material from which the fibers are made, with the resultant differences in qualities, characteristics, and uses of the finished product, has necessitated arbitrary terms to identify them. In the majority of cases these designations are registered trade names of the manufacturers. Among the leading products identified in this manner are acetate rayon, oralac, arnel, bemberg, celanese, celeperm, chromespun, dacron, cynel, fiberglas, fortisan, lurex, naugahyde, nylon, orlon, saran, and valon. Distributors usually label their products with the fiber name, and in the finished product state the proportions of each type.

Ramie. This is a fiber which is sometimes used as a substitute for flax and is commonly known as china-grass. It is coarse, strong, and durable.

Jute. This is a fiber that resembles linen and comes from the interior of the stalk of a tall plant that grows in India. It is used for burlap bags, twine, furniture webbing, and for bindings and backings of the cheaper grades of rugs and carpets. The fiber is very long and does not stretch. The short fibers are used in the manufacture of wrapping paper.

Hemp. This comes from a plant that grows in many countries located in temperate zones. It produces a strong coarse fiber and is used for fabrics, ropes, and sacks.

Asbestos. This is a mineral which is of a fluffy consistency and in weaving must be combined with cotton to produce a fabric. Its only advantage is in its fireproof qualities, for which it is used where local laws require such protections, as in theater curtains.

Lurex. Is a metallic thread that is nontarnishable and made with a gold or silver finish.

Fiberglas. Is a yarn produced from glass.

Leather. While this material is not a textile, it is extensively used in decoration for upholstery, table covers, and other purposes. There are many varieties, the best for upholstery uses being cow and steer hide. The hide is taken off the carcass by cutting the length of the belly so that the center of the hide is from the back of the animal. The best-wearing portion and the most interesting grain of the hide is taken from this part. The quality depreciates along the edges of the hide so that these portions are used for surfaces that receive the least amount of wear, such as the outside of backs and arms of chairs and sofas. A cowhide contains about 50 square feet of leather, but due to its irregular shape, one must count on about 25 per cent wastage in its use. Leather can be finished in almost any color and is furnished in several grades. Genuine leather hides are usually sliced into four layers, the outer layer being the most durable. These are graded in order from the outside and are known as Top Grain, Deep Buff, Split, and Slat. As leather is a product of nature, there are always irregularities in the surface of the top grain, but these do not affect the wearing quality and are a proof of the grade. Leather of course has a distinctive odor that makes it easy to identify.

Artificial leather. This is the name given to a cotton fabric coated with a cellulose solution, dyed, and stamped to imitate various leather grains. It is not durable for heavy upholstery use, but has been applied to purposes in which wear is not a consideration, such as walls, draperies, table covers, screens, bookbindings, and small articles. The imitation is generally obvious and it is advisable to avoid using this material in the better grades of decorative work.

Fiber tests. All fibers may be tested by means of chemistry, but these methods require laboratory equipment that is too complicated except for the manufacturer. There are several simple tests any one may make that are reasonably satisfactory. In testing any textile, a sample length should be taken of both the warp and weft thread, each of which should be un-ravelled to verify whether the yarn has been made of two fibers. The most easily made test is by burning the end of each thread with a match. The following results will be noticed:

Pure silk burns slowly and produces an animal odor. When the flame is extinguished, the end of the thread shows a small bead. *Weighted silk* often will not burn, but an applied flame will produce a hot metallic ash that disintegrates upon touching.

Wool burns more slowly than silk and produces a noticeable animal odor like singed human hair. The end of the thread usually curls into a small ball.

Cotton burns with a flash, is completely consumed and smells like burning paper. A grayish ash remains when the flame is extin-guished.

Linen burns slowly and smells like charred wood. No ball is left.

Synthetic fibers. These are more difficult to test by the burning method than natural fibers; the difference in ashes is due to the various chemical elements. Rayon yarns burn rapidly and leave a slightly charred but brittle end. Some of them melt as they burn and small sparks appear. The acetate types sometimes have a pungent odor.

There are other tests for certain fabrics. The moisture test can be made to distinguish linen and cotton. If water is dropped on linen, the spot appears translucent; if dropped on cotton, the spot is more opaque. The broken ends of a cotton yarn are fuzzy in appearance while those of linen are pointed. As linen threads are stronger than cotton threads of the same size, it requires greater strength to break them. The feeling or touch test requires experience and is not always accurate, but is sometimes the best way to distinguish between silk and synthetic fibers. Cloth tests are not as important as they were formerly, as yardage is today usually marked by the manufacturer as to its proportional content.

Weaving

There is little fundamental difference between the earliest known hand looms and the machine looms found in up-to-date factories. The principle of the loom is quite simple. The *warp* threads (those that go the full length of the material) are stretched taut around drums, so that a great number of yards may be woven. They are unreeled from one drum, and the finished cloth is rolled around a second. These warp threads are con-trolled overhead by *heddles,* originally bars of wood. The heddles are threaded with strings or wires on the ends of which are loops—one loop for each warp thread. For a plain weave, they are so arranged that by raising one heddle, every other warp thread is lifted. A second heddle controls the alternate warps. As the heddle lifts the alternate warp threads, an opening called a *shed* is made. Through this passes the shuttle holding the *filler* thread (the thread that goes across from selvage to selvage; sometimes called the *weft* or *woof*). The first set of warp threads are then lowered, the other set lifted, and the shuttle sent through the shed again. The weft or filler threads are pushed down tightly against each other by a kind of comb arrangement. All weaves are variations of this simple process. To make patterns, the warps are lifted in groups according to the design for that particular fabric.

Though there have been many improvements added to looms, the power loom invented in the early 19th century, with but few basic changes, is in operation today. The pattern to be woven is drawn on squared-off paper, each square representing a warp and a filler. Cards are then made with corresponding holes punched in them. The hooks controlling the lifting and lowering of the warp threads are maneuvered through these holes. For a simple pattern with a short repeat there are not very many cards; but for an intricately designed brocade, the complexities of the weaving machinery seem too great for the layman to follow. A loom can even handle two series of warps and two series of fillers.

Of the simple basic weaves there are three general divisions: plain or taffeta weave, twill weave, and satin weave.

Plain or taffeta weave. In this weave, the filler thread crosses the top of alternate warp threads. One thread over and one thread under, with both warp and filler of the same weight and size, makes a plain weave. Two or more over and under an equal number of warp threads makes a *basket weave*. A variation of the taffeta weave is seen in the *rep* weave, in which either the warp or filler thread is heavier than the other, which produces a corded effect.

Twill weave. In the twill weave, each warp thread runs over two and under one filler thread. The adjoining warp thread skips different fillers to produce a diagonal effect. Many variations of this weave are possible, but in all of them the diagonal or herringbone effect is produced, as in denim and serge.

Satin weave. In this type, the warp threads skip four to seven fillers. The filler threads are often finer than the warp and are practically invisible on the right side of the textile, so that the long floats of the warp produce a smooth, shiny surface. The filler threads dominate the back of the fabric. A variation is seen in sateen, made from mercerized cotton, in which the filler threads dominate the face of the fabric.

The combination of plain, twill, and satin weaves produces most of the familiar textiles, including damasks and brocades. There are also four important weaves of a slightly more complicated nature.

Plain or Taffeta Weave	Sateen Weave
Twill Weave as in Denim	Twill Weave as in Serge
Satin Weave	Basket Weave

COMMON TYPES OF TEXTILE WEAVES.

Leno weave. This is a loose weave in which two warp threads are twisted together and around a filler thread to form a kind of knot that keeps the warp thread from slipping. This makes an openwork fabric like marquisette or net. The weave is sometimes incorrectly called "gauze."

Pile fabrics. These are made with two sets of warp or filler threads. In velvet, one set of warps combined with the filler makes a plain but solid

Fragment of gros-point needlework showing a typical Rococo pattern.

backing, while the second set of warps makes an upright loop known as a *pile*. These warp threads are run over a wire and then caught down to make the loop. For cut velvet, the loops are all cut as the wire is withdrawn. If the wire is withdrawn without cutting the loops, the resulting fabric is called an *uncut velvet* or *frisé*. Floor coverings made in this manner were formerly known as moquettes. Velvets are sometimes woven face to face and cut apart to produce the pile.

Handmade tapestry. In making this fabric, filler threads of different colors on bobbins (spools) are wound about the warp threads by hand, according to a design or pattern produced by the filler threads only. These threads are not carried the whole distance across the width of the loom, but are cut off and left hanging on the underside of the tapestry when the thread of each color has played its required part in that portion of the pattern. In antique tapestries, the warp threads were usually made of wool. Gold and silver threads were often used in the filler to give sparkle to the design. The whole process is extremely costly and handmade tapestries are only produced in a very few places in the world today.

Gros-point and petit-point needlework. These are types of embroidery made on a fine net background. The pattern is produced by cross-stitches of different colors sewn with thread and needle diagonally across adjoining squares of the net. Gros-point averages 144 stitches to the square inch and petit-point about 400. Either wool or silk may be used to make the stitches.

Printing and Dyeing Textiles

The earliest known textile designs were painted by hand and antedate woven patterns by many centuries. Today, various methods of pattern printing are used.

Direct printing. For this type of printing the color is applied directly to the cloth. It can be done by hand with pen or brush, or with wooden blocks, each of which prints one color and a certain section of the design. This system is known as *block-printing*. When copper-plate printing was originated, it was considered quite efficient, but was soon superseded by roller printing. At first the rollers carried only the outline of the design, which was later filled in with the necessary colors. Designs are now etched on copper rollers, one roller for each color and for a certain section of the pattern. The last roller prints the background color. Some fabrics are printed on the warp threads only. These are known as warp or shadow prints, and the design has a mottled or faded appearance.

Resist and extract printing. An old method of producing patterned fabrics, a variation of which is still in use, is the process known as *resist-dyeing*. It was employed when a pattern of small light motifs was desired on a large dark background in one color. The effect was produced by coating the portions of the fabric to be left white with wax or clay. The entire fabric was then dyed. Wherever the coating had been applied, the fabric "resisted" penetration of the dye. Upon removal of the wax, a white pattern was left on the dark ground. In modern reproductions of this type of fabric, the procedure is exactly opposite from the former method, and is called *extract printing*. After the entire fabric has been dyed, a chemical is applied to certain portions, which removes the background color, and forms the desired pattern. In both methods, an effect of great charm is achieved by the slight irregularities and color variations in the finished product.

Stencil and screen printing. Textiles are sometimes printed by means of stencils. The stencils are made of paper or metal with a hole cut in them to fit a certain portion of the pattern. When they are placed on the cloth in the proper position in relation to the pattern, the dye is pressed through the opening by means of a rubber strip called a "squeegee." The stencil is then moved to the same position in the next repeat. If the pattern is elaborate, many stencils are required, making the process very slow and costly. As a substitute for this, *screen-printing* was invented in the early years of the 20th century. In this process the stencil consists of a large sheet of fine silk stretched and mounted on a frame that is the same dimension as the whole repeat and width of the fabric. The yardage is laid flat on a long table. The number of frames required is the same as the number of colors in the pattern. The complete pattern is drawn on each framed stretch. Each stretch is completely varnished except for the portions of the pattern that are of the same color. The complete series of frames produce stencils for every color for an entire repeat of the pattern. These frames are then carefully and consecutively placed over each repeat and the dye is brushed or squeezed through the unvarnished portion of the pattern. When all the frames have been used for the full length of the fabric, the stencilling or screen printing is complete. Some of the most charming silk and cotton fabrics are made in this manner. The process permits longer repeats than cylinder printing and a more flexible use of color resembling that of the former hand-blocked processes.

Dyeing. Several different methods of dyeing materials are commonly practiced. *Stock-dyeing* is a process of dipping the raw fibers in a vat of dye before the thread is spun. *Yarn-dyeing* consists of dipping the threads before weaving, as in plaids and striped effects. Cross-dyeing is sometimes used for fabrics of mixed wool and cotton. The wool or cotton yarn is dyed before weaving. After weaving, the whole fabric is dyed again. This method is used only where the dye for one fiber will not be effective on the other. *Piece-dyeing* or dip-dyeing consists of dipping the whole fabric after weaving.

Textile Period Patterns

Textiles of antiquity. Historians claim that weaving was well known some five to six thousand years before Christ. The earliest authentic records come from Egypt, where, as a result of the Egyptian burial customs, almost complete evidence of their mode of living has been preserved. In the tombs were placed many objects of daily use, including clothing; and the walls of the tombs were decorated with scenes from the daily life of the Egyptians. Among the extant wall-paintings is a picture of a loom then in use (about 2500 B.C.). It is very simple, and yet is not unlike hand looms which are used to this day. Fragments of actual cloth from about that date have also been found—linens, finer than anything that can be made today. The Egyptians were also familiar with cotton and wool, and with silk brought from China. The lotus was the favorite pattern motif.

The neighboring peoples of Assyria and Babylonia were equally advanced in the art of weaving; but few of their textiles have been preserved. The most famous Assyrian pattern is known as the *hom* or tree-of-life.

As a slender stem or a rugged tree, it has reappeared down through the centuries. The ancient Persians copied the pattern, which eventually found its way to India, and finally was exported in the painted cottons to England where it had a most important influence on English textile and wallpaper designs.

Greece did little to advance the art of textile weaving. Many of the finest Greek fabrics were woven on the island of Crete, where expert weavers from the East and from Egypt gathered. The intricacies of these woven or painted patterns are clearly defined on the picturesque Greek vases. Though the early Roman emperors in the first centuries of the Christian Era were lavish in their use of rich fabrics, very few were created under their régime.

Byzantine textiles. Before the days of the Mohammedan conquest Byzantium (later Constantinople) was the Eastern center of the Roman Empire. The powerful emperors felt that to maintain their prestige they must have rich fabrics, not only for clothing but for presents, and for a display of wealth and power. It was for the Emperor Justinian in the 6th century that the Nestorian monks smuggled from China the priceless silkworm cocoons and the seeds of the mulberry tree on which they feed. But for his desire to excel all the rich potentates of the East, the silk industry might never have been introduced into Europe. Influenced by both Persia and China and with a heritage of early Egyptian art, the Byzantine patterns were rich and colorful. Christian symbolism was introduced, though the *rondel* served as the enclosing form. The patterns were formal and symmetrical, including fantastic animals and birds, particularly the elephant. By the 11th century the long, sweeping ogival bands, which were later so important in Italian design, came into existence.

Chinese textiles. The Chinese used handsome silks for textiles long before the people of the Mediterranean had any knowledge of them; in fact, they alone could make silk, for no one else knew its secret. Tradition states that the fine thread of the silkworm was discovered and the cocoon unravelled by a Chinese empress (about 2690 b.c.). Having spun the thread (a secret they guarded jealously), they wove the silk into rich and beautiful textiles. Silk textiles are still in existence that were made by the Chinese in the 2nd century b.c. Since that time, unsurpassed silks of every description have been made. Satin embroideries and brocades were produced with colored and metal threads and many silks were enriched with hand-painted decorations. Hand-blocking of patterns also dates from a very early period. Textiles were also made of hemp, linen, wool, and cotton. Beautiful damasks and tapestries produced during the Ch'ing period (1644–1912) are still available in the markets. Their patterns were filled with religious symbolism derived from their various faiths—Confucian, Buddhist, or Taoist. The royal dragon, peacocks, the swastika, various flowers, and the conventionalized cloud and wave are among the best-known motifs, and usually all of them were arranged in compact, well-planned designs.*

Japan is now almost as famous as China for silks, though Japan produces entirely different weaves and patterns. Japanese textile motifs have less religious significance, and often include figures, particularly lovely ladies with weird headdresses and long, sweeping kimonos. Cherry blossoms and plum blossoms are typically Japanese, and even their sacred mountain, Fuji, finds its way into their designs.

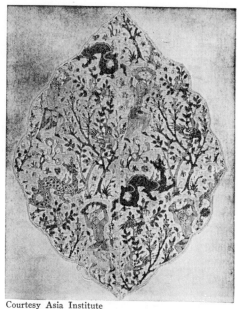

Courtesy Asia Institute

A 16th century Persian velvet panel showing Alexander hurling a stone at a dragon. Gold ground with red and green pattern.

Persian textiles. The influence of Persia on textile design has been almost as strong as that of China. The Persians inherited from Assyria and Babylonia a sound sense of design, and were excellent craftsmen as well. They made many of the fabulous brocades so important in the romantic tales of old Persia, although they imported many others from China. These priceless fabrics, as well as bales of raw silk, were brought over the long caravan routes to such great trading centers as Bagdad. Naturally, the Persian princes selected the rarest and most beautiful silks for their own use, and in turn they sent back to China textiles of native manufacture, to show the Chinese weavers the patterns and weaves they found most appealing. The silk velvets and brocades woven in Persia during the Safaid period (1502–1736) are the most sumptuous that have ever been produced. They were used for clothing, wall hangings, and even for the tents of military officers. Patterns of this period often reproduced the most delicate effects of the contemporary miniaturists, adjusting their techniques, however, to the textile medium and taking advantage of the rich sheen of the silk pile and contrasting it with metal threads. Brocaded satins, taffetas, and twills were also produced, and embroideries and tapestries were made in silk. In the 17th and 18th centuries, Persia and India made the hand-

* See Chapter VIII for description of Chinese decorative forms and motifs.

Typical painted Indian cotton or Palampore, showing the tree-of-life pattern adapted from old Persian designs and transmitted to England during the 17th and 18th centuries.

blocked or painted cottons known as *palampores* for which a great demand developed in western Europe, where they were often called *persanes* and *indiennes*. Extraordinary fabrics were also made of the wool of the Cashmere and Angora goats. The most typical pattern motifs consisted of flowering trees, cypresses, poppies, roses and other floral forms, and the pomegranate. Real and imaginary animals were often shown. The camel, sphinx, dragon, horse, dog, and deer were frequently combined with bird forms such as peacocks and hawks. Landscapes and rocks were also used. Hunting and coursing scenes were often represented showing turbaned horsemen following the hounds. Practically all the early designs up to the 7th century were enclosed in circles (rondels) or lozenge forms, the more familiar ones being arranged in doublets with the figures facing or turning their backs to each other.

Courtesy Asia Institute

A 16th century Persian velvet showing all-over pattern of red poppies on gold ground.

Other Islamic textiles. In the Mohammedan countries that were ruled by the Sunni sect, such as Turkey and Spain, textiles were not enriched with the naturalistic motifs used in Persian design, due to the Prophet's ruling that there must be no representation of living things. Inspiration turned to geometrical and abstract forms and to the use of the flowing Arabian script quoting the wisdom of Mohammed. Small phrases lent themselves to filling the old rondel, and so satisfied two needs: praise of Allah, and a worthy design. The most perfect examples of highly conventionalized Mohammedan design are to be found in Spain. Flowing arabesques, geometric figures, and interlacing lines, were all woven into heavy, brilliantly colored silks. Gold and silver thread made them even more elegant. The elaborate ceremonial and social existence led by the Sultans and Caliphs required accoutrements of great splendor and the weavers of the period furnished brilliantly patterned textiles for all purposes. When the Moors were driven from Spain in 1492, the Spanish weavers turned to Italy for new patterns. The native initiative disappeared and Italian patterns were either exactly copied or at times were combined with some of the Moorish geometrical forms that seemed adaptable to Christian requirements. The most outstanding examples of Renaissance textile weaving in Spain were the ecclesiastical vestments which were woven for specific dignitaries and ceremonies. Great collections of these are still to be seen in the Spanish museums and monasteries.

Italian textiles. Sicily was the leading textile center during the 12th century. The Mohammedans, stopping there briefly, had bequeathed their conventional patterns to the weavers gathered from both Egypt and Byzantium. From this mixture of tongues and religions a new style finally evolved. Palermo was famed for beautiful silks spotted with glistening

Fragments of 15th century Spanish silks showing the Mohammedan influence in geometrical and abstract patterns.

LEFT: *An early Sicilian silk showing Byzantine influence in the use of pairs of conventionalized animals.* RIGHT: *A typical 15th century Florentine velvet showing the elongated S-scroll combined with the artichoke motif.*

gold. The patterns were less severe than the Mohammedan or Byzantine, despite the stylized motifs set within the elongated ovals.

The weavers were driven from Sicily in the 13th century, and many migrated to Lucca in northern Italy. There, many of the most precious church silks were woven with patterns of saints and angels. For the first time, the faces of these figures were woven of white silk, and the rest of the fabric was heavy with gold and color. At the same time, in Florence, the master craftsmen were turning out amazing weaves and patterns. With the beginning of the 15th century came the Renaissance—that revival of interest in all the arts—with Florence as a cultural center. The patterns definitely marked as Florentine include the elongated S-scroll which, of

Courtesy Metropolitan Museum of Art

A 13th century Lucca silk with Gothic religious pattern of angels and stars.

course, developed from the ogee curve. Combined with the early floral forms was the well-known pomegranate or artichoke. The pomegranate, originally an essential part of all Persian designs, was unfamiliar to the Italian weavers, but they felt its similarity to their own artichoke. Very soon they had transformed the motif from a pomegranate to an artichoke, and it became one of the dominant motifs of the Renaissance. The Renaissance vase, in various forms, first holding the artichoke and later all the important floral forms, was almost equally popular. By the 16th century it held an enormous bouquet of fairly naturalistic flowers. The royal crown was often worked in, suspended in a bouquet or seeming to hold together two of the sweeping serpentine bands.

Venice had so many facets to its artistic life that sometimes the importance of its weavers is overlooked. As Venice was an important seaport, rare fabrics from all over the world were assembled there, and the native weavers drew their designs from these rich foreign fabrics. Particularly influenced by the Chinese patterns, they scattered small flowers about, after the oriental fashion, and to give order to this arrangement, they borrowed from Persia the set patterns which helped to stabilize the whole design. Venetian velvets, too, were famed, particularly those that were small and intricate in pattern. One fashion that must be credited to Venice is the *ferronnerie* velvet, with its finely drawn design which resembles delicate wrought iron.

Italian Renaissance velvets of the 16th and 17th centuries, showing the small pattern where the design appears in cut pile on a smooth background. Usually the background and design are in contrasting colors, and they are commonly known as Genoese and Venetian velvets.

The fourth of the great weaving centers of Italy was Genoa, which was particularly famous for its velvets. The beautiful 16th century *velours-de-Gênes* (Genoese Velvet) with its jewel-like coloring was in demand all over Europe. This was woven in a small all-over pattern and while the cloth was originally intended for clothing, it was appropriated by the upholsterers in whose work it was extensively used. The multicolored floral pattern known as the jardiniere velvet was set against a light satin ground, and had several heights of pile as well as uncut loops included to give greater variety.

French silk textiles. France, prior to the Renaissance, had expended all her artistic effort on the development of beautiful architectural forms. She had bought all of her valuable textiles from Italy or Spain. About the middle of the 15th century France began to weave tapestries in Arras. Lyons was established as a silk center by Francis I in the early years of the 16th century. The early designs were mainly Italian in feeling, for many of the finest weaves were imported from Italy. Gradually, influenced by the extravagant court life of France, the patterns became more luxurious, less severe, and more feminine in appeal. Tapestries, vastly important in the decorating of a great hall, were made in various weaving centers. But it was not until the reign of Louis XIV in the 17th century that distinctive French fabrics, quite free from Italian influence, were woven.

The Baroque style of Louis XIV textile design was impressive, with its heavy garlands of fruit and flowers. The bold, large-scale, florid patterns, which were seen in velvets and brocades, were indicative of the grandeur and display of court life. Toward the end of the 17th century the designs were slightly subdued. Flowers became more naturalistic and patterns less complicated. Tapestries were important, and to Louis XIV and his minister Colbert can be credited the success of the Gobelins works in Paris.

Seventeenth century velours-de-Gênes with multicolored floral pattern raised on a light satin ground.

The King bought the factory at Gobelins, supported it with royal grants, and limited its productions to royal use. Also to this king, who ruled so long, must be attributed a great setback to textile development in France. When Louis signed the revocation of the Edict of Nantes in 1685, a great number of skilled weavers who were Huguenots were forced to flee France. Though the French weaving industry continued to thrive, keen rivalry was felt with the countries to whom the weavers and other artisans had fled.

Typical Louis XIV velvet showing baroque pattern of symmetrical large flower and fruit forms.

Louis survived several changes of style, and the graceful patterns known as Louis XV or Rococo were well established before the old king died. To the reign of Louis XV belong all the romantic frivolities that took such a hold on the French people of the 18th century. Never have more beautiful silks been made, with more intricacy of weave, than were then produced on the looms of Lyons. There seemed no limit to what the weavers could do. The patterns were charmingly disordered and lacked the splendor of

Louis XIV fabric showing densely compressed patterns and conventionalized floral forms.

Louis XV brocade with typical pattern of bouquets of garden and field flowers and lace.

Typical chinoiserie in the style of Pillement, with dainty Chinese figures, Rococo scroll, and small-scale floral forms. About 1785-1790.

the previous century. Lace motifs grew in popularity and did, indeed, provide a suitable background for the playful patterns. Long streamers of ribbon were entwined with cupids and turtledoves in asymmetrical designs with scrolls and abundant flowers. Importations from the Far East set the vogue for the adaptation of Chinese patterns, known as chinoiseries, which are so typical of this era. Everything was light and dainty in scale, color, and texture, and the curved line dominated all design.

Another reversal of style occurred in the third quarter of the century, when the Neo-classical forms were introduced as a result of the Pompeian excavations. The curves were replaced by straight lines. Stripes were over-

Philippe de la Salle brocade of the Louis XVI period showing naturalistic baskets of flowers, ribbons, and wreaths.

patterned with fragile little bouquets of flowers in natural colorings. In more magnificent brocades all the classical details that had become so important in furniture and architecture came into prominence. These were often combined with bows and arrows, the symbols of Cupid, and with bow-knots with loose floating ends of ribbon. Later came the elaborate patterns with groupings of musical instruments or agricultural implements. Philippe de la Salle was one of the greatest silk designers whose composi-

Early Empire brocade reflecting the classic influence in the use of the wreath and classic motifs.

tions were shaped by a sweeping classicism. His intricate designs are sometimes overnaturalistic, but they are justly famous as the turning-point that led away from the miniature patterns of the mid-18th century. He was the advance spirit of the Directoire, which was to be the next significant French style.

After the wave of fine classicism had subsided because of the dominating force of Napoleon, there was another violent change of patterns in France. Although Napoleon favored

Louis XVI brocade with delicate sprays of flowers worked over stripes.

certain aspects of classicism, he was insistent that all traces of his royal forerunners be obliterated. The forms of republican Rome rather than the more refined motifs of democratic Greece appealed to him. The well-known Napoleonic motifs which appear in the patterns of this period include eagles and torches, wreaths with the imperial letter "N," the star and bee, and Egyptian motifs.

Oberkampf's toiles-de Jouy. From the early years of the 18th century efforts had been made in France to imitate the delightful printed cottons that had been imported from Persia and India, but it was left to one man to manufacture these types of materials successfully and popularize them to such an extent that there has existed almost a continuous demand for them ever since their introduction.

Christophe-Philippe Oberkampf.

Christophe-Philippe Oberkampf, a Bavarian, established in the year 1760 a cotton print manufactory in the village of Jouy near Versailles. Public interest in decorating had greatly increased at that time, and as the cost of silk fabrics was extremely high, it was obvious that a cheaper substitute would find a ready market. Oberkampf was a man with a persuasive personality, great business integrity, an artist and excellent salesman, and he had an uncanny intuition for the pulse of public taste. His first efforts were to imitate the foreign prints, the

Courtesy Metropolitan Museum of Art

Typical toile-de-Jouy entitled "Le Petit Buveur," manufactured at Jouy about 1770.

rising demand for which was beginning to surpass the supply. By frequent personal contacts with his aristocratic customers, he could advise his designers as to the motifs that would appeal to a public who maintained a high degree of connoisseurship. As his fame grew, he enlarged his plant and his patterns became more ambitious. He turned from copying Eastern repeat motifs to produce patterns that were more representative of his time and public. He commenced to make patterns having large repeats

Post-Revolutionary toile-de-Jouy designed by Jean-Baptiste Huet. The design shows the classic influence in the costumes of the figures, the ornaments, and the geometric arrangement of the motifs.

which showed groups of peasants or aristocrats dressed in their particular clothing in activities associated with their daily interests. He also pictured bourgeois scenes, fables, and historical events. These prints were made in one color only—red, blue, plum, or green, and hand-blocked on a natural cream-colored background. This general type of pattern he continued to produce for nearly the whole period of the existence of his factory. To maintain his sales and record his patriotism, he was quick to take advantage of the political changes in France; the discoveries of Pompeii strongly influenced his designs, and the ornamental motifs introduced by Percier and Fontaine after Napoleon's accession were immediately adapted to his printed products. His later machine-made products have short repeats and are the small floral motifs that are known as "mignonette" and "picoté" designs.

The printing process was at first entirely by the hand-block method, but by 1770 cylinder printing commenced and his output increased enormously. It is on record that he claimed that with cylinder printing one man could do the work of forty hand-blockers. He employed many able designers, the most famous and gifted being Jean-Baptiste Huet who worked for him from 1783 onwards. Huet's designs were full of grace and animation, with humor often added, and after the Revolution he evolved the architectural and geometrical backgrounds against which were placed medallions, classical figures, and delicate arabesques. In 1783 the factory became a "Manufacture Royal," permitting the use of the arms of the King as a trademark. Oberkampf died in 1815 and the factory continued under various owners until 1843, when, lacking the managerial inspiration of the founder, it finally closed its doors. Some of the original Oberkampf cylinders are still in existence and many copies have been made from them. All the original Jouy prints were marked on their selvage with the words "bon-teint," meaning fast dye. Toiles-de-Jouy following the original traditions are among the most popular decorative cottons today.

Jean-Baptiste Huet.   *Joseph-Marie Jacquard.*

The Jacquard loom. The second greatest name in French textile manufacturing is that of Joseph-Marie Jacquard, who was born in 1752 and died
in 1834. His contribution to the decorative arts was the invention of a
power loom to weave elaborate colored patterns in imitation of handmade
brocades, brocatelles, and tapestries. The loom bearing his name was later
adapted to the weaving of pile fabrics and floor coverings. The story of
Jacquard's achievement is a record of hard work and ambition. He was
the son of a poor weaver whose trade he inherited. For years he wove
busily but without financial success, and he lived in extreme poverty. During the French Revolution he was called out with the troops of Lyons.
After the war he returned to his meager trade and spent long nights working on his invention. When it was first shown to the public in 1801, it was
instantly acclaimed. But his victory was not yet complete, for his machine
aroused the antagonism of the Lyons weavers, who destroyed one of the
first Jacquards in a public square. Soon, however, the opposition faded,
and by 1812 there were 11,000 Jacquard looms in use in France.

English textiles. To understand the chintzes, hand-blocked linens, and
crewel embroideries for which England is so justly famous, it is necessary
to go back to the early days of cotton in India. It is from India that England borrowed her patterns and her technique. India and cotton have gone
hand in hand from as early as 2000 B.C., though no actual pieces of cloth
of that period are still in existence. But it is certain that instead of weaving
patterns, they used paints and dyes to produce their designs. It is also a
known fact that cotton was not woven to any extent in Europe until the
13th century. At about the same time, the merchants of India began to export their gay chintzes, first to the ports of the Eastern Mediterranean,
then to Venice, and finally to Portugal. From there the traders carried
them to France and England.

Typical English chintzes of the late 18th and early 19th centuries, showing designs of English floral sprays adapted from the Indian printed calicoes.

The printed cottons caught the fancy of the English, and they tried in vain to reproduce them. They soon discovered it was simpler to send their designs to India and have them made there. In the 17th and 18th centuries rival trading companies brought in such quantities of printed cottons that both England and France decided to protect the home industry by excluding the "indiennes," as they were often called. There were several early efforts to establish cotton mills in England, but it was not until after the revocation of the Edict of Nantes, when French refugees settled in England, that there is evidence of an important print works. In the early part of the 18th century, the first large plant was set up in Manchester, and from that day to this, Manchester has remained the center of England's great cotton industry.

By the end of the 18th century, Indian patterns were out of style, and England was making designs that were distinctly adapted to cotton. The large central floral spray was, of course, derived from the original Indian pattern, but the flowers were truly English. Porcelain motifs copied from real porcelains came into vogue, and later, with the revived interest in classicism, many classical motifs were included. This was particularly true during the Adam period, when delicate classical figures and arabesques, based on Pompeian motifs, were produced in chintz and lampas to harmonize with the Wedgwood and Kauffmann productions.

The English patterns of the early 19th century (Regency period) were not so ostentatious as the French, though a definite relationship between the two is apparent. Realism in pattern design was brought to the fore, but England's chintzes and hand-blocked linens are far more outstanding than any of her woven fabrics. The Victorian period of the mid-19th century

Cotton print picturing famous Americans in allegorical scenes. Made about 1800, and probably of English origin.

produced some interesting printed fabrics, mainly of realistic flower forms. Naturalism and sentimentalism were the dominant characteristics of these designs.

Modern textiles. Many manufacturers in Europe and America continue to reproduce period textiles with both woven and printed patterns for which there is a persistent demand, but the chemical and scientific discoveries and inventions of the early years of the 20th century have been responsible for great changes and novelties in decorative textile manufacturing. The production of rayon now almost equals that of cotton; the possibilities of nylon are vast, and fiberglas and tinsel are extensively em-

Decorative sampler showing cross-stitch work on a net background.

ployed as yarns. These synthetic fibers are used alone or combined with natural fibers. The synthetics are not considered substitutes, but have many advantageous qualities of their own. Manufacturers label the ingredients of such materials, as each can make its contribution to the economy, comfort, and beauty of the home.

The standard textiles such as taffeta, satin, velvet, and brocade are often produced with rayon yarns and nylon has been used for nets and satins. It is however, in the so-called novelty weaves that the synthetic fibers have been used in the most interesting manner. In these weaves, the accent has been placed upon texture rather than pattern, perhaps due to the realization that textiles can be of interest to the touch as well as to the sight.

In the production of novelty fabrics a great number of variations and combinations of fibers, yarns, and weaves have been used. A rough surface has usually been the principal aim in weaving decorative textiles. The methods employed to produce these effects are many. Among them are those of alternating coarse and fine yarns in either the warp or weft; producing yarns by twisting coarse and fine threads or threads of different colors; using loosely spun nubbed (knotted and irregular) threads; weaving heavy ribbed or rep effects by great contrast in the size of warp and weft; and completely changing the character of parallel yarns, by introducing tinsel, fiberglas, or spun rayon. The structure of the fabrics however, remains standard plain, twill, satin, pile, and leno weaves.

Many interesting drapery and upholstery textiles are hand-woven by

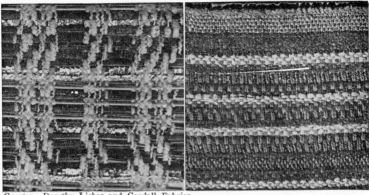

Courtesy Dorothy Liebes and Goodall Fabrics

LEFT: *Handwoven bamboo, cotton, and metal for screens and blinds.*
RIGHT: *Handwoven cotton textile.*

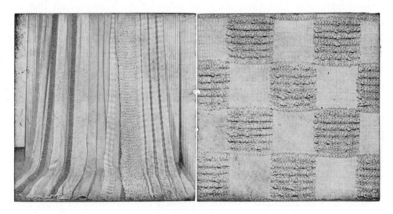

LEFT: *Machine-made and handwoven textiles in cotton, silk, and nylon.*
RIGHT: *Machine-made reproduction of handwoven textile.*

MODERN TEXTILES.

talented individual weavers. These fabrics are woven on special order and while their cost is comparatively high, they are often used in the better class of decorating work. In the weaving, both natural and synthetic yarns are used and almost any pattern can be produced. Interest has been attained by adding loose or curled fringes to the surface of the fabric in either vertical or horizontal stripes or in spotted arrangements. The field of the fabric is often sparkled by a thread of nontarnishing gold or silver tinsel. Other weavers are making beautiful hand-blocked or screen-printed fabrics in both repeat and large-panel designs; the majority of these are floral or foliage effects at large scale. Many beautiful sheer materials are woven with various fibers in irregular net and lattice effects.

It is difficult to recognize a definite trend in modern pattern design. A great variety of sources have been developed with mixed results, but on the whole textile designers have given careful study to their projects, and motifs have been delineated so that intervening spaces have been of as much interest as the motifs themselves. For all-over patterns, there has been a tendency toward the use of abstract and geometrical forms in both woven and printed interpretations. Motifs taken from nature have been both realistic and conventional. Tropical trees, plants, and flowers have been frequently used. Contemporary events, and sports and games, such as riding, yachting, bathing, tennis, card-playing, picnicking, and other activities, have been represented or symbolized. Landscapes, garden scenes, city streets, and buildings; and the automobile, airplane, and other machines have often served as pattern inspiration. Humor, sarcasm, and caricature have been drawn upon. Plaids, tweeds, basket weaves, and stripes have also had their share of popularity. There often has been a noticeable tendency to exaggerate the scale of motifs. Color schemes have been infinite in variety and color. Intense and neutralized hues, strong and mild contrasts have been used to cover every requirement. Many textiles have been fused or coated with vinyl plastic for durability and ease of cleaning. In the fused types the weave is visible. In the coated types the plastic is opaque in plain colors or embossed to imitate leather or other patterns. The latter type is very serviceable for upholstery purposes.

The Uses of Textiles

The uses of standard weaves are given below. Many of these are now woven in both natural and synthetic yarns or in a combination of the two.

Glass curtains:
 Chiffon, dotted swiss, gauze, lace, marquisette, muslin, net, pongee, poplin, scrim, voile.
Casement curtains:
 Gauze, muslin, pongee, poplin, shantung, taffeta.
Unlined draperies:
 Broché, casement cloth, celanese, cellophane fabrics, chintz, cretonne, India prints, monk's cloth, novelty fabrics, oiled silk, pongee, taffeta, terry cloth.
Lined draperies:
 Broché, chintz, cretonne, crewel embroidery, damask, faille, hand-blocked linen, India prints, lampas, moiré, novelty fabrics, sateen, satin, silk velvet, taffeta, velours, velveteen, vinyl fused fabrics.

Medium-weight upholstery coverings:

Armure, leather, brocade, brocatelle, chintz, corduroy, cretonne, crewel, embroidery, damask, lampas, moiré, novelty fabrics, sateen, satin, taffeta.

Heavy-weight upholstery coverings:

Brocatelle, crewel embroidery, damask, denim, frisé, haircloth, lampas, mohair, moiré, monk's cloth, moquette, novelty fabrics, petit-point, plush, rep, satin, tapestry, twill, velours, velvet, velveteen, vinyl coated fabrics.

When one particular fabric is entirely satisfactory in a room, being suitable in weave, pattern, and color, it is sometimes difficult to know what other fabrics to combine with it. First of all the textures must be friendly, for a rough-and-ready novelty fabric will never be at home with a delicate brocade. All the finer silks—brocades, damasks, taffetas, silk velvets—are harmonious, but a denim or a coarse rep would be a jarring note, if used with them. With the latter, cretonne or India prints or monk's cloth may be combined. With fine chintz, splendid cotton or wool damasks, lustrous sateens, and some of the finer novelty weaves are harmonious. With an expensive hand-blocked linen, brocatelle and velvet may be used. With the rough textures which are modern, the shiny surface of satin is effective as a decided contrast. In general, it is wise to combine like with like, avoiding too strong contrasts except for very modern effects.

It is also necessary to be exceedingly careful of scale, for a large and bold pattern (brocatelle, for instance) would be overwhelming in combination with one that is fine and dainty (French broché). There are some fine geometric patterns which will harmonize with spreading floral forms, and there are some small all-over designs which can be used with highly stylized forms. In general it is wise to keep the scale of all the fabrics fairly close together, and, of course, in harmony with the scale of the room.

The selection of a pattern for a room should harmonize with the use and character of the room itself, and should correspond to the character of the occupant. It is disconcerting to introduce too many different patterns in various parts of the same room, particularly if the patterns are large or very obvious. As a rule, where a patterned rug is used, it is best to employ upholstery coverings of plain materials, and vice versa. Also, a patterned wall is usually as much patterned surface as any room can stand, and calls for a restricted use of patterned materials for draperies or upholstered surfaces. Patterns in self-tones, as in damasks, may be used with other more strongly contrasting materials.

The beauty and color in a pattern are best shown by contrasting the pattern with plain surfaces. Where surfaces are plain, however, it is essential to give them interest of color or texture, or both.

The basic principles of selecting decorative textiles require a thorough understanding of the subtle balance between variety and monotony, between contrast and similarity, which must be part of the ability of the true artist.

The popularity of decorative textiles is as subject to the whims of taste and fashion as are all other objects or materials of room furnishing. Decorators cannot be concerned solely with the practicality of a material for some particular use. Style changes must be considered, and these are always reflected in the current price of the goods, which may later be found marked down.

Names and Types of Textiles

The majority of names applied to decorative textiles have become standardized, and are well understood by all manufacturers, wholesalers, decorators, and by the public in general. From time to time, however, trade names are introduced for special types or combination weaves that become popular, and these eventually become standardized themselves. Usage and the fact that sometimes they are not legally protected causes them to become common property. Many standard textiles are now composed of synthetic as well as natural fibers. The principal textile terms are given below:

~~~~~~

Glossary of Textile Terms

~~~~~~

Appliqué. A pattern that is cut out and sewed or pasted on the surface of another material.

Armure. A kind of cloth with a rep background. The raised satin pattern, which is not reversible, is made of warp threads floated over the surface. The pattern usually consists of small, isolated, conventional motifs arranged to form an all-over design. A good upholstery material.

Artificial leather. A substitute for leather which is made by coating a cotton fabric with a nitrocellulose preparation. This surface is then stamped to simulate the surface of real leather. Many varieties are made, which are generally known by trade names. Widely used, at present, for cheap grades of upholstery.

Batik. Javanese process of resist dyeing on cotton, using wax in a design, then dyeing cloth, after which wax is removed. The method is practiced by modern de-

signers on silks and rayons, and imitated in machine printing.

Block print. Fabric printed by hand, using carved wooden blocks. Can be distinguished from modern printing with metal rollers or screens by the marks of the joining of the pattern printed by different blocks. Screen printing has now been substituted almost entirely for hand blocking in the United States.

Bobbinet. See Net.

Bouclé. Plain or twill weave in wool, rayon, cotton, silk, or linen. Distinctive by its small regularly spaced loops and flat irregular surfaces produced by the use of specially twisted yarns.

Braid. A strip composed of intertwining several strands of silk, cotton, or other materials. Used as a binding or trimming.

Broadcloth. Twill, plain, or rib weave, of wool and spun rayon, and cotton and rayon or silk. The cotton or spun rayon fabric has fine crosswise ribs.

Brocade. A kind of weave; also, a finished silk cloth which, although made on a loom, resembles embroidery. The background may be of one color or may have a warp stripe, and its weave may be taffeta, twill, satin, or damask. A floral or conventional pattern in slight relief is usually multicolored and is produced by the filler thread. It is woven on a Jacquard loom, and the threads that do not appear on the surface are carried across the width of the back. The finest old handmade brocades all included threads of real gold or silver. Excellent for draperies and upholstery, particularly in period rooms.

Brocatelle. A heavy silk fabric resembling a damask, except that the pattern appears to be embossed. The pattern (usually large and definite) is a satin weave against a twill background. Made with two sets of warps and two sets of fillers, it is not reversible, as the linen backing produced by one set of filler threads shows plainly. Its uses are similar to those of brocade.

Broché (pronounced bro-shay). A silk fabric similar to brocade. The small floral designs, which are quite separate from the background pattern, are made with swivel shuttles to resemble embroidery. The filler threads not in use are carried only across the width of the small design, and not across the entire back as in brocade.

Buckram. A strong jute cloth of plain weave, finished with glue sizing. It is used as a stiffening for valances, for interlining draperies, etc.

Burlap. Plain weave of cotton, jute, or hemp. Heavy, coarse, and loosely woven, in a variety of weights, and used for sacks, the backs of floor coverings, inside upholstery, etc.

Calico. A term formerly used for a plain woven printed cotton cloth, similar to percale. Its name is taken from Calicut, India, where it was first made.

Cambric. Plain weave linen or cotton. True linen cambric is very sheer. It is named for the original fabric made in Cambrai, France. Now coarser fabrics are called cambric and used for linings, etc.

Canvas. A heavy cotton cloth in plain weave. It may be bleached or unbleached, starched, dyed, or printed. Used for awnings, couch covers, and whenever a coarse, heavy material is required.

Casement cloth. A lightweight cloth originally made of wool and silk in plain weave. Now made of cotton, linen, mohair, silk, wool, rayon, or a combination of any two. Although usually neutral in tone, this material may be had in colors and is popular for draw curtains.

Cashmere. A soft wool textile made from Indian goat hair. The same breed of goat is now grown in the United States.

Chenille. A type of woven yarn which has a pile protruding all around at right angles to the body thread. The yarn may be of silk, wool, mercerized cotton, or rayon and is used for various types of fabrics.

Chiffon. A descriptive term which is used to indicate the light weight and soft finish of a fabric, as in "chiffon velvet"; also, a sheer, gauzelike silk fabric.

China silk. Sheer plain weave fabric which is nearly transparent, and is dyed in various colors.

Chintz. A fine cotton cloth usually having a printed design. Chintz originated in India in the 17th century, and was called "chint," which means spotted. Practically all modern chintz is *calendered* or glazed, which makes it more resistant to dirt. In washing glazed chintz, the glaze is lost and cannot easily be renewed. The shiny surface and stiff texture produced by glazing also add to its charm. Chintz may be printed by blocks, copper plates, screens, or rollers, or it may be plain, in various colors. It is widely used for draperies, slipcovers, lamp shades, and upholstery.

Corduroy. A cotton or rayon cut pile fabric with ridges or cords in the pile which run lengthwise. Extensively used for upholstery, especially in modern treatments.

Crash. This is a term that includes a group of cotton, jute, and linen fabrics having coarse, uneven yarns and rough texture. Used for draperies and upholstery, and is often hand blocked or printed.

Crepe. A descriptive term applied to a large group of materials that have a crinkled or puckered surface, which may be produced by highly twisting the yarn in weaving or by a chemical process. The materials are made of cotton, wool, silk, or a combination of fibers, woven in any basic weave.

Cretonne. A heavy cotton cloth with printed pattern similar to chintz, though the designs are usually larger and less detailed. The background may be plain, or a rep weave. The name comes from the

Normandy village of Creton, where it was first produced. It is usually unglazed. Useful for draperies and upholstery.

Crewel embroidery. A kind of embroidery with a pattern of varicolored wools worked on unbleached cotton or linen. The spreading design covers only a part of the background, and usually includes a winding stem with various floral forms. It was used extensively during the English Jacobean period for upholstery as well as for draperies. The designs were often inspired by the East Indian "tree-of-life" motif.

Damask. A kind of Jacquard weave; also a fabric with a woven pattern similar to brocade, but flatter. In damask any combination of two of the three basic weaves may be used for the pattern and the background, provided that the weave of the pattern differs from that of the background. The pattern is made visible by the effect of light striking the portions of the fabric in the different weaves. Usually both warp and filler are of the same weight, quality, and color, though it may be woven in two colors. The pattern effect is usually reversible. Originally made of all silk, damasks are now made of linen, cotton, wool, and any of the synthetic fibers, or of combinations of any two. The name originated with the beautifully patterned silks woven in Damascus during the 12th century and brought to Europe by Marco Polo. Damask is widely used for draperies and upholstery.

Denim. A kind of heavy cotton cloth, of a twill weave. Usually a small woven pattern is introduced or warp and filler may be in contrasting colored threads. Originally called toile-de-Nimes. Used for upholstery and draperies.

Dotted Swiss. See Swiss.

Duck. A closely woven cotton fabric, sometimes called awning stripe or awning duck, of plain or ribbed weave. The stripe may be woven in, or painted or printed on one side only. Often given protective finishes against fire, water, and mildew. Similar to canvas.

Embroidery. The art of decorating a fabric with thread and needle. Its origin is a source of conjecture, but the form known today was developed in Italy during the 16th century. Handwork embroidery is little done today, and consequently most embroideries used in interior decoration antedate machine production.

Faille. A kind of fabric with a slightly heavier weft than warp, producing a flat-ribbed effect. It is often all silk and lusterless. Used for trimmings and draperies.

Felt. A material that is made by matting together and interlocking, under heat and pressure, woolen fibers, mohair, cowhair, or mixed fibers.

Fiberglas. Trade name for fabric or fine filaments of glass woven as a textile fiber. It has great strength, yet is soft and pliable, resists heat, chemicals, and soil. It is used for curtains.

Filler. Threads which run crosswise of fabric from selvage to selvage. Same as weft.

Flannel. Wool or cotton twilled fabric of coarse soft yarns, napped. The ends of the fibers are loosened by revolving cylinders covered with bristles. It is not a pile fabric. Used for interlinings.

Fringe. Trimming for draperies and upholstery. Threads on cords are grouped together in various ways, and left loose at one end.

Frisé. (pronounced free-zay). Also written *frieze*. A pile fabric with uncut loops. The better quality is made with two sets of fillers to provide greater durability. Patterns are produced by cutting some of the loops, by using yarns of different colors, or by printing the surface. As it is used chiefly for upholstery, it is made of wool, mohair, or heavy cotton. The name comes from the French *frisé*, meaning "curled."

Gabardine. Hard-finished twill fabric, with a steep diagonal effect to the twill, which is firm and durable.

Gauze. Thin, transparent fabrics made of leno or plain weave or a combination of the two. Formerly made of all silk, it is now made of cotton, linen, wool, mohair, synthetic fibers, or combinations. Especially useful for glass curtains.

Gingham. A lightweight, yarn-dyed cotton material, usually woven in checks or stripes. Useful for trimmings, draperies, and bedspreads.

Grenadine. Leno weave fabric like marquisette, but finer. Plain or with woven dots or figures.

Grosgrain. Ribbed or rep silk produced by weaving heavier filler threads so that they are covered with close, fine warps. Used for ribbons and draperies.

Gros-point. See Needlepoint.

Guimpe. Narrow fabric, with heavy cord running through it, used for trimming furniture, draperies, etc., as an edging.

Hair cloth. A kind of cloth with cotton, worsted, or linen warp and horsehair filler. It is woven plain, striped, or with small patterns and is manufactured in narrow widths. As it is very durable, it is used for upholstery. It was popular during the mid-19th century in England and America.

Homespun. A term applied generally to hand-loomed, woolen textiles. It is also a trade name given to imitations made on power looms. Useful for curtains and upholstery in informal types of decoration.

India print. A printed cotton cloth made in India or Persia, with clear colors, and designs characteristic of each country. The many colors are printed on a white or natural ground. Useful for draperies, bedspreads, wall hangings, etc.

Indian Head. "Permanent" finish cotton, smooth and lightweight. Colors are vatdyed and guaranteed fast. Shrinkage is reduced to a minimum. The trade name is so familiar that it is becoming known as a special fabric.

Indienne. French interpretation of the Indian printed cottons which were being imported into France in the late 17th century and during the 18th century. French designers produced them to supply the demand for this type of fabric at a lower cost than that of the imported originals.

Jardinière velvet (pronounced zhar-deen-yare). A handsome silk velvet with a multicolored pattern resembling a flower grouping set against a light background. The weaving is most intricate, as there may be several heights of velvet and uncut loops set against a damask or satin background.

Jaspé (pronounced zhas-pay). A streaked or mottled effect in a fabric, produced by uneven dyeing of the warp threads. The name is derived from its resemblance to jasper.

Khaki. A heavy cotton twill fabric of an earthy color.

Lace. An openwork textile produced by needle, pin, or bobbin by the process of sewing, knitting, knotting (tatting), or crocheting. Real lace is a handmade product, but in the late 18th century, machines were invented to imitate the hand productions. Probably first made in Greece,

lace manufacturing received a great impetus in Renaissance Italy, and particularly in Venice. Among the principal types are *filet,* embroidered on a net; *reticella,* a combination of drawn and cut work; Valenciennes, Cluny, Duchesse, and Chantilly—elaborate bobbin-made patterns in which the ornament and fabric are identical; Irish, principally of the crocheted variety, although Limerick is made on a net and Carrickmacross is cut work, Brussels lace is of several varieties. Nottingham lace is a general term used for machine-made productions, particularly inexpensive lace curtains made in one piece.

Lampas. A patterned textile with a compound weave having two warps and two or more fillers. The distinguishing feature is that the pattern is always a twill cr plain weave, the background in satin or plain weave, or both, and may be in two or more colors. Philippe de la Salle made it famous and it was much woven in the 18th and 19th century, so that the pattern is usually classical in inspiration. It is similar to a two-colored damask.

Leno. Type of weave in which pairs of warp yarns are wound around each other between picks of filler yarns, resulting in a net effect. Various versions of this weave are used for glass curtain fabrics, etc.

Marquisette. A sheer cloth having the appearance of gauze and woven in a leno weave. The cotton, silk, rayon, nylon, glass, or wool thread is usually hard-twisted to give it greater serviceability. An excellent glass curtain material.

Matelassé. Fabric with two sets of warps and wefts. Its embossed pattern gives the effect of quilting. Imitations are stitched or embossed.

Mercerized materials. Materials that have a lustrous surface produced by subjecting the material to a chemical process. The cloth is treated in a cold caustic alkali bath while held in a state of tension. By this treatment the yarn is changed from a flat ribbon-like shape to a rounded form, making the cloth more lustrous, more durable, and more susceptible to dye. Mercerized cotton has a silky appearance. The process is called after its originator, John Mercer, an English calico printer.

Metal cloth. A fabric the surface of which has a metallic appearance. It is made by weaving cotton warp threads with tinsel filling yarns. The latter are made by winding strips of metallic substance around a cotton yarn. Creases cannot be removed from this material. Useful for trimmings.

Mohair. A yarn and cloth made from the fleece of the Angora goat. The fiber is wiry and strong, making the most durable of all textiles. It is now woven in combination with cotton and linen into many types of plain, twill, and pile fabrics. Widely used for upholstery.

Moiré (pronounced mwa-ray). A finish on silk or cotton cloth which gives a watermarked appearance. Woven as a rep, the marks are produced by engraved rollers, heat, and pressure applied to the cloth after it has been folded between selvages. The crushing of the ribs produces a symmetrical pattern along the fold. The pattern is not permanent, as cleaning and pressing tend to remove it. When made of synthetic fibers moiré holds the marks better than when made of all silk.

Monk's or friar's cloth. A heavy cotton fabric of coarse weave. Groups of warp and weft threads are interlaced in a plain or basket weave. Used for hangings and upholstery in informal rooms.

Moquette. An uncut pile fabric similar to frisé. It is woven on a Jacquard loom and has small, set patterns of different colors. When used for upholstery, it is made of mohair, wool, or heavy cotton. A coarse type is used for floor coverings.

Muslin. A plain-woven, white cotton fabric, bleached or unbleached. Used for sheeting and other household purposes. Originally woven in the city of Mosul.

Needlepoint. An old-fashioned cross-stitch done on net, heavy canvas, or coarse linen. The threads are wool. The effect achieved is that of a coarse tapestry. *Petit-point* and *gros-point* are two variations of this embroidery. Petit-point is very fine, made on a single net, and has about 20 stitches to a lineal inch. Gros-point is coarse, made on a double net, and has about 12 stitches to the lineal inch.

Net. Open weave fabric. There are various types, as follows:
Bobbinet. Machine-made net with hexagonal meshes.
Cable net. Coarse mesh.
Dotted Swiss. A net with small dots.
Filet net. Square mesh, used as base for embroidery. Handmade variety has knots at corners of meshes, machine-made net has no knots.
Maline. Has a diamond mesh.
Mosquito net. Coarser than others, of cotton.
Novelty net. Made in a variety of effects.
Point d'Esprit. Cotton net with small dots over its surface in a snowflake effect.

Ninon. Often called triple voile. Sheer rayon used for glass curtains, made in various weaves.

Nottingham. A machine-made lace curtain material. First made in Nottingham, England.

Novelty weave. General name for a variety of modern fabrics, having unusual textural effects produced by using warp and filler of different size, color, or fibers, nubby yarns, or the introduction of tinsel, metallic threads, or even cellophane. Rayon and cotton are especially adaptable.

Nylon. Generic term for a protein-like chemical which may be formed into bristles, fibers, sheets, etc. Has extreme toughness, elasticity, and strength. Its fibers are used in almost all types of textiles where silk and rayon have been used in the past.

Oilcloth. A fabric having a cotton base that has been coated with a preparation of linseed oil and pigments. Its finish may be smooth, shiny, dull, or pebbled. Used for table and shelf coverings and other household purposes.

Oiled silk. A thin silk that is waterproofed by a process of soaking the silk in boiled linseed oil and drying it. It was formerly used only for surgical purposes, but is now used as a drapery fabric, particularly for kitchen and bathroom curtains.

Organdy. A lightweight, crisp fabric of muslin construction woven of very fine cotton threads. It may be white, piece-dyed, or printed, and is used for trimmings and glass curtains.

Paisley. Printed or woven design in imitation of the original Scotch shawl patterns made in the town of Paisley.

Palampore. Hand-painted or resist-dyed cotton, chintz, and calico, made before the invention of block-printing for fabrics. Original tree-of-life prints were so made in India.

Panné. A term applied to pile fabrics having a shiny or lustrous surface. This appearance is produced by having the pile pressed back.

Percale. Plain closely woven fabric of muslin in dull finish, which may be bleached, dyed, or printed. Similar to chintz.

Persane. Term used to describe the French 18th century printed cottons that had designs inspired by Persian originals.

Petit-point. See Needlepoint.

Picoté. A type of pattern design consisting of small floral or other motifs surrounded by numerous minute dots to soften their silhouette.

Pile fabrics. See Velvet, Velours, Frisé, Moquette, Plush, Terry cloth.

Piqué. A heavy cotton fabric with raised cords running lengthwise. Used for trimmings, bedspreads, and curtains.

Plain weave. A basic weave in which warp and weft are of the same size, and alternate over and under each other.

Plissé. Name refers to a method of printing on plain weave rayon or cotton which produces a permanent crinkled surface in stripes or patterns.

Plush. A fabric with a long pile. Made like velvet, the nap is sometimes pressed down to form a surface resembling fur. It may be made of silk, wool, cotton, or any synthetic fiber. Extensively used for upholstery.

Point d'Hongrie. Needlepoint having a design vaguely resembling an irregular series of chevron forms or V shapes usually made with silk and used for chair upholstery.

Pongee. A fabric of plain weave made from wild silk in the natural tan color. It is very durable and has an interesting texture. Used for draw curtains. The name is derived from a corruption of two Chinese words which signify "natural color."

Poplin. A fabric similar to a lightweight rep. It is made with a heavy filler, producing a light corded effect across the material. Cotton, silk, wool, synthetic, or combination fibers may be used in its weaving. A trimming and drapery fabric.

Quilted fabric. A double fabric with padding between the layers, held in place by stitches that usually follow a definite pattern.

Ratiné. Name of yarn, and of fabric, in plain or twill weave. Owes its coarse, spongy, nubby texture to the knotlike irregularities of the yarn used in the warp.

Rayon. A trade name for a synthetic fiber having a cellulose base. Originally highly lustrous, it can now be handled as a lusterless thread. It is more lustrous, stiffer, and less expensive than silk. In combination with silk, wool, or cotton its possibilities are limitless. Textiles manufactured of rayon are known by various trade names.

Rep. A plain-weave fabric made with a heavy filler thread giving a corded effect. A warp rep is made with heavy filler threads, producing a ribbing across the material. A filler rep uses coarse warps and the ribbed effect is vertical. Rep is unpatterned and reversible, and may be made of cotton, wool, silk, or synthetic fibers. Used for drapery and upholstery purposes.

Sailcloth. Very heavy and durable fabric, similar to canvas. Lightweight sailcloth is often used for couch covers, summer furniture, etc.

Sateen or satine. A fabric, imitative of satin, with a lustrous surface and dull back. It is made with floating weft threads and is, therefore, smooth from side to side. It is usually made of cotton, the better quality being mercerized.

Satin. A basic weave; also, a fabric having a glossy surface and dull back. The whole face of the fabric seems to be made of warp threads, appearing smooth and glossy. No two adjacent warp threads are crossed by the same weft thread, and the skip may vary from 8 to 12 fillers. Because of the length of the warp floats, it is not an extremely durable material for heavy usage. It may be made of all silk, but is stronger when linen or cotton wefts are used. Used extensively for upholstery and draperies. There are several different types as follows:

Antique satin. Dull, uneven texture, heavy, and rich looking.

Charmeuse. Organzine warp and spun silk weft.

Hammered satin. Treated to give the effect of hammered metal.

Ribbed satin. Bengaline and faille woven with satin face ribs, giving a lustrous, broken surface. May have a moiré finish.

Scrim. A sheer fabric made like a marquisette, but with coarser cotton, wet-twisted thread. Sometimes a cheaper variety is not wet-twisted, which causes it to thicken when laundered. Used for curtains and needlework.

Serge. Silk, wool, cotton, or rayon in twill weave, with a clear and hard finish.

Shadow prints. Also called warp prints. Fabrics with a pattern printed on the warp only; the filler is a plain thread. When woven, the design is blurred and indistinct.

Shantung. A heavy grade of pongee. It is usually made of wild silk, cotton, or a combination of both.

Sheer. General name for diaphanous fabrics.

Shiki. A heavy silk or rayon rep made with irregular sized filling threads.

Spun silk. Silk yarn made from waste fibers from damaged or pierced cocoons and weaving mill waste. Heavier and less lustrous than reeled silk.

Strié (pronounced stree-ay). A fabric with an uneven color, streaked effect produced by using warp threads of varying tones. A two-toned effect may be given to taffeta, satin, or corded upholstery materials by this process, same as Jaspé.

Swiss. A very fine, sheer cotton fabric which was first made in Switzerland. It may be plain, embroidered, or patterned in dots or figures which are chemically applied. It launders well, but has a tendency to shrink. Often used for glass curtains.

Synthetic fibers. These are made from various chemical compounds and are used as yarns in modern textile weaving. They are known by trade names given to them by individual manufacturers. Combinations of natural and synthetic yarns are often used. Among the leading types are those known as rayon, bemberg, celanese, dacron, fortisan, lurex, nylon, and orlon.

Taffeta. The basic plain weave. Also, a fabric woven in that manner. The fabric is usually made of a silk fiber with warp and weft thread of equal size. It is often weighted with metallic salts. Useful for trimmings and draperies.

Tapestry. Originally a hand-woven fabric with a ribbed surface like rep. The design is woven during manufacture, making an essential part of the fabric structure. Machine-made tapestry is produced by several sets of warp and filling yarns woven with the Jacquard attachment which brings the warp threads of the pattern to the surface. Machine-made tapestry can be distinguished from hand-woven by its

smooth back and the limited numbers of colors used in the pattern.

Tarlatan. A thin, open cotton fabric of plain weave which is almost as coarse as a fine cheesecloth. It is sized, wiry, and transparent, and made in white and colors. It cannot be laundered.

Terry cloth. Heavy loosely woven uncut pile fabric, as used in bath towels.

Theatrical gauze. A loosely woven, open cotton, or linen fabric. Because of its transparency and shimmering texture, it is used for window draperies.

Ticking. Closely woven cotton in twill or satin weave. It usually has woven stripes, but they may be printed. Damask ticking is also made in mixed fibers used for mattress covers, pillows, and upholstery.

Toiles-de-Jouy. Famous printed fabrics produced at Jouy, near Paris, by Philippe Oberkampf, from 1760 to 1815. Modern reproductions continue the typical design of landscapes and figure groups in monotone of brick red, blue, or other colors on a white or cream-colored background. Effectively used for draperies, bedspreads, and wall hangings.

Toiles d'Indy. Printed cotton and linen of floral or pictorial design, which began to be imported into France during the latter years of the 17th century from India and Persia.

Tussah silk. Wild silk, from cocoons of worms which have fed on oak or other leaves. Light brown in color. Used for pongee, shantung, shiki.

Tweed. Originally a woolen homespun material made in Scotland. Now the term is applied to a large group of woolen goods made from worsted yarns; they may be woven in plain, twill, or herringbone twill weaves.

Twill. A basic weave; also, the fabric woven in that manner. The weft thread is carried over one warp and under two. Sliding along one to the left on each row, still going over one and under two warp threads, a diagonal ribbed effect is achieved. A herringbone pattern is a variation of this weave, with which squares and zigzags can also be made.

Velours. A general term for any fabric resembling velvet. It is the French word for velvet, but has been so misused that it no longer has a definite meaning.

Velvet. A fabric having a thick, short pile on the surface and a plain back. A true velvet is woven with two sets of warps, one for the back, and one for the pile which is made by looping the warp thread over a wire which later cuts the loops. Cheaper velvets and some chiffon velvets are woven face to face and have two backs using two warps and two fillers. The pile is made by slicing apart the two pieces of fabric. Velvet may be plain, striped, or patterned. It may be made of all cotton, linen, mohair, synthetic fibers, or silk, though it is seldom woven with all silk threads. The finer quality may be used for draperies, and the heavier for upholstery. There are several variations as follows:

Brocaded. Pattern made by removing part of the pile by heat and chemicals.
Embossed. Pattern imprinted by rollers.
Façonné. Same as brocaded velvet.
Moquette. Uncut velvet with large Jacquard pattern.

Panné. Pile pressed down in one direction by rollers under steam pressure.
Plush. Velvet with deep and thinly woven pile, often with crushed effect.
Upholstery velvet. Heaviest type, with a stiff back and very thick pile.
Velveteen. A fabric which is sometimes called cotton velvet. It is not woven with a pile, but like a heavy sateen, with the weft threads floated loosely over the warp. It must then be sheared to produce a fine close pile. It is ordinarily made of cotton, and is suitable for upholstery.
Vinyl Fabrics. Textiles fused or coated with vinyl plastic. In the coated types the vinyl is opaque and the surface is printed or embossed.
Voile. A light, transparent fabric of plain weave used for glass curtains. Hard-twisted thread is used to make it durable. It is usually piece-dyed, striped, or figured, and can be made of cotton, wool, silk, or any synthetic fiber.

Handmade Tapestries

The word "tapestry" is very loosely used in the decorating trade, but as correctly used it refers only to a hand-woven fabric. The term "real tapestry" is now expressly reserved to designate hand weaving.

Tapestries are made both in all-over patterns and in pictorial subjects. Pictorial tapestries are of prime importance as wall hangings, but are sometimes cut into smaller pieces for upholstery coverings or for small panels. The design is the essential element of esthetic value in a tapestry; materials and workmanship, while important, are secondary to the design. The chief material used in tapestries is wool, though most modern tapestries have cotton warp threads. In antique tapestries silk was sometimes used in parts, and gold and silver threads were occasionally added to give greater brilliancy.

Tapestry is distinctly a rep weave, and the warp threads of the fabric are strongly accented, a feature that distinguishes it from cross-stitch needlework. In a very fine tapestry, the warp threads are spaced about 24 to the inch, while in the coarser grades there may be as few as 8. The weft threads are woven between and around the warp threads, and are pushed together with a comb, so that the warp is completely hidden; they do not run across the fabric, but are used only so long as their particular color is needed in the pattern; they are then tied in a knot and their ends hang loosely at the rear. The tapestry is reversible if the loose ends are cut off.

The art of tapestry weaving in Europe was encouraged and developed

Courtesy Metropolitan Museum of Art

ABOVE: *Fragment of a late 13th century French crucifixion tapestry, showing the earliest type of European tapestry design. Ten colors are used with very simple gradations, and an extraordinary effect is attained by flat tones.* BELOW: *Very large hunting tapestry made about 1500. There is no perspective foreshortening, and the horizon line is near the top of the pattern.*

by the return of the Crusaders, who had learned much concerning it in Constantinople and the Orient. There were many similarities between early medieval European tapestries and Near Eastern art forms, notably the similarity of their pictorial compositions to Persian miniatures. It was natural that tapestries should become a popular form of wall decoration in northern countries. Fresco work, so prevalent in Italy and other warm climates, could not be practiced in western Europe, because freezing temperatures tended to crack the plaster. Tapestries not only added color and pattern to an interior, but the heavy wool from which they were made helped to retain heat in the rooms of the medieval castles.

The earliest efforts at weaving these textiles were made in Paris, during the 14th century. Of the tapestries woven at this time, very few still remain.* The city of Arras in French Flanders soon took the lead, under the patronage of the dukes of Burgundy, and held it during the whole of the 14th century, and until Louis XI pillaged the town in 1477. The center of tapestry weaving then moved to Tournai, Belgium, which had become increasingly important in this field. It is extremely difficult, however, to assign the source of many 15th century tapestries definitely to either Arras or Tournai. Decisions are mainly based on pattern and style. Tapestries were undoubtedly woven throughout this period in other small towns and it is also highly probable that travelling weavers stopped to work wherever a commission was offered, making almost impossible any positive identification as to source of manufacture of many early tapestries. By the end of the 15th century and during the 16th century, Brussels held a leading position in the field. While French artists carried on the medieval tradition of excellence of design and workmanship until well into the 16th century, they eventually fell under the influence of the Renaissance painters. Technically, the quality of French work was maintained at a high level of excellence, but the competition of the Brussels weavers, who were being increasingly patronized, caused a decline in French tapestry production during the latter half of the 16th century. Looms were also established in Bruges, Enghien, Lille, Fontainebleau, the Loire valley, Antwerp, and Delft. The art was given renewed encouragement in France by Henry IV, in the early 17th century, by the importation of Flemish weavers to work both in Paris and in the provinces. The Gobelins looms in Paris, which had been established about 1446 by two brothers of that name, were consolidated with several other small private looms in the same neighborhood and became a huge state institution and Royal Manufactory under the patronage of Louis XIV in 1662. In the early years of its existence, furniture and other objects connected with the decorative arts were made as well as tapestries. Louis appointed his Minister of Fine Arts, Charles Le Brun, as Director and chief designer. These looms were manned by both French and Flemish weavers, and, with their enormous output, during most of the 17th century they shared the honors with the looms at Brussels. Later Beauvais and Aubusson came under royal support, and with the aid of the finest artists that France could produce, tapestries of wondrous beauty and weave were made to furnish the homes of the nobility and to enrich the walls of the churches and public buildings. When Louis XIV was forced to close temporarily the Gobelins works in 1690, due to financial difficulties, the production of the Beauvais factory, still under royal patronage, took a definite upward trend. Upon the reopening of the

---

* These include the tapestries of the Nine Worthies, made in Paris, now in the possession of the Metropolitan Museum in New York, and the series of the Apocalypse, from Angers. With the exception of some fragmentary German pieces from the 12th to 14th centuries, and a few other French examples, these are the oldest European tapestries known.

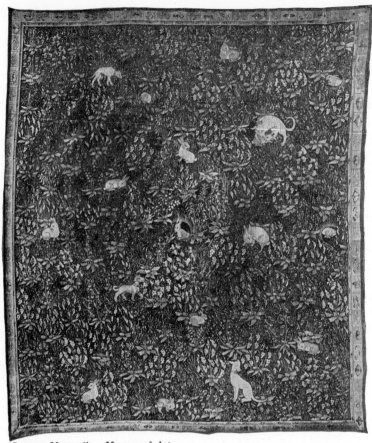

Gothic millefleurs garden tapestry with a very simple border. The various domestic animals are used as a note of surprise in the pattern.

Gobelins between 1694 and 1699, the Renaissance fashion of Beauvais was well established, and the Gobelins weavers were forced to follow a style very different from that of their earlier work. In the 18th century, Beauvais, Gobelins, and Aubusson were all great centers of the art, which, from the design standpoint, had lost a considerable amount of its earlier dignity and grandeur as the tendency developed to reproduce oil paintings rather than to accentuate in the pattern the substance of the textile medium.

Looms were soon started in the other countries of Europe. Particularly noted were those of Mortlake, Merton, Barchester, and Windsor in England. Germany, Spain, and Italy also were centers of production.

The use of the term *arras* as synonymous with tapestry in England * is

* See *Hamlet,* Act III, Scenes 3 and 4.

significant of the importance of the town of that name in connection with the art. *Arrazzo* in Italian is also used as a synonym. In the United States the term "arras" is used as a designation of a tapestry of the Gothic period.

Gothic tapestries. As a rule, Gothic tapestries are of the *millefleurs* variety. The translation of the French word is "thousand flowers," and refers to the fact that the background or other portions of the picture are covered with numerous small bushes, plants, flowers, and leaves. Many of these bushes have small animals of various types crouching upon or under them. It is a general conception that most millefleurs tapestries were woven in the region of the Loire about 1500. Evidence suggests, however, that many of them were woven by itinerant workers.

Though Gothic tapestries cover a wide range of subject matter, they are distinct and easily recognizable because of special characteristics in their design. The laws of perspective were considered unadaptable, and pictorial depth, distance, and atmosphere were not rendered. Consequently, in Gothic tapestries objects behind other objects do not appear reduced in size, nor do they become fainter in tonal value; shadows are absent or are only vaguely suggested; the ground often appears to fold up toward the observer; horizon lines are close to the top of the composition; and the design as a whole resembles a flat-colored line drawing, with little or no gradations in the coloring or rounding of forms. The general effect is stiff and conventional, though beautiful and dignified. The range of colors is very limited, there being sometimes as few as 20 different dyes used, whereas the Gobelins factory at the present time uses thousands of different colors. Machine-made tapestries are usually limited to a maximum of 28 different colored threads although very few have this number.

The subject matter of the pictorial tapestries of the 15th and early 16th centuries invariably tells a story rather than creates a picture with an important central figure or dominating motif. Distortion of figures and objects and other artistic license are often resorted to, with a resultant lack of relationship in the scale of both objects and persons in the same plane.

The subject matter of the Gothic work also simplifies its identification. Religious subjects were paramount. Biblical, allegorical, and ecclesiastical personages were often pictured in a setting of Gothic architectural forms. Scenes of pastoral, agricultural, and courtly life were often represented. Many Gothic tapestries were made showing the unicorn and other animals chased by hounds and hunters. These are known as "hunting tapestries." In the series known as "The Lady With the Unicorn," from the Cluny Museum in Paris, the subject matter is allegorical. The lady is flanked on one side by a lion, symbol of bravery, and on the other by the unicorn, symbol of purity. She stands on an island of deep blue on a rose ground, both of which are covered with flowers and animals.

Costumes often facilitate the dating of a tapestry, and a careful study

French Gothic tapestry of the last quarter of the 14th century, probably from the workshop of Nicolas Bataille.

One of a set of the most famous tapestries in the world, the "Lady with the Unicorn" series. It was woven during the end of the 15th century.

of this feature is well worth while. Men of the 15th century had short hair and wore long pointed shoes. Their vests were usually of a different material from their sleeves, or else they wore plaited jackets with full sleeves. Their legs were covered with close-fitting tights. The women wore high, pointed headdresses known as *hennins,* and their full skirts hung in stiff folds. In the 16th century, the men wore their hair "bobbed," and eventually grew beards. Their legs were covered with short, full trousers which were slashed.

The majority of Gothic tapestries did not have frames; although some were enclosed with a narrow border carrying out the millefleur idea.

The great beauty of Gothic tapestries lies in the qualities in which they are unlike paintings, and not in the qualities in which they resemble them. They are distinctly textile patterns, and never attempt to compete with a painted decoration. In other words, it is the design interest, not the pictorial interest, which makes them superior to later weaves that followed more closely the modelling and detail of the painted *cartoon.* They are the most valuable tapestries on the market today, partially because of their rarity and partially because they are considered the finest examples of the art of tapestry weaving.

Renaissance tapestries. The transitional period between the Gothic and the Renaissance showed tapestry patterns in which details of the two periods were mixed. Often Gothic architectural forms were combined with human figures dressed in Renaissance and classic costumes. The perspective of the pictures improved. The horizon line was lowered below the middle of the picture, and distance and atmospheric effects were introduced. Shadows and highlights were shown in greater contrasts and borders became much more important than in the Gothic period. More detailed modelling and rounding of draperies and clothing was attempted, and both Roman and Gothic letters were used.

The tapestry weaving of the Renaissance assumed its definite character when Raphael made for Pope Leo X a series of cartoons illustrating the Acts of the Apostles. Raphael was not a weaver, and knew little of the art of weaving or of tapestry texture. The greatness of the artist as a painter misled the world, and caused the critics of his day to admire the work that was executed from these cartoons. As a result, the Acts of the Apostles tapestries are more valuable as pictures than as masterpieces of tapestry weaving. Though Raphael and his patrons were Italians, this set was actually woven in Brussels; the originals are now in the Vatican, after having been stolen and subjected to other vicissitudes. They are perhaps the most famous tapestries in the world, and have been copied many times, the copies being owned by most of the chief museums of Europe.

Tapestry weaving was introduced into England under James I. The Mortlake works were the earliest, and employed Flemish workmen, who produced much excellent work, though their designs were copied from

Magnificent example of a 17th century Brussels tapestry with a pictorial composition enclosed by a heavy frame. The pattern shows a strong relief with vivid color-value contrasts. The subject shows Antony viewing Cleopatra on her barge.

foreign sources, including the Raphael cartoons. The looms at Merton and Windsor are more recent, most of their work having been produced during the 19th century.

The Flemish looms were the most important during the early Renaissance. They produced a great quantity of work, particularly during the 17th century under the leadership of Rubens and Teniers. The former produced designs of great vigor, showing high relief effects of warlike subjects or tempestuous scenes. Wide borders of foliage and architectural motifs usually surround the central composition Although of immense decorative value, the tapestries were merely woven paintings and helped to crush the art of tapestry weaving. Teniers' subjects were nearly all pastoral or village scenes and may be easily recognized. In addition to Rubens and Teniers, countless individual weavers sprang up in all parts of Flanders, who, although gifted with expert technical knowledge and craftsmanship, were utterly lacking in artistry of design. These weavers produced the thousands of tapestries of varying merit which are often sold in the auction market as "Flemish Verdures" or *Verdure tapestries,* which sometimes show human beings and animals of extraordinary shapes.

Courtesy Parke-Bernet Galleries, Inc.

Courtesy Metropolitan Museum of Art

TOP: *Brussels Teniers tapestry, "Dancing Harvesters," woven about 1720.* BOT-
TOM: *Brussels verdure tapestry, showing Renaissance characteristics.*

A magnificent 17th century Gobelins tapestry showing Diana bathing, woven in wool and metal threads and having all the characteristics of Renaissance design.

Flemish workers were imported into other countries, including Spain, Germany, and Italy, though the industry in these countries never assumed very great importance. Italian tapestries of the earlier periods are scarcely distinguishable from the Flemish. Later they assumed a character of their own, and in the Baroque period, they took on the same characteristics as other contemporary arts.

Under Louis XIV and his successors, French tapestry weaving finally became even more important than the Flemish. This largely resulted from the royal support given to the Gobelins works on the banks of the Bièvre River near Paris. The water of this river was, and still is, said to have exceptional qualities for dyeing, although modern chemists have denied this claim. The Gobelins factory developed into one of the greatest producers of this class of work. It was taken over by the French Crown in 1662, and is still owned by the French government, for which it works exclusively. The output of the Gobelins works during the period of Louis XIV, in contrast to Gothic work, showed pattern full of relief, with elaborate naturalistic shadows, fine gradations of color, strong color contrasts, atmospheric effects, low horizon lines, and a definite composition of subject matter, always with a central or important point of interest, instead of a loose distribution of decorative motifs or figures placed over the whole surface of the textile. The tapestries, in imitating paintings very faithfully, lost greatly in textile character and texture quality, though they were still rich and decorative. Borders were often imitations of wide gilt carved picture frames, and subjects were usually mythological or historical, replacing the religious subjects of earlier times. The Gobelins tapestries were made on both the high-warp and low-warp loom. In the former the weft threads were vertical to the pattern and the outline of the design was drawn on the warp threads. In the low-warp loom, the warp threads are horizontal to the pattern and the weaver follows a cartoon that is placed behind the weft threads. In both cases the tapestry is woven from the rear side.

Under Louis XV, pastoral, amorous, and garden scenes, executed from the paintings and designs of Watteau, Boucher, Fragonard, and other popular court painters, were much in demand. Many tapestries were woven in small panels for use as chair- and sofa-back upholstery coverings. *Vignette* patterns, in which a small scene or portrait was surrounded with a large patterned frame, were also introduced at this time. The frame became more important than the picture that it enclosed. Ornamental patterns of this, and the subsequent, period followed the general character of painted and carved motifs.

The Beauvais tapestry works were at first a private enterprise, but were later taken over by Louis XIV, and are still a French government factory. The early work was mainly of the verdure type, though, later, various subjects were produced. For a time rugs, too, were manufactured, but this was discontinued during the French Revolution. The looms of Aubusson, in central France, are said to be of very ancient origin. They manufacture rugs, and tapestries for furniture up-

Eighteenth century French tapestry showing the typical use of garlands of naturalistic flowers and the vignette framing a pastoral scene.

Eighteenth century French tapestry showing the use of the arabesque fancifully combined with naturalistic flowers.

An Aubusson tapestry designed by Jean Lurçat in 1938, showing the revival of tapestry weaving as an independent art. The subject is "Harvest Time."

holstery and wall hangings. Their work is produced commercially for the general market.

Modern tapestries. Until recent years tapestry weaving has been largely confined to reproducing antique patterns, which, because they have been uninspired imitations, have lacked the spirit of original creative work. While skillful in technique, they have often been poorly designed. A few attempts have been made to weave modern patterns, but the cost of producing a handmade tapestry is so high and the demand has been so small that tapestries of this type have not yet been made in any considerable quantity. There has been, however, an effort to revive tapestry weaving as an art in France, and a return to the creative spirit of the Gothic period, with Aubusson and Gobelins looms in the vanguard. Such artists as Gromaire, Lurçat, Dufy, and Matisse have endeavored to rejuvenate one of France's oldest industries. Technicians in other fields have given of their knowledge and experience, and have approached the problem in a new light, not merely copying old patterns, but applying the earlier sense of fantasy and poetic feeling to contemporary designs, with results that attempt to equal the Gothic productions in freshness, vigor, and sincerity of artistic effort. They are designed on the hypothesis that tapestries should afford modern man a glimpse of unreality and a means of escape from the pressures of the machine era. Since modern rooms frequently possess large areas of unrelieved wall space, these disciples of the use of modern tapestry urge its restoration to a prominent place in the decorative plan, as a source of texture, color, and pattern interest. Such usage would be comparable to that of the Gothic period, in which the hangings brightened the severity of stone walls. The weavers have adhered to the truest traditions of textile weaving, and one realizes that these productions are woven designs, not paintings. The stereotyped efforts of the 19th century seem dwarfed by these new productions, whose vitality and integrity offer a promising future to an ancient art.

The use of tapestries. It has often been said that a room in which a tapestry hangs is already furnished. It is indeed true that such a room needs little else from a decorative point of view, so rich is the effect. A large tapestry is such an important object in any room that it should always have the place of honor and should be so hung that it is not only properly lighted both in natural and artificial light, but that it may be seen at a distance, also, to obtain fully its best effect. Needless to say, its full beauty is only brought out by contrasting it with plain surfaces, whether these be wall treatments, upholstery materials, or floor coverings. The use of tapestries as decorative features in contemporary rooms has reached a low ebb, but this fact in no way denies the fact that the art of weaving reached its apex in this medium.

Tapestries should be arranged to hang freely, the effect of the textures gaining greatly from the irregular folds into which they naturally fall. This method also allows them to be dusted and cleaned with facility or to be removed quickly in case of fire. If tapestry is tightly stretched on a frame, it loses much of its character; and to cover it with glass is to destroy its effect almost completely, as well as to furnish a breeding place for moths, which are its greatest menace.

Bibliography

BENDURE, Z., AND PFEIFFER, G., *American Fabrics.* The Macmillan Co., New York, 1947. Their origin and history, manufacture, characteristics, and uses. Well illustrated.

CANDEE, H. C., *Weaves and Draperies, Classic and Modern.* Frederick A. Stokes Co., New York, 1930. A complete illustrated history on this subject.

CLOUZOT, H., AND MORRIS, F., *Painted and Printed Fabrics.* Metropolitan Museum of Art, New York, 1927. Fully illustrated history of printed cottons in England and America.

CLOUZOT, H., *Le Décor Modern dans la Tenture et le Tissu.* C. Massin et Cie., Paris, 1929. Modern designs for textiles and wallpapers.

DENNY, G. G. *Fabrics.* J. B. Lippincott Co., Chicago, 1936. Revised edition. A small, inexpensive book giving definitions of fabrics, practical tests, and classifications.

FLEMING, E., *An Encyclopedia of Textiles from the Earliest Times to the Beginning of the 19th Century.* E. Benn, Ltd., London, 1928. Brief text with color plates and many photographs.

GLAZIER, R., *Historic Textile Fabrics.* B. T. Batsford, Ltd., London, 1923. A short history of the tradition and development of pattern in woven and printed fabrics. Illustrated.

Hunter, G. L., *Decorative Textiles*. J. B. Lippincott Co., Philadelphia, 1918. Out of print. Illustrated text covering all decorative fabrics.

Hunter, G. L., *The Practical Book of Tapestries*. J. B. Lippincott Co., Philadelphia, 1925. Fully illustrated text.

Lewis, E., *The Romance of Textiles*. The Macmillan Co., New York, 1937. An interesting romantic approach to the history of textiles from the earliest times.

Maciver, P., *The Chintz Book*. William Heinemann, Ltd., London, 1925. Illustrated text.

Priest, A., and Simmons, P., *Chinese Textiles*. Metropolitan Museum of Art, New York, 1934. An introductory study of this field.

Taylor, Lucy D., *Know Your Fabrics*. John Wiley and Sons, Inc., New York, 1951. A study of standard and historic types of fabrics, and their correct usage in decorative work.

Thomson, W. G., *Tapestry Weaving in England from the Earliest Times to the End of the XVIIIth Century*. Charles Scribner's Sons, New York, 1914. Illustrated text.

Thurston, V., *A Short History of Decorative Textiles and Tapestries*. Pepler and Sewell, Sussex, England, 1934. Illustrated text with history of hand weaving from the earliest times.

Von Falke, O., *Decorative Silks*. Wm. Helburn, Inc., New York, 1922. Beautifully illustrated text.

Wingate, I., *Textile Fabrics and Their Selection*. Prentice, Hall, New York, 1947. An excellent description of decorative fabrics with an explanation of the manufacturing and their fibers. Well illustrated.

CHAPTER XII

DRAPERIES, SLIPCOVERS, AND UPHOLSTERY

Draperies

As one enters a room, the windows and their treatment are, as a rule, the first features that are noticed. For practical reasons, windows are necessary for light and ventilation. Architecturally, they relieve the monotony of unbroken wall space both on the exterior and interior of the building. Physically their transparency relieves the eye muscles by occasionally permitting them to focus on a more distant view than the interior walls themselves permit.

The majority of windows are rectangular in shape and, if undraped, create pronounced hard, straight lines in a room. If for no other reason, therefore, curtains are necessary to soften the severity and to serve as trimming of the outline of the window frame and opening.

Window curtains also have very important decorative purposes to fulfill. They may serve in the place of window shades to maintain privacy, may assist in eliminating an undesirable view, may soften and regulate the amount of light that is permitted to enter a room, and act as a connecting link between the windows and walls. Lastly, because of their size, draperies also form an important element in the color scheme of a room, and may be used either to extend the color of the walls or to accentuate it by being treated in contrasting color, texture, or pattern.

The three types of window draperies. In the finest decorative work in domestic interiors, there are usually three sets of curtains to every window, but more frequently only two sets are used, and in simple rooms even one is permissible. Where three sets are used, there is first a thin material that is placed nearest the glass. This is known as the glass curtain or *sash curtain* and may be hung straight, tied back, or arranged to draw.

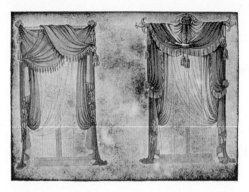

Designs for window draperies taken from George Smith's "Cabinet Makers Guide," 1825.

Over the sash curtain is often placed a medium-weight material, usually called the *draw curtain*. As the name implies, this should be arranged to draw by means of a pulley at the side. These curtains may take the place of the window shade, and should be sufficiently opaque to exclude the view and light when closed. The third set of curtains is generally known as the overdraperies, the purposes of which are primarily decorative; but if they are made to draw, the inside draw curtains may be eliminated. Overdraperies, as a rule, consist of a pair of curtains, plain or draped, with or without a *valance* or cornice board across the top. Overdraperies are generally hung to cover the top and side trim or casing of a window. In rare instances, where the window is large and the woodwork of great interest, or where the window jamb is deep, the overdraperies may be hung inside the trim.

Period draperies. As original draperies of 17th and 18th century rooms are almost nonexistent, it is necessary to search documents for information. Contemporary descriptions are vague on matters concerning designs, but often give full details as to materials. In the accurate restoration of period rooms required by museums and owners of old houses, it is always interesting to use the original designs for window draping. The most authentic documents for research are the paintings and engravings of interiors by Vermeer, Hogarth, Boucher, and others, and the books on interior design that were published between 1750 and 1850.*

Dutch and English paintings of the 17th century show rather simple window draperies usually hung to the sill and set within the jambs of the window. The purpose was functional rather than decorative. In the early 18th century, floor length draperies without a valance were common, and were hung straight to draw. Many weaves and patterns were used, depending no doubt upon the wealth of the owner and the character of the room. In some paintings, shaped valances accentuated with galloons or fringes are indicated.

---

* Most of the information concerning these matters has been obtained from Sheraton's *Director* (1793), George Smith's *Household Furniture* (1808 and 1826), Ackerman's *Repository of the Arts* (1806–1840), and Nicholson's *Practical Cabinet Maker* (1826). Sketches for draperies were also published by Chippendale, Ince and Mayhew, and Thomas Hope. There were also many French books on this subject published in the 17th and 18th centuries.

The state-beds of this period still in existence at Versailles, Fontainebleau, Hampton Court, and elsewhere indicate not only the importance of draperies for warmth, but the necessity for impressive bed adornment due to the custom of receiving guests before arising. These beds had corner posts crowned with an elaborate cornice from which hung a silk valance composed of overlapping swags, festoons, cascades, and jabots enriched with cut or molded fringes. The headboards were often enriched with silk sunbursts. Single or double full length draperies were held back during the daytime with tasselled ropes. The bed draperies were made to match those of the windows.

Valances apparently did not become common until the middle of the 18th century and they never entirely displaced the exposed pole or rod. The straight rod was treated with ornamental end motifs or enriched with a leaf or rosette ornament. Some rods were bent into graceful curves or frankly given the shape of a cupid's bow. Sliding rings were used or the rod served as a support for an overthrow swag. Carved

Drapery designs made by Sheraton, 1793.

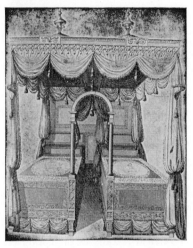

Sheraton's original design for twin beds made in 1793, called by him "A Summer Bed in Two Compartments."

wooden, or hammered brass cornices were enriched first with Rococo, and finally with classical detail. Draped valances in many designs often hung from a visible rod or from ceramic or metal rosette supports. Draperies were held back with ropes or hung over ornamental pins. When rich effects were desired, each window was treated with three or four pairs of draperies, a profusion that was only possible by alternating the method of hanging or the height of the tie-backs; in these treatments there were often an excessive use of swags, trimmings, and tassels, producing a lavishness that is impractical for present day application.

Drapery design. While many of the original period rooms had excessively rich and complicated drapery treatments, the present tendency

Drapery designs in the Chinese manner, made by Sheraton, 1792.

is toward simplicity. Before the use of modern heating devices, draperies were depended upon to maintain the temperature of rooms, but other considerations now guide the drapery designer. It is difficult to give any general rules for drapery designs, because of the great variety of window shapes and the numerous requirements and limitations in various types of rooms. The important points to consider are line, proportion, materials, colors, pattern, and scale. The line is formed by the silhouette and the folds of the curtains themselves, and by the method in which they are hung. It is always advisable to avoid square effects in window treatments. The windows should usually appear to be a vertical rectangle that is twice as high as it is wide. Groups of windows should be treated either as a series of vertical rectangles or if long enough, the horizontal line should be accented. Draperies should never overhang the wall at the sides of the window if such a treatment produces a square effect. Overdraperies should be hung to the floor in the great majority of cases. The window-sill height may be acceptable in small cottage interiors, or where, because window-seats, radiators, or other fixed objects interfere, it is impossible to hang the overdraperies to the floor. For very rich effects it is often advantageous to extend the curtains so that about one foot of the material rests on the floor.

Overdraperies may be hung straight or they may be tied back to introduce a graceful curved line, to contrast with furniture or architectural forms in which straight lines dominate. The tie-back should not be placed in the center of the length of the curtain, but usually looks best when placed one-third the distance from either top or bottom; this proportion may vary, however, under some conditions. Tie-backs should harmonize in color or material with the curtains they serve. Where pairs of windows

*Different types of drapery designs: (1) taffeta draperies, French-headed with
satin looped through tie-backs and tops; (2) satin swag and jabots,
taffeta curtains, Venetian blind; (3) gray satin, French-headed with blue
binding, Venetian blind; (4) informal stretched chintz valance board
with contrasting binding, draperies same; (5) wooden valance board,
moldings painted predominating colors in chintz, Venetian blind; (6)
mirror valance with wooden moldings, taffeta curtains with crystal
tie-backs.*

Different types of drapery designs: (1) damask, satin, or chintz drapery, tie-backs of same material; (2) formal treatment with two-color satin swags, silk fringe; (3) treatment for bay window with window seat—silk gauze curtains, shirred valances with silk swags; (4) treatment for arched window—damask, satin, or chintz held back with mirrored tie-backs.

Different types of drapery designs: (1) informal treatment for bedroom, organdy curtains held back with taffeta bows; (2) draperies and shirred valance of taffeta, glass curtains of sheer celanese or marquisette; (3) voile curtains with plaited ruffle; rod, rings, and tie-backs of crystal.

exist, an interesting treatment may be obtained by considering them as a single composition, tying back one curtain in each window only and permitting the other to hang straight. In such cases, the straight curtains may be made in a lighter weight or plainer material from that of the curtains that are tied back.

Windows are sometimes treated with sheer materials used as over-draperies. This is a saving in cost but is also done in expensively decorated rooms and is especially suitable where large windows exist with interesting views. In such cases soft sheer materials such as ninon, voile, and marquisette are used. The curtains may be hung straight to draw or they may be tied back. If the window proportion is suitable the top of the curtains may be hung with a sweeping overlap. Small cottage windows are also often treated in this manner, but the material is usually a heavier net or organdy. In informal rooms organdy and other crisp textiles are often edged with large ruffles which also may be used for tie-backs and a single or double row used at the top as a valance.

Sash curtains are usually made of translucent textiles such as gauzes, marquisettes, nets, ninon, dotted Swiss, point d'esprit, casement cloth, and organdy. They may hang free from a rod at the top or may be stretched between two rods. They are usually shirred with from 100 to 200 per cent fullness. The free-hanging type should be finished at the bottom with an edging or small fringe. There should usually be a double stitching of the hems so that a channel is made through which a rod may be slipped,

Where windows are close to each other the center division may be mirrors and the draperies designed as a unit.

leaving a small amount of material to extend beyond the rod. On French doors and windows, sash curtains often do not cover the entire glass area, but are run sufficiently high to exclude the view from the outside but permit the entrance of light; these are sometimes known as *brise-bise,* a French word that can roughly be translated "wind screen."

Valances, cornice boards, and drapery supports. The term "valance" refers to the horizontal decorative treatment that is usually applied to the top of a pair of draperies for the purpose of giving a more finished appearance to the framing of a window; it also serves the practical purpose of screening the hardware and traverse cords. Valances may also serve to improve window proportions and structural defects; low windows may be increased in apparent height by placing the valance partly on the wall above the window, keeping the lower line of the material a little below the top of the window opening; narrow windows may be made to appear wider by extending the valance beyond the trim at each side, so that the drapery will cover part of the wall. Windows of different heights may be made to appear to have the same dimensions by altering the proportions by these methods. The height of a valance should be approximately ⅛ of the total height of the window treatment measured from the top of the valance to the floor level.

Careful consideration must be given to valance designs, as a badly proportioned valance may ruin the decorative effect of a window. Valance treatments may be elaborate or simple as required to harmonize with the character of the room, and in their design a great variety of both materials and forms may be used. Textile valances are the most common, and the

Wide plate-glass windows treated with Venetian blinds and sheer draperies that can be drawn to cover the entire glass area.

type of textile may differ from that of the draperies, but should never be of lighter weight. Valances may be made of other materials than textiles. Colored silk or rayon ropes are often draped in the shape of a swag. In rococo treatments, plaster molded into ornamental forms such as swags, cupid's bows, scrolls and leaves, and other motifs create interesting effects. In place of the cloth valance, solid materials are often used either in rectangular shapes or curved forms, according to the design required in the style of the room; in these cases the valance is usually called a "cornice board" or just a "cornice." The materials used for this purpose include wood-moldings, shaped compo-board and plywood sheets, colored or painted glass, mirror, pressed brass, wallpaper, leather, and cork. Some of these materials must be mounted on a stiff board backing. Cornice boards vary in height but are usually between 4 and 10 inches, depending upon their length and the height of the window. The design, location, and dimensions of a cornice board or valance should always be tested by making a facsimile in wrapping paper, placing it in its proposed position, and judging its proportions from a distance.

Cloth valances are generally hung from a wooden box or support that is screwed to the trim, but the valance itself may follow a variety of forms. It may be a stretched textile applied to a thin plywood backing, and it may be rectangular, scalloped, or the top or bottom line may be cut into any desired shape. If the valance is other than rectangular it is known as a "shaped valance." The majority of cloth valances are shirred or arranged with French or box plaits. Valances may also be designed in single, double or triple swags, in which cases it is usually advisable to add a *jabot* at each end. With swag valances the supporting feature at each end may be hidden, or the swags may be drawn through an ornamental ring or thrown over a pin decorated with a rosette or ornamental head. The appearance of cloth valances is improved if the lower line is edged with a *guimpe*, grosgrain ribbon, edging, or fringe. When patterned materials are used for stretched valances it is important to balance the pattern so that the largest motif is in the center or two similar motifs are spaced equidistant from the center.

Valances and cornice boards should always be constructed to return to the wall surface at their ends, covering the edges of the drapery and the outside molding of the trim. The inside dimension is usually made 2 inches longer than the over-all trim width at the top of the window. Valances and cornice boards should be covered if possible with a piece of thin wood to serve as a dust cap.

While valances are advisable for most windows, they are often omitted in the following cases: (a) if the side draperies are hung to meet in the center of the window head, shirred or plaited and fixed in that position and are tied back to produce a graceful curve; (b) in windows that reach the ceiling where no convenient space is left for a valance; (c) in low-ceilinged rooms where a valance would accentuate the insufficient height; (d) in very wide windows, where a long valance would create an undesired long horizontal line; (e) where a rebate or groove has been built at the top of a window frame to hide the drapery hardware; and (f) where an elaborate cornice or pediment crowns the window trim. Valances are often omitted with casement windows that swing inwards, due to the fact that they interfere with the movement of the sash, but in these cases this disadvantage may be avoided by hanging the valance on the wall so that it clears the sash, or the valance and drapery may be hung on a metal rod that is hinged at the side of the window to permit the draperies to swing with the sash itself.

When valances are not used, the equipment for hanging the draperies remains visible. If a metal or wooden pole with curtain rings is used to support the draperies, it is advisable to paint it the same color as the wall. Ornamental pole-ends or finial forms are often added to wooden or brass poles and wrought iron rods should be treated with end motifs. Rods and supporting devices are usually made as inconspicuous as possible. An excellent substitute for the rod is the device known as the aluminum I-beam track, which can be laid straight or bent into almost any shape, and may be attached to the ceiling, wall, or valance board. The flanges of the small I-beam serve as a guide for sliding wheels placed at intervals and from which drop a ring, which in turn supports the drapery hooks. Another useful device is the wooden or metal molding designed with one to

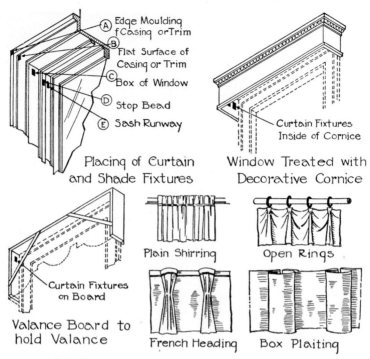

Placing of Curtain and Shade Fixtures

- (A) Edge Moulding f Casing or Trim
- (B) Flat Surface of Casing or Trim
- (C) Box of Window
- (D) Stop Bead
- (E) Sash Runway

Window Treated with Decorative Cornice

Curtain Fixtures Inside of Cornice

Valance Board to hold Valance

Curtain Fixtures on Board

Plain Shirring

Open Rings

French Heading

Box Plaiting

MISCELLANEOUS DETAILS OF DRAPERY CONSTRUCTION.

three grooves for gliders attached to a tape to which is sewn the drapery. The most inexpensive drapery supports are ordinary brass extension rods supported at their ends by small brackets, the draperies being hooked to sliding rings or shirred on the rod itself. There are several other devices which serve for this purpose. Draperies are made to draw by a system of cords and pulleys known as a "traverse."

Headings. Both valances and draperies may be given interest and, at the same time, organization and symmetry of folds by means of headings, plaiting, or shirring.

The *French heading* is probably the most satisfactory treatment, and consists in gathering the material in small folds about 6 inches apart and sewing the folds together usually 4 or 5 inches down from the top of the curtain; the folds then continue down the full length of the drapery, and are permanently fixed at a reasonably even spacing; the curtain is thus given a more tailored appearance. *Box-plaiting* consists of a similar spacing and start of folds, except that the head is not gathered, but doubled and pressed flat and sewed in that position. Plain *shirring* starts the folds at irregular intervals and is accomplished by sewing rings on the underside of the head of the curtain and sliding them on a small rod. Small weights evenly spaced along the bottom hem of curtains are some-

Sheer draperies with cord valance leaving pattern interest to Aubusson rug.

Tate and Hall, Decorators; Drix Duryea, Photographer

times used to make them hang properly, particularly if the material is unruly, as are glazed chintz and organdy.

If draping without a valance is desired, one or both curtains may be hung so as completely to cover the trim at the top of the window. Sometimes both curtains are arranged to cover the whole width of the window at the top, and are tied back to form an overlap. This is desirable when lightweight or transparent materials are used.

Drapery materials. The greatest latitude is observed today in the types of materials that may be used for window curtains and draperies. For sash curtains, the more usual fabrics are net, lace, voile, marquisette, gauze, fine casement cloth, and organdy. The materials used for draw curtains and overdraperies are frequently of types similar to each other, although, as a general rule, the draw curtains should be lighter in weight than the overdraperies. For these purposes, fabrics may be divided into three classifications—light, medium, and heavy. The lightweight materials include taffeta and reps made of either silk or cotton. In the medium group are included chintz, cretonne, linen, satin, moiré, cellophane, silk damasks and brocades, permatex, and oilcloth. The heavy group includes the coarse linens, antique satin, wool and cotton damask, brocade, brocatelle, corduroy, velvet, velveteen, and suède cloth. There are also many fabrics of heavy novelty weave both with and without patterns, of a distinctly modern character that are useful for rooms done in a modern manner or for period rooms in which a modern touch is desired.

To indicate the extremes to which some leading decorators have gone for the sake of novelty in window treatments, materials such as cowhide, patent leather, painted wood and tin, metal cloths, sheet aluminum and copper, rope, and hand-painted and stencilled silks have been used.

Inexpensive draperies may be made of theatrical gauze, sateen, mull, ticking, or almost any other cheap material. When the textile itself has little interest, it is essential that the colors and color scheme be well worked out and of unusual harmony. Paper draperies are sold by the department stores and large mail order houses, but this material cannot be considered for serious or permanent decorative work.

For informal American Colonial and English types of decoration, there is nothing more appropriate than chintz. In the more formal variations of these styles, silk damasks and brocades may be used. Velvets, wool damasks, and heavy brocades lend themselves well to early Italian and Spanish rooms. Eighteenth century and early 19th century rooms may be treated with silks and printed cottons in patterns that are consistent with the periods. In Victorian rooms all kinds of satins, damasks, and reps may be used, and chintz, as well, if it is Victorian in pattern. In modern rooms, cellophane, corduroy, permatex, and the coarsely woven modern fabrics of nylon and rayon are the most usual types of textiles used, although other modern materials heretofore mentioned may be employed if extreme novelty is desired. Striped materials are sometimes used for overcurtains, but if the color contrast of the stripes is strong, they are apt to cut up the wall space too much. Vertical stripes give a higher appearance to the room, whereas horizontal stripes have the reverse effect. The type of material to be used for window draperies depends entirely upon the general character of the room and the style of the furniture. Formal rooms call for satins, damasks, silks, and brocades. Simple rooms call for linens, chintzes, and inexpensive materials that are effective and cheerful in appearance.

The choice of plain or figured textiles. There can be no fixed rule as to when figured or plain materials should be used for overdraperies. Patterns unquestionably produce a gay effect; plain materials are more restful. The choice of either is a matter of taste. Visual fatigue and monotony should both be avoided, and perhaps the different rooms in the house should be treated with varying materials in order to introduce the variety that is necessary for good decoration. A rule that is followed by many decorators is to use plain drapery materials in rooms with patterned walls, and vice versa. Draperies should always contrast with the wall in some manner; if pattern is not used to foil a plain adjoining surface, contrast can be introduced by color, tone, or texture. A certain amount

Wide windows that are separated by mullions may be treated in subdivisional draperies that operate concurrently by a single traverse.

of interest and variety is always obtainable by trimming draperies with color-contrasting fringes, borders, or edgings. Valances and draperies may also be made of different materials.

The use of too many patterned surfaces in a single room is undoubtedly contrary to the best decorating standards. Floors, walls, and upholstery materials must be carefully considered for proper pattern balance. The number of windows in a room may also influence the decision as to whether a patterned material should be selected for the draperies. Numerous windows will not stand the profuse repetition of a strong pattern.

If patterned materials are to be selected, the most minute attention must be given to the character, subject matter, and scale of the pattern, so that it will be suitable to the character, use, and size of the room. When several rooms are so arranged that they may easily be seen together, as is sometimes the case in apartments, their color schemes may be linked by the use of similar colors in each room in a different arrangement or quantity.

In choosing drapery materials when both glass curtains and overdraperies are used, each kind should be carefully considered in its relation to the other, as to both color and texture. With silk taffeta or rep draperies, the glass curtains should be fine net or gauze; with chintz, a coarser net, voile, or organdy; with linen or cotton rep, a heavy net or casement cloth. Curtains made of spun glass and nylon have greater durability than other types. In general the weight of the sash curtain corresponds respectively with the weight of the overdraperies, and the heavier the overdrapery, the heavier the sash curtain required.

Drapery linings. The lining of draperies adds to their durability, reduces fading, permits them to hang better, and gives them a weightier appearance. All heavy materials should be lined with sateen or a more expensive material in a color that harmonizes with the curtain and with the color scheme of the room. Elaborate curtains are frequently lined with satin. When curtains are made of lightweight silks they should be interlined with soft white canton flannel. Black cambric is sometimes used for this purpose, but, if the draperies are accidentally dampened by rain, they are apt to absorb the dye of the cambric. When best quality workmanship is required the drapery should be hemmed by hand, but linings may be hemmed by machine and should be made about 1 inch smaller on all sides than the drapery itself. The lining should be stitched to the hem of the drapery by hand at about 6 inch intervals with a thread of the same color as the drapery itself. Draperies that are to be visible on both sides should be double-faced or lined with the same material as the drapery itself.

Glazed chintzes are sometimes better unlined, as the effect of light shining through shows them at their best. Lining them with a thin silk, however, gives them a much longer life and protects them from the sun. It is well to hold any material against the light before determining what lining should be used.

Trimmings. The majority of curtains require a trimming or edging to give them a more finished effect. There are many varieties furnished by trimming manufacturers, and there are constant changes in style and fashion, so that at times the use of certain types is discontinued or revived.

Chintzes and lightweight drapery fabrics are often edged with a narrow single or double strip of cloth that may or may not be accordion-plaited. Piping or welting, used both for draperies and for upholstery trimming, consists of strips of materials wound around a small cord. Narrow grosgrain ribbon is also used for edging lightweight fabrics, and ruffles of various sizes may be used as a finish for organdies and swiss. Narrow bands of woven strips or tapes known as guimpes and *galloons* are also used for trimming of the heavier materials, such as velvets and damasks; these are made in gold and colored patterns in tinsel, silk, wools, cottons, and cellophane, and are used for both draperies and upholstery work.

Fringes have a very wide range of variety in size, color, and material. The principal types are the cut, uncut, ball, tassel, and mould. Among the cut and uncut fringes are those known as bullion, bouclé, moss, chenille, scallop, and chain. Ball fringes are made in silk, wool, cotton, wood, and crystal. In the group of tassel fringes there are scalloped, looped, cascaded, and braided types. The molded fringes consist of elongated

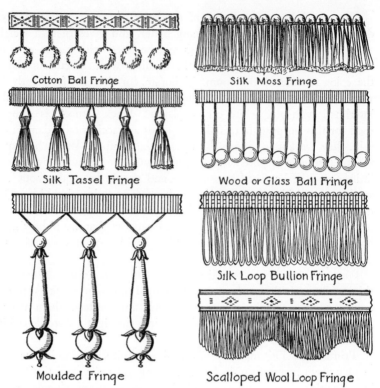

Examples of various types of fringes used for draperies and upholstery work. The loop, moss, tassel, and cotton ball types are also used for slipcovers.

wooden turnings usually wound with silk. The moulds come in diverse shapes such as pendants, drops and balls and are often hung from a galloon by an interlacing network of twisted strands of silk; they are also often combined with tassels. Mould fringes were used on draperies during the 18th and 19th centuries. They are elaborate and usually expensive, since they must be made in part by hand.

Tie-backs. Tie-backs may be made in the same material as the curtains, or they may be in rope or other contrasting materials. Their selection depends upon the style of the curtain and the texture of the fabric.

The usual kind of tie-back is a flat-shaped belt made of the curtain material, lined with sateen, and interlined with buckram so that it will retain its shape. A small ring is sewn on each end and caught in a hook put into the window casing at the desired height.

Cord and tassel tie-backs are effective. Wood and metal arms are sometimes used. Cloth and rope tie-backs are often looped over an ornamental pin which is screwed into the window trim. Ornamental pin-heads, forming a rosette, hand, or mask, may be obtained in crystal, mirror, brass, carved wood, gold leaf, paint, or other material.

Drapery measurements. Accurate measuring is of the utmost importance both in ordering materials for draperies and in making the draperies themselves. For the height of a curtain, the distance from the floor to the top of wood trim should be taken, with the extra allowance for hems added to this figure. Allowances for headings and hems depend upon the style of the curtains. When lightweight materials are used, a 3-inch or 3½-inch hem at the top is required. For heavyweight materials, a 4-inch heading should be used. The hem at the bottom should be 2 inches deep and of triple thickness of material. A good general rule is to allow 8 inches of material extra for the top hem and 6 inches extra for the bottom. If the overdraperies are to rest on the floor, allow an extra 12 inches. In the commercial types of ready-made draperies, there is less allowance for hems than stated.

As many textiles used for draperies and curtains have a tendency to shrink when cleaned or washed, it is always better to err in giving them ample length when newly hung and to have both top and bottom hems of sufficient size to alter them if necessary. Sash curtains should have at least a 15-inch allowance for this purpose. Overdraperies look best when there is sufficient material for ample folds; skimpy fullness always looks badly. Extra fullness is not objectionable. Drapery fabrics are usually made in 36-inch or 50-inch widths. A general rule for proper draping is to have the sum of the widths of both draperies approximately twice the width of the space they are to cover. This is what is known as 100 per cent fullness. As an example, if a window including the trim on each side equals 36 inches in width, the sum of the width of both draperies should be 72 inches, or each drapery should be of 36-inch material. In a window that is 4 feet wide, or 48 inches, the drapery on each side should be of 50-inch material. In wide windows it is sometimes necessary to use 1½ or 2 widths of material for each side.

When measuring for overdraperies that have a large repeat pattern, extra material should be ordered to take care of the pattern. At least one extra repeat should be ordered for each individual curtain, so that each curtain will have the individual features in the pattern at the same height above the floor when hung. Zigzagging of large patterns is not advisable. The bottom of a repeat should start at the bottom of each curtain used in the same room.

Window shades. The most widely used method to secure privacy and control of daylight in a room is by the ordinary roller shade operated by an interior coil spring and hammer catch. The preferred material for this type of shade is the pyroxylin-impregnated cotton, a material that is durable, washable, fire- and weather-resistant, and does not crack or fray at the edges; it is furnished in various colors and with hand-blocked designs. Roller shades should be hung between the window jambs on supports screwed to the sash stop-bead; they may also be hung to the front of the window trim, but this requires a roller that is 4 inches longer. Shades should be ordered 9 inches longer than the window opening.

Venetian and woven-wood blinds. The use of this type of window screen dates from the time of ancient Egypt and they have been used in all periods of decoration. They consist of slats supported by tapes and controlled by cords. Their principal advantage is that they permit ventilation while maintaining privacy and light control, and their shadow may create an interesting interior pattern. Glass curtains may be omitted when Venetian blinds are used.

Wooden slats vary in width from 1 ⅝ inches to 2 ⅜ inches, depending on the width of the window. They are furnished in all colors and stains with cotton tapes to match or contrast. Water and sun tend to crack the paint, which requires frequent renewal. Slats are also furnished in galvanized steel, plastic, aluminum, and cardboard. The steel slats are sturdy and durable, but heavy. Plastic slats are slightly curved in section and are available in nonfading impregnated colors. Aluminum slats are slightly curved for greater strength, are lightweight, flexible, and furnished in natural finish and many colors, and are perhaps the most satisfactory. Plastic tapes that may be cleaned with a damp cloth may be obtained. Cardboard slats are inexpensive but are not durable. There are also blinds with removable slats, a convenience for repairing, but requiring a mechanism which sometimes presents difficulties.

For large windows it is advisable to have a center as well as side tapes. Slats are usually hung from a metal or plastic cornice or box which contains the operating hardware. If Venetian blinds are hung on the face of the trim, they should overlap the jamb 2 inches on each side; if hung between the jambs they should be ¼ inch narrower.

There is another general classification of blinds known as woven-wood types. These include bamboo, flat wooden slats, and a handmade type combining thin, flexible wooden strips and vinyl plastic in a basket weave. All of these types are decorative; they all are designed to reduce glare and permit adequate ventilation, but none of them gives complete privacy. They are operated as a roll that lowers to the window sill.

Bamboo blinds are available in various styles. An expensive but formal type is made of very thin strips of bamboo bound closely together. Others more informal in character are made of wider strips, either from the outside or the inside bark; the former presents an irregular, varied surface in both the color of the strips and their width; the latter is more standard in these respects. Bamboo blinds are available in widths up to 10 feet.

Blinds made of bound wooden slats operated as the bamboo ones have long been used for porches and outdoor rooms. With beveled edges, narrow slats and decorative finishes, they may also be used indoors. These are available in widths up to 15 feet 8 inches, with slats $\frac{3}{8}$ inch or $\frac{7}{8}$ inch wide. Finishes include paint and weather-resistant wood stains.

For modern rooms vertical blinds are available in a wide range of colors. They are made of rayon strips stretched on vertical louvre-type frames and operated by a single control rod, in much the same manner as horizontal Venetian blinds. The strips are removable for laundering, and may be rehung on the frames while still damp. Since the fabric is translucent, these blinds cut down glare without shutting out light entirely. Strips are also made of plastic for nurseries, kitchens, and bathrooms.

Slipcovers

Slipcovers offer many excellent opportunities for introducing color and pleasing design into a room that would otherwise appear dull and cheerless. They add an informal atmosphere in either summer or winter months and also serve for re-covering shabby or uninteresting furniture that does not harmonize with the other decorations. Slipcovers are valuable, also, for the protection of furniture.

There are two types of slipcovers to be taken into consideration: the temporary ones used during the summer months, and the ones that form part of the permanent decorative scheme of a room. The latter may properly be used throughout the year provided they are well-tailored and fit snugly over the furniture, and provided the material harmonizes with the decorations already existing in a room.

When choosing material for slipcovers, the character of the room should be considered, as well as the type of the chair or sofa to be covered. In general, so far as the pattern is concerned, the same principles should be applied as when selecting any other type of upholstery material. The laws of harmony and contrast should be considered.

As a rule, slipcovers should be made of the medium-weight fabrics, such as glazed and unglazed chintzes, plain and printed linens, cretonnes, plain and striped taffetas, satins, sateens, and silk and cotton reps. Other materials which are often suitable are mohairs, plain and striped poplins, ginghams, and linen crash. Patterned fabrics may be found in practically all of the above-mentioned weaves to harmonize with period or modern rooms. There are also many plain modern fabrics with interesting novelty weaves and textures that are restful and in excellent taste for slipcovers in either period or modern rooms. The majority of plain fabrics require contrasting colors in the piping or *welting* to give them additional interest. Where economy is to be considered and no particular style is to be adhered to, there are many varieties of inexpensive cretonnes with all-over flower patterns which are always in good taste. Checked ging-hams and percales are smart and effective for covers for small boudoir chairs, and can be found in striking color combinations. For sun porches and semi-outdoor rooms, striped awning material is very durable and makes striking and colorful slipcovers. There are also waterproof glazed chintzes and rubberized materials that are practical for such rooms. Slip-covers should be dry-cleaned to prevent shrinkage.

For the purpose of obtaining unity in a room, some of the furniture covers may be in the same material as the curtains. In many instances, a colorful glazed chintz that has been chosen for the curtains may be re-peated in slipcovers for one or two chairs or a sofa, with cushions made of a plain material, either plain glazed chintz, taffeta, or satin in colors appearing in the chintz pattern. Plain glazed chintz is a particularly good choice for use in rooms where wallpaper and a patterned rug have been used.

In selecting slipcovers as well as upholstery materials, the shape of the piece to be covered must be considered in selecting a pattern. Chairs and sofas that are mainly rectangular in form may be covered with stripes and plaids as well as irregular all-over patterns, but curvilinear furniture must always be covered in irregular patterns or with those that have im-portant motifs that can be centered on a seat or back. It is dangerous to use different patterns to cover the largest chairs and sofa. If a chintz is used for both draperies and upholstery it is better to use the same material for both. Slipcover materials should always be of a firm and closely woven type. Sleazy fabrics do not hold their shape or position, are apt to tear at the seams and to permit dust to infiltrate. Slipcovers may have a flounce or kick-plait at the bottom, the latter requiring box-pleated corners so that it can not be stretched. The upholstered slipcover is tied or tacked to the underside of the seat, which holds it firmly in place and accounts for its popularity. Seams are finished with either a welt, cord, or piping, or are just bound. The welt is the most usual edging. The self-welt is made out of the fabric itself cut on the bias, or a ready-made or special welt may be obtained in a color contrasting to the slipcover ma-terial. For added interest a moss, chenille, or short cut fringe may be used in the seams. Fringes are especially advantageous where plain color fab-rics are used.

Measuring for yardage. An approximate method for finding the yard-age of material required for a slipcovered chair with a back not over 33 inches in width using 36-inch material uses measurements taken as fol-lows. Place the end of a string on the floor at the back of the chair, carry it up the back, over the top, down to the seat, and down to the floor. Do the same from the seat over each arm and down to the floor. Measure around each cushion. Add 12 inches for tucking into the crevices if required, and 2 inches for each hem. If the pattern is large and requires centering on the back and seat, add one repeat of the pattern. Add all these figures together. For a 6-foot sofa, take the measurement twice from the floor over the back and seat and down to the floor. When 50-inch material is used, deduct 20 per cent from these measurements.

Measurements for upholstery may be taken in the same manner, although the kick-plait or flounce is usually omitted. Leather supply houses recommend an order of 125 square feet of leather for a 6-foot sofa and 55 square feet for a large leather chair; these figures allow for the customary 25 per cent wastage in cutting and fitting.

Accurate measurements for slipcovers and upholstery are difficult to take and it is always wise to oblige the tradesman who is to do the work to take his own measurements. The disadvantage in this system is that the tradesman is usually very liberal in his allowances and he is not careful in regard to wastage, so that it is always a wise precaution for a decorator to be able to check the yardage.

The safest way for a beginner to make a slipcover is first to prepare a pattern out of cheap muslin, fitting and cutting it on the piece of furniture. Ample allowance should be made for seams. The material should first be pinned in place on the larger surfaces, the corners and irregular portions should be patterned afterwards. If tucking around seats is required, ample material should be allowed for this purpose. When the complete pattern is in place, it should be basted and the seams clearly marked by tailor's chalk. Much information may be gleaned by examining an existing well-tailored cover and studying its construction by turning it inside out. Slipcover fabrics should be tested for shrinkage or washed before they are made up.

One of the most important points to remember in the making of slipcovers is that they should have a strictly tailored appearance. They produce a very untidy effect, and their wearing quality is greatly lessened, if wrinkles are in evidence or they do not fit tightly. It is very difficult for an amateur to cut and make a professional-looking cover; proficiency comes only after considerable experience.

Upholstery

One of the most prosaic subjects concerning which a decorator should have a thorough knowledge is that of the construction and materials used in upholstered furniture and sleeping equipment. These are among the most important articles of home furnishing that the average family selects, and a guarantee of comfort in the home is as essential a part of a decorator's service as the advice regarding the appearance.

In the finest decorating work, upholstered furniture should be custom-made, but if cost precludes this, the decorator should investigate the character of ready-made stock, should be able to recognize the earmarks of quality and be able to discuss intelligently the specifications of the intended purchase with the manufacturer or salesperson. The laws of many states require that labels be attached to all upholstered products, giving information as to the internal contents, but this requirement is not universal. It is quite possible that externally two upholstered pieces may look alike, yet one may have twice the durability of the other, due to the differences in the internal materials and construction. The slightly higher cost of one may be entirely offset when measured in years of comfortable service.

Co-relating upholstery textiles. In decoration, upholstery textiles must first be considered from the angle of their cost, suitability, and durability, but their relationship to the ensemble of the room depends mainly on their pattern and color. Walls appear as backgrounds to chairs and sofas placed against them, and floor coverings must be considered in their effect upon free-standing pieces. Contrast of upholstery materials with their backgrounds is usually advisable, and it may be obtained in any one or more of the usual methods, such as texture, tone, color intensity, hue, or the use or omission of pattern. As upholstery coverings are secondary color areas to walls and floors, the color brilliancy of the former may be increased. Care must be taken to avoid an excessive use of patterned upholstery in a room, and particularly if wallpaper or a patterned floor covering is used. An excess of plain surfaces is less objectionable than an excess of patterned ones; the former is restful and may be given interest by variations in texture and color. Stripes and plaids produce a medium degree of animation and are less disturbing than elaborate patterns and harmonize well with both these and plain colors. Plain colored upholstery usually looks best and may be given greater interest if contrasting colored welting cords or chenille fringes are used with it. Patterns and weaves should be in character with the style of the room and with the character and scale of period furniture. Large all-upholstered sofas and chairs may be used in rooms that are otherwise treated in a period style, and such pieces are not necessarily required to be covered in period patterned textiles. All the large upholstered pieces forming conversation groups do not have to be covered in the same materials, but some attempt at balance should be made. Where a sofa faces two chairs, the sofa may be in a different material from the chairs, but the chairs should be treated in a manner similar to each other, and unity is always increased if by the use of welting, fringes or patterns there is some repetition of colors in the facing units. The use of several different chintzes in a room is usually inadvisable. When draperies consist of a strongly patterned chintz, the same chintz may be used on some of the larger upholstered pieces but a different patterned chintz is disturbing. In wallpapered rooms, a better effect is attained by using plain, striped, or plaid upholstery coverings in colors that repeat some of those used in the wallpaper. It is better to attempt to distribute the patterned textiles used for furniture evenly, rather than to concentrate them at one point.

Upholstered furniture. Integrating cushions with the framework of furniture dates only from the time of the Renaissance, and the modern all-upholstered chair was first made in France in the middle of the 19th century and was called a "comfortable." This type eliminated the bergère. Its origin may have been inspired by the Turkish divan, and it was the first seat that permitted one to take a semireclining position. Since that time many changes and improvements have occurred.

The decorator is often obliged to purchase ready-made upholstered furniture in which the construction and stuffing are entirely hidden from view. There are always visible a few clues as to quality; but the reputation of the dealer must be the principal guarantee. The price range is always an indication, and most upholstered furniture is sold with a label indicating the wood of the framework and the ingredients of the padding. In the best grade of upholstery, cushions are soft and fluffy and are made mostly of down; in cheaper grades cushions are made with springs, covered with a padding, but these may be easily felt by pressing with the hand. If any wood is exposed, the kind is easily identified and the quality of carving and finish would indicate the general type of materials and construction used throughout the piece. Ready-made upholstered furniture is usually sold "in the muslin" so that the decorator may select his own surfacing material.

In the best type of decorating work, upholstered furniture should be custom-made. Thus the decorator may establish his own standards and reputation, by specifying the materials and supervising the construction of any piece for which he is responsible. He should therefore have an intimate knowledge of this subject.

Upholstery construction. *Frames.* The first essential for a quality upholstered seat is to have a properly made frame to build upon. These should be made of kiln-dried poplar, birch, soft maple, gum, or sycamore. Harder woods such as oak, ash, and hickory have a tendency to split under excessive nailing. Frames should be assembled with spiral grooved dowels, tenons, screws, and the best glue; nails should never be used. Triangular corner blocks should reinforce the four inside corners of the seat frame.

Webbing strips intended as support for springs should be of pure jute, 4 inches wide for seats and 3½ inches wide for backs; the strips should be placed on 5-inch centers, tightly stretched, interlaced, turned over 1½ inches at each end, and stagger-nailed with 7 nails to the underside of the

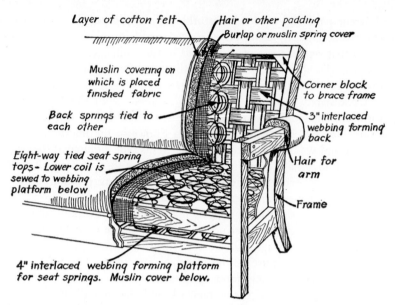

Layer of cotton felt

Hair or other padding

Burlap or muslin spring cover

Muslin covering on
which is placed
finished fabric

Corner block
to brace frame

Back springs tied to
each other

3" interlaced
webbing forming
back

Eight-way tied seat spring
tops - Lower coil is
sewed to webbing
platform below

Hair for
arm

Frame

4" interlaced webbing forming platform
for seat springs. Muslin cover below.

Diagram showing detail of construction of an upholstered seat.

seat rails. Wooden slats are sometimes used in place of seat webbing, but these produce a less comfortable support. In springless seats the webbing strips should be as close as possible. The best quality webbing is usually indicated by the insertion of four colored threads in the warp. In inexpensive furniture the webbing is often omitted and two steel bar supports, to each of which is attached three springs, are nailed to the seat frames.

Springs should be placed as close to each other as possible but should not touch. They should be firmly sewed to the webbing or stapled to the slats. In the latter case a strip of webbing should be placed on each slat to prevent rattling. Small chair seats should have a minimum of nine and large chairs thirteen. Davenport seats usually require thirty-six. They should be made of 9- or 11-guage wire of a height to suit the seat. Back springs may be smaller and made of finer guage wire. The bottom coil of springs should be firmly sewed to the webbing or stapled to the wooden slats. The springs should be compressed to fit the curve of the seat and held firmly in place by French 8-ply twine stretched in two cross and two diagonal directions. Each cross-cord should be tied in two places to the top coil, making a total of eight knots for each spring. The ends of each cross-cord should be firmly knotted to nails on the framework. The springs should then be covered with 10½ ounce burlap or canvas as a foundation for the stuffing. The softness of a seat depends in part upon the number of springs, the amount of compression, the guage of the wire, and whether they have wide (soft) or narrow (stiff) center coils. The final comfort depends upon the quality of the cushions.

Filling materials. Inexpensive types of upholstery are filled with cotton felt, kapok, Spanish moss, sisal, tow, sea grass, and excelsior. All of these materials should be avoided in high-grade work. Curled horsehair is considered best, cattle tails next, and finally hog hair, which is short and must be mixed with a longer fiber. These materials should be evenly laid over the canvas, covered with a layer of cotton felt, over which should be stretched

An upholstered chair showing method of construction when using rubber cushion and back.

a sheet of unbleached muslin, which is tightly nailed to the seat rails and serves both to relieve any strain on the finishing material and prevent a filtration of the hair. Latex or foam rubber is also extensively used now as a substitute for stuffing or springs or both; it has many advantages among which are its lightness, softness, buoyancy, durability, freedom from moth or vermin attack, and shape-holding quality.

Cushions are best made from a mixture of 80 per cent down and 20 per cent goose feathers, although some manufacturers use less down than this and others advise a 50–50 mixture. Goose feathers are curved and springy while duck feathers have little strength or resiliency. Chicken and turkey feathers should always be avoided. Feather cushions should always have an inner casing divided into four separate compartments to prevent shifting and lumping. The cheaper grades of cushions have inner springs of 2½ inches in diameter and 3½ inches high, made of 12- to 15-gauge wire. These should be in individual pockets and covered on all sides with several layers of ¼-inch cotton felt (not wadding). As cushions receive most of the wear of a seat, they should always be covered on both sides by the finishing material. In first quality products seat cushions made of down and feathers are 4½ inches high.

Piping and tufting. Piping is used for the upholstery of curved forms such as the interior surface of rounded chair backs and arms. The stuffing is tacked to the wooden frame every few inches in vertical strips and projects in the intervening space so that the finished upholstery appears as a row of pipes. Tufting is a method of holding the stuffing in place by carrying twine or small metal chains through the cushion or back and attaching the ends to a cluster of threads called a tuft or to a button. This causes a depression in the surface of the upholstery.

Draperies, Slipcovers, and Upholstery 509

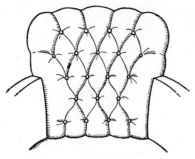

Finishing materials. After the interior upholstery is finished the final covering is applied. This should be stretched tightly and nailed to the framework. Nails with ornamental heads may be used. Ordinary tacks should be covered with a guimpe. Seams should be avoided if possible, or they may be treated with welting, cording, or fringes. The webbing of the seat bottoms should be undercovered with burlap and after the finishing material is in place, black glazed cambric for dust-proofing and to prevent loose penetration of particles of the stuffing, should be nailed to the underside of the framework.

Sketch of chair back showing a combination of piping and tufting.

Sleeping Equipment

This classification includes mattresses, box springs, and pillows. Mattresses have been used since the dawn of civilization, but box springs with helical supports were not common until the middle of the 19th century. Springs of woven twisted-wire sheets were introduced about 1875, but these are now only used in inexpensive beds and they have neither the comfort nor lasting quality of the helical spring types. At the present time, the most comfortable bed is considered to be a box spring supporting a mattress made of hair, latex (foam rubber), or innersprings. Individual taste dictates which of these interior materials shall be used, and all are good if quality and workmanship are of the best.

Mattresses are made with three types of edges, called imperial, roll, and plain. The "imperial edge" produces the most sturdy construction and is identifiable by two padded rolls or upholstery pipes that run around the mattress, and four rows of visible stitching along the edge; the "roll edge" is similar in appearance but has only two rows of visible stitching; the "plain edge" has no roll and no edge-stitching except at the seams which are often taped. The edges of all well-made mattresses should have small screened ventilators to permit the circulation of air.

Stuffing materials vary greatly. The best stuffed mattresses are 5½ inches high and contain 4½ inches of curled horse tail hair, and are padded top and bottom with 1 inch of lamb wool. The wool, however, is often omitted. Cotton felt is used in commercial grades and loose cotton and kapok in the cheapest types; the latter lose their resiliency, produce lumps, and have little durability. The latex mattress, developed about 1938, is soft and has great resiliency and durability; the thicker sizes only should be used and covered with a ticking.

Many people prefer the innerspring types of construction, but of these there are many grades. In general the comfort of this type depends upon the number and resiliency of the springs. For a double-bed size (4 feet 6 inches wide) the best contain

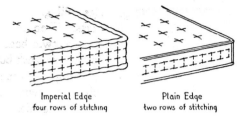

Imperial Edge
four rows of stitching

Plain Edge
two rows of stitching

Sketch showing difference in the construction of the Imperial and plain edge mattress.

900 interwoven cylindrical 4-inch springs and for a single-bed size (3 feet 3 inches wide) 650 springs. Some of the innerspring type have separate springs, each in a muslin pocket intended as a silencer; the pockets are sewn together but have a tendency to deteriorate. All innerspring mattresses should be tufted with short metal chains that pierce the cover and are attached to buttons. The cheaper grades of innerspring mattresses have from 180 to 504 hour-glass shaped springs joined by metal clips or helical wire strips. When few springs are used, each is necessarily a heavy gauge wire, which results in less resiliency and comfort. Spring mattresses should be strongly braced along their edges with a thoroughly padded wire or metal strip, and should have on the top and bottom, tufted pads of hair or cotton felt. All mattresses should be covered with 8-ounce ticking and all but the latex type should be tufted with twine held by cotton tufts to keep the stuffing in place. The majority of states require mattresses to be tagged with a label indicating their contents.

Box springs, when custom-made, should be constructed with a strong wooden frame. Commercial types have metal frames. The helical springs should be hour-glass shape, made of 9½-gauge wire and 9 inches high when used with a hair or latex mattress and 7 inches high with an inner spring mattress. Double beds should have 72 springs, single beds, 54, and studio beds, 45. Springs should be tied with twine as in the best quality upholstery seats (see page 508). Other suitable, but less comfortable, methods of joining the springs are by clips and wires. Springs should be covered with a 1-inch tufted pad of horsehair or cotton-felt and enclosed in a tufted ticking on top and sides and on the bottom with black cambric or muslin.

There are two shapes for box-spring sections, the plain and rabbeted. The plain type fits within the side boards of the bed and rests on the bed slats or metal angle irons, or when no bedframe exists can be furnished with legs. The edges of the rabbeted type are designed with a shelf that rests on the top of the bedframe. Beds that have a frame but no footboard should be equipped with the rabbeted type, but the plain box-spring with

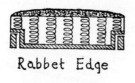

Rabbet Edge

Single Border

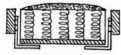

Single Border Dropped

Sections showing three ways of supporting a box-spring on the side boards of a bed.

legs will give the same effect if no bedframe exists. When a single decorative headboard is used for twin beds placed closely to appear as a double bed, each box-spring should be on casters and hinged to the side of the headboard, to enable it to swing open for convenience when making the bed.

Pillows may be stuffed with any of the materials that are used in upholstery cushions. The best quality pillow is filled with 80 per cent down and 20 per cent goose feathers. If down filled, it will weigh about 1½ pounds, if filled with goose feathers alone, it will weigh 2½ pounds, and a chicken or turkey feather-filled pillow will weigh 3½ pounds. A down-filled pillow, if pressed, will quickly spring back to its original shape, and chicken quills can easily be felt by pressing the pillow with the fingers. In a damp climate pillows are less resilient. Standard pillow sizes are 20 inches $\times$ 26 inches, 21 inches $\times$ 27 inches, and 20 inches $\times$ 36 inches. Ticking should be of the 8-ounce type, although other closely woven materials may be used. The 6-ounce ticking makes a softer pillow, but is less durable.

Bibliography

BAST, H., *New Essentials of Upholstery*. Bruce Publishing Co., New York. Excellent illustrated handbook.

PICKEN, MARY BROOK, *Sewing For The Home*. Revised and enlarged edition. Harper and Bros., New York, 1946. Contains clear step-by-step instructions, illustrated by diagrams, for making various types of slipcovers, draperies, etc.

SEAGER, C. W., *Upholstered Furniture*. The Bruce Publishing Co., New York, 1936. An excellent illustrated handbook.

STEPHENSON, J. W., *Practical Upholstering*. Hall Publishing Co., New York, 1950. Well-illustrated handbook giving the fundamentals of fine upholstering work.

STEPHENSON, J. W., *Drapery and Slipcover Cutting and Making*. Revisions and additions by Stephen Fridek and Wm. O. Hall. Hall Publishing Co., New York, 1950.

CHAPTER XIII

FLOOR COVERINGS

![decorative rule]

F loor coverings were probably woven in Egypt before 3000 B.C. Pictorial records show that in early times, patterned fabrics were
placed before the Pharaohs' thrones and only royal personages or suppli-
cants were allowed to tread or kneel upon them. Biblical writers, Homer,
Horace, Pliny, and other ancients, mention them. During the Islamic
expansion, and particularly in Persia, where highland sheep provided a
fine, long wool, the weaving of rugs* was developed over hundreds of
years into an artistic culmination that occurred in the 16th century. These
Asiatic floor coverings were sometimes in tapestry weave, but the majority were pile fabrics woven on a loom composed of two beams between which were stretched the warp threads; colored threads of wool
or silk were knotted to the warp to form a pile pattern that sometimes
was composed of as many as 1000 knots to the square inch. When the
knotting was completed, the ends were sheared to produce an even surface. Fabrics of this type were also used for tent walls, wall hangings,
partitions, awnings, camel saddles, bed mats, covers, and portieres.

During the Middle Ages, the floors of many of the castles in northern
Europe were spread with rush and dried grass. Tradition states that
Moors from Spain entered southern France in the 13th century and
established the first rug looms in Aubusson. Spanish rugs were brought
to England in 1255 as part of the dowry of Eleanor of Castile. Carpets
were exported from Turkey to England in the 15th century where they
inspired an effort to copy them, and a magnificent rug was woven for
Elizabeth in 1570. Holbein painted members of the court of Henry VIII
and often showed Oriental rugs as floor coverings or table covers. In 1608

* The English word *rug* of Anglo-Saxon origin is akin to "rugged" and "rough" and
the early meaning was "coarse" or "shaggy." Its correct application is therefore to a pile
fabric, but custom has associated it also with tapestry weaves. The word *carpet* is of Latin
and Old French origin and was derived from a word that referred to the cleaning of wool.
Today the two words are often synonymous, but it is perhaps convenient to apply "carpet"
to the floor covering that extends to the wall and completely covers the floor. Machine-made
carpets are usually known as "broadlooms" and are made in strips of wide dimensions.

513

Henry IV of France employed several Persian weavers for looms that he established in the Louvre, and the Savonnerie factory was founded in 1618. The revocation of the Edict of Nantes in 1685 forced many French weavers to emigrate to Flanders, and Brussels, already a tapestry-making center, became famous also for its looped pile floor coverings. Rug-weaving guilds were established in England in the 17th century and in 1740 production was accelerated by the absorption of Flemish emigrants, who introduced the Brussels type of carpet weaving and who established what was later to become a great British industry. A few years later French weavers from the Savonnerie factory went to England and improved the design of English floor coverings. Weaving of these fabrics had meanwhile started at Kidderminster and Axminster.

Hand looms were used until 1839 when the first power loom based on Arkwright's, Cartwright's, and Jacquard's inventions, was adapted to rug weaving. From this time, the industry spread rapidly to other centers in Europe and America.

Machine-made Rugs and Carpets

Classification. By far the most popular types of floor coverings used today are the commercial carpets that come within the classification known as Chenille, Wilton (Brussels and ingrain), Velvet (tapestry), Axminster (moquette), and rugs of the luster type.

These names designate the various looms upon which carpets are woven and the method of construction of the fabric. On the early looms all carpets were woven in strips 27 inches wide, this being the length of the old Flemish measuring unit known as an "ell." Large sizes had to be made by sewing the narrow strips together. Strip carpeting is now made 27 and 36 inches wide, and in what are known as broadlooms, which are produced in standard widths of 9, 12, 15, and 18 feet, and in other special widths, and of almost any reasonable length. Plain and patterned rugs with borders are also woven in many standard sizes and chenille weaves are available in widths up to 30 feet.

A carpet is judged by the depth of pile, the closeness of weave (*i.e.,* the number of picks, wires, or rows per inch), and the quality and selection of wools used. A high-grade worsted Wilton will have 13 wires to the inch, a medium-grade, 11; a high-grade wool Wilton will have 9½ wires per inch, a medium-grade, 8. On the other hand, a high-grade Axminster will have 11 rows, and a low-grade, 5. But the most important factor in the construction of a carpet is the quality and selection of the wools used.

Carpet wool. Wools from which carpets are woven in the United States are imported from Scotland, the Argentine, China, Italy, Afghanistan, Spain, Tibet, Persia, Egypt, Syria, India, Turkey, Irak, Iceland, and Russia. Australian and American wools are too fine and soft for use.

The wool as received, known as "wool in grease," is sorted, scoured in a mild solution of soda ash, and rinsed. It is then passed many times through a carding machine, which removes burrs and other foreign matter and separates the wool fibers. A mechanical comb separates the long, thin, straight fibers of the carded wool from the short, curly fibers, called "noils." The long fibers, twisted together on high-speed spinning frames, are known as "worsted yarn." The wool remaining after the selection of the worsted yarn, spun on a spinning jack, is called "woolen yarn." It is a soft, bulky type. Selected worsted yarns are used to weave worsted Wilton, worsted Chenille, and handmade carpets of the highest grade. Cotton yarns also are used in the cheaper grade of rugs.

Due to the inadequacy of wool production throughout the world, the enormous need for such fibers, and their constantly increasing cost, many American manufacturers are now using synthetic fibers in rugs still identified by the standard rug-weave names. The fibers are used both separately and in combination with natural ones. To reduce costs, weave structure has also been simplified by omitting the woven cushion of rugs and coating the underside of knots with a plastic to hold the pile threads in place. This results in a lighter weight and less luxurious textile. The comparative durability of some of the synthetic fibers is open to question, and some do not hold dyes as well as the natural ones.

Chenille carpets are so called from the manner of their construction. The word "chenille" is from the French word meaning caterpillar. A furry ribbon, or "caterpillar," is used as a weft in weaving a Chenille fabric, the fur protruding between the warp threads to form the surface nap. Chenille weave is always distinguishable by its heavy wool back, which no other carpet has. It is distinctly a luxury product, costly, extremely durable, and soft under foot.

While Chenille floor covering was developed in Scotland as early as 1839, it was not produced in quantity in America before 1916. Since that time, domestic manufacture of this type of carpet has been so perfected that it is comparable with, and in no way inferior to, those imported from Scotland and England.

Chenille carpeting is always made to order, with the exception of a limited number of plain broadloom carpets which are issued each year by the mills. It has consequently many advantages. It can be had in any color, since the wools are dyed for the job; it can be made in any design or in any shape, employing as many colors as desired; and it can be woven seamless up to a width of 30 feet, without limitation as to length.

It is possible to produce Chenille in a variety of grades, depending upon the height of pile and the closeness of weave. It is often true that a

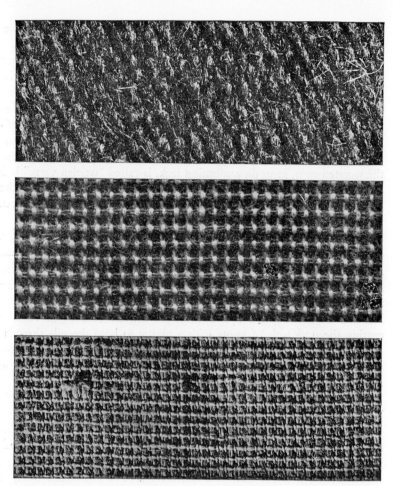

UPPER: *The back of a typical chenille carpet showing the heavy wool weave.* MIDDLE: *The back of a medium grade Axminster carpet having six rows per inch and showing the characteristic ribbed texture.* LOWER: *The back of a medium grade Wilton carpet having eight and a half wires per inch and showing a comparatively even texture.*

Chenille made of the finest worsted yarn, closely woven, with a smooth, velvety surface, has a comparatively low pile, while another with a high pile of a luxurious appearance may be made of a rough, soft woolen yarn, more loosely woven, and is consequently of a considerably inferior quality to the first carpet and sells for a lower price.

Wilton carpets were first woven by hand in Wilton, England, where were made 27-inch Brussels carpets with a low-looped pile. The pile was eventually cut and the rugs became known as Wiltons. They are now woven on the Jacquard loom. The Wilton loom is much on the order of the tapestry loom, but with the Jacquard mechanism attached. This mechanism consists of a number of frames or cards in which holes are punched in the same manner as on a music roll, indicating the pattern to be woven. These frames, when threaded with yarn and attached above the loom, lift to the surface the colored yarns which are to appear in the design, at the same time depressing all yarns not appearing. These depressed yarns thus become buried in the back of the carpet, adding to the durability of the fabric and to its softness and resiliency. With the Jacquard attachment it is not possible to use more than five or six colors in a design. However, by a process of "planting" yarn in the back of the carpet, this number may be increased with half-tones of the colors used in the card.

The Wilton carpet is generally regarded as a standard of high quality. The carpet trade considers that no finer carpet can be woven than the worsted Wilton. Toward the end of the 19th century the worsted Wilton was the carpet most in use in fine homes. It was made in narrow widths, either plain or patterned, closely woven, with a low erect pile and a fine, silky texture. Worsted Wiltons are even now seldom made in broadloom widths.

The wool Wilton is made in many grades. Even when woven with a high pile, the woolen yarn is softer, the tufts larger, and consequently the design woven is less fine in detail than in worsted carpets. A special type of Wilton is known as Saxony because it was originally woven from Saxon yarns; these are tightly twisted and give exceptionally long wear; the carpet is very soft and heavy and lies flat.

A *Brussels* carpet is woven on a Wilton loom, and is in fact a Wilton carpet with an uncut pile. An *ingrain,* or Scotch carpet, on the other hand, while woven on a Wilton loom, is a flat, pileless fabric that is woven like a plain weave cloth from predyed yarn. It is a reversible fabric and sometimes different colored threads are alternated in the warp to add to its textural interest. While the ingrain carpet was very popular during the Victorian period, it has fallen into disuse because it lacks the wearing qualities of pile floor coverings.

Velvet carpets. The majority of plain broadloom carpets made today are woven on the Velvet or tapestry loom. A Velvet carpet of good quality closely resembles the Wilton in external appearance. It has a cut pile, but does not have wool buried in the back, and therefore has not the resiliency or good wearing qualities of the Wilton. As the wool is almost entirely on the surface, there is great economy of material in its weaving, which accounts for its lower cost.

In patterned weaves this loom has not the limitations of colors imposed by the Jacquard loom. The different colors to be used in a Velvet pattern are first printed on the yarn before it is woven, causing the pattern to have a slightly indefinite outline. Some Velvets have their patterns printed after weaving and others are made with a twisted thread of two colors. The yarn used must be of consistently good quality throughout in order properly to take the various dyes. Velvet may be used where there is not too much traffic and where there are definite budget limitations. It is woven in widths up to 18 feet.

Tapestry carpet is a Velvet carpet with an uncut pile. It is seldom used today, though it was actually the forerunner of the popular Velvet weave. It is sometimes called a hooked type because of its resemblance to some of the handmade products. By varying the height of loops, interesting textural effects are obtained. The name is a misnomer as the weave has no similarity to a hand-woven rep tapesiry.

Axminster carpets. These were first woven by hand in 1755 by a man named Witty in the village of Axminster, England. The modern machine-made Axminster carpet is produced in greater volume than any other weave today. It is woven only up to 18 feet in width. It is distinguishable by a coarse, stiff jute back, and by the fact that the fabric can be rolled lengthwise but not crosswise.

The Axminster bears the closest resemblance to a hand-tufted carpet, in its construction. The tufts are inserted mechanically and bound down in the weft, but not knotted. No wool is buried in the back. The tufts are clearly visible on the face of the carpet, and the weave permits an unlimited number of colors and designs. The majority of Axminsters are now made with only 8 rows of tufts to the inch. Carved types showing self-tone patterns in contrasting high and low pile heights are now being produced, and patterns are also made by contrasting twisted and loose piles of the same height, which produces a carved appearance. Axminster is woven in many different qualities but in general costs less than the Chenille or Wilton. It is very suitable for residential use but cannot compete with the other types for heavy duty in public places.

Luster-type rugs, woven of worsted or wool yarn on wide looms, have soft cotton backs. They are washed in a chemical solution of caustic soda and lime which produces a high luster. While approximately 20 per cent of the original color is taken out with this washing, the remaining color is absolutely fast. These rugs were originally known as "American Oriental" or "domestic Oriental," terms which have been discarded. They are usually less expensive than original Oriental examples, but are advantageous for those who cannot afford the genuine. Made in a variety of patterns as rugs in stock sizes, this type is also being produced in plain carpets. Their construction may be of the Wilton, Axminster, or Velvet type. They are comparatively inexpensive, durable, and serviceable, and in good taste if a good quality is selected in a color that harmonizes with the rest of the room. The Oriental patterned weaves of machine manufacture are generally not selected for rooms where connoisseurship must be expressed. The fault lies in the fact that in carpets of this type, repeats are too accurate and mechanical in appearance and lack the softness, mellowness, and individuality of the hand-made product. In other words, machine-made "Orientals" are imitations, and any object included in such a category should be avoided on ethical grounds.

Handmade Rugs and Carpets

In this group of floor coverings are included the pile and tapestry weave rugs that are made in Europe and America on hand looms. Many of these are among the finest quality rugs that it has been possible to make. The designs vary from the traditional patterns to ultra modern conceptions. These types originated during the historic periods and have been produced continuously to the present time, the patterns changing to correspond to the tastes of the times in which they were made. There are three variations in the method of making the pile surfaces. The most durable is the hand-knotted type in which the knot is the same as the extremely tight Ghiordes or Turkish knot with both ends of the knot left in a vertical position to form the pile. The hand-tufted pile is produced by a yarn that first runs loosely under and over three or four warps and only one end rises vertically to create a pile. As the pile of a hand-tufted rug is easily pulled out, the threads are usually held in place by applying glue, rubber or synthetic latex solution to the back. The fine hooked rugs are technically similar to the country-made types and are formed by pushing two ends of a short length of wool through a canvas backing to form the pile. The difference between the fine and country-made types is in the character of the pattern and the quality of the dyes and materials that are used. These rugs are generally made to order to any specified size and shape, and their possibilities as to patterns, color, and texture are limitless. As made today, they constitute the finest and most expensive grades of merchandise.

Savonnerie rugs. These rugs are the aristocrats of Western weaves. They were first woven near Paris in 1618, and in 1625 the factory came under government ownership. The production has been continuous since that year, with only short interruptions due to war or economic conditions. In 1826 the looms were moved to the Gobelins factory, but in the 19th century similar rugs were woven elsewhere and the name is now applied to a general type of rug rather than one definitely woven at the Gobelins. The rugs are always pile fabrics made by hand in the same manner as the Oriental types, but the patterns are French and the motifs have followed the changes of the various French periods. The rugs are usually in large dimensions and suited to elaborately decorated rooms. Patterns are consistent with the rug sizes, colors are rich and strong with dark

Mid-19th century Aubusson rug in tapestry weave.

backgrounds. The warp is usually of linen and the pile of the pattern is usually slightly higher than that of the field. Thick yarns are used in their making.

Aubusson rugs. Rugs have been woven in the town of Aubusson, France, since the Middle Ages, at which time they probably had an Oriental influence in their patterns. During the late Gothic period, mille-fleur types were woven, but from the time of Louis XIV the patterns followed, at an enlarged scale, the French textile designs. Colors as a general rule were light in tone, or slightly neutralized for faded effects. The weave has always been that of a heavy, coarse tapestry and the term "Aubusson" is now applied to rugs of this type regardless of whether they were woven in the town of that name. Linen and wool warp threads were used until the middle of the 19th century after which time cotton was substituted. The Aubusson production has always been large and there are many 18th and 19th century examples available. The production continues today on a large scale and many are woven to order. Period

Samples of fine quality American made hand-knotted rugs in modern designs produced by combinations of high-pile and tapestry weaves.

patterns are reproduced and during recent years the designers have endeavored to produce patterns that reflect contemporary thought and culture.

Moquette carpets. The term "moquette" is applied to the French 27-inch strip hand-loomed carpets. It is similar to the Axminster in weave. There are two types; the *moquette velouté* has a cut pile and the *moquette bouclé* has an uncut pile. The strips are usually treated with a small repeat motif. One of these carpets made with a special pattern was presented to George Washington by Louis XVI of France and is now in the banquet room at Mount Vernon. Carpets under this classification have also been made by machine methods.

Modern hand-knotted rugs. Weavers in several European countries, particularly those of Scandinavia and a few in the United States are now making extraordinary floor coverings in contemporary patterns by the hand-knotted process. These are unquestionably the finest floor coverings being made today. The Ghiordes knot is used, the finest quality wools and dyes are selected and the patterns have been made by designers of international reputation. The Scandinavians have specialized in producing what is known as the Flossa or Rya weave; this is an alternating pile and tapestry surface, in which high pile strips about one inch wide are separated by about one inch of plain tapestry weave; the pile bends over with a shaggy appearance and covers the tapestry strip. The Scandinavian patterns often show modernized peasant design characteristics. There are hand-knotted rugs woven in New York City that in spite of higher production costs than in Europe are sold at a lower price than the European productions due to tariff protection. These are so beautifully designed that they can only be considered as works of art. Structurally they are woven with a tightly tied Ghiordes knot and they are the most durable of all floor coverings. They are suitable for luxurious types of interiors and are made of the finest imported wools. Modern patterns are produced by both color variations, contrasting pile heights and textural effects, and consist of geometrical, abstract and naturalistic subject matter. Rugs of this type are necessarily made to order.

Carved rugs. Carved rugs, sometimes known as *sculptured* or *embossed rugs,* have been an important 20th century contribution to rug weaving. They are a type of rug made by hand in the United States, India, Indo-China, Canada, Puerto Rico, and other countries and are known by various trade names, but are, because of their construction, usually a form of hooked or tufted rug. They are made on a strong, closely-woven cotton back by a process of pushing woolen yarn through the fabric from the back by means of a looped needle or hook. This process leaves yarn loops on the face of the carpet, in a depth of nap regulated by the hook, and these loops are then sheared to a smooth surface or left uncut, according to the texture desired. It will be seen that this process allows a great variety in quality of wool used, depth of pile, closeness of tufting, design and color, as well as in texture. Plain and twisted yarns are used in a combination of cut and uncut tufts. Some of these rugs achieve their patterns solely by the manner in which they are sheared, so that they have been called *carved* rugs. They are available in all standard rug sizes, as well as in *broadloom* rolls which may be cut to any desired length. It is possible to make them in any color or pattern desired, but the majority of colors and patterns are nonperiod in character. Some patterns are produced in self-tones by shaving the pile to different lengths so that the pattern itself has a high pile and the field is short. Machine-made reproductions of these rugs are now made. A self-tone rug of this type is particularly suitable where plain carpet would be monotonous and a colored pattern excessive, and it is adaptable to any historical or modern type of interior.

Peasant rugs. There are many European countries where governmental authorities or societies established for the promotion of arts and crafts have developed native peasant industries. Many of these efforts have been applied to rug production but with varying degrees of success. Exportation has been handicapped by political and economic conditions. In some cases these rugs have been made from designs made in the United States to appeal to the American market. The cheap labor of China and India has been used for both the reproduction of European patterns and native patterns. Czechoslovakia, Finland, and the Scandi-

Modern hand-tufted, carved, and hooked rugs.

navian countries have produced interesting rugs using their native peasant motifs. Granada in southern Spain produces the Alpujarra rugs with delightful little animal and floral motifs woven in contrasting cut and uncut pile. Sardinia has made rugs for generations showing unique arrangements of animals and geometric figures in black, yellow, and red. Morocco furnishes small rugs with a loosely woven shaggy pile in natural colored wools and geometrical patterns. The mountaineers of the Balkan countries, Greece, and Yugoslavia also produce rugs in which the Oriental influence is in evidence.

Homemade Rugs

Needlepoint rugs, sometimes called embroidered rugs, are rare but they are the aristocrats of the homemade types. They have been made in Europe since the early years of the 18th century and the early housewives of America produced them in varying qualities of design. The most durable were made with a heavy wool yarn sewed in a cross-stitch pattern on a heavy net or canvas foundation cloth. Designs varied from copies of fine English and French patterns to characteristic peasant and farm motifs, the latter type being produced in New England and in the German settlements in Pennsylvania. Some of them were made in a single

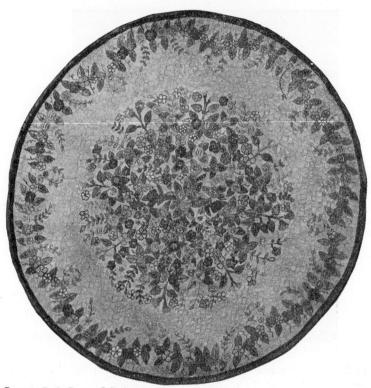

Early 19th century American hooked rug showing an unusually fine floral pattern.

piece and others made in squares that were sewn together. The value of such rugs if in good condition depends upon their color and pattern. There is little in the art of rug weaving that surpasses them in interest, and even at the present time they are made for home use by women who appreciate their charm and value. They are seldom found through usual supply sources and they are a challenge to the housewife and decorator who is looking for the unusual. It is said that approximately three hours time is required to make one square foot of such a rug.

Hooked rugs. These are the most interesting of the homemade types. They were produced in many European countries but their most prolific manufacture has been in New England and Nova Scotia. They may therefore rightly be considered an American product. The process of manufacturing is very simple. A design is outlined on a piece of coarse canvas or burlap (old feed sacks were often used), the fabric is then stretched on a frame, and strips of colored rags or short yarns are pushed through it, by means of a hooked needle, to form a pile and pattern. The pile may be cut or left uncut and the fineness of the weave depends upon the fineness of the foundation cloth. Patterns vary according to the artistic ability of the maker, who was usually a housewife; they include floral, patriotic, rural, humorous, and geometrical motifs; crudely represented houses, barnyard scenes, and ships are frequently shown; mottoes and bits of homely philosophy were often introduced; the words "Welcome" or "Beware of the Dog" were frequently woven on door mats. In many of the rugs

Mid-19th century hooked rug, showing humorous subject matter, typical of many of the period.

are woven quaint figures and ingenuous warnings or laments similar to the one showing two youthful lovers in a cushion-bedecked hammock captioned with "Caution! Endearing Words Are Sweet to Hear, as Many Have Found to Their Sorrow." And another with "Your Son Dear Mother is Now my Mate, So leave us Be & do not Tinker. I'll Run my Home, Hook, Line, & Sinker." In a few cases, designs have been obviously inspired by French rug patterns. Some interesting rugs were made of small squares sewed together, each square showing a different motif. As care was not taken in the selection of the cloth fragments, and many of the rugs were made from remnants of clothing, the dyes varied greatly in quality. Many colors were used in the patterns, but the most interesting compositions were the floral designs in light tints or those with black backgrounds. Variations in pile height were frequently introduced, the pattern being higher than the field. All shapes were produced. Collectors usually prefer the closely hooked, uncut pile types showing handsome bouquets and wreaths.

The hooked rag rug was not extensively made until the middle of the 19th century, so that it cannot be called a Colonial product, although it harmonizes well with all types of informal interiors. Handmade hooked rugs continue to be made in the Northeastern States but they are also produced in China, Puerto Rico, and other places. Imitations in a Brussels weave are now made on the Jacquard loom. There are also rugs of this type made of long cotton or wool strands which produce a shaggy finish.

A special type of hooked rug, first made in England, and later by the American colonists, was known as "turkey work," a name derived from the fact that the rugs were crude imitations of those from the Orient. Colored woolen yarns were pushed through a canvas cloth, and in some instances the pattern only was produced in pile, the background being an unfinished portion of the foundation cloth. These fabrics were used both for upholstery and floor coverings and were made by those who wished to imitate the Oriental rugs of their more opulent neighbors.

Rag and braided rugs. The rag rug was the original Colonial home-made rug. These were mostly made on a loom by farmers' wives. The materials consisted of old scraps of wool, cotton or linen, which were cut on the bias into narrow strips, and sewed together, regardless of color, to form a long strand. Two or three of these strands were usually twisted to form a weft yarn that was woven in plain weave on a linen or cotton warp. The looms were narrow so that the finished strips had to be joined to make a wide rug. There was no pattern and the fabric was reversible.

Another type of rag rug was the patchwork variety. In this kind, scraps of cloth were cut to fit floral or geometrical patterns, and sewed to a foundation cloth in an arrangement that resembled a mosaic. There was sometimes a padding introduced to add weight to the finished product. Many interesting patterns were made in this manner, but the rugs were not as durable as the pile types.

The braided rugs were made from twisted rag strips that were braided together into a sort of rope. These were then sewn into an oval or round shape; a few were rectangular. Usually no pattern was attempted, but some show concentric bands in alternating colors.

Rugs were also produced by knitting strands of rags into narrow strips and sewing the strips together. Crocheted rugs were made of the same materials in circular or oval shapes. Other methods of making fancy floor coverings were also used by the Colonial housewives; floral rosettes were made by superimposing small concentric circles of different colored cloths, each slightly smaller than the one below; these were sewed together on a foundation cloth. Sometimes the rugs of this type were made in patterns that resembled overlapping laural leaves or elongated diamond shapes.

Navajo rugs. The early Spanish settlers of the Southwest taught rug weaving to the Pueblo Indians, who in turn communicated their knowledge to the nomadic Navajos of Arizona and New Mexico. As the Spaniards also introduced sheep to these Indians, the ancestry of these rugs may be directly traced to Moorish and Oriental sources. The Navajo rugs were woven in plain weave and were used as blankets, clothing, and mats. They were woven in natural colored wools with black, white, or gray striped patterns. The Mexicans furnished red cloth to the Indians, who unravelled it and rewove the yarn into their blankets. They eventually obtained a red dye from a tree bark, and bartered for indigo, and these colors were then introduced in their patterns. By the middle of the

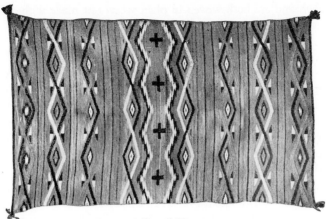

Navajo rug or blanket. Red background, pattern in white, blue, and yellow.

19th century chevron, zigzag, and diamond motifs and symbolic forms were often combined with straight border stripes. Navajo rugs are now made from commercial yarns and chemical dyes. Old patterns are repeated but colors have become unlimited and many light tints are used. Strong tonal contrasts in pattern and field are typical. The rugs are made only in small sizes, but they are gay in their effect and very adaptable to informal rooms.

Numdahs. These are an informal type of felt rug made in East India. They often are enriched with embroidered bird or floral designs.

Fiber, Flax, and Other Rugs

These include floor coverings that are made in materials of lower cost than wool and are intended mainly for porch, terrace, and other summer uses. They are frequently used, however, as a substitute for the more luxurious pile rugs in interiors of temporary use or where a low budget for decorating is necessary. The group includes the following:

Fiber rugs. This is a general name given to floor coverings that are made of paper pulp twisted into a yarn. The pulp is woven into either a plain or twill weave and may be used for both warp and weft or it may be combined with one of the other fibers such as wool, cotton, or sisal; the latter is a fiber that is grown in Java and the West Indies. These rugs are usually reversible. Simple striped patterns or textural effects are produced by alternating the colors or kinds of fiber. Coconut fiber is also used for small rugs. These are produced in both natural colors and dyed fiber, and are both woven in plain weaves or made with a pile; they are coarse in appearance and primarily suitable to porch use.

Linen rugs. Interesting and durable rugs up to 12 feet in width are made of coarse flax fibers. These are good for either interior or exterior use. They are the heaviest linen weave and are made in a variety of textures, weaves, and patterns, are reversible, and are issued in standard sizes under various trade names.

Rush and grass rugs. These vegetable fibers cannot be twisted but strands are made by combining them with cotton yarns. The fibers are tough and taken from weeds that grow in Europe and the Far East. They are then woven usually in a plain weave and either left in the natural colors or patterns are stencilled, sprayed, or painted on them. Occasionally small squares or other shapes are woven and sewed together to make large sizes. Grass rugs are usually varnished for protective purposes.

Thread and thrum. A flat, pileless carpet woven up to a width of 16 feet. It has a thick cotton warp, a thin wool weft, and has the general appearance of a tapestry weave. It is usually made to order in special colors.

Synthetic Floor Coverings

Among the floor coverings made from combinations of synthetic materials may be mentioned vinyl, linoleum, rubber, cork, and asphalt tile.

Vinyl is a plastic used extensively for floor tiles. It has a hard, slightly resilient surface and is reasonably resistant to denting, scratches, grease and acid stains. It is very suitable to heavy wear and particularly in kitchens and other service portions of a house. It is manufactured in variously dimensioned square and rectangular tile sizes of ⅛th and ¹⁄₁₂th inches in thickness, and in many colors, marbleized and woodgrained effects. It can be laid in patterns of contrasting shapes and colors and is often alternated with ceramic tiles or brass strips. It is also used as a binder in making tiles of cork, asphalt and asbestos.

Linoleum is a synthetic material made by pressing wheat flour, cork, asbestos, oil or other substances together to form a sheet. It is manufactured in rolls 6 and 9 feet wide and the standard thickness is ⅛th of an inch. Other thicknesses are available. Plain colors, strié and marbleized effects are popular with decorators but an unlimited number of patterns are available in printed and inlaid types. The inlay penetrates the entire thickness of the material and is more durable than the printed variety. Many novel cut-out pattern arrangements and borders in contrasting colors are possible. The material is durable, resilient and comparatively inexpensive. Linoleum can be laid on either a wood or cement floor. In laying linoleum, a felt paper lining and special adhesive should be used.

An interesting inlaid linoleum made from a special design and used in a traditional foyer. Any design may be produced in this material to correspond with the character or style of the room.

Rubber tile. Made of a rubber composition and resilient to the step, rubber tile is often used as a substitute where marble floors are desirable. It is made only in stock colors, which include a great variety of marbled types. Sheets are made 24 by 36 inches, and can be cut to any smaller size. The possibilities in pattern design are practically unlimited in this material. Rubber tile may be laid on any type of floor surface.

Cork. A popular material for floor covering, particularly in modern rooms. It is made ⅛ inch, ¼ inch, and ½ inch thick for floors, and in thin sheets for walls. The bulk of cork floor and wall covering is made in one of the three stock shades of brown, though it may also be stained to a variety of colors. The material is very resilient and is an excellent silencer. It may be laid on either concrete or wood. It is necessary to keep it waxed in order to preserve its surface.

Asphalt tile. This is a very serviceable type of flooring material, the principal advantage of which is that it can be furnished in an unlimited number of floor designs and a multitude of colors. It is nonporous and easy to maintain and is excellent for kitchens and commercial institutions where floors are exposed to greases and oils. The material is virtually fireproof and the colors are fade-resistant. It is furnished in differently dimensioned squares and strips that come in ⅛ inch or ³⁄₁₆ inch thicknesses. It is less expensive than rubber tile and can be laid on either a wood or concrete floor. Its disadvantage is that it scratches more easily than either linoleum or rubber.

Oriental Rugs

In the Orient the art of weaving rugs dates from the days of King Solomon. The history, romance, tradition, and poetry associated with the looms of the East recall the names of Croesus, Cyrus, Alexander the Great, Omar Khayyam, Genghis Khan, and Tamerlane, to say nothing of more modern mortals. The luxurious productions of the Eastern weavers have been in demand for the homes of Western civilization since the days of Marco Polo and the development of the earliest systems of long distance transportation.

Previous to about 1875, the utmost care was taken in the weaving of rugs in the Orient, particularly with regard to design, material, workmanship, and permanency of dyes. Rugs woven prior to that date are usually considered antiques. Since the development of modern transportation facilities, the demand for Oriental rugs has increased to such an extent that their manufacture has become commercialized. Although Oriental rugs are still made on hand looms, as in earlier times, quantity production in factories has been attempted, with less experienced craftsmen, a speeding of effort, a cheapening of materials, and the use of aniline instead of vegetable dyes. The most salable antique patterns, however, with all their conventions and symbolisms, continue today to be blindly repeated by the makers.

The older rugs were made in the homes of the inhabitants, the designs passing from father to son and being preserved with great care. Some of the modern rugs are of nomad origin and are still produced by the old methods; but the majority are today made on a commercial scale. Antique Oriental rugs are generally of great beauty, and are seldom obtained except at very high prices, and are rarely seen except in museums and the homes of wealthy collectors.

Classification. There are six main classifications of Oriental rugs, and less than fifty common kinds. The majority of these are named after their probable birthplace or the towns from which they are imported. The name of a rug does not guarantee quality, as both superior and inferior grades are made in all places. The important essential ingredients in all rugs are design, material, and workmanship, and of these, from the decorator's standpoint, design—which includes color—is by far the most important. The six classifications are Persian, Indian, Turkoman, Caucasian, Turkish, and Chinese.

Persian rugs are profusely decorated with a great variety of flowers, leaves, vines, and occasional birds and animals woven in a free-hand manner and considerably conventionalized with purely decorative intent. They generally have an all-over pattern, and the ground is almost entirely covered. The colors are soft and delicate, blending with one another in a

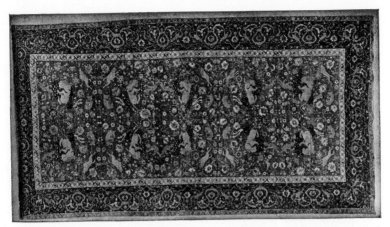

Persian rug of early 16th century, showing animal pattern with claret ground. Details accented by a silver thread.

Persian rug of 17th century, probably Kerman. Tree design with claret red ground and light-colored pattern.

most pleasing manner. Many of the patterns start from a central medallion. The lines of the patterns are always graceful. Among the most popular of the Persian rugs are the *Saraband,* whose entire field is covered with a repeating pattern of palm leaves, such as are used on an Indian shawl design, with a rose or blue ground; the *Ispahan* or *Herat,* having a coarse pile showing an intricate, stately design on a claret ground; the *Hamadan,* a camel's-hair rug with a coarse weave in light browns, reds, and blues;

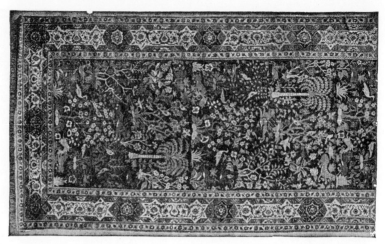

Indian rug of the early 17th century. Animal and foliage pattern on a dark red ground with star border.

Turkoman rug of the 19th century. Beluchistan, with light tan field and red border. The pattern in vivid colors shows the typical crudely drawn geometric figures.

the *Kerman* and *Kermanshah,* with a fine pile in soft cream, rose, light blue, and other pastel colors; the *Sarook,* having a fine pile in dark reds and blues mixed with lighter colors; the *Bijar,* as thick as two or three ordinary rugs; the *Polonaise,* a delicately colored antique silk rug; the *Sehna,* the closet-woven small rug with a minute pattern; and the *Fera-ghan,* usually produced with a small all-over design of flowers or conventional forms arrayed in rows.

Indian rugs are those in which flowers, leaves, vines, and occasional animals are woven in a naturalistic manner. In the earlier rugs, of which few remain, the weavers drew the flowers as though they were botanical specimens. In the later Indian rugs many copies of Persian patterns were made, but the copies are always easily recognized. The colors in these rugs are often brilliant. In broad generalization, the two classifications of Oriental rugs that are decorated almost exclusively with flowers are the Persian and the Indian, and their style and patterns are so distinct that their identification is comparatively easy. The leading place names associated with Indian rugs are *Agra, Lahore, Kashmir,* and *Srinagar.*

Turkoman rugs, comprising the products of *Turkestan, Bokhara, Afghanistan,* and *Beluchistan,* are red rugs with web fringes, or apron ends woven in kindergarten patterns—squares, diamonds, octagons, stars, and crosses. The forms are nearly always of pure geometric linear design. They are closely woven, with a short firm pile. That the wild tribes of these localities should dye their wools in the shades of blood and weave the designs of childhood is fitting and logical.

Caucasian rugs, also the product of a wild section of Central Asia, differ from the Turkoman rugs chiefly in being dyed in other colors than blood red, in omitting apron ends, and in being more crowded, elaborate, and pretentious in geometric linear pattern. The Caucasian weaver's distinction as the Oriental cartoonist, the expert in wooden men, women, and animals, is well deserved. He holds the Oriental rug patent on Noah's-ark designs. Incidentally, Mount Ararat and Noah's grave, "shown" near Nakitchevan, are actually located on the southern border of the Caucasus.

Some of the design forms resemble snow crystals, others are not unlike the patterns of the Navaho and other American Indian blankets. The eight-pointed star is a great favorite, and forms borrowed from the Persian are occasionally used. Borders are often wide and important. The designs are bold and the colors brilliant and strongly contrasted, imitating mosaic effects. The principal rugs of the Caucasus are those of *Daghestan, Shirvan, Soumak, Kuba, Ghendje,* and *Cashmere,* the last generally attributed to India.

Turkish rugs, sometimes called *Asia-Minor,* are of both geometrical and floral design, but can be distinguished from Persian and Indian products by the ruler-drawn character of their patterns. They often show quasi-botanical forms, angularly treated. Turkish rugs that contain the patterns common to the Caucasian and Turkoman families can be recognized by their brighter, sharper, and more contrasting colors. The key to the identification of this most difficult rug family is to be found in the Turkish prayer rugs. To know Turkish rugs, one must see many of them; to know the other families, one need see only a few. *Ghiordes* was famous for making prayer rugs. *Bergamo* was justly esteemed for its shaggy rugs of individual designs. Many rugs actually made in the interior are attributed to *Smyrna,* a port town. The *Anatolian* and *Armenian* rugs are also classified with the Turkish.

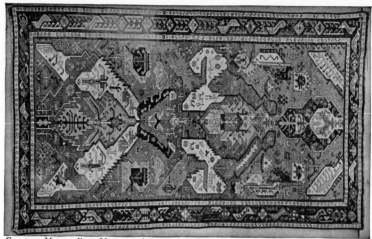

Caucasian rug. A late 18th century Soumak with rose-red ground and pattern in gray, green, white, and yellow, showing jagged-edged medallions and highly conventionalized animals and figures.

Seventeenth century Turkish prayer rug from Asia Minor. Bright red ground and deep blue border showing influence of 16th century Turkish floral carpets.

Chinese rugs can be recognized instantly by their colors; these are determined by their backgrounds—the reverse of the Persian method, which is to make the design the principal color medium. The Chinese colors are probably best described as lighter and softer colors of silk—dull yellows, rose, salmon-red, browns, and tans, the design usually being in blue. The

Turkish rug. Early 17th century, Armenian. Dull red ground showing leaf forms in compartments in indigo and ivory. Conventionalized dragon motifs also shown.

Chinese were the original manufacturers and dyers of silk, and they applied their silk dyes to their rugs.

The older Chinese rugs frequently show designs influenced by the Buddhist, Taoist, and Lamaist faiths. Symbolism was of the utmost importance. The Precious Things, The Hundred Antiques, The Fragrant Fingers of Buddha, the peony, the waves and clouds of eternity, the mythical dragon, the fabulous lion, the heavenly dog trying to devour the moon, the horse, the bat, the butterfly serving as the symbol of Cupid, the temple bells, and other distinctive features are found in the patterns.

The best periods of antique Chinese rugs were the K'ang Hsi (1662–1723) and the Ch'ien Lung (1736–1796). The patterns of these periods have been extensively copied ever since they were originated, but unfortunately commercialism has entered the field and many of the modern Chinese producers have disregarded the old traditions and created patterns solely to appeal to an uninformed European and American public.

Weaves and knots. The majority of Oriental rugs are woven with knots, the ends of which are cut off, forming a pile. There are two kinds woven without knots. They are *Khilims* and *Soumaks,* the latter sometimes called *Cashmere* rugs. Khilims are Oriental tapestries. The design is obtained by frequent changes of weft colors. The face and back of this rug appear to be alike. The best of Khilims, known as *Sehna,* are rightly among the most desirable of Oriental weavings. Khilims are thin and light in weight, but are often quite durable. They can be attractively used for table and couch covers and for wall hangings.

The Soumak rug, from Shemakha in the Caucasus, and not from India as is commonly supposed, has three parts to its weave. In addition to the

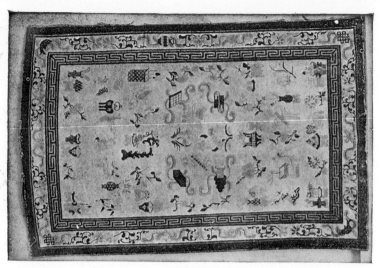

Chinese 18th century Ch'ien-Lung rug. Cream-colored ground and pattern in two shades of yellow and blue. The field is covered with Taoist symbols.

warp and weft, which form only the basis of the fabric, the pattern is made by a stitch woven in and out between the warp threads. The stitch passes over four warp threads, back under two, forward over four again, and so on, making a smooth surface. The ends of the threads are left loose on the back, as on a Cashmere shawl; this has caused these rugs to be known incorrectly as Cashmeres.

The third type, or *knotted rug,* is the one most generally used. Here the weft is a mere binder, the entire surface, or pile, being formed by the ends of threads knotted around the warps. Two types of knot are used, the Ghiordes or Turkish, and the Sehna or Persian. The former is used in Turkey, the Caucasus, and parts of Persia, the latter throughout the greater part of Asia, including China, Turkestan, Beluchistan, and most of Persia.

To make the Ghiordes knot, a short piece of thread is laid across two warps, and the ends are carried down outside and up between them, and pulled tight. In the Sehna knot, one end is treated in this manner, but the other passes down between the two threads and up outside. In either case the pile is of wool, but the warp and weft may be of wool, cotton, or a mixture of the two, or occasionally of camel's hair or silk.

In addition to these Oriental knots, there is another used by Spanish weavers that is called a single knot. To produce this knot, each warp thread is completely circled by each pile thread, the two ends of the latter being brought upward to form the pile surface. There is a separate weft system of threads that serves to hold the warps together.

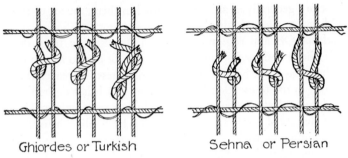

Ghiordes or Turkish   Sehna or Persian

DIAGRAM SHOWING MANNER OF TYING KNOTS IN ORIENTAL RUGS.

Fibers and materials. A great variety of materials is used in the making of Oriental rugs. Wool is the all-important textile of the industry; cotton, the base and binder; hair and silk, the occasional materials. Hemp, jute, and linen are also used in their manufacture; but to be a real judge of rugs, one must be a judge of wools. Wool is a modified form of hair, distinguishable from it by its softness, curl, and elasticity, and by the microscopic overlapping scales of its surface. It is sometimes impossible to determine whether an animal fiber is wool or hair, because the one by degrees merges into the other. Fine wool has as many as 2,800 scales to the inch. Poor wool has not more than 500. This makes a difference in Oriental rugs in the absorption and retention of dye.

The best wool is taken from the shoulders and sides of the young sheep, goat, or camel. Wool taken from old, undernourished, or dead animals is of second and third grade. The importance of the quality and condition of the wool in Oriental rugs is accentuated by the possible effects of the processes that are applied to finish them for the market. These processes, known as washing or treating, are the application to new rugs of various chemical solutions that diminish the strength of the raw dyes and colors. If carelessly applied, these solutions actually consume the fabric. When applied to good wools and dyes, they do little or no damage. As practically all modern Oriental rugs are treated, the buyer must concern himself to secure rugs that have been wisely treated.

Dyes and coloring. The dyes used exclusively in the East until a comparatively few years ago were vegetable and natural dyes. The vegetable dyes were obtained from leaves, flowers, roots, berries, bark, and nuts. Cochineal is the stock example of a natural insect dye. These were the materials that made Oriental rugs famous, and the recipes were carefully guarded secrets. Substitutes have been found for every dye, however. Alizarin dye is an artificial dyestuff obtained from coal-tar. Aniline, invented in 1856, has gradually eliminated the natural dyes. Many of the aniline dyes are as permanent as the natural or vegetable dyes. If the color schemes, designs, and wools of the Oriental rugs woven today were as satisfactory generally as are the dyes used in them, the art of rug weaving would be on a very high plane.

Defects. Oriental rugs may have defects resulting from the depredations of heels and moths, and from the dry rot due to age and salt water; and they may have holes, cuts, and crookedness in weave. Old rugs that are worn to the foundation in sections are much less desirable for service than those with the pile of fair depth which is worn evenly. The deep and serious defects of a rug are easily detected by holding it to the light, and by examining its back. Heavy beating to clean a rug, quickly ruins it. Light beating with a wicker mat is allowable. Sweeping and vacuum cleaning can do little harm, if not too vigorously applied.

Values. There are three possible values in every Oriental rug—the utility value, the art value, and the collector's value. The utility value depends entirely upon the durability of the fabric as a floor covering. The art value depends upon the color and design rather than upon the texture. The collector's value depends upon the rarity of the art value. It follows that Oriental rugs are valued and priced according to individual worth, and that the honest dealer can neither ask more than a rug is worth nor confess attempted extortion by radical price reductions. The fairness of the price is proportionate usually to the honesty of the dealer. To judge the quality of an Oriental rug is a matter requiring considerable study, and the amateur will be well-advised not to attempt this without the aid of an expert or a dealer whose reputation is unquestioned.

The use of Oriental rugs. It has often been stated that a room in which a large and beautiful Oriental rug is used needs little else in the way of decoration. Certainly it needs little else in the way of patterned surfaces. As a consequence, plain or inconspicuously patterned coverings for chairs and sofas are usually necessary to avoid confusion and to act as a foil and contrast. From a decorative angle, the dominant colors in an Oriental rug should set the color scheme for the room and should be recalled in the draperies, upholstery coverings, and walls, if possible. Oriental rugs should be used only in formal rooms. They are suitable for all the sophisticated types of decoration that are based upon the historic periods.

Selection and Laying of Rugs and Carpets

In nearly all rooms of the house, with the possible exception of entrance halls and sunporches, it is preferable to cover the floor with rugs, carpets, or other forms of covering. Floor coverings add warmth, dull the noise of footsteps, help silence any possible echo, and by their pattern, weave, or color, make an important contribution to the general scheme of decoration.

Floor coverings should generally be considered as backgrounds for the furniture, and although patterned materials may be used, these should never be obtrusive. Strong color contrasts between pattern and field are psychologically uncomfortable to tread upon, and as a general rule plain-colored floor coverings should be subdued in tone. The floor covering, whether patterned or plain, should always have its color or colors repeated elsewhere in the room. A floor covering that is in a colored pattern usually will not permit the use of other important colored patterns on the wall or larger pieces of upholstered furniture. Plain rugs and carpets have been woven only since about 1900 and they have consistently grown in popularity since that date. Texture mottling, pepper and salt effects made by twisting different colored threads in the pile, and patterns produced by contrasting pile heights have served to give them surface interest.

The question frequently arises as to the relative merits of rugs and carpets. Formerly rugs were preferred because they could be easily removed and cleaned, but to some extent the vacuum cleaner has eliminated this objection. The wall-to-wall carpet must be cut to fit the room, which may make it unsuited to the shape of a new one in case of removal. There are, however, wide carpets sold under trade names that are manufactured with a coating of latex on their backs which prevents ravelling in case the fabric has to be cut; these carpets may be patched in any part, or added to without a visible seam, and mosaic patterns may be easily introduced in contrasting colors. This type eliminates the principal disadvantage of wall-to-wall carpet. If parquet flooring is used in a room, many persons prefer rugs that leave a border showing the woodwork, although this tends to make a room look smaller. All-over carpets are generally recommended for rooms in cold climates. The choice between a rug or a carpet is eventually a matter of individual taste.

Carpets should be sufficiently large to fit the dimensions of the room up to the baseboard. Where breaks occur in the shape of the room, around hearths, and elsewhere, the carpet should be cut to fit, and the cut edges should be thoroughly sewed to prevent ravelling. As broadloom carpets come in stock widths, one can usually be found to correspond closely to the width of a room. Any length is obtainable.

It is advisable to have carpets laid over a layer of felt, ozite, or other inexpensive manufactured products that are made for this purpose. The extra layer of felt adds to the softness and durability of the floor covering.

Domestic carpets come in a very wide range of colors, and the color effect of a pile fabric changes according to the direction from which one looks at it, and the amount of light thrown upon it. As the pile has a tendency to bend sideways, the color effect is much darker when one looks into the pile than when one looks at the side of it. This condition must be considered in deciding in which direction a carpet should be laid. As a rule, neutral-colored, dark-toned floor coverings are the most satis factory from every point of view. Greater novelty and more up-to-date effects may be carried out in white and light pastel shades, but because of the fact that such colors rapidly become dull from dust, they must be frequently cleaned and the expense of upkeep is high.

Bibliography

BODE, W., AND KUEHNEL, E., *Antique Rugs from the Near East* (tr. Riefstahl). E. Weyhe Co., New York, 1922. Illustrated text.

CLIFFORD, C. R., *Rugs of the Orient.* Clifford and Lawton, New York, 1911. Illustrated text.

DILLEY, A. U., *Oriental Rugs and Carpets.* E. Weyhe Co., New York, 1936. An authoritative treatment of this subject, beautifully written and thoroughly illustrated.

FARADAY, E., *European and American Carpets and Rugs.* Grand Rapids, 1929. An illustrated history of hand-woven floor coverings of Europe and modern machine-made carpets of Europe and America. Some color illustrations.

HACKMACK, A., *Chinese Carpets and Rugs* (tr. Arnold). La Librairie Française, Tientsin. A good concise text with excellent plates, some colored. Good diagrams of Chinese symbols and their meanings.

HOLT, R. B., *Rugs, Oriental and Occidental, Antique and Modern.* A. C. McClurg and Co., Chicago, 1927. An illustrated handbook on this subject.

MAYERS, F. J., *Carpet Designs and Designing.* F. Lewis, Ltd., London, 1934. Good text illustrated with diagrams, halftones, and color prints.

O'BRIEN, M., *The Rug and Carpet Book.* M. Barrows and Co., New York, 1946. An excellent handbook on domestic and imported floor coverings for the layman.

Tapis Anciens de la Chine. Henri Ernst, Paris, 1932. Twenty fine colored plates.

TATTERSALL, C. E. C., *A History of British Carpets.* F. Lewis, Ltd., London, 1934. A complete and illustrated treatment of this subject from the introduction of the craft until the present day.

WALKER, L. LeB., *Homecraft Rugs.* Frederick A. Stokes Co., New York, 1929. Excellent text illustrated with diagrams and color plates.

CHAPTER XIV

WALLPAPERS

The invention of wallpaper was a very fortunate occurrence in the history of the decorative arts, because it permitted people of small means to enrich their walls with gay patterns—a decoration which before had only been possible with painted murals or expensive fabrics.

It is hard to know exactly when wallpaper was first made. Records state that it was used in China as far back as 200 B.C. All old Chinese wallpaper was hand painted, and the system of hand painting was maintained well through the 18th century. Chinese wallpaper was imported into France and England in the early years of the 16th century. At that time the Oriental painted papers came in small rectangles about 12½ by 16½ inches. The Chinese patterns were made without a definite effect of light and shade; flat tones were used with contrasting colors; and birds and flowers were popular subjects. After 1750, landscape effects were produced in false perspective.

The Dominotiers. The demand for a cheap patterned wall decoration increased greatly in Europe after the importation of the Chinese examples. A guild of painters and papermakers known as the Dominotiers was established in France in the latter half of the 16th century to create a domestic substitute. The Dominotiers produced papers that imitated marble graining, and also made papers covered with small hand-painted or stencilled patterns and grotesques.

During the 15th and 16th centuries, the wealthy classes in Europe were covering their plaster walls with wood, tapestries, and leather. In the 17th century the walls of the palaces were hung with brocades, velvets, and damasks. Le François in 1620 introduced a method of imitating brocaded velvets in paper. Paper made in this fashion was known as flock paper. A textile pattern was printed in varnish on paper sheets; powdered wool was then scattered over the pattern, and when dry, the result looked remarkably like velvet. Flock papers were made in England in 1634.

An example of an original painted Chinese scenic paper similar to those brought to America on the trading ships in the middle of the 18th century and used in the Colonial rooms of the period.

Papillon's influence (about 1688). Jean Papillon, a Frenchman, was the first to make paper designs in repeating patterns that would match on all sides when the separate sheets were pasted together. Papillon produced his patterns by carving them in large wood-blocks, covering the blocks with the necessary pigments, and then pressing them against sheets of paper. In this way he could make a much greater quantity of patterned paper than by painting each sheet separately. By using separate blocks for each color, he could print any pattern in any number of colors desired. Papillon is the real inventor of wallpaper as it is known today.

Madame de Pompadour used both flock papers and Papillon designs and had much to do with popularizing the use of wallpaper in France during the mid-18th century. As this was the period of the famous chinoiseries and singeries in French art, many of the wallpaper patterns were made with similar motifs and subject matter.

Reveillon's productions. In 1752 Reveillon started a wallpaper shop and factory in Paris. With the increasing demand for cheaper types of wall decoration, he produced pictorial hand-blocked panels that were intended to replace the paintings that were being used in the fields of wood panels, then popular in French interior decoration. Small panels and vignettes were also designed for overdoor and overmantel trumeaux. Reveillon was a remarkable craftsman and made some of the most beautiful wallpaper patterns ever produced. Many of the original hand-blocks made by Reveillon are in existence today and have been used in making reproductions of his work. At times he employed designers to assist him, some of whom had also worked for Oberkampf, the manufacturer of toiles-de-Jouy. Among them was Huet.

Reveillon's factory was partially destroyed during the French Revolution, and he was forced to flee to England, where he died in 1795. His factory was later operated by Jacquemart and Benard, who continued his processes with designs in the Directoire and Empire feeling.

Jackson and later manufacturers. John Baptist Jackson was one of the most important persons connected with the wallpaper industry in England. He studied and worked in Paris under Papillon, and in Venice, and opened a factory in Battersea, England, in 1746. He was particularly known for his pictorial panels framed in hand-blocked representations of stucco forms designed in a rococo manner. The subject matter of his panels was selected from Venetian and Roman landscapes and French engravings.

During the latter years of the 18th century, scenic papers were produced in France and Alsace by Joseph Dufour and Jean Zuber. These greatly differed from the earlier pictorial papers that were intended for small panels only. The scenic papers were made in a series of connecting

Examples of French wallpaper. LEFT: *An interesting early Louis XIV flock paper in an all-over pattern with cream ground and grayish brown design.* RIGHT: *A Louis XVI wallpaper showing a dainty pattern of natural flowers and cupids very similar to contemporary textile designs. The pattern is attributed to Jacquemart and Benard.*

Courtesy Nancy McClelland

Louis XVI wallpaper used to cover a screen. The design is attributed to Reveillon and consists of arabesques and medallions in colors on a tan ground.

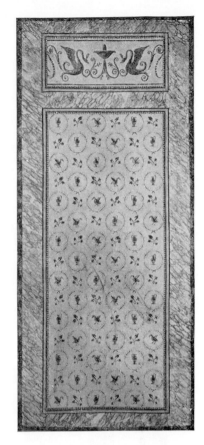

Publisher's Photo Service

Interesting wallpapers. LEFT: *French Empire paper much used in early 19th century American homes. The background is pumpkin-colored and the scenes are said to represent the King of Rome playing in the gardens of Versailles.* RIGHT: *Paper made to imitate marble. The panel inset of alternating medallion and foliage motifs and the small top panel are framed with strips of moldings and marbled paper.*

strips that were intended to cover the entire wall space of a room from the top of a low dado to the cornice or ceiling.

From 1800 until 1850 scenic papers were printed from hand-blocks. The popularity of the scenic designs spread over the whole of Europe and America. A great variety of subject matter was produced, such as land-scapes, seascapes, town views, places, and events. Because the invention of this type of wallpaper occurred at a time when the classic arts were being revived, many patterns showed classical ruins and mythological figures. The papers were made in both colored and *monotone* effects and so intricate were many of the designs that 3,000 wood-blocks were neces-

Paper designed by John Baptist Jackson and dated 1786. Notice the Rococo scrolls used to frame the panels, and the characteristic scene of Roman ruins.

Colonial paper in the hall of Hamilton House, South Berwick, Maine. The repetition of the arch motif is softened by the intertwining garlands. The design of this paper is similar to that used in Paul Revere's home

sary to produce them. The paper stock used in their manufacture was made entirely from linen rags, which explains the lasting qualities of some of the antique examples.

Wallpaper was first printed in America about 1739 by Plunket Fleeson of Philadelphia, who built up a considerable business in domestic wares because of the high duty imposed on the imported article.

Printing long rolls of paper in all-over patterns was begun about 1800. Machine printing on cheap paper started about 1840, at which time thought in the development of patterns ceased, and all efforts were placed upon methods of lowering the cost of manufacturing. It has only been during the 20th century that a renewal of the appreciation of merit in wallpaper design has been noticeable.

Modern manufacturing methods. There are three processes of making wallpapers in general use today. The ordinary commercial types are printed by the cylinder process. Strips of paper of the required width are run through presses that are furnished with as many metal rollers as there are colors in the pattern. Each roller prints all the parts of a pattern that are in similar color. A careful setting of the rollers is required so that an accurate registry occurs for all the pattern subdivisions and colors. The speed of the press requires the use of colors that dry rapidly, but heat is supplied to the moving strip of paper to aid in this process. The second method is by the old hand-block method in which each motif in a repeat is imprinted by hand-pressing a separate wooden block engraved with a portion of the pattern in the proper position. The third method, which is now largely substituted for hand-blocking, is by the silk-screen process. A wooden frame the full size of a pattern repeat is made for each color of the pattern. On each frame is tightly stretched a sheet of silk. On each stretch are drawn the parts of a pattern that are to be printed in the same color; the remaining portion is then heavily varnished. A paper strip is laid flat on a long table and each repeat is printed by applying to it the series of frames, and painting the unvarnished portions of each with the required pigment that seeps through the silk. The colors are allowed to dry between the application of each frame, and it is possible to overprint any of them with other opaque colors to produce highlights or additional shadows in the motifs. Overprinting is not possible with cylinder presses, so that hand-blocked or screen-printed papers are more interesting in appearance and are of course more costly to produce.

Wallpaper sizes. Scenic wallpapers are made in series of separate strips, 19 inches wide and 6 to 10 feet long. A different number of strips composes each complete set. If there are not sufficient strips in a single set to cover the walls of a room, it is necessary to use additional strips or to cover only a portion of the walls of the room. In repeat patterns made by the hand-block process, the repeat may be longer than in machine-made

Courtesy Nancy McClelland

*Beautiful paper frieze of classic design that is a reproduction of plaster orna-
ment in the Petit Trianon, Versailles.*

papers, where the repeats must be the same length as the circumference
of the roller that prints them. This dimension may vary, but in most
papers of this type the repeat has been standardized at 14½, 18, or 21
inches. French commercial papers are usually ½ meter or about 19 inches
wide. English papers are 22 inches, and American papers vary from 20
to 21 inches in width, which dimension includes a selvage that must be
trimmed before use, reducing the width of the paper to 18 inches. A few
American papers are made 30 inches wide. Wallpapers are sold by the
roll, which always consists of exactly 36 square feet. Papers are delivered
in what is known as a *bolt* or *stick* or *bundle* which may consist of 1½,
2, or 3 rolls.

Figuring quantities. In ordering scenic wallpaper, the exact perimeter
of the walls of the room should be figured in inches. The width of the
doors and windows should be deducted. This length should be divided by
the width of each strip; the result will give the number of strips required.
In ordering all-over patterned wallpaper by the roll, the square foot area
of the walls to be covered should be figured. The percentage of wastage
in cutting and hanging wallpaper is very great. Each strip must be in one
piece for the full height of the wall. Patched strips are not permissible.
Patterns must be matched for adjoining strips, and much cutting is often
required around doors, windows, mantels, and other architectural features, so that a considerable allowance must be made for such wastage. It

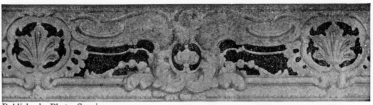

Interesting Victorian cornice frieze of flock paper with grisaille pattern on an orange-red background.

is therefore the custom in figuring the number of rolls required for a wall area, to divide the number of square feet of the wall area by 30 instead of 36 to give the number of required rolls. It is, however, customary to subtract from this quotient ½ roll for each normal size door and window. As papers are sold in uncut "bolts," "sticks," or "bundles," the total number of rolls ordered must be evenly divisible by the number of rolls that the manufacturer supplies in each bolt. As an example, if the desired paper is furnished by the manufacturer in 3 rolls to a bolt, and the room calls for 26 rolls of paper, it would be necessary to order 27 rolls or 9 uncut bolts, because 27 is exactly divisible by 3. A slight excess in the required amount is always desirable for future patching or repairs.

Preparation of walls. For reasons of protection it is advisable to put a lining paper on the wall before applying the finer papers. This protects the finished paper from absorbing discoloration from the plaster, and usually prevents the showing of cracks that may appear. Both the lining paper and finished paper should be applied with butt joints rather than overlapping joints.

When very expensive antique or scenic wallpaper is used, the walls should always be covered in advance with muslin, and the paper glued to the fabric. This will permit removing the paper without tearing, if occasion for this should arise. Valuable wallpaper may be *sized* (covered with a coating of glue or gelatin) and then shellacked with white shellac. This protects the paper from dirt, dust, and finger marks and permits gentle washing with a damp rag. Care should be taken in applying the size to prevent the colors from running, as many wallpapers are printed with water-color or tempera paints that dissolve when liquids are used. The shellacking tends to give the paper a warm yellowish tone, gives it a slightly antique appearance, causes the colors to be more brilliant, and to be blended in a more harmonious effect.

Character of patterns. The most expensive wallpapers are the pictorial panels and scenic types. All-over repeating patterns come in unlimited numbers of subjects and colors, although each pattern is usually made in only a few different color schemes. Appropriate wallpaper patterns may

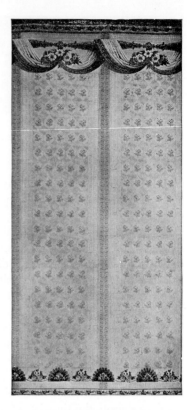

French wallpapers. LEFT: *Eighteenth century paper with an all-over design of salmon-pink pomegranates and green stems on a yellow background.* RIGHT: *Directoire paper in which a spot pattern alternates with vertical stripes. The drapery frieze and base-border motifs are added features.*

now be had for any room in the house. Floral and leaf patterns are the most common, and usually the conventionalized forms are in best taste. Too great realism is inadvisable. Many striped, abstract, and textile patterns may also be found. Where walls are completely covered with paper it is sometimes advisable to create an effect of variety by using extra borders at the top or baseboard of the room or around door and window trim. Many borders are made that correspond to special wallpaper patterns, and panel effects may also be produced by border strips. In this arrangement, the wallpaper is used inside the panel and the stiles are covered with a contrasting plain paper or one which corresponds to the background of the patterned paper.

Papers are also made to imitate marble and wood graining. This type should be applied in stiles and panels arranged in the same manner as real marble or woodwork.

Courtesy Nancy McClelland

One of a series of historic scenic papers known as "Venetian Scenes," which were produced in grisaille or sepia. Many papers of this type were hand-painted as well as printed by the hand-block process.

Courtesy Museum of Fine Arts, Boston

Scenic paper known as "The Seasons," taken from a house in Hanover, New Hampshire, and properly used above a dado.

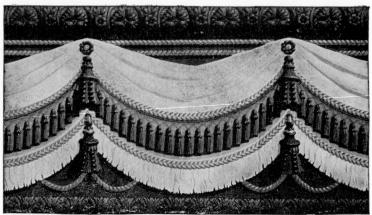

Drapery frieze paper in mauve, gold, and blue. An early design by Dufour, before he turned to making scenic papers.

Wallpaper reproductions of architectural features are also obtainable. Column, pilaster, dado, arch, and cornice effects have been extensively used to good advantage by leading decorators. These forms necessitate a careful advance design for the layout so that the wall composition will be agreeable. Various trellis patterns are also available for rooms requiring an outdoor effect. Waterproof wallpapers are available for use in bathrooms or places that are apt to be damp.

In addition to wallpaper, thin wood *veneers* are now obtainable in rolls and may be applied to the walls in the same way that paper is. As this is a comparatively new material, the effect is usually modern in character.

Certain photographers specialize in making what are known as "photo-murals." These consist of enormous paper enlargements of photographs, drawings, prints, or other pictures. The enlargements are in black and white, but they may also be tinted in colors so that they have an effect on a wall similar to a scenic paper or mural decoration and, of course, have the advantage of being unique.

The use of wallpaper. A room that is treated with wallpaper needs less furnishing and fewer accessories than one whose walls are treated in a plain color. The wallpaper, particularly if it be a scenic type, becomes the most prominent decorative element in the room. The stronger the colors and contrasts of the pattern, the more outstanding is the effect, and if they are too sharp, the walls, instead of remaining a background for the furnishings, protrude into the decorative scheme.

Wallpaper makes a room gayer in appearance and more restless in effect. Many wallpapers fatigue the eye if one is constantly forced to look at them. This point, therefore, should be seriously considered before

Drix Duryea, Photo-Muralist

One of the great uses of photo-murals is in producing enlargements of actual scenes from nature. Such a feature is particularly appropriate (ABOVE) *in the office of a travel bureau.* BELOW: *An entrance lobby decorated with photo-murals which are enlargements of drawings made in the classical manner. The photographs are framed with a wallpaper border which is also used as a cornice and base decoration and door trim enrichment.*

Moldings and borders are extremely useful for giving a finished appearance to an all-over paper design or for creating the effect of panelling. They are available in many widths, colors, and patterns.

making a choice between wallpaper or plain-colored walls. To counteract this disadvantage some rooms are treated with wallpaper on only part of the wall area, although there must be a logical reason for using it in this manner. Pictorial panels and scenic papers are the best to use for this purpose.

Wallpapers in pale or neutral colors, monotones, patterns showing a large area of background, or papers in which the pattern and background are close in tonal value are more suitable for covering entire walls in rooms of constant use such as bedrooms and living rooms. Wallpapers of patterns that contrast strongly with their backgrounds may be used to advantage in entrance halls, passageways, guest rooms, and other portions of the house less permanently occupied. Patterns having vertical stripes tend to give a higher appearance to a room, but, if the color contrast of the stripes is strong, the effect may become very fatiguing.

Wallpaper patterns may conflict with other wall decorations such as pictures, wall sconces, and hanging objects. If one desires to use the latter with wallpaper, it is necessary to use a wallpaper of delicate colors and rather small-scale pattern; or, if this is not possible, to use only pictures that are large enough not to be lost in the pattern of the paper. Rooms in which wallpapers are used usually require very few other patterned surfaces. In order to attain optical relief and contrast if a wallpaper has a prominent pattern, drapery materials should preferably be in plain colors

Type of wallpaper with small figure scenes, garland frieze, and base border, popular in America during the early 19th century. The subject of this paper is "Blind Love."

or inconspicuous patterns and the draperies themselves designed with simple edging, fringe, or ruffling of a different hue. The same idea may be carried out in the upholstery materials, although it is less important to maintain simplicity of surface in the upholstery than in the window draperies.

It is usually wise to allow the colors of the wallpaper pattern to fix the color scheme for the whole room by distributing the wallpaper colors in the furnishings, draperies, and trimmings.

The scale of a wallpaper pattern is of the utmost importance. While there is no unalterable rule regarding this matter, generally speaking small patterns are used for small rooms and large patterns for large rooms; but much depends upon the pattern and its strength of tonal value. Experience and a test of a large sample of the paper in the room where it is to be placed is the only safe method of determining whether the scale of the pattern appears too large or too small. The subject of the pattern must also be considered from the point of view of suitability to the character of the room. Small samples of wallpaper tested on a white plaster wall are apt to be lighter in appearance than they will be when the walls are completely covered with the paper, and the room furnished and curtains hung. For this reason it is advisable to select a paper that appears a little too light in the sample.

In order to be sure of making a good selection, it is perhaps wise to obtain a paper that is a copy or close imitation of an antique design. However, many excellent modern designs have been produced. In recent years there has been a great increase in the appreciation of good design on the part of both the manufacturers and the public. As the range of patterns in wallpaper is exceedingly wide, it is impossible to give a complete list. In the early part of the century, English and French wallpapers were usually in colors and patterns that were superior to the machine-made papers produced in the United States; but, at the present time, there are many manufacturers and individuals in the United States who are producing screen-printed papers of exquisite design and coloring. Since 1945 Japanese grass paper, also called grass-cloth, has become increasingly popular in this country although it is not inexpensive. During moments away from work in the fields, oriental peasants have for generations diverted themselves by weaving together fibers of grass or ramie creating a slightly rough textured effect. Today grass-cloth is frequently used as a substitute for wallpaper. It is available in many colors.

There are many other uses for wallpapers in addition to surfacing walls. Niches or closets may be lined with them, drapery valance boards and head boards of beds may be given pattern interest, or a bright colored pattern may be introduced under the glass of a dressing table top. Laundry and wastepaper baskets may be covered. Drawers and cabinet shelves may be lined. Door panels may be enriched. Screens may be covered, and wallpaper borders, friezes, and door trims may be added to painted rooms. These uses are particularly adaptable to informal and inexpensive types of decorating.

A brief list of some of the most popular types follows:

1. Plain colors.
2. Small-scale all-over patterns.
3. Spot patterns composed of evenly distributed stars, dots, rosettes, or other small motifs.
4. Stripes, both narrow and wide, in two or more colors.
5. Plaids, checks, and cross patterns.
6. Geometrical forms, consisting of interlacing lines forming squares, rectangles, triangles, diamond shapes, waves, circles, and ellipses.
7. Human, animal, and bird all-over patterns.
8. Floral and verdure effects in all-over patterns or in vertical strips.
9. Imitation textiles, tapestries, wood, marble, plaster, stone, and tile.
10. Chinese wallpapers and tea-papers.
11. Abstract designs in all-over repeats.
12. Architectural papers.

13. Pictorial panels and scenic papers.
14. Panels, borders, and moldings.

Bibliography

ACKERMAN, P., *Wallpaper, Its History, Design and Use.* Frederick A. Stokes Co., New York, 1925. Illustrated text.

CLOUZOT, H., *Tableaux-Tentures de Dufours et Leroy.* Librairie des Arts Décoratifs, Paris, 1930. Illustrations of historic scenic papers, with an introduction by Clouzot.

CLOUZOT, H., AND FOLLOT, C., *Histoire du Papier Peint en France.* C. Moreau, Paris, 1935. Excellent photographs and color plates.

DONNELL, E., *The Van Rensselaer Wall Paper and J. B. Jackson.* Metropolitan Museum of Art, New York, 1932. An illustrated study.

Fleurs, Oiseaux et Fantaisies par J. Pillement. H. Ernst, Editeur, Paris, 1924. Beautiful color plates of the works of this designer.

KATZENBACH, L. AND W., *The Practical Book of American Wallpaper.* J. B. Lippincott Co., Philadelphia, 1951. Valuable information to the consumer concerning the selection and use of wallpapers.

McCLELLAND, N., *Historic Wall Papers.* J. B. Lippincott Co., Philadelphia, 1924. A standard reference work giving a thorough treatment of the subject, with excellent illustrations.

SUGDEN, A.V. AND EDMONDSON, J. L., *A History of English Wallpaper, 1509–1914.* Excellent illustrated history.

CHAPTER XV

PICTURES

Pictures and books are the most significant external clues to the intellects of their owners. Conversely, for a decorator, these objects are the most useful to express an individual's personality in a room. A decorator is seldom concerned with books, but is often consulted in regard to pictures because these usually are part of permanent furnishings. Discretion must be used in choosing pictures for others. The satisfaction of an owner should far outweigh any decorative consideration. Pictures are to be enjoyed, and must be of interest to those who live with them; the pleasure may be that of connoisseurship, memory, amusement, or any message that conveys a worthy reaction.

If delight is not felt in viewing a picture, it will become boresome and undesirable. To the average intellect, interest in a picture is in the subject matter or literary aspect, but as connoisseurship improves, the composition, structure, form, rhythm, design, color, and deeper meaning will be appreciated.

Mosaic and mural decorations were produced in all early periods of art, but it was not until the 13th century in Italy that pictures were made to hang on walls. From this origin all the arts of modern graphical representation have evolved. After the invention of printing, many methods were developed to produce pictorial decorations in quantity. The science of photography has added to these. Each medium has its relative merits and deficiencies.

Pictures should be selected on the basis of taste, and to develop this quality, a knowledge of the history, techniques, and processes of the pictorial arts is necessary. It is impossible here to give more than a cursory outline of these subjects, and it is recommended that the student read in addition one of the many standard reference books. A list of more specialized volumes is given at the end of this chapter.

The Historical Schools of Painting

No one can claim to be cultured without a knowledge of the art of painting. Modern efforts in this field cannot be intelligently judged without information concerning the works of the past that have influenced and reflected the thoughts and activities of humanity.

Italian painting. Italy's wealth during the Middle Ages was derived largely from her trade with the Orient, and in each city leaders competed in externally expressing their power and grandeur. The purchase of works of art was one of their methods, and great opportunities developed for the artists who excelled in reflecting the philosophy, religion, and needs of their particular patrons. Cities vied with each other and all their citizens discussed the relative merits of the masters. The church, too, used the artist to explain its dogmas and history to the people. These developments in different localities are today known as schools of painting. In Italy the principal centers of art were in Florence and Venice, although minor schools existed in all other large cities.

The painters of the Renaissance were not greatly influenced by the arts of antiquity and the Middle Ages, although a minor sequence may be traced. It was obvious, as early as the beginning of the 14th century, that there was an attempt to break away from the traditions of Byzantine conventionalism and Gothic mysticism, and approach the spirit of realism and classicism that had been buried for centuries. Many of the artists, however, lacked sufficient knowledge of anatomy and foreshortening, and the painters of this period are generally referred to as *primitives*. To Cimabuë of Florence, who was born about the year 1240, is usually attributed the title of the first of modern painters, although no authentic pictures by him are known. Duccio (1255–1319) and Simoni Martini of Siena painted in a style closely related to that of the Byzantine mosaics and Gothic illuminated manuscripts. Both had probably been taught by Byzantine artists who had visited Florence about 1260. Duccio was the first Italian painter to enlarge the Biblical manuscript illustrations and make them suitable for use as wall decorations. In these early examples, flat symbolical figures are shown in brilliant colors on gold backgrounds, with the emphasis on the expression of religious emotion.

The Florentine, Milanese, and Umbrian schools. Giotto (1276?–1336?), who according to tradition, was discovered by Cimabuë, was the first naturalistic painter in Italy, and by his emphasis on broad structural form in his religious frescoes, he started the movement toward realism, naturalism, and the third dimension that was later to dominate the entire Florentine school. He was the first painter to paint from observation. His motto was "Follow Nature." Giotto lived shortly after St. Francis of Assisi

"The Death of St. Francis," by Giotto.

"Spring," by Sandro Botticelli.

had reacted against the tyranny of a misguided church, and he endeavored by means of his art to promote the Franciscan doctrines, and to lead the people back to the simplicity of Christ's teachings. He painted some of the frescoes in the Church at Assisi, built in honor of the Saint. His aim was to tell the truth, although he lacked knowledge of the laws of perspective. He was a friend of Dante, whose portrait he painted on a wall of the Bargello in Florence. Giotto had many disciples, the greatest of whom were Masaccio, a realist, who 100 years later studied perspective with Brunelleschi, the architect of the dome of the Florence cathedral, and Ucello, who profoundly researched in mathematics and painted battle scenes with converging lines and cubical forms. Fra Angelico * (1387–1455), the Dominican monk, also eloquently interpreted the teachings of St. Francis. He prayed before commencing each picture, and, as this pious mentality was dominated by the cloister, he never permitted himself a secular approach. The faces of his Saints and Angels are visions of purity and his paintings sing the exaltation of Christian philosophy. Donatello (1386–1466), the sculptor, revived a waning naturalism and influenced painters who followed him. The jovial Fra Filippo Lippi, an exact antithesis of Angelico, who claimed he was only flesh and blood, combined both strength and tenderness in his work that consisted mainly of chronicles of contemporary Florentine life. Verrocchio (1435–1488) was the first to paint landscape, light, and air. He was also a sculptor and modelled the equestrian statue of Colleone in Venice. Botticelli (1444–1510), a creative genius, who was a contemporary of Lorenzo the Magnificent and Savonarola, turned to pagan mythology, and painted "Spring," a perfect thesis for Humanism, earthly joys, and pleasures. Lorenzo saw no inconsistency in hanging paintings of Venuses next to mournful Madonnas. Thus the road was paved for Leonardo da Vinci, Michael Angelo, and Raphael.

Leonardo (1452–1519), of Vinci, a pupil of Verrocchio, was one of the greatest geniuses who ever lived, yet he was humble in self-appraisal. Tormented by a seething, creative instinct, he was author, philosopher, painter, sculptor, metalworker, inventor, scientist, musician, architect, mathematician, designer of firearms, mechanical and structural engineer, physicist, and geologist, and in all his activities he was far in advance of his times. He was a superb draftsman and a master of light, color, perspective, and anatomical forms. He discovered secrets that would have completely revolutionized contemporary thought if his enormous number of manuscripts had been published. His emotions were entirely controlled by his intelligence and self-discipline. Many of his paintings were unfinished or have been destroyed. His "Madonna of the Rocks" in the Louvre was the first painting to interpret the Virgin as a human being rather than a celestial character; she watches her Child with tenderness, but the halo and symbols of divinity have disappeared. For his crumbling "Last Supper," an oil on plaster painting in Milan, he takes the moment when Jesus says, "One of you shall betray Me," and every face and figure portrays this tragic moment; it is one of the greatest pictorial studies in profound psychology. Tradition states that his portrait of Mona Lisa was painted shortly after the wife of Giaconda had lost a child; the sphinxlike smile has had numerous explanations, but if the assumption is correct, it was perhaps due to the fact that Leonardo is supposed to have

* His true name was Guido di Pietro da Mugello. He was only called Fra Angelico after his death.

*Florentine school of the High Renaissance. "Madonna with St. Anne,"
by Leonardo da Vinci.*

employed musicians and jesters to create a momentary diversion for one
who was buried in grief. The portrait is one of the greatest ever painted,
and breathes as a living spirit. Leonardo worked for a long period for
Ludovico Sforza of Milan and died in the Chateau at Amboise, France,
while in the employ of Francis I.

Michael Angelo Buonarroti (1475–1564) was sculptor, painter, architect, engineer, and poet. He was the greatest artist of Florence, and perhaps the greatest the world has ever seen. Tireless, his titanic mentality
crushed the comparatively meager efforts of all other artists of his time
and ended the Florentine school. He considered himself primarily a
sculptor, and his paintings largely reflect this self-appraisal. He was all
absorbed in representing the superman, whose figure was heroic, muscular, vital, and physically perfect. His women, too, were Amazons lacking
in feminine appeal. He was the first to paint nude figures in extraordinary
contortions, floating through the air, or incredibly foreshortened. He used
the human figure to express intense thought. Tradition was abhorrent to
him and serenity unknown. In 1508, the Pope commissioned him to decorate the ceiling of the Sistine Chapel. For four years he lay on his back
on a scaffold to paint 10,000 square feet of plaster surface. He covered it

"Holy Family," by
Michael Angelo.

with figures from the Old Testament, prophets and sibyls in disconcerting attitudes expressive of superhuman energy. In his old age he worked for seven years to paint "The Last Judgment," covering the end wall of the Chapel, in which he shows a colossal Christ and a terror-struck Virgin in the presence of a combat of naked giants singularly lacking in Christian manners. Michael Angelo left few paintings and they are mostly in Italy. His creations have been compared to the Greek, but Greek figures are static, while Angelo's are in a state of turbulent movement or restrained power. It is perhaps advisable here to recall that Michael Angelo also designed the dome of St. Peter's in Rome, not only a fantastic engineering feat, but the greatest creation of the Renaissance.

Correggio was the painter of the Counter Reformation, and aided the Jesuits in making Catholicism attractive, joyful, and mystic. His pictures have more emotional than intellectual appeal.

Raffaelo Sanzio (1483–1520), known as Raphael, one of the most versatile and prolific of all artists, was born in Urbino, where in his youth he decorated pottery. During his short life he became architect of St. Peter's, mural decorator of the Stanza and Logi of the Vatican, official inspector of the antiquities of Rome, designed tapestries, and in his spare time was a prolific producer of easel pictures. His nature was sweet, gracious, and sensitive, and he has been called divine. Although an Umbrian, his best work was done in Florence and Rome. He borrowed ideas from many painters, but he was himself a master of composition. Highly imaginative and intellectual, he ranked high in illustrative ability; but his pictures are sometimes cold in color and lacking in virility. He painted

"Holy Family," by Raphael.

many devout subjects, but lived at a time when art was losing its religious importance. He was idolized by an adoring group who overwhelmed him with orders, and his reputation has not suffered in nearly five centuries. Some of his greatest paintings were made during his association with his model "Bella," who was the inspiration for many of his Madonnas; in presenting this subject, he arranged his group in a triangular pattern and represented the Virgin with an expression that mixed sensuality with the ethereal. His greatest Madonna was the Sistine in Dresden. In "La Belle Jardiniere," Mary sits in a meadow, the two children against her knees; her face is tender and human, but lacks a virginal quality. The "Fire in the Borgo," one of his murals in the Vatican, shows violent, muscular, nude figures that indicate the influence of Michael Angelo. In portraits painted shortly before his death, he retains his innate refinement, but avoids sublimity for more earthly facial characterizations. His untimely death at 37 years of age stupefies the imagination as to his potential production if he had lived twice as long.

The Venetian school. The magnificence of life in Venice was reflected in the work of its artists. The brilliant sunshine of the Adriatic accentuated the hue on every surface, and trade with the Orient added to the color consciousness of every individual. It was natural that the Venetian painters saw color as the dominant element in pictorial design. Accurate drawing, perspective, and anatomy were considered secondary to the emotional appeal of color symphonies. The subjects of the Venetian painters were avowedly religious; but, actually, they represented the splendor and pomp of the costumes, pageants, and social gatherings of the people. Women were portrayed as young and beautiful, and the men, strong, vigorous, and handsome. Stress was laid upon worldly joys, in contrast to the idealism of the Florentines. In the 15th century, Jacopo Bellini and his two sons painted monumental religious and historical frescoes that were serene and majestic. Giovanni Bellini, one of his sons, was the teacher of both Giorgione and Titian; in painting the nude he subordinated interest in the form to the beauty and sensual appeal of the flesh. This thought dominated all later Venetian painters.

Giorgione (1478?–1510) was the first Italian to paint a frankly carnal

"Concert Champêtre," by Giorgione.

picture. His allegorical "Concert Champêtre" shows an idyllic group of two nude women listening to the lutes of two dressed musicians; in the distance is a poetic background of trees and luminous clouds. In the character of the landscape treatment and in the naturalistic subject matter this picture was a model for many later artists. Giorgione understood humanism, the moods and feelings of man, and how they are affected by the moods of nature. He was a genius in the use of color, and as a portraitist had the capacity to represent the innermost thoughts of his models. His life was unfortunately short, but his student, young Titian, finished many of Giorgione's uncompleted works.

Titian (1489?–1576) inherited his master's magical use of color and surpassed him in imagination. Living to a ripe age, he painted every kind of subject with an intense love of life. There was a feeling of gaiety in most of his pictures, and even in his religious groups one can detect a semblance of pagan ardor. His portraits reflect a profound psychology as well as a rich understanding of technical possibilities. He was a friend of popes, princes, and politicians, who lavished favors upon him. He decorated many of the public buildings in Venice and painted the nobility of Italy. His interpretation of "Christ at Emmaus" is very different from that of Rembrandt, the figures being set in a palatial room with the Emperor Charles V as model for the figure of Luke. The "Portrait of a Man

"Venus and Adonis," by Titian.

with a Glove" shows Titian's ability to portray character, in its treatment of a sensitive youth gazing at a life he seems unable to understand. Titian strongly influenced the work of Rubens, Velasquez, and Reynolds.

The Counter Reformation of 1545 changed the character of painting as well as of architecture and decoration; the purpose was to revitalize a sagging faith, and the painters set out to overawe and dazzle their public. Tintoretto (1518–1594), the pupil of Titian, carried on the ideas of Michael Angelo in figure painting. He was called "Il Furioso" because of his speed in painting, which sometimes resulted in carelessness. His "Paradise" in the Ducal Palace at Venice is the largest painting in the world, and contains over 400 figures. He also painted portraits of many of the Doges. Veronese (1528–1588), who was born in Verona, but lived in Venice, was noted for his draftsmanship, rich use of color, a tendency toward silver effects, and for his custom of placing groups of figures in elaborate architectural settings. His enormous "Marriage Feast at Cana" in the Louvre is one of his best known.

Caravaggio (1569–1609), considered a Neapolitan, was self-taught, but naturally gifted. Little influenced by his contemporaries, he rejected idealism and chose a naturalistic representation of the more vicious aspects of life. He painted murders, brawls, and ugly events in the lives of the dregs of humanity, and used a violent lighting that accentuated the brutality

"Venus and Mars," by Paolo Veronese.   *"Boy Bitten by a Lizard," by Caravaggio.*

of the incident. He was the first realist and also one of the first artists to paint out-of-doors, at which times he attempted the atmospheric effects that were later solved by the French Impressionists. His masterpiece is the "Death of the Virgin," now in the Louvre. He had a strong influence upon the work of both Ribera and Goya in Spain.

Tiepolo (1696–1770), the great 18th century artist, was the final exponent of the luxurious life of Venice. He continued to paint the processions and pageants and the tottering superiority of the aristocratic classes, and his work strongly influenced Goya, Delacroix, and others.

The Venetian school's contribution to art was very great; its gay and human character had a more universal appeal but was less profound than the intellectualism and sublimity of the Florentine. It became, however, the fountainhead for many later schools, and was far more influential in the 19th century than the painters of Florence, whose only disciples were the short-lived Pre-Raphaelites of England.

Flemish and Dutch schools. The northern schools of painting developed concurrently but independently of Italy. Membership in the Hanseatic League and the French civil wars had brought wealth to the Low Countries. Brilliant courts had been established at Ghent and Bruges during the 14th century and these cities had become the intellectual centers of Europe. They had been centers of manuscript illustration during the Middle Ages and it is generally acknowledged that the first successful use of oil as a painter's medium * was introduced about 1426 at

* Until this period, painters used tempera, mixing their pigments with gum and the whites of eggs.

"The Sacrifice of Abraham," by Giovanni Tiepolo.

Bruges by the brothers Hubert and Jan van Eyck. These men were portraitists of supreme talent, and painters of religious subjects, who established the first naturalistic tendencies in art in contrast to Gothic conventionalism. Critics frequently state that in "John Arnolfini and His Wife," painted by Jan in 1434, perfection in art was established in its first example; the picture is today one of the most popular in the National Gallery in London. The supreme work of these two brothers was the "Adoration of the Lamb," an altar-piece in Ghent.

The van Eycks were followed by Van der Weyden and Memling, both idealistic religious painters. Bosch (c. 1462–1516), with a lugubrious imagination, painted monstrosities and diabolical nightmares that both repel and attract the eye. Pieter Breughel (c. 1525–1569) of Brussels and his two sons introduced the painting of landscapes, agricultural scenes, and ghostly subjects, using great inventiveness. Other Flemish artists popularized subjects related to jests, satires, and intimate activities of the people, and were the precursors of 17th century Dutch *genre* painting. Those who visited Italy became saturated with concepts of splendor, and offered to the burghers of Antwerp richly colored decorative subjects that prepared the way for Rubens.

Rubens (1577–1640), born in Antwerp, was the most prolific painter who ever lived. Of magnetic personality and supreme intellect, he numbered among his friends scholars, scientists, and kings. As a diplomat and painter, he visited Italy, and twice went to the Court of Spain where he met Velasquez. Charles I of England heedfully listened to his advice and knighted him. Rubens, bursting with health and vitality, with the aid of

100 apprentices, produced over two thousand paintings. His representations of historical and allegorical events, hunting scenes, and tournaments are astounding narratives that twirl in tempestuous patterns of colors, lines, and forms, his seductive nudes are robust and sensual; his rollicking "Kermess" in the Louvre pictures a remarkable composition of roistering villagers, protesting maidens, and mischievous children. Twice happily married, he frequently painted portraits of himself, his wife, and children, richly costumed and blissfully clasping hands. His "Descent from the Cross" in the Antwerp Cathedral is generally considered his greatest work, though such a designation is difficult considering his vast production. If

National Gallery, London

"Jan Arnolfini and His Wife,"
by Jan Van Eyck.

his pictures lack the psychological depth of those of the Italian masters, he was not surpassed in the other elements of painting. Every great museum in the world is replete with examples of his work.

The gigantic mentality of Rubens left no single inheritor of all his capacities. Teniers (1610–1690), his pupil, continued to paint kermesses, drinking scenes, and peasant jests, that were often reproduced as tapestries. Van Dyck (1599–1641) inherited Rubens' elegance of style, but specialized in aristocratic portraiture that featured, with exquisite technique, details of silken fabrics, fine laces, and trimmings. Most of Van Dyck's work was done in England, where he flattered the nobility and prepared the way for the 18th century native portraitists.

In 1648, the Dutch part of Flanders was liberated from Spanish domination and free to worship in the Protestant faith. With the establishment of the East and West India Companies, Holland captured the lion's share of the world's carrying trade, and the burghers, who benefited, organized the guilds and began to build themselves elaborate homes which needed pictures. Religious and mythological subjects were frowned upon under the new church dogmas, the people preferring genre paintings showing small-dimensioned views of street scenes, interiors, country activities, and phases of their middle class life. Steen and de Hooch under Flemish influence used painstaking craftsmanship in showing tavern groups and interiors. Cuyp, Hobbema, and Ruysdael painted charming landscapes that later influenced the English School. Artists were also commissioned to paint "corporation pictures" showing group portraits of guild members.

"The Harvesters," by Peter Breughel the Elder.

"Wolf and Fox-Hunt," by Peter Paul Rubens.

Franz Hals (1580–1666) was the first Dutch artist to achieve fame and a lasting recognition. A man of joyous temperament, he transferred his viewpoint on life to the canvas with a full brush and glowing colors. His paintings, though lacking in depth, vibrate with vitality and a good humor that borders on the theatrical. Hals had the gift of catching a momentary expression, and suitably adapting the color and composition to the subject; he became the outstanding interpreter of jocularity in art. In the characteristic "Laughing Cavalier," a soldier stands with a quizzical expression, the details of his clothing minutely rendered; he is about to burst into uproarious laughter. Hals drank heavily and lived recklessly, which eventually dulled his artistic sense; his works as a result are sometimes heavy in coloring, carelessly executed, and disorderly in composition.

"The Earl of Warwick," by Sir Anthony Van Dyck.

Rembrandt van Rijn (1606–1669), one of the greatest intellects of his age, combined realism with a mystical approach, searching beneath the surface of everyday things for inner meanings. Little is known of his private life, except that it was full of sorrow. His wife Saskia, a prominent young woman, who figures in several of his early paintings, died young, leaving one son. Though at fifty Rembrandt became bankrupt, this only seemed to increase his spiritual qualities and he toiled indefatigably till the end of his life to satisfy his creditors. While he never visited Italy, a baroque quality in his work shows study of the Italian masters, but his work was simpler and more sincere. He preferred character to beauty. It is said the only book he read was the Bible. His paintings are not only Dutch; they indicate the struggles of all humanity. His subjects were greatly varied, including corporation pictures, landscapes, and portraits, and, contrary to Dutch tradition, many Biblical scenes. He painted for both rich and poor, gave interest to the most commonplace subjects, and had an extraordinary power of expressing character.

His major contribution to the art of painting was the development of an artificial and unique technique of handling light and shadow, called

"The Merry Company," by Franz Hals.

"Portrait of Himself," by Rembrandt.

chiaroscuro. It was a luminosity of his own invention. Lines were subordinated and the main subject was left in shade, with masses merely blocked in, but a strong highlight emphasized the upper portion of the composition. The light areas were treated in rich colors and explicit detail, as in the "Man With a Gold Helmet," in which the chasing on the helmet stands out as if in relief. Transitions from light to dark were gradual, and the shadows were painted in red; the result was to accent and to lift an ordinary subject to a higher plane of interest.

His most widely discussed picture is the misnamed "Night Watch" (1642), showing a company of crossbowmen readying for a daytime march. The figures are actual portraits, but he subordinated the individuals to the whole pattern, and pleased no one. From this time his fortunes began to ebb. The "Supper at Emmaus" reverently and dramatically depicts Christ before the ascension. He is seated frontward at a table, and His face is illumined by a ray of light from an upper window; with Him are two seated disciples and a serving lad whose figures contrast, in less detail and in semidarkness. Rembrandt painted many self-portraits and frequently used his wife as a model. His etchings have probably never been surpassed; this was a field almost unexplored before his time. Recognizing the limitations of the technique, he modified his style to suit lineal reproduction, and drew portraits, landscapes, and Biblical subjects.

Jan Vermeer (1632–1675) was probably the "Little Dutch Master" of greatest stature next to Rembrandt. About 40 paintings of his have been authenticated,* the major portion of which are interior scenes with an uncanny feeling of spaciousness. Like Rembrandt, he created a lumi-

* During World War II, Vermeer's paintings were remarkably counterfeited.

nosity for his own convenience. His subject matter usually shows a woman at some household task; there is usually a window, a wall area broken by a map or picture, and, in the foreground, objects arranged with logical relation to the whole pattern. Analysis of the "Young Woman at a Casement" and "The Lacemaker" shows carefully contrasted linear and spatial relationships, yet so natural in structure, that one is unaware of the planning involved. This handling of inanimate objects eventually led to a later interest in *still-life* painting.

"Officer and Laughing Girl," by Jan Vermeer.

In the 18th century, Holland produced no genius but in later centuries Van Gogh (1853–1890) the Post-impressionist, and Mondrian (1872–1944) the non-objectivist came under French influence but each developed strong individualism in his work.

German painting. The art of painting was never as extensively practised in Germany as in the other countries of Europe. The early Renaissance produced three great painters, but a further development was prevented by the disasters of the religious wars. Dürer (1471–1528) of Nuremburg is often considered the equal of Michael Angelo, but most of his masterpieces were in the medium of engraving, etching, and woodcuts. He was also a water-colorist. His portraits are intense and earnest, and reflect the morality of Luther and Erasmus, who were his friends. He was the first to interpret the Italian Renaissance to the people of northern Europe. Hans Holbein, the younger (c. 1497–1543), in the opinion of many, is unrivalled in portraiture. He lived in Basle, where he became famous for his pencil sketches. His woodcut series known as "The Dance of Death" are today popular throughout the world. He visited England and was the guest of Sir Thomas More, whose portrait he is supposed to have painted. Henry VIII authorized him to paint his fourth wife, Anne of Cleves. The collection of Holbein's chalk sketches at Windsor Castle show him at his best. Much of his work has been destroyed, and he is judged by his smaller productions. He was frank in his treatments and never modified his subjects by unusual lighting. Cranach (1472–1553) was greatly influenced by Luther and painted many religious pictures. He was, however, primarily noted for his nudes, who appear both naïve and humorous, but with graceful figures that lack the corpulency of the typical Teutonic women. The German painters of later centuries had illustrative abilities but never reached the profundity of

"Melancholia," an engraving by Albrecht Dürer.   *"The Plowman," a woodcut by Hans Holbein.*

thought or technical expertness of those of other countries. Under the totalitarian regime, when any evidence of imagination was designated as "degenerate," German art reached its lowest ebb.

Spanish painting. The art of painting in Spain began at the time of the Renaissance and was first influenced by Caravaggio, the Italian realist. With a few exceptions, Spanish artists have retained realism as a characteristic feature of their work, and at times have carried its conception to a thundering climax.

The 16th and early 17th centuries produced Ribera and Zurburan, both of whom painted gloomy religious themes, featuring emaciated friars and aged men with shrunken faces, who typified the asceticism of the Church of the period. The next two centuries produced four geniuses who are unsurpassed in art history.

In 1576 a Cretan whose name was Domenikos Theotocopoulos (1541–1614) arrived in Toledo after having studied with Titian in Venice. His surname in Greek can be translated "Of the Mother of God," but as a foreigner he was derisively nicknamed "El Greco." He soon became more Spanish than the natives themselves, and after his abilities and loyalty were recognized, the Toledans covetously remarked, "Crete gave him life, but Toledo, the brush." Vexed at the accusation that he painted too much like his master, he developed an individual style of great originality. He was frequently commissioned by the Church authorities, and many of his paintings are of austere religious subjects inspired by a Jesuit fanaticism. In these he shows an elongation of the human figure and a gravity of facial expressions, producing mystical and melancholy effects that are accentuated by the use of sombre, greyed tones, with puzzling highlights and deep shadows. His greatest work is considered to be "The Burial of Count Orgaz" in a chapel of Santo Tomé in Toledo; this picture is in two parts, the lower part is ultrarealistic and represents the corpse being lowered into its sarcophagus by magnificently caped Cardinals, surrounded by the Count's former friends; the semicircular upper portion is in forceful contrast by its idealism, and shows the presentation of his soul to Christ, the Virgin, St. Peter, and the angels; the two conceptions integrate a work of emotional power that has seldom been

Courtesy Metropolitan Museum of Art

"View of Toledo," by El Greco.

surpassed. El Greco was also a landscapist of dramatic force; his favorite subject being the City of Toledo viewed from an adjoining hill; his "Toledo in a Storm" is ghastly in effect and shows the elements of nature during their most vicious moments. El Greco has had an enormous influence upon modern painters.

The second of the four was Velasquez (1599–1660), a Portuguese, born in Seville, who lived to be the supreme genius of Spain, and one of the most gifted painters in all art history. When he was 36 years old, he became Court Painter for Phillip IV and never left the King's service. Velasquez was not interested in the visions or asceticism of El Greco, nor the religious and political turmoil that surrounded him, but concentrated mainly on pomp and splendor. He was ultranaturalistic in his interpretations and as a technician he has perhaps been equalled but never surpassed. His portraits show a penetrating psychology. Countless times he painted the King with the Hapsburg jaw, in every costume, aspect, and mood. With remarkable skill he produced charm in the enamelled faces of the ladies of the Court, and his children's portraits exquisitely reflect the innocence and sincerity of childhood, combined with a dignity that befits royal birth. His greatest works are in the Prado in Madrid. The "Maids of Honor" is a mirror reflection of the artist's studio showing him in the process of painting the Infanta surrounded by her maids, dwarfs, and dog, and a mirrored reflection of the King and Queen in the rear of the room. His outstanding historical picture is the "Surrender of Breda," a beautifully patterned composition showing the Dutch general graciously handing the keys of the city to the Spanish conqueror,

"The Maids of Honor," by Velasquez.

who is surrounded by his officers and a guard of proud lancers; the burning city, immersed in a violet atmosphere, forms a background that gives
a fantastic illusion of air, space, and distance. His superb, life-size "Crucifixion" is awesome in its effect. In "The Drunkards," painted in his youth,
one clearly sees the influence of Caravaggio in combining mythology with
contemporary life; Bacchus is being crowned by peasants whose faces are
extraordinary characterizations; the group is painted in a soft golden
light as though it were being seen through a glass of clear wine.

Murillo (1617–1682), the pupil and friend of Velasquez, was also
from sunny Andalusia, but his paintings differ greatly from those of his
master and his tenderness contrasts strongly with the bloody existence
that surrounded him. His style is perhaps oversentimental, but reflects
great religious devotion and human sympathy, and it appealed tremen-
dously to the Spanish masses, who worshipped him for his spirituality.
The faces of his celestial figures reflect a divine love, and he enveloped
them in glowing lumination. He made the poverty of the people seem
poetic and affectionately painted the street gamins of Seville. His representations of the infant Jesus appeal to a universal mother love. Repeatedly and peerlessly he painted the "Immaculate Conception," the great-

"The Drunkards," by Velasquez.

est of which is in the Louvre. His work fails to show the power of that of his predecessors, but his technique and warmth enkindle a loyal enthusiasm, and his place in Spanish art is unique.

The last of the great quartet was Goya (1746–1828), the graphical realist of his age, who produced a complete pictorial history of Spain when her politics were at their most corrupt level. Born to low life, he rose to be the most famous Spaniard of his time. His youth was replete with escapades, and vigilant monks just prevented his elopement with a nun. He married and had twenty legitimate children. His magnetic personality finally gathered around him the greatest people in Spain. He was painter, etcher, water-colorist, and designer of tapestries. His genius was manifested in his paintings of the lower classes and his deep insight into contemporary Spanish life. His dance scenes reflect all the gaiety of these moments, and suggest the lightheartedness of Fragonard. He was both a caricaturist and powerful satirist. He castigated the degenerate Court of Charles IV by painting the pompous King and his dominating wife with repulsive facial expressions. In a series of etchings known as "The Caprices," he lashed at the vices of society, and, in another series, he courageously depicted the atrocities of the French troops during the Napoleonic war, in spite of the fact that he had been appointed court painter to Joseph Bonaparte. His famous paintings were those known as the "Maja Nude" and "Maja Dressed," believed to be the Duchess of Alba, with whom Goya was in love. It is said that the Duchess is the only royal nude model in art history. Goya painted her reclining body in flesh tones that vibrate with emotional tenderness. Tradition states that he hurriedly painted her clothed in the same pose, when her husband announced his

"Adoration of the Shepherds," by Murillo.

intention of visiting the studio. Both pictures now hold the position of honor in the Goya room at the Prado in Madrid. He was a prolific painter of portraits of the Spanish aristocracy. Goya's daring greatly impressed Delacroix and the Romanticists of France. He was a hundred years ahead of his time and, as such, was an important influence in the work of many later artists.

Spanish painting of the late 19th and early 20th centuries is represented by Sorolla and Zuloaga, both of whom tried to continue the great traditions of Spanish art. They were delightful colorists, but superficial in their conceptions. The more modern trends are seen in Sert, the muralist; Dali, who paints nightmares well, but in the manner of Bosch; and Picasso; the latter is an internationalist and an experimentalist, influenced by the French school, who has assumed leadership with able, but sometimes questionable results, but his work is so powerful that a definite change in the art of painting will probably result. Miró is a leading surrealist and humorist.

The English schools. During the 16th century, when the continent was producing its great masters of painting, the English were not sufficiently convinced of their own artistic capabilities to support and promote a native talent; they knew only the work of foreign artists. Henry VIII invited Holbein to his Court, and under Charles I, in the early 17th century, Van Dyck painted the British nobility in a manner that is a feast for the eyes. Rubens also visited England in 1629 for both diplomatic and artistic reasons, and was listened to with the utmost reverence. Puritanism, however, relegated art to the infernal regions, and created a hiatus in the development of a national school that was not counteracted until, with brilliant technique, Lely reflected some of the sensual qualities of the Court of Charles II.

Hogarth (1697–1764) was a spontaneous development in English art. Whistler called him "the only great English artist." At least he was the first of importance and came upon the scene when England was interested only in the Italians, Flemish, and Dutch. Hogarth was unimpressed by foreigners, but was vitally interested in the homes and haunts, the

"The Nude Maja," by Francisco Goya.

"La Gallina Ciega," by Francisco Goya.

qualities and vices of the middle classes. His talents, both as engraver and painter, permitted him to interpret what he saw with wit, entertainment, and satire. As moral narratives, he produced the series known as "A Harlot's Progress," "The Rake's Progress," and "Marriage à la Mode," in which each final picture shows the calamitous end of the unrighteous. His family groups known as *conversation pieces* were painted like snapshots of stage sets during the progress of a drama, but he skillfully discloses the personality of each individual. His scintillating portraits thor-

"Shortly after Marriage," by William Hogarth.

oughly reveal the character of his models, and those of David Garrick, the Shrimp Girl, Peg Woffington, and himself with his dog "Trump," show an economy of brushwork that astounded his contemporaries. He painted many members of his own family and it seemed that the plainer the appearance of his model, the stronger was her chance of being painted. His reputation has suffered from the tendency of historians to dwell upon the subject matter of his pictures. In 1753 he wrote the controversial "Analysis of Beauty," in which he claimed the most beautiful line in nature to be an elongated S-curve, a form that he used constantly and which ever since has been called by artists "Hogarth's Line of Beauty." Hogarth's style was not appropriated by later painters, but he aroused the creative consciousness of the English artists.

Reynolds (1723–1792) aided in establishing the Royal Academy in 1768, and became its first president. He lectured on his theories and on the proper training for artists, and urged a thorough study of drawing, color, and composition, and a complete understanding of the history of painting, before creative or imaginative efforts were undertaken. The public, however, demanded portraits, and he and his contemporaries, Gainsborough (1727–1788) and Romney (1734–1802), painted in the Van Dyck tradition, with minor influences of Rubens and Titian. Gainsborough produced several delightful landscapes, but to keep himself

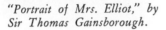

"Portrait of Mrs. Elliot," by Sir Thomas Gainsborough.

Lady Hamilton as "Nature," by George Romney.

alive was forced to paint "potboilers"; * his exquisite portraits of Mrs. Siddons, Mrs. Graham, and "The Blue Boy" are the best known. Romney was in love with his model Emma Lyon, who later became Lady Hamilton and eventually the mistress of Lord Nelson; he portrayed her in innumerable characterizations. He also painted historical pictures of which the best known is "The Death of Wolfe." The reputation of these three artists rests upon their immortalization in exquisite colors of the charm and refinement of a wholesome aristocracy, and their ability to make women appear more beautiful than they probably were. Reynolds' pupils and successors, Raeburn, Hoppner, and Lawrence, were worthy of their master, but their lives overlapped the decline in art that commenced in the first quarter of the 19th century.

At the turn of the century, a Suffolk lad named Constable (1776–1837), who loved his countryside, taught himself to paint independently of the aristocratic school of London. He specialized in landscapes and painted with a sincerity that had been previously unknown. The public was slow to accept his work, but he was convinced that his ability to catch the luminous atmosphere in both stormy and fair weather would eventually be rewarded. He won medals at the Paris Salon in 1824 and was a strong influence in the establishment of the Barbizon school. He is looked upon today as the originator of modern landscape painting.

* The term "potboiler" was originated by Gainsborough and, ever since, has been used by artists to refer to paintings made to appeal to the public taste and not those that the artist wished to paint.

"The White Horse," by John Constable.

"Fishing Boats Entering Calais Harbor," by J. M. W. Turner.

Turner (1775–1851) was a poet who lived in a dreamland. He was a genius in his field and an accident in art history. He lacked education; was uncultured, personally offensive, and friendless; but he was bewitched with the mystery and beauty of light, sky-expanse, and water reflections. He painted the atmosphere of landscapes with a broad palette, indicating stationary objects with a blurred effect. He was studied by contemporary French landscapists, and his last works may be considered precursors of the Impressionist movement. Bonington (1802–1828) studied and lived in France. He unfortunately died before his full maturity, but left several delightful landscapes and portraits.

Courtesy Wildenstein and Co., Inc.

"Woman with Red Lily," Fontainebleau School.

During the middle of the 19th century English painting fell into a state of triviality temporarily relieved by the "Pre-Raphaelite Brotherhood" of Hunt, Rosetti, and Burne-Jones, who turned to medievalism with Botticelli as their God. They were defended by Ruskin, but world thought was soon to discard eclecticism and to search for new artistic interpretations. With the approach of the 20th century, the English artists looked for inspiration from across the Channel.

Early French painting and the school of Fontainebleau. With the 16th-century decline of Italy's Eastern commerce, France struggled for the cultural leadership of Europe. The northern countries for a time showed brilliance, and Spain had her geniuses, but France in the 18th century finally emerged to dominate the arts, a position she has never relinquished.

During the Gothic period, French painting was largely limited to altar decoration and religious manuscript illustration. As early as the 13th century, however, exquisite miniatures were painted to illustrate the new secular romances and scientific treatises. The printing press eventually served to exterminate this beautiful art. Fouquet, in 1455, made his charming pictures for the "Book of Hours" and was the first painter in France to use sensual subject matter; in his "Virgin and Child" he impiously showed Agnes Sorel, the King's mistress, as a carnal and provocative Madonna. During the 16th century the Clouets painted royalty with pale and reticent faces. The "School of Fontainebleau," under the leadership of Primaticcio, an Italian, gave evidence of the reaction from

"Landscape," by Claude Lorrain.

"Embarkation for Cythera," by Jean Antoine Watteau.

medieval asceticism in producing many unsigned paintings of Diane de Poitiers and other Court beauties, who seemed intent upon giving their contemporaries complete information concerning their physical charms.

French Baroque and Rococo painting. The Louis XIV period commenced with the work of Claude Lorrain and Poussin, who painted vistas of shimmering waters and luminous clouds seen through settings of dark trees and ruined temples. The latter also produced murals of pagan and Christian subject matter. The King frowned upon the Le Nain brothers, who portrayed peasants in their daily activities. Le Brun was appointed Director of Fine Arts, and under his tyrannical authority, absolute power was glorified and individualism was stifled. Historical events and symbolical groups became the subject matter of all paintings, and a cold, spiritless art developed. At the King's death the French burst into a gaiety that long had been smoldering and the painters once again could paint as they desired. Watteau (1684–1721) quickened the pulse with his exquisite colors in the portrayal of a gallantry that implied that all life had been dedicated to love; his "Embarkation for Cythera" (1717) represented young aristocrats leaving for an isle where Aphrodite could be eternally worshipped. Art was

Courtesy Wildenstein and Co., Inc.

"The Bath of Venus," by François Boucher.

Copyright the Frick Collection, New York

"Storming the Citadel," by Jean Honoré Fragonard.

now for the beautiful women of the Court, and their approval was sufficient adulation. Boucher, often vulgar, but never dull, used light blues and pinks and the sinuous curves of the period in depicting boudoir scenes or voluptuous women engaged in frivolous pastimes. Lancret and Pater imitated the "Fêtes Champêtres" of Watteau. Fragonard (1732–1806), in such paintings as the "Storming of the Citadel," painted alluring beauties

ABOVE LEFT: *"The White Pot,"* by
Jean Chardin. ABOVE RIGHT: *"Roman Ruins,"* by *Hubert Robert.*
BELOW: *"The Death of Socrates,"*
by *Jacques Louis David.*

whose virtue was a mockery. His paintings were delightful but reflected
the superficiality of the period and lacked intellectual depth. The 18th
century established an initiative in France that has caused her to be the
nucleus of creative effort in many of the arts to the present day.

Neo-classicism. Classical influences in painting were introduced some
ten years before Louis' death, and were partly the result of the importation of Piranesi's engravings of Roman ruins, and, of course, the influence
of the Pompeian discoveries. The public had already begun to weary of
the license of the Rococo period, and Louis XVI endeavored to appear as
an honorable family man. Marie Antoinette turned at least outwardly to
the simple life, and carried on the patronage of the arts. The painters
applied their talents mainly to a portraiture that expressed purity and
refined sentimentality. Greuze, Nattier, and Vigée Le Brun produced
delicately colored portraits in oil and pastel, indicating perhaps a glint

of regret on the faces, and Quentin Latour, the pastellist, was noted for the winsome expression of his models. The independents were Fragonard and Chardin; the former, as muralist, continued to paint amorous scenes and was accused of corrupting public morals; the latter, under Dutch influence, produced remarkable compositions showing kitchen utensils, floral groupings, and genre pictures representing informal home scenes; his technical ability was at its best in his renderings of the satin costumes of the period. Hubert Robert painted fanciful views of classical ruins demanded by a public entranced by antiquity.

David and Ingres. The Revolution was not only to change the social and economic life of France, but also to smother all former concepts of the art of painting. The horrors of the period began to be recorded in oil. In the early years of the 19th century, under the influence of David (1748–1825), the Art Director for Napoleon, there was ushered in a ponderous solemnity and classical severity. David was imbued with a delirium for the antique. Enormous paintings of scenes from Greek and Roman history and mythology were made, and Napoleon's military victories were recorded. David's portraits of Madame Recamier and others showed the sitters in Greek-inspired costumes and settings. Official dictatorship of the painters once again provided abundant production but little evidence of imagination.

Ingres (1780–1867), a pupil of David, dominated painting until the middle of the century; he was a superb draftsman, but produced frigid pictures and tinted line drawings that were the last gasps of his master's concepts. Portraits, seraglio scenes, and Greek goddesses were portrayed with a bloodlessness that confounded nature; he failed to grasp the changes that were occuring in life and art, and his critics accused him of trying to extinguish the sun.

Romanticism and reaction. Delacroix (1798–1863), a protesting contemporary of Ingres, inspired by the warmth of Rubens, turned to romanticism, vigor, and vibrant color; his ideas fell like a sledge hammer upon the conservatives who were still floundering in Hellenic dreams, and he split the art world of Paris in two. He had lived through the Revolution of 1830, and, impregnated with a passion for liberty, he fought with feverish energy to re-establish the traditional glory of France. His realistic "Liberty Leading the People" remains one of the great dramatic masterpieces of all times. He visited Morocco and painted many exotic Eastern subjects, the most famous of which is "The Jewish Wedding," which was later copied by Renoir. The greatness of Delacroix was acknowledged only on his deathbed by the visits of those who had disdained him.

By 1830 most of the arts had begun to feel the paralyzing effects of the Industrial Revolution. The painters alone maintained vitality and reacted

"Madame Leblanc," by Jean-Auguste Ingres.

"The Abduction of Rebecca," by Eugene Delacroix.

to the changed conditions. The aristocratic patrons had been displaced by a wealthy bourgeois whose understanding of the arts was meagre. The Salon was established to find a new market for the artists' work. Only a few intellectuals had grasped the meaning of the democratic developments and confusion reigned in the art world. The day of the individualist was at hand.

Courbet (1819–1877), of humble birth, was working unobtrusively in the Provinces as the first of the French realists. He disregarded classicism, idealization, and romanticism and wished to produce a living art by painting what he saw around him —placid landscapes and rude peasants. His famous remark was, "Show me an angel and I will paint one." He had no love for accuracy of detail and often applied his paint with a palette knife. His political view; eventually caused him to be ostra cized by the Salon and to flee the country, but his devotion to nature remained as an influence upon a host of followers. Another individualist of exquisite refinement was Corot (1796–1875), who concentrated on dawn and twilight landscapes showing distant dancing nymphs and satyrs. He arose often to see the sun creep over the horizon; at noon he "saw too well." In a self-appraisal he remarked, "Delacroix is an eagle, but I am only a lark singing songs in my gray clouds," but his misty forest scenes, rendered with an intentional lack of precision, greatly influenced his successors. The third great individualist was Daumier (1808–1879), who for many years was a lithographer and a poignant cartoonist who satirized Parisian officials, city life, and the classical tradition that lingered. This early experience had taught him to penetrate deeply into human foibles and to say much with few

Courtesy Wildenstein and Co., Inc.

"Two Boats on a Beach," by Gustave Courbet.

Courtesy Wildenstein and Co., Inc.

"The Plough," by Jean Corot.

Courtesy Metropolitan Museum of Art

"Actualités," lithograph by Honore Daumier.

lines and simple masses. When he commenced to paint, he eliminated unnecessary detail, and his color range tended toward monochromaticism.

The Barbizon school. While the individualists were working, Theodore Rousseau (1812–1867) and Jean François Millet (1814–1875), struggling with poverty, settled, about 1836, in peaceful Barbizon near Fontainbleau. The former wandered through the forest and painted the splintered tree trunks, windswept branches, and weird rocks; his style was often crude in the use of thick dark slabs of paint, but his versatility was shown also in paintings done in minute detail and light tones. Millet concentrated on the life of the peasant; endeavored to dignify the glory of labor, and promote sympathy for the agricultural classes. "The Angelus" is among the best of his pictures. By 1865 Barbizon had become the center of an enraptured group. Corot and Courbet were early visitors and were followed by Daubigny, Diaz, Dupré, Manet, Monet, and Degas. Troyon and Bonheur, the animal painters, also settled there. This group, later to be called the "Barbizon school," became known for their impressions of nature rendered in simple techniques. The fields, tranquil waters, village streets, and daily activities of the lower classes were established as suitable material for interpretation. Thus these painters paralleled the democratization that was occurring in other fields of thought.

The Impressionist school. This name was inappropriately applied in 1863 to a loosely knit group of young French artists, some of whom had been associated with the earlier realists and social propagandists. They concentrated on subject matter of the period, but their distinguishing mark was their attempt to apply to painting the principles of light refraction. The most important were Pissarro, Manet, Degas, Cezanne, Monet, Whistler, Sisley, Morisot, and, later, Renoir, Gauguin, and Seurat. The theory was that as color is produced by light rays, it was more important to paint the light that enveloped an object than to paint the object itself. As the character of daylight constantly changes, it seemed logical to paint a rapid visual impression that subordinated composition, silhouette, and detail. By juxtaposing on the canvas short strokes or dots of pure spectrum colors, a blending would occur by fusion of light rays rather than by mixing pigments on the palette, and the results would be more vibrant and luminous.* The Salon authorities regarded these policies with opprobrium, and from 1874 to 1886, the group conducted exhibitions known as the "Salon des Refusés," which were at first greeted by jeers, but eventually established the movement in the eyes of the public. Many of the group were gifted with extraordinary ability and versatility, and as they matured, it was impossible to restrain their individualism.

The Post-impressionists. Interest in Impressionism was at an end by 1886, and many of the leaders had begun to enjoy the fruits of their struggle. A new generation was coming up to take their place, and those who had been associated with the movement began to proceed along highly individual lines so that the term Post-impressionism hardly classifies a cohesive trend, but rather implies a rebellion from former interests. If any concerted conception was finally indicated it was a disregard for natural appearances and natural coloring, and this intentional indifference eventually led to Cubism, Futurism, Abstractionism, and the later 20th century explorations. Many artists of the late Barbizon school, who had adopted Impressionism for a time, later discarded both ideals for the individualism upon which their fame rests. All, however, were forceful in their results. A brief list of the leaders with a description of the general character of their work follows:

Manet (1832–1883) was wealthy and cared little for others' opinions. He had been early influenced by Goya, but was the backbone of Impressionism. His technique was that of a full brush with few strokes to attain his effects, and that of placing a concentration of light upon the important feature in his pictures. He painted portraits, Spanish scenes and figures, boating and garden scenes, and subjects taken from everyday life. He permitted his models to take unexpected poses. His "Olympia" (1865) portrays a brazen courtesan, which he painted without idealization as a protest against the sentimental nudes then in vogue;† his "Dejeuner sur l'herbe" (1863) shows two undressed girls picnicking on the banks of the Seine with two fully clothed men, an event that was not uncommon among the models and art students of Paris. Both pictures at first caused a tumult of protest but hang today in the Louvre.

Degas (1834–1917), though associated with both Barbizon and the Impressionists, proved to be a thorough individualist and the greatest drafts-

---

* Greens were obtained by juxtaposing dots of pure yellow and blue, greys by using small areas of complementary hues, etc. Shadows were in colors complementary to the color of the object that cast them. Large areas of adjoining complementary colors would intensify each other and give greater vitality to the picture as a whole. Pictures painted according to these principles had to be viewed from a distance. Turner, the English artist, had used these methods as early as 1825, and must be considered a direct ancestor of the French group, some of whom had carefully analyzed his work.

† Particularly those of Bougereau, Gerome, and Cabanel.

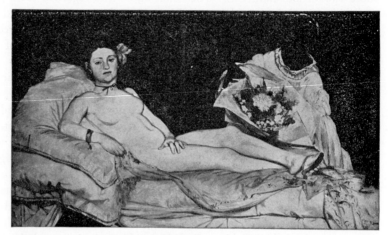

"*Olympia,*" *by Edouard Manet.*

"Four Dancers," pastel by Edgar Degas.

"Landscape," by Paul Cezanne.

man and decorative painter of his time. He worked in both pastel and oil. From Japanese prints he adopted the high, diagonal viewpoint and the abrupt cutting of his compositions by the picture frame. Colors in his pastels often resemble multicolored fireworks. Photography aided him in becoming a master of the portrayal of motion. His subject matter included portraits, landscapes, race track, and ballet scenes, and nudes casually washing themselves, or stepping from the bathtub.

Cezanne (1839–1906) must rightly be classified as an Impressionist due to his deep interest in the scientific aspects of color. His early work was influenced by El Greco and Delacroix but his later productions were highly individualized. His rugged applications of vivid pigments and carelessness in drawing caused him to be ridiculed by the critics, and, in 1879, he retired to his native Aix and courageously worked in seclusion for many years. His ability was unique in the simple handling of masses and planes that were given depth by the use of dark shadows and outlines. He sought to indicate the internal structure of a thing rather than the external form, thus leading the way for the later cubists and abstractionists. He carefully studied the anatomy of landscapes and seascapes and interpreted them in glowing tones. Fearful of women, he produced few nudes, but painted his uncomely wife many times. His still-lifes of fruits and vegetables have rarely been surpassed. His methods revolutionized painting, and, although his leadership was not recognized until 1904, he is considered today one of the greatest contributors to the de-

"By the Seashore," by Pierre-Auguste Renoir.

"The Bather," by Pierre-Auguste Renoir.

velopment of the art. He has been the greatest single influence in art in the first half of the 20th century.

Monet (1840–1926) was primarily a landscapist interested in transitory effects. His trees and buildings were often little more than a blurred mass, and it was after his "Impression at Sunrise" was exhibited in 1863 that the term Impressionist was applied to his group. He painted Rouen Cathedral seventeen times, under different light conditions, and always the form was indistinct and seemed trembling, but the colors glistened whether they were the purples and grays of a moisture-laden day or the reds and yellows of a brilliant sun. One of his best known pictures was an interior view of St. Lazare railway station,* a banal subject that he glamorized by a delicate luminosity that was diffused by smoke, steam, and a dawn-lit atmosphere. He appealed to the esthetic emotions by color rather than by subject matter. He was a leader of the "Pleinairists" who believed in working out-of-doors instead of in the studio. Sisley (1840–1899) and Pissarro (1831–1903) were his close counterparts.

Renoir (1840–1919) was influenced by Rubens and the Venetian school and was content to be an Impressionist for but a short time. He was interested in the interplay of colors caused by flickerings of sunshine and shadow, and his tone harmonies are attained by innumerable light refractions, in which hue melts into hue and produces a vibrating effect. The surface of his pictures is satin-like in quality. His subject matter was rooted to the innocent joys of life and particularly to those that were typical of his native France. One feels the

* In the Art Institute of Chicago.

"The Nativity," by Paul Gauguin.

bloom of pulsating youth and a lust for life in all that he painted. He was skillful in the representation of bare flesh; his nudes in bizarre poses are indicated with a discreet refinement, and are a pure tribute to nature. His portraits attain the utmost in charm and his flowers and trees reflect a sensitivity that embodies the redolence of Spring. One of his most expressive paintings is the "Luncheon of the Boating Party," * in which he entrancingly portrays the innocent gaities of a youthful gathering on a sunny summer's day. His style was unique and was not adopted by later artists.

Henri Rousseau (1844–1910) was a government customs inspector who painted as a pastime. In his youth he had visited the Mexican jungles, and on returning to France, he reproduced such scenes from memory with vivid, though naïve, imagination. Due to his lack of technical training, his work was primitive in character, but of excellent decorative quality. He is today considered an individualist of unusual talent.

Gauguin (1848–1903) had a Peruvian mother and in his youth shipped as a seaman to tropical ports. He was later a banker in Paris and pursued painting as a hobby. He soon became depressed with the sordidness of money-changing and felt a creative urge. In 1881 he turned to painting as a life work. Rejecting all previous theories, he became the most radical of the Impressionists and retired to Brittany to be close to nature. Disillusioned by the conventions of civilization, he fled, in 1891, to Tahiti to

* In the Duncan Phillips Gallery, Washington, D. C.

Pen and ink drawing by Vincent Van Gogh.

become part of the life of the South Seas, and there produced his most characteristic paintings. He loved the tropical colors, the brown-skinned natives, the luxurious landscape, and the romance of primitivism. His paintings are decorative and non-realistic. Figures are molded in attitudes to fit a preconceived pattern and they have a timeless, dignified calm. He applied pure color in broad flat areas and in flowing curves with only a suggestion of depth. The influences of Oriental arts are obvious and there are resemblances to medieval tapestry and stained glass design.

Van Gogh (1853–1890), a Dutchman who worked in France, was considered a Post-impressionist. He first worked as a picture dealer in Paris, later becoming a preacher in mining towns, and it was only during the last eight years of his life that he turned to painting with a passionate devotion. At first he followed Dutch tradition, but later was inspired by Millet, Delacroix, and Daumier, and finally moved from realism into an expression of turbulent emotions. His life was essentially tragic, a fact apparent in all his work; colors are violent, forms deliberately contorted, and even inanimate objects seem to twist with abnormality. His unusual textural effects were produced by applying the paint with palette knife, fingers, or by stippling. His brush strokes were sometimes in obvious curves. At times he adopted the pointillism of Seurat and, later, joined an incompatible Gauguin in southern France where he painted landscapes, still-lifes, portraits, and figure studies. He was not concerned with representing externals, but with hidden meanings, and often he appears to lean toward a madness that was deliberate and more than imaginary. At one time he cut off his own ear and he finally committed suicide. Typical examples of his work include "Sunflowers," "Houses at Arles," and "Cypresses in the Moonlight." His style was too personal for imitation and he left no inheritors of his art theories.

Seurat (1859–1891). Seurat's active production did not come until the end of the Impressionist period, when many artists were beginning to investigate new paths. He was not only inspired by the Impressionists' formulas, but was the supreme example of the "pointillist" group, whose painstaking technique was to eliminate all brush strokes and create effects by the most minute juxtaposed dots of spectrum colors. He is sometimes called a Neo-impressionist and believed that opaque objects should be made to vibrate, as well as the atmosphere. He was a student of space

"La Grande Jatte," by Georges Seurat.

"The Sofa," by Henri de Toulouse-Lautrec.

relationships, studying his paintings as a pattern design. He also was conscious of the necessity that the painter avoid photographic competition and he endeavored to introduce elements that the camera could not imitate. He tried to reduce painting and the use of color to scientific formulas. His subject matter, which was considerably conventionalized, included park scenes, groups of bathers, and circuses. He was not a prolific producer. His greatest work, and one in which his flawless abilities are evidenced, is "La Grande Jatte," * which shows a group of holiday-makers on a river bank near Paris, a subject typical of the period, full of local color, and having a nostalgic appeal.

Toulouse-Lautrec (1864–1901), a talented bohemian who was influenced by Daumier, Degas, and Goya, concentrated on decorative satire, finding rich subject matter in the sordid cafés and dance halls of Paris. The fact that he was a cripple may have accounted for his cynicism. He was an excellent draftsman, but a mediocre colorist, and observed outstanding characteristics with penetrating clarity; in recording them he used the tricks of exaggeration of the caricaturist. One also notices in his work the influence of Japanese prints, and he is considered the originator of the modern poster. "At the Moulin Rouge," one of his most typical paintings, is in the Art Institute of Chicago.

Matisse (1869–1954) was the leader of the "Fauves" (wild beasts), who, after 1900, reacted vigorously against Impressionism. He was an expert draftsman, but ignored detail, and his credo is "Simplification, Organization, and Expression." He was a painter, sculptor, and lithographer, and his paintings have an extraordinarily decorative quality with flat-patterned compositions in pure colors that dazzle the eye. The subject matter is often borrowed from Persian, African Negro, or Polynesian figures; textile patterns; and ceramics; and is usually joyful and sensuous in character.

Rouault (1871–1958) has been called a psychologist and a mystic because of his austere religious figures, sad-faced clowns, bedraggled prostitutes, and leering judges. During his early apprenticeship as a stained-glass worker he learned of the luminosity of colors separated by dark lines, and he usually maintained this technique in his work.

Utrillo (1883–1955) has concentrated on painting the Montmartre section of Paris. His technique is rough, but clever, and his colors tend toward neutralized tones; his affection for the subject matter is so intense that he has almost captured the odors as well as the poetry and romance of the district, and his paintings have had a strong appeal to Francophiles.

Picasso (b. 1881) was born in Malaga, Spain, and studied art in Barcelona and Madrid, but became a resident of Paris in 1904. Of all artists

* In the Art Institute of Chicago.

Courtesy Art Institute of Chicago

"Daughter of the Artist," by Henri Matisse.

"The Guitarist," by Pablo Picasso.

Courtesy Museum of Modern Art, New York

"Guernica," by Pablo Picasso (1937).

he has probably produced the greatest variety of theories, techniques, and conceptions, which he claims are neither experiments nor researches, but merely the application to canvas of his thoughts and feelings. His purpose in each painting seems to be to relieve himself of a momentary emotional desire. He avoids naturalism as being the opposite of art, has concentrated on abstractions and form, and believes that good art is timeless. In painting symbols of thought, emotion, or internal structure, he only hints at the representation of externals. In his etching "Weeping Woman," he has endeavored to delineate a visual impression of internal feelings, and vaguely indicates the woman herself. His style changes seem to be exploratory, rather than evolutionary, and under such theses he disregards all canons of the past. Picasso is an exquisite draftsman, but frequently subordinates this quality in his work. His early years were a struggle for recognition and, in his Blue Period, he painted beggars and a miserable humanity in bluish tones, exemplified by the "Old Guitarist" in the Art Institute of Chicago. This was followed by a Rose Period, when his outlook on life appeared to be more cheerful, and he turned to examine Greek and Negro sculpture. From 1913 to 1920 he was the leader of the Cubists, who attempted to simplify all natural forms to the shapes of cubes and geometrical solids as a protest against photographic exactitude. For a time he was interested in *collage,* where for the purpose of textural effects, paper and other materials were used in his compositions. He also reintroduced what is known as *simultaneity* in art, a term used to indicate the concurrent presentation of two or three sides of an object, such as an overlapping profile and full face to give a comprehensive view, or multiplied legs and arms to convey the idea of motion. This technique had previously been used by the ancient Egyptians. His "Guernica," painted after the German destruction of the peaceful inhabitants of that Spanish city, carries in gray, black, and white, a stylized symbolism of all the horrors of war, using the conventionalisms of El Greco in an exaggerated form. In later years he has attempted many other styles and techniques. Much of his work has been grotesque or surrealistic, with unrecognizable subject matter. Picasso has also worked as an etcher, sculptor, and ceramist, and by common consent has been the most powerful influence in art since Cezanne.

There were several other artists who collaborated with Picasso during the Cubist period, although each contributed a personal element, and some of them eventually branched in other directions. Among these were Braque, who considered a canvas to be a flat surface that deserved a flat pattern, and Duchamp, who attempted to paint motion in the "Nude Descending the Stairs," a picture that received notoriety in the Armory Show in New York in 1913. Picabia and Leger had similar approaches. Other artists proceeded along more independent lines, and there have been many theories and "isms" since the days of Cubism. Most of these have been of short duration, such as Futurism, based on pure abstraction; Dadaism, inspired by Negro sculpture; and Surrealism, an attempt to interpret the subconscious. Vorticism was of English origin.

Other painters who have worked along individual lines or paralleled the Parisian movements are Derain, Vlaminck, Dufy, Laurencin, and Segonzac of France; Miro and Dali of Spain; Klee of Switzerland; and de Chirico of Italy. Some critics of the productions of the last few of these men are of the opinion that these artists have intentionally blasphemed the sanity of the public although well-known authorities have accepted their work. Rivera and Orozco were foremost Mexican muralists with a social consciousness and a deep sympathy for oppressed humanity. They were equipped with a complete historical knowledge of painting and were energetic and imaginative. They specialized in reviving the art of the true fresco and decorated many public and private rooms in Mexico and the United States. Their paintings are usually on a tremendous scale and magnificently composed. The subject matter is related to the activities of the industrial age, with details and technique that reflect a mixture of the fierceness of native Indian character and the serenity of a European inheritance. The middle of the 20th century has witnessed a vigorous resurgence of every manifestation of

Collection Museum of Modern Art, New York

"The Agrarian Leader Zapata," by Diego Rivera (1931).

art in Mexico, and it is possible that here as well as other Latin American countries will be the center of a new Renaissance.

Résumé of French painting. It is impossible to summarize the contemporary movements in painting because of their complexity and the constant flux that characterizes them. One is still too close to obtain a rational perspective. The only exact statement that can be made is that all the movements differ in approach and technique. All seem to have a horror of photographic form, and, in their production, the same principles have been used by which all great art has been created. There have been honesty and integrity in the work of the leaders, although some have undoubtedly pursued extremes of fantasy. Much modern painting is difficult for the uninitiated to understand, but it is perhaps a source from which the next generation will draw inspiration. In the struggle for renown there often appears an effort to shock the public; reputations are falsely gained and confidence is often misplaced; yet no one can afford to consider genuine efforts as valueless, and logic dictates the necessity to permit the future to pass final judgment.

American Colonial painters. In early Colonial days American inhabitants were adjusting themselves to a new life, and no time was available for art. As time passed, and a degree of security had been attained, there arose a demand motivated by family pride, for "face-painting," a crude form of portraiture. Self-taught artists known as "limners" would peddle canvases on which they had already painted a headless figure to which they could add the face of any purchaser who would sit as a model. These

"Portrait of Samuel Verplanck," by John S. Copley.

journeymen also undertook any other painting job in the offing, whether it was the house itself, a carriage, or a sign. Gustavus Hesselium (1688–1755), a Swede, was probably the first foreigner to arrive in America for the purpose of making a living as a portrait painter; his technique was crude, but he showed a feeling for characterization John Smibert, a Scot who had lived in Italy, arrived in America in 1729. His group portrait painted shortly afterwards, of "Bishop Berkeley and His Entourage" * shows a sense of characterization and composition that technically surpasses the art of the limners. Contemporary with Smibert was the English emigrant Peter Pelham, whose chief importance lies in the fact that he was the stepfather and teacher of John Singleton Copley (1737–1815), the first great American-born painter. The work of the Colonial period culminated in the many portraits of Copley. In his "Lady Wentworth" the textures of materials are smoothly handled and a great refinement of line and detail is apparent. Copley, disapproving of the American Revolutionary ideals, left in 1774, never to return. After this he was considered an English painter, and, although he advanced technically, his late works lack the interest and character of those painted during the American period.

Benjamin West (1738–1820), born in Pennsylvania, went to Rome as a young man and then to England, where he became the second president of the Royal Academy. Although West was primarily a portrait painter he also produced a few historical and mythological subjects that were conceived in a romantic style that later influenced Delacroix. His painting of the "Death of General Wolfe" created a sensation in showing contemporary uniforms rather than the Roman togas that until then had been used in historical paintings. During his residence in London, West taught many Americans, among them Charles Wilson Peale, Gilbert Stuart, and Samuel F. B. Morse, in whose work the impact of West is most strongly reflected.

Charles Wilson Peale (1741–1827) studied under both Copley and West and settled in Philadelphia, where he took an active part in the Revolution. He painted many military portraits and his 14 pictures of

* In the Yale Art Gallery, New Haven, Connecticut.

Washington show him in a more natural manner than those of Stuart, though the latter's have been more extensively reproduced. In 1805 Peale aided in founding the Pennsylvania Academy of Fine Arts. He was a capable draftsman, a harmonious colorist, and able at characterization. His brother James was a miniaturist, and of his 11 children, all named for famous artists, Raphaelle painted still-lifes, Titian painted animals, and Rembrandt (1778–1860) painted historical pictures and portraits, several of them posthumous, of Washington. Robert Fulton (1765–1815), Thomas Sully (1783–1872), and Samuel F. B. Morse (1792–1872) were the last of the realistic portrait painters. It was an indication of the changing economic and cultural interests of the nation that both Fulton and Morse eventually turned to scientific invention. During the second quarter of the 19th century, the daguerreotype temporarily submerged the art of portraiture, and wealthy Americans began to import European "old masters."

American primitive and folk painting. From the 18th century to the present day, America has had her amateur artists, most of whom have painted as a result of a creative urge, and for the purpose of having pictures to decorate their own homes. The middle classes had little access to professionally made pictures or prints, and what the amateurs produced was remarkably harmonious with the rest of their furnishings. Journeymen-painters, and house-owners probably produced many of the pictures, but it was a custom for the young ladies of the family to study "art" in their finishing schools, and upon graduation, they proudly exercised their modest faculty for useful purposes. The pictures that have endured were seldom signed and are mostly of anonymous origin. Most of the early folk painting was produced east of the Mississippi Valley, but Virginia, Ohio, western Pennsylvania, New England, and the Hudson River sections were replete with picturesque views, and seemed to appeal to the artistic instincts of their inhabitants, who were especially prolific in this type of work. The pictures varied considerably in technical proficiency, but were usually naïve and vital in character, and were conscientious efforts. A lack of knowledge of perspective often produced entertaining results. Logical contrasts of highlights and shadows seemed sometimes to be disregarded, drawing was usually poor, and colors often unnatural. A lack of study of relative proportions caused children's faces to be too large for their bodies or legs too short for a torso. Every conceivable subject was painted—portraits, landscapes and seascapes, village and city scenes, important public and church buildings, farmhouses, naval and military battles, ships, race horses, and religious groups were the most common. Many of these old pictures are collector's items and are useful today in carrying out the decoration of informal rooms. They are honest representations of a definite period of American culture and should be

"Delaware Water Gap," by George Inness.

"Gulf Stream," by Winslow Homer.

distinguished from the work of modern painters who capitalize on the crudity of the style.

The Hudson River school. As a result of a developing nationalistic spirit, the building of the Erie Canal, and the romantic influence of such writers as Cooper and Irving, there developed in the early 19th century a group of landscape painters known as the "Hudson River School." The literature and interests of the day were reflected in the West Point and neighboring landscapes of Asher B. Durand (1796–1886), Thomas Doughty (1793–1856), and in the panoramic New England views of Thomas Cole (1801–1848). These men acquired a realistic technique, and, in the grays and browns that had been used by Claude Lorrain, fervently expressed their love of American scenery. Frederick E. Church (1826–1900) painted the natural wonders of both North America and South America. The "Heart of the Andes," now in the Metropolitan Museum of Art in New York, is an outstanding example of his work. He was the great champion and illustrator of the life, and the vast spaces, of the West. This school culminated in the work of George Inness (1825–1894), Homer Martin (1836–1897), and Alexander Wyant (1836–1892), who were perhaps the first Americans to paint landscapes in which the artist's conception dominated the importance of the subject matter. Although as young men these three painted in the traditional manner of their predecessors, there is an influence of the French Barbizon school, and, in Inness' "Peace and Plenty," in the Metropolitan, and other paintings, there is a tendency to omit detail to articulate more clearly the moods of nature.

Mid-19th century American painters. Despite the continued tendency on the part of the wealthy to buy the works of European artists, an artistic consciousness mounted after the close of the Civil War, and several individualists produced work that was indigenous in more than its subject matter.

Winslow Homer (1836–1910) as a young man made two trips to Europe, but there is little evidence of this in his work. At first a successful illustrator for *Harper's Weekly,* in 1884 Homer retired to a small cottage on the coast of Maine and devoted the remainder of his life to depicting and interpreting the local scene. His realistic paintings acquired a distinctive force by careful organization and strong contrasts. He is considered one of the greatest of marine painters.

Thomas Eakins (1844–1916) was a painter of American life. After a trip to Europe in his youth, he returned to Philadelphia, his birthplace, where he taught at the Academy of Art and painted athletes and portraits. More an interpreter, than a reproducer, of realism, Eakins combined bold contrasts in values with serious themes. Having no social ambitions, he preferred painting people characteristic of various elements in society; although greatly criticized in his own day, he finally received recognition. He was a pioneer in scientific methods and among his pupils were John Sloan and William Glackens.

James McNeill Whistler (1834–1903), although born in Massachusetts, was disgusted with the ignorance evidenced by the patrons of art in the 1870's, and went to France and England, where he came under the influence of Courbet, Degas, and the early Impressionists. Opposing the

"The Writing Master," by Thomas Eakins.

"Mrs. Leyland," by J. M. Whistler.

popular and realistic snapshot technique, Whistler painted in near monotones, "Harmonies," "Arrangements," and "Nocturnes." These titles are descriptive of his interest in juxtaposition of lines, masses, surfaces, and tonal values. His "Mother" is composed in a pattern in gray and black. His interest in tonal unities and contrasts is apparent by the fact that the field of etching was as alluring to him as that of painting. As in the paintings of Degas, many characteristics of Japanese prints are apparent in Whistler's work. He decorated the "Peacock Room" now in the Freer Art Gallery in Washington.

Albert Ryder (1847–1917) shunned society and became a recluse in New York City, stating, "The artist needs but a roof and a crust of bread, and his easel and all the rest God gives him." Born in New Bedford, Massachusetts, he was attracted by the sea, the night, the moonlight, and fishing boats, and became a poet in paint. Although he had little formal training, and a certain clumsiness of technique forced him to omit many details of drawing, his paintings as a whole convey, in comparatively abstract terms, the power and mysticism of nature. He is sometimes called "the last of the Romanisticts."

Mary Cassatt (1845–1926) lived most of her life in France. Her work tended toward impressionism, and was strongly influenced by her friends Renoir, Degas, and Manet, whose admiration for her genius was unlimited. She was noted particularly for her portraits of women and children, subjects that she interpreted with unusual delicacy, simplicity, and charm. She also worked as an etcher and pastellist. She took an active interest in promoting collections of art in the United States, and was often called upon to act in an advisory capacity to wealthy American collectors.

Late 19th- and early 20th-century American painting. The last third of the 19th century witnessed the great industrial, economic, and scientific changes in America, and these forcibly affected the artists. The large public art museums were established in New York, Boston, Philadelphia, Chicago, and Cincinnati, and these began to be filled with the work of the European artists of the past. The American artists struggled with little recognition or support, and such men as Childe Hassam, John Twachtman, Alden Weir, Frederick Carl Frieseke, Jonas Lie, and Maurice Prendergast, most of whom had studied in Paris, endeavored to create an indigenous art influenced by the French Impressionists; but, the buyers of pictures continued to look across the Atlantic. At the turn of the century there was a tendency to catch the American pulse in art by means of subject matter. Historical, political, economic, and social changes began to be reflected by these same artists and by others who were equally energetic, honest, and capable. Several painters formed themselves in groups to promote their work and ideas. Robert Henri, Arthur B. Davies, George Luks, William Glackens, John Sloan, and George Bellows were among them. Some of these were members of the "Ashcan School," a designation given to them because they frequently painted backyards, deserted streets, and city slums. Great variety in style occurred. Realism, romanticism, and fantasy were among the methods adopted in the search for an American expression. Etching and lithography were used as well as oil and water color. The attempts, however, were only partly successful, and the public remained somnolent.

The Armory Show of 1913. One of the most important events in American art history occurred in 1913 when the leading American painters, co-operating with foreign artists, organized an International Exhibition of Modern Art in New York City, now known as the "Armory Show." The Americans for the first time saw a large collection of the work of Cezanne, Renoir, Van Gogh, Picasso, Duchamp, and other notable painters from Europe whose pictures were hung side by side with the leading American radicals. The exhibit received much advance publicity and the impact of the opening day was tremendous. Crowds flocked through the doors and the front pages of the newspapers were filled with the news. Many visitors were angered; others laughed, and others cried, "At last." But the consensus of opinion was that American art would never be the same. The following observation, written by Frederick J. Gregg and quoted from the catalogue of the exhibit, is significant: "There can be no life without change, as there can be no development without change. To be afraid of what is different or unfamiliar is to be afraid of the truth and to be a champion of superstition." It was the beginning of a new art movement in the United States. It awakened the public from its lethargy, and revitalized the painters, sculptors, architects, decorators, and industrial designers.

20th-century trends in American painting. Since the "Armory Show," painters in the United States have made a sincere and energetic effort to find an American idiom. There has been much confusion, but confusion is typical of the thought of the century. In general, however, the painters have followed one of three parallel paths. One group has endeavored to interpret the local scene in a realistic manner, using their own instinctive emotional and intellectual capacities; another group, of equal talent but less imagination, in search for a market, has unblushingly imitated the styles of some of the old masters; and a third group, inspired by the abstract processes of Picasso and Braque, have used fantasy, internal structure, symbolism, iconography, simultaneity, or humor in their interpretations. Many of the latter group have created patterns of unrecognizable or highly conventionalized subject matter, to which are given provocative or obscure titles that cause one to pause and contemplate. Techniques in all groups have varied from the extremes of immaculate drawing and sharp cleanliness to the roughest of smudges. Mediums have been oil, water color, and pastel. Subject matter has generally reflected political, social, and economic changes. The world wars, the depression of the 1930's, labor conditions, industrial and agricultural developments, and city growth have been basic themes from which details have been masterfully portrayed. The pleasures, pastimes, joys and sorrows of the people, valleys and mountains, seas and streams, homes and resorts, nudes, and still-lifes have also been universally mirrored. Artists have consistently increased in number, following a greater public consciousness as to the meaning and importance of the work of the painter in the daily life of the individual.

Without classification in the groups above mentioned, some of the recognized leaders whose paintings are exhibited in the museums throughout the United States are Thomas H. Benton, Louis Bouché, Charles E. Burchfield, John Steuart Curry, Stuart Davis, Charles Demuth, Guy Pène du Bois, George Grosz, Edward Hopper, Walt Kuhn, Yasuo Kuniyoshi, John Marin, Reginald Marsh, Abraham Rattner, Charles Sheeler, John Sloan, Franklin Watkins, Max Weber, and Grant Wood. These have been followed by such abstractionists as William Baziotes, Jackson Pollack, Hans Hofmann, and Robert Motherwell.

Miscellaneous Types of Pictures

The rarity and cost of great paintings have forced the decorator to use minor works of art in various mediums to enrich the walls of rooms.

There are many original works of secondary quality, and many methods of quantity production in the pictorial and graphic arts have contributed greatly to decorative room treatments. A knowledge of available material is essential.

As a general rule, reproductions of the works of great artists are only to be considered for the walls of rooms if they are done by graphic processes such as engraving and etching, in which the engraver himself has put something into the work in translating it into a medium that is different from the original picture. But even reproductions by such processes tend toward poor taste, because so many have been made that the saturation point in their use has been reached, making them common in character and their use unoriginal. In spite of the greatness of da Vinci's "Mona Lisa" and Hals' "Laughing Cavalier," it is advisable to avoid the use of reproductions of them or similar ones in any medium. The same is true of reproductions of the work of many of the more recent American painters, many of which have a popular appeal and false prestige attained by modern commercial methods.

There are many forms of inexpensive pictures done by professional and amateur artists that are not only good works of art but are also of decorative value because they are sincere efforts to produce the pictorial interpretation of their periods. Many of these examples are not only beautiful but have also the interest and charm that comes from accuracy and care of delineation, subject matter, naïveté, romance, sentiment, or humor.

In the following pages are given brief descriptions of various types of pictures made by professional and amateur artists that are available, suitable, comparatively inexpensive, and in good taste when used in their proper places.

Water colors. These were the earliest type of brushwork pictures, and are made of pigments soluble in water. It was the method employed by the Chinese and Persians. The true water color is technically called an *aquarelle,* and is produced with a transparent color mixed with water. As the mixture is usually applied to white paper, the whiteness of the background affects the tonal value of the color and plays its part in the final effect. Aquarellists must work rapidly and surely, as it is difficult to alter a color when once it has dried. In *gouache* the pigment is first mixed with a white zinc powder to make it opaque. It is then thinned to the proper consistency with water and is applied to the paper or other background; but it is sufficiently opaque to completely cover the surface, so that only the pigment shows. *Tempera,* a very old process, is similar to gouache except that the pigment is combined with a thin glue or with white of egg instead of water. It is, today, extensively used in poster work, designs for magazine covers, and commercial advertising. Water color is used as a medium by itself and to color or tint drawings or engravings.

Drypoint etching, "Limehouse," by James McNeill Whistler.

Practically all the famous artists have produced in this medium as well as in oil, and it is universally used at the present time. Water colors make delightful decorations, and must be judged on an art basis.

Woodcuts. These were the earliest means of making prints. The line design is drawn or pasted upon a pearwood block and the necessary furrows are cut out with a knife or graver, to leave only the line in relief. Woodcuts are used for impressions upon paper and textiles. Lines are bold, and prints may be made in black or color. The great period of woodcuts occurred in Germany during the life of Albrecht Dürer (16th century). However, excellent woodcuts are extensively made today. In wood-engravings lines are cut in a boxwood block. The design is printed from the untouched surfaces. In woodblocks, the block is cut away to leave the design intended. The surfaces are inked and pressed on paper. In color printing, separate blocks are used for the various colors.

Etchings. Impressions from line drawings made upon copper plates. The design is cut through varnish with a needle. Acid bites the exposed copper, making sunken lines, a method practised since 1513. Many of the great Renaissance masters worked in this medium, and it is a method constantly used today for the production of black-and-white drawings covering all subjects. Recent foreign etchers of distinction include Cameron, McBey, Zorn, Segonzac, Matisse, Forain, and Marcoussis. The leading American etchers are Whistler, Pennell, Arms, Eby, West, Lewis, and Benson.

Steel engravings. Line and wash effects produced by parallel and fine intersecting lines cut on a steel plate, sometimes with mechanical aids for drawing lines. A process particularly popular for book illustrations and wall pictures during the 19th century. Black-and-white prints, sometimes hand colored. The process is used when large editions are required.

Dry points. A copper plate is scratched by a very sharp steel tool with a tapering point, used like a pencil. Sunken lines result, and a "bur" is turned up which prints richly unless cut off. The plate is inked all over and then wiped clean, so that only the ink remaining in the lines prints. Sometimes a tone is left on the whole plate. Black-and-white line drawings are made by this process. Rembrandt used this method extensively for making sketches, and it has constantly been used since by etchers. More recent artists who have used this method are Cameron, Rodin, Forain, Bone, Blampied, and Nevinson.

Mezzotints. An early process similar to engraving, but producing tonal and wash effects rather than line drawings. The plate is "rocked" by a many-toothed tool until evenly roughened. The design is procured by scraping and burnishing the higher lights. When the surface has been inked all over and wiped, the ink is retained by the roughnesses and leaves the scraped and burnished surfaces in varying degrees. On paper the print shows an almost lineless design in soft velvety black-and-white effects. Brilliant productions were made by this process in England during the 18th century, when the works of the English portrait painters were reproduced. Many reproductions were also made of Morland's paintings, showing pastoral scenes and figure compositions.

Aquatints. A process similar to the mezzotint, but permitting very subtle and delicate effects in color. The design is put on copper through a process of roughening the plate by acid "biting." Popularized in England at the end of the 18th century for reproducing paintings of views, naval engagements, and sporting subjects.

Lithographs. A system of reproduction introduced in 1798. Impressions imitate the character of chalk drawings in black or color. Prepared soapstone is drawn on with a greasy crayon and then chemically treated. Ink rolled onto the wetted stone "takes" only where the crayon has touched, and prints only therefrom. Extensively used for both illustrations and posters, but many of the great artists—particularly Daumier, Gavarni, Bellows, and Matisse—have produced works in this medium in every variety of subject.

Monotypes. Oil paintings on glass or copper transferred to a sheet of paper by pressure. The subjects are usually flowers and landscapes.

Linoleum cuts. Similar to woodcuts, but coarser in detail. Original plates cut in linoleum.

Original drawings. In pencil, pen, pastel, and crayon. They are, of course, of varying merit depending upon the artist, and an appraisal of their value either as works of art or as decorations must come from ex-

Drix Duryea, Photographer

Early 19th century English coaching print.

Courtesy The Art Institute of Chicago

Swedish Bonader painting, or wall hanging of the early 19th century, typical of folk or peasant arts of Europe.

perience. They have been made in all periods and are extensively used today in decoration.

In addition to pictures produced by the
foregoing processes, there are prints of two
special types of subject that may be considered particularly valuable for decorative
use: sporting prints and Audubon prints.

Sporting prints. Hunting, coaching,
fishing, and sporting scenes made from
original oil paintings in England and
France during the 18th and 19th centuries.
Most of them were engravings colored in
part by hand. The prints were made for
wide distribution to the general public,
who were as interested in hunting as were
the great landowners. The works of Alken,
Herring, Sartorious, and Wolstenholme
were particularly notable. Many of the
prints today are more valuable than the original paintings. Many reproductions have been made.

*"Wild Turkey," an original
painting by John J. Audubon.*

Audubon prints. Magnificent life-size, hand-colored aquatints of hundreds of species of American birds, made by the great naturalist and engraved and colored by Havell in London, between 1828 and 1837. Limited quantity and of considerable value. Many worthless reproductions.

Peasant paintings and folk art. Paintings on wood, canvas, paper, velvet, and glass, of naïve and quaint subject matter, made by peasants and
amateurs in Europe and America.

Wool ship pictures. Made by British seamen in the early years of the
19th century. Subjects consist mostly of ships and views of foreign ports.
Embroidered in coarse bright-colored yarns. Flags are usually conspicuous.

Embroideries. Made in needlepoint and silk during all historic periods
of decoration, usually by women.

Samplers. Sample embroideries, usually made by children. Local
scenes, alphabets, poems, and patterns. Made during the 18th and 19th
centuries in Europe, North America, and South America.

Velvet paintings. Local scenes and portraits, often of a mortuary type.
Made in England, France, and America during the early years of the 19th
century.

Bead and shell pictures. Extraordinary combinations of colored beads
or shells to form scenes or patterns. Placed on a fabric background.

Silhouettes. Extraordinary technique developed by cutting profiles in

Currier and Ives lithograph, "The Rocky Mountains."

paper and pasting them on white or colored grounds. Figures, portraits, flowers, and other subjects in black and colors. First made as a popular pastime at country fairs. Very popular as decorations in the Biedermeier period.

Wax silhouettes. In relief, usually showing portraits in profile, sometimes clothed in lace and jewelry. Popular in 17th century Germany and 18th century France and England.

Tinsel pictures. Started as a fad for both men and women in England in the 18th century. Composition produced by colored cut-outs of figures and flowers combined with bright-colored tinsel and lace, with jewelry often added. Shakespearean characters were popular as subject matter. Tinsel pictures were often applied to screen decoration during the 18th and 19th centuries in England and France.

Images populaires. Cheap engravings, crudely drawn, colored by hand, and made in all European countries. The "vues d'optiques" are of French architectural and garden subjects, with windows cut out so that candlelight would show through the openings. The "Epinal" pictures in France glorified Napoleon's victories. Many religious prints were also of this nature.

Glass paintings. Done in oil on the reverse side of the glass. Many of these paintings are of extraordinary beauty, while others are primitive in character. The best were made in China, but fine ones were produced in France and England during the 18th century. The subjects show great variety. Many amateurs in the United States made them during the Federal period, showing naval battles and historic scenes.

Currier and Ives. Colored lithographs of early 19th century American scenes. Very popular among farmers, and now valued for historical record. Great range of subjects: farm scenes, historical, sporting, and hunting events, early Western range views, early railroad scenes, portraits of presidents, and many others.

Courtesy Metropolitan Museum of Art

Stumpwork picture, English, about 1680, "The Judgment of Paris."

Photo Reproductions. In color, of modern paintings. Remarkable imitations of every detail, including the brush strokes and paint shadows. Inexpensive and excellent substitutes for original works, providing mass production is not begun.

Colored engravings. Made during the 19th century. Subjects: flowers, costumes, animals, portraits, historic scenes, and scenes of adventure. Often decorative and very inexpensive.

Stumpwork. Embroideries showing figures padded to form a relief effect. Popular during the Restoration period in England.

Serigraphs. Excellent reproductions of paintings made by the silk screen process.

Picture Framing

The framing of pictures is a matter of great importance. Etchings, water colors, oil paintings, Japanese prints, pencil drawings, and photographs all require varying types of frames. Some are better under glass, some without; some require ornate frames, others the simplest ones possible. The frames of a generation ago were almost invariably bad. They were too heavy and elaborate, often overloaded by shadow boxes, and in many cases were more important than the pictures they contained. Furthermore, these frames were of plaster and not of carved and gilded wood, as were the beautiful frames of the 18th century. Designs were poor and of a commercial character. At present antique frames are much in demand for both genuinely old paintings and prints.

Oil paintings, particularly by the old masters, demand rich frames. Gilt frames are usual, and properly so, as gold helps to harmonize rich color without competing with it. Whatever the type selected, care should be taken to keep the gilding dull. Italian frames of the Cinquecento were

Courtesy Mrs. Paul C. Downing; Samuel H. Gottscho, Photographer

Joseph Platt, Decorator; Drix Duryea, Photographer

Picture hanging. ABOVE: *two or three pictures of similar size and subject matter appear best when hung symmetrically at eye level and properly composed with the furnishings.* BELOW: *when pictures of various sizes are
hung in mass as shown in this room, they serve as an all-over pattern for
the wall, and while a balanced arrangement is desirable, it is not always
possible.*

usually architectural in design, flanked by columns or pilasters, the top usually centered or with a pediment, and the whole design ornamented with arabesques in relief. No better type could be found, particularly for religious subjects. The design is that of an altarpiece, for which purpose most of these paintings were made. The Renaissance in Spain produced very fine frames. The workmanship and scale of detail were possibly cruder than in Italy and France, but their striking originality has always had a marked decorative appeal.

As a rule, oil paintings should be framed without mats or glass, although today narrow borders, either painted or covered with natural-colored linen, are in vogue. Logically, modern oil paintings require simpler frames than do the old masters, although antique frames are often used on ultramodern pictures.

Pictures made on paper require glass for protection, as they grow dirty and cannot be cleaned. There are, however, many possible types of frame, varying according to the character of the picture. For colored reproductions of the old masters, the frames may be very similar to those that would be used for an original. As a matter of fact, reproductions of famous paintings are rarely seen today in well-decorated interiors; if one is particularly fond of a masterpiece of the past, however, there is no law of taste which forbids that a photograph of it be hung. Decorators have encouraged their clients to buy genuine antique paintings of a decorative nature, even though these pictures may be third or fourth rate—that is, providing the client cannot afford the best. It is felt that period rooms should be hung with contemporaneous originals or at least with well-executed copies.

Portrait photographs, travel views in photography, and others of this class may be framed in simple mouldings with or without mats; however, it is inadvisable to hang them on the wall. Frames for portrait photographs should have adjustable stands for table use. With less body than oil paintings, water colors should be framed more simply; their frames should be of the simplest type, usually of natural wood, with little or no ornament; if the picture is small, a mat is usually advisable. For pencil sketches, equally simple frames are advisable. If the drawing has a considerable expanse of paper left blank around it, no mat is necessary.

In conformity with French taste and an equally French medium, pastels may be framed with gilt moldings, although a natural wood is entirely suitable. Eighteenth century French prints and drawings should be framed with rather wide ruled paper mats, typical of the framing of the Louis XVI period. The artist's name and the title of the drawing were invariably lettered within a decorative cartouche on the matting. For modern prints, etchings, lithographs, etc., mats are ordinarily used. The mat should be cut out to fit the print, the opening being large enough to

This arrangement of pictures of various sizes is agreeable in appearance and well related to the furniture composition.

show the plate-mark and the signature. Prints also look well framed in black lacquer with narrow gold beading or in natural, unstained wood. Some etchings approach the strong tones of painting and should be framed with relatively heavy moldings. Frames are today made of varied materials. Glass, mirror, chromium, richly grained veneers, cork, and even stretched fabrics are used. The forms of the moldings themselves vary from the conventional curves to flat splayed surfaces.

Picture Selection and Hanging

Pictures should first be selected from the point of view of their satisfaction to the owner; but to the decorator, it is important to consider the quantity needed, the size and scale of each, their relationship to the wall composition, the colors, and the frame.

Rooms whose walls are decorated with murals, scenic paper, or strongly patterned wallpaper do not usually require a great amount of additional pictorial enrichment. If pictures are hung on wallpaper, they should be sufficiently important in size and effect not to be lost in the background. Hung pictures are at their best against a plain neutral surface.

If an owner has selected a painting as an important decorative feature,

When prints of similar size and subject matter are used for pictorial enrichment, they should be arranged in an orderly composition resembling a repeating wallpaper pattern.

it is advantageous to repeat the colors of the painting in the color scheme of the room. Small pictures can not be used for this purpose, and unless they are unusually inharmonious with the selected color scheme, they may be considered as color accents or disregarded. It is agreeable to relate the subject matter of pictures to the character and use of the room, as well as to the interests of the owner.

As a general rule, instinct will designate what wall areas should be hung with pictures or other decorative objectives such as mirrors, clocks, and sconces. One should feel that a space appears empty before a decision is made to fill it. Walls upon which many pictures are hung are, of course, more restless in appearance than those that are treated sparingly with pictorial decoration. A picture of unusual decorative or esthetic value should be given ample wall area. The Orientals frequently hang but one picture in a room, and that one, of great beauty, is hung in the most significant space and is changed from time to time for the sake of variety. If several pictures are hung on a wall, they should not be placed indiscriminately, but arranged in a simple geometrical grouping such as a rectangle, straight line, or triangle. Where numerous pictures of varying sizes and shapes are used, composition in balance is difficult, and it is then usually advisable to mass them in close proximity so that they "count" much the same as a mural decoration or scenic wallpaper.

Pictures may often be used advantageously to create an effect of balance in wall composition, where a symmetrical arrangement of furniture forms is not attainable.

The more usual method of hanging pictures is to place them singly or in small groups in important wall spaces or panels or above mantels or furniture. Groups of three should usually be balanced with the largest picture in the center or two pictures should be of equal size. A better effect is obtained if the pictures in the same groups are similar in character and color value. Oil paintings and water colors hung in close proximity are usually inharmonious unless similar in tonal values, and colored pictures hung close to black-and-white drawings or reproductions have an appearance of inconsistency. Unsymmetrical groups of pictures may be arranged in wall spaces that are not on the central axis of the room or in cases where pictures must accommodate themselves to adjoining furniture that is irregular in shape. Small pictures look best when hung at eye level. Large paintings that must be viewed from a distance may be hung at a greater height.

It is advisable to avoid showing the wires necessary for picture hanging. Pictures should be hung from nails or hooks that are driven into the wall behind the picture itself, and the picture should be hung as flat as possible against the wall. This can be done by placing the screws near the top of the frame.

Bibliography

Abbot, E. R., *The Great Painters in Relation to the European Tradition.* Harcourt, Brace and Co., New York, 1927. Fully illustrated text.

ARMS, J. T., *Handbook of Print Making and Print Makers*. The Macmillan Co., New York, 1934. A very complete text, fully illustrated.

Art Studies, Medieval, Renaissance, and Modern. Edited by members of the Departments of Fine Arts at Harvard and Princeton Universities, 1929. Excellent illustrated text.

BARNES, A. C., *The Art in Painting*. Harcourt, Brace and Co., New York, 1928. Excellent illustrated treatment of the development of painting.

BARR, A. H., *Cubism and Abstract Art*. Modern Museum of Art, New York, 1936. Illustrated brief history of the modern movement toward abstract design.

BARR, A. H., Editor, *Masters of Modern Art*. Simon and Schuster, New York, 1954 Excellent illustrations.

BERENSON, B., *Florentine Painters of the Renaissance*. G. P. Putnam's Sons, New York, 1909. Authoritative text.

BLISS, D. P., *A History of Wood-engraving*. E. P. Dutton and Co., New York, 1928. Illustrated comprehensive study of the history of wood engraving.

CHENEY, S., *Expressionism in Art*. Liveright Publishing Corp., New York, 1934. Illustrated text treating the modern movement.

CORTISSOZ, R., *The Painter's Craft*. Charles Scribner's Sons, New York, 1930. Illustrated collection of essays on European and American artists.

CRAVEN, T., *A Treasury of Art Masterpieces*. Simon and Schuster, New York, 1939. Beautiful colored reproductions with descriptive text.

DOERNER, M., *The Materials of the Artists and Their Use in Painting* (tr. Neuhaus). Harcourt, Brace and Co., New York, 1934. A comprehensive book on the technique of painting.

EARP, T. W., *The Modern Movement in Painting*. The Studio Publications, New York, 1935. Text on the Impressionist and Post-impressionist schools of painting, illustrated with color plates.

Encyclopedia of Painting, edited under the auspices of the Metropolitan Museum of Art, New York, 1955. An excellent alphabetical listing of artists and art subjects with many colored illustrations.

HAMERTON, P. G., *Etching and Etchers*. The Macmillan Co., London, 1876. Out of print. A standard illustrated work.

HIND, A. M., *A Short History of Engraving and Etching*. Houghton Mifflin Co., New York, 1908. Illustrated text.

MARLE, R. VAN, *The Italian Schools of Painting*, 17 Vols. M. Nijhoff, The Hague, 1923–1935. Illustrated histories of the various schools from the 6th to the end of the 13th centuries.

MATHER, F. J., JR., *History of Italian Painting*. Henry Holt and Co., New York, 1923. A comprehensive survey of Italian painting with illustrations.

MATHER, F. J. JR., *Western European Painting of the Renaissance*. Henry Holt and Co., New York, 1939. An excellent description of these types.

REWALD, J., *The History of Impressionism*. Museum of Modern Art, New York, 1946. An authoritative and detailed study.

REYNAL, N., *Modern French Painters* (tr. Roeder). Brentano's, New York, 1925. Excellent illustrated text.

ROTHENSTEIN, J., *Nineteenth Century Painting*. The Bodley Head, Ltd., London,

1932. Discussion of 19th century English and French painters.

SMITH, K., *An Outline of Modern Painting in Europe and America*. W. Morrow and Co., New York, 1931. Good illustrated text.

SOBY, J. T., *After Picasso*. Dodd, Mead and Co., New York, 1935. Illustrated general background of the newer painting.

SOBY, J. T. *Contemporary Painters*. Museum of Modern Art, New York, 1948. An excellent handbook.

STOKES, A., *Landscape Painting*. J. B. Lippincott Co., Philadelphia, 1925. Illustrated text.

TAYLOR, FRANCIS H., *Fifty Centuries of Art*. Harper and Brothers, New York, 1954. Excellent colored illustrations.

WEITENKAMPF, F., *How to Appreciate Prints*. Charles Scribner's Sons, New York, 1932. Illustrated text.

WEITENKAMPF, F., *The Quest of the Print*. Charles Scribner's Sons, New York, 1932. An illustrated text on collecting prints.

WILENSKI, R. H., *Masters of English Painting*. Hale, Cushman, and Flint, Inc., Boston, 1934. An excellent illustrated history.

WILENSKI, R. H., *French Painting*. Hale, Cushman and Flint, Inc., Boston, 1931. An excellent illustrated survey of this field.

CHAPTER XVI

PAINTS AND PAINTING

The subject of paints and painting is so intimately related to effective and tasteful color use that a technical knowledge of the processes and the methods of obtaining desired results is essential as part of the equipment of all decorators.

Plain painting is distinctly a trade, but in its higher forms it may approach the borderlines of art, and it invariably requires consummate craftsmanship. There are so many variations in quality of both material and workmanship that much experience is necessary before expert technical or intelligent supervisory ability may be acquired. The decorator seldom handles a paintbrush himself, but he should know the language of the painter and the names of the various finishes and effects, and should have a reasonable amount of information concerning the mixtures and applications necessary to produce them.

Paint materials. Good oil paint must be made of a mixture of materials which give it a proper working consistency. It should be opaque, its pigments should be as nearly nonfading as possible, and the proportions of the various chemicals used to produce it should be such that it has the greatest durability for its particular use.

Paint is a mixture of a base, a pigment, and a binder or vehicle. The base, except for very dark paints, is *white lead,* which gives the paint its covering quality. The pigment or pigments give the paint its color and decorative quality. The binder serves to cement the pigment to the base and to the surface to be painted, and to make the consistency of the paint suitable for spreading evenly over a surface. In interior paints linseed oil is most commonly used as a binder, although varnish, glue, or casein are also used for special purposes. A cheaper grade of paint is made by adulterating the linseed oil with fish oil. A small amount of *turpentine* or benzine may be added to a paint mixture to dilute it in order to create a thinner layer to cover a larger surface area, to increase its rate of drying, and to give greater penetration of the pores of the surface to be painted. Special drying chemicals that may be added in small quantities are oxide of cobalt, iron, lead, manganese, and metallic salts; these materials also produce a harder finished surface.

In addition to white lead as a base for paint mixtures, it is usually wise to add a percentage of zinc oxide. Lead has a tendency to turn into a fine powdered chalk after it has dried for two or three years. The addition of pigments lessens this tendency. Zinc oxide may also be used as a base, but paint made of this material will eventually crack, which makes it difficult to repaint over such a surface. The majority of painters advise, as a paint base, a mixture of about 30 per cent zinc to 70 per cent lead; this is claimed to overcome the defects of both materials. Titanium oxide, a very white pigment, is often combined with zinc oxide, in the proportion of 20 per cent zinc oxide to 80 per cent titanium oxide. It has excellent hiding power, and stands up well under exposure. This pigment is frequently used by paint manufacturers for ready-mixed interior and exterior paints and enamels.

The selection of oils to be used for paint mixtures is of the utmost importance. There is nothing better than pure linseed oil for a binder, although linseed oil has a tendency to turn yellow, and when a white painted surface is desired only a small quantity should be used for interior work. It is very essential to use only the products of reputable manufacturers of linseed oil, as there are many adulterated products on sale.

Pure linseed oil may be obtained in its raw or boiled state. When raw oil is used, it is necessary to add a japan drier to the paint mixture. Boiled oil dries more rapidly by itself.

Calcimine is another word for tempera, or opaque water-color paint. It is usually made of a very finely ground chalk, known as whiting, and a powdered pigment mixed with a binder of water and glue or casein. Calcimine is comparatively inexpensive, but is without the permanency of oil paint, and because of its water base is unwashable. If the glue is made of casein, a protein of milk, it becomes insoluble when dry, so that the finished surface is theoretically washable, but as many ready-mixed paints of this type have an insufficient content of this material, they do not fulfill this claim. Casein dries to a hard surface and only one coat need be used.

Lacquers are made of pigments mixed with solutions of pyroxylin and ethyl or alcohol, combined with a plasticizer to increase adhesion. They are very hard when dry, adhere firmly to any surface upon which they are applied, and dry rapidly. Enamels are not as hard as lacquers and are made of mixtures of pigments and varnish.

Varnishes are made of gum or resin mixed with oil, turpentine, alcohol, ether, or chloroform. They are transparent or translucent and may be mixed with a limited amount of pigmentation. They dry quickly with a glossy finish, but rubbing and polishing increase their reflecting qualities. If varnishes are mixed with liquid rubber or gutta-percha, they may be used on flexible surfaces such as leathers or textiles.

Stains are made of thin pigmented liquids that are easily absorbed by the materials upon which they are applied. As wood graining varies in density, portions of wooden surfaces absorb stains with different degrees of rapidity; the natural color of the wood is altered and the texture and graining of the wood is accentuated.

Fluorescent paints are made of substances containing radioactive ele-ments that have luminous and high reflective qualities.

Paint mixtures and coverage. For interior work one gallon of paint will cover approximately 400 superficial feet, but this will vary according to the character of the surface to be painted. On rough surfaces or materials which are highly absorbent, the coverage of paint may be considerably less. Thin paint will go further than thick paint, but will have less opaqueness. Paint spreads further on smooth surfaces such as metalwork than it does on rough surfaces such as wood. Second-coat work requires less paint for the same area than first-coat work.

The usual proportions of materials used in making paint for interior work are as follows:

> 100 lb. pure white lead
> 1 gal. raw linseed oil
> 2½ gal. turpentine
> 1 pt. japan drier
> Pigments as necessary

The above mixture produces about 6½ gallons of paint. Each subsequent coat should have a little less turpentine and more linseed oil. For a glossy finish the final coat should have about 3 gallons of oil to 1 pint of turpentine. An *eggshell* or semiflat finish should have 1 gallon of oil to 2 gallons of turpentine and a flat finish should be mixed with 3 gallons of turpentine without any oil whatsoever. The use of zinc and lead in equal parts for a final coat of paint produces a white finish.

In rooms painted in light colors it is usually advisable to use a dull or mat finish for the wall paint. When rooms are to be finished in dark colors, an eggshell or semiflat finish is advisable because of its greater capacity to reflect light. The majority of paint manufacturers supply ready-made paints in a great variety of colors. Care, however, should be taken in selecting such materials, and the reputation of the manufacturer is often the only guarantee of quality, as many adulterants are now used, and the ingredients are not always indicated on the labels of the containers. Ready-made paints often fade rapidly, particularly when exposed to the sun, and also tend to become brittle and crack when dry.

Synthetic paints. For many years the majority of house paints have been made with a base of white lead and oil, and these materials are still considered superior for surfaces subject to weather erosion, wear, and friction. Developments in chemistry have, however, produced several synthetic materials that indicate superior advantages for interior paints. These products are sold under trade names, but most of them are produced from alkyd enamels or latex rubber solutions.

Surfaces painted with either of these synthetics are washable. One coat application is sufficient except on newly plastered walls, and they are fast drying and easy for the novice to apply. The alkyds are made in flat, semi-gloss, and high-gloss finishes, and withstand dampness well in kitchens and bathrooms. The latex types are also produced in a variety of finishes; they tend to leave brush marks but may be patched more easily if surfaces are damaged.

Both types are supplied in ready-mixed hues, and variations may be obtained by mixing these with standard pigments. Color retention and fugitiveness are the same as for the lead and oil bases. Quality in these paints is best judged by considering the reputation of the manufacturer.

Synthetic paint production is subject to constant improvements due to new discoveries, and there are optimistic claims about future developments. The use of polyvinyl acetates appears promising.

Pigments. The majority of first class painters prepare their own colors from pigments furnished by a reputable manufacturer. If the finished color is to be light in value, the pigments are slowly added to the mixture of the base and binder with constant tests and color comparisons with the desired sample. Colors have a tendency to dry to a slightly different hue than when wet, so that if an exact match is required, it is necessary to permit the sample to dry until the gloss has been eliminated. If dark colors are to be mixed, it may be necessary to add a great deal of pigment, so that usually it is better to start with a ready-mixed paint that is close to the color desired, and to which additional pigments may be added.

The following palette will be found sufficient for most types of work.

REDS

Alizarin crimson—A strong red with a bluish cast. A coal-tar color that mixes poorly with earth colors, such as sienna, ochre, or chrome yellow. Good for producing rose and violet hues.

English vermilion—A brilliant red with a yellowish cast. Made from chromate of lead. Does not mix well with cadmium and ultramarine.

Carmine—A brilliant red made from cochineal insects. Strong for tinting.

Indian red—An earth or metal color with a brownish cast. Not good for combination with yellow or blue.

BLUES

Prussian blue—A strong tinting blue, very dark with a greenish cast. Good for producing brilliant greens when combined with yellow.

Cobalt blue—A strong blue with a reddish cast. Good for mixing.

Cerulean blue—A strong blue with a greenish cast.

Ultramarine—Sometimes called French blue. It has a reddish cast and makes a beautiful purple when mixed with alizarin crimson.

YELLOWS

Cadmium—An excellent yellow that mixes well with all colors except chromes and American vermilion. Makes good greens or oranges. Should not be used with white lead. Manufactured in four tones: pale yellow, cadmium yellow, deep yellow, and orange.

Chrome—A color made from lead derivatives manufactured in four tones: light, lemon, medium, and orange. Does not mix well with ultramarine.

Yellow ochre—An earth color with a reddish brown cast. Excellent for producing tans, creams, buffs, and olive green.

GREENS

Viridian, also known as Emeraude—A very brilliant green with a yellowish cast. Excellent for mixing with all other colors.

Emerald green—A very brilliant green with a bluish cast.

BROWNS

Raw sienna—Very similar to yellow ochre. Has high tinting strength.

Burnt sienna—A dark reddish brown with characteristics similar to raw sienna. An earth color.

Raw umber—A dark greenish brown of great tinting strength. Produces very clear tints when mixed with white. An earth color.

Burnt umber—Characteristics similar to raw umber but darker and bluer.

Van Dyke brown—A dark rich purplish brown with high tinting strength. Very transparent. Its tints have a lavender cast.

BLACKS

Lamp black—Made from the smoke of burning oils. A jet black that is good for producing grays when mixed with white.

Ivory black—Made from bone charcoal. Excellent to use as a solid color.

WHITES

White lead—An excellent base for all colors. Has a tendency to turn yellow with age.

Zinc white—A permanent white, used by artists. Mixes well with all colors. Has a tendency to become brittle if exposed to the weather.

Titanium—An excellent opaque base for interior work. Retains its whiteness; should be mixed with 20 per cent zinc oxide.

Permanency of pigment colors. The chemical constituents of pigments are derived from a great variety of animal, mineral, and vegetable sources; and many synthetic or aniline colors have a coal-tar origin. Some of these have a tendency to fade or to change hue. It is essential to know the nonfugitive pigments when permanent color work is planned. Some pigments are fugitive only when combined with certain others. The quality of pigments made by the different paint manufacturers varies greatly, so that no accurate indication may be given as to the permanency of all colors. In general, however, the list given below may be followed:

Permanent—Raw sienna, burnt sienna, ultramarine blue, cobalt blue, raw umber, burnt umber, yellow ochre, Van Dyke brown, ivory, lamp black, vermilion.

Semipermanent—Chrome yellow, green, cadmium yellow, Indian red, Venetian red.

Fugitive—Carmine, crimson lake, madders, Prussian blue, cerulean blue.

White lead makes a poor chemical mixture when combined with ultramarine blue, cobalt blue, English vermilion, and chrome yellows. When using oil paints, it is better to combine these pigments with zinc white for tinting.

Plain wall painting. In the painting of interior plaster walls, there are three conditions that may exist: new walls; old walls that have already been painted; and walls that require the removal of wallpaper before paint can be applied. Plaster should be thoroughly dry before any attempt is made to paint it, and it is often wise to cover a plain plaster wall with a coating of thin varnish, shellac, or size to prevent the chemical stains, which often develop in new plaster, seeping through the several coats of paint and causing a discoloration in the finish. Some painters prefer to apply a size after the first coat of paint has been completed. If there are cracks in a plaster wall—and they often occur in new walls as well as old ones—the cracks should be "cut out" and "painted up." Cutting out means that the crack should be widened with a sharp tool so that the inside of the crack is slightly wider than its appearance on the surface. Filling up refers to filling the crack thoroughly with plaster. The fact that the crack is narrower on the wall surface creates a safer binding for the patch. It is wise to shellac the crack before the plaster filler is added. After adding the plaster, it should be smoothly trowelled, then sandpapered so that it is as smooth as the wall itself, and finally shellacked again. Old walls should be washed with soda and water before the cracks are sealed. When old paint has fallen off, leaving depressions, these are usually "sparkled," or filled up with a special preparation which dries quickly and makes a very smooth patch when sandpapered. "Sparkled" areas must also be treated with shellac or size to prevent greater penetration of the paint than in surrounding areas.

If cost is not a prime consideration, plaster walls should first be canvassed. This procedure excludes all possibility of visible wall blemishes, and is permanent. The permanency is not to be overlooked in the final cost, as the canvas may be repainted many times without the necessity of patching the plaster. There are several different grades in canvas wall coverings. Muslin and "Sanitas" make excellent surfaces for painting and may be applied to the wall with ordinary wallpaper paste.

In painting plaster walls, whether canvassed or otherwise, the first coat of paint, known as the *priming coat,* should have a considerable amount of oil used in the mixture so that the porous surface of the muslin or plaster will be thoroughly filled with both oil and pigment. After each successive coat of paint is applied, and before it begins to dry, it may be *stippled.* A stipple-brush is about the shape of a large scrubbing brush, with bristles three to four inches in length. While one man lays on the paint, another should follow him almost immediately, going over the freshly painted surface with short rapid blows of the stipple-brush. This eliminates the irregularity and streaks of the brush marks, and evens the surface. If the paint is thin, the stippling will not show; but in cheap jobs, the custom is to apply thick coats of paint to save labor, and the stipple marks may be very noticeable and may produce an undesirable rough texture. The same effect may also be achieved by use of the stippling roller, which is about 2 inches in diameter, with a handle, and covered with a coarse pile fabric, such as a small piece of rug. Stippling is usually done only on plaster walls, not on wood.

The subsequent coats of paint should not be applied until the priming coat is entirely dry. Three coats in all are necessary in order to produce a satisfactory result, although many decorators advocate more. Usually four coats should satisfy a most fastidious client.

Suggestions for mixing paint colors. There are no scientific formulas for mixing pigments to produce other colors. One cannot state either what quantity, volume, or weight of paint to use to obtain a desired result. This is due to the fact that the chemical ingredients of certain pigments have stronger *tinting values* than others, so that relatively less of those pigments must be used in mixtures. The production of colors by pigment mixtures must be done by the trial and error method of visual examination.

In trying to obtain a certain color by a paint mixture, the decorator is usually matching another color or producing a color that will be suitable for some part of a room or one that will harmonize suitably with the other hues of a tentative color scheme.

One usually starts with a container of white paint. It is usually advisable to obtain the final colors first in a small quantity, as errors in mixing large quantities are sometimes costly. Pigments should be added slowly and tests of the color should constantly be made on a flat piece of cardboard or wood and these should be held in their final position on wall, ceiling, or elsewhere.

In matching colors, it is advisable to look at the original and the new mixture through a "color window." This is merely a hole of about 1½ inches diameter cut out of a sheet of white paper. The two colors should be placed directly adjoining each other and compared through the hole. The white paper prevents either color from being influenced by any nearby color and the differences in hue, chroma, and tone of the two colors are easily distinguishable.

In selecting colors for walls from small samples one should always keep in mind the fact that the color is to be used in a large area and will appear more brilliant in its mass than it will in the small sample.

The constituents of mixed colors are usually more easily identified by comparison with other colors, i.e., a greenish blue will look greener when placed next to a pure blue, and a certain red will look bluish or yellowish when placed next to a pure red. One can also identify the respective degree of neutrality or tonal value of a color by this same method.

For example, if one compares a group of any four varied examples of painters' pigments in which yellow dominates, one will immediately notice that one appears greenish (blue tinge), another appears to have an orange cast (red tinge), another will appear lighter (white tinge), another will appear grayer or more neutralized (violet tinge). These four colors may be made identical by adding a small amount of the complement * of their respective tinges.

To the first add orange, to the second add green, to the third add yellow, and to the last add yellow and white. The addition of the complement in each case counteracts the original tinge. This principle may be followed in making all mixtures for matching other colors. A small sample of the mixture should be tested by looking at the two samples in very close contact through a color window. The comparative tinge of the mixture should be noted and corrected by adding more pigment of its complement.

Colors are light and dark only by comparison in the same light. The term light and dark is largely a relative term. While white is always light and black always dark, there are many intermediate tonal values that are hard to identify relatively unless they are seen in contrast with colors of other tonal value when they will accentuate each other.

In mixing colors with white, gray, or black pigments one will usually find that the resultant colors turn slightly blue. There is an unseen bluish

* See Chapter XXIV for explanation of this term.

element in these neutral pigments. Mixing any of these pigments with blue, the additional tinge is not visible; but mixing them with red or yellow, a purplish or greenish tinge will respectively be noticeable. This must be corrected in such mixtures by the addition of a slight amount of orange or yellow in the first case and orange or red in the second. The exact amount of the complement to be added must be estimated by observation and trial and error. There is no scientific method of exactly accomplishing this correction.

It is usually advisable to use very little gray or black in any mixture as the brilliancy of the hue will be dulled. The best neutralized tones are obtainable by mixing complementary colors. Very dark colors, however, are only possible by using a black pigment which dulls the brilliancy of the hue.

To obtain light neutral colors it will be found advisable to start with the white pigment, which may be neutralized with any complementary mixture (red and green) to the approximate tonal value required. After this is done a small amount of the pigment of the desired hue may be added.

Yellow pigment must be neutralized cautiously as it turns green immediately when black or gray is used. The addition of red will turn it brown. Violet, which turns yellow into tones of mustard, is the best color to use. Browns are fundamentally a mixture of orange and black, but either yellow or red usually dominates in the mixture. These tinges may be counteracted by adding the missing one. If blue is added to a brown, the color neutralizes rapidly toward dark gray and appears cold. The addition of black pigment to any hue causes the hue to neutralize or disappear very rapidly so that only small quantities of black should be added slowly to any mixture.

As the most intense yellow has the lightest tonal value of any brilliant hue, the addition of any other hue darkens the tonal value of the mixture. Conversely strong pigment colors of the red or blue families lighten their tonal value when yellow is added.

Removing wallpaper. Wallpaper must be thoroughly soaked before any attempt is made to remove it. In order to accomplish this, a large calcimine brush and warm water are used. When the paper has absorbed all the water it can, it should be let stand for a few minutes until the paste has been softened by the moisture. The paper may then be scraped with a putty knife and easily removed. When valuable or antique wallpaper must be removed, it is advisable to obtain the services of a professional, as it is a very long and difficult procedure. The usual method is to hang large steaming cloths about four inches from the wall over a large portion of the wall at the same time. The dampness from the cloths will eventually be absorbed by the paper or muslin upon which all valuable paper is mounted, and the paper may then be carefully pulled off the wall, strip by strip. When all traces of paper and paste have been removed from a plaster wall, the wall may be treated as new and the painting procedure carried out as heretofore described.

Calcimining. Calcimine may be applied in one coat only; when a surface has been previously treated with a coat and is to be repainted, the old layer should first be removed by means of a large sponge and warm water. It is often customary for economical reasons to treat ceilings with this material, but this should not be done in work of good quality, and as labor costs in applying calcimine are only slightly less than in applying oil paints, there is only a minor economy in using this material.

Painting and staining wood surfaces. In painting woodwork, if the wood has a rough grain it should first be "filled" with white lead or one of the many standard fillers. It should then be entirely covered with a coat of shellac to seal the absorbent surface. Over this sealing coat of shellac the wood may be painted in the same manner as a plaster wall surface. Where it is desired to apply a coat of stain to woodwork, it is necessary first to apply a filler that is the same color as the stain. The surface need not be shellacked. The stain may be purchased from any paint store or it may be prepared with a thin oil base mixed with pigment.

Glazing and antiquing. It is often advisable to apply a finishing coat of thin color to the whole or parts of a wall in order to give the surface greater interest and a slight variation in effect. This is usually called glazing or antiquing. Such finishes are numberless in their elaborations, but the plainer effects are simple to apply.

The customary procedure is to apply over a thoroughly dried, light neutral-colored surface, a film of color of the consistency of water. The medium is usually of oil and turpentine, and a small amount of pigment is added to the mixture in the desired strength. For antiquing, walls are usually glazed with umber, which, more than any other color, seems to produce a satisfactory illusion of age.

Other tones, however, are also used for antiquing. A smooth glaze may be applied with a large brush over a whole painted surface and then stippled. In other glazes the brush marks are intentionally left visible. The latter are known as streak glazes and they are produced by a large calcimine brush.

Plain glazes may be softened or modulated by means of a soft cloth, sponge, or cheesecloth, but care should be taken not to produce artificial effects unrelated to antique rooms. Simple, unostentatious glazes are to be recommended. It is very easy to overglaze a surface, and such an effect is always artificial, vulgar, and in bad taste. Proper antiquing is almost imperceptible.

Glazing is particularly adaptable to panelled rooms and should be used to make the paint and woodwork appear slightly dusty. As dust invariably occurs in panel corners and on certain portions of moldings, it is advisable to put a slightly darker tone in these places. In antique panelled rooms, it was customary to wash the paint in the most accessible portions of the panel fields. This caused the centers and lower portions of the panels to be slightly lighter in tone than the tops and corners. A realistic imitation of this natural condition may often be introduced to advantage, but much discretion must be used to avoid a false effect.

Glazing is sometimes produced by means of a spatter finish that consists of covering the surface evenly with small dots of pigment that are complementary in hue to the surface color. This may be done by using a sprayer or by gently finger-snapping the hairs of a large paint brush toward the surface until the required effect is obtained. This treatment neutralizes the color of the original paint, but should be done most carefully and consistently, and never excessively. The dots should be very small and indistinguishable when viewed from a distance of six feet. Neutralizing done by this method leaves a more vibrant effect than when the paint is originally mixed with neutralizing pigments and the method resembles that employed by the Impressionist artists of the 19th century.

Plaster effects. Certain types of rooms require the walls treated in the effect of rough, sand-finished plaster. The textural charm of old walls of this type is well known, and if mellowed by age, they have an unusual appeal and are exceedingly durable. If existing walls are not of this type, the painter may be called upon to cover the wall with one of the many patented surfacing materials, to produce the desired effect. It is essential, however, that the degree of roughness and irregularity of the old walls be imitated exactly. Many of the old plaster walls consisted of a coating applied to rough stonework, and the unevenness of the stones produced slight variations in the plaster surface. The plaster, although it often gave the appearance of having been applied carelessly, had irregularities which were never intentional or self-conscious in appearance, nor was the aim to produce a crude or unfinished result. Many incompetent and unintelligent craftsmen have, in recent years, under the spell of early Italian and Spanish types of decoration, resorted to effects that have produced walls completely devoid of taste and understanding.

The preparation and application of the patented materials used for the effect of rough plaster are simple. The material, in the form of a flour-like powder, is mixed with water and, in some cases, with oil. Powdered color may be added to the mixture, thus finishing the wall in one operation. It is also possible to apply the white, colorless plaster—a thick pasty substance—alone, and when it is thoroughly dry, to add the desired color by means of a thin glaze, to give the effect of age.

For applying the plaster, a trowel or brush is customarily used. For textural variations, all sorts of implements may be employed. These plasters, as a rule, will not crack, and if cracks do occur, they may be easily

Louis Bouché, Decorator

Fine example of a marbled wall designed in panels and enriched by a painted mirror.

filled. Most commercial products for this form of decoration are fast-drying, very hard, and permanent.

Graining and marbling. Economic conditions, short leases, and frequent changes of residence today often require substitution for the more expensive materials of decoration. While, judged purely from the point of view of esthetic morals, such substitutions are indefensible, they are often practical and necessary. Within this class of work comes the graining or marbling of surfaces to imitate natural wood or real marble. Such work is a highly developed craft, and can by no means be accomplished by the amateur, but painters and artists in all periods have been able to develop an extraordinary technique in this line. Although it would be impossible for the average decorator to do this type of work himself, it is his duty to design the surface of the wall in panels, planks, or other divisions that would be consistent with the material that he wishes imitated.

Wooden wall panels are made a certain size and shape, according to their period, and they are held in place by moldings and stiles. If they are imitated by applied moldings on a plaster wall for economy's sake, the proper design and layout must be carried out.

A wall covered in full or in part by marble (such as a dado or baseboard) is actually covered by marble slabs about one inch thick and of varying sizes. The marble joints are always visible, and if the desired effect is to be imitated in paint, the marble slabs, stiles, panels, and other parts with visible joints should be carefully imitated.

Wood or marble graining always ends with each separate piece of wood or marble. In the adjoining piece the graining commences in a different pattern or direction.

To be in good taste, painting made to imitate wood or marble must create a complete illusion, and the work must be very realistic.

Antiquing of wallpaper. Painters are often called upon to give wallpaper an antique, mellow effect. This softens the colors and draws them together. If the wallpaper pattern is printed in water color (tempera), the paper should first receive a coat of gelatin size, followed by a coat of shellac. The glaze itself may be in oil or turpentine, and the procedure is the same as antiquing painted surfaces.

Metal leaf. The use of silver and gold leaf surfaces in decoration has become popular in recent years. These effects are also part of the painter's work. Aluminum leaf is generally used in place of silver, as it is less expensive and does not tarnish. The application of metal leaf is accomplished by first applying a *gold size* to the surface to be treated. This is allowed to dry to a thick consistency, and the leaf is then applied to the size and allowed to dry thoroughly. It is best to varnish metal leaf for protection. Metal leaf is usually glazed over the varnish for antique effects.

Bibliography

BUSTANOBY, J. H., *Principles of Color and Color Mixing.* McGraw-Hill Book Co., Inc., New York, 1947. Useful information for house painters.

VANDERWALKER, F. N., *The Mixing of Colors and Paints.* Frederick J. Drake and Co., Chicago, 1939. Excellent text on the mixing and use of paints for interior decoration and house painting.

CHAPTER XVII

CERAMICS AND GLASSWARE

T he smaller decorative accessories of a room contribute to its character and color scheme, fill the empty spaces, arouse curiosity,
express dignity, provoke humor, and reflect the culture, judgment, and
interests of the owner.

Among the most useful articles to accomplish these ends are the clay
products of the kiln broadly known as *ceramics,* a term that includes
both pottery and porcelain. The productions of this craft cover a large
field in both design and quality, and only the principal ornamental
varieties can be included in this chapter.

Ornamental Pottery

The majority of civilized countries have produced their own varieties
of ornamental pottery, and each type has shown a gradual evolution in
quality and design as new materials and processes of manufacture have
been discovered or new influences contributed to the imagination of the
craftsmen. Pottery making, both as a practical and fine art, dates from the
earliest periods of civilization. Egypt, Babylon, Crete, Greece, Rome,
ancient China, and Europe during the Middle Ages produced vast quantities of extraordinarily beautiful examples, but as practically all pottery
made previous to the Renaissance is extremely rare and unavailable, this
chapter will include only the important varieties produced since 1500.

There are three principal types of ornamental pottery; these are differentiated by the character and quality of the clay from which they are
made and the amount of firing to which they are submitted. Ordinary
earthenware is heavy, soft, porous, and opaque; the simplest example of
it is the common brick or red garden flower pot. The first *firing* produces
what is known as the *biscuit,* and many ornamental pieces are left in this
condition. The finish at this point is dull and the color, depending upon

the clay, a tan-colored or red terra-cotta. The biscuit, if desired, may be finished with a scratch or painted pattern and finally covered with a thin coat of transparent glaze by additional firing. *Stoneware* is a very hard, close-grained, nonporous pottery, which may be either white or colored, glazed or unglazed. It is sometimes slightly translucent in its thinner parts. The commonest example of stoneware is the ordinary pickle or preserve jar, but fine decorative pottery of this type has been made in Germany and England. *Porcelain* is the finest kind of pottery, and was first made in China. For centuries European potters attempted without success to discover its chemical contents and to imitate it, but it was not until 1711 that porcelain was first made in Europe, when the clay known as *kaolin,* used by the Chinese in making porcelain, was discovered in Germany.

The pottery made from kaolin is known as true or *hard-paste* porcelain. The clay is a clear white, and after firing, produces a very hard, thin, translucent, and sometimes semitransparent ware that rings with a bell-like sound when struck with the finger. An imitation porcelain known as *soft-paste* was made in Europe before the local discovery of kaolin. Some of the finest soft-paste porcelain was made during the 18th century in the Rouen, St. Cloud, Mennecy, and Sèvres factories near Paris. The Sèvres factory did not make true porcelain until 1768. Soft-paste porcelain is more creamy white, more translucent, and more fragile than hard-paste porcelain.

Kaolin was discovered in Cornwall, England, about 1755, and in Limoges, France, in 1768, and its discovery completely revolutionized English and French ceramic pottery production. In the latter part of the 19th century, the English potters added bone ash to their porcelain mixture and developed "bone porcelain," which is midway between hard-paste and soft-paste porcelain in whiteness and hardness.

There are several additional technical terms used in connection with the making of pottery which should be understood before proceeding upon a study of the various types. These terms, with definitions, are given herewith:

China. A hard translucent porcelain body containing a large percentage of bone ash. The term was originally applied by Europeans to the Oriental porcelains, and was later adopted as a designation for any porcelain product as distinguished from pottery or earthenware.

Enamel. A glassy substance used for painting on pottery and porcelain after it has had a preliminary coating of glaze. After the pattern is finished, the piece is again fired and the enamel is fused to the original glaze. The colors are made from gold, silver, iron, tin, lead, and other compounds.

Firing. Turning clay into pottery by great heat in a kiln.

Glaze. A thin coating of glass fired on pottery, giving it a glossy appearance.

Hard-paste. A term applied by European potters to a pottery clay made with a base of kaolin, a material used by the Chinese in making true porcelain, and not discovered in Europe until 1709.

Luster. A pottery decoration producing metallic hues formed by thin layers of gold, copper, silver, etc.

On-the-glaze colors. Refers to colors applied on top of glazed ware, such as the enamels used in majolica pottery.

Paste. A term used to denote the body of the pottery. Soft paste was produced by an artificial or glass mixture, hard paste by felspar and kaolin.

Salt glaze. A surfacing of thin glass for pottery produced by throwing salt into the oven while firing.

Slip. A watery clay of various colors used for surfacing pottery by dipping the piece in a bath.

Soft-paste. A term applied by European potters to a mixture of clay and ground glass that was used to make an imitation porcelain before the European discovery of kaolin.

Transfer printing. An inexpensive method of printing one-color patterns on pottery. The pattern or picture is first printed on paper from a copper-plate engraving and then transferred to the pottery from the paper.

Underglaze color. A term applied to a mineral pigment used for pottery decoration that may be applied before glazing and that will resist the high temperature needed to melt the glaze.

Since many pieces of old chinaware are still in the market and can be used to decorative advantage in both period and modern rooms, a brief description, for identification purposes, of the important types produced since 1500 in Europe, the Orient, and the United States is given in the following pages.

Spanish ceramics. The Mohammedan potters of Persia, Mesopotamia, and Egypt excelled in their art which in the 9th and 10th centuries was transmitted to the Spanish Caliphate of Cordova. Here, for the first time in Europe, tin glazes and such ceramic refinements as luster were used. The Kingdom of Granada and later, Valencia, became the centers of production. The best known examples of the luster earthenware, called Hispano-Mauresque, are represented by tall amphora-shaped vases known as Alhambra vases, as well as by large platters bearing coats of arms of kings and princes. The decoration of the vases consists of Arabic inscriptions, beautifully executed arabesques, and, in a few instances, of stylized animal forms. Hispano-Mauresque ware was coveted all over the continent. The ships carrying it from Valencia to Italian ports made a halt on their way at the island of Majorca, from which derives the Italian term Majolica, which is now generally applied to tin-glazed and enamelled earthenware.

Pottery and porcelain. (1) Chinese K'ang Hsi porcelain plate. (2) Persian Rhages ware, 13th century. (3) Nevers pottery, Persian influence. (4) Persian plate, 14th century. (5) Hispano-Mauresque plate. (6) Italian Capo-di-Monte plate. (7) Italian Doccia porcelain. (8) Rouen pottery, oriental influence. (9) Sceaux pitcher of the 18th century. (10) K'ang Hsi famille noire porcelain vase.

Although the production of Hispano-Mauresque luster ware, with its remarkable and indescribable sheen and iridescence, reached its zenith in the 14th and 15th centuries, it has been carried on, based on traditional models, without interruption to the present day.

Glazed floor and wall tiles were also introduced by the Moors. The rooms of the Moorish palaces and smaller dwellings invariably had tile wainscots to a height of about four feet, covered with interlacing and geometrical patterns. Openings between rooms were often trimmed with tile borders and small patterned tiles were used on floors. Seville became proficient in the 15th and 16th centuries in the output of beautiful polychrome tiles decorated with flower and abstract motifs, often showing a fusion of Mohammedan and Renaissance motifs.

In the 16th century Spain had to yield its ceramic prominence to Italy. Yet Talavera de la Reina and other kilns near Toledo produced attractive tiles and domestic ware, decorated with figural subjects, including scenes taken from contemporary life, in blue and white, in blue and ochre, or in green, blue, white, and brown.

The establishment founded by Count Aranda in 1727 at Alcora produced throughout the 18th century a very fine faïence tableware partly inspired by current French taste, but Spanish in character. In Catalonia, wall tiles known as azulejos were often painted with entertaining scenes showing groups of people engaged in sports, amusements, dancing, or drinking the newly discovered beverages of coffee and chocolate, or humorous pictures of bullfights, boating scenes, incidents associated with Don Quixote, and other events. Religious pictures painted on tile were frequently used as altar decorations in churches.

After his accession to the throne of Spain in 1759, King Charles III transferred to Madrid the entire porcelain factory and staff of artists of the Italian manufactory of Capo di Monte, which he had founded in 1743 when he was King of Naples. In Spain this ware was known as Buen Retiro after the royal residence, where the new plant was set up around 1760, and in which were produced beautiful figurines and groups made of soft paste. Walls and ceilings of entire rooms in the palaces of Madrid and Aranjuez are covered with huge plaques of this porcelain, and figurines are supported on ornamental wall-brackets. These were features of decoration that admirably lent themselves to the modelling of spirited rococo rooms.

There have always been many small local kilns in southern Spain that make pottery for the peasants, who frequently decorate the walls of their rooms by covering them with ornamental plates or bowls and with water jars. Carried by the donkeys in the country districts and contributing so much to the picturesque landscape, these jars have maintained the same design for over two thousand years.

Italian ceramics. The pottery of the early Renaissance in Italy was a development and elaboration of the Hispano-Mauresque ware, which the northern Italians began to copy in the 14th century. The actual body of the pieces was made in the same manner as the Moorish product. The great development in pottery design occurred during the first part of the 16th century. Platters, urns, bowls, apothecary jars, and other pieces were elaborately hand-painted in strong-color patterns of scrolls, festoons, flowers, leaves, arabesques, cherubs, dolphins, masks, grotesques, and scenes taken from the Scriptures and Roman history and mythology. Heraldic devices and portraits were also occasionally used. The large panels made by the della Robbias, described in Chapter III, were extensively used for wall decoration, and figure patterns were often built into the walls of the room. The della Robbias also produced circular panels in high relief framed in leaf and fruit wreaths.

Courtesy Metropolitan Museum of Art

Fifteenth century glazed terra-cotta plaque by Luca della Robbia.

It is said that Raphael in his youth was employed to decorate the pottery made in his birthplace, Urbino. Other localities where 16th century Italian majolica was made were at Castel Durante, Faenza, and Caffagiolo. Much of this pottery was exported to other European countries.

The colors used in nearly all majolica ware were limited to light blue, orange, mulberry, green, and black. The patterns were usually applied over a pinkish white slip.

During the 18th century, the Italian potters followed the styles of France and Germany. The works at Venice were founded in 1719; at Florence in 1735; at Doccia in 1737; at Capo di Monte in 1743; at Portici in 1771; and at Naples in 1773.

The first attempt to make porcelain in Europe was made in Venice, in the latter years of the 15th century. In the early years of the 16th century the Medici family supported these efforts, which produced a translucent ware that they frankly called "counterfeit porcelain," but which is now known as "Medici porcelain." The examples were usually dishes, platters, and ewers. The colored patterns are taken from both Renaissance and Oriental sources. There is very little of this ware in existence today, but at the time it was being produced it served as an inspiration for the later makers of soft-paste porcelain in France.

Dutch ceramics. The craft of pottery making was introduced into Holland by the Spaniards at the time when Flanders was a Spanish possession. Production eventually concentrated in the city of Delft and this name has usually been applied to all the ceramic production of Holland. A high standard of quality was maintained by a trade organization of artists and craftsmen known as the Guild of St. Luke, founded about 1610.

Delft table and ornamental ware had a remarkably brilliant and heavy glaze and was particularly noted for its blue colors and decorations used on a white field. Conventional patterns and town and landscape scenes were also represented. The patterns were painted before glazing and firing, a method of decorating known as *underglazing*.

The Dutch factories endeavored to imitate the Chinese and Japanese wares during the 18th century, but not with a great degree of success, because of the improvement of transportation facilities and the eventual cheapness of the real Oriental ware. Their manufacture of porcelain was also unsuccessful. Delftware was exported into England to a large extent during the early years of the 18th century and was much sought after by English collectors. Many pieces, such as apothecary jars and drug pots, were made for commercial use. Small flat tiles were manufactured for fireplace facings and other architectural uses. The English eventually imitated delftware in their own factories.

French ceramics. The first great Renaissance potter in France and one of the greatest craftsmen of all times was Bernard Palissy (1510–1589), who started work in Saintes in Brittany in 1539. Palissy, previous to that year, had been a glass painter. He experimented long and suffered much privation and hardship before discovering the materials and processes for making ceramics. He lost all his savings in these experiments, and it was only after he had, in his frenzy, burnt up the chairs and tables in his house for fuel, that he succeeded in producing the wonderful enamel for which his pottery is noted. He lived in troublous times and was eventually imprisoned for embracing the principles of the Reformation.

His work was strongly influenced by the Italian majolica ware, which he at first tried to imitate and eventually improved upon. He drew his inspiration for modelling and coloring largely from nature; sea animals and plants, fish, crabs, shells, coral, and seaweed, were naturalistically represented. Religious and mythological subjects were occasionally used. The value of original Palissy pieces is so high that many forgeries have been made. The original ware has a reddish-yellow tint to the white areas, and the reds are of poor quality. The glazes are usually crackled.

At the same time that Palissy was working, a group of potters in St. Porchaire, near Saintes, were producing heavy, ornate vases and other useful articles in the Italian style. These are sometimes known as Henry II ware, because some are decorated with the monograms or crescent symbols of Diane de Poitiers. Others, however, show motifs that were used in the Francis I period. Similar wares were also produced at Nantes, and in the mid-17th century, copies of both St. Porchaire and Nantes wares were made at Nevers.

Ornamental tiles were made in the city of Rouen in the middle of the 16th century, but it was not until 1644 that the first pottery factories were founded in this city, and faïence was made, supposedly in imitation of the pottery made in Faenza, Italy; actually, however, it was quite different.

Pottery and porcelain. (1) Rouen plate. (2) Marseilles plate. (3) Vincennes vase. (4) Moustiers plate. (5) Sèvres vase. (6) Blue and white Staffordshire plate. (7) Majolica Urbino plate. (8) Sèvres jardinière. (9) Chelsea candlestick. (10) Delft teapot.

Rouen pottery was delicate and more refined in size, proportions, and pattern than the early Italian ware. The best period occurred between 1720 and 1740. The platter designs were done in blue, green, and yellow and usually followed a wheel-and-spoke radiating form, produced by small flowers and conventional shapes, with arabesques, cornucopias, and arrows. This was followed by patterns of rococo and Oriental influence.

Edme Poterat, who worked in Rouen, in 1673, was the first Frenchman to make soft-paste porcelain, and a few years later Pierre Chicaneau established a factory in St. Cloud where a similar product was produced. Small objects were made that were decorated both in low relief and flat enamel colors in patterns of both Oriental and French origin. This factory was later carried on by his heirs and finally closed its doors in 1766. Other establishments for manufacturing soft-paste wares were founded at Lille in 1711, Strasbourg in 1720, Chantilly in 1725, and Mennecy-Villeroy in 1735. Still later the factories at Sceaux, Orleans, Arras, and Tournai were established. The material called "soft-paste" was fragile, chipped easily, and lacked solidity, so that the making of large objects was difficult, and the wares produced by these early factories were largely limited to plates, saucers, cups, vases, snuffboxes, cachepots, cane handles, small human and animal figurines, and grotesque and humorous motifs. The patterns were usually carried out with a Chinese feeling.

Between 1664 and 1770 the French East India Company imported great quantities of pottery and porcelain into France. Many of these pieces were made by Oriental workmen, in factories specially established by the company near Canton, China, to make objects that had a particular appeal to the French market. The motifs usually consisted of floral forms applied to a bluish off-white ground. A large amount of this ware is still in existence and is called by its French designation, *Compagnie des Indes*.

The most important of the French ceramic factories was established at Vincennes on the outskirts of Paris in 1738. Madame de Pompadour took a great interest in the production of this factory and induced Louis XV to become one of the principal stockholders. In 1753 the King granted the firm the privilege to use the words *Manufacture Royale de Porcelaine de France* in connection with its name. The factory produced soft-paste table and ornamental ware that was decorated with Chinese and floral patterns, and in 1747 made the first biscuit or unglazed ware. The omission of the glaze enabled the potters to obtain, with much greater accuracy, the minute detail of the sculptor's model. About the middle of the century, the factory became famous for the production of small soft-paste flowers that were mounted on wires and combined with metal leaves; these were used as bouquets and as decoration for candelabra, clocks, and table ornaments. The factory employed able chemists, and in 1749 first produced the ground color known as *bleu-du-roi* (royal blue), and in 1752 a remarkable turquoise blue. In 1756 the factory moved to a building constructed by Madame de Pompadour at Sèvres, and the ware was thereafter called by that name. In 1757 the Sèvres factory developed the pink ground color known as "rose Pompadour," sometimes miscalled "rose du Barry," and later on "yellow jonquil," green, and many other colors. For a time it was the only factory in France permitted to decorate its wares with gold.

Pottery and porcelain. (1) Ch'ien Lung porcelain vase. (2) Majolica Gubbio lustered plate. (3) English slip ware platter. (4) Majolica Urbino plate. (5) Lowestoft bowl. (6) Delft pottery vase. (7) French Palissy pottery. (8) Italian Doccia porcelain. (9) Delft pottery vase. (10) Whieldon statues. (11) Strasbourg plate.

The most capable painters, sculptors, and craftsmen were employed at Sèvres. Boucher the painter for a time was hired in an advisory capacity. The King used the products for gifts to his friends and foreign potentates, and they soon became regarded as the finest made in Europe. Enormous quantities of table and ornamental wares were sold to the reigning houses and noble families of countries as far away as Russia. Every sort of useful and ornamental designs were made, many of them decorated with miniature paintings in the style of Watteau and Boucher, while in others the ornament was inspired by the Orient. The general character, forms, and surface enrichment closely followed the art style of each period. Pompeian patterns were introduced when the Neo-classic trend occurred, and these were followed by the Greek and Roman forms of the Empire. In 1768, kaolin was discovered near Limoges, France, and immediately thereafter the Sèvres factory began to produce the hard-paste true porcelain. The factory has continued with various interruptions to the present day, the French government still acts as its patron, and its products are sold to the public.

A ware called *Vieux Paris* is today frequently seen in antique shops. Most of it was made during the 19th century; it is enriched by patterns, ground colors, and painted miniatures, but the craftsmanship is crude in every element of its design. It has little to do with the art of ceramics, and it can be entirely classified as a commercial product.

An important type of French decorative accessory was the terra-cotta statues made by Claude Michel, known as Clodion, who was born in Nancy in 1738. He was a sculptor of great ability who won the grand prize of the Royal Academy in 1759, which permitted him to study in Rome. When he returned to France, he made terra-cotta reproductions of his figures in his own kilns. He had been impressed with the unrestrained character of the art of his period and specialized in modelling groups of amorous nymphs and satyrs that were in great demand as ornaments in the interiors of the latter portion of the 18th century. Clodion died in 1814.

German wares. German pottery is perhaps most interesting due to the fact that it was in this country that hard-paste porcelain was first made in Europe. Augustus, the King of Saxony (1670–1733), was a great collector of Oriental wares, which were exceedingly costly to buy, and the idea occurred to him that possibly he could discover the secret of the hard material in which the finely detailed Oriental objects were produced. In 1709 a chemist in Dresden named Bottger discovered a clay that was similar to the Chinese kaolin. He attempted unsuccessfully to keep the formula a secret, and called the material "Arcanum." The King immediately aided in establishing a factory to produce porcelain ware at Meissen, about 14 miles from Dresden. Bottger died in 1719, but under the two directors Herold and Kandler the Meissen factory was in full swing by 1720, and was producing a large amount of colored and glazed ware in designs that imitated the Chinese examples. By 1740 the influence of the Rococo style of France was felt and much ornamental porcelain was produced in this style, often enriched with miniature scenes that were copies of the paintings of Watteau and Lancret. A great variety of objects was produced. Tableware, beautifully modelled figurines, statuettes of real and imaginary persons, and vases were made.

The Meissen factory was followed by those at Nymphenburg in 1747, where floral patterns, imitation chintz designs, wooden-ware reproductions, and chinoiseries were produced, and at Berlin in 1751, which factory was supported by Frederick the Great. Other factories were established at Furstenberg, Frankenthal, Vienna, and Ludwigsburg. All the German factories made similar designs and produced both glazed and biscuit wares. The most usual patterns were colorful floral and trellis motifs, which were both surface painted and in relief. Other motifs were imitations of mosaic and chintz patterns, gold scrolls, and birds. The Chinese, Sèvres, and later the English Wedgwood wares were extensively copied. On the whole, the Germans were excellent chemists and technicians, but lacked imagination in design.

Hausmalerei was pottery that was decorated by independent artists and amateurs working in their homes. Plain pieces were furnished by the kilns, and after being decorated were returned for glazing and further firing. Unfortunately many of the amateurs produced forgeries in imitation of the work done in the better factories. The Meissen ware suffered particularly with this abuse, and adopted the crossed swords as a symbol of its own productions. Many interesting patterns were created, however, from 1725 to 1750, with Chinese motifs, landscapes, ruins, flowers, birds, hunting scenes, arms, trophies, and mythological subjects; but, the excellence of technique in the drawings depended upon the talent of the individual, and, as a result, this type of ware varies greatly in quality.

Early English pottery. One of the most important developments in the history of decorative ceramics occurred in England, and was started in the early years of the 17th century. Previous to this period, utilitarian pieces had been produced with little or no thought of decorative effect.

Most of the 17th century pieces were heavy earthenware coated with what is known as *slip,* which consisted of a deep orange-colored mixture of clay and water. When dried, this preliminary coating was covered with another yellowish-white slip. The whole object was then covered with glaze, after which a crude and naïve pattern was scratched upon the surface with a sharp stick, the scratch being sufficiently deep to expose the underlying orange color. The glaze occasionally showed touches of green and red. The decoration often included the name of the owner, a date, and a verse or motto. Other ornaments used were rosettes, *fleurs-de-lis,* shields, armorial bearings, initials, and grotesques. Thomas Toft, who lived around 1670, was the best-known master of ornamental slip ware. He produced cooking vessels, pots, porringers, saucers, basins, bowls, dishes, jars, candlesticks, and cups.

Toward the final years of the 17th century, much Delft and Oriental pottery was imported into England. This paved the way for the English potters to turn out goods of similar lines. Much of the English delftware was made at factories in Lambeth, but the painting of the English pieces was inferior and the body was coarser than in the Dutch originals.

The early years of the 18th century were given over to experimentation and to analysis of the Oriental products and to a greatly increased public and collector's interest in the porcelain of the Orient. As rewards increased, many skilled artists and sculptors were attracted to the industry. Easier transportation and improved technical facilities in firing made it possible to obtain and use clays from foreign countries. It was therefore no longer necessary to work native clay.

As compared to the early pottery, the porcelain made in England was always lacking in originality of decoration and form. It is perhaps only natural that with an avowedly imitative product, the ornament should also be copied. The decoration of English porcelain in the 18th century falls into four periods of imitation: first, the period of Oriental influence; second, that of the Dresden style; third, the Sèvres influence; and last, the classical revival, which everywhere seems to have been the prelude of esthetic decadence.

English pottery made after 1740 is generally classified according to the town or locality where it was manufactured or by the name of the craftsman who made it.

Bristol, Bow, Chelsea, and Derby wares. In these towns, factories were established between 1744 and 1755 which were active until 1810. There was a close similarity in the productions of these factories, and at times two or more of them were combined under the same ownership.

Those in charge of production and management were men of excellent taste and exceptional initiative. Considering the crude artistry and craftsmanship of their predecessors, the directors of these works were responsible for an immense advance in the English pottery industry along both technical and artistic lines.

Industry in Bristol seems to have flourished as early as 1652, when Delft earthenware was first imitated. Bristol continued to be noted for its reproduction of Delft pieces as late as the middle of the 18th century. Wall tiles were made, as well as the usual plates and bowls. Transfer printing is said to have been introduced as a method of ornamenting Bristol ware, about 1757. Several early attempts to make porcelain were initiated in Bristol, but it was not until about 1770, at the time that the Plymouth factory was absorbed by the Bristol, that this ware was successfully made. The Bristol works closed their doors in 1782. Bristol porcelain is exceedingly hard and durable; it is milk-white, with a cold glittering glaze. Biscuit wares were also manufactured. Tableware, figures, and

Pottery and porcelain. (1) Dresden statuette. (2) Sèvres biscuit ware. (3) Ralph Wood statue, "Vicar and Moses." (4) Worcester mug. (5) Wedgwood table jasper ware. (6) Wedgwood cream ware plate. (7) Worcester plate. (8) American Bennington ware pottery teapot. (9) Staffordshire rustic figures. (10) Wedgwood ornamental jasper ware. (11) Derby plates and dish. (12) Bristol teapot and cream pitcher. (13) Liverpool pitcher. (14) Worcester bowl and jar.

ornamental plaques were produced. Much of the painted ornament was in the Chinese manner. The products of the factory at Dresden strongly influenced the Bristol modellers.

The Bow factory, sometimes known as "New Canton," was always associated with the making of porcelain. It is supposed first to have been organized in 1744, and in 1776 to have merged with Derby. Bow ware shows many variations in the quality of the body. Many white figures and painted statuettes were made. The painted types of chinaware were usually of Chinese character, in both underglaze and overglaze enamels. The subjects include bamboo or plum branches, partridges, grotesque animals, and sportive boys with small red flowers in gold and other colors. The early tableware was frequently edged in brown. The glaze of Bow wares now is often discolored and iridescent. Bow ware is mainly of a useful type, the ornamental forms having been left to the Chelsea factory. As compared with Chelsea ware, the bulk of the Bow productions are coarser in texture and rougher in decoration.

The Chelsea factory is supposed to have made the first piece of soft-paste porcelain in England, about 1745. A small milk jug was produced during that year, when the Chelsea works were controlled by two French-men most of whose employees were likewise French. This French man-agement lasted until 1763, during which time the productions of table-ware, vases, and ornamental figures were often inspired by Chinese and Dresden forms, the finish being in a creamy paste with a satiny texture. Other types clearly showed the influence of Vincennes and Sèvres, with rich ground colors such as dark blue and claret, and panels painted with pastoral scenes, bouquets, exotic birds, heavy gilding, and extravagant rococo vase handles and bases—in a word, overdecoration. In 1769 the Chelsea factory was sold to some Derby potters, whose work was mostly in the Japanese taste (*Kakiyemon*) with paintings of flower sprays, in-sects, and other old Japanese patterns.

Of the figures for which the Chelsea works were so justly noted, the earliest were the undecorated examples, not always distinguishable from the Bow examples which they probably imitated. Next in date to these came the statuettes with quiet coloring and little or no gilding. Last came the richly decorated and heavily gilt pieces. Portrait pieces were modelled from statuary, pictures, and prints, and first-rate artists were employed in their production. Snuff bottles, scent flasks, flowers, and seals were also among the daintiest of all the Chelsea wares. Many of these bore gallant French inscriptions.

From 1770 until 1784, during the Derby-Chelsea period, the original wares of both factories continued to be made; but finally the rococo forms gave way to the colder effects of the classical revival, while in the decora-tion lapis lazuli, Derby blue, gold stripes, medallions, and biscuit reliefs made their appearance.

Transfer-printed Chelsea ware was of rare occurrence, although pos-sibly some Chelsea porcelains were sent to Battersea to receive the trans-fers.

The Derby factory probably started about the year 1756, under the ownership of a man named Duesbury. An auction sale held by his order describes the goods of the Derby works as a "curious collection of fine figures, jars, sauce-boats, services for desserts, and a great variety of other useful and ornamental porcelain after the finest Dresden models." This statement gives an idea of the variety of goods sold and of the character of their design. In 1758 the factory was enlarged. In 1770 it combined with the Chelsea factory, and in 1776 the combination bought up the Bow works.

The best period of the Derby production was from 1786 to 1811. Figures were always a specialty of the factory, although much tableware was also made. Flower paintings and particularly roses were favorite ornaments. Japanese designs were also used. The shapes of vases showed the influence of the classic revival, and landscape paintings were resorted to for ornament with meager success.

A beautiful biscuit ware was made during the best period, and the groups and figures made of this body constitute the finest ornamental productions of the Derby factory. Very skillful artists and modellers were employed. Other specialties of the Derby factory were the use of brilliant lapis-lazuli blue and of delicate lace trimmings of a realistic character on figures in contemporary costume. Transfer printing was introduced in 1764, but was not extensively favored.

Lowestoft (1757–1802). The history of the Lowestoft porcelain factory has suffered greatly for want of records, and many absurd legends have been told concerning its output. It was founded by Robert Browne, and was of sufficient importance to have a London warehouse. The ware was a soft-paste porcelain similar to that produced at Chelsea and Bow, but of varying quality. The designs were largely copied from Worcester productions or from Chinese porcelain. There was very little modelled ornamentation, although occasional relief patterns were used. Much porcelain was also made in China and distributed by the East India Company in Europe through the Lowestoft factory. This type was enriched with both Western and Oriental motifs and is known as Oriental-Lowestoft. Many jugs, flasks, dishes, and inkpots made at the Lowestoft factory were inscribed with the words, "A trifle from Lowestoft."

Worcester (1751–1840). The Worcester productions were very similar to those made at the Derby and Chelsea factories, and it was advertised that workmen from the latter places were employed in making them. The Worcester factory, in spite of frequent changes of ownership, maintained a group of highly skilled employees who kept the quality of their product on an extremely high plane over a long period. The moulds of good models were kept, and many of the early models were repeated in later years with a new color treatment.

Printing on porcelain by the transfer process was first accomplished at

Worcester about 1757. Engraved pictures and portraits were thereafter directly applied to the surface of the pottery, lowering the cost of producing the patterned surface. Hand painting was renewed, however, after 1768.

In 1788 King George III visited the works, and thereafter the ware became known as "Royal Worcester."

Miscellaneous factories. Among the other types of English porcelains were those produced at Longton Hall, Coalport, Liverpool, Rockingham, Pinxton, Nantgarw, and Swansea. Many of these smaller factories were started by former employees of the larger organizations, and their output was similar in quality and design to that of the factories where their owners had served apprenticeships.

Staffordshire potteries. Staffordshire, a county of about 30 square miles, has been for centuries a most important locality for the production of earthenwares. This has been true because of the quality, variety, and color of clays that are found in the vicinity. Because of the cheapness and availability of the basic materials for making pottery, there have always been thousands of free-lance potters located in this district. Many homes have their own kilns which have been inherited from one generation to another. As a result of this long experience, the average Staffordshire potter has developed a high degree of technical ability; but he has, with few exceptions, failed to develop the same degree of esthetic knowledge and appreciation in the modelling of his forms. The result has been that the average product turned out by the Staffordshire kilns has a provincial character in its shape, and its ornamentation and coloring cannot in any way compare with the very beautiful output of Chelsea and Derby. The better grades of pottery made in Staffordshire are usually known by the individual names of their makers.

In the early years of the 18th century two Dutchmen, John and David Slers, became famous in the English pottery industry for their red, black, and salt-glazed stoneware produced at Bradwell Wood. John Astbury and Twyford learned the Slers' secret, and started a factory at Shelton where they made a fine earthenware of red, buff, yellow, fawn, orange, or chocolate color with relief ornaments that were sometimes lightly touched with purplish brown, the whole coated with a fine lead glaze. Salt-glazed products became common about 1720, and many teapots were made in this manner to compete with Oriental importations that were sold at a high price. The manufacture of salt-glazed ware, little of which was for ornamental purposes, was discontinued after 1780.

"Cream ware" was first made by Thomas Astbury, son of the previously mentioned John, about 1725. Variegated wares, including the fine "marbled" or "agate" wares, were at their best between 1740 and 1756 and were made by several Staffordshire potters. "Clouded wares" are most commonly associated with the name of Thomas Whieldon, who produced between 1740 and 1780. These were wares with a cream body colored by metal oxides dabbed on with a sponge, giving a mottled effect suggestive of tortoise shell. They were also known as Rockingham ware. The shapes were varied and original, but often more quaint than beautiful; the cauliflower, pineapple, and apple supplied the motifs. The cauliflower design seems to have enjoyed considerable popularity.

Thomas Whieldon was of considerable importance to the pottery industry because many of his assistants later went into business for themselves. Josiah Wedgwood was his partner from 1753 to 1759; Aaron Wood, block-cutter, occasionally worked for him; and Josiah Spode, Robert Garner, and William Greatbach were his apprentices. Several different types of luster ware were produced in Staffordshire toward the end of the 18th century. The Spode factory made luster ware with copper, silver, steel, and gold.

An immense number of figures were made in Staffordshire, the bulk of them being for cottage decoration and of a crude or rustic character. Portraits were modelled from life and pictures. Toby jugs, allegorical figures, sentimental arbor groups, and humorous subjects were produced in color, black, and cream ware. The figures made by Ralph Wood in the third quarter of the century are particularly well known. Others who made Staffordshire figures were Voyez Nealeolo, Enoch Wood, Wood and Caldwell, Wilson, Lakin, and Poole. Walton, Salt, and Dale were the best known Staffordshire potters of the 19th century.

Wedgwood ware. By far the most important name connected with the potteries of Staffordshire is that of Josiah Wedgwood, who in 1759 inherited a pottery at Burslem near Stoke-on-Trent. In 1769 he opened his celebrated factory in Burslem which he called "Etruria." Wedgwood was a genius of intense energy; he was one of the first men to unite art and industry. He was a remarkable chemist and antiquarian and sought the most beautiful specimens of antique pottery as models. He employed the best talent available and was willing to pay for it.

As he lived in the age of Robert Adam, he took advantage of the classical influence that spread over England, and produced pottery that harmonized with the Adam designs for furniture and decoration. He introduced several new types of pottery and was constantly alive to new opportunities. Wedgwood's greatest fame rests upon his *jasper ware,* a dull white biscuit capable of being colored and ornamented. The colors of the field were blue, olive green, black, lilac, or sage. The ornaments invariably were white, and usually showed Greek ornamental motifs or figures draped in graceful robes. This particular product obtained immense popularity for interior decorative purposes. As separate free-standing shelf and table ornaments, as panel insertions in walls, mantels, and door trim, and as furniture appliques in the designs of Hepplewhite and Sheraton, the jasper ware was used repeatedly. One of the most famous of the Wedgwood pieces was his reproduction in jasper ware of the famous "Portland vase," a glass relic of an unknown art found in a sarcophagus in Rome and now in the British Museum. John Flaxman, the sculptor, worked for Wedgwood and was responsible for the design of many of the most beautiful examples of jasper ware.

Wedgwood was also noted for his terra-cotta ware colored to resemble porphyry and other stones. *Basalt ware* was the name for a black biscuit in imitation of the Egyptian stone by that name. "Queen's ware," made originally for Queen Charlotte, wife of George III, was the original cream ware for which Wedgwood obtained royal patronage in 1765. The use of Queen's ware spread with amazing rapidity over almost the entire civilized world. *Agate ware* had a mottled or marbled finish in imitation of the stone by that name; the ornament thereon was usually painted in a remarkable imitation of gilded bronze.

Transfer-printed pottery. Until about 1750 all English pottery decoration was done by hand. A method of transfer-printing pottery was discovered by John Sadler, a Liverpool printer, in 1754. The method involved transferring a design to paper from an engraved copper plate coated with pigment, and from the paper to the pottery, which was then refired. This was similar to the decalcomania process. The early pieces were printed over the glaze, producing crude and impermanent designs. The process was extensively used, however, to guide the enamellers, who filled in the black outlines with cobalt blue. Josiah Wedgwood regularly sent his "Queen's ware" to Liverpool for decoration from 1756 to 1794. In 1780, in Worcester, a man named Turner discovered a method of underprinting the designs with oily pigment, making possible a softer and more permanent effect. Turner also originated the "Willow" pattern, later to become the most popular transfer-printed design.

Josiah Spode, recognizing the possibilities of the new technique, hired two men from Worcester to teach him the method, and commenced production in 1783, using as a base an inexpensive white earthenware. After his death in 1797, the business was carried on by his sons and William T. Copeland, and the new commercially-produced pottery gained even greater popularity between 1800 and 1850, with over 700 different designs made especially for the American market. Spode's "blue and white" Staffordshire was the most widely produced, and the best of its kind, although it was also available in pink, red, green, black, and other colors. Transfer wares were soon also being manufactured by Whieldon, Enoch Wood, James Clews, William Adams, Minton, and others.

After the War of 1812, the potters concentrated on the American market, and numerous scenic and city views of the United States were produced. Historical scenes, political events, and famous persons were depicted. Social and political satire and romantic scenes of birds, gardens, and ruins were also popular.

The interest of "old blue" ware is chiefly due to its historical subject matter. It is distinguishable from hand-painted pottery by the gaps and overlaps in the design left by inaccurate joining of the papers used to transfer the pattern. Even on the finest examples a narrow white line or a slight overlapping shows at these points. The standards of excellence are the clarity of the picture and the accuracy with which the parts of the design match. The transfer-printing process greatly reduced the cost of ornamental wares, and caused less demand for the hand-painted types. As a result, the evolutionary development of fine porcelain making practically ceased by the middle of the 19th century.

American pottery. Useful pieces of pottery were made in all the colonies shortly after the first settlements of the 17th century. Little, however, of any decorative value was produced.

The earliest pottery of interest was produced in Pennsylvania by Germans about the middle of the 18th century. This was a slip decorated with crude scratch carving, and was known as *sgraffito ware*. The body colors were red, brown, and cream. The slip was green, pink, and blue. The color of the body showed through the *scratch-carved* ornament on the slip covering. The subjects of the ornamental motifs consisted of strange humans and animals and flowers, with dates, names, and inscriptions. The Pennsylvanians also produced a ware with a marbleized finish. The forms produced were all for useful purposes. Connecticut and Massachusetts also produced pottery, beginning with the middle of the 18th century, when the decoration as well as the practical value of an object began to be considered.

The developments in America in fine pottery and porcelain making were greatly handicapped by English importations, both before and after the Revolution, and the popularity of the imported types often obliged the American craftsmen to imitate them, and to disguise their origin by omitting the stamp of their own names or factory marks. The popularity of the Oriental and French productions also increased the financial difficulties of the American producers. Vast quantities of English transfer-printed wares flooded the American market after the American Revolution.

About the third quarter of the 18th century several English potters who were equipped with technical training acquired in some of the English firms came to America. From this period onward, more successful attempts were made to produce china of a better quality, and there was a corresponding improvement in design. By 1800 the industry had spread to practically every important city in the United States. The most interesting American pottery, from the point of view of design, was made in

Vermont. John Norton at this time produced utilitarian terra-cotta objects and a salt-glazed stoneware in Bennington, Vermont, where kaolin had been found. He also later produced an imitation of English cream ware and Whieldon's Rockingham ware; the latter often having a classical appearance in its modelling. The Bennington factory frequently changed hands, and reached its best period between 1847 and 1857, when both utilitarian and ornamental objects were produced, usually in the brown mottled tortoise-shell finish, although green and yellow colors were also used. Designs on the whole were heavy, quaint, and often humorous in appearance, and the glaze was rich, brilliant, and uniform.

Daniel Greatbach, who came from England about 1839, worked for various American potters, and is said to have been responsible for several of the most interesting designs produced at Bennington. The hound-handled pitcher was one of these. In this piece the body was decorated with a hunting scene, the handle formed by the curved body of a greyhound. Toby jars, cows, poodles, lions, coachmen bottles, flasks, candlesticks, toy banks, hot-water bottles, cuspidors, and table and toilet ware were other forms that were made.

The Bennington factory also produced light-colored wares and a small amount of soft-paste porcelain. A Parian ware, first produced in England in 1840, having somewhat the color and texture of Wedgwood jasper, was another popular product. The shapes and ornamentation were in biscuit finish, and usually showed leaf and flower forms, however, and did not in any way resemble the sophisticated classic art of the original Wedgwood.

The first true porcelain made in the United States was produced in Jersey City, New Jersey, in the early years of the 19th century. Both porcelain and earthenware thereafter were made in Kaolin, South Carolina; Trenton and South Amboy, New Jersey; East Liverpool, Ohio; Baltimore, Maryland; and several other places, in all of which English or French wares were poorly imitated. The results were artistically crude and many of the productions were of a commercial type. The majority of these potters lasted but a short time, and by the end of the century there was very little production in the ceramic field in the United States that could be classified as art.

Chinese pottery and porcelain. The history of pottery and porcelain making in China is as old and wondrous as the history of China itself. From 1100 B.C. through the 18th century, this art showed a slow but consistent development, reflecting the spiritual and religious changes of China and her rulers. Since the 18th century, though fine porcelain is still being made, the art has deteriorated, through a lack of originality, into a rather mechanical imitation of past excellence.

At first the ancient potter molded the clay to make necessary utensils, mortuary pieces, and vessels for the honored dead. In later centuries, when the Chinese had acquired an unsurpassable technical skill, the art of the craftsman, under royal patronage, was dedicated to fashioning exquisite pieces for adornment of imperial palaces and temples of worship.

To appreciate this art fully and to comprehend its significance, one must be familiar with the cultural background of China, with its sacred customs, ritual, and religion. Symbolism is the essence of Chinese decoration; it permeates every field of Chinese art and remains a mystery to the uninitiated. Every piece of ornament has a story behind it which is familiar only to the student of art. The presence of the Eight Immortals and the God of War in a pattern imparts a mysterious significance which can only be interpreted by Chinese mythology. However, certain designs are more simple in their connotations. For instance, a bundle of books is emblematic of scholarship. Ribbons tied in bow-knots on books or baskets of flowers have a religious significance. The ever-present dragon is representative of the emperor and divine power, and the *kylin* signifies good and wise government.

The most popular ceramic designs, however, were floral motifs inspired by the blossoms and flowering shrubs in Chinese gardens, and these were repeated through all periods of Chinese art.

As the potters created for their emperor's favor, the names of the reigning dynasties designate the different styles of the potter's art in China. The last two styles, the Ming and the Ch'ing, are the most important to the decorator of today, because they are practically the only styles of which examples are still available to the general public. The earlier productions are so scarce that they are only to be seen in museums or in valuable private collections; although in recent years burial jars and ornamental forms have been excavated from some very early graves. The important dynasties for the production of pottery and porcelains are:

1. SOUTHERN SUNG PERIOD (1127–1280).
   Golden age of landscape painting and refinement in pottery. The earliest porcelains were made to imitate bronze forms, and crackle glaze was first discovered and used.
2. YUAN-MONGOL PERIOD (1280–1368).
   Less vigorous art. Old traditions followed.
3. MING PERIOD (1368–1644).
   Art followed past models, especially T'ang dynasty (618–907), but there were some great artists. A great period in architecture. Fine pottery and porcelains were made, particularly celadons, polychromes, and blue-and-white ware. Exportation of pottery to Europe.

4. CH'ING-MANCHU PERIOD (1644–1912).
Great age of porcelains, jades, and cut stone, with elaboration of form and decoration of pottery. Extensive trade with Europe.

The last two Chinese dynasties were those that greatly influenced Western art in the 18th century, because of the exportations of pottery to England and France.

The Ming dynasty (1368–1644). During the Ming dynasty all the arts received great encouragement from the emperors. The advancement in the making of porcelain was designated by a greater variety of beautiful colors. Plain-colored glazes, which had, in previous dynasties, furnished the chief decoration, were supplanted in popular favor by monochrome pattern decorations, although the plain glazes continued to be used side by side with more ornate pottery. New motifs such as birds and fish were added to the old floral patterns. This was the period of the blue-and-white porcelains, in which flower patterns in several shades of blue were placed on a cream-colored field and the whole covered with a glaze of a very faint bluish tinge. These were the porcelains that were popular with the Europeans and that had a great influence on English porcelain. Occasionally the colors were reversed and white flowers were placed on a blue background. In the latter part of the Ming period, additional variety in the technique of color decoration was developed, and the beginning of polychrome decoration was evident in Ming enamelled ware and in Ming "three-color" ware, which took its name from its patterns wrought in the combinations of three colors. These colors were usually selected from a palette of dark violet-blue, turquoise, aubergine-purple, yellow, and white.

The Ch'ing dynasty (1644–1912). In the Ch'ing dynasty the emperor K'ang Hsi (1662–1722) and his grandson, the emperor Ch'ien Lung (1736–1795), were deeply interested in the making of porcelain, and encouraged an extensive trade with European countries. The potters of this time excelled in technical perfection. A great variety of porcelains were produced, including the blue-and-white patterns previously discussed. The most typical of these was the familiar hawthorn jar, showing the hawthorn blossom falling on a background imitating a pattern of crackled ice. The design symbolized the passing of winter and the coming of spring. These jars were presented as gifts on the New Year's Day of the Chinese, and were filled with candy, tea, or preserved ginger.

The polychrome decoration, which had been introduced in the Ming period and which was a process of painting enamel colors of various delicate shades on the original glazed piece of porcelain, produced the most glorious creations. The enamel paints were applied to the surface of the piece, which had already been glazed, and then the colors were made more permanent by means of refiring at a temperature lower than the original firing, as the enamel colors could not stand the high degree of heat necessary for firing the body of the piece itself.

The potters in this period created the porcelains now known by their French names of *famille noire, famille verte,* and the *famille rose,* these names being derived from their background colors. The *famille noire* is a rare black porcelain decorated with gold or painted with brilliant enamel colors. *Famille verte* designates a porcelain of rich green background with applied colored decoration in transparent enamel. *Famille rose* is a precious porcelain with a background of a beautiful rose color, made from gold, and upon which enamelled colors are painted. Sometimes the rose shades were applied on a fine white porcelain. The Chinese perfected beautiful purple and yellow glazes, but these are extremely rare. The yellow or *famille jaune* was used mainly to adorn imperial palaces.

Such a variety of decorative designs and amazing colors has never been equalled, and the decorations include a great variety of flower patterns in their natural colorings placed on the background colors described above. Other patterns were made showing scenes of domestic life, court scenes, historical and mythological subjects, the familiar dragon and phoenix bird of the most gorgeous plumage, landscapes, sacred mountains, butterflies, insects, the Buddhist emblems, and many others too numerous to mention.

In these two periods the zenith of this art had been reached, and it is hard to imagine man capable of producing more beautiful creations. It is perhaps only natural that the Chinese of the last two hundred years have created little, in their efforts to imitate the beautiful floral patterns and rich glowing colors of the Ming and Ch'ing potters.

Glassware

Products made of glass have both useful and ornamental functions. Most glass products have been made for table use, but lighting fixtures, candelabra, candlesticks, lamps, and ornamental vase forms have been produced in practically all glass-making centers. As a rule, glassware has less surface pattern and texture than china, and its principal interest is in its shape and color.

The composition of glass consists of sand or silica, plus various bases such as soda, potash, lime, or oxide of lead.

Nearly all antique glass forms were made by blowing while the glass was hot, soft, and malleable. When blown to the required shape, each piece was placed on an iron rod called a *pontil*. After cooling, it was removed from the pontil, and there remained a roughness known as the *pontil mark* where it had rested on the rod. The age of glass may be judged by this mark; the rougher or larger the pontil mark, the older is the piece of glass.

Glass is never perfectly transparent. It is always slightly tinted, although the tint is sometimes only visible to the expert. Colored glass is produced by the addition of a metallic oxide to its composition. Glass, when struck, should ring clearly with a long, diminishing sound. Very old glass is usually heavy and does not have a continuous ring. Antique glass is very often covered with invisible scratches.

Glass may be ornamented by cutting, engraving, painting, enamelling, gilding, and pressing. Crystal is a glass made of flint and lead oxide. It is very hard and is usually cut into prismatic forms to produce a sparkling effect.

All of the nations of antiquity produced useful and ornamental types of glassware in the forms of bottles, flasks, vases, cups, and oil and perfume containers. Many of these examples have through age or long burial attained an iridescence of great beauty, and they are highly prized by collectors.

Venetian glass. Venice has been known for its glass production since the Middle Ages. During the high period of the Renaissance and thereafter, Venice was acclaimed by the whole world for the high quality of its glassware, which included ornamental as well as useful pieces, mirrors, and beads. The major portion of Venetian glass was made in Murano, a suburb of Venice, where glassware of fine quality is still produced, and although other localities in Italy had glass furnaces, their products are all called Venetian.

Venetian glass was exceptionally light and delicate. Most of it was the product of the blowpipe. Because of its thinness it was never cut, but was modelled into extraordinary shapes, made in every variety of color, and ornamented with applied forms resembling dolphins, flowers, wings, stems, and leaves. Much of the Venetian glass was enamelled and gilded in pictorial, foliage, or abstract patterns. Other surface finishes included net, crackled, marbled, lace, and spiralled effects.

Through the migration of Venetian workmen to neighboring countries and especially to Flanders, imitations of Venetian ware became widespread, and this fact, combined with improved materials and processes for glassmaking in other countries, eventually ruined the Venetian industry.

German and Bohemian glass. At first Venetian forms were reproduced in German and Bohemian work, although they were slightly heavier in appearance than the originals. The Germans invented a very hard form of glass which they were able to cut into many shapes and also to enrich by engraving and stippling. Ornament and figures in both incised and relief effects were produced. Beakers, wine glasses, cups, flasks, and figures were made.

Irish and English glass. Irish glass is usually known as Waterford, taking its name from the famous Waterford works, but it was also made in Belfast, Dublin, and Cork. It was exceptionally hard, and was usually ornamented by cutting. The cut motifs consisted of diamonds, stars, festoons, nailheads, pineapples, beads, and other shapes. The older examples showed shallow-cut ornamentations; the later examples were cut deeply. As a rule this glass was the plain, transparent type, although a few pieces were made in color. Waterford glass was extensively used for chandeliers, lighting fixtures, and tableware.

English glass was made at Bristol, Nailsea, and other places. It was particularly noted for its color and for its cut and painted decoration. Two especially famous features of Bristol glass were its deep blue tones and the spiral stems on drinking glasses. The Nailsea glass was made largely in imitation of Venetian models. Many colors were produced, with a great variety of intricate patterns. Stripes, waves, and threads, both within the glass itself and applied to the body, were used as ornamental motifs. Bristol glass is considered superior to Nailsea, but because of considerable interchange of workmen, great similarity often exists.

Early 17th century tavern drinking glasses were also made at various places in England. These glasses were frequently decorated with humorous mottoes and pictures.

American glass. Useful pieces of glass were made in the southern colonies as early as the date of the first permanent settlement. It was not until 1739, however, that ornamental pieces were first made in New Jersey.

Stiegel glass. The most famous American glass was made by Henry William Stiegel, a German who came to America in 1750. Stiegel was a romantic figure, and many myths have been written concerning his activities. He started an iron foundry at Elizabeth Furnace, Pennsylvania, made *firebacks* and stoves, prospered, and expanded his business to considerable proportions. In 1762 he purchased land in Lancaster County, Pennsylvania, called it Manheim after the German city of that name, and endeavored to develop a real estate business. Land was slow in selling, and he was forced to establish a local industry to attract buyers. He knew the glass-making industry and started a glass factory. Operations commenced in 1763. Personal extravagance caused Stiegel to be thrown into the debtor's prison in 1774. His fortunes varied thereafter, and he died in 1785.

From 1763 to 1770 Stiegel made window glass and various types of bottles and hollow ware at both Elizabeth Furnace and Manheim. In

Cockatoo Tumbler
Enamelled in
Colors by
Stiegel

Venetian Glass

Waterford Glass
Sugar bowl →

Fluted Tumbler
by Stiegel

Sandwich
Glass Lamp

Irish Cut Glass Pitcher

Hurricane
Glass

Setting Hen of
Sandwich Pressed Glass

Sandwich Glass
Candlestick

EXAMPLES OF EUROPEAN AND AMERICAN GLASSWARE.

1769 Stiegel started the manufacture of flint-glass—the first of its type in America—at Manheim, and many experienced apprentices were brought from Bristol, England; Cologne, Germany; and Venice, Italy. In the few years that this factory was in operation, many beautiful pieces were made, following English and Continental prototypes. Quaint, useful, and decorative objects of every kind, in clear glass, opaque white, emerald green, amethyst, brown, and sapphire blue, were produced. Etching was occasionally employed as decoration because the glass was comparatively soft and easily treated in this manner. He also made an interesting enamelled glass covered with colorful German peasant patterns of leaves, berries, and parrots. His perfume bottles, sugar bowls, and flower vases were particularly in demand.

Stiegel was a spendthrift and had poor business judgment, and after the collapse of his undertakings, many of his employees organized their own factories and made the same kind of glassware that had been formerly produced by Stiegel. Factories were established in Zanesville, Ohio; New England; and New York. European wares similar to the Stiegel types also began to be imported from the early years of the 19th century, with a result that there is probably more imitation ware of the Stiegel type than there are original pieces. Due to the short existence of the Stiegel factory, it is doubtful that he could have made all that is attributed to him.

Jersey glass. In 1739 Caspar Wistar established a glass factory in the southern part of New Jersey. It was carried on by his son, Richard, until the Revolution. Several brothers by the name of Stanger also started a glass factory in the same section, probably just after the Revolution. The productions of these factories were known as "South Jersey" glassware, and consisted mostly of useful pieces such as window glass and bottles.

Individual workmen in these factories, in their free time, became interested in blowing more ornamental forms, the majority of which were heavy, crude, and elementary in appearance. Interest was obtained by color and shape and with occasional applied ornament in swirls, crimpings, and threads. This glassware is sometimes known as "Wistarberg" ware.

Midwestern glass. Window glass, bottles, and table and ornamental ware were made after the Revolution in the vicinity of Pittsburgh and the Ohio River. Most of this glass imitated the Stiegel ware.

Sandwich glass. Table and ornamental ware were made in Sandwich, Massachusetts, between 1825 and 1885 by Deming Jarves. The enormous output of this factory was only possible by employing cheap methods of manufacturing. Most of the Sandwich glass was enriched by pressing into moulds which produced an imitation cut pattern. This product is known as *pressed glass* and is easily recognized by the lack of sharpness to the edge of the ornament or pattern. The early glass made at the Sandwich factory is considered the best, as the moulds were comparatively sharp when first used. The outer surface of the early glass was frequently covered with a lacelike stippling and tracery causing considerable sparkle. Some blown glass products were made. Other types were the striped, threaded, mould-blown, clear, colored, overlaid, and milk glass.

Many of the Sandwich pieces were enriched with political symbols and portrait heads. Ornamental pieces were made to imitate animals. Their cats, dogs, ducks, and setting hens were used as souvenirs and premiums by commercial houses, to be given away with a purchase of goods. Whale-oil lamps, candlesticks, doorknobs, drawer pulls, decanters, mugs, and tableware were also produced in clear glass, cloudy effects, and colors. Jarves also tried at one time to make etched glass patterns. The quality of his ware was good, and much of it was exported to foreign countries. Sandwich glass, although not correctly speaking a Colonial product, is frequently used, due to its informal character, as a decorative accessory in all American period types of rooms.

During the 19th century, factories in Ohio, Pennsylvania, New York, Kentucky, Virginia, and Maryland manufactured bottles and flasks for various purposes, many of which have become collector's items, due to their color, shape, or unusual design. They were made in yellow, amber, various greens, aquamarine, sapphire blue, pink, red amber, amethyst, lavender, and moonstone, the latter now very rare. The flasks were of both opaque and clear glass, decorated with ribbed, swirled, or diamond designs, or made in the shape of violins and log cabins. Among the most desirable to the collector are those decorated with historical or political themes, pictures of famous persons, masonic emblems, and American eagle or other patriotic designs.

Modern glass. The art of the glass-workers was developed to an extraordinary degree during the latter years of the 19th century. In Bohemia, France, and Sweden, glass designers concentrated their efforts on inventing new forms, types, and colors. Louis Tiffany of New York developed an iridescent glass of great brilliance and luster. In the early years of the 20th century Lalique of Paris produced a luminous, transparent glass, ornamented by pressing and by alternating polished and dull surfaces. He designed tableware, ornaments, and lighting fixtures. Many of his designs were sculptural and architectural in character.

Today, Swedish Orrefors glass, with its engraved figures and patterns, is considered one of the finest of contemporary productions, as is the output of the Steuben factory at Corning, New York, which is noted for the purity of its crystal. The Corning factory produces both utilitarian and ornamental glass, with fine cut and etched patterns executed from designs of Sidney Waugh and others, and structural glass products. The latter, consisting of heavy slabs and bricks, are priced for popular consumption, and the future will probably witness a more extensive use of these forms both for practical and decorative purposes.

Bibliography

Anscher, E. S., *A History and Description of French Porcelain* (tr. Burton). London, 1905. Illustrated text.

Barnard, H., *Chats on Wedgwood Ware*. Frederick A. Stokes Co., New York, 1924. Illustrated text.

Buckley, W., *European Glass*. Houghton Mifflin Co., Boston, 1926. Illustrated text on the history of glassmaking.

Burton, W., *A General History of Porcelain,* 2 Vols. Cassell and Co., New York, 1921. Illustrated history with color plates and photographs.

Chaffers, W., *Marks and Monograms on European and Oriental Pottery and Porcelain*. Reeves and Turner, London, 1932. An illustrated handbook for collectors.

Cox, W., *Pottery and Porcelain*. Crown Publishers, New York, 1944. A comprehensive description of all types.

Eberlein, H. D., and Ramsdell, R. W., *The Practical Book of Chinaware*. J. B. Lippincott Co., Philadelphia, 1925. Fully illustrated text.

Glass. A catalog of a special exhibition prepared by various members of the staff of the Metropolitan Museum of Art, New York, 1936. A brief illustrated summary of glass-making from ancient Egyptian to modern times.

GUILLAND, W. G., *Chinese Porcelain.* Chapman and Hall, Ltd., London, 1902. Illustrated text.

HANNOVER, E., *Pottery and Porcelain: II, The Far East* (tr. Rackham). Ernest Benn, Ltd., London, 1925. Illustrated text.

HAYDEN, A., *Chats on English China.* Frederick A. Stokes Co., New York, 1904. Out of print. Illustrated text.

HOBSON, R. L., *A Guide to the English Pottery and Porcelain.* British Museum, London, 1923. Illustrated text.

HOBSON, R. L., *A Guide to the Pottery and Porcelain of the Far East.* British Museum, London, 1923. Illustrated text.

HOBSON, R. L., *The Later Ceramic Wares of China.* Ernest Benn, Ltd., London, 1925. Illustrated text.

HONEY, W. B., *European Ceramic Art.* Van Nostrand Co. Inc., New York, 1950. Excellent illustrated listing.

JANNEAU, G., *Modern Glass.* The Studio, Ltd., London, 1931. Illustrated text.

KNOWLES, W. P., *Dutch Pottery and Porcelain.* Charles Scribner's Sons, New York, 1919. Illustrated text.

LLOYD-HYDE, J. A., *Oriental Lowestoft.* Charles Scribner's Sons, New York, 1936. Illustrated text.

MOORE, N. H., *The Old China Book.* Frederick A. Stokes and Co., New York, 1903. Out of print. Illustrated text on English pottery and porcelain.

MOORE, N. H., *Old Glass—European and American.* Frederick A. Stokes Co., New York, 1924. Illustrated text.

NORTHEND, M. H., *American Glass.* Dodd, Mead and Co., New York, 1926. An illustrated thorough treatment of this subject.

RACKHAM, B., *A Book of Porcelain.* Adam and Charles Black, London, 1910. Text with color illustrations.

ROHAN, T., *Old Glass Beautiful.* Mills and Boon, Ltd., London, 1930. Good simple text with illustrations on English and Irish glass.

CHAPTER XVIII

METALS AND HARDWARE

M etals, as used in art and industry, have varying physical characteristics that limit the forms into which they may be fashioned and
define the character of their enrichment. To a certain extent, each historical period of art has featured certain structural and ornamental metals.
The Egyptians knew the processes of making objects in iron and bronze.
The Greeks and Romans cast magnificent statues in bronze, made metal
furniture, and produced many household utensils and toilet articles in iron
or copper alloys. During the Middle Ages in Europe great care and effort
was expended by the metalworkers and locksmiths in the production of
hardware, gates, screens, and grilles for the cathedrals. Heavy wooden
doors were hung on elaborately scroll-patterned hinges, which served for
protection as well as operation. Silver and gold jewel-boxes, reliquaries,
crucifixes, and other religious objects were produced in exquisite perfection in the uncounted hours of labor contributed by the monks in their
cells.

During the Italian and Spanish Renaissance, less importance was given
to the decorative effect of hinges and locks, but many of the greatest
sculptors contributed their efforts in the design of bronze door handles
and knockers, andirons, lanterns, gates, and lighting fixtures; and the
Plateresco period of art was named in honor of the Spanish silversmiths
whose work so influenced craftsmen in other materials.

In Italy, during the Renaissance, were also produced those extraordinary miniature reproductions of classical statuary that were used as
household ornaments. These statuettes were made by the cire-perdue or
"lost-wax" process, so named because the original wax model of the figure
was lost in making the bronze casting. Very intricate models were made
in wax, delicately tooled, and then covered with a layer of fine clay which
was left to harden. When dry, the clay was heated and the melted wax
permitted to run out through a small hole, leaving a beautifully finished

mould in which to pour the liquid bronze. When the bronze cooled, the clay mould had to be broken and removed, leaving the finished product, but only after both the model and the mould had been destroyed so that it was impossible to produce another casting without having the sculptor make another model. (See illustration, page 128.)

Among the many great names associated with the metalwork of 16th century Italy were Sansovino and his pupil, Vittoria, noted for their ornamental bronzes, and Benvenuto Cellini, known for his work as goldsmith, jeweller, sculptor, and medalist.

The pinnacle of the metal arts in France occurred simultaneously with her high period of decorative work. The production of the gilded bronze furniture ornaments, clocks, andirons, and other objects in ormolu reached near perfection in design and finish under the great ciseleurs, Gouthière and Caffieri, during the middle of the 18th century and, with the exception of the work of Odiot and Thomire, began to decline in quality and design in the early years of the 19th century.

The use of metals in the interior decoration of both England and America has followed similar lines. In the 17th century most of the hardware in both countries was made in wrought iron, although in England far more thought was put upon design than in America, where the village blacksmith usually made a latch, bolt, or hinge with utility as the only consideration. Fireplace accessories were also made of iron, although in the more elaborate homes in England brass ornaments often enriched the baser metal. During the 18th century both brass and iron were used for hardware and irons and firetools, and far greater elaboration was given to ornamental details. The 18th century was also the great period of silver tableware and ornaments in both countries, and France exported shelf clocks and ornaments in ormolu that were designed especially to appeal to the English and American public.

The metals used for decorative purposes. In the decorative arts ten different elementary metals are commonly used. These are iron, copper, tin, lead, zinc, chromium, aluminum, magnesium, silver, and gold. Certain of these metals, lacking needed qualities, are frequently combined with others to form what are known as *alloys;* in each case a product is obtained that has the advantages of both the combined metals. The principal alloys are bronze, a combination of copper and tin; brass, a combination of copper and zinc; and pewter, a combination of tin and lead. Sometimes a small quantity of a third metal is added to these alloys for special reasons. The more valuable metals, such as gold and silver, are often used for surfacing or plating baser materials. Chromium, a very hard gray-white metal, is seldom used in its pure state, but is usually alloyed with another metal or used for surface plating. Zinc, a very soft bluish-white metal, is used for roofing and for alloys. Aluminum and magnesium are both extremely lightweight metals that are nontarnishing, resist corrosion, and maintain a polished surface. They are used as alloys, coating materials, and in solid form. Both are used extensively in airplane, automobile, and furniture construction, and for cooking utensils and kitchenware.

The physical characteristics of iron. Iron is the most abundant of all metals, and is found in larger or smaller quantities in almost all rocks, earth, and water. It has been known and prized from very early times. Articles made of it have been found in Egypt, Nineveh, ancient China, and Roman Britain. The iron of commerce is never entirely pure, but always contains a little carbon, silicon, sulphur, and phosphorus. All iron objects are likely to rust when exposed to damp air, but do not change when in protected places. Iron may be kept from rusting by coating it with a nonoxidizing material such as tin, zinc, or brass. Commercial iron is produced in three principal varieties—cast or pig iron, wrought iron, and steel. The principal chemical difference between these three materials is in the percentage of carbon that is contained in them. Cast iron contains the most carbon, steel the next amount, and wrought iron the least. The amount of carbon greatly affects the strength, character, and working qualities of the material.

Cast iron comes from the blast furnace in small bars or pigs. These bars may easily be liquefied under sufficient heat, and when in such condition, may be poured into a sand mould to form various useful shapes. Cast iron is exceptionally brittle, cracks easily under a blow, and is not subject to bending. It is not used to any great extent in the decorative arts, as articles manufactured by this process are coarse in finish. Ornamental firebacks and facings, stoves, and fireplace accessories are the principal decorative uses for cast iron.

Wrought iron is softer than cast iron and has less carbon and other impurities in it. It is not brittle and may be hammered into bars, rolled into plates, or drawn into wires. It can be hammered or bent to almost any shape and holds the shape to which it is bent. For this reason it is called a malleable material (derived from Latin, *malleus,* a hammer). Wrought iron may be welded; that is, separate pieces may be joined together by hammering when they are red-hot.

Wrought iron has many uses in the decorative arts. From bars are made grilles, gates, railings, furniture, andirons, tools, lighting fixtures, hardware, brackets, braces, and ornaments. From sheets of various thicknesses are made fireplace linings, cheap hardware, and lighting fixtures. Wrought iron objects are often coated with brass.

Steel is a variety of iron with a hardness that is halfway between cast and wrought iron, and it has some of the physical characteristics of both. Steel is lighter in weight and has a finer grain than iron; it is subject to a high polish; it may be tempered and is, therefore, elastic, and when slightly bent, springs back to its original shape. Steel is decidedly malleable at a high temperature and hardens greatly by sudden cooling. Steel is used principally as a structural material, but owing to the fact that it may now easily be worked by electrical processes, it is used for many of the same decorative purposes as wrought iron. The alloying of chromium with iron or steel will prevent rust, and the polished alloy will retain its luster. Much iron hardware and furniture, many metal bathroom accessories, table objects, and other useful and decorative pieces, are now made of an alloy of iron or steel and chromium, or are covered with a coating of the latter because of its nontarnishing quality. Steel that is alloyed with 10 per cent to 20 per cent chromium is called *stainless steel,* and is used for cutlery.

Copper is a soft, orange-colored, tarnishing, but non-rusting metal, which is considered everlasting. It was one of the first metals known to man and was used before iron. It is said the ancient Egyptians cut their granite with copper chisels which they hardened by a method now unknown. Nearly all the nations of antiquity used copper alloys in the making of articles of household use, weapons, coins, and statues.

Copper is much used in the industrial and decorative arts because of its strength and the ease with which it may be worked. It may be cast or hammered into desired shapes. It is often alloyed with gold or silver to harden these metals, or it may be alloyed with nickel and zinc for making German silver.

Because of its durability, copper is extensively used in decoration for the production of small ornamental objects or for structural objects that do not have to endure excessive strain. In its variations of brass and bronze, it is useful for hardware, lighting fixtures, statues, table ornaments, clocks, vases, pedestals, fireplace accessories, screens, grilles, kitchen utensils, and similar objects.

Brass has a bright yellowish appearance and is susceptible to a high polish. It tarnishes easily and is consequently often protected by a coat of shellac which, however, will not entirely prevent it from changing color. Brass requires much polishing to keep it bright.

Bronze can be cast with great ease and in the most delicate patterns, and may be finished in a great variety of styles and colors. For these reasons it is more largely used in the manufacture of metal ornaments, statues, and finished hardware than any other material. The surface finishes are obtained by dipping the object in baths of various acids, but these finishes are only light veneers, and disappear if the object is exposed to the weather or frequently handled.

Both brass and bronze may be rolled into very thin sheets, after which spun, hammered, or repoussé forms and surfaces may be produced.

Objects that are cast in bronze and treated with ornament in relief may have the ornament sharpened or undercut by hand chiselling or chasing. The ormolu used on French 17th and 18th century furniture was finished in this way, the bronze finally being coated with gold by a mercury process that was very dangerous to the workmen. The ornament on fine bronze hardware is always hand-chiselled, which is responsible for its high cost. The finish of hardware that has not been touched by handwork is called "commercial."

Brass and bronze are both used as base materials for decorative and useful objects that are coated in gold or silver.

Tin and lead are metals used in alloys, and are too soft for practical purposes when used alone. They are nonrusting. Lead is often used for garden statues and ornaments and occasionally for appliqués on woodwork.

Miscellaneous decorative metal objects. There are many kinds of metal objects valued for their design and workmanship even though the material from which they are made may not be "precious." Many of these objects have great decorative value, while others must be placed in the "collector's" class. There are many books concerning every type of metalwork, and those interested should obtain those upon the particular subject in which they may be interested, as space does not permit a full description here.

Some of the more interesting special types of decorative metalwork are described briefly in the following pages.

Table silver. Most of the antique silver that is available today to the decorator is of English and American origin. The English have always been great workers in this metal, and, to a certain extent, portions of the family fortunes were kept in the form of useful and display articles made by the silversmith. In times of stress and warfare, taxes could be paid by melting down the ancestral ware.

In addition to the design forms, which help to approximate the date of manufacture of English silverware, the law was very particular in requiring that each piece be carefully marked with the maker's name, the *hallmark,* identifying the purity of the silver, and the date letters, giving the year of manufacture. As a result of these legal requirements, all English silver can be very accurately identified by comparison with the published tables of marks.

Though museums contain fine examples of Gothic and Jacobean production, there is very little that is sold today that was made earlier than 1700. The introduction of tea, coffee, and chocolate drinking in the middle of the 17th century contributed greatly to the quantity and quality of work produced by the silversmith.

During the Queen Anne period, most of the silverware was plain, the beauty being in the gracefulness of the contour. Gradually, engraving or hand chasing was introduced in simple border patterns and coats-of-arms, and eventually the whole piece was covered with arabesques and other forms. Repoussé work was also used for enriching the surface.

During the early Georgian period, the influence of Sir Christopher Wren and William Kent was carried into the silversmith's shop, and architectural forms became common. By the middle of the 18th century, the rococo and Chinese influence of Louis XV designs had crossed the Channel. Symmetry and balance gave way to elaborate scrollwork and fantastic patterns.

Under the influence of the Adam brothers, a return to simple lines occurred, with the motifs returning to the classical architectural forms and ornaments that are characteristic of the period. Straight lines, graceful Grecian curves, and chaste decoration predominated. Many pierced or perforated patterns were also used. The classic style continued during the early years of the 19th century in its more cumbersome Regency interpretation.

Almost the entire American Colonial output of silverware came from New England, New York, and Pennsylvania, and many of the silversmiths were of Dutch and Huguenot origin. The Americans followed the English patterns, but much of the charm of American silverware is dependent on its simplicity of line and graceful form and the absence of the over-ornamentation which mars the beauty of contemporary European work. American silver cannot be identified as easily as the English. While the maker's name or initials were usually stamped in an inconspicuous place, there was no law to require accurate marking of quality or date of manufacture. The silversmiths themselves, however, held their own reputation and integrity of importance and maintained a standard of quality in all that they produced. On American silver from 1837 the letters "C" for coin and "D" for dollar were used on all silver of not over 10 per cent alloy. The word "sterl" was first used on Irish silver during the 18th century, and in 1865 it became obligatory to use the word *sterling* on all American silver productions of a standard quality.

There are many names associated with the making of silverware in America, among them being John Coney of Boston (1655–1722), Cornelius Kierstead of New York (1674–1753), and Paul Revere of Boston (1735–1818). The productions of Revere were all characterized by astute craftsmanship and refinement of design, although, as a result of Longfellow's poem, he has received perhaps more credit than was his due, since the work of many other silversmiths was quite the equal of his. The high prices at which his productions are sold frequently reflect a superior sentimental value rather than one of design or workmanship.

The finest American silverware is seen in tankards, beakers, mugs, caudle and candle cups, porringers, punch bowls, kettles, tea, coffee, and chocolate pots, inkstands, salvers, sauceboats, and tazzas.

Silver Porringer 1700

Silver Teapot

Silver Caster 1725

Silver Beaker 1650

Silver Tankard 1750

Silver Punch Bowl by Paul Revere

Silver Teapot by Paul Revere

Silver Sauce Pan by Revere

Pewter Plate

Pewter Caster

Pewter Porringer

Pewter Beaker

Pewter Teapot

Pewter Lamp

Pewter Sugar-bowl

Pewter Jug or Flagon

Pewter Whale-oil Lamp

EXAMPLES OF AMERICAN SILVER AND PEWTER.

Pewter. This alloy has often been called the poor man's silver. It has been made and used for table and ornamental ware since the early days of history in the Orient, Europe, and America.

Because of the softness of the material, objects made in pewter must depend upon their shape and mellowness of color for their interest. Engraved ornamentation is occasionally introduced, particularly on the French examples. Some repoussé or hammered ornament is also seen. Pewter cannot be used for objects intended to contain hot liquids.

American pewter is far more rare than English, as many of the American pieces were used in the manufacture of ammunition at the time of the Revolution. When china began to be imported from the East and was finally made in Europe, pewter was discarded except for use in public inns, where it was valued for its resistance to hard usage.

The forms made from pewter covered every type of container, drinking vessel, dish, candlestick, and lighting fixture. Pewter objects today are valuable decorative shelf accessories for informal and provincial types of rooms.

Sheffield plate was first made in 1742 in Sheffield, England, as a substitute for silver, and as such, gradually drove pewter out of use. Old Sheffield plate was made by fusing a sheet of silver ⅛ inch thick to a sheet of copper 1 inch thick. After successive rollings, the fused materials were reduced to a thin sheet of metal in which the proportion of silver and copper remained constant. The thin sheet could then be hammered or spun into the required shapes. The majority of pieces of Sheffield plated ware were for table use. Salvers, trays, cake baskets, urns, candelabra, and candlesticks were the usual pieces produced, although practically everything that was made in silver was later reproduced in the plated ware. The plate was engraved or enriched with added relief ornament. Where engraving was required, a piece of solid silver was sometimes inserted, as the silver plating was not sufficiently deep to be pierced by the engraver's tools. Sheffield plate was not made by the original process after 1830, when *electroplating* was substituted for coating copper. Old Sheffield plate is in demand by collectors because of the peculiar luster given to the silver by the copper body underneath.

Firebacks. Firebacks are made of cast iron and vary considerably in degree and quality of the finish. The 18th century French firebacks and some of the earlier English examples were far more finely modelled than the American Colonial ones. The French firebacks were ornamented in the relief patterns typical of each period. In the English and American firebacks many of the castings were made by local ironworkers who had little sculptural ability. The motifs used were of a very wide range, and many were of exceptional interest, reflecting local thought or persons. Human figures, ships, mythical creatures, historical scenes, family events, flowers, trees, humorous subjects, coats-of-arms, and many other motifs were used. It is difficult to identify the age of a fireback by the pattern, as many patterns were repeated for generations. The names of the makers and the date of casting are occasionally seen. Paul Revere and Stiegel of Philadelphia were the two best known of the Colonial ironworkers who made these articles.

Brass and copper objects. Many small objects, even of great antiquity, are still available to the collector in the antique shops of Europe, but the

Dinanderie, Ewer

Knight on Horseback Flemish 14th Cent.

Early English Cast-iron Andiron Early 17th Cent.

Early English Cast-iron Fireback 1650

Cast iron Hobgrate English - 18th Cent.

Brass Andirons English - Early 18th Cent.

Steel Basket Grate English – Late 18th Cent.

Colonial Brass Andiron →

Colonial Brass-headed Andirons

Hessians Colonial Cast-iron Andirons

Colonial Fender of Cut Brass

Colonial Brass Door Knockers

EXAMPLES OF ENGLISH AND COLONIAL METALWORK.

purchase of ornamental brasses in the United States is largely limited to objects of household use and furnishings of the Colonial period.

If copper articles are kept polished, their warmth of color and patina may contribute greatly to the character and the decorative effect of a room intended to reproduce a style that is consistent with their use. Among objects made of brass and copper and suitable for interior decoration are clocks, candlesticks, candelabra, and oil lamps; fireplace accessories such as andirons, fenders, warming pans, fire covers, coal scuttles, and tools;

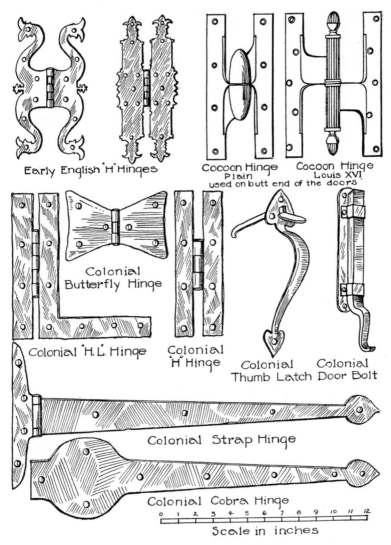

Early English 'H' Hinges

Cocoon Hinge
Plain
used on butt end of the doors

Cocoon Hinge
Louis XVI

Colonial
Butterfly Hinge

Colonial 'H.L.' Hinge

Colonial
'H' Hinge

Colonial
Thumb Latch

Colonial
Door Bolt

Colonial Strap Hinge

Colonial Cobra Hinge

Scale in inches

EXAMPLES OF DOOR HARDWARE.

kitchen and cooking appliances such as caldrons, kettles, and skillets; table utensils such as jugs, water pots, drinking cups, tankards, and other flagons.

Among the more fanciful ornamental objects made of brass and copper were lighting fixtures, water jugs, cisterns, perfume bottles, bowls, strange birds, winged dragons, and imaginary animals made during the Middle Ages in Dinant, Flanders. These have been given the name of *Dinanderies*.

Hardware. Many decorators give too little thought to the hardware

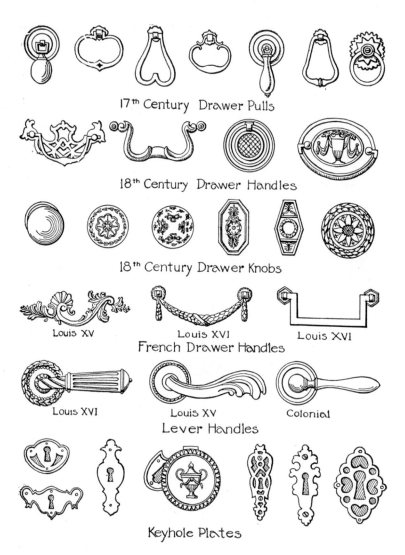

17th Century Drawer Pulls

18th Century Drawer Handles

18th Century Drawer Knobs

Louis XV   Louis XVI   Louis XVI

French Drawer Handles

Louis XVI   Louis XV   Colonial

Lever Handles

Keyhole Plates

EXAMPLES OF FURNITURE AND DOOR HARDWARE.

used in a room, and yet the selection of practical and ornamental metal-work for the proper mechanical operation of such features as doors, windows, and drawers is of the utmost importance so far as comfort and convenience are concerned. From the decorative standpoint, hardware should be given equal consideration with the selection of any of the other smaller accessories.

Most of the hardware that was used for period rooms and furniture was of the surface variety, which means that the metalwork was visible and placed on the face of the woodwork. Under such a condition it was important that both the design and workmanship of the metalwork be harmonious with the style of the architecture of the room, and the craftsmen, having pride in their workmanship and ability, produced by hand, hardware of great beauty. Much of the modern machine-made hardware is of the mortise type, a term referring to the fact that portions of the hardware are inserted in specially cut holes or grooves in the wood; while mechanically satisfactory, such pieces do not play an important part in the enrichment of the room.

Although hardware must be primarily functional in design, in each historical period it was either silhouetted or surface-ornamented in patterns that harmonized with the architectural and decorative treatment. The wrought iron pieces were given interest by their shape and hammer marks; the thin brass pieces, by repoussé ornament (a surface relief pattern produced by hammering the metals either on the front or rear); the heavier brass and bronze pieces, by cast relief ornament additionally finished by hand chiselling and filing, called *chasing,* which produced sharper edges and undercuts than was possible by the casting process alone.

There are unnumbered varieties, sizes, qualities, and mechanical designs for hardware, and the manufacturers' catalogs appear very confusing to those who are not accustomed to this branch of decorative equipment. While a decorator should have a knowledge of the ornamental forms of metalwork that may be required for certain types of doors or furniture, the mechanical design should be checked by a manufacturer's representative or hardware dealer. Serious and quite unexpected errors may easily be made in the proper sizes and types of hinges and locks to be used, even under the simplest conditions.

The great majority of rooms today are furnished with the ordinary, commercial stock-pattern types of hardware, but in the best decorative work the hardware is specially designed and made to order. The latter type is, of course, far more costly and requires more time to produce. A description of the many available types of hardware used by decorators would occupy too much space for the purposes of this book. The reader must be referred to the commercial catalogs of hardware dealers or to the craftsmen who make special-order hardware and metalwork. Illustrations of the more common types of hardware are shown on pages 675 and 676.

Students of decoration should acquaint themselves with the following terms and articles:

> Locks (tumbler and cylinder)
> Bolts (plain, cremorne, and espagnolette)
> Escutcheons (keyholes and pushplates)

Hinges (butt, cocoon, strap, H, HL, butterfly,
   double acting, and secret)
Handles (knobs, levers, and drawer pulls)
Latches (surface and secret)
Sash fittings (locks and adjusters)

Bibliography

AVERY, C. L., *Early American Silver*. D. Appleton-Century Co., New York, 1930. Excellent illustrated text.

BURGESS, F. W., *Chats on Old Copper and Brass*. Frederick A. Stokes Co., New York, 1914. Illustrated text.

Burlington Fine Arts Club Exhibition of a Collection of Silversmith's Work of European Origin. London, 1901. Illustrated text.

BYNE, A. AND M. S., *Rejeria of the Spanish Renaissance*. The DeVinne Press, New York, 1914. Collection of photographs and measured drawings with descriptive text.

BYNE, A. AND M. S., *Spanish Iron Work*. The Hispanic Society of America, New York, 1915. Excellent illustrations.

CLOUZET, H., *La Ferronnerie Moderne*. C. Moreau, Paris. Thirty-six plates of modern ironwork.

CONTET, F., *Documents de Ferronnerie Ancienne*. F. Contet, Paris, 1908–1909. Series of portfolios containing photographic plates of ironwork in France.

FERRARI, G., *Ile Fero*. U. Hoepli, Milan. Italian ironwork.

GARDNER, J. S., *Ironwork, Part I, From the Earliest Times to the End of the Medieval Period*. Victoria and Albert Museum, London, 1914. Illustrated text.

GOTTERELL, H. H., *Pewter Down the Ages*. Hutchinson and Co., Ltd., London, 1932. Illustrated survey of pewter from medieval times to the present day.

HOWARD, M., *Old London Silver, Its History, Its Makers, and Its Marks*. Charles Scribner's Sons, New York, 1903. Illustrated text.

JACKSON, C. J., *Illustrated History of English Plate*. Country Life, London, 1911. The most authoritative text written on the subject. Very expensive, but usually available in large public libraries.

JONES, E. A., *Old Silver of Europe and America*. B. T. Batsford, Ltd., London, 1928. Illustrated text.

KERFOOT, J. B., *American Pewter*. Houghton Mifflin Co., New York, 1924. Illustrated text.

PETTORELLI, A., *Il Bronze e Il Rame nell'Arte Decorativa Italiana*. U. Hoepli, Milan, 1926. Illustrated history of Italian bronze.

SONN, A. H., *Early American Wrought Iron,* 3 Vols. Charles Scribner's Sons, New York, 1928. Text illustrated with plates from the drawings of the author.

CHAPTER XIX

LIGHTING AND LIGHTING
FIXTURES

The general problem. The planning of artificial lighting presents a problem that requires both practical and esthetic considerations. The average room needs light for general illumination and special lights for particular areas or activities. The lighting equipment and fixtures must be consistent with the style of the decorations, must contribute to the desired character and atmosphere, and must be adequate for the purpose of the room.

Scientific lighting by electricity is a comparatively modern development, and it has been greatly handicapped by the persistence of the traditions associated with the candle and oil lamp, which have been used since the beginnings of civilization. The early designers of electric lighting fixtures could not resist the temptation of thinking in terms of the long established types of holders, and did not at first realize the basic differences between the small flame and the incandescent filament. A flame must be reasonably isolated from adjoining areas for fire prevention, it requires air for combustion, and must be placed where it may be easily lit or extinguished. The glare of a one-candle power flame is not so intense as to cause eye-strain, but for proper lighting there must be a sufficient number of units to compensate for the small quantity of light produced by each. With these limitations, the practical considerations were often more important than decorative effects, although from the beginnings of art history beautiful candlesticks, torches, candelabra, and lamps have been produced.

With the introduction of electricity, many of the limitations of flame lighting were eliminated and an entirely new basis of lighting made possible. Other limitations, requirements, and possibilities had to be met, however, such as the necessity for preparatory wiring, the placing of numerous electrical outlets and controls, the excessive glare from strong spots of illumination, the existence of heat but with little danger of fire, and the possibility of introducing different color effects.

Lighting engineering. Due to advances in electrical illumination since Edison's invention in 1879 of the first practical incandescent lamp, it is impossible for any one but the specialist to grasp the progress that has been made or keep in touch with the frequent technical developments. The decorator who is called upon to furnish elaborate electrical layouts should call upon the lighting engineer for assistance. Many of the modern lighting methods are of the "architectural" type, i.e., they must be integrated with the architecture and structure of the room, and require that special arrangements or equipment be planned in advance of construction, or that structural alterations be made in an existing room. The manufacturers of electrical equipment have done much research on these subjects and free literature and consultation service are available to those who are interested. The subject can be outlined here only in the briefest manner, leaving to the judgment of the reader the selections that may be adaptable to some particular installation. A room that is to be decorated in any of the historic styles should be equipped with such of the newer forms as may be adaptable, providing they do not conflict with the harmony of style of the room. Contemporary living requires the lighting efficiency and dramatic effects that are only possible with properly designed and distributed electric lighting equipment.

Electrical wiring. One of the most important features for the proper lighting of every room is to have an abundance of supply sockets or baseboard plugs. These are inexpensive to install, add greatly to the flexibility of the lighting layout, permit a greater use of portable lights, and facilitate subsequent changes in the lighting arrangements. In planning for new lighting it is advisable and economical to confer with a lighting specialist during the blue-print stage. The average electrician is not a lighting expert. If a specialist is not available, a good general rule to follow, in the location of outlets, is that no point along a wall should be over 6 feet from a wall- or base-plug, and there should be one or more double base-plugs on each side of a room. Each room is always a special problem by itself, and common sense, as well as theory, must guide in the planning of its illumination. Furniture arrangement should be considered, but as furniture is likely to be moved about, an ample supply of electrical current should be planned for in all locations. Proper lighting is not only a matter of quantity of light, but its proper distribution, as well. All outlets if possible should contain double plugs, and one side of each plug should be controlled by a switch placed at the entrance of the room to control the general illumination; the other side should be left for the lights needed for special purposes.

Electric bulbs and tubes. There are two classes of electrically produced light in general use today. The most common is the incandescent filament bulb that, according to its size, gives a glow of varying degrees of intensity. The basic principle of this light has undergone only minor changes since its original invention; technical improvements, innovations, and size variations, however, have been introduced to provide greater efficiency; it is used for both spot and flood illumination. Three-way bulbs are also available, providing different strengths of lighting from the same bulb at the option of the operator.

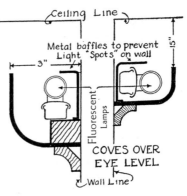

Cross-section of two types of coves using fluorescent tube lights.

The incandescent lamp produces warm yellow rays of light, except when the bulb is of colored glass.

The second most usual light source is the fluorescent tube, which consists of translucent glass filled with a gas that becomes luminous when used as a conductor of electricity, and which produces a very small amount of heat. The glass tubes are furnished in a variety of straight lengths, from 6 inches to 8 feet, and are from 5/8 inch to 2 inches in diameter, each size consuming a different amount of current. Ring and other shapes are also manufactured, and various colors are available.

The preference in using incandescent or fluorescent bulbs, or both, for lighting any one room, depends upon the specific problem involved. A room entirely lighted by fluorescent tubes may appear cold and uninviting, because of the absence of red and yellow rays; and if such an appearance is undesirable, it may be counteracted by using one of the colored varieties. Fluorescent light is extensively used for dramatic effects in both residential and commercial installations, and it is particularly valuable for lighting general areas rather than specific spots. It has a tendency to distort colors because of its cold quality; therefore lighting engineers do not advise its use where food is prepared, or in women's bath or powder rooms where make-up is applied. Incandescent light is not as adaptable as fluorescent, but is used to better advantage in rooms that are decorated in any of the historic styles and for spot lighting and portable lamps. The initial cost of properly installed fluorescent lighting is considerably more than that of a comparable incandescent installation, but operating costs are lower, and the life of the fluorescent tube is longer than that of an incandescent bulb.

Methods of lighting. Types of electrical lighting are classified by the manner in which the light rays are directed to the object to be illumined. These are *direct, indirect,* and *semidirect.* Direct lighting is the type that

A section of cove for installation over windows and doors or around the entire perimeter of a room. Fluorescent tubes are mounted in a small metal trough which can be painted to match wall or wood trim.

is produced by most table and floor lamps, the light from which shines directly down on the object or on a limited area. This type produces sharp shadows, strong contrasts of light and dark, and, if the light source is improperly shaded, it is likely to produce a strong glare. Direct lighting is usually combined with other types. Indirect lighting is that in which the light is directed to the ceiling, cove, wall, or another surface, from which it is reflected into the room, the immediate light source usually being shielded from view. Indirect lighting creates almost no shadows, and if used alone is flat and uninteresting, but is unexcelled for a general glow or illumination; it is more costly in current than direct lighting because a reflection is never as strong as an original source of light. Semidirect lighting is a combination of the first two methods, in which a portion of light shines directly on an object or surface, and a portion is reflected. An example is the floor or table lamp containing a concealed bowl of diffusing glass, which directs the light up to the ceiling for reflection and general illumination, but also allows some of it to shine directly downward on a table, reading chair, or other area. The best arrangement of lighting for domestic use combines these methods, so that there is a general illumination by reflections but sufficient direct light to produce enough shadows for interest, without sharp contrasts that fatigue the eye, and enough direct light to provide for reading, writing, games, and other special purposes.

Below are outlined the principal methods of illuminating by electricity.

Cove lighting consists of placing a continuous series of fluorescent tubes in a groove or trough placed on one or more walls of a room about 12 inches from the ceiling. It is an indirect type and throws the illumination on the ceiling.

Recessed ceiling lights are often used in low-ceilinged rooms although they have the disadvantage of producing a glare near the eye level. A pocket of the proper dimensions is cut into the plaster ceiling to hold the bulbs or tubes and this is covered with diffusing glass or "egg-crate" *louvres* that screen a direct view of the light source. The louvres may also be used to direct the light in other than a downward ray and to illumine side walls, special furniture, or show cases. The recesses may be in isolated locations, in circular or rectangular shapes, or may consist of strips running

Courtesy Kurt Versen; Hedrich-Blessing, Photographers

A room with general illumination produced by cove lighting and recessed ceiling lights.

Courtesy Hamby and Nelson, Architects; Dan Cooper, Decorator

An example of valance lighting giving general illumination. This is supplemented with a portable lamp and bedlight.

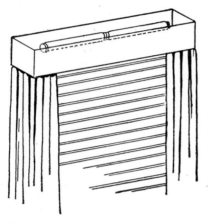

Lamps mounted back of valance board.

the length of the room, around the room, or in places where special illumination is required. This type is used mainly in commercial installations.

Cornice lighting is similar to cove lighting and may sometimes be placed underneath a cornice projection, in which case the light is thrown downward, or on top of a door, window, or overmantel cornice, in which case the light is thrown upwards. The source of light should be screened from direct view.

Valance lighting consists of tubes placed behind a valance board or cornice to throw light both upward for ceiling reflection, and downward for direct drapery or window illumination. It is dramatic in effect and is frequently used in domestic types of decoration. The idea may be extended by carrying the lights down the sides of the drapery to the floor, a feature that is easily carried out if the draperies are hung in a recess, but which requires the construction of an extra box shield at the side if the draperies hang in the usual manner.

Furniture lighting. Bookcases, shelving, mirrors, glass cabinets, and wall niches may be lighted by incandescent or fluorescent lamps installed in strategic hidden locations adjoining or in various parts of the framework. Such lights are usually directed toward the back of shelving to illumine standing objects or accessories. The tops of tables, cabinets, bookcases, and mantel shelves may be treated with illuminated glass panels to light objects placed upon them, and to add to the general illumination by ceiling reflections. Dining room tables that have a permanent location may have a glass-covered hole cut in the middle, under which may be placed a spot light that throws its rays upward to a mirror on the ceiling, which returns them without glare at an angle to the top of the table itself.

Flood and spot lights are used in different ways to highlight limited areas, paintings, or other important objects. These lights may be built into the walls, may be placed behind ornaments, or may be placed in visible positions with their reflectors painted the wall color. The light source and rays should be kept either above or below eye level. If placed under furniture, spot lights should have a covering lens to protect the eyes from glare. Holders for lights are often furnished with swivel brackets or gooseneck arms so that they may be directed to any point.

Vase and urn lights. Strong incandescent bulbs may be placed in vases or urns that are large enough to conceal them completely. Their vertical rays are reflected from the ceiling. The tops of such vases should be above eye level.

Ceiling down-lights are miniature spot or flood lights wholly or partially recessed between the ceiling and floor boarding above, and are used for dramatizing and highlighting certain portions of the room, such as dining, coffee, and card tables, or some important decorative object or grouping. These lights may be equipped with louvres to prevent a diagonal glare.

Ceiling drop lights. These are used mainly in commercial types of decorating. They are usually de-

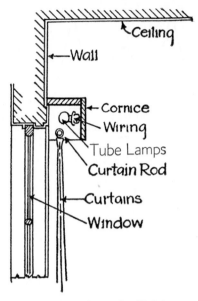

Cross-section of cornice lighting at window.

signed to supply both direct and indirect lighting. If the bowls are of translucent glass or plastic, they are apt to produce a glare that destroys the full effect of the colors and decoration of a room. They should preferably be used only in high-ceilinged rooms and they should be kept well above the level of the eye. An infinite variety of designs of this type have been produced for special purposes. They are often useful in kitchens, pantries, bathrooms, and other working portions of the house or shop, but in these cases should be supplemented by lights over specific working areas.

Portable lamps. Nearly all rooms require one or more portable lamps for flexibility in the lighting plan. These may be used either as general illumination by rays directed toward the ceiling, or for reading, writing, and card-playing by the downward type, in which case they should be fitted with disk reflectors. Lights throwing their rays upward should be fitted with diffusing bowls and the tops of their shades should be above the level of the eye.

Lighting of period rooms. In the lighting of rooms of a period character, both old and new methods of lighting are usually employed. Original period rooms were lighted by table and floor lamps, candlesticks, ceiling candelabra, and wall sconces. Table and floor lamps are adaptable to electrical uses because their shades may be designed to screen the glare of a strong bulb or to direct the rays as desired. Real candles are frequently

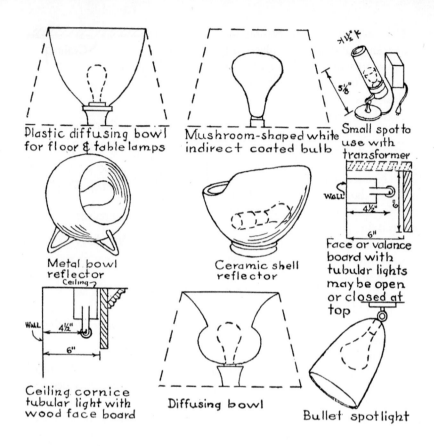

Plastic diffusing bowl for floor & table lamps

Mushroom-shaped white indirect coated bulb

Small spot to use with transformer

Metal bowl reflector

Ceramic shell reflector

Face or valance board with tubular lights may be open or closed at top

Ceiling cornice tubular light with wood face board

Diffusing bowl

Bullet spotlight

Fixtures and equipment used for modern lighting.

used on dining tables and in other places. Elaborate ceiling candelabra are only used today in high, formal types of period rooms, and leading decorators now attempt to retain their period character by using the smallest of electric bulbs (¼ candle power) which are placed in wired wax candles. A natural candle effect is well imitated in this way, but the illumination is decorative only and is not sufficient for practical use. If the design of the candelabra permits, small spot or flood lights are hidden in it, and these reflect their lights to the ceiling to produce the real illumination. Electrical wall sconces are difficult to use for practical light because if the bulbs are unshaded, they produce a direct glare; if shaded in front only, a strong purposeless glare occurs behind them on the wall, smothering the detail of the fixture; and if an opaque shade is used, the light is too meagre to reflect on the ceiling and its downward rays are in a poor position for utility purposes. If wall sconces are necessary to carry out a period type of decoration, it is better to consider them as decorations only, use the ¼-candle-power bulb with real candle,* and depend upon other sources of light for the main illumination of the room.

In adapting modern lighting to period rooms, cove, cornice, valance, furniture, spot, flood, and portable lamps with period bases are practical, and the occasional use of ceiling down-lights for objects or areas of special interest.

Lamp bases and shades. The actual size and shape of a standing floor or table light has little to do with the amount of light that may come from the fixture. Design alone should be the main influence in the size, shape, and material of the base and shade. The wattage of the bulb alone affects the amount of light produced, but the amount of illumination, in spite of strong wattage, will be modulated by the shade itself and by the wall color. A small lamp with a strong bulb may give far greater illumination than a large fixture with a weak bulb. The position of the bulbs or tubes within the shade also will affect the amount of illumination. The spread of the illumination from any shaded source of light is limited by the angles that the source makes with the upper and lower rims of the shade. Bulbs when placed near the top of a shade, throw rays at a wide angle upward and a narrow angle downward, and vice versa.

A lamp base should harmonize with the style and character of a room. In formal and accurate period reproduction rooms, vases, candlesticks, oil lamp supports, sculptured figures, and architectural details such as miniature columns in metal, ceramics, glass, wood, or marble are suitable. In informal types of rooms, there is sometimes a tendency to use any small object as a base for a shade. Some of these have had a humorous aspect, such as coffee grinders and children's toys, that are hardly logical and are of questionable taste.

The contemporary tendency has been to use holders that are primarily functional and reflect their purpose. These usually consist of jointed or gooseneck metal arms that serve practical purposes. They are particularly suitable for offices, stores, and other commercial types of decorating, or for residence rooms that are not furnished in a strictly authentic historical style. They are of minor consequence to the appearance of a room, but they are efficient and serviceable.

There are well-made lamps for different purposes that are produced by leading manufacturers that are known as "certified" and patented designs. These may be attached to almost any form of base. They consist usually of a glass bowl or metal reflector which softly diffuses the light over the area around the lamp and give a direct light downward for special use.

* Real candles with socket inserted for a small bulb are available.

The bowls are made of unbreakable materials and they protect the eyes from a glare at the top of the lamp. Some of these lamps have a louvre at the top to reflect the upward light in any desired direction. Both bulbs and tubes are used for the light sources.

Lamp shades are a matter of taste, but plain materials are usually preferable. Silks, parchment, heavy paper, plastics, tortoise shell, and suede should be lined with a light warm color to obtain efficient reflection. A small amount of exterior trimming is advisable. Opaque shades of tin, leather, tole, or other materials are very suitable, because of the elimination of glare. Light sources should always be out of the line of vision. It is difficult to present any rule for proportioning the size or shaping the silhouette of a lamp shade, but various patterns may be made in paper and placed in position for the eye to judge their correct scale, size, and shape. Too much importance cannot be given to the quality of workmanship in making a shade and its frame. Badly constructed shades made of inferior materials are a poor economy.

The top of the shade of standing floor lamps should be at 5 feet from the floor. The bottom of the shade of a desk light should be 16 inches above the desk. Dressing table lights should have the center of the bulb about 16 inches above the table. A library table lamp should have the bottom of the shade about 40 inches above the floor and the shade about 11 inches high, with the bulb about in the middle of the shade to screen it.

Location of fixtures in period rooms. If it is impractical or too costly to undertake the architectural changes often necessitated in introducing modern lighting, the decorator is limited to a large extent to the use of traditional light sources. A plan of the layout of lighting should be made in advance to locate the fixtures and electric outlets.

The distribution and strength of lighting in any room depends upon the purposes, size, and shape of the room, the height of the ceiling, and the positions of the permanently located furniture. General and specific illumination should be evenly distributed. A few strong lights may give ample general lighting, but such an arrangement is not as decorative, practical, or easy on the eye as the use of several smaller light sources placed in various parts of the room. The exposure of light sources or strong reflections on walls or ceilings tend to close the retina of the eye, which causes the less illuminated areas of the room to appear too dark, and their contribution to the decorative treatment is lessened. Too many visible points of illumination, such as table and floor lights, may appear confusing to the decorative effect.

Central ceiling lights are usually inadvisable except in the working portions of a house, or where ceilings are high and they contribute to the period character of the decoration. Examples would be the use of crystal or metal chandeliers in elaborate French, Georgian, and other historical types of decoration, but even these are best treated as decorations with extremely low bulb wattage with the principal light produced by hidden spot lights giving indirect illumination.

The disadvantage of wall sconces has been mentioned in a previous paragraph, but if wall lights cannot be avoided, their position and size should be agreeably related to the general wall composition and a closely similar distribution should be made on opposite walls. It is never wise to place a wall sconce in the center of a panel or in any position that would interfere with a more important feature of decoration, such as a picture, bookcase, or secretary desk. If the design of the wall sconces consists of candle sockets, small opaque shades should be used, permitting the light rays to be thrown both upward and downward.

In a living room of average size, four table or standing lamps should be adequate if each contains a bulb of 100 watts strength, and additional smaller lights should be arranged for writing, reading, piano, games, or other special purposes. Many arrangements for bed lighting are possible, and their choice is a matter of taste. The best dressing table lights are small strong standing lamps on each side of the mirror. For attractive dining table lights of a period character there is nothing that can surpass the ordinary candle without a shade; the candlelight should be well above the eye level of a seated person. If all the lamp shades in a room are similar, a monotonous effect is produced, yet there should be enough relationship between them in color and design to create a harmonious effect.

In general, light sources should be hidden or screened, and standing lamps should be of a height so that the bulb and the interior of the shade is not in evidence.

Special uses of illumination. The "mood" of a room may be altered by changing the color of its illumination, using differently colored bulbs, tubes, shades, or screens as desired. Extreme theatrical effects should be avoided in residential decoration. Architectural features or defects may frequently be accentuated or hidden by the addition of extra illumination in the more interesting portions of a room or less illumination in the less attractive ones. The problem of the lighting specialist is more than that of giving visibility. He can emphasize or suppress form; accentuate composition, line, or scale; lend mystery, dignity, or gaiety to the character of a room; correct or alter the appearance of decorative elements, give comfort to the eye at all times, and add greatly to the charm and satisfactory appearance of the general scheme.

Color absorption of light. Wall colors have a definite effect on the amount of wattage required in a room. Light colors, in general, give a greater percentage of reflections and get the most out of the light used. Dark-colored walls and fabrics soak up light. The following table shows the percentage of reflection given by different colors when they are illuminated by white light. Relative percentages may be estimated for other colors. The surfaces are assumed to be in a dull finish giving a diffused reflection. Highly polished surfaces slightly increase the percentage of reflection. Surfaces reflect the color of their own hues. Excessive dirt, dust, or grease on ceilings or walls wastes light. Wall colors in the list below reflect the percentages indicated:

White	85%	Intense Yellow	60%
Ivory	75%	Light Green	55%
Light Gray	65%	Dark Brown	10%
Dark Gray	15%	Dark Blue	5%
Tan	60%	Olive Green	10%
Black	5%		

To be properly lighted, the average room in a dwelling requires from 1 to 3 watts of electric current per square foot of floor space, if transparent bulbs are used. The smaller figure is low, the higher gives great brilliance. The choice will depend upon the color of the ceiling and walls, the efficiency of the fixtures, the color of the bulb, and the purpose of the room. The lower wattage is suitable for rooms with light-colored walls; the higher wattage, for rooms with very dark walls. Bulbs transmit the percentages of original light shown in the table below. The amount of wattage may be approximated where colored bulbs are used.

Transparent	70%	Red	10%
Light Amber	65%	Green	15%
Dark Amber	35%	Blue	5%

Period Lighting Fixtures

The use of original and reproduction period lighting fixtures is perhaps less common today in rooms of distinct period design, because practically all period fixtures were designed for candles, and the beauty of detail of an old and well-made fixture may be lost in the glare of the electric bulb. Certain types of period fixtures, such as ceiling chandeliers in large rooms and table and shelf lamps, will probably continue to be used for some time to come, until lighting engineers have developed a satisfactory solution of electric illumination.

In practically all countries since the time of the Renaissance, candles have been held by hanging candelabra, floor standards, table candlesticks, hanging lanterns, or wall brackets; or illumination has been produced by the oil lamp. The materials used for the making of these objects have differed somewhat in each style, but the forms and ornamental detail used in the design of many of the light holders and lamps have been borrowed from, and correspond in character to, the typical motifs used in the painted and carved ornamental forms of the architecture, furniture, and other arts of each period.

Italy and Spain. The lighting fixtures of the early Renaissance in these countries were inspired from the superb torches and lamps that were constantly being discovered in the excavations of the ruins of antiquity in Rome. Architectural forms and ornamental details were the basis of the design of the most elaborate light holders. Scrolls, brackets, amorini, and the acanthus leaf enriched the structural forms. Plain and polychromed wrought iron, cast brass and bronze, silver and gilded wood, and colored Venetian glass and Byzantine enamels were the principal materials used for structure and ornament. The bent and twisted wrought iron, hammered into graceful curves, was enriched with exquisitely modelled rosettes and foliage.

During the 17th century, the metal lighting fixtures were given some of the resplendent forms of Baroque and Rococo styles, with bulbous vase shapes ornamented with voluptuous repoussé work and gadrooning.

The work of the Spanish craftsmen closely followed Italian tradition, but the pierced metal patterns inherited from the Moors often gave to the Spanish productions a native character, and the prevalence of gold and silver permitted the use of these metals for the occasional enrichment of both iron and bronze in the form of hammered leaves and rosettes.

Toward the end of the 17th century, the Italians introduced the crystal chandelier and the mirror-back sconce. Rock crystal was used at first for pendants, but owing to its excessive cost and the extraordinary ability of the Venetian glass-workers, cut crystal glass was soon used as a substitute. As glass became popular, the use of iron and bronze lessened. During the 18th century, the Italian productions were almost exclusively borrowed from French designs. Capo-di-Monte figures and pottery often formed the central motif of wrought iron candleholders.

France. The French architects and decorators designing for Louis XIV were strongly inspired by Italian luxury, and the crystal chandelier was adopted as the proper method of illumination of practically all the large rooms at Versailles. Gilded and carved wood and the ormolu of the period were used in the making of appliques (wall sconces) and the elaborate girandoles (multiple candlesticks) of the period.

The rococo influence of the mid-18th century was reflected in the asymmetrical and curvilinear ormolu designs for the smaller appliques suitable to the Louis XV rooms. Candle supports and arms began to be attached to such pieces of furniture as writing desks, wall mirrors, and clocks. Vases and urns in marble and ormolu were treated with stems covered with exquisitely wrought flowers and leaves and ending in candle sockets. Silver and silvered bronze were also used as materials for richly designed appliques and girandoles, while tole, sheet brass, and pewter were introduced for the more simple and inexpensive types of lighting fixtures. The Chinese influence was brought into the field of illumination, and the rare imported porcelains were mounted on ormolu bases and arranged with candleholders. Exquisite chandeliers and appliques were made in metal stem and foliage patterns and enriched with colorful enamel flowers and surface decoration.

Toward the end of the 18th century the more intimate character of room decoration called for a reduction in the size of lighting fixtures, and the designs became almost jewel-like in color and finish. The restless curves of the preceding period gave way to the more subdued lines and detail inspired by the classic forms of Herculaneum and Pompeii or by pastoral and sentimental motifs that reflected the thought of the nobility at the moment. Ormolu and silvered bronze, gilded wood, crystal, marble, alabaster, and tole continued to be used for lighting fixture designs. Dresden and Sèvres biscuit ware and colored porcelains contributed their share for candle supports and sconce back-plates. Dressing tables, beds, secretaries, spinets, inkstands, and a multitude of other objects had their own metal arms and sockets for holding candles. Oil lamps were given respectability by being moved from the kitchen and barnyard to the salon and bedchamber. The ornamental forms in carved wood, paint, and cast and wrought metal were human figures, cherubs, garlands, bowknots, sheaths and arrows, classic columns and broken shafts, fluted vases and urns, and the other design motifs typical of the Neo-classic period.

During the Directoire and Empire periods, there was a continuation in the use of the same general types of fixtures, the details of design changing, however, as in all the arts, toward greater severity, with a more profuse use of classical and Egyptian forms. The imperial eagles, cornucopia, griffins, sphynxes, satyrs, swans, flames, frets, honeysuckles, and anthemion forms were most common.

England. The lighting fixtures of England from the time of the Renaissance were of the same general type as those used in France. Hanging chandeliers, wall sconces, lantern floor standards, and table candlesticks were used. For materials, silver, enamel, and crystal were used for the more elaborate fixtures; but brass, pewter, mirror, mahogany, pottery, and iron were employed for the more common types. The Flemish and Dutch influence in design was seen in the gadrooned ball and baluster stems used both for the chandeliers and candlesticks. Many of the candlesticks were equipped with large grease pans. The Chinese influence made itself felt about the middle of the 18th century, and toward the end of this century the pottery factories of Chelsea, Derby, and Staffordshire produced an innumerable variety of candleholders in realistic coloring. Many

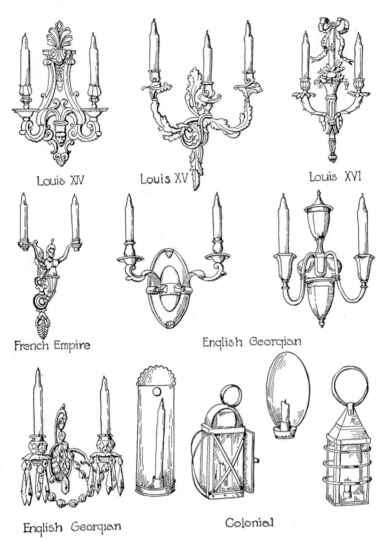

Louis XIV   Louis XV   Louis XVI

French Empire   English Georgian

English Georgian   Colonial

EXAMPLES OF PERIOD LIGHTING FIXTURES.

wall sconces and table lights were made in plain and colored Waterford glass. Repoussé silver and Sheffield plate were popular materials used for English fixtures. Both metal and wooden frames enclosed the mirrors used as back-plates for wall sconces. Reflectors for the candle light were a common feature.

Under the Adam, Hepplewhite, and Sheraton influence, the lighting fixtures of the room became more closely allied to the general scheme of decoration, and the gilded bronze, carved wood, and glass or composition ornament were often combined with the cameo forms of Wedgwood

Bronze and
Marble Candelabra

Gilt and Crystal Sconce

Astral Lamp

'Betty' Lamp

Lanterns

Tin Wall Sconce
With Glass Reflector

Tin Student Lamp   Glass Lamps   Glass Candlestick   Brass Lamp

EXAMPLES OF COLONIAL LIGHTING FIXTURES.

jasper ware. Silver continued to be dominant as a material for table lights. The swags, garlands, scrolls, festoons, paterae, vase forms, and floral sprays that were executed as architectural and furniture ornament were used in lighting-fixture design. Plain and convex wall mirrors were often combined with candle brackets.

America. The early lighting fixtures of the American colonies were of the simplest type. There were few experienced designers or metalworkers who could fashion a candleholder or oil lamp into any form surpassing functional needs, but the very lack of sophistication of design contributed to the charm of the product. Candles were homemade and were a luxury. The oil lamp burning sperm oil, lard, and grease was, from the time of the earliest settlement, a popular colonial accessory. The early Betty-lamp hanging from the mantelshelf, and tracing its ancestry back to Egypt and Rome, burned a ready flame for the lighting of candles, fires, or smokers' pipes. The Betty-lamp was made of iron or copper, and for table use was later supported by an arm rising from a base. Iron and brass lanterns of little elegance were also common through the early years of the 18th century, and these were often fitted with transparent horn instead of glass. The farmer's home was usually equipped with small wooden shelves, brackets, or hanging beams as candle supports and a discarded wagon wheel, hung parallel to the ceiling, served as a chandelier.

Candlesticks were made of iron, tin, and pewter; and candlestands with adjustable arms and with tripod or circular bases for floor use were made of wrought iron and wood, and were frequently furnished with snuffers.

After the middle of the 18th century, the more opulent householders imported their lighting fixtures from England and France. Silver, cut glass, pottery, brass, and bronze became more common materials in the American interior. Wall sconces with elaborate back-plates were popular, and polished tin, pewter, and mirror reflectors served to increase the illumination.

With the beginning of the 19th century and the increase in wealth and luxury of the early republic, the lighting fixtures that were made in America were based on French Directoire and Empire designs and on the English, Adam, Sheraton, and Hepplewhite forms. The glass hurricane shade, made large enough to completely enclose a candlestick and protect it from drafts, was a frequently used fixture. Glass candlesticks and lamps were made in the Wistar factory in New Jersey, and in Sandwich, Massachusetts.

Bibliography

Artificial Light and Its Application in the Home. McGraw-Hill Book Co., New York, 1932. A practical treatment of this subject illustrated with drawings and photographs.

HAYWARD, A. H., *Colonial Lighting.* B. J. Brummer Co., Boston, 1923. Illustrated text.

HENRIOT, G., *Encyclopédie du Luminaire,* 6 Vols. Les Editions Guérinet, Paris, 1933–1934. Portfolios of examples of all styles and times.

The General Electric Company furnishes through its retail sales outlets various pamphlets giving information on contemporary lighting layouts.

CHAPTER XX

WALL TREATMENTS AND
BACKGROUNDS

I n an examination of the methods of treating the walls of rooms over a period of the last two hundred years, one notices that there has been a gradual but constant tendency toward simplification. In the 18th century, walls often were elaborately decorated with architectural wood-work and carved or painted ornamental features. As such, these backgrounds dominated the character of the decoration of the room, and were of greater importance to the design than the furnishings and accessories. In the later years of the century, several external conditions developed that caused a reduction in the relative importance given to wall treatments. Both the French and American revolutions greatly lessened the aristocratic patronage of the arts, and interest in decoration spread to the middle classes, who could not afford the hand-painted and panelled rooms that had preceded these events. With wealth less concentrated, the artists and craftsmen made an effort to produce imitative materials and types of decorating that would maintain elaborate effects by cheaper methods. This was the motivation behind the production of wallpaper, printed textiles, marbleized surfaces, grisaille painting, transfer-printed ceramics, and similar substitute materials.

There were also other reasons for the elimination of wood-panelled walls. The introduction of coal as a fuel substitute for wood reduced the size of the fireplace and eliminated the necessity for lining walls with woodwork for purposes of insulation.* With the development of rail-roading in the middle of the 19th century, coal could be easily transported

---

* Toward the end of the Middle Ages, the increase of population in Europe and the growing scarcity of fuel as a result of the destruction of the available forests, caused the invention of the iron stove in the 15th century, and the tile stoves of northern Europe in the 16th and 17th centuries. The former were cast and often bore reliefs of biblical scenes or armorial and arabesque designs. The latter were beautiful specimens of the ceramic arts, and the early ones show traces of Moorish design. Many are preserved in the museums at Oslo, Amsterdam, and elsewhere.

Hare and Coolidge, Decorators; Drix Duryea, Photographer

A wall treated in wood panelling of English design produces a vigorous and dignified effect.

Wanamaker, Decorator; Drix Duryea, Photographer

The sinuous curves in the wall panels of this French room produce an effect of dignified gaiety tending slightly toward sentimental and feminine characteristics.

*A simple and inexpensive effect in informal rooms may be obtained by cover-
ing the walls with slightly stained knotty pine planks and harmonious
and attractive stock furniture. If the furniture is well selected and distributed, a tasteful room will be produced.*

from distant mines to every home, and with the introduction of central
heating, the plaster wall came into its own.

Since the opening of the 20th century, social and economic changes
throughout the Western world have caused less sentiment to be attached
to the word "home." Whereas formerly, houses were used by several
generations of the same family, ease of transportation and communication
have tended to make the home less of a pivotal center. The introduction
of apartment house living has contributed to this movement. Many persons have developed nomadic habits that have lessened their interest in
permanent or costly types of decorative treatments. In the average room
of today there is less thought allotted to the decoration of walls than to
any other part of the treatment or furnishings of the room.

A few exceptions to this condition occur. Certain people have the
means and desire to use antique wooden wall panels of either European
or American provenance and there is no doubting the charm of these
decorative treatments if the balance of the furnishings permit modern
conveniences and living conditions. In many cases, the antique woodwork
is limited to a single wall, an overmantel decoration, or a built-in cabinet
or bookcase. Reproduction of period wall panelling is seldom advisable
due to the inability of the average American craftsman to produce these
forms correctly, or the painter to create the mellowness of the original
treatments. The custom of applying wooden moldings to plaster walls to
attain a period panelled effect is a decorative falsity and always unsatis-

A spot pattern wallpaper does not protrude and is often sufficiently gay for bedroom use. In this room it serves admirably as a background for the informal peasant furniture.

Inez Croom, Decorator; Richard Averill Smith, Photographer

Backgrounds of rooms used only occasionally or for short periods of the day may be comparatively lively in pattern and color interest, especially if the furnishings are of simple design.

factory. Wallpaper strips in molding designs are more permissible as an honest type of decoration in itself.

Exclusive of wood panelling and wallpaper * there are five usual methods for treating or decorating walls in use today. These are:

> Plain paint
> Textural effects
> Mural decorations
> Draped or stretched textiles
> Natural and synthetic materials

Plain painted walls. Plaster painted in solid colors is by far the most usual and least expensive method of giving interest to a wall. Such walls are practical, clean, and economical. There is but little labor of upkeep, they may easily be changed, and they make a suitable background for most household possessions. The surfaces are restful to the eye, and interest may be added by accessories hung on the wall and varied at will. Plain walls produce an excellent contrast or foil for interesting furniture or architectural trim, and the avoidance of the subdivisions created by panelling permits greater variation in the arrangement of furniture and accessories. In the best decorative work walls are usually covered with muslin before being painted. The cloth permits plaster cracks without affecting the painted surface, and prevents spots that occur from the chemical disintegration of the plaster penetrating the paint.

The finish for a painted wall may be dull, glazed, antiqued, or stippled. Glazing or antiquing may be applied by rubbing a thin coat of umber and turpentine in either irregular spots or in a vertical stroke, but the contrasting color should be only just visible or it will appear too artificial. It is usually preferable to give dark colors a slight sheen and maintain a dull or eggshell finish for light tones. Stippled effects produce a textural interest, but they are not used in the better grade of work. The advantage of stippling is in the fact that it hides the brush strokes and produces a more even appearing surface. It can be done with a coarse stippling brush or roller. Tinted calcimine is less expensive than oil paint, but cannot be washed and is, therefore, much less durable. Calcimine is used for quick temporary effects.

If the architectural trim of a room is of little interest or is poorly designed, or if doors are badly distributed in the wall composition, it is advisable to make such features as unobtrusive as possible by painting them the color of the walls. If the designing and distribution of the woodwork are good, this may be accentuated by causing the woodwork to contrast in color with the wall. Additional color interest may be obtained by striping certain moldings or the ornament of the wood trim.

* See Chapters IX, XIII, and XXII for additional information on the use of these materials.

A small bathroom with the walls treated with a mural showing a perspective view of French gardens, giving the effect of greater spaciousness to the room.

Coloring is sometimes produced by spraying walls with a paint spray. Gradations in colors may be produced by this means. Stepped effects in wide horizontal stripes are also occasionally seen. In both cases the darker values are placed at the lowest portion of the walls and the lighter tones at the top. Walls may also be painted in wide vertical stripes, the alternate stripes being similar in color but varying slightly in tonal value, so that a strong contrast is not apparent.

The selection of a paint color for the walls of a room should most emphatically be made at the same time as the selection of the textiles to be used for draperies or upholstery purposes. It is usually advisable to select for the wall color one of the lighter or more neutral tones used in the textiles, in order that there may be a chromatic harmony. One must also keep in mind that a color seen in a small sample of paint may be entirely unsuitable for use in as large an area as the walls of a room. Large painted areas must be more subdued in tonal brilliancy than smaller areas, and small spots of color seen in a textile pattern may be entirely too strong on a large surface.

The amount of daylight in a room will also affect the decision as to

Courtesy Gardner E. Campbell

Original Colonial overmantel mural decoration showing a view of the surrounding landscape and painted in a naïve manner by a journeyman painter.

the color depth. Rooms that have ample sunlight may be painted in dark tones with a semiglaze. Rooms with only a small window area or with little natural illumination should be brightened by having the wall surfaces covered in light warm tones.

Ceilings may be calcimined or painted white or off-white. An agreeable effect is obtained if the ceiling is treated in a lighter tint of the color used for the walls. Increase in color interest may be obtained by painting the ceiling a color contrasting, either in hue or in value, with the walls. Ceilings that are painted in a color darker than the walls or treated in gold or silver leaf tend toward a modern effect. If a definite color is used for the ceiling, it should be repeated elsewhere in the decoration of the room.

Using two or more colors on the walls in the same room is always logical if the materials are different, such as wood panelling on one wall, and plaster on the other, or if one wall is treated with wallpaper and the other with paint. A plaster wall may be painted a different color than the woodwork. Where wallpaper is used in part of a room, it is advisable to paint the remaining plaster walls with the lightest and most neutral color used in the wallpaper. The wall area can often be painted the wallpaper-background color, or even more neutral in chroma. Where all walls are to be painted, decorators may use two colors; the window wall is generally painted in a lighter tonal value than the opposite wall. In a double-use room (living room-dining room) an apparent division is often made by painting the walls different colors, and indicating the different

Original Colonial mural decoration of unusual charm, in a house in East Setauket, Long Island.

uses thereby. Walls should not arbitrarily be painted different colors, but may be if there is a logical reason for so doing.

Textural surfacing. The pleasing irregularities left by the impressions of the plasterer's trowel in rooms of the past have long fascinated decorators and architects. Rough plaster or stucco walls are suggestive of Early Italian, Spanish, English, American, and peasant types of interiors.

In the more commonplace modern work, zealous craftsmen have produced rough plaster wall surfaces with little discretion. Overcoarse and objectionally artificial effects are frequently seen. The appearance of such plaster work is often aggravated by the addition of badly blended, sponge-painted colors. Moderation in the roughness of textural surfaces is essential for good taste. Rough plaster effects may be produced by the painter with patented composition materials intended for this purpose.

Imitation stonework. Stone and other forms of masonry effects may also be imitated by the skilled plasterer. The principal responsibility of the decorator in such work is in the design of the imitation *stone-jointing*. The average plasterer, not being a stonemason, is apt to lay out or *scribe* the joints in the easiest way, which results in an unnatural stone effect. For interior work, stones are usually smoothly surfaced and of similar sizes, approximately 12 inches high and 24 inches long, resembling cut

Mural by Louis Bouché; Drix Duryea, Photographer

Typical panel mural in a country house. The size of the room permitted the use of strong contrasts, and the subject matter was in harmony with the owner's hobbies.

ashlar. Much variation from these dimensions will seriously affect the scale of the wall. The joints of real stonework are both horizontal and vertical. The vertical joints alternate with each course of stone so that one vertical joint is never directly above the one below it. In arches, the jointing should indicate stones of approximately the same size as used in the walls, there should be a keystone in the center of the arch, and the jointing should all point to the center of the spring-line.

Imitation in decoration, never considered good art, may be occasionally excusable on economic grounds; but it is an unpardonable sin if the imitation is poor. The reproduction of superior materials with inferior ones should be done so carefully that the uninitiated fail to notice the deception.

Travertine and Caen stone are the two stones usually imitated in plaster. Travertine is light brown in color and is filled with imperfections which appear as deep furrows on its surface. Caen stone is yellowish in appearance and exceptionally smooth. Real Travertine comes from Italy and Caen stone from Normandy. Both are used for walls and floors in public buildings and in semipublic rooms of residences, such as entrance halls and lobbies. Caen stone was used in 18th century French styles because of its softness and ease of carving. When it was used for exterior construction, however, the exposure to rain caused it to harden considerably.

Mural decorations. In wall treatments, mural decorations include fresco paintings, applied canvas wall paintings, stencils, and other painted patterns. Pictures or patterns produced by any of these methods are, as a rule, more expensive than pictorial paper; but the advantage in the work of the artist is in the novelty and uniqueness that is obtainable. A painted picture or pattern more genuinely reflects the character of the occupant, cannot be copied in quantity, and may exactly fit the room in subject matter, scale, size, and color. Many householders value the ownership of things that are unavailable to others, and the fulfillment of such desires contributes to the support of artists.

The art of the mural decorator is as old as architecture. The artists of Egypt, Greece, and Rome developed it to a high degree of perfection. The walls of nearly every room in Pompeii were treated with mural decorations, and the artists of the Middle Ages carried it on for those of the Early Renaissance. Fra Angelico, Raphael, Titian, Tintoretto, Veronese, Perugino, and Pinturicchio have left unsurpassable masterpieces, and the roll of honor continues down through the great French and English painters of the 18th century. There are many painters in America who have produced remarkable work along similar lines in recent years. As a result, a revival of the art of the mural decorator has occurred, and many decorators are depending upon this type of wall treatment for unique effects in all types of rooms. From the bathroom and boudoir to the public rooms of the house, murals are often featured.

Good qualities in a mural decoration. For a domestic interior, a mural pattern, whether pictorial or otherwise, should be reasonably pale in color value. Contrasts of light, shade, and shadow should be gentle. The picture should never appear to jump off the wall. Too great naturalism in representation should always be avoided, and conventionalization and stylization are greatly to be preferred. Colors should be comparatively flat and drawings should be simple. Lineal flourishes are disturbing as a background. It is always advisable to relate the subject matter of the pattern or picture to the personality of the owner of the house or to the use of the room, and to see that colors are used which establish the color scheme of the room and may be recalled in the rest of the furnishings. Of recent years, however, many rooms have been painted with abstract motifs.

Mural decorations need not necessarily cover every wall in a room. It is often advisable to limit such paintings to important areas, such as an overmantel or one end of the room. Painted decoration may also be concentrated over doors or in specified wall panels. It is always well to

Mural decoration showing a complete wall painted with architectural forms, the panels treated with vignette figures in grisaille.

Murals by Rudolph Guertler

In this small dressing room both the walls and the door panels are covered with painted vignette patterns in the Chinese manner.

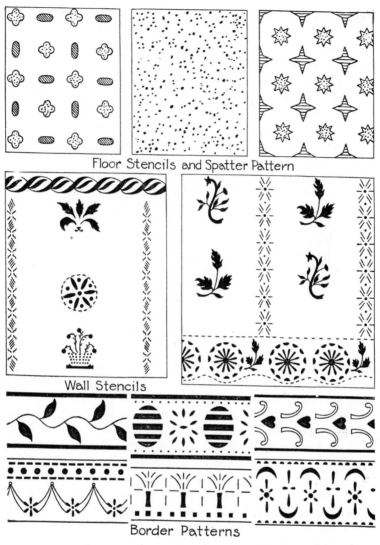

Floor Stencils and Spatter Pattern

Wall Stencils

Border Patterns

EXAMPLES OF COLONIAL STENCIL ORNAMENT.

use a low dado in a room where a painted wall decoration is to be introduced, so that no portion of the picture will be below a table top or sofa back. In small rooms it is possible to produce an impression of greater size through the use of perspective and atmospheric effects in a mural composition.

In period rooms, both the character of the picture or pattern and the technical execution should be in harmony with the style, although many painters of talent are able to give an interesting and harmonious modern interpretation to antique subject matter.

A type of mural decoration frequently used is known as a grisaille painting. This term refers to a picture painted in one color only. Grays and buffs are generally used for this purpose. During the Louis XVI period, grisaille paintings were very common, and the painters developed extraordinary ability in imitating low relief sculpture by indicating natural highlights and shadows as though the illumination of the picture came from the direction of the windows of the room.

Mural decoration is not necessarily limited to formal interiors. In early Colonial farmhouses, many murals were used; in these the painting was crude, but it was in harmony with the architecture and decoration. The interior walls and woodwork were often lavishly treated with landscapes, farm scenes, and flowers. The journeyman painters who were called upon to paint both houses and fences, portraits and murals, could hardly be expected to exhibit excellence of technique. Many of these compositions, however, had a naïve appeal and great decorative charm.

Mural decorations may be produced by true fresco work or by oil painting on a canvassed wall. The latter system is most often used today. Fresco work is done on wet plaster with colors made from powder mixed with white of egg. The plaster absorbs the color for a considerable depth, and the pigment becomes an integral part of the wall and a permanent decoration that cannot be removed. Because of the technical difficulties encountered in fresco work, it is not often attempted today except in large public buildings. The painting of a mural decoration on canvas may be done in the artist's studio, the canvas being applied to the wall after the artist has completed his work. If the owner moves, the picture may be dismounted and transferred to a new location.

Stencil work is produced by piercing or cutting a pattern in a sheet of thick paper, applying the paper to a wall surface, and painting the area of the cutout pattern. One color only can be used for each stencil sheet, so that the pattern is always in a flat tone, and therefore conventionalized. Border and all-over wall patterns are very frequently painted in this manner, for by this means the labor of drawing the patterns on the wall is avoided, and as many repeats as may be required are easily produced. Many interesting stencil patterns are found in peasant and in American Colonial interiors.

Textile-covered walls. The use of textiles for wall coverings dates from a period of great antiquity. Textiles served to give greater warmth to the stone-walled rooms, to introduce color and pattern, and to create an air of friendly hospitality. During the Gothic period, tapestries, embroideries, and loosely woven patterned fabrics in wool and linen were attached to hooks or rods and allowed to hang in loose folds. During the

The architectural features of a room may often be accentuated with wall-paper or painted decoration placed in important locations. The pilasters and dado cap were in this instance painted in a naturalistic manner.

Renaissance, lustrous damasks, brocades, and brocatelles were stretched on the wall areas, and during the latter years of the 18th century, patterned moiré silks, cotton toiles, Chinese painted silks, and painted East Indian cottons were placed in the large panels of the architectural woodwork as a substitute for the more costly carvings or painted decorations. In the more important dwellings of the American Federal period, imported silks and printed cottons often covered the wall areas. The use of textiles as wall coverings is less common today because of their fragility and the difficulty of keeping them clean. The rarity of their use, however, makes them a novelty. They are particularly suitable for boudoirs and dressing rooms where the cost of upkeep is not a serious consideration.

When textiles are to be stretched, they should be mounted on a light-weight wooden frame that exactly fits the wall area or panel that is to be covered. This permits ease of dismounting for cleaning purposes. In certain types of extravagantly decorated or exotic rooms, the walls may be covered wholly or in part with loosely hung textiles attached to hooks or a rod placed near the ceiling. The folds should be ample and evenly spaced. Heavy silks and velvets are often used for this purpose. Inexpensive cottons, such as toiles and ginghams, may be pasted to the wall in the same way as wallpaper.

Although not strictly a textile, decorated leather may be included in this group of wall decorations. Leather, being a particularly warm material, was used to line many of the rooms of the castles of the Middle Ages and early Renaissance, and its use for wall covering has continued to the present day. Much of the antique leather used for walls was elaborately painted; but more suitable for the enrichment of this material were the embossed and tooled designs sometimes used. The embossing consisted of patterns in low relief produced by hammering or pressing the back of the leather. The tooled ornament was made by hammering a motif on the front of the leather by means of a small die. Gold leaf was usually placed on the portion of the leather to be tooled, and was made to adhere to the surface by slightly heating the die. In modern leather wall effects, tooling and embossing are not used for decorating, but natural-colored parchment, pigskin, horse- and cow-hide are applied to wall surfaces in small squares or rectangles. Pony, sheep, and goat pelts have also been used, but because of the difficulty of keeping them clean and mothproof, such wall coverings are perhaps impractical.

Natural and synthetic wall materials. There is a tendency today either through intention or unavoidable circumstance to find rooms in which the various walls and ceilings are made of two or more different materials. In many dwellings, certain portions of the interior walls are structural and built with permanent materials and must for reasons of economy remain as an element in the decorative treatment of the room in which they are located. Ceiling surfaces often vary from the walls due to the introduction of acoustical materials that have a rough texture. In modern planning, it is often possible to subdivide rooms by means of sliding or folding partitions that are made of materials that differ from the wall surfaces. The popularity of built-in cabinets covering an entire wall area, and glass wall surfaces substituting for windows, add to the variability of walls in the same room. These features create a problem that did not exist to the same extent in historical types of rooms in which similar types of walls were pierced by doors and windows and compositional unity was attained by similarity of treatment on all four sides. The decorator must accept conditions such as these and must select and arrange the movable furnishings to harmonize with the permanent walls and partitions that have been installed by the builder of the house.

Among the permanent natural and synthetic materials that are used for the inside surfaces of exterior walls and partitions the following may be listed:

> Masonry
> Plywood
> Wood veneers
> Synthetic sheet materials

In contemporary design, simplicity of wall treatments is accentuated with interest given by textural effects such as shown in this wood veneer.

The modern interior is less concerned with symmetry in composition than with utility, as is indicated in this dining room lit by clerestory windows.

In the interior of this remodelled barn the structure is left exposed and forms the interest in the wall treatment.

Decorators are often confronted with rooms that have walls in part or entirely of masonry that cannot easily be changed. These walls may consist of cut or uncut field stone, ashlar, concrete or cement-blocks, brick, or various types of tile. Stone is often used for fireplaces and chimney-breasts and it is best in these cases to leave the stonework in its natural finish. Concrete or cement-blocks, if used structurally, usually form walls that are 8 or 16 inches thick, and as these materials are moisture-absorbent in the majority of climates, they require a furred interior finish wall of plaster or other material, built with an air space between it and the blocks. In warm and dry climates, or where walls are well protected by a roof overhang, block walls may be treated with either a water or oil paint. Bricks and tiles are produced in an infinite variety of colors, textures, and sizes, and there is no objection to using them in their natural finish, if they are of good quality and color; otherwise a coat of paint is preferable. Masonry materials have a degree of permanence that does not exist in the majority of wall surface treatments, and they have the added advantage of low cost of upkeep.

The use of plywood sheets for walls is now very common. This material is produced in a great variety of woods, qualities, and textures, and is usually furnished in panels that are 4 feet wide and from 8 to 16 feet in length, and from ¼ to 1 inch in thickness. The largest production is of Douglas fir, the grain of which is uninteresting and requires painting, but many rare and exotic woods are available that can be used in their natural finish. Among these are gum, mahogany, knotty pine, walnut, oak, elm, cedar, and others. These laminations are made with plastic adhesives and they are split-proof and warp-resistant, and some are fireproofed. They may be installed as lining over existing plaster walls or may be applied directly to the structural studs of a partition. Plywood may be used in whole sheets or cut into any size squares and rectangles and laid in alternating grain directions. A flexible type is available that may be applied to curved surfaces. Aluminum strips or matching moldings may be used to cover joints and corners, but this is not always necessary. A veneer of these natural woods is also available mounted on cloth to be used in the same manner as wallpaper, on dry plaster, or wooden surfaces. These veneers are $\frac{1}{85}$ of an inch thick, and are available in 18- or 24-inch widths, and 8-, 10-, and 12-foot lengths.

Plywoods are particularly useful in the decoration of stores, offices, and commercial establishments, and for making flush panel doors, cabinets, and furniture. They are a permanent type of wall decoration and their upkeep is limited to an occasional waxing.

The synthetic sheet materials are made of plastic and kraft paper under high pressure. They are available in numerous plain colors suitable to interior finish and in wood-grain, linen, marble, and other effects. They do not stain or scratch and are heat-resistant. Certain types are also burnproof. The sizes are 4×8 feet. These materials are extremely durable and are easily kept clean. They are furnished in both satin and glossy finishes.

Other materials suitable for wall treatments are a plastic that looks like leather, small 1-inch squares of wood that are furnished on flexible sheets for application to either flat or curved surfaces, cowhide leather tile, and cork tile.*

* Information concerning plywood and synthetic sheet materials and veneers may be obtained from any lumber yard, or from the United States Plywood Corporation, with offices in the principal cities of the United States. The trade names used by the various manufacturers are weldwood, flexwood, checkwood, micarta, formica, masonite, bakelite, vinylite, and others.

Bibliography

ALLEN, E. B., *Early American Wall Paintings*. Yale University Press, New Haven, 1926. Photographs of authentic paintings with descriptive text.

BAYES, W., *The Art of Decorative Painting*. Charles Scribner's Sons, New York, 1927. An illustrated treatment of all phases of decorative painting.

GUSMAN, P., *La Décoration Murale à Pompéi*. A. Morancé, Paris, 1924. Fine collection of color plates.

GUSMAN, P., *Panneaux Décoratifs et Tentures Murales de XVIII Siècle*. C. Massin, Paris. French introductory text to a series of plates reproduced from original works.

HALE, G., *Fresco Painting*. W. E. Rudge, New York, 1933. Illustrated text on the technique of fresco painting.

MACON, G., *Château de Chantilly (Les Singeries)*. H. Laurens, Paris, 1925. Illustrations.

MARANGONI, G., *Decorazione Murale, Pietre Lavorate, Mosaico, Pavimento Artistico*. Casa Editrice Ceschina, Milan, 1928. Italian text illustrated with recent Italian work.

McCLELLAND, N., *The Practical Book of Decorative Wall Treatment*. J. B. Lippincott Co., Philadelphia, 1926. Excellent illustrated text.

CHAPTER XXI

INTERIOR TRIM AND WOODWORK

It is essential for decorators to understand the structure and design of the interior architectural features that are covered by the word "trim." This term is applied most commonly to the woodwork in a room, but it may also refer to the ornamental details in formally designed interiors made of stone, marble, or other materials. The stone detail used for this purpose is usually similar to that of wood. In rooms of period influences, the tendency is to design the detail of the trim upon the customary classical architectural forms. In rooms that have plywood, synthetic, or built-in cabinet walls, the standard trim is often omitted as unnecessary, and the same is true when doors and windows are built with metal frames. It is then primarily in rooms based upon historical types where trim is used, and the term, in general, covers the following features:

Door and window trim
Baseboards, picture moldings, and
    chair rails
Doors and windows
Cornices and coves

Mantels
Built-in cabinets
Dadoes, wainscots, and panelling
Flooring

All period rooms that have been based on Renaissance design have used some or all of the above details. The differences have been in the local interpretations of the classical detail, the materials used, and the finish given to them. Variations between the Italian, English, French, Hispanic, and American uses of these forms have also been in their proportions, the frequency of use, and particularly in the sections and shapes of the moldings, and the general character of the ornament.

Door and window trim. This term refers to the strip or frame, composed of moldings in wood or other material, that is used to give a finished appearance to an opening in a wall and to cover up the space

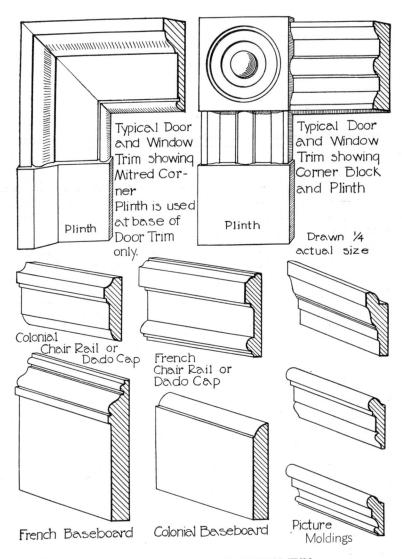

Typical Door and Window Trim showing Mitred Corner
Plinth is used at base of Door Trim only.

Plinth

Typical Door and Window Trim showing Corner Block and Plinth

Plinth

Drawn ¼ actual size

Colonial Chair Rail or Dado Cap

French Chair Rail or Dado Cap

French Baseboard

Colonial Baseboard

Picture Moldings

EXAMPLES OF SIMPLE TYPES OF WOOD TRIM.

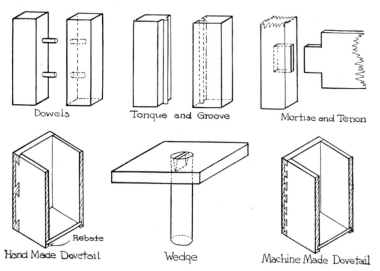

Dowels

Tongue and Groove

Mortise and Tenon

Hand Made Dovetail

Rebate

Wedge

Machine Made Dovetail

VARIOUS METHODS OF WOOD JOINERY.

that exists between the structural wall itself and the finished jamb of the opening. A finishing trim is usually placed on both exterior and interior faces of the wall, and the moldings are placed only at the top and at the two sides of the opening. In door openings, the trim may run all the way to the floor, or at the bottom it may butt against a *plinth* or plinth-block that is placed on the floor for the purpose of making a convenient intersection of the trim and *baseboard* of the room. In window openings the trim is usually cut off at the *sill*. If the window is of the French type and runs to the floor, the plinth is sometimes used.

Window and door trim is usually treated with moldings that correspond to the style or design of the room. It is only left plain where the most inexpensive and simplest effects are desired. The width and design of the trim is also influenced by the size of the opening.

For the average interior door opening, which is 2 feet, 8 inches wide and 7 feet high, a trim that is 4½ inches wide is sufficient. A narrower width looks scant, and anything over 5 inches appears heavy. The moldings commonly used for trim are inspired by the architrave of a classic entablature, although variations are often made, and in each period style the silhouette of the moldings (called section) differs. Trim should be mitered at the top corners. This means that the head or top and sides should be cut to meet at an angle of 45 degrees. Properly made trim should be locked by mortise-and-tenon or joined by a dowel or wooden *spline*. A less expensive type of trim may be assembled by means of a square *corner block,* the trim itself being cut off at right angles and forming a *butt joint* against the block at each corner. The outer molding of the trim should project sufficiently far from the wall to catch the chair rail and the baseboard, if no plinth-block is used. Examples are shown in the illustration on page 716. When a room is panelled in wood, the door and window trim may be very narrow or may be omitted, as the edge of the panelling itself acts as a substitute for the trim.

Because of the excessive cost of carving, trim moldings today are usually unornamented, except in very elaborate work or where an accurate reproduction of a certain period room is required. If trim is to be painted, it is best made of white pine or whitewood. If it is to be left in a natural color, it should, of course, be of the same wood as the rest of the woodwork in the room.

Baseboards. The baseboard is used to give a finish to the lower part of a wall and to cover the crack between the plaster wall itself and the floorboards. It has also a practical value in protecting the wall when the floor is being cleaned. A plain ⅞-inch board about 4 inches high is sufficient as a baseboard, but moldings are usually added at the top of the board for richer effects. Baseboards may vary in height up to 12 inches, and may be made up of several boards that overlap or join by moldings. Examples are shown in the illustration on page 716.

Picture moldings. Many rooms are furnished with a picture molding, which, as its name implies, is intended to create a continuous projecting support around the walls of a room for picture hooks. It serves also to give a finishing line to the upper portion of the wall. The picture molding may be as small as 1 inch in height, or, in large rooms, 3 inches, and should be curved at the top to receive the picture hooks. The present custom in hanging pictures is to place a hook or nail in the wall behind the picture so that no wires are visible, and when this method is used, there is no practical need for the picture molding. The picture molding, if used, should be placed about ¼ inch below the ceiling, or it may, if desired, be placed several inches from the ceiling to give a lower appearance to the room. Where a coved surface connects the wall and ceiling, the molding is placed at the base of the cove and the color of the ceiling should be carried down the wall to the top of the molding.

Chair rails and dado caps. The term *chair rail* was originally applied to the molding placed on a wall and running around a room at the height of a chair-back to protect the plaster from damage. A molding may still be used for this purpose, but in the design of many period rooms the term has become interchangeable with the word *dado cap,* indicating a narrow molded board used around the room at the height of an ordinary dado (2 feet, 6 inches from the floor) or at window-sill height. If the effect of a complete dado is necessary to fulfill design requirements, the dado cap, the baseboard, and the plaster wall between them may be painted the same color, and the area of the wall above the cap may be treated with a similar

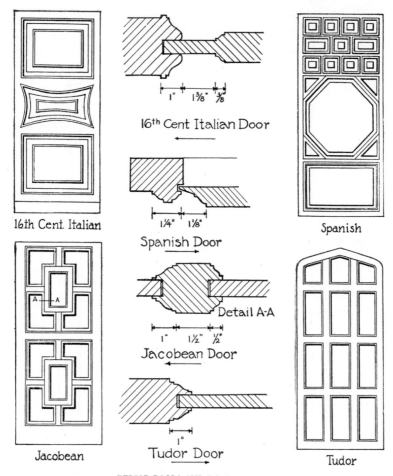

16th Cent Italian

16ᵗʰ Cent Italian Door

Spanish Door

Detail A-A

Jacobean Door

Tudor Door

Jacobean

Spanish

Tudor

PERIOD DOORS AND DOOR MOLDINGS.

or contrasting color, or may be papered. The projection of the moldings of a dado cap should be less than that of the outside moldings of the trim used for the openings. The moldings of the dado cap usually butt against the door and window trim.

Doors. The majority of doors are now machine-made, and are manufactured in quantity. The usual door is assembled by means of stiles, rails, and panels. A molding covers the joint between the panel and stile and accentuates the panel shape. The cheaper grade of doors is constructed of solid wood. The better grade is built up of a core composed of small strips of wood arranged so that the grain of each piece runs in a different direction. The core is then covered with a veneer of finishing wood. Such construction prevents warpage and shrinkage. Doors composed of solid rails are usually 1⅜ inch thick. Built-up doors are slightly thicker.

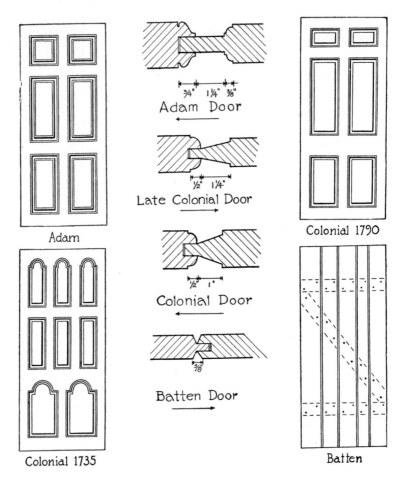

PERIOD DOORS AND DOOR MOLDINGS.

Each period had its own particular design for door panels, and characteristic examples of these, with the detail of the molding shapes, are shown on pages 719, 720, and 721. Period panelled doors other than Colonial are not held in stock by the supply houses and must be made to order. Doors for use in modern rooms are often made without panels, built up on a plywood core, and covered with one large sheet of veneer; these are called flush-panel doors. Doors known as *calamine* are made of sheet metal and are used for fireproofing purposes. They may be made in any design and finish. In contemporary rooms doors are often made of thick plate glass or polished sheet metal.

Windows. The decorator usually has little to do with the installation of the windows in a room, but the character of a window often influences the selection of furnishings and wall treatments.

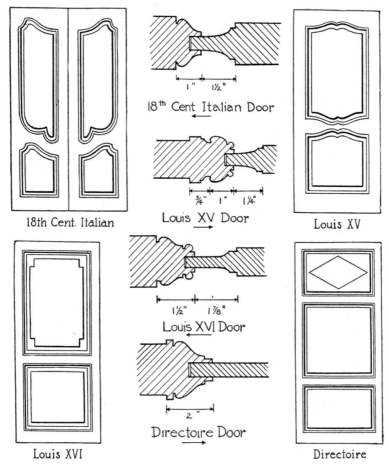

18th Cent. Italian

18ᵗʰ Cent. Italian Door

Louis XV Door

Louis XV

Louis XVI

Louis XVI Door

Directoire Door

Directoire

PERIOD DOORS AND DOOR MOLDINGS.

There are two important types of window sash, the *double-hung* or sliding type, and the *casement*. In the latter type the sash is hinged at the side and may swing either inward or outward. English casements usually swing outward, while French and American casements usually are hung to swing inward. The outward swinging casement is more weatherproof, but interferes with outside screens. Inward swinging casements are apt to interfere with draw curtains. Casement windows that start at the floor are usually called French windows.

In the majority of rooms of period type the window sash is subdivided into small panes of glass separated by what are known as *sash bars*. In the period styles before 1700, the small, rectangular, diamond-shaped, or round pieces of glass were usually held in place by lead strips. After 1700, glass sizes increased and were usually rectangular in form. Wooden sash bars held them in place.

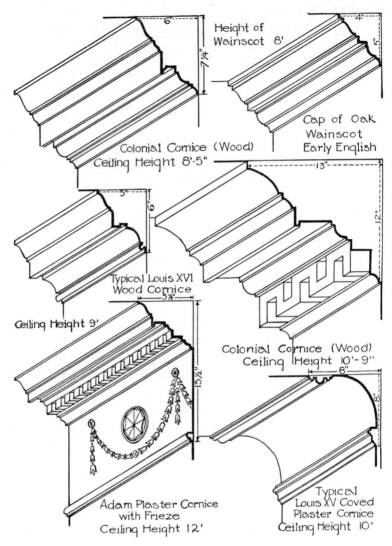

Height of Wainscot 8'

6"

7¼"

Colonial Cornice (Wood)
Ceiling Height 8'-5"

4"

5"

Cap of Oak
Wainscot
Early English

5"

6"

Typical Louis XVI
Wood Cornice

13"

12"

Colonial Cornice (Wood)
Ceiling Height 10'-9"

Ceiling Height 9'

5¾"

15½"

Adam Plaster Cornice
with Frieze
Ceiling Height 12'

8"

8"

Typical
Louis XV Coved
Plaster Cornice
Ceiling Height 10'

TYPICAL CORNICE AND COVE DETAILS.

Early glass was made by hand, and each piece varied somewhat in texture and tint, so that an interesting glass surface is nearly always seen in old windows. The modern machine-made window-glass lacks the interesting irregularities and tints of the old types. Plate glass should be used for the large picture windows or glass walls that are now in common use.

Cornices and coves. Nearly all formal period rooms require some sort of cornice or finishing molding at the top of the walls. The picture mold-

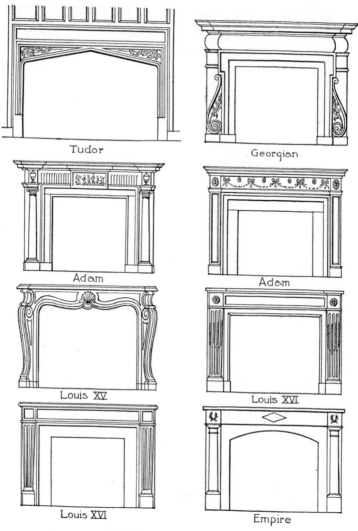

Tudor

Georgian

Adam

Adam

Louis XV

Louis XVI

Louis XVI

Empire

COMPARATIVE MANTEL TYPES.

ing is sufficient for low-ceilinged, informal types of rooms. A complete entablature is seldom necessary except in high-ceilinged and very formal architectural treatments. Cornices may be made of wood or plaster and are shaped according to the principles of the cornices of the classical entablatures.

The total height of all moldings in the usual classical cornice runs from $\frac{1}{10}$ to $\frac{1}{20}$ the total height of the wall. A good average proportion to use is about $\frac{1}{14}$ of the wall height. In this space should be the bed-moldings, fascia, and crown moldings. In large cornices, the moldings are

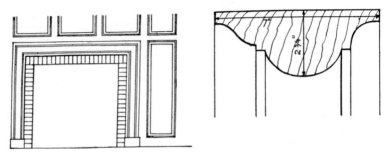

MANTEL WITH DETAIL OF BOLECTION MOLDING TRIM.

more numerous than in small cornices and a great variety of molding forms is permissible. Examples of period cornice forms for variable room heights are shown on page 722.

In rooms that are not designed on period principles, cornices are considered unnecessary. A finishing line is sometimes introduced at the top of the wall by means of a plain wood, glass, metal, or painted band.

In French rooms, the cove was frequently used alone or in connection with a simple cornice form. A cove is a rounded surface connecting the wall and the ceiling, and should be made of plaster rather than wood. By the use of a cove the ceiling appears to be carried down the wall for a short distance, and a lower effect to the room is obtained if the color of the ceiling is also used on the cove. The cove often is bordered by a simple group of moldings. The plain cove is often introduced as a light reflector in modern lighting layouts.

Mantels. The fireplace with its enrichment, called the mantel, is often the most important decorative element in the fixed architectural treatment of a room. Until about the middle of the 16th century, the majority of European rooms had the projecting, hooded type of fireplace, but with the introduction of the countersunk opening in the wall, the ornamental trim and mantelshelf began to be used.

In practically all the later period styles the mantel was designed on architectural principles. The fireplace opening was treated with either a simple architrave trim, similar to the type used for the doors and windows, or a heavy bolection molding on three sides, without a shelf, or with side supports, such as columns, pilasters, brackets, or caryatides, surmounted by an entablature.

It is important to have a mantel properly proportioned to the size and scale of the room. The decorative effect of many rooms has been ruined by a poorly selected mantel. In English and Colonial rooms of average height, the mantelshelf was usually from 44 to 54 inches from the floor. French 18th century mantels were from 36 to 48 inches in height.

If the mantel itself is made of wood, the fireplace opening should be

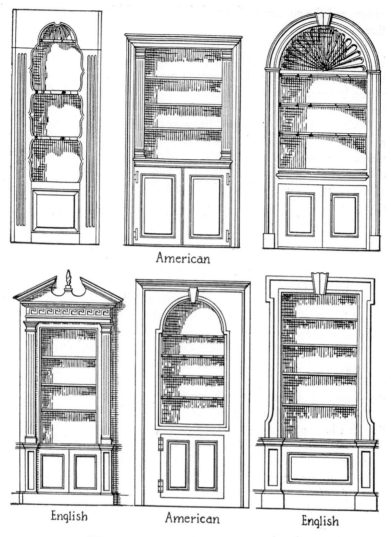

American

English American English

EXAMPLES OF BUILT-IN NICHES AND CABINETS.

faced with a fireproof material such as brick, stone, or tile. Colored marble may be used for more formal treatments. In mantels for modern
rooms, the shelf is often omitted and the opening is treated very simply,
often without special accentuation of any sort.

Each period style had its special type of overmantel treatment, usually
architectural in character and additionally enriched by trumeaux, mirrors,
carvings, or paintings. The fire opening was invariably treated with andirons or a grate. Cast-iron firebacks were also used in many styles of deco-

ration, and the customary fire tools helped to add interest to the composition.

Typical designs for mantel types are shown on page 723. Others may be seen in the chapters on the period styles. With the introduction of modern methods of heating, mantels are not so necessary today as formerly, but many people look upon the hearth as the symbol of home, and the fireplace still may have its functional value.

Niches and built-in cabinets. In many early Italian and Spanish rooms, a shallow niche was cut into the wall for practical and ornamental purposes. The form was usually arched at the top and treated with shelving. Shutters were introduced and painted with a colorful pattern. The rear of the niche was either lined with bright tiles or painted as a contrasting color accent for the neutral walls.

In the English and French styles of the 18th century, architectural importance was given to the niche, which often became a storage cabinet or was used for the exhibition of items of collector's interest. The framework was of wood and the design was consistent with the other architectural treatment of the room.

During the English Adam and Regency periods, the niche was often placed in the plaster wall, and consisted of a narrow semicircular arched form without trim. The space was filled with a copy of an antique statue. In the Colonial and Federal periods, the niche or built-in cabinet was made of wood and occupied the recesses or corners of the room. It was designed with or without doors, and its trim harmonized with the rest of the woodwork. Examples are shown on pages 725 and 727.

Dadoes, wainscots, and panelling. There are few types of wall decoration that have greater dignity and charm than well-designed wood panelling. Rooms treated in this manner radiate comfort and warmth, and produce a feeling of permanency. The insulating advantage of wooden walls is no longer important and the excessive cost has lessened their popularity, but to some extent modern plywood sheets have taken the place of panelled walls where a natural wood surface is desirable as a background.

Wood panelling is closely associated with period types of wall treatments and may be either limited to a dado or a complete wainscot. The former was usually an architectural feature imitating the detail of a classical pedestal carried around the lower portion of the walls of a room; it was usually between 2 and 3 feet high, depending on the height of the room, and had a cap-molding at the top, a baseboard at the bottom, and the center portion was designed in panels consistent with the style. The purpose of the dado was to cover the area of a wall that might receive the greatest wear, but it had a design value in accenting the horizontal and lessening the apparent height of a room. The dado was either painted or

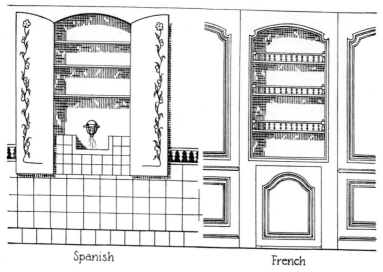

Spanish   French

EXAMPLES OF BUILT-IN NICHES AND CABINETS.

left in natural wood color and contrasted in color or appearance with the treatment of the plaster wall above it. The wainscot usually covered the entire wall from floor to ceiling and was designed with a dado and cornice with a panelled area between. This method of treating walls has been used in all period styles, and in all types and character of rooms. It is as adaptable to the farmhouse interior as to the most formal type of city dwelling.

Each of the period styles from the Gothic to the 19th century produced its own type of wood panelling that varied in the shape and size of the panel, the character of the molding used to frame the panel, the kind of wood that was used, the treatment of the surface of the woodwork, and the type and character of the ornament.

Because of the structural limitations of wood, dadoes and wainscots must be designed as skeleton framework composed of stiles and rails, usually forming rectangular frames. The frames are then filled in with wooden boards or panels. In the Gothic period, the edges of the stiles and rails were sometimes grooved with a molding and in English and French wall panelling during the 18th century a molding was usually added to the framework. The panel itself was held in a groove cut into the stile and rail. In the English Gothic, Elizabethan, and Jacobean periods, the panels were usually rectangular, vertically placed; the width was seldom over 12 inches, and the height about 3 feet, and one plank only was used in each panel. The stiles and rails were from 2 to 3 inches wide and had a small cyma or ovolo molding cut along their edge. The panel was sunk below the stile. The multitude of small panels produced a decorative effect

Interior Trim and Woodwork   727

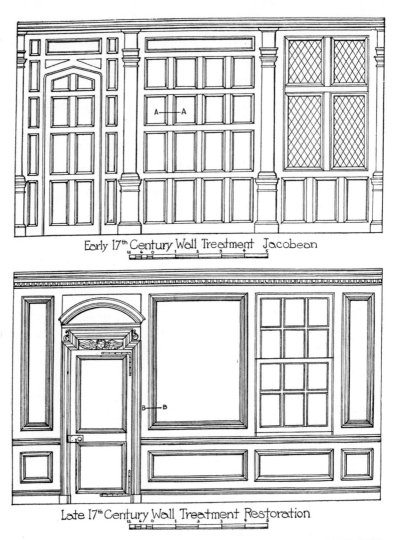

Early 17th Century Wall Treatment Jacobean

Late 17th Century Wall Treatment Restoration

TYPICAL EXAMPLES OF ENGLISH WOOD-PANELLED WALLS. SEE DETAILS PAGE 729.

that was rather primitive and at times monotonous. The panel field was often carved with a linenfold, *lozenge,* or arabesque. A simple cornice was introduced at the top, although classic proportions played no part in governing the designs.

In England during the late 17th and early 18th centuries, oak, walnut, and knotty pine were used for wall panelling, and panels became much larger. The rooms were designed with a low dado and a cornice, and the panels ran the full height of the wall between these two finishing features.

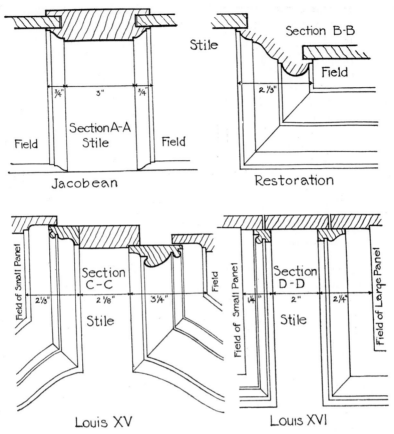

DETAILS OF CONSTRUCTION OF WOOD-PANELLED WALLS SHOWN ON PAGES 728 AND 730.

The stiles and rails were about 4 inches wide and a heavy bolection molding bordered the panel field in such a way that the field was actually about 1½ inches in front of the stile.

In the latter part of the 18th century, wood panelling was less used in England, but when introduced, large panel sizes were used and a return was made to the sunk panel with a heavy molding. The stile continued to be about 4 inches in width. The woodwork was usually painted.

In the 18th century French periods, the wooden walls were elaborately carved, and during the Louis XV period, the panels themselves assumed curved shapes. The stiles used in the French work were much narrower than in the English examples, and an entirely different effect was produced. French stiles and rails average 2 inches in width. The silhouette of the largest molding was also more complicated, the French often using an ovoid form. In French rooms wide panels often alternated with nar-

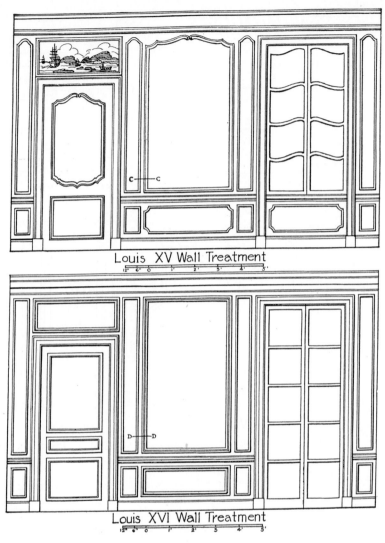

Louis XV Wall Treatment

Louis XVI Wall Treatment

TYPICAL EXAMPLES OF FRENCH PANELLED WALLS. SEE DETAILS PAGE 729.

row ones, and the moldings were reduced or increased in size to harmonize in scale with the width of the panel. A great effort was made to maintain symmetry in the design. In high rooms, panels were superimposed and were always placed above a dado and carried up to a cornice or a cove. The field of the panel was either carved, painted, or treated with a textile, wallpaper, or mirror. In the Louis XVI style the panel molding was often of the simplest variety, and additional accentuation of the frame of the panel was produced by painted stripes contrasting in color

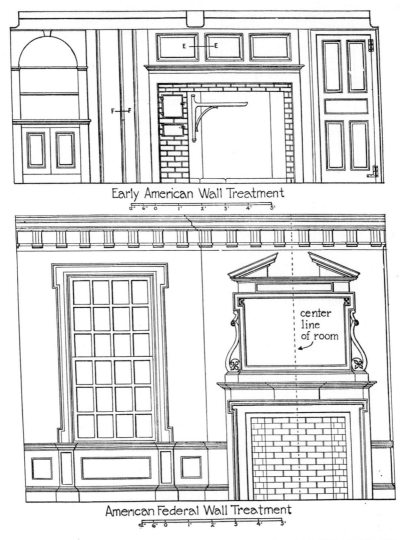

Early American Wall Treatment

American Federal Wall Treatment

center
line
of room

TYPICAL EXAMPLES OF AMERICAN WALL TREATMENTS. SEE DETAILS, PAGE 732.

with the color of the balance of the woodwork, or by the use of gilt.

In Early American rooms, one or more of the walls was lined with pine planks running the full height of the room, or arranged horizontally as clapboards. The planks interlocked by tongue and groove, and a molding was run on the edge of each plank. When panelling was introduced in the first quarter of the 18th century, the panels were small. Stiles varied in width from 2 to 10 inches. Under the Wren influence, more formal panel designs were introduced and panels became larger. The wood

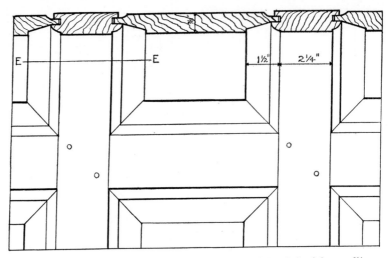

Actual construction and shape of moldings used in Colonial panelling.

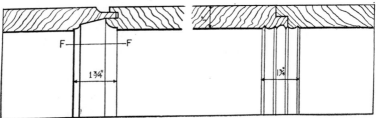

Actual shape of moldings used for Colonial plank walls.

DETAILS OF CONSTRUCTION OF WOOD-PANELLED WALLS SHOWN ON PAGE 731.

panelling in America was often limited to the interior partitions or fire-place wall only. The other walls were finished in whitewashed plaster or wallpaper. Examples of typical panelled walls with the actual molding silhouettes are shown on page 731 and above.

Applied moldings. Wood-panelled walls may be inexpensively imitated by applying wood moldings to a plaster wall or to one that has first been covered with muslin. The disadvantage of this treatment is in the fact that it has been greatly overdone, and at best is but an imitation of real panelling and is at present frowned upon by better designers. If for reasons of economy it is necessary to substitute this method for real wood-work, it is important that the arrangement, shape, and moldings used exactly simulate the form and design of correct structural wood panelling. When walls are treated with applied moldings, it is necessary to introduce a dado effect and treat the upper portion of the wall with a simple cornice. The moldings used to form the panels should be adequate in size and with the proper silhouette or section.

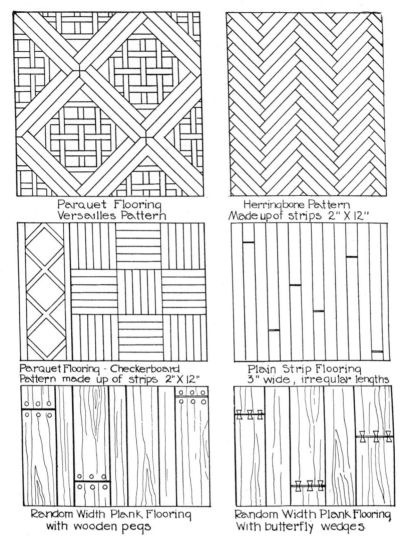

Parquet Flooring
Versailles Pattern

Herringbone Pattern
Made up of strips 2" X 12"

Parquet Flooring - Checkerboard
Pattern made up of strips 2" X 12"

Plain Strip Flooring
3" wide, irregular lengths

Random Width Plank Flooring
with wooden pegs

Random Width Plank Flooring
With butterfly wedges

EXAMPLES OF TYPICAL PATTERNS FOR FLOORING.

In work of this character, rectangular panels are usually preferable, although a few simple curves introduced at the top of some of the panels will produce a Louis XV or French provincial feeling. Many successful rooms have been done in this manner—the walls have been grained to imitate oak or pine or painted to imitate various colored marbles. If graining or marbling is used, it is essential to reproduce the correct joints and intersections of the natural materials. As antique wood panelling was usually joined by wooden pins, the tops of these may be indicated in their probable positions. Marble often shows a thin cement line at the joints; an imitation of this structural feature should also be painted.

Flooring. There are three principal types of wood flooring: the plank, the commercial strip, and the parquet pattern. Oak is the usual wood used for flooring, as it is hard and durable. White pine was extensively used during the Colonial period, but it is a soft wood and splinters easily if cut with the grain. Pine planks were of great width.

In the early English and French rooms, the floors were often of stone and tile. Where wood was used, the random-width oak plank was generally used, with pins or dovetails to hold the planks firmly together. In nearly all 18th century formal European rooms, oak parquet patterns were used. These can be made of thicknesses from ⅜ to ⅞ inch. Various parquet patterns are shown on page 723. In addition to those illustrated, parquet patterns often consist of 4- to 10-foot squares.

In modern commercial work, the floor material has little to do with the appearance of the room, because it is usually covered with a rug or carpet. Oak flooring is made in narrow strips 2 to 3 inches wide, ⅞ inch thick, and each strip interlocks with the adjoining one by means of a tongue and groove.

Many different woods are now used for flooring, but none is more serviceable than quartered oak. Southern pine, maple, cherry, birch, mahogany, and other woods are used for elaborate parquet patterns. The rising cost of wooden flooring materials has caused a considerable increase in the use of synthetic sheets and plastics for floors, many of which have certain advantages. Linoleum and cork squares also make very satisfactory materials for this purpose and are suitable in residential interiors as well as for commercial use.

Cabinet Woods

All wood is divided into hardwoods and softwoods. By definition, hardwood comes from the broadleaf trees, including oak, walnut, maple, and birch, while softwood comes from the evergreen trees, such as pine, hemlock, fir, and spruce. Some of the so-called softwoods, however, are actually harder than some varieties of hardwood, so that this classification is not entirely accurate. It is true, however, that nearly all the fine woods for furniture and decoration come from the hardwood group.

The grain of wood is produced by the manner of its growth, being usually formed by the annual rings and medullary rays, which in some varieties are very conspicuous. The method of sawing the trunk of the tree has a great effect upon the appearance of the graining in the lumber. In some woods, particularly oak and mahogany, the medullary rays produce a striking pattern obtained by *quarter-sawing* the lumber (sawing

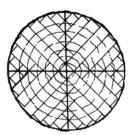

Method of quarter sawing toward the center of the trunk and at right angles to the annual rings.

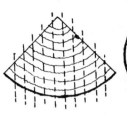

The quartered trunk in the position it is run through the saw and showing the successive saw cuts.

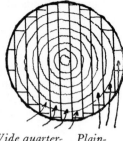

Wide quarter-sawed planks are cut across the whole tree trunk.

Plain-sawed planks cut from the edge of the trunk.

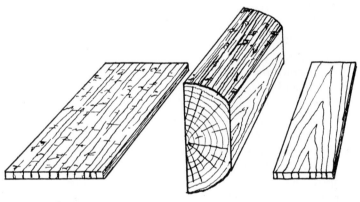

Grain effect of a quarter-sawed plank cut through the center of the trunk.

Grain effect of plain-sawed wood cut from the edge of the trunk.

METHODS OF CUTTING THE TRUNK OF A TREE FOR QUARTER- AND PLAIN-SAWED GRAINING.

toward the middle or heart of the tree trunk), though in most varieties of wood these rays are too small to affect the appearance. The term "quarter-sawing" comes from the early practice of longitudinally dividing a log into quarters and sawing each quarter into boards by cuts that run toward the center of the log. Quarter-sawing frequently produces the better graining, and such lumber has less tendency to shrink and warp. Boards that are not cut toward the center of the log are called *plain-sawed* or flat-grained lumber and the grain on the top of the board approaches an elongated oval or V-shape in appearance. Usually plain-sawed lumber is cheaper than the quarter-sawed, because it can be cut with less waste;

and in some kinds of wood, such as ash, chestnut, or elm, it has a better figure.

Wood to be used in building must first be seasoned, either by air-drying or kiln-drying. This removes most of the sap in the wood and causes a considerable shrinkage across the grain. Wood not sufficiently seasoned tends to warp and twist when used; and the same trouble occurs when woodwork is placed in a building before the masonry and plastering have had time to dry. If woodwork must be placed in its final position in a room before the plaster is thoroughly dry, the back should be painted with some impervious substance, such as asphaltum or lead and oil.

The best wood comes from the heart of the trunk of a tree and from the lowest portion of the trunk. The heartwood is usually darker in color than the sapwood or outside portions.

Interior trim is usually made of solid wood. Furniture is made of solid wood, but flat surfaces such as panels and table tops are often veneered. Veneer consists of thin sheets of wood about $\frac{1}{16}$ inch thick that are selected and cut for the beauty of their graining. The sheets of veneer are glued and pressed to the foundation surfaces of the furniture, the latter sometimes called the *carcase* or *core*. In antique furniture the veneer was cut by hand and was often $\frac{1}{8}$ inch thick. In modern machine-made furniture the veneer is cut by saw or knife and is sometimes only $\frac{1}{32}$ inch thick. Many modern veneers are cut by the rotary process. These are known as rotary veneers. They are peeled off in a continuous layer from a rotating log and have the advantage of being produced cheaply and in large sheets. The thinnest sheets are glued to muslin and sold in rolls like wallpaper. They are applied to walls much in the manner of wallpaper and are popular in contemporary work.

Very handsome grained surfaces may be obtained by cutting veneers from portions of a tree in which the growth of the fibers is irregular. *Crotch veneer* is obtained from forks in the tree trunk or where large branches join the trunk in a Y-shape. The graining often appears as a pattern resembling a V-shape or a cluster of plumes. This is called the crotch figure or more often "crotch mahogany" or "crotch walnut," according to the kind of wood. Such veneers are usually matched so as to produce a panel with a symmetrical pattern in the form of an approximate square or diamond. *Burls* are large wart-like excrescences on tree trunks. They contain the dark piths of a large number of buds. Throughout the burl, the fibers are very irregularly contorted, so that the grain cannot be said to run in any particular direction. Burls may occur on almost any species, but walnut, ash, cherry, and redwood burls are among the most highly prized in furniture woods. *Bird's-eye* cut or veneer is somewhat similar to burl, but is caused by local sharp depressions in the

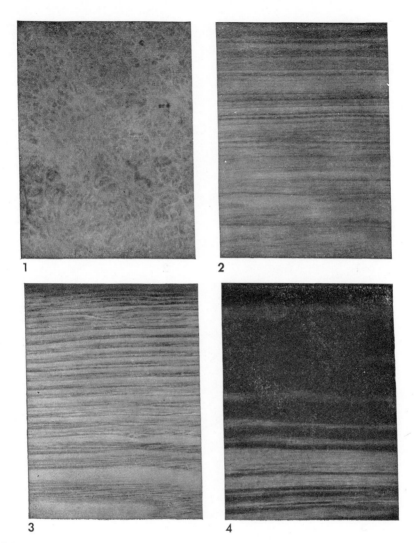

Cabinet woods. (*1*) *Amboyna burl; color, rich yellowish-brown with yellow and red markings.* (*2*) *American black walnut; straight-grained; color, yellow-brown with dark brown streaks.* (*3*) *Plain-sawed chestnut; color, light tan.* (*4*) *Macassar ebony; straight-grained; color, coffee-brown with black streaks.*

annual rings, accompanied by considerable fiber distortion. The bird's-eye figure is confined almost exclusively to maple, and it occurs in only a small percentage of trees; its effect is that of a series of circlets resembling rather remotely a bird's eye. *Butt-wood veneer* is taken from the junction of the larger roots with the stem of the tree, where the fibers are greatly

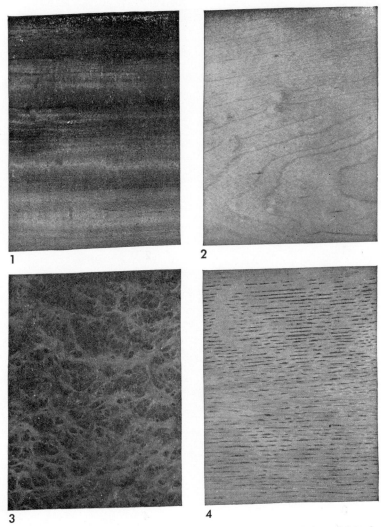

Cabinet woods. (1) Cuban mahogany; straight-grained; color, light red-brown with dark red streaks. (2) American maple; straight-grained; color, light tan. (3) California redwood burl; color, red-brown with darker red-brown markings. (4) Quarter-sawed oak; color, light tan.

distorted, producing cross figures, mottle, and curly grain. Pollard veneer or wood is cut from a tree that has been constantly trimmed at its top so that its growth is diffused into many small shoots. The shoots produce knots in the grain which add to the decorative value of the wood.

The idea that veneered furniture is cheaply made has long since passed. The present use of veneer gives added strength to furniture construction and prevents warpage. The modern method consists of gluing thin strips of veneer to plywood made of three, five, or more layers of wood glued together. The grain of each ply, as the layers are called, runs at right angles to the adjoining ply. Since wood is stronger the long way of the fiber and shrinks more across the grain than with it, this method of laying the grain of one piece across the grain of the adjoining layer helps to equalize the strength and to prevent uneven shrinkage which causes warping. Veneered furniture of the past and present often represents the highest attainment of the cabinetmaker's craft.

Veneered woods are often enriched by marquetry patterns in which the sheets of wood for the pattern and the field are cut together so that they exactly fit each other.

Many varieties of wood are used for interior finish, cabinetwork, and furniture. Among the hardwoods, oak is the most important, others being walnut, maple, birch, ash, chestnut, while among the softwoods the most important are white pine, cypress, and redwood. Local conditions often make possible the use of woods that are little known to the general public, and the varieties are so numerous that no list can be complete. The rare woods are, as a rule, used for veneers only. On pages 741–744 are given brief descriptions of the important woods used for cabinetwork or interior trim.

Woods used in furniture construction. Oak is the most common wood used for furniture construction and finish in both solid and veneered surfaces. Its hardness, strength, finish, and adaptability make it suitable for all grades of furniture. White oak rather than red oak is preferable where a natural finish is desired. Chestnut is used mainly for cores for veneered surfaces such as table tops and drawer fronts; it is soft and light, dries easily and warps and shrinks little. Yellow birch is another very common furniture wood; it is strong and hard and holds its shape, takes stain and enamel well, and is often used as a substitute for mahogany and walnut. Rosewood (jacarandá), while less popular today than during the 19th century, is excellent for piano-cases, handles and small objects. West Indian mahogany, due to its color and beauty of grain, is used for all types of high-grade furniture, often on veneered surfaces, although many antique pieces were made in solid lumber. In the less conspicuous parts of the cheaper grades of furniture, red gum or birch are sometimes used as substitutes for mahogany. Walnut has long been popular as a furniture wood; it is hard and strong with a rich color and luster, comparatively free from warping, and has good gluing qualities; it is used for both solid and veneered construction. Beech is used for furniture that is to be painted or stained; it bends easily and is therefore particularly adapted for curved parts such as arms and backs of chairs; it is also extensively used for the unseen portions of furniture, such as drawer sides, runways

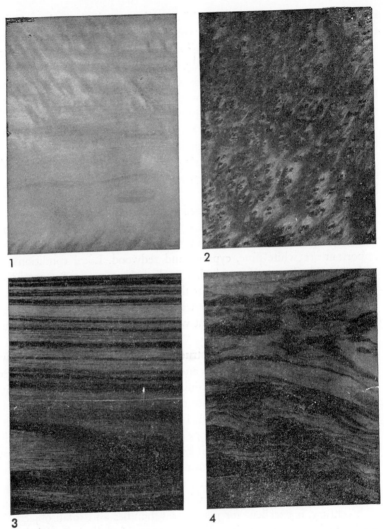

Cabinet woods. (*1*) *East Indian satinwood; straight-grained; color, blond.* (*2*) *Madagascar thuya burl; color, red-brown with darker brown markings.* (*3*) *Brazilian tulipwood; straight-grained; color, light yellow with red-orange streaks.* (*4*) *Olivewood; straight-grained; color, light brown with dark greenish-brown irregular streaks.*

and frames; it is strong and hard but has a greater tendency to warp than other woods. Maple is one of the principal American furniture woods and is usually given a natural finish, for which reason the curly or bird's-eye figure is preferable. Maple is hard and strong and has good gluing properties. Red gum has recently become one of the leading furniture woods of this country. The heartwood has a beautiful figure and deserves recognition under its own name, although when stained, its grain has the appearance of walnut or mahogany. Gum is of a medium hardness that makes it easily worked in machines. The rare imported woods such as amboyna, satinwood, tulip, cocobolo, avodire, thuya, kingwood, and zebrawood are used principally for veneered surfaces in the more expensive types of furniture.

~~~~~~

Glossary

Woods Used in Cabinetwork

~~~~~~

Acacia. A light brown hardwood from Australia and Africa. In ancient times it was used by the Eastern nations for religious and sacred buildings; today it is used for furniture and for architectural and ecclesiastical woodwork.

Aceitillo. West Indian hardwood with fine grain, somewhat resembling satinwood in color and appearance. Used for furniture.

Amaranth. A dark purplish wood imported from South Africa. It is usually fine-grained and figured, and is much used in contemporary furniture.

Amboyna. A rich brown wood, highly marked, with yellow and red streaks. Much used for modern cabinetwork and veneering. It is of East Indian origin.

Apple. A light-colored, fine-grained wood used for furniture. It is suitable for staining or natural finish.

Arbor-vitae. An evergreen tree of the genus Thuya, native to North America and eastern Asia. An excellent building and furniture wood.

Ash. A blond wood with a handsome figure and pleasing texture, which, because of its hardness, is not extensively used for interior work, though it can be used to produce very rich effects. It is well adapted to dark stained effects.

Avodire. A blond wood with strong, dark brown vertical streakings. It has a fine texture and is much used for modern furniture, for veneering purposes.

Bamboo. A woody, perennial plant that grows in tropical regions. The wood is used for furniture, ornaments, building purposes, pipes, paper-making, and food.

Baywood. An alternate name for Honduras mahogany, which is lighter in color and softer than the Cuban or Spanish mahogany. Its fine marking makes the wood useful in veneered work.

Beech. A pale straight-grained wood much used for flooring and furniture. It resembles maple and birch, and can be similarly used.

Birch. A fine-grained wood, strong and hard, usually a light brown in color. It requires no filler, takes paint and stain well, and can have a natural finish or be stained to imitate walnut, mahogany, and other more expensive woods. It is much used for doors and trim as well as for flooring, where it competes successfully with oak.

Black walnut. In spite of its extensive use at a period when design was at its lowest level, it is one of the most beautiful woods grown in this country. It has a rich color, takes a high polish, and shows a very handsome figure. It is fine-grained enough to allow intricate carving, though its open pores call for the use of a filler in finishing. It is among the more expensive woods, because of wasteful cutting thirty to fifty years ago; but it can still be found in the market in fair quantity, and for furniture it is unsurpassed for richness of effect.

Boxwood. A light-colored, fine-grained wood used for marquetry.

Butternut. Called also white walnut; resembles black walnut in all respects except color, and may be similarly used, where a lighter effect is desired. It works easily, is hard and durable, and has a handsome figure, formed by the annual rings. In some sections it is used for flooring and ceiling, elsewhere for interior finish and furniture. The trees grow throughout the United States.

Cedar. A name applied to several woods that are fine-grained and fragrant. The North American cedar is a juniper; the West Indian is of the mahogany family. The wood is used for chests and lining clothes closets, cigar boxes, and pencils. Persian cedar, or nanmu, is an eastern hardwood used for building.

Cherry. A durable hardwood of a reddish-brown color, which is produced only in small quantities, the trees being usually too small for lumbering. It is often used to imitate mahogany, which it greatly resembles, and is used for marquetry and inlay.

Chestnut. A softwood, sometimes white and sometimes brown, which resembles plain oak, but has a coarser grain. Where a quartered effect is not desired, it can take the place of oak and is generally much less expensive. Because of its strongly marked rings and coarse grain, it is unsuitable for fine detail.

Circassian walnut. A brown wood with a very curly grain, one of the handsomest finishing woods, which comes from the country near the Black Sea. It is used largely for furniture and panelling, and is very expensive.

Cocobolo. A dark brown wood with a violet cast. It takes a highly polished finish and is used for modern furniture.

Coromandel (also called coromandel ebony and calamander). A hard dark-brown wood with black stripes that grows in India and China and is much used for furniture.

Cypress. A wood with a light brown color, though it varies considerably according to its origin. It is a very handsome wood for interior use, quiet inexpensive, adapted to all types of finish, and remarkably free from warping and twisting. This last property recommends it for kitchen use, or wherever heat and moisture are met. Cypress is too soft for flooring, though occasionally so employed, and too weak for structural timber; but for finish, few woods can equal it. It may be given a natural finish, or may be painted or stained to give almost any effect that may be desired, including imitations of many

of the expensive hardwoods. A special treatment, to which cypress alone seems adapted, is so-called *sugi* finish, an imitation of Japanese driftwood. It is produced by charring the surface with a gasoline torch and rubbing off the charcoal with a wire brush. The spring wood burns away and the harder summer wood remains, leaving the grain in strong relief.

Deal. A term used in England for designating standard merchandising dimensions of fir and pine lumber. In the United States it is generally applied to southern yellow pine, and in Canada to northern soft pine. The word is sometimes used as a misnomer for pine wood itself.

Douglas fir. A western wood that resembles white pine as to its physical properties, but has, in addition, a very handsome curly grain that makes it more suitable for natural or stained finish. It is strong and durable, works easily, and is adaptable to almost every type of use. It is, moreover, fairly inexpensive, being produced in great abundance, probably more than any other single species. There are several other species of fir, but they are of relatively little importance. It is used extensively for large plywood or laminated sheets.

Ebony. A handsome dark heartwood of a tropical tree. Black ebony or *gabon* comes from Africa, is hard and heavy, takes a high polish, and is used for furniture and inlay. *Macassar* ebony is a coffee-brown wood with black streaks, and is used for modern furniture. Coromandel and striped ebony are names that are also applied to macassar ebony. Ebony is sometimes red or green.

Elm. A strong and tough wood, with a less interesting figure than most other hardwoods. When treated with stain and polish, however, it makes a fine appearance. Because of its durability, it is used in large quantities for furniture, and its use for interior work might well be more extensive.

Eucalyptus. A pale reddish-yellow figured wood, much used in modern decoration, and also in shipbuilding. It is also called oriental wood or oriental walnut.

French burl. A term applied to a walnut that comes from Persia. It has small warts or knots that form on the side of the tree when young, giving the lumber an interesting curly grain. It is much used for cabinetwork.

Fir. See Douglas fir.

Gum. See Red gum.

Harewood. Its common name is English sycamore. It has a fine cross-fiddle figure and is much used today for cabinetwork, particularly after it has been dyed a silver gray.

Hemlock. It is little used for finish, particularly in the eastern states. The western hemlock, however, is a far better wood than the eastern variety, and can be used for finish wherever strength, lightness, and ease of working are desirable. It greatly resembles white pine, and may be used in a similar manner.

Hickory. An American tree of the walnut family. Its wood is hard, tough, and heavy and is not used for decorative purposes.

Holly. A light-colored, fine-grained wood used for marquetry.

Jacarandá. See Rosewood.

Kingwood. A dark brown wood with black and golden yellow streakings. It comes from Sumatra and Brazil and is a fine cabinetwood.

Korina. A wood resembling primavera, and having a light yellow color. Used for wall veneers.

Laurel. A dark reddish-brown with a pronounced wavy grain. It takes a high polish and is much used for modern furniture.

Mahogany. A wood with a beautiful reddish color and handsome grain which has long made it a favorite for furniture. It is imported from South America and the West Indies, the various islands of which produce several distinct species. The best of these is found in Santo Domingo, and is sometimes known as Spanish mahogany. White mahogany or primavera has a creamy color and comes from Mexico. Mahogany is easily worked, takes a high polish, and warps and shrinks but little. Honduras mahogany is known as baywood. In addition, mahogany for various purposes comes from Cuba, Africa, Nicaragua, Costa Rica, and the Philippines.

Maple. A wood similar to birch, though usually lighter in color. It is adapted for the same uses, including flooring. Straight-grained maple is one of the handsomest woods for interior finish, while the curly

or bird's-eye varieties are used for veneered furniture. It is very hard and strong.

Myrtle. A blond wood with fine markings. It is much used in cabinetwork for inlay and veneer.

Nanmu. A wood used in China for building and decoration. It is aromatic and turns a deep rich brown with age. It is also called Persian cedar.

Oak. This is the most important of all woods for interior use. It may be sawed, either plain or quartered, the latter being generally preferred for fine work, because of the striking pattern produced by the medullary rays. Plain oak is less expensive, because there is less waste in its production, and it is used for the less important features, or where durability rather than beauty is the chief consideration. Oaks are divided into over fifty species, but the differences in the wood are not great. They are all hard, durable, and very similar in grain. The wood lends itself well to carving of all kinds and is also well adapted to panelling. Because of its open grain, oak should be treated with a filler before applying stain or varnish. English and French oak have finer graining than the American variety.

Olive. A light yellow wood with greenish-yellow figures. It takes a high polish and is popular for inlay purposes.

Palisander. A brown wood with a violet cast. It comes from Brazil and the East Indies and is much used for modern furniture.

Pearwood. A pinkish-brown, finely grained wood that is frequently used for inlay and fine cabinetwork.

Pine (white). Known sometimes as soft pine, this was once the most important of softwoods, and is still used in large quantities, though its price is now rather high. It works easily and is used for both structural and finishing purposes, though it is nearly always painted, its texture being of little interest. The leaf of the trees has short needles.

Pine (yellow). Called hard pine, it has several species varying greatly in strength and other properties. In general it is stronger and harder than white pine. It makes good and cheap flooring, trim, doors, and furniture. For interior finish, its natural yellow color is not very pleasant, but by the use of dark stains, effects are obtained that are little inferior to dark oak. Yellow pine grows in Georgia and the Carolinas, and the leaf of the tree has long needles.

Primavera. A blond, smooth wood with a handsome figure, it is sometimes known as white mahogany. It takes a high polish and is much used in contemporary decoration. Comes from Mexico.

Red cedar. A wood little used for decorative purposes, though great quantities are used for making shingles and lead pencils. Its chief use as a finish wood is for the lining of clothes closets and chests. The small use made of cedar for finish is doubtless the result of its great variation in color, ranging from a decided red to almost white. Both colors are often found in a single piece, the heartwood being red and the sapwood white. Its odor is also too pungent for constant association.

Red gum. A handsome, fine-grained wood, of a reddish-brown color. *Sap gum* is the sapwood of the same tree, and is much lighter in color. Red gum is much used for veneered doors, as well as for general interior finish, though its use has only become general in recent years. It may be used as a base for white enamel, or may be stained to imitate a variety of other woods, including walnut, mahogany, and maple, while selected specimens may even be found to imitate the striking figure of Circassian walnut. The figure of red gum varies in different trees, and it must be selected according to the use intended. In addition to various stained finishes, it may be given a natural finish by the use of wax, producing a handsome satiny effect that wears remarkably well.

Redwood. A wood of a very handsome and uniformly red color, extensively used on the Pacific Coast, though seldom seen in the eastern states. It takes stain and paint readily, and can be obtained in very wide boards because of the great size of the trees. It is used for interior trim.

Rosewood. A fine reddish-brown wood with black streakings. There are many varieties, of which the most popular is Brazilian rosewood, called *jacarandá*. It takes a high polish and is much used for fine cabinetwork and for musical instruments.

Satinwood. A light blond wood with a satiny finish and a handsome figure, used for finishing only in the finest work. It is largely used for furniture, and particularly for inlay and parquetry. Satinwood is cut from various species of trees that grow in India, Florida, and the West Indies.

Snakewood. A yellow-brown or red-brown wood with dark spots and markings. It is popular for inlay work.

Spruce. A variety of pine closely related to the fir. Important ornamental tree with a soft, light, straight-grained wood used for interior and exterior construction and for sounding boards of musical instruments.

Sycamore. A wood that ranges from white to light-brown in color. It is heavy, tough, and strong, and handsome in appearance. It is extensively used for finishing work.

Tabonuco. A light-colored, beautifully grained West Indian hardwood used for furniture.

Teakwood. A wood that is yellow to brown in color, often with fine black streaks. It is more durable than oak and is used for shipbuilding as well as for furniture.

Thuya. A dark red-brown wood from North Africa. It takes a high polish and is much used in contemporary cabinetwork. Arbor vitae is of the same genus. The wood was known to the Chinese and Greeks.

Tulipwood. A light yellow wood with red streaks. It comes from Brazil and is much used for ornamental inlay.

Walnut. A light brown wood taken from trees that grow throughout Europe, Asia, and Africa. Much used for cabinetwork. There are English, French, and Italian varieties. The American walnut has a coarser grain than the European varieties and is often called English walnut or black walnut. The hickory tree has a similar wood and leaf, and is often called a walnut in the United States. See also Butternut and Black walnut.

Whitewood. The trade name for poplar and cottonwood. There are several species, but all are characterized by a uniform grain of little interest, so that the wood is used mainly for shelving, interior parts of furniture, and cores in veneered work. It is soft and works easily, but is durable in ordinary use, excellent for painted surfaces.

Yew. A close-grained hardwood of a deep red-brown. It is a European evergreen and thrives especially in England. Frequently used in cabinetwork where an elastic quality is desirable.

Zebrawood. A light golden-yellow wood with dark brown stripes. It is used for ornamental cabinetwork.

Bibliography

BEVERIDGE, T. J., *English Renaissance Woodwork*, B. T. Batsford, Ltd., London, 1921. Excellent measured drawings, chiefly of the period of Sir Christopher Wren. Good for tracing and design work.

DALY, C., *Historical Motifs of Architecture and Sculpture,* 2 Vols. Wm. Helburn, Inc., New York. Scaled drawing of French woodwork, mantels, and architectural and decorative details.

KNOBLOCH, P., *Good Practice in Construction.* Pencil Points Press, New York, 1925. Scale drawings of architectural woodwork.

KOEHLER, A., *The Identification of Furniture Woods.* U. S. Department of Agriculture, Washington, D. C., 1926. Excellent treatment of woods with illustrations.

Measured Drawings of Woodwork Displayed in the American Wing. Metropolitan Museum of Art, New York, 1925. Portfolio of scaled drawings of the woodwork exhibited in the American wing.

PAYSON, W. F., *Mahogany, Antique and Modern: A Study of Its History and Use in the Decorative Arts.* E. P. Dutton and Co., New York, 1926. Illustrated series of essays on various uses of mahogany.

PELTON, B. W., *Furniture Making and Cabinet Work: A Handbook.* D. Van Nostrand Co., New York, 1949. Instructions and step-by-step drawings for furniture construction.

RAMSEY, C. G., AND SLEEPER, H. R., *Architectural Graphic Standards for Architects, Engineers, Decorators, Builders, and Draughtsmen.* J. Wiley and Sons, Inc., New York, 1951. An encyclopedia of dimensions.

SHAPLAND, H. P., *The Practical Decoration of Furniture,* 3 Vols. Ernest Benn, Ltd., London, 1926–1927. Good illustrated text.

TANNER, H., *English Interior Woodwork of the XVI, XVII, and XVIII Centuries.* Architectural Book Publishing Co., New York. Reprint. Measured drawings with descriptive text.

TIPPING, H. A., *Grinling Gibbons and the Woodwork of His Age.* Country Life, London, 1914. Illustrated text.

WARNE, E. J., *Furniture Mouldings.* Ernest Benn, Ltd., London, 1923. Measured details of English furniture moldings. (Full size.)

WEAVER, SIR L., *Laminated Board and Its Uses.* The Fanfare Press, London, 1930. Illustrated study of modern furniture and decoration.

WELLS, P. A., AND HOOPER, J., *Modern Cabinet Work: Furniture and Fitments.* J. B. Lippincott Co., Philadelphia, 1924. Illustrated account of theory and practice in the production of all kinds of cabinetwork. Working drawings, photographs, and original designs.

PART FOUR

SELECTION, ARRANGEMENT, AND HARMONY

CHAPTER XXII

STANDARDS OF TASTE
AND DESIGN

W orks of art must be judged on the basis of the conditions of life existing at the time and place they were produced. The requirements of people, the purposes of artists, the character of materials, and the efficiency of tools alter with the years. One cannot properly appraise the quality of former masterpieces by modern standards of criticism; the critic must revert to the thought and knowledge of the period during which they were made and examine the reasons why things were done as they were. The proportions of Greek temples were not chosen arbitrarily; they were dictated by the structural limitations of marble. The French rococo rooms were intended to enhance the charm of women, and contribute to the gaiety that was a necessary reaction from the solemnity of the previous regime. The Greek Revival in America was the political and artistic effort to establish a republican form of government, the only models for which had been the Greek and Roman philosophies. The impressionist painters of the 19th century were concerned with the analysis of the rays of light, and the methods of adapting their scientific principles to the use of pigments. Contemporary designers are dominated by changes in economic conditions, scientific developments, considerations of function, efficiency, convenience, and comfort, and they relegate the former concepts of beauty to secondary importance. Each art during each period of civilization was evolved from circumstances that produced the particular visual characteristics by which it may now be recognized. The exact conditions were never repeated. There was a reason for everything, and the criteria by which any art production of today must be judged are entirely different from those of former periods.

A common standard of criticism and appraisal may be established by consideration of the following questions: What is the artist attempting to do? Is it worth doing? Has he done it well, considering his tools, materials, and cultural level? It is obvious that no artist is born with a full knowledge of his art. A study of the history of his medium is essential if he wishes to make a contribution. A painter with integrity cannot paint today like Michael Angelo nor can a musician compose like Beethoven. Imitation is not art. An artist must have an intelligent understanding of every important effort of previous artists in his field. History is not a list of events and dates, but a record and analysis of significant causes and effects; its roots and branches must be minutely examined. The great artists of the past were saturated with the wisdom of the ages and the problems of humanity, and understood the psychology of their times and patrons. The results are on record. The artist of today must understand the conditions of the present to enable him to create that which is suited to, and representative of, modern life. His duty is to produce beauty and contentment for the people of his time. He cannot create by rules alone; by that process he merely struggles in obscurity. His intentions and intellectual caliber must be high, and the roots of his knowledge must extend deep into the recesses of the human thoughts and activities of contemporary existence.

The motive in any artistic effort must be honest and sincere, and not influenced by fear, vanity, snobbishness, or the desire to produce a false effect. There must be no meretricious intent. The efforts of peasants, children, and savages are frequently works of art. Though these may be on a lower level than the productions of great artists, they are the result of entirely honest endeavors. The esthetically virtuous artist may lack technique in his medium, but he is unlikely to produce anything in poor taste so long as he avoids imitation. Technical proficiency adds to the quality of a work of art, but the absence of such does not disqualify the work from this classification. The artist may take advantage of previous ideas, but he must definitely add something of his own. Instead of imitating effects, he must search for the principle that made them original.

Taste in the decorative arts. The art of designing interiors is justified on the basis of its contribution to human contentment. The competent designer aims to produce that which will cause both psychological and practical satisfactions. His decisions must fulfill the purposes of the room and at the same time be a pleasure to contemplate. The art is inexact and perfection can seldom be achieved, due to the variations in human needs and to financial, structural, and other restrictions. The rules of pure design must be applied to their limit in the conception of any proposed decorative scheme, but there is an intangible quality that will occur, regardless of material conditions or perfection of line, detail, and color. This is generally described as "taste," and it is the keystone of any esthetic production.

Philosophers of every era have endeavored to define taste in its relation to the arts, but have found the subject perplexing. Dictionaries generalize by stating that taste is a sense that permits one to distinguish artistic excellence, or reflects the ability to discern fitness, beauty, and order. But these definitions are incomplete, because they do not explain what constitutes excellence. As taste is a mental quality, it is not intrinsic in the materials or forms of a work of art, and its apparent presence is dependent upon the emotional reaction that an observer feels as a result of the intelligence and intellect that an artist imparts into his work. It is thus closely allied to the expression of personality. Beauty and taste are co-related but exist independently.

It is commonly stated that matters of taste are not arguable. Persons who are initiated, however, usually have similar feelings and opinions about a work of art, and time always establishes its eventual status. Taste, however, is transient and evolutionary; it is influenced by changed conditions and the normal desire to escape from boredom or monotony. Often what is considered good taste today is condemned tomorrow, and what is acceptable in one place is rejected elsewhere. Taste is not necessarily a product of gentility of birth, intellect, or opulence; but it usually grows on the top branches of the trees of culture and refinement, and it is part of an instinct that is reflected in the words, actions, and creative efforts of an individual. Its presence or absence may be seen in any work of an artist. It includes a sensitivity that enables one to distinguish the true from the false. Problems of pure design can be solved by established formulas, but the intangibles are the elements that differentiate superiority from mediocrity. Taste may be as much in evidence in the most simple of decorative compositions as in the most elaborate or extravagant. Wealth often hinders its expression, because there is an urge toward ostentation. The most inexpensively furnished room often will indicate the good taste of its owner. Discriminative ability will enable one to pick from a mass of available articles those that display beauty of color, texture, line, and artistic integrity, even though of moderate cost. A room that reflects a simple, but good, taste denies ignorance, and possesses an atmosphere that is charged with personality. A single accessory or picture of quality in a room becomes a light that indicates the gentility of the owner.

Taste is not solely expressed by the proper selection of individual features of decoration. It is also in evidence in grouping, proportion, and composition. There must be an orderly arrangement of details that suits the function and design of the room, and is agreeable to look at. Every object also should be located so that the activities conducted in the room may be carried on with convenience, comfort, and efficiency. The daily habits and individual needs of those who are to occupy the room should be studied. Walls as well as furnishings should contribute to esthetic, psychological, and practical requirements; architecture, materials, colors, and patterns should be made to play their part.

Features that are pretentious, ostentatious, or vulgar should be avoided, and good taste precludes the use of pictures, ornaments, or patterns that are oversentimental in subject matter or arouse emotions of pity, sorrow, or sympathy. Trivialities that may be described as "pretty," "cute," or "whimsical" reflect an intellectual superficiality.

The decorations of a room should not reflect a self-conscious effort on the part of its designer. Every room should appear natural and mellow and look as though it is used by someone who enjoys it. When the impress of the decorator's hand is too much in evidence, the work does not reflect the taste of his client. Decorative features that are introduced for the sole purpose of making a startling impression should be used with great discretion. Naturalness is as desirable in the decorative arts as in the personality of an individual; it is a component part of a charm that captivates by its inherent quality. Self-consciousness is in evidence when historical or identical forms have been used excessively, or with too great accuracy for "correctness." A constant repetition of ornamental motifs for the purpose of unity indicates mental immaturity. Good decoration is not produced by "packaged schemes" that cannot contain the necessary elements of individuality or taste, or by the use of manufacturers' suggestions for unity of forms and colors. One of the current insults to the esthetic intelligence of the public is the offer of "suites of furniture," and the advice of paint manufacturers and color consultants as to "the" popular colors to be used. The adoption of such conceptions merely reflects a paucity of intelligence or mental laziness, and no good can result. The manufacturers and the public are equally to blame for this condition.

In rooms that must be impersonal, such as transient hotel and club apartments, a more tasteful result may be obtained by designing for an imaginary individual. Occupants prefer such rooms even if they do not reflect their own ideas, and there is always the possibility of featuring local interests or activities in the details.

In commercial establishments, such as offices, shops, hospitals, and restaurants, there are always important functional or economic limitations that affect the character of their decorative treatment, but the element of taste and fitness may be reflected in a degree that is consistent with their use. Such rooms are usually intended for specific class levels for which there are standards of quality. Every business deals in merchandise of a certain grade, or it caters to customers or clients of a definite social, financial, or intellectual type. The details of decoration in interiors for these purposes may vary from features intended for glaring publicity and theatricalism to expressions of dignity and refinement that screen the obvious business activities; but, the designer, if imbued with taste, will not avoid its inclusion in his decisions.

Style. There are two definitions of the word "style" when used in reference to art forms. One refers to a definite trend in the character of art productions during a particular era, and in a specific locality. These are the so-called Period Styles of architecture and the decorative arts that are recognizable by the materials, forms, colors, and textures that were used. Each style was developed by social, political, philosophical, economic, scientific, and other influences; it reached a peak when it best fulfilled the needs of its epoch, and as external conditions changed, began a decline. Its ebb was usually followed by a transitional period as new influences were introduced, and finally a new style would take its place.

Style, in the other sense, refers to features that are approved as elegant or fashionable at some particular time. The word "fashion" is perhaps more suitable, because it has a transient meaning. Fashions are temporarily popular and often illogically introduced; they destroy themselves, because popularity is dated, and the designers promote new ideas that cause existing fashions to be outmoded. Fashion has been pithily defined as a method to make things obsolete before they wear out. Catering to a desire for change, manufacturers introduce novelties to increase trade. Good fashions merge themselves into the style of the period; the inconsequential quickly pass to oblivion. Fashion has little to do with good art, as the latter is universal and eternal. It is the duty of the artist to be able to distinguish the permanent from the transient, and the good from the bad.

During the early years of the 20th century, nearly all architectural and decorative design in the United States was based on a predetermined style. Buildings, interiors, and furnishings imitated as closely as possible the types of the past. Style was reproduced, but without originality, and in many cases the public was forced to accommodate itself to manners of living that existed centuries before. Taste was saturated with eclectic formulas; new concepts were discouraged and were relegated to the lowest type of commercial use. The imaginative artists and designers were often considered dreamers or worse. The critics were unable to recognize the obstructions to the evolution of the decorative arts caused by an eclectic philosophy. The external appearances of former styles were forcibly adapted to new living conditions and the basic principles from which these styles had evolved were overlooked.

Art cannot be produced by these methods, nor can a people be satisfied by failing to give them the advantages of new developments. Styles of decoration must evolve from fundamental influences and cannot be merely imitative. The beautiful and utilitarian forms and objects of past generations may continue to be used only if no superior production of the present may be substituted for them. This superiority, however, is not limited to form or utilitarian value. It may be psychological, and the world is full of persons whose personalities and intellectual interests may best be expressed in decoration by objects produced in former times. Many an owner of an 18th century New England farmhouse prefers to surround himself with the earmarks of Colonial design. A Francophile may prefer the use of rococo art. A ranch-house owner may have a passion for Indian relics. But the use of such details in decorative work does not today create a period room. Modern elements encroach surreptitiously. The academically pure styles of the past are gone forever. There was too much that is unadaptable to life today and there is too much of the new that is necessary to have it excluded. The all-upholstered chair or sofa is a comparatively modern invention; its use spontaneously expresses modernism. The 20th century style does not exclude the antique (nor even a reproduction if unavoidable); but, the style of today is created by logical reasoning and not by imitation. Simplicity, utility, convenience, comfort, economy, and the advantages or beauty of new materials or equipment are the modern dictators of design. Even in traditionally planned rooms, such considerations cannot be avoided, and if old furnishings or patterns seem best to satisfy their owners, then these should be used if reasonable harmony of design is maintained. Prejudices in favor of, or against, certain features, should be disregarded if they do not coincide with common sense. It is dangerous to follow the crowd blindly. Features should not be introduced or omitted because "It is being done" or "It is not being done any more." Quality in the decorative arts reflects imagination. Imitation may be a form of flattery, but it also indicates a vacuous area in the mentality of the imitator. There should be an avoidance of the use of poorly made objects of any type, or of inferior reproductions of stylized furniture or accessories. Features that have been manufactured in such quantity that they have become the common property of shopwindows, magazine illustrations, or homes, in general, should never be used. There should be a definite reason for every feature of a room; each should contribute to a practical, esthetic, or psychological purpose. Nothing that is superfluous should be used.

The charm of the twentieth century interior is its flexibility. Freedom of expression is the goal and anything is possible if it fulfills the requirements of use and harmony. The Styles as directives are destructive of the development of a style. Taste and individuality are the intangible essentials; functionalism, the practical; and pure design, the esthetic.

The expression of personality. In appraising the quality of the decoration of a room, it is difficult to establish fixed standards of judgment. The interiors of the mansion, small city apartment, cottage, farmhouse, office, hotel, or business establishment differ greatly; yet all are subject to the extremes of decorative quality that are independent of the cost of production. In planning residential decoration, an essential requirement is to reflect the personality of the owner. In an owner-decorated room this element is almost always visible. Refinement, culture, ignorance, and ostentation are self-evident. An intelligent stranger who enters a room the first time should be able to read the character of the owner at first glance. The inner meaning of the decorative treatment should be caught rather than the external effect. When a decorator plans a room for a client, the interests and character of that person should be carefully analyzed in advance. An owner should feel mentally and physically comfortable in a room, and should be surrounded with things that please him. The decorations of a room are subject to as many characteristic expressions as are typical of individuals. Dignity, sophistication, informality, gaiety, maturity, youth, masculinity, femininity, and many other characteristics may be indicated. The quality of the harmony, and consistency of the major details, the types and subject matter of furniture, textiles, and accessories will indicate the personal interests and cultural level of the owners.

A room need not always be serious in appearance. Humor has its place in decoration, and an amusing detail lifts a room above too sober a level. Humor may be introduced most easily in pictures, ceramics, metalwork, textiles, wallpapers, and minor objects.

The designer must guard himself against popular slogans, consider their merits and to what extent they should influence his decisions. A universal application of similar ideas in decoration tends toward lack of individuality, a deficiency that has often been noticed in modern interiors. The term "functionalism" can lead to an excess of utility at the sacrifice of soul. "Open-planning" can easily lead to lack of privacy. "A machine for living" must be considered with caution and "bringing the garden into the house" is not always an advantage. In spite of the economic savings in "rooms for double and triple use," this principle eventually may prove detrimental to family life. Similar formulas produce identical answers. All human beings differ, and each has individual requirements that may be interpreted in decoration to produce a personalized interior.

Contrast and variety in design. A design is an orderly arrangement of lines, forms, masses, colors, or textures, forming a unified composition. There are no rules of eternal validity for combining these elements, but custom and habit have established certain principles which, when applied, produce effects giving the degrees of satisfaction that people call beauty. Interest is primarily attained by the introduction of contrast and movement. A design without these features is dull and monotonous; with them in excess it lacks unity and becomes confusing and restless.

Every object has line, area, or mass. Contrasts are produced by various methods. Lines may be straight, curved, and irregular; line directions may be vertical, horizontal, and diagonal. Movement is created by the use of curved lines. Straight lines have a static effect. Dominance of curvilinear lines and forms produce what is generally termed a rococo effect, and may become easily fatiguing. Straight lines and particularly horizontal lines are restful. Areas are created by lines forming a silhouetted enclosure of any shape or size. Masses and surfaces are large and small, light and heavy, narrow and wide, tall and short, or flat and curved. Textures are smooth, medium, and coarse. Colors vary in hue, tone, and chroma. Surface treatments may be plain or covered with elaborate patterns.

The artist's function is to introduce just the proper amount of contrast and movement in his design to create the effect that he desires, and to avoid the extremes of dullness and confusion. No rule may be given for the use of these contrasts. The artist must judge when they are lacking or carried to excess, but their proper use and proportion is the basis of all good design.

Collections and hobbies. Many persons have hobbies or make collections of special types. It is well to indicate these interests, but they should be exhibited with regard to their decorative value and shown in arrangements that compose with the ensemble of the room. No room should have the appearance of a museum. Crowding of details is confusing. Table cabinets and built-in or free-standing cabinets may be used to contain rarities, and certain types of collectors' items may be hung on walls. If a collection is large, it is better shown in a special room with a few pieces selected as accessory decorations in other places.

Following is a short list of collectors' items that have been used decoratively. Many collections are limited to special types, such as literary autographs, etchings or paintings by particular artists, porcelains of a single country or subject, Colonial flasks, Roman glass, antique watches, or miniatures.

Antique globes
Antique playing cards
Antique toys
Autographs and letters
Barometers and thermometers
Butterflies
Buttons
Coins and stamps
Curiosities
Daguerreotype cases and pictures
Dolls and marionettes
Etchings, lithographs, etc.
Fans
Firearms

Firebacks
Fishing equipment
Flasks and bottles
Glassware
Lead soldiers
Miniature furniture
Miniatures
Musical instruments
Old butter moulds
Old maps
Old valentines
Paintings
Paper dolls and cutwork
Paperweights

Pewter and silver
Pottery and porcelain
Primitive arts
Samplers
Scientific instruments
Scrimshaw work
Sculptured figures

Sea shells
Ship models
Snuffboxes
Sports accessories
Swords and daggers
Toy music boxes
Watches

Bibliography

CHAMBERS, F. P., *The History of Taste*. Columbia University Press, New York, 1932. An account of the revolutions in art criticism and theory in Europe.

LYNES, RUSSELL, *The Tastemakers*. Harper and Brothers, New York, 1954. An excellent outline of the history of taste in the United States from 1830 to modern times.

PARKER, D. H., *The Principles of Aesthetics*. Silver, Burdett and Co., New York, 1920. An analysis of the nature and meaning of art.

SALYER, O. M., *Revolt in the Arts*. Brentano's, New York, 1936. A survey of appreciation of art in America.

CHAPTER XXIII

WALL COMPOSITION

The term *composition* in its reference to spatial or flat design implies an arrangement of related lines, areas, or masses that appears orderly and produces a unified effect. Unity is obtained if each part contributes a share to the grouping as a whole. The relationships may be through position, shape, size, color, texture, material, relative interest, or any combination of these.

There are two compositional problems in the treatment of interiors. They are, first, the wall areas and, secondly, the floor areas. The wall areas are composed by a combination of architectural features and movable furnishings. The floor composition is primarily a matter of furniture arrangement. There is a close relationship between the two problems, as certain objects must necessarily be considered in connection with both. Perfect solutions are not always possible, as many rooms have structural elements or fixed architectural features that prevent a faultless arrangement. The designer must attain a satisfactory balance between function, convenience, comfort, and pure design, and must often sacrifice certain of these elements to contribute to the better application of the others. His aim must be to approach perfection within practical limits and possibilities.

In the composition of walls there is a different approach in the classical and the contemporary theories. In rooms that are intended to reflect any of the historical types, the major principles of classic design must be given a reasonable degree of consideration, but modern conceptions permit more flexible arrangements. Irregularities in room shapes, broken walls, and open or fluid plans complicate the solution of wall compositions and make classical standards impossible of application. There are many advantages to this new approach.

Rooms of a normal shape are rectangular and have four walls. Each wall must be studied as a separate problem in design, but there must be an interrelationship or similarity of treatment between all of them. In a wall composition the fixed elements may consist of doors, windows, mantels, trim, built-in furniture, or other features. The wall materials and textures also must be considered if they cannot conveniently be altered, and lighting and heating equipment is often a visible necessity. The hanging elements may be pictures, lighting fixtures, mirrors, or other accessories and decorations that usually are removable. The movable standing elements that are related to the wall composition consist of furniture, the permanent location of which is on the perimeter of the room at the intersection of the wall and floor; these include pieces such as bookcases, cabinets, secretary desks, wall tables, sofas, sideboards, consoles, and chairs. The problem of the wall composition reduces itself to the arrangement of the hanging and movable elements so that they will create a unified effect with the fixed elements. The separate parts must produce the appearance of a single entity.

The principles of wall design. In the language of design, a wall of a room is a vertical plane limited horizontally by the intersections of floor and ceiling and vertically by the corners of the room or by other breaks in the plan. These lines are basic and features forming other lines must harmonize with them. Diagonal lines disturb the appearance of equilibrium, and conflict with the essential structural forms of the room. Wall design must be considered, therefore, as a study of the possible combinations and intersections of horizontal and vertical subdivisions.

Traditional rooms are usually simple in shape and the walls are pierced by comparatively small windows and doors. Furniture and decorative features may be introduced in their relationship to the full dimensions of each wall area, or to short wall-lengths or panels between openings.

In contemporary residential architecture walls are more frequently broken both vertically and horizontally. Large windows decrease wall areas, and usually must be unobstructed; irregularities in plan, such as alcoves, niches, and large openings to adjoining rooms, decrease wall lengths. Walls are often pierced by long horizontal and clerestory windows that reduce the height of the solid portions; or they are of the folding, sliding, or movable types in glass, opaque materials, or textiles; or are storage cabinets that have sliding or swinging doors. The composition of these walls is created by the structure of the room, and movable features are difficult to introduce for further interest. Only where a fixed wall area exists, may a grouping of furniture or accessories be placed against it.

Horizontal divisions of a wall. In classical design the most agreeable wall effects were produced by three horizontal divisions of unequal height. The Pompeian walls were so laid out, and practically all of the formal rooms of historical periods. Such a decision was, perhaps, purely arbitrary or related to the subject of pure design, but it was exemplified in the proportioning of the classical architectural orders. The column was divided into base, shaft, and capital; the entablature was organized into architrave, frieze, and cornice; and the pedestal was organized into base, shaft, and capital. The whole order was divided into column, entablature, and pedestal, and in each case the horizontal proportions of the various parts were of unequal height. As walls for period rooms are based on classic fundamentals, the principle of unequal horizontal wall divisions may be carried out in their design. Dividing a wall into horizontal elements causes the wall to appear lower than it actually is. Strong horizontal accentuation is therefore inadvisable for low walls, but is necessary for walls that are too high in appearance. The divisions shown in diagram 1 of the illustration on page 761 are best for low walls (7 feet 6 inches or under in height). The divisions shown in diagram 2 may be used for walls higher than 7 feet 6 inches. These are the two simplest arrangements. In these examples, the important thing to note is that the subdivisions are of unequal height, thus producing variety of effect. In diagram 1, only baseboard and picture molding are indicated. Nearly the whole wall is left plain in its undecorated condition. Both the baseboard and the picture molding are so small that they are comparatively unimportant in the composition, and are placed there only for reasons of utility. The wall really "counts" as a plain surface without subdivisions, and therefore is a unit by itself. Interest must be added through hanging objects or wall furniture. In diagram 2, a greater emphasis has been placed upon the subdivisions, which now become more important; but the classic rule is maintained by varying the height of each subdivision, producing thereby contrasting horizontal proportions. The lines at the top of the wall indicate a cornice. The lines at the lower portion of the wall indicate a dado. The subdivisions of the dado are also of irregular heights. The cornice is approximately $\frac{1}{14}$, the dado is $\frac{4}{14}$, and the remainder of the wall is $\frac{9}{14}$ the total height from floor to ceiling. Other irregular horizontal divisions could be used, producing both variety and contrast, but the greater the number of parts, the less unity is obtained. Five divisions would have a less unified effect than three.

In rooms that are not based on classic precedent, the arrangement may be different. There has been some intentional effort by modern designers to avoid compositions that recall too strongly the principles of classicism. The result has been that irregularity of horizontal divisions in wall design has frequently been discarded for divisions of equal height. This, however, is a negative approach to design. Horizontal divisions, if any, should only be introduced for a logical reason, such as the introduction of built-in features or an unavoidable change in materials. Walls need not be subdivided horizontally at all, in which case they are similar to diagram 1 of the illustration shown above, and there is no need of a line giving a border finish at the top of the wall. If, for design requirements,

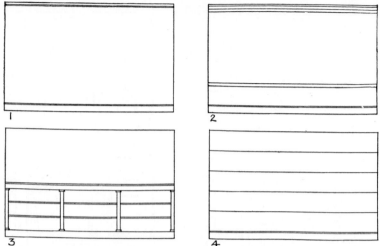

Horizontal subdivision of walls. ABOVE: *Examples of the classical method.* BE-LOW: *Examples of a modern method which avoids classical tradition. Many modern rooms have no horizontal wall subdivisions.*

a line is necessary at the top of the wall, it may be introduced by using a band of wood, metal, mirror, or contrasting color in paint or paper. The baseboard is low and is usually introduced for practical reasons.

Walls that are not designed for period rooms may be cut into two equal horizontal parts by means of built-in furniture, as shown in diagram 3 of the illustration above. Another method is to divide the wall into a series of bands of equal or graded heights, as in diagram 4. The bands may be produced by contrasting painted colors, by metal or wooden strips, by wood inlay or marquetry, or by other means. In all cases, however, the effect differs from the classic traditional arrangement.

Walls are sometimes structurally broken by beams, coves for lighting, horizontal windows, balconies, or exposed stair-runs, all of which establish limits of design. They are also often divided horizontally by the introduction of built-in furniture, and proportions are regulated by necessity. Cabinets are placed under window sills. Upholstered seats are built to regular heights. Bookshelves may run only half the height of a wall or may be carried to the ceiling. Book backs become part of the wall composition and each row becomes a horizontal feature.

In general, a room in which there is an accent placed on horizontal lines is considered more restful than when the vertical predominates; but, in any room, interest is attained by the punctuation of the horizontal elements by vertical motifs.

Vertical divisions of a wall composition. A wall is divided vertically by its architectural features. Doors, high windows, mantels, arches, shelv-

TYPICAL WALL COMPOSITIONS SHOWING VERTICAL DIVISIONS BY SYMMETRICAL
BALANCE.

ing, or the use of the classical orders fix the composition of a wall in such
an unalterable way that only small areas between such features can be
considered for additional treatment.

In the historical styles, walls were often panelled, and the custom in
formal rooms was to vary the width of the panels in a symmetrical distribution to maintain verticality in their proportions (see diagram 5 on

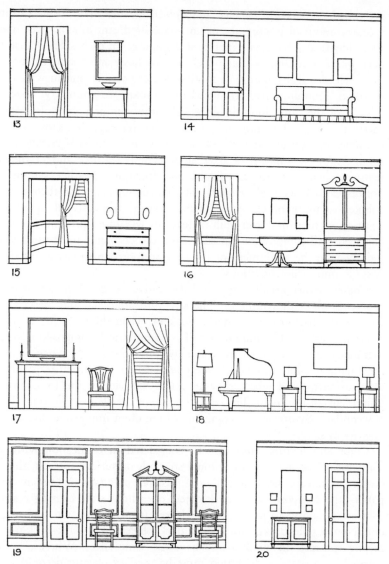

TYPICAL WALL COMPOSITIONS SHOWING VERTICAL DIVISIONS BY OPTICAL BALANCE.

page 762). If the wall was pierced by doors or windows, the designer generally attempted to compose or balance the panelling with such openings to aid in the symmetry of the treatment as shown in diagram 20 on this page. If vertical divisions were fixed by existing features, there was always an attempt to balance these by the use of wall furniture or hanging objects.

There are two types of vertical balance possible for every wall. They are called *symmetrical balance* and *optical balance.* The former assumes a central motif of importance or an unaccented central axis, with one or more identical subordinate motifs or groupings on each side. Optical balance refers to a composition which approaches symmetrical balance but in which identical subordinate motifs are not possible, and in which such motifs or groupings are introduced to approximate symmetry. Diagrams 5 to 12 of the illustration on page 762 show common examples of symmetrical balance. Diagrams 13 to 20 of that on page 763 show common examples of optical balance. As will be seen in these illustrations, the groupings are composed of fixed architectural features and of movable features, such as pictures, mirrors, and furniture. Neither symmetrical nor optical balance is always attainable in room design, but their use contributes to unity of effect and tends toward formality of appearance. Existing architectural and built-in features will often prevent a perfectly balanced wall composition; in such cases the decorator must use his own judgment in the attainment of the nearest approach to symmetry that is possible under the conditions.

Contemporary architectural and decorative design does not primarily concern itself with symmetry. The structure, function, and materials determine the background composition, and, when these are logically considered, it is of little importance if a symmetrical composition results. Symmetry is not avoided intentionally, but occurs only when it is the most natural solution. Features are placed where the structure permits or calls for them, and where they are most suitable for the functional requirements of the room. The consideration of the elements of pure design is secondary. Symmetrical arrangements are often impossible due to complex room shapes.

Color and texture must also be considered in connection with wall composition, because, by their tonal strength or surface interest, they increase or decrease the noticeability of forms or objects which are an actual part of the composition. A dark object on a light wall, causing a strong contrast, "counts" to a far greater degree in a composition than a pale object on a pale background, or a dark object on a dark background. Strong contrasts in textures also have the same effect. Where a wall is covered by a pattern, discretion must be used in placing decorative features against it. A mural or scenic paper should not be hidden by any object. A wallpaper with a large scale or strongly contrasting pattern should not have small pictures or other objects applied to it, as their detail will be lost. A paper with a pattern that is in delicate tones, scale, and color may have additional features hung on it or placed in front of it, but care should be taken that the objects contrast sufficiently in size and color.

The dominant motif. In a wall composition, it is usually essential to have a dominant motif. The importance may be given to the motif by

Examples of optical balance. ABOVE: *A difficult wall composition in which balance has been agreeably attained by introducing pictorial interest on one side of an axis to counterbalance an existing vertical window on the opposite side.* BELOW: *Balance obtained by furniture groups of similar mass and height used as subordinate motifs to a larger central motif.*

its position (in the center or at the side), its size, height, color, or degree of interest. Other motifs in the composition should be subordinated to the dominant motif.

As an example, the dominant motif may be a mantel and overmantel treatment in the center of a wall. If there is sufficient space on either side to introduce additional motifs, these should be similar to each other and smaller in effect than the central motif. Whether or not they should be horizontal or vertical in line is the designer's option.

Generally speaking, square and circular forms are not as agreeable to the eye as rectangles or ovals. The former shapes lack direction of line, which the eye demands. The eye likes to travel, it seeks variety and new things to look at, but likes to know where it is going. It therefore appreciates rhythm, balance, and direction in a composition. It must first grasp the important point from which it starts, then wanders to the subordinated motifs, and finally feels satisfied at the finishing point.

Wall compositions produced by groups of accessories such as pictures or ornaments need not necessarily have a central or dominant motif. Certain wall areas may best be treated with a horizontal or vertical row of features, all of which are of similar shape and size. An example of this would be a row of six or eight framed pictures placed above a long table or a vertical row on each side of a door or window opening. Other small collections of objects may be arranged in a circle, square, or other geometrical form on the wall with or without furniture below. Small objects may be evenly distributed over a plain wall area in much the manner of a repeating pattern, with no dominant point of interest. This arrangement gives equal importance to each of them. Picture collectors often cover their walls with pictures of various types and sizes. If the collection is too large for composed arrangements, the pictures should be hung close together, and spaced equidistant so that none dominates, thus forming an approach to an all-over pattern.

Contrast of vertical and horizontal lines. In connection with the composition of a room, certain real or imaginary lines are formed by the proper grouping of objects. To avoid monotony, it is necessary to vary both the direction of these lines and their character. There are certain objects that create vertical lines, and other objects that create horizontal lines. Vertical lines are usually produced by windows with straight draperies; by doors; by high pieces of furniture, such as secretary desks, cabinets, highboys, bookcases, and floor lamps; or by such groupings as a console with a picture hung above it. Horizontal lines are produced by long, low objects such as dadoes, long sofas, low desks, long tables, square-backed chairs, and grand pianos. It is essential to have in the same room features that produce both vertical and horizontal lines. These should be as evenly distributed as possible on opposite walls, so that such walls will

A wall symmetrically divided by architectural motifs, with a nicely balanced contrast of straight and curved forms, here produces a room of unusual refinement.

balance each other and the room will not appear too important on one side. An agreeable arrangement is usually reached by placing a horizontal form between two vertical ones or a vertical form between two horizontal ones.

Contrast of straight and curved lines. In addition to a variation and contrast in line direction, similar contrasting effects should be obtained in the character of the line. Straight lines should be relieved by curved lines. An excess of straight lines gives the room a stiff, uncomfortable look. An excess of curves produces a restless effect. Straight lines are produced by the architectural forms, by doors and windows, by square case furniture, and by panelling, pictures, and other rectangular pieces. Curved lines may be made by tying back the draperies, by introducing swags or other curves in valances, by arched forms for openings, by scroll and curved pediments and furniture tops, by curved or circular mirrors or picture frames, and by table tops and furniture with curved, serpentine, or bombé fronts.

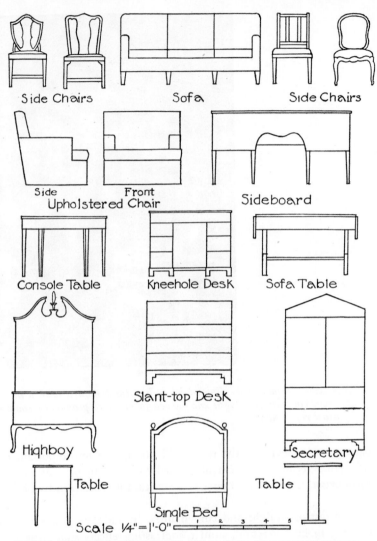

Side Chairs Sofa Side Chairs

Side Front
Upholstered Chair Sideboard

Console Table Kneehole Desk Sofa Table

Slant-top Desk

Highboy Secretary

Table Table

Single Bed

Scale ¼"=1'-0"

TYPICAL FURNITURE OUTLINES FOR USE IN WALL COMPOSITION STUDIES.

No rule can be made that would indicate exactly the number of straight or curved forms to introduce, but the artist will instinctively feel when an agreeable balance and contrast is reached, taking into consideration the degree of dignity or gaiety that he wishes to express. Straight lines, particularly horizontal ones, give one a feeling of repose. Curved lines produce the effect of movement and vivacity.

Surface contrasts. In addition to contrasts of line, there should be contrasts in surface treatments. Plain surfaces may contrast by the hues, tones and chromatic values of colors, or by patterns or texture. A room may be

Thedlow, Decorator; Emelie Danielson, Photographer

A library in the modern Neo-classic style, showing a nicely balanced wall com-position producing an effective background for two rare Italian primitive paintings.

treated throughout by plain wall and floor areas, and plain drapery and upholstery materials. The vitality of the room will depend upon the relative brilliance of the colors that are used; but, in the treatment of such a room, it is usually advisable to retain neutralized values with colors selected according to the rules of chromatic distribution. Where materials change, as with trim and plaster walls, it is usually advisable to change the color. With dark walls, the trim, if it deserves to be accented, may be painted the same hue in a slightly lighter tone or vice versa with light-colored walls.

Drapery treatments are part of the wall composition and the drapery materials should usually contrast with the walls by pattern, hue, or tone. Plain draperies when used with plain walls are quiet and dignified in effect. Patterned draperies are gayer in appearance. With patterned walls it is always advisable to use plain drapery materials that recall one of the colors in the pattern.

The same principle should be carried out in contrasting upholstery materials with floor coverings. Both may be plain for dignified effects, but should contrast by hue or tone. The use of patterned floor coverings in combination with patterned upholstery materials is confusing and tiring

McMillen, Decorator; Samuel H. Gottscho, Photographer

An oval room with a simple but unusual decorative treatment. The painting by Matisse, hung on a glass panel, and the combination of direct and indirect lighting are notable. The pale gray walls act as a foil for the red lacquered furniture.

In this connection, it is difficult to make rules that are inviolable. The experienced designer introduces such variations as may be of interest, but the beginner will find it safer to follow the traditional methods.

In the use of minor objects with pattern interest, such as ornamental screens and collections of colored ceramics, it is always best to place them against plain backgrounds.

Scale and proportion. The human eye, by habit, becomes accustomed to definite dimensions of certain objects in daily use. Some of these dimensions are fixed for human convenience, others for practical or economical reasons, and still others by chance. Everything is considered large or small by comparison only. In matters relating to design, forms that are larger than the average are spoken of as being large in scale. Scale, therefore, refers to the size of objects in comparison to the size customarily seen. The ordinary interior doorway is 7 feet high; one that is 8 feet high is large in scale. The average step is about 6 inches high, a chair seat is approximately 17 inches high, a human face averages 9½ inches from the chin to the top of the head and the average man is something under 6 feet in height. If any of these dimensions are larger either in nature or in reproductions, the object is said to be large in scale, and under reverse conditions, the object is small in scale.

Children's rooms are usually treated with undersized furniture and bright color accents. The composition and arrangement is often limited by small dimensions.

Samuel H. Gottscho, Photographer

In this small room, the pattern interest is limited to the lacquered chest and chintz slipcover, the colors of which are repeated in the wall and drapery.

The eye has unconsciously become accustomed to seeing the architectural orders in certain proportions. The cornice of an order averages about 7 per cent of the total height of a column and entablature; on a wall, a proportion close to this will be found to be a suitable one in designing a cornice for a room. In a room 9 feet high designed in a classical manner, the cornice should be approximately 6½ inches high. A variation from this dimension will make the cornice appear either large or small in scale.

There is a proper scale for everything used in a room, whether it be the architecture, the furniture, the accessories, the patterns, or the texture of objects. The decision as to the proper scale must come from the experienced eye, and it is of the utmost importance in good design and decoration.

Proportion is correlated to scale, but is a less technical term, and is frequently used in referring to the size and shape of forms and masses in relation to their ideal dimensions. One speaks of "good" and "bad" proportions.

It is not only necessary that all the details of room decoration should be in correct scale to the size of the room, but they should also be in proper relationship and proportion to each other. Small rooms should preferably be furnished in the smaller types of furniture, with consistent patterns for wallpapers and textiles. Large pieces of furniture are unsuitable to small rooms. Upholstery materials with large patterns are unsuitable to use on small chairs or for draping small windows. Small-scale objects in a large room look insignificant, and do not contribute to the composition. A careful consideration of the scale and proportion of every feature to be introduced in a room is an essential part of good decorating.

Quantity balance. It is necessary to study the correct quantity of furnishings and patterns used in any room. A room should never look overfurnished or underfurnished. Rooms that are crowded with details are confusing to live in. Excess of patterned surfaces produces the same result. There should be felt a definite need for every object placed in a room, so that if the object is removed, the space appears bare, with something obviously missing. With the tendency of contemporary designers to eliminate maintenance costs and labor of upkeep by building storage space in the walls, the furnishing of some rooms has been limited to a few seats and convenient tables crowded in one corner. This results in the room's appearing underfurnished, and does not seem to be taking advantage of the allotted space. Either the room should be smaller or it should have additional pieces. The distribution of furnishings should appear approximately equal throughout the floor area and all walls should be equally interesting. If it is possible, opposite walls should be composed along similar lines, or at least should have an equal degree of interest.

*A formal room arranged with a standard conversational grouping around the
fireplace. This distribution is always suitable to traditional types of decorating. The vertical and horizontal lines are nicely balanced and the
pattern interest is entirely in the wallpaper.*

*Symmetry is of little importance in contemporary interiors where function and
simplicity of treatment are paramount.*

Mary E. Dunn, Decorator of Nancy McClelland, Inc.

In this informal French adaptation the antique patterned wallpaper dominates the design. Plain draperies and textured rug are subordinated to the background and furnishings. Agreeable surface, textural, and line contrasts are introduced.

Résumé. The elements of wall composition that must be considered are given in the list below. With interest produced by proper contrasts, the artist must analyze his design and decide whether the suitable variations are carried out to the necessary degree for his purposes.

Reflection of personality
Functional considerations
Horizontal subdivisions
Vertical subdivisions
Line direction
Line character

Patterned and plain areas
Proper scale of all details
Desired symmetry
Balance of furniture distribution
Color balance
Harmony of furniture

CHAPTER XXIV

FURNITURE ARRANGEMENT

T he study of the arrangement of furniture is a problem of floor composition. It must be approached less from the point of view of line,
form, and mass than from practical considerations of convenience and
use. Common sense must be the guide in its solution. The changes that
have occurred in living, due to the shifting of economic standards in recent years, have affected both the number, size, and use of rooms, which,
in turn, have presented new problems in the study of space. The concentration of activities has required a distribution of furnishings that primarily answers efficiency of use, often at the sacrifice of appearance. At
the same time, the variety in the character of rooms, the preferences of
occupants, the choice of the traditional versus the new, and many other
important influences must be considered in any plan, and the decorator
must be prepared to offer the best.

There are many rooms that were formerly important in the average
home that have practically disappeared. The old fashioned parlor is never
seen and even the "salon" intended for the sole purpose of entertaining
is extremely rare. The average good-size dwelling or apartment of today
may contain a living room, dining room, master and children's bedrooms,
bathrooms, and a service portion. If the owner is sufficiently affluent, there
may be a guest-room, library, study, music room, nursery, recreation
room, sunroom, and minor accommodations such as dressing and powder
rooms. The reverse trend, however, is more common, in which rooms are
used for double and triple purposes. This has been carried to the ultimate
limit in the one-room apartment, in which living, sleeping, and eating
must be carried on with such flexibility as is possible in the daily requirements of a single individual or young married couple. It is not an uncertain prophecy to state that the modern eventually becomes traditional,
and it is impossible to turn the clock backwards. Efficiency is today more

important than outward appearances, and honesty in decoration has superseded theatrical effects.

The arrangement of furniture and equipment in business offices and commercial interiors presents so many special problems that its analysis must be excluded from a text of this character. It is even difficult to present principles of furniture arrangement for residential interiors that have universal application. The following suggestions, however, will be found of value in the traditional type of room:

1. Furniture should always be arranged with the purpose of the room uppermost in thought.
2. Individual pieces should be placed so that they are convenient, their use is obvious, and they are not interfered with by other pieces.
3. Pieces should be distributed for noninterference of circulation. Door openings and passageways should be kept free of obstruction.
4. Furniture should be placed in its relation to architectural or mechanical features, so that there is no interference with their operation. Attention should be given to the swing of doors, the opening of windows, and the operation of electrical or heating devices.
5. The location of movable pieces of furniture should be carefully studied for their compositional relationship to the fixed architectural features—doors, windows, built-in furniture, alcoves, niches, mantels, panelling, etc.
6. An agreeable balance of high and low pieces of furniture should be introduced and co-ordinated with high windows and doors and other fixed vertical and horizontal features.
7. The quantity of furniture should not give the effect of either underfurnishing or overcrowding.
8. The distribution of furniture should be relatively even. In a long room, one end should not appear crowded and the other bare, nor should one wall appear more crowded than the others.
9. If the plan permits, opposite walls should have similar groupings, or at least they should appear evenly balanced in quantity or interest.
10. Pictorial surfaces (scenic papers, mural decorations, tapestries, and large hanging pictures) should not be hidden by furnishings to a point that their visibility is marred.
11. Furniture should be related in scale to the size of the room. Small rooms, in general, should be furnished with details of refined design. Large pieces of furniture, creating heavy shadows or dark spots, are inadvisable except in large rooms.
12. Furniture placed with lines parallel to the walls creates greater unity than when placed in diagonal positions.
13. Some seats should always be located to take advantage of natural light and view (if any).
14. In general, the center of a room should be kept clear for circulation.

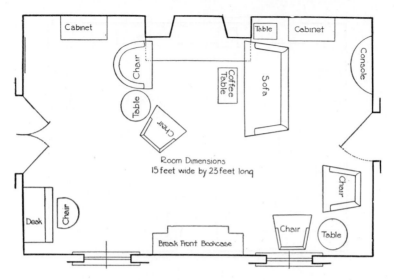

Room Dimensions
15 feet wide by 25 feet long

CONVENTIONAL METHOD OF INDICATING WALLS, WINDOWS, DOORS, MANTEL,
AND FURNITURE ARRANGEMENT.

The smaller a room, the more obvious becomes the furniture arrangement, because of the fewer possible choices of position for each piece. The small room, however, is unlikely to permit a perfect arrangement of furniture, as there is less opportunity for studied compositions, and, in placing the furniture, the decorator is often obliged to select the lesser of two evils.

Living rooms. A living room must today fulfill many functions. It must be planned for many activities formerly associated with the parlor, salon, withdrawing room, or library. The family use it as a common meeting place, and in it receive friends in either formal or informal manner, but it is often used for reading, game-playing, lounging, home-study, music and television, conversation, working, bookkeeping, and other purposes. It must be flexible for both parents and children; arranged for father to interview business acquaintances, mother to receive club guests, daughter to develop romance, and the young people to roll back the rug and rollick to the latest Latin-American dance rhythms. To accomplish all these ends, the dominant notes must be simplicity, avoidance of a cluttered appearance, careful location of permanent or heavy seats, and the maintenance of a clear area in the center of the room.

The average room requires a "conversational group," usually consisting of as large a sofa as the floor space will permit, and two comfortable seats arranged with necessary tables for placing refreshments, smoking supplies, books, and, perhaps, lamps. There may be additional comfortable chairs for resting and one located with proper natural or artificial light

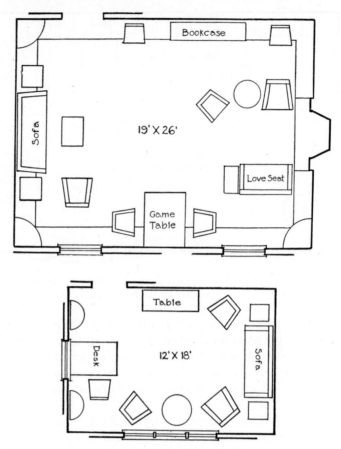

EXAMPLES OF FURNITURE ARRANGEMENT IN TWO LIVING ROOMS OF DIFFERING
SHAPE AND SIZE.

for reading. The majority of living rooms require one table of good size
or a desk for working and writing, and either a built-in or movable bookcase. There should always be several lightweight chairs that may easily be
moved for special occasions, and in traditional rooms, console or wall
tables may be added for useful or decorative effect to cover wall surfaces
that appear bare.

The tendency in contemporary design has been to build in much of
the furniture. Long seats, bookcases, and storage shelving have become
part of the architecture of the room, resulting in fewer movable pieces and
a less crowded appearance. The adherents of this theory claim benefits in
room flexibility and savings in cost of upkeep and cleaning. The question
resolves itself into a matter of taste and personal preferences.

A tentative arrangement of furniture should be considered from the point of view of wall composition, but changes should be considered to co-ordinate this with the practical location of floor pieces.

Generally speaking the location of the largest pieces of furniture should be first considered and the others according to their respective sizes. The placing of a large sofa, forming a part of the conversational group, must nearly always be the first decision. In rooms that are over 13 feet wide, this may be placed at the side of a mantel, vertical to the wall and faced with comfortable chairs or a similar sofa in conjunction with utility tables. In narrower rooms it is usually necessary to place a sofa with its back to the wall and flank it by chairs facing each other. Only in a very large room where ample floor space exists should a sofa face a mantel. In rooms of irregular or long shapes or those in which no mantel exists, it is often most convenient to keep a corner or an end of a room for the conversational group, leaving the rest of the area free for other activities. Only in very large rooms may two conversational groups be introduced, although a secondary minor group may sometimes be located so that the seats may be easily added to the main group. If such space exists it is usually preferable to use it for furniture intended for other activities. Sofas do not have to be a central feature of the furniture arrangement. Diagonal positions of any long pieces of furniture are usually inadvisable. Angular or curved sofas are best located in corners. Sofas, being long and low, may often form an agreeable wall composition with flanking high pieces of furniture or vertical windows, and a picture, mirror, or other wall decoration hung above.

Tables should be used only where there is a functional need for them; and they should be of a size, shape, and height that suits their purpose. A table that is larger than necessary wastes floor space. There should be a table near all large upholstered seats for holding books, and smoking or refreshment accessories. Writing table-desks may be placed with their short side to a wall near a window for better natural illumination, and should have a suitable lamp with an opaque shade. Console tables or cabinets serve a decorative as well as useful purpose and are generally placed against wall panels; ornaments or standing lamps or objects hung on the wall above them should be related in scale and composition to flanking features. Game tables of the folding-leg type are best for storage when not in use. Permanent game tables should not be used unless essential.

A piano presents a problem in the decorative treatment of any room. It is required when there is a musical member of the family, but is not a contribution to appearances. In an average room there is generally little choice for its location. It is usually advisable to place a piano in a part of the room that is least suitable for other groupings. Grand pianos are preferable to uprights for their musical quality. Practical considerations sug-

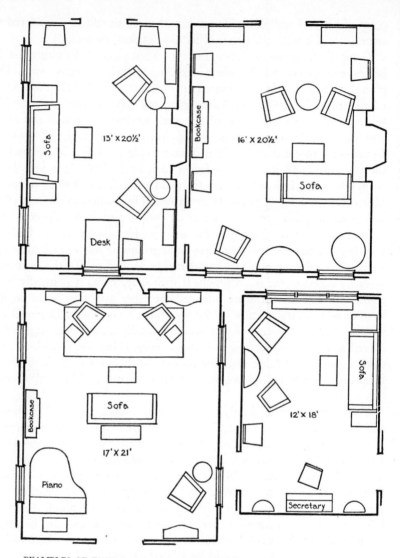

EXAMPLES OF FURNITURE ARRANGEMENTS FOR LIVING ROOMS OF VARIOUS
SHAPES AND SIZES.

gest that the keyboard and music rack should receive natural light if possible. The right side of a grand piano should be placed toward the audience or the center of the room, so that the lid may be opened in the proper direction. The curve on the right side also gives more space to the room. The spinet models are satisfactory for amateurs, but the shortened wires, fewer octaves, and reduced sounding boards make them unsuitable for serious music, and while they may be used when space is lacking, they are not more decorative than the large models. Piano cases should always be functional in design and should never show period detail. The use of antique pianos, spinets, or harpsichords that have lost their musical quality should not be countenanced.

Mechanical musical instruments, radios, and television sets may be given the importance in location that an owner attaches to them. Their value, however, is their sound and screen view, and if possible the machinery case should be inconspicuously located, or built in a wall or closet. The majority of stock cabinets furnished for such machines do not contribute to a tasteful scheme.

Bookcases may be part of the wall composition or may be free standing. They are usually among the larger furnishings of a room and their location should be considered before the small pieces. A detail often overlooked is the decorative effect that may be obtained with books. Those bound in bright colors with gold tooling or titles, have the same decorative interest as a mural decoration or painting. Drab or dilapidated books have quite the opposite effect. The preservation of fine books requires the use of glass doors for bookcases, especially in cities where dust is collected, but the use of glass dulls the decorative effect of the books, and causes a disagreeable reflection of light. In bookcases that are built in the wall, the lower shelf should be about 2 feet 6 inches from the floor, with a closed cabinet underneath. In rooms under 9 feet in height the shelves should be carried to the ceiling or to the underside of the cornice. In high rooms the top shelf of built-in bookshelves is often placed at hand-reach level. Small shelves for books of current use are often inserted in cabinets, under table tops, in wall panels, and wherever a convenient place can be found.

On pages 778 and 780 are shown layouts for several living rooms of different sizes and shapes. In each one, the view of the mantel is comparatively free, and a conversational grouping of chairs and sofas has been assembled about the most important feature. Free circulating space has been considered, and the walls balance symmetrically, when possible. The principles indicated in these arrangements may be followed in the majority of living rooms.

Dining rooms. In the average rectangular dining room, there are two pieces of furniture that are commonly arranged in standard positions. The table is customarily placed in the center of the room, and the sideboard is placed in the center of one of the long walls. If there is a mantel, a balance may be obtained by placing the sideboard directly opposite. The sideboard or dresser is generally the most important piece of furniture in the room, and should be a center of interest. The display of silver, fruit, or flowers on the top of a sideboard should be restrained, and only unusually interesting china, pewter, or silver should be displayed on shelving or dresser. The serving table should be placed near the door to the pantry. A screen

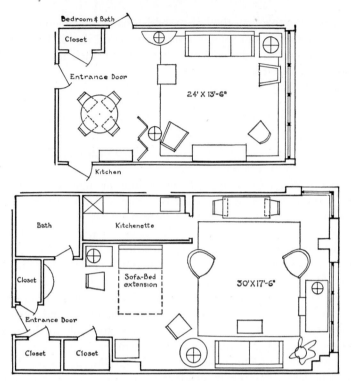

EXAMPLES OF FURNITURE ARRANGEMENTS IN TYPICAL DOUBLE-PURPOSE
ROOMS.

may be used to partially hide the pantry door if desired. With the modern
tendency of subordinating dining space by the use of alcoves and niches,
or by using the end of a living room near the door to the service portion,
there have been numerous designs and inventions introduced for space-
saving and eliminating the cost of a special room for dining that is used
only a part of the time. The most economical is the dining table that folds
upward into a wall panel. The wall panel may contain shelves and crockery, or it may be an opening into a kitchen for passing food to the diners.
In small houses a shelf is often arranged in an opening in the partition
between dining area and kitchen. A sliding panel closes the opening when
not in use. Dining areas may be separated from the living portions of a
room by sliding or folding walls or wooden curtains hung from a ceiling
track, or by high storage cabinets.

There is a considerable choice in the shapes of dining room tables. The
square or rectangular top is usually more pleasing in appearance, but the
circular form is more flexible to use. Center pedestal legs are more convenient for the sitters, but they do not have the decorative value of corner
ones. Gate-leg tables may be used where the style permits, but their sup-

ports interfere with the comfort of those seated. Dining tables vary in width from 24 to 54 inches.

All dining room chairs should be practical and strongly built. They are forced to stand much wear and handling and they should be covered with a material that can be cleaned easily. Armchairs may be used at table ends if desired.

Bedrooms. If a bedroom has been properly designed by the architect, there should be only one place for the location of a double bed—the center of a wall. Single beds may be placed with either their headboards or their sides against the wall. The latter position will often appear to give a greater amount of unoccupied floor space. Several practical points should, if possible, be taken into consideration in locating a bed. It is better for a person not to face a window when lying down; and proper ventilation should be obtainable without a direct draught on the sleeper. If the room is small, it is better to place a bed so that it does not divide the room in two, but leaves what vacant space there is at one end or one side. If the bed is ornamental in character and space is sufficient, it should be placed so that on entering the room one may obtain a direct view of the headboard, rather than the side of the bed. Twin beds, if parallel, should be placed at least 16 inches apart, or they may be hinged to a single headboard and furnished with wheels so that they can be swung at an angle for convenience in making the bedclothes.

Style in bed design is as varied as in the design of any other kind of furniture. The four-poster was designed to carry the canopy and curtains that were essential for warmth and comfort. The French often placed their beds in alcoves, over which curtains were drawn at night. In many cases an alcove was actually built around a bed, and closets were introduced at its side to fill the occupied space. In others, a large crown or canopy was placed high upon the wall over the center of the bed; from this hung curtains that were drawn back during the day.

There is a modern tendency to give less decorative importance to headboards and footboards. Many decorators prefer to omit these entirely, using only a box spring and mattress supported on a wooden or textile-covered framework. The decorative effect is obtained by featuring a handsome bedcover and ornamental pillows or a draped canopy or wall mirror.

The bureau, dresser, chiffonier, or chifforobe may be placed where convenient, applying as far as possible the rules of wall composition. A night table next to the bed, for lamps or books, a comfortable chair, small chairs, and a chaise-longue or sofa should be used, if possible. Separate dressing rooms with dressing tables, cabinets, closets, drawers, and other storage spaces are always advisable, if space permits.

Halls. The furnishing of an entrance hall, foyer, or stair hall depends entirely upon the size of the space to be furnished. Sometimes such a room is merely a landing for the stairs or an inside vestibule with coat closets; while in a large house this room may be of the utmost importance. In the latter case, the rules to follow in its furnishing are much the same as for the living room, except that there is usually a little less of the personal touch. It is more in the nature of a reception room, where less intimate visitors may be entertained.

When the entrance hall is very small, as it often is in city apartments, a small table and mirror may fill all the space that is not used for passage. Coat and hat racks or hooks and cane and umbrella stands should be in closets. The entrance hall of the average residence generally permits a symmetrical grouping of chairs and one or two ornamental pieces of furniture. It is often convenient to use a wall or console table for this purpose; if the hall is of sufficient size, a large sofa may also be introduced. Above the console table may be placed a picture, mirror, or other hanging.

The secondary rooms. The treatment of libraries, sunrooms, porches, nurseries, recreation rooms, boudoirs, dressing rooms, and powder rooms is a matter of selecting furnishings suitable to the purpose of the room and arranging these according to the principles of wall composition and convenience.

A library is intended for the storage of books and conveniences for reading, writing, and studying. It is advisable to have built-in bookshelves if possible, and the best arrangement is to place them above low cabinets. Shelving should be carried to the ceiling in most cases. If the ceiling is too high, cabinets for unused documents may be built above the reach level. Bookshelves should not be so long that they sag when filled. They should be about ¾ inch thick, and not over 3 feet long. Lighting arrangements should be made so that titles may be easily read. A writing or study desk and a reading chair or two should be located near daylight, with proper lights for evening use. A sofa and tables for magazines and for smoking and drinking equipment should be used, if there is space. The accessories, such as pictures or ornaments, should reflect the interests of the owner. Literary prints, autographs, maps, etchings, and other pictures of either serious or humorous character may be used.

The sunroom is intended primarily to take advantage of the sun on cold winter days. It also gives an opportunity to bring part of the garden into the house when outdoor living is inclement. Southern exposure is taken for granted, and the profuse use of winter plants and flowers is logical. Sunrooms should be treated informally, with permanent floors in tile, brick, or linoleum. Inexpensive waterproof floor coverings may be used. The furniture may be limited to seating accommodations and small tables. Lounging furniture and dining and game tables are usually introduced. Garden furniture in metal, wicker, and reed is suitable, and upholstered furniture covered with informal or waterproof materials is always attractive. If there is a view through the sunroom windows, the furniture should be arranged to take advantage of this feature.

The nursery and child's playroom is intended for many uses. It sometimes serves for eating and sleeping as well as for playing, and a careful layout of both built-in features and movable furniture is essential. Decorations may be of a comparatively temporary and inexpensive type, since changes will be necessary as the child grows. In the furniture arrangement, every advantage should be taken of the sunlight, and the storage shelves and cabinets should be placed in the darker portions of the room. The room should be planned so that there will be a proper place for all toys or equipment, to impress the child with system and order. Simplicity in all features, and plain, washable surfaces and materials are essential. The scale of everything in the room should be suited to the child's age. The principal decorative interest of a child's room should be in color, although suitable patterns may also be used to a limited degree. Excess of pattern is just as fatiguing to the young person as it is to the adult.

The recreation room should be furnished with strong, durable furniture, and the general treatment of the room should lend itself to easy care and cleaning. Cheerfulness, gaiety, and humor—and theatrical effect, if desired—may be expressed in the decoration. There should be ample storage space for the equipment of the various indoor and outdoor games, pastimes, and hobbies of interest to the family. What furniture outside of game equipment is used should be for comfort and rest. This is an especially adaptable room for the radio or television set.

Dressing rooms and powder rooms are primarily rooms for utilitarian purposes. Usually small, they should contain every convenience required in their use. Triple mirrors, dressing tables, closets, comfortable chairs or sofas, and ample illumination are necessities. Since they are for temporary use, they may be gay in character, but should not be too personal.

Studying furniture arrangement. A perfect arrangement of furniture, entirely suitable to the purposes of a room and satisfactorily fulfilling all requirements, is frequently an impossibility because of some local condition or because of the shape of the room. It is often necessary to balance one evil against another, and the decorator must use his own judgment as to which is the lesser.

When a decorator wishes to study the possibilities of furniture arrangement in a room, the best method is to lay out on a piece of paper the floor plan of the room, giving the exact dimensions in all directions. This is generally done at a scale of ¼ inch to 1 foot. A distance of 1 inch on the plan is then the equivalent of 4 feet. The windows and doors must be correctly located, and the correct width marked upon the plan. It is also customary to show the direction of the swing of doors, or of casement windows if these are used. This is important, so that space may be left

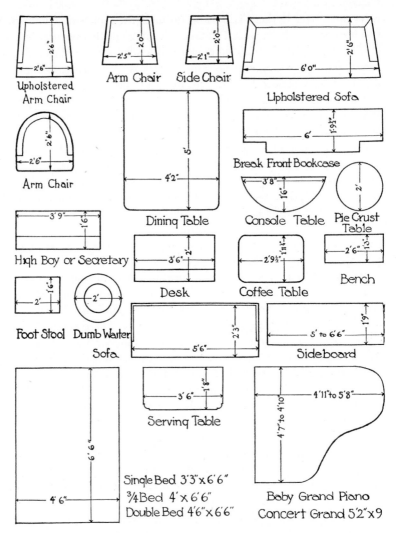

Upholstered Arm Chair

Arm Chair Side Chair

Upholstered Sofa

Arm Chair

Dining Table

Break Front Bookcase

Console Table

Pie Crust Table

High Boy or Secretary

Desk

Coffee Table

Bench

Foot Stool Dumb Waiter

Sofa

Sideboard

Serving Table

Single Bed 3'3" x 6'6"
¾ Bed 4' x 6'6"
Double Bed 4'6" x 6'6"

Baby Grand Piano
Concert Grand 5'2" x 9

CONVENTIONAL METHOD FOR INDICATING FURNITURE IN PLAN FOR STUDYING
FURNITURE ARRANGEMENTS. SCALE: 4 FEET EQUALS 1 INCH.

for the doors or windows to open without interfering with the furniture. A typical floor plan made on this scale is shown on page 777. The furniture may be indicated by small pieces of cardboard which may be moved around at will until the most suitable arrangement is decided upon. In drawing the furniture for this purpose, it is only necessary to indicate the shape and size of the floor area that each piece of furniture would cover. The pieces of cardboard may then be marked with the names of the pieces of furniture that they are intended to indicate. After a satisfactory arrangement of the furniture has been decided upon, a pencil line may be drawn on the plan around each piece of cardboard, thus producing a permanent sketch.

The advantage of a study of this kind is in the fact that it not only solves a furniture arrangement, but indicates the number and kinds of pieces that will be required and their dimensions. There are many types of furniture, such as dining tables, bookcases, cabinets, and sofas, that vary greatly in the size of different models. A furniture plan as above outlined is the most convenient method of finding the dimensions that will be suitable for particular cases.

CHAPTER XXV

COLOR AND COLOR SCHEMES

The source of color. Science has proved that all color comes from rays of light. The white rays of sunlight may be separated as they are in the rainbow or mechanically subdivided by a prismatic lens giving a colored band called a spectrum. (The dominant *spectral colors* in the rainbow are usually called violet, indigo, blue, green, yellow, orange, and red; but there are many intermediate hues.) Conversely, a combination of all spectral colors produces white. This does not hold true for paint colors; when paint colors corresponding to the spectral colors are mixed, the result is a dark gray.

Each material in nature has the capacity of absorbing one or more of the subdivisions of a ray of white light. The rays that are not absorbed are reflected to the human eye, and the object then is said to be the color of the nonabsorbed rays. A leaf, for example, absorbs the red rays and reflects only the blue and yellow rays, making it appear green. An exception is seen in the chemical compounds known as *white lead,* zinc white, and titanium, which absorb no rays and therefore reflect all the rays of light causing them to appear white to the human eye. Carbon or soot from a wick flame absorbs all the rays and therefore appears black. If in a dark room, a red light is thrown on a green leaf, the leaf will absorb the red light. Since there are no blue or yellow rays thrown upon it, the leaf will reflect no rays but will appear black, even though the surrounding areas may appear red. If a white light is thrown on the leaf it will appear green, reflecting the blue and yellow rays contained in the light.

Rays coming from artificial light have the same general characteristics as those coming from the sun, except that they are but an infinitesimal fraction of the sun's rays in strength.

The sun's rays have other characteristics besides those of color. The most important of these are the heat-rays, which increase toward the red end of the spectrum. Fortunately, the atmosphere absorbs and tempers many of these rays; otherwise, habitation on the earth would be unbearable. The sun's rays are hottest when the atmosphere is of least depth. Since the sun is directly above us in summer, its rays then reach us through the shortest distance of atmospheric depth; but in winter the sun is at a low angle, and its rays penetrate a greater atmospheric depth, giving us a lower temperature. Red and yellow light rays are stimulating and promote life and growth in nature. The sun's rays also contain an actinic property that causes chemical changes. The blue, violet, and green rays affect the photographic plate, cause skin to tan and textiles and paint to fade. They are the destructive rays of sunlight, preventing growth and causing disintegration. The peculiar distribution of these rays explains the apparent inconsistencies in the values and effects of various colors in the photograph. A shade of yellow or red will photograph much darker in appearance than a blue of similar strength. Other properties in light rays are brought to practical use in motion picture sound films, in the X ray, in electronics, and in the mechanics of radio activity.

The color problem in interior decoration. A knowledge of the original source of color is useful to the colorist in helping him realize the importance and influence of light upon any color scheme he may develop for a particular purpose.

The decorator produces his color scheme by using objects or surfaces in natural color, such as woodwork and marble; or materials, the colors of which have been selected by the manufacturer and are limited in range, such as in porcelains, textiles, and wallpapers; or surfaces that are to be colored by paint, stains, or dyes for which the decorator has an unlimited range of selection. The problem is to select colors to develop a harmony that will be pleasing in appearance and produce a desired psychological and emotional reaction upon those who observe it, and one that will be suitable for the purposes of the room and co-related to the amount and quality of the natural or artificial light that is available. Many attempts have been made to reduce the principles of color harmony to a formula by means of charts. These have been found to be of limited value to the decorator. Charts are not used by experienced artists, and their use by the beginner has the danger of preventing development of ability in color selection by methods of reasoning and visual reactions. Designers of textiles, wallpapers, and posters may sometimes use charts for preliminary tests of color combinations because in such designs colors are used in comparatively small areas and are visualized in the same light. The decorator has a more complicated problem, inasmuch as colors used in a room are on surfaces that stand at a variety of angles, vary in texture, and receive different degrees and character of light. There are too many considerations that a decorator has to meet to permit the use of a limited mechanical chart in the selection of a color scheme. Interior decorators must use a set of guiding principles that will enable them to accentuate the desired character of the room, and contribute to its functions and the psychological satisfaction of its occupants.

Color characteristics. Pigment colors have four characteristics. These are known as *hue, chroma, tonal value,* and *finish. Hue* refers to the color itself, such as red, blue, yellow, green, etc. The hue is the same whether it is a light or dark variation or a dull or brilliant one; pink is a red hue; lavender is a purple hue. Chroma or *chromatic value* refers to the relative degree of intensity, brilliancy, or saturation that exists in a color. A ripe tomato is a red hue of a brilliant chroma; the majority of flowers are in colors of brilliant chromatic values. A brilliant pigment may be dulled or neutralized until it becomes almost a gray by adding to it a pigment of the color that is directly opposite to it on a standard color wheel. If this is done in specific amounts, one obtains definite steps or degrees of neutralization of that color. The most neutral step is very close to a gray that has been slightly tinged by the original color, and it is possible to arrange a row of samples of any hue, each of which is slightly more or less brilliant in chroma than its adjoining one.* If a color sample chart of this type is made, showing stepped or graded examples of a hue between gray and its most brilliant state, the steps can be numbered or lettered in an arbitrary but consecutive manner for purposes of convenience, and the series shows the degrees of neutrality of that particular hue. The various pigment colors cannot all be divided in exactly the same number of chromatic values or degrees of neutrality because some are lighter than others. The most brilliant yellow is very light compared to the most brilliant blue or red, and the former neutralizes very rapidly so that the same number of steps of neutralization is not possible. *Tonal value,* sometimes merely called *tone* or *value,* is the relative degree of lightness between an *off-white* and an *off-black* of any hue. A pink is a light tonal value of red, an ivory is a light tonal value of yellow or orange, and a brown is a dark tonal value of orange. Light tonal values are often called *tints* and dark values are often called *shades.* Tonal values of any hue may be graded arbitrarily in relatively even steps between the extremes of white and black. *Finish* is a quality of pigment colors and refers to the presence or absence of a luster, gloss, sheen, glaze, or other light reflection of a surface. In the absence of a glossy surface, the finish is called *mat.* Metals such as gold and silver, silk textiles, enamel paints, and glazed ceramics reflect light rays, and the portion of the surface upon which the ray shines appears a different color from the portion that does not come directly within the reflection of the light ray.

* This is an arrangement resembling the notes of a piano scale, which are sounds that have been standardized for convenience. Intervening sounds exist, but cannot be played on a piano and are considered unnecessary for most types of music. The stringed instruments such as the violin can produce the so-called quarter tones.

The *complement* of any hue is the hue or combination of hues that is lacking in the original color to produce the complete range of colors in the spectrum. In a Color Wheel, complements are always shown in sectors directly opposite to each other. A simplified example is as follows:

Hue	Hue(s) forming complement	Complement
Red	Blue and yellow	Green
Orange	Blue	Blue
Yellow	Red and blue	Violet
Green	Red	Red
Blue	Red and yellow	Orange
Violet	Yellow	Yellow

Colors also have certain commonly accepted qualities, the origin of which may have a scientific basis, or may be due solely to mental association. Orange and its adjacent colors are known as *warm,* and their use in decoration contributes to the warmth, gaiety, and cheerfulness of a room. These colors may be used in rooms with northern exposures to give the effect of sunshine. Blue and its adjacent colors are *cool* and are supposed to be advantageous in counteracting excess warmth or sunshine, although this would seem to be only a psychological condition. Certain colors are called *distant* or *receding;* these are the light tonal values in general and the variations of greens, blues, and violets, colors that are recommended for small rooms to give the effect of larger space. Other colors are considered *near* or *approaching;* these include those of dark tonal values and particularly the derivations of red and orange. As green is the middle color of the spectrum, it is considered to have the most restful effect of any hue. This quality has caused its use in hospital rooms.

The term *subtle* is often used in describing a color; it is applied to grayed variations of mixed primary hues that sometimes appear to change color under different lighting or conditions. One is not always sure of their ingredients. The word, as applied to color, is in popular use, but has no scientific application.

The strong chromatic values of all hues are more exciting and fatiguing in their effect than those that are neutralized. A restful effect is obtained best by the use of grayed values on large plain areas and mild tonal contrasts in patterned surfaces. In general more satisfactory results in decoration are obtained by using mixed colors rather than the pure primary pigments: red, yellow, and blue.

Classification of colors. An infinite number of colors can be produced with pigments by combining red, blue, yellow, black, and white in varying proportions; but, there are, in practice, only 24 basic hues of full chromatic value with a sufficient variation to be perceptible to the eye. When hues are neutralized the adjoining colors often cannot be differentiated.

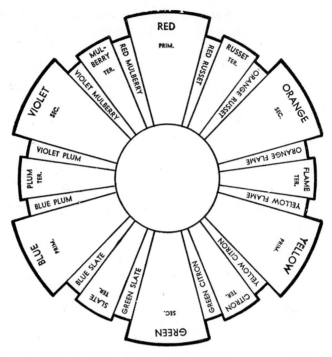

Color wheel showing the 24 basic colors in their proper relationship. Colors that are complementary are opposite each other. This arrangement is for the mixture of pigment colors only. Colors from light-rays vary in their complements from those shown above. The arrangement is for hues of full chroma or equal tonal value. Each hue is subject to an infinite number of neutralized gradations toward both white and black. The wide segments indicate the primaries and secondaries; the medium sized segments indicate the tertiaries and the smallest segments indicate the quaternaries.

Since each of the basic hues can be neutralized to at least 40 noticeable and different tints or shades, there are about 1,000 different and easily distinguishable colors available to the decorator.

The 24 basic hues may be divided into what are termed *primaries, secondaries, tertiaries,* and *quaternaries.* These divisions, indicated on the color wheel above, are as follows:

3 Primaries: Blue, red, and yellow.

3 Secondaries: A combination of any two primaries:

> Violet, a combination of blue and red
> Orange, a combination of red and yellow
> Green, a combination of yellow and blue

6 Tertiaries: A combination of a secondary color with any additional quantity of one of its constituent primaries. The generally accepted designations are:

> Plum or blue violet
> Mulberry or red violet
> Russet or red orange
> Flame or yellow orange
> Citron or yellow green
> Slate or blue green

12 Quaternaries: A combination of a tertiary with either its constituent primary or secondary. There are no standardized names for these intermediate hues and they vary only slightly from their adjoining hues. They may best be designated by coupling the name of the tertiary with its additional admixture, such as blue plum, violet plum, yellow citron, greenish citron, etc.

One may, in theory, continue indefinitely the combinations in varying proportions of these 24 basic hues, but the results would differ so slightly that for practical purposes they may be disregarded. It should be noted, however, that it is only possible to combine colors that are close to each other on the color wheel to produce another color of strong chromatic value. If opposite colors are combined, they neutralize each other and the result will approach a gray.

Other colors with which a decorator has to deal are the grays. These can be produced either by mixing the three primary pigments in approximately equal quantity, or by combining black and white in various amounts to produce different tonal values of gray. In mixing the three primaries with white, it will be found almost impossible to prevent one of the colors from dominating, and this is particularly noticeable in the lighter tints, so that each gray will differ slightly in hue. White is of course extensively used by decorators, but usually in an off-white tint. Pure white is rather glaring. White harmonizes with almost any combination of stronger hues. Black should be used with discretion. It is best employed in generally dark color schemes where its strongly contrasting value does not make it too striking. It can be used in small areas, such as trimmings, edgings, weltings, and ornaments, to accentuate the adjoining hues.

Discrepancies between theory and practice. The three pigments red, blue, and yellow, when combined in paint colors will produce a dark gray. Two of them mixed in approximately equal quantities will produce other definite colors (orange, green, or violet). But if the third is added, the original combination will become neutralized or approach a gray. This is what is termed neutralization by a complement, and each step toward gray is called a degree of neutrality of the color. Neutralization by means of a complement will tend to darken the tonal value so that it is almost always necessary to add some white if the same tonal value is required. This method of neutralization tends to maintain the chromatic strength of a color to a greater extent than by adding a gray or black pigment as described below. It is for this reason often preferred by artists. Since practically all house paints are pigments added to white lead as a base, this causes them to become tints, and, as a general rule, tints are used for the great majority of interior color schemes.

Pigment colors may also be neutralized by the addition of gray, black, or white. Black pigment should be used sparingly in neutralizing pigment colors, since it has the darkest chroma of all and tends to submerge the chromatic value of the other hues very rapidly. Some gray and black pigments contain a small amount of blue. When they are mixed with yellow they have a tendency to produce a greenish hue. To counteract this, a small amount of orange—the complement of blue—must be added to the mixture. When gray or black is mixed with red, the red will sometimes turn purplish. Yellow or orange must then be added. Browns, which are made most simply by mixing orange with black, may turn yellowish or reddish, depending upon which color dominates in the particular orange pigment used. A small amount of blue may be added to a brown mixture, but too much will cause the warmth of the brown to disappear.

Because the chemical constituents of pigments differ, the mixing of paint colors does not always work out in practice as the theory would indicate. There are, for instance, many different blue pigments, some having a slight tinge of green and others having a slight tinge of red. The mixture of these tinges with a second color would give a slightly different result. The only accurate method of obtaining desired hues by mixing different colored pigments is by trial and error and the correction of unwanted tinges by adding their complements.

As colors are increasingly neutralized they become more harmonious with each other, because they gradually approach the same color, i.e., white, black, or gray. The degree of neutralization in colors that are to be used in close proximity is a matter for the judgment of the artist, who must take into account the color effect he wishes to produce. He must avoid monotony, but introduce relief and variety only to a point where they do not begin to fatigue. *There is no more important point for the decorator to keep in mind in planning color schemes for rooms than the analysis of the degree of neutralization of the colors that he intends to use.* The combination of large areas of colors having strong chromatic values in interior color schemes invariably become offensive and tiresome.

Color terminology. The most confusing detail in the study and use of color is in finding a method for naming the hues and their variations of chroma and tone, by which one can intelligently convey in words a reasonably accurate idea of what color the speaker has in mind. The number of colors that can be produced by mixing pigments is unlimited and no complete standardization of names is possible, and one cannot carry an exact color in one's mind. The names of colors convey slightly different impressions to every one and even manufacturers' pigments using the similar designations vary greatly in hue.

There are several common systems for naming colors, but all are arbitrary, and, in spite of the fact that an infinite number of colors exists in nature, the colors used in commerce and art probably do not exceed several hundred. In addition to the popular systems of color designation, there have been several organized for standardizing names, and these, though not official, are practical and have been accepted by many of the largest business organizations in the United States. The popular systems are three in number and are as follows:

1. Using the names of the common hues such as red, blue, yellow, orange, green, purple, etc., and designating a dominant tinge if necessary (reddish or grayish purple) or associating an adjective or the word tint or shade. (Light tint of green, pale green, shade of dark bluish green, etc.)

2. Using a romantic name for sales purposes or popular appeal, by using the names of flowers, fruits, gems, and other natural objects, or using French names. (Plum, orange, rose, amber, emerald, cerise, beige, taupe, etc.)

3. Using the name of a painter's pigment. (Ultramarine, Sienna, Ochre, Vermilion, Van Dyck Brown, etc.) See Chapter XV on Paints and Painting.

There are two major commercial systems of color identification, the promoters of which publish color charts that organize the spectrum into a fixed number of hues, and show a reasonable number of the chromatic and tonal values of each. The systems are known by the names of their creators, Munsell and Ostwald. The color charts have become standardized and are extensively used throughout Europe and America. Instead of a name, there is an identification number or letter applied to each color, which if learned conveys reasonably well a mental image of each hue and its tone and chroma. These systems have nothing to do with methods of harmonizing colors, but are only for establishing specific color designations.

The most frequent romantic terms used by decorators for color designations are given below:

Absinthe	Amber gray	Apple green	Ashes of roses
Adam green	American beauty	Apricot	Aquamarine
Amber	Amethyst	Ash gray	Aubergine

Bay	Cucumber	Moss green	Rose pink
Beige	Delft blue	Mulberry	Rose pompadour
Blue	Dusty pink	Navy blue	Royal purple
Bottle green	Ecru	Nile green	Ruby
Brick red	Eggplant	Nutmeg	Russet
Brown	Eggshell	Ochre	Salmon
Buff	Fawn	Off-white	Sapphire
Burgundy	Flame	Olive green	Scarlet
Café-au-lait	Flesh pink	Oyster white	Shell pink
Canary	French gray	Parchment	Silver gray
Candy pink	Garnet	Pea soup	Sky blue
Celadon	Havana	Peach	Slate
Cerise	Heliotrope	Pearl gray	Smoke gray
Chartreuse	Henna	Periwinkle	Stone gray
Chestnut	Indigo	Pink	Tan
Chinese red	Jade green	Plum	Tangerine
Chocolate	Juniper	Pomegranate	Taupe
Citron	Lavender	Pompeian red	Tête-de-negre
Colonial blue	Lettuce	Powder blue	Tobacco
Colonial yellow	Lilac	Primrose	Turquoise
Copper	Lime	Pure gray	Verdigris
Coral	Maroon	Putty	Verdure
Cream	Mauve	Red-pepper	Violet
Crimson	Mimosa	Robin's-egg blue	Wedgwood blue

The Munsell system of color designation. The Munsell system is perhaps most practical for decorators' use and is described herewith:

The various hues of spectrum colors are arranged in a Color Wheel, each hue being indicated in its most brilliant chroma near the outside circumference of the wheel. The hues are then neutralized in graded steps toward the center of the wheel, until they all approach a neutral gray circle at the center. There are ten superimposed wheels, arranged according to 10 steps of tonal values, the darkest at the bottom (black), and the lightest at the top (white). Each wheel limits its colors to those of a single tonal value.

The regular editions of the *Munsell Book of Color* * contain 40 hues, each showing tonal values from 2 to 8 with their corresponding chroma scales. These are not subdivided into primaries, secondaries, tertiaries, etc., as described in this text, so that it becomes necessary to make an arbitrary selection to correlate them with the triangular subdivision of red,

* Published by the Munsell Color Co., Baltimore, Md. Student charts are also available and will be found extremely useful for all students of decoration. In ordering ask for N.Y.S.I.D. Standard Charts of primaries, secondaries, and tertiaries. These are furnished with unmounted chips, but instructors should have a mounted set which the students may use as a model. Mounted sets are available, but are considerably more expensive.

blue, and yellow, and their combinations in creating a 12- or 24-hue color-wheel. A 12-hue color wheel (primary, secondary and tertiary hues) that is light in tonal value (Munsell value 7) and gray in chroma value (Munsell value 2) can be set up as follows:

Common color name (N.Y.S.I.D. Standard)	Munsell color number	Munsell hue name	Munsell initial indication
Red	5	Red	R
Russet	10	Red Yellow-Red	RY-R
Orange	15	Yellow Red	YR
Flame	20	Yellow-Red Yellow	Y-RY
Yellow	25	Yellow	Y
Citron	35	Green-Yellow	GY
Green	45	Green	G
Slate	60	Blue-Green Blue	B-GB
Blue	70	Blue Purple-Blue	BP-B
Plum	80	Purple-Blue Purple	P-BP
Violet	85	Purple	P
Mulberry	92.5	purplish Red-Purple	pR-P

Student charts are obtainable for each of the above hues. There are spaces for seven of the tonal values on each hue chart. Black is 1, off-black 2, off-white 9, and white 10, the intervening tones being numbered from 3 to 8 inclusive. The chromatic values are shown for each hue at each tonal value; the second chromatic value is an off-gray, and the brilliancy increases in even steps as far as available pigments will permit. The brilliant chroma colors are indicated by the high numbers 10, 12, 14, etc. The indication for each sample chip is marked in the manner of a fraction, such as $2/6$, which indicates the 2nd tonal value and 6th chromatic value of a particular hue. The light tones are placed at the top of each chart, the dark tones at the bottom. The grayed chromas are placed at the left side in a vertical line and those of increasing brilliance toward the right.

There are many advantages in using an orderly system of color samples. Other colors can be easily recorded by comparing them to the chips. The graded chips are also useful in classifying colors under any illumination as light or dark, neutral or strong, or as light and neutral, dark and neutral, light and strong, dark and strong, etc. With these color samples as reference chips it is easy to visualize or describe color harmonies that are developed by applying certain rules in an orderly system of color identification and nomenclature.

Principles of color harmony. The methods used for selecting colors for room interiors differ from those that apply to other branches of art and industry. The painter and illustrator select colors that are to be used within a small area and their purpose is to delineate and accentuate subject matter. The advertising artist wishes to call attention to what he has to say and uses brilliant colors for this purpose. The industrial designer thinks of the suitability of his color selection for his product and its potency in sales appeal. The decorator, however, wishes to create a mood or atmosphere that is suitable for the use of a room. He deals mainly in backgrounds for human beings and his selections cannot be protruding elements in a decorative scheme. While certain hues must be used according to requirements and taste, the consideration of these is less important than the chromatic or tonal values that are to be decided upon. While the painter's colors cover a small area of canvas, the decorator's problem is complicated by the fact that he is confronted with a great number of surfaces that vary in size, texture, material, and lighting.

There are some persons who have a better "color sense" than others. They react emotionally to colors and are able by instinct to select agreeable color combinations for decorative use. Emotional judgments are often uncertain and it is always advisable to have a logical reason for any selection and to compare such a selection with established principles. Empirical formulas have been evolved for use in developing color schemes for rooms. Such formulas are not limited by exact boundaries and must be considered only as a general guide to a safe result, if not one that shows evidence of virtuosity.

In planning the color scheme for any room a preliminary consideration must be given as to its degree of vitality, or chromatic key. Whether the use and purpose of a room requires neutral or semibrilliant chromatic values, and whether its lighting requires a tonal key of light, medium, or dark values. Interest in a color composition is attainable by contrast and variety of color areas, hues, chromatic and tonal values, and the use or elimination of patterns. It is advisable to make a tentative plan as to what and where these contrasts are to be introduced. The unity of a color scheme is more easily attained by few colors. The use of one color only would produce a monotonous effect, and many colors create confusion. The artist therefore must make his decision as to how many colors may be used to create interest and variety and yet avoid chaos. There should always be a dominant color in a room. Two colors should not be used in equal areas. White, gray, and black may be used in small areas and need not be counted as extra colors in a scheme; their tendency is to give greater unity to divergent hues.

It is usual for planning purposes to subdivide a room into its component areas of color distribution as follows:

Dominant areas—Wall, floor, and ceiling.
Medium areas—Draperies, large upholstered furniture, bed covers, etc.

Small areas—Small upholstered furniture, chair seats, pillows, table covers.
Accents—Welting, fringes, small accessories, small pattern motifs in wall-papers and textiles, flowers.

The general rule that is applied in reference to the chromatic value of these areas is called the "Law of Chromatic Distribution." This is as follows: *The larger areas should be covered in the most neutralized colors of the scheme. As the areas reduce in size, the chromatic intensity may be proportionately increased.*

A color scheme is usually created by the treatment of the dominant and medium areas of a room. The smaller areas and accents are less important to the general effect of the scheme, although greater unity is attained by several repetitions of the same hue accents in various parts of the room. For example, a bright color used as welting for a sofa could be repeated in a wallpaper pattern or in a porcelain ornament.

There are various combinations that are possible in color schemes, as follows:

One hue scheme—One hue used throughout with contrast obtained by suitable variations in tone and chroma.

Neutral and one hue scheme—Where dominant and medium areas are gray or white and one contrasting hue is introduced in small and accent areas.

Analogous scheme—When a complete scheme is limited to any three adjoining hues on a 12-color wheel, and distributed according to the law of chromatic distribution.

Complementary scheme—Where complementary hues are used for the dominant and medium areas and are generally repeated in higher chromas in the smaller areas. In schemes of this type, practice has proved that the use of exact complements is less agreeable than the use of complements that are tinged with the same hue (i.e., in a red and green scheme, it is better to have both hues slightly tinged with either yellow or blue. A red-russet harmonizes more agreeably with a green-citron, or a red-mulberry with a green-slate).

The use of the color wheel. The chart on page 797 describes a color wheel of 12 hues in a chromatic and tonal value that has proved to be average usage in colors for the background areas of a room. The hues have been identified by their common names and by their Munsell chart designation. All are 7th tonal value and 2nd chromatic value by Munsell standards. This means they are medium light colors and strongly neutralized. They may be conveniently used as wall colors for any room. By adding white to a paint matched to any of these colors, an 8th or 9th tonal value may be obtained. The 3rd, 5th, 7th, and 8th tonal values of gray are shown on the lower line of chips and a tonal identification may be made with any color sample by comparison with any of these chips. Rooms that are poorly lighted should have backgrounds in the 8th or 9th tonal value. No wall should be pure white. The 9th tonal value of any hue may be considered as an off-white. If a dark wall is desired for a room, it is inadvisable to use one that is no darker than the 5th tonal value as shown in the line of grays, and a semigloss finish is necessary. The 2nd chromatic value of any hue has been found to be the strongest that is suitable for large areas such as walls and ceilings. More brilliant chromas for such areas are too definite in hue to be agreeable. If the Munsell charts are available, it will be found that 4th and 6th chromatic values are the most brilliant that may be used for the secondary color areas of a room. Accents may of course be in the most brilliant chromatic values. Ceilings are usually painted in an off-white of the wall hue, although this tonal value is not essential. Plain floor coverings may be in 4th or 6th chromatic values, as dust and usage tend to neutralize them.

In addition to their use in selecting wall paint, the neutral colors and values may also be used in the selection of the backgrounds of wallpapers and textiles. For textiles intended for draperies, slightly brighter colors may be used than for wallpapers, as the shadows caused by folds tend to neutralize the colors of the fabric.

In mixing pigments for light tones, it is advisable to start with white paint and slowly add the colored pigments until the proper tone and chroma is obtained.

Symbolism and psychology of colors. Colors unquestionably have a psychological effect and produce certain thoughts or emotions. Whether this is due to some inborn element in the human mind or whether it has merely developed through long association is not known. Theatrical producers have studied the association of colors with emotional reactions to a greater extent than other artists, but decorators have, though to a less extent, used the generally accepted associated thoughts. Light, cool colors, such as turquoise, robin's-egg blue, lavender, and light foliage-greens suggest quiet, freshness, and repose. The light, warm colors, such as tan, cream, ivory, pale yellows, and apricot, suggest cheer. Pleasure and excitement are created by brightly lighted areas, and depression is aroused where visibility is low. Mystery and romance are stimulated by meagre illumination, and vulgarity by strong lights. The bright warm colors, such as orange and red, suggest excitement and exhilaration. The darker colors are more dignified, richer, and more vigorous in appearance. A room may be cheerful or gloomy, friendly or cold, according to its predominating hues, and a very definite "mood" may be produced by color treatment. Colors also have different appeals to persons of opposite sex. Men as a rule prefer darker tones than women.

The symbolism of certain colors is frequently called the "language of color," and a knowledge of the ideas associated with certain colors is useful to any decorator.

White—Purity, peace, faith, joy, cleanliness.
Red—Passion, anger, warmth, gaiety, martyrdom, revolution.
Blue—Restfulness, coolness, sky, constancy, truth.
Black—Darkness, despair, sorrow, mourning.
Green—Spring, hope, restfulness, coolness.
Yellow—Warmth, cheerfulness, fruitfulness, jealously.
Gray—Humility and penance.
Purple—Justice, royalty, depression, suffering, church color.
Gold—Royalty, luxury, power.
Pale blue—Male child.
Pink—Female child.

Effect of distance and area upon color. In considering a surface that is to be colored, it is necessary to consider the distance from which it is to be viewed, as a colored surface that is near by will appear more brilliant and darker than the same surface when placed further away. The neutralization of the more distant surface is due to the interposition of the atmosphere, and while this is of minor importance in a small room, it should be seriously considered in rooms of large size.

Colors appear stronger in their chromatic values when covering large areas than when used on small areas. This is an optical illusion, and if areas are visible at the same time and it is desired that they appear similar, it is wise to equalize the effect by painting the large area a slightly lighter tone of the same color.

Colors affected by adjoining colors. A scientific fact of importance in relation to color surfaces is that they are greatly affected by adjoining or surrounding colors, and appear to change in color and value when certain other colors are close to them. A test can be made by taking two small squares of red. Place one on a purple background and one on an orange background. In each case the red square will appear to be tinted with the omitted primary color. The red placed on the purple background will appear tinged with yellow. The red on the orange background will appear tinged with blue.

The value of colors is also greatly influenced by adjoining color values, and a color may be made to appear either light or dark by contrast. Adjoining contrasts of light and dark colors accentuate the tonal values of each. A white object placed against a colored background will cause the background to appear dark, and, conversely, a dark-colored object placed against a white background will accentuate the tonal values of both surfaces; the white will appear lighter and the dark object will appear darker.

To illustrate this point, the illustration on page 802 shows the divisions

Diagram showing effect of adjoining tones or colors. Band B is actually the same color for its entire length, but it appears darker at the top in contrast to the light values of bands A and C. The dark values of A and C at the bottom of the bands cause B to appear light. The stepped gradations of A and C appear lighter where they adjoin the next darker step. Each step is actually a flat tone.

of gray tones. Bands A and C show a stepped series of flat tones in juxtaposition, light at the top and dark at the bottom. Band B appears to be graded in the reverse manner and looks dark at the top and light at the bottom. As a matter of fact, band B is a flat tone throughout its entire length, and if a sheet of paper is used to cover up the graded bands A and C, the even tone of band B will be seen. By this experiment it is obvious that colors may be made to appear either lighter or darker according to the tonal values of the colors adjoining them. These tests show the importance of working out complete color schemes for rooms in advance, so that samples of all the colors to be used in a room may be seen at the same time. They also illustrate the importance of analyzing the size of the intended areas to be covered and the influence of neighboring colors on one another.

The effect of natural light on colors. The quality of light is perhaps the first thing the trained decorator considers in planning the color scheme of any room—whether or not sunlight enters the room, and for what portion of the day it is there. In rooms that are particularly sunny, it is advisable to subdue the sunlight. Thus, in rooms with a southern exposure, it is the custom to use the cool colors. This will not only help soften the glare, but it will help give an agreeable effect in the heat of summer, when the sun actually becomes a problem. The decorator will then have an opportunity for variety in the use of the warmer colors in rooms or portions of the house that face north, thus bringing warmth and the effect of sunlight where it is most needed.

The next most important point in planning a color scheme is the consideration of the quantity of light which penetrates the room. The number, location, and size of the windows will have to be carefully studied, the kind of material that is to be used for draperies and sash curtains, and the area of the window that may be covered. Needless to say, darkening a room by partially or completely covering the source of light darkens the appearance of every color in that room, and often so neutralizes them, that a cheerful color scheme is turned into an uninteresting or gloomy effect. The quality of light in a room largely governs the choice of colors. but the tonal value of those colors will depend upon the amount of light penetration permitted by the curtain treatment, and upon the amount and character of the artificial light, if the room is for evening use.

These are very important features to consider, and they accentuate the importance of trying out color schemes in advance in the actual room where they are to be placed, and under conditions as similar as possible to those finally to be encountered. Many colors absorb so much light that it is impossible ever to have a bright room when they are used. An example of this may be found in a room panelled to the ceiling in dark oak. Both the material and the color reflect very little light; and while this may not be a disadvantage in some types of rooms, it may be a serious one in others. The decorator must consider in advance the amount of light he can afford to sacrifice in a drapery treatment in order to carry out the color effect he may be planning.

The effect of artificial light on colors. A treacherous element in interior decoration is artificial light, with its effect upon colors. The use of artificial light in theatrical productions is well known, and the remarkable changes upon a stage that can suddenly be made with a spotlight are common knowledge. Such changes may be pleasing or exceedingly disagreeable to the eye, and an understanding of the general theory of artificial light, particularly that of the common electric light, is necessary if the best results are to be obtained.

The ordinary electric light casts a warm light yellow or orange glow, but these colors may be altered by using slightly tinted or colored bulbs, and light of almost any color may be produced with modern electric illumination. It is impossible to describe the exact effect of different colored lights upon various colored surfaces, owing to the great number of hues that may be produced and the variability of the brilliance of the light. In general, however, the following results have been proved:

WALLS WITH RED AS A DOMINANT PIGMENT

Yellow light makes them appear red-orange.
Blue light makes them appear purple.
Red light makes them appear gray.

WALLS WITH BLUE AS A DOMINANT PIGMENT

Yellow light makes them appear green.
Blue light makes them appear gray.
Red light makes them appear purple.

WALLS WITH YELLOW AS A DOMINANT PIGMENT

Yellow light makes them appear gray.
Blue light makes them appear green.
Red light makes them appear orange.

WALLS WITH GREEN AS A DOMINANT PIGMENT

Yellow light makes them appear bluish green.
Blue light makes them appear yellowish green.
Red light makes them appear gray.

In general a light thrown on a wall of a similar color tends to neutralize the color, owing to the fact that all other colored objects in the room are given the same tint as the wall color, so that there is less contrast for the color of the wall, and it therefore appears to lose part of its tonal value.

The color of electric bulbs may be also influenced by the color of the shades or the shade linings.

If a room is intended for evening use to a greater extent than daytime use, a preliminary test should be made showing the effect of the intended artificial light upon the color scheme.

The effect of texture on colors. Rough textures, because of the great number of small shadows produced, make colors appear darker than do smooth surfaces. Very smooth textures that have a glaze or sheen reflect light and cause colors to appear lighter than would be the case with a dull finish. It is important to keep this point in mind in selecting colors for any large areas in a room. A pile carpet may give entirely different color values when seen from different directions, depending upon whether one looks into the pile or at the side of the pile. A wall may be painted a much darker tone, if a glazed finish is used. Dull-finished painted surfaces must always appear darker than glossy-finished ones.

Colors used in period rooms. Each of the historic periods of art has had its characteristic color scheme. In the periods of antiquity, this was in part due to the limited number of permanent pigments; but in the 16th century pigment chemistry began to be developed and in recent years there has been a great expansion of pigment production from a great variety of sources. During the Egyptian, Greek, Roman, and Gothic periods the most used colors were rather strong in primary and secondary hues; but with the Renaissance neutralization commenced. In Italy and in 17th-century France the colors used for walls and textiles were rather dark. In the tapestries of the late Renaissance a great many neutralized browns and greens were seen. Spanish Renaissance colors were usually brilliant primary and secondary hues, although those used by El Greco, the painter, were off-grays, and generally sombre tones. In 18th-century France, color schemes ran toward pale tints of neutralized colors for the large areas of woodwork and walls, while in textile patterns so-called pretty tints of the primary and secondary colors were extensively used. Patriotism dominated the Directoire period, and strong reds, whites, and blues were the rule. Under the influence of David in France, in the early years of the 19th century, considerable severity marked the use of color, and many of the color schemes show a dominance of off-grays and blacks. Some Empire textiles, however, show rather brilliantly colored backgrounds with pattern motifs in dull gold. Josephine had a more cultivated taste and undoubtedly influenced the colors for the interior of Malmaison which are in pale dull blues and grayed purples, medium dull browns, and flesh colors. The English colors of the 18th century are generally well neutralized and tend toward darker values than the French. The Wedgwood pottery colors are typical of these with neutralized blues, greens, browns, and black. The Adam colors are dull blue, pale yellowish green, light gray, lavender, and other tints that harmonized with the light satinwood and Angelica Kauffmann decorations. During the Victorian period—the so-called mauve decade—colors were often dark, such as eggplant, bottle-green, tobacco brown, and dull red and purple. American Colonial colors for woodwork show a great range of hues from light to dark and well neutralized. In provincial and peasant interiors colors were largely limited to textiles and painted decoration and were usually bright and gay. The general trend of all modern coloring for interiors is toward the use of very few colors, mainly in large areas of light, strongly neutralized tints.

But occasional dark backgrounds are used where there is ample illumination in the room. Brighter colors are used for small accents.

Color schemes from textiles and papers. The need to key a room to the hues introduced in textiles and wallpapers limits somewhat the selection of color schemes. While this may appear to be a handicap, it is a great advantage to the beginner, inasmuch as it often limits the number of possible color schemes for a room, requiring the consideration of but a few, and so simplifying the selection.

After a color scheme for a particular room is abstractly formed in one's mind, and after the general character, scale, dimensions, and orientation have been taken into consideration, the textiles and wallpaper (if wallpaper is to be used) should first be decided upon. It is a hopeless task to approach the wholesaler of these materials without something definite in mind in the way of cost, quality, color, and pattern. Several samples should be selected and brought to the actual room in which they are to be used, and a final decision should then be made before any paint colors are chosen.

The reason for this is perfectly obvious. The colors in textiles and wallpapers are limited and fixed, while paint may be mixed by an experienced painter to any color desired. The error in reversing this process is obvious. If multicolored materials are used, it is customary to repeat some of the same colors in other portions of the room. If chintz curtains are to be employed, for instance, it is often advisable to select the most neutral tone in the chintz pattern as a paint color for the walls of the room, using possibly a slightly lighter or darker tone for the trim. Other colors may be used in either plain or striped materials for the upholstered pieces, while the floor covering may be an Oriental rug of similar tones or a plain rug of one of the drapery tones.

Developing a color scheme. The most practical method for working out a color scheme is to build it up from some existing textile, floor covering, wallpaper, picture, or other surface color, using the more neutral values for the large areas and properly proportioning the additional colors. This scheme is not possible in every case, and a decorator must arbitrarily develop in his own mind a composition that will be suitable, taking into consideration the size and purpose of the room, the amount of light, frequency of occupancy, and other conditions that have already been mentioned.

If Munsell charts are not available, small books of color samples are usually obtainable from paint stores, or one may purchase elaborate color sample books at artists' supply houses. A decorator may prepare a color scheme with water-color or tempera paints, mixing them with a white pigment to make them opaque. On page 807 is shown a sample chart for preparing a color scheme for a single room. The size of each color sample

Color for Walls

Color for Floor Coverings

Color for Upholstery of Large Sofa

Color for Draperies

Color of Wood Trim

Colors for Small Chair Coverings

Color Accents for Accessories or Patterned Surfaces

Sample chart for the presentation of a color scheme. The spaces should be filled in with paint or actual samples of textiles, wallpaper, etc., following general rules laid down for planning a color scheme for a particular room.

is proportioned to the relative area of color distribution in the average room. The walls and floor are indicated in the largest squares, with secondary areas and color accents in the smaller ones. This chart may be traced and used in its actual size, or it may preferably be doubled in size and drawn on a sheet of heavy paper. Sample color schemes may also be worked out with paint in combinations with actual textile and wallpaper swatches, if such are available.

Important points to remember. Any two hues may be used together if they are at the proper degree of neutralization. They should preferably contrast in tonal and chromatic value. The largest areas should be the most neutral, secondary areas of an intermediate chromatic value, and small areas and accents brightest.

It is preferable to have three steps in tonal value in one room. With light walls and dark floors, draperies and upholstery should be an intermediate value. With dark walls and an intermediate tonal value on floor, furnishings should be light, etc. With this principle, contrasts are orderly and maintain unity with variety and interest.

When bright and multicolored patterns form the basis for a color scheme, the bright colors may be repeated in the large areas (walls and floors) but in a neutralized value. Do not use over three hues for the large areas. The repetition of hues in various parts of the room aids the unity of the scheme.

In general, it is more simple to harmonize colors that approach each other, i.e., yellow-greens with yellow-reds, and blue-greens with blue-reds, etc.

Uninteresting color schemes are usually those of insufficient contrasts. Contrasts that are too strong are not restful. The colorist must decide the proper relationships.

Neutral colors are formal. Brighter values are more informal and gay. A neutralized color appears more neutral in a small area than it does in a large area.

If color contrast is lacking in a room, contrasts should be obtained by other methods, such as texture, line direction, line character, size and shape of furnishings, plain and patterned surfaces, and furniture and accessory interest, etc.

In working with house-painters' pigments, burnt sienna, burnt umber, raw sienna, and raw umber are good neutralizers for all colors. In the former two, the red-orange quality also acts as a warming agent for violets, grays, and whites.

Procedure and résumé. There is no procedure in planning the color scheme for a room that is applicable to all cases. A decorator must often start by considering some existing feature or piece of furnishing that cannot be changed and from which the balance of the scheme must be developed. He must also consider the general purpose of the room and the preferences of the owner. He must decide in advance whether the room is to be gay and young in character or dignified and mature. Other considerations must be the size of the room, the degree of formality, the frequency of use, the purpose of the room, and the amount and type of illumination. These points should influence him as to whether a warm or cool scheme is preferable, whether a light, medium, or dark tonal effect would be most suitable, and if and where patterns are to be used.

The general procedure would then be about as follows:

1. Consider the general color character to be expressed and decide tentatively which type of scheme is to be used.
2. Consider the amount of natural or artificial light to determine in general the tonal values of the main areas.
3. Distribute the tones or patterned surfaces in their respective locations. See that they are evenly balanced throughout the room, and that an orderly, but not excessive, contrast occurs between important color areas such as draperies and walls, upholstery and floor covering, and upholstery and walls.
4. Select the definite hue families and patterns for each area, starting with the largest and ending with the accents. Use the tertiary and quaternary hues for backgrounds if possible.
5. Make a final decision as to tonal and chromatic values for all surfaces. Walls and ceilings should seldom be stronger than a B chromatic value and may, at choice, range from 5th to the 8th tonal value in a light room and preferably a 9th tonal value in a room with little light.
6. Obtain samples of all colors and materials and examine them in their final lighting conditions. Visualize the areas in which they are to be used and keep in mind that colors covering large areas appear in stronger chromatic values than the same color in small samples.
7. Color accents should be distributed as far as possible in all parts of the room.
8. Dark colors reflect greater light if they are finished in a semigloss.
9. Keep all color schemes as simple as possible. Usually three different colors for the dominant and medium areas are sufficient.

Bibliography

Biren, F., *Selling with Color*. 1945. An excellent analysis of the use of color in industry.

Bossert, H., *An Encyclopedia of Colour Decoration from the Earliest Times to the Middle of the XIXth Century*. V. Gollancz, Ltd., London, 1928. Colored illustrations with explanatory text.

Burris-Meyer, E., *Colour and Design in the Decorative Arts*. Prentice-Hall, Inc., New York, 1935. A thorough illustrated treatment of color and design in all fields of art and applied art.

Burris-Meyer, E., *Contemporary Color Guide*. Wilhelm Helburn, Inc., 1947. Sample color schemes.

Carpenter, H. B., *Color: A Manual of Its Theory and Practice*. B. T. Batsford, Ltd., London, 1933. Excellent study of color with good color illustrations.

HOLMES, J. M., *Color in Interior Decoration*. The Architectural Press, London, 1931. A thorough treatment of color and its application in interiors.

Munsell Book of Color. Munsell Color Co., Baltimore, Maryland. Separate charts showing variations of each of forty hues of the Munsell color system.

Glossary of Decorative Art Terms

The following abbreviations are used to indicate the sources from which the technical terms defined in the glossary are derived or the particular fields in which they are used:

arch., architecture
cab., cabinetwork
carp., carpentry
Fr., French
It., Italian

Lat., Latin
O.F., Old French
orn., ornament
pot., pottery
Sp., Spanish

In addition to this general glossary, the student is referred to the glossaries on special subjects as follows:

Textile terms, page 464
Ceramic terms, page 637
French furniture and decorative art terms, page 230
Structural and cabinetmaking woods, page 741
Painter's pigment colors, page 626
Arichitects, artists, craftsmen, etc., listed at the
end of each chapter of Part I.

Abacus (arch.). The slab that forms the uppermost portion of the capital of a column.

Abstract design. Patterns or motifs that are not based on forms inspired from nature.

Acanthus. A large leaf conventionalized by the Greeks for ornamental use, as in the capital of the Corinthian column.

Acroteria. Blocks at the apex and lowest points of a pediment, often with carved ornament.

Agate ware. A type of pottery resembling agate or quartz. Made in England during the 18th century by Wedgwood and other potters.

Alabaster. A fine-grained stone with a smooth milk-white surface. Used for ornaments and statuary. Slightly translucent.

Alloy. A mixture of two or more metals; for example, brass is an alloy of copper and zinc.

Amorini (It.). Childlike figures, such as cupids or cherubs. Used for ornamental purposes, especially during the Italian Renaissance.

Amphora. A Greek vase form. A large, two-handled earthenware vessel with a narrow neck and usually an ovoid body, used for the storage of grain and other products.

Anta (pl. antae). A type of projecting pier similar to a pilaster placed behind a column at the end of a side-wall of a Greek temple. The base and capital differ from those of the column; also used in Egyptian architecture.

Antefix. An upright conventionalized spreading leaf or fanlike ornament used in classic art.

Anthemion. A conventionalized honeysuckle or palm leaf ornament or pattern seen in Greek decoration.

Antimacassar. Knit, crocheted, or embroidered doily placed over upholstered chair back to protect it from the Macassar oil hair-dressing commonly used during the mid-19th century.

Antique. A work of art which, according to United States law, must be at least 100 years old.

Applique. An ornament that is applied to another surface. Also, a wall sconce.

Apron. A board placed at right angles to the underside of a shelf, sill, seat, or table top.

Apse. The semicircular or angular extension at the east end of a basilica or Christian church. It is typical of Continental cathedrals only. The English churches have rectangular ends.

Aquatint. A method of engraving on copper by the use of a resinous solution of nitric acid.

Arabesque. A scroll and leaf pattern with stems rising from a root or other motif and branching in spiral forms. It is usually designed for a vertical panel, and the sides resemble each other.

Arca (Sp.). Chest.

Arcade. A series of adjoining arches with their supporting columns or piers. The arcade usually forms a part of the architectural treatment of a corridor or passageway.

Arcaded panel. A panel whose field is ornamented by two dwarf piers or columns supporting an arch form. Particularly used in early English Renaissance woodwork.

Arch. A structural feature spanning an opening, supported at the two ends, and composed of several wedge-shaped parts. An arch form is usually curved but may also be flat. Sometimes an ornamental form resembling a structural arch. Concrete arches are monolithic.

Archaic. Primitive or antiquated. In reference to Greek art, it denotes the primitive period of development from 1000 to 480 B.C.

Architect's table (cab.). Combination drawing-table and desk, with an adjustable lid that lifts to make a slanting surface.

Architrave. The lowest part of the three principal divisions of a classical entablature, corresponding to the lintel; usually molded. It is directly supported by the columns and supports the frieze. The term is also used to define similar moldings used as door or window trim.

Arcuate (arch.). Archlike in form. Arched.

Argand lamp. Lamp invented by a Swiss named Argand, in 1783. Had a round wick with provision for the introduction of air inside the wick as well as around the outside.

Arras tapestries. Tapestries manufactured in Arras, France, during the 14th and 15th centuries. Their fame was so great that the name of the town is sometimes used as a synonym for handwoven tapestries of Gothic design.

Arrazzi. Italian name for the town of Arras, France. In Italy, sometimes used as a synonym for a Gothic tapestry.

Arris (arch.). The sharp edge formed by the meeting of two surfaces coming together at an angle. An example is the angle formed by the two sides of a brick. More specifically the sharp edges occurring between two adjoining concave flutings of a column shaft.

Artesonado (Sp.). Moorish woodwork or joinery, usually made of Spanish cedar. It is soft and fine-grained, somewhat like red pine.

Artifact. Any article of great antiquity, made by man, especially prehistoric stone, bone, metal, or clay objects.

Ashlar. Masonry constructed of flat-surfaced stones with straight, clean-cut jointing.

Astragal (arch.). Small torus molding.

Astral lamp. Oil lamp with swinging tubular arms, generally furnished with an Argand burner. Used in the early 19th century.

Atrium. The principal central room or courtyard of a Roman house, with a central opening in the roof.

Attic (arch.). In classical design, a low wall above a cornice or entablature, usually ornamentally treated with statuary or inscriptions.

Axminster. A pile carpet with a stiff jute back; the weave permits a great variety of colors and designs.

Azulejos (Sp.). Wall tiles produced in Spain and Portugal, painted with scenes of sports, bullfights, or social and amorous groups.

Baldachino (It.). A canopy resting on columns, usually built over an altar.

Ball-and-claw foot (cab.). A furniture foot cut to imitate a talon or claw grasping a ball. Of Chinese origin, the motif was greatly used in English 18-century furniture.

Ball foot (cab.). Any foot or leg terminating in a ball. A loosely used term.

Baluster. An upright support which is made in a variety of turned forms. In general it curves strongly outward at some point between the base and the top; commonly an elongated vase or urn shape. Used for the support of hand railings and for furniture legs or ornament. A spindle.

Bambino (It.). Child or baby, or the representation of such in any art medium.

Bamboo-turned. Wood turnings in mahogany and other woods that imitate natural bamboo forms.

Banding (cab.). Strip of veneer used as a border for table tops, drawer fronts, etc.

Bandy-legged (cab.). Literally, "bow-legged." Old inventories mention such legs; the lay term for cabriole leg.

Banister. Same as baluster.

Banister-back chair. A late 17th century American chair with back uprights consisting of split turned spindles or flat bars.

Baptistery. A separate building or part of a church used primarily for the rite of baptism.

Baroque. A style of architecture, art, and decoration which originated in Italy during the late 16th century and spread to other parts of Europe. It is characterized by large scale, bold detail, and sweeping curves. It was followed by the Rococo style and overlapped it.

Barrel vault. See Vault.

Basalt. Dark green or brown igneous rock, sometimes having columnar strata. Egyptian statues were frequently carved in this material. The name is also applied to a black porcelain invented by Josiah Wedgwood.

Basalt ware. Black vitreous pottery, made to imitate the mineral of the same name.

Base (arch.). Any block or moldings at the bottom of an architectural or decorative composition, particularly a series of moldings at the bottom of the shaft of a classical column.

Base molding. A molding used on the lowest portion of any object or surface.

Baseboard (carp.). A board placed at the base of a wall and resting on the floor; usually treated with moldings.

Basilica. In Roman times, an oblong, three-aisled building used as a hall of justice. The central aisle, or nave, was higher than the side aisles and was usually pierced with windows placed above the roof of the side aisles. This plan formed the basis for later Christian churches.

Basket weave. A textile weave in which the warp and weft are usually of large threads of similar size and in which the weft crosses the top of alternate warp threads.

Bas-relief (Fr.). See Relief.

Batik. A process of decorating fabrics by applying a design to the surface of the cloth in hot wax. The cloth is then dipped into a cool vegetable dye which is absorbed by the unwaxed portion. After the dye is dried, the wax is washed off in hot water. The name is applied to all fabrics so treated.

Bay (arch.). The space between columns or isolated supports of a building. A bay window is one placed between such supports and usually projects outward from the wall surface.

Bay window. A large projecting window that is polygonal in shape. If it is curved or semicircular, it is usually called a *bow window*.

Bead. A molding ornament that resembles a string of beads. Sometimes called *pearl*.

Beaker. Tall drinking vessel with slightly flaring sides.

Beam. A long piece of timber or metal used to support a roof or ceiling, usually supported at each end by a wall, post, or girder.

Bell turning. A type of turning that is used for furniture legs and pedestal supports shaped approximately like a conventional bell. Common in the William and Mary style.

Bevel. The edge of any flat surface that has been cut at a slant to the main area.

Bird's-eye veneer. A thin sheet of wood with fine circular markings caused by fiber distortions in the growth of the annual rings of the tree. It is most frequently found in maple.

Biscuit or bisque (pot.). Pottery that has been fired once and has no glaze or a very thin glaze.

Blackamoor. A statue of a Negro used for decorative purposes during the Italian Renaissance and revived in the Victorian period.

Bleach. The process of removing the original color or of whitening a fabric by exposure to air and sunlight or by the chloride process.

Block-front. A treatment of case furniture in which the front surface is articulated by a central panel sunk between two slightly raised surfaces of equal width. Often seen in English and American 18th century furniture.

Block-printing. A process of producing a colored pattern or picture on paper or textile by wooden blocks, each one producing a portion of the pattern in a single flat color.

Body (pot.). The clay or other material of which a piece of pottery or porcelain is manufactured, as distinguished from the glaze or finish later applied.

Bolection moldings. A series of moldings which project sharply beyond the plane of the woodwork or wall to which they are applied. A *bolection panel* is a projecting panel as opposed to a *sunk* panel.

Bonader. Wall hangings of peasant subject matter, painted on paper or canvas. Made in Sweden or by Swedes in America, and used to decorate homes on feast days.

Bonnet top (cab.). In cabinet work, a top with a broken arch or pediment, or a curved or scroll top with a central finial motif in the shape of a flame, urn, etc.

Border pattern. A continuous running motif used in the design of bands, borders, and panel frames.

Boss (orn.). The projecting ornament placed at the intersection of beams or moldings. It is often a carved head of an angel, flower, or foliage motif.

Boston-rocker. General term formerly applied to any chair with curved supports. Synonymous with *rocking-chair*.

Boulle work (cab.). Marquetry patterns in tortoise shell and German silver or brass, introduced by André Charles Boulle, and used as furniture enrichment in the 17th century.

Box-plaiting. Pressed folds in a fabric, sewed in place in series, as in a drapery.

Bracket (arch.). A flat-topped underprop which projects from a wall or pier and forms a support for a beam or other architectural member above it.

Bracket foot (cab.). A low furniture support which has a straight corner edge and curved inner edges. It was used in 18th century English and American furniture. In the French bracket foot the outer corners are curved. It is a stunted cabriole form.

Brasses. General term referring to cabinet hardware such as drawer-pulls and escutcheons.

Brazier. One who works in brass; also a pan with feet, for holding embers and used as a stove for heating rooms until the 19th century.

Breakfront. Cabinet piece the front of which has one or more projecting portions.

Brewster chair. A chair named for Elder Brewster, one of the first settlers of New England. Has rush seat and turned spindles.

Broadloom. A term of the carpet trade referring to carpets manufactured in wide strips (9, 12, and 15 feet and over).

Broken pediment. A triangular pediment that is interrupted at the crest or peak.

Brussels carpet. A carpet with a looped woolen pile and a cotton back.

Buffet (Fr.). A cabinet for holding dining table accessories; also a table from which food is served.

Bulbous form (cab.). A stout turning resembling a large melon; used for furniture supports during the early Renaissance in England, France, and Italy.

Bun foot (cab.). A furniture support that resembles a slightly flattened ball or sphere. Common in Dutch furniture.

Bundle. The unit in which wallpaper is delivered. In the trade in the United States a roll is 36 square feet of paper, but paper is delivered in bundles of 1½, 2, or 3 rolls.

Burl. A curly-grained wood surface or veneer cut from irregular growths of the tree, such as the roots or crotches. Very common in walnut.

Butt joint (cab.). A type of joint in which the squared end of a plank meets the side or end of another plank head to head or at right angles.

Butterfly table. A popular name for a small drop-leaf table used in the American colonies; the raised leaf was supported by a board bracket cut to resemble a butterfly wing.

Buttress (arch.). An exterior support built against a wall. Particularly seen in Gothic architecture, where it was introduced as extra masonry to resist the heavy thrust of the arched stone roof of the building.

Butt-wood veneer. Veneer that is cut from the part of the tree where the large roots join the trunk. It has fine curly and mottled markings.

Cabriole. A term used to designate a furniture leg or support that is designed in the form of a conventionalized animal's leg with knee, ankle, and foot; used particularly in France and England during the 18th century.

Caen stone. Limestone of a yellowish color, with rippled markings, found near Caen, in Normandy. Often used in French architecture and decoration.

Calender. A process imparting a smooth, impermanent surface to cotton goods by pressing the cloth between cylinders.

Calligraphy. In general, beautiful penmanship; specifically the brush-stroke work done by the Chinese for reproduction of the written characters of the Chinese language.

Camber. A slight upward bend or convexity; a slight rise or arch in the middle.

Camel back. Chair back of late Chippendale or Hepplewhite style, the top rail of which was in the form of a serpentine curve.

Cameo. A striated stone or shell carved in relief.

Candelabrum (pl., candelabra). A branched candlestick or lamp stand.

Canopy. A draped covering suspended over a piece of furniture, as over a bed or a seat of honor.

Canterbury (cab.). Ornamental stand having compartments and divisions for papers, portfolios, envelopes, etc.

Cantilever. A beam supported near the center and weighted at one end. The other end projects without apparent support. Used structurally for the support of projecting balconies, eaves, etc.

Canton china. Original blue-and-white china imported from the Far East from the 17th century until the Sino-Japanese War, 1938. A traditional staple in Chinese ceramic history.

Capital (arch.). The decorative crowning motif of a column or pilaster shaft, usually composed of moldings and ornament. The most characteristic feature of each classical architectural order.

Carcase or core (cab.). The structural body of a piece of wooden furniture which is covered with a veneer.

Cartoon. The term used to designate a drawing or design made for reproduction in another medium, as the original design for a rug, tapestry, or painted mural decoration.

Cartouche (orn.). A conventionalized shield or ovoid form used as an ornament, often enclosed with wreaths, garlands, or scroll-like forms.

Carved rug. A rug with the pile cut to different levels to produce a pattern.

Carver chair. A type of Early American chair.

Caryatid (arch.). A column carved in human form, used as a supporting motif in an architectural composition.

Case furniture. Any furniture used to contain objects, such as desks, bookcases, hutches, cabinets, etc.

Casement window. A window hinged at the side to swing in or out.

Cassapanca (It.). A long wooden seat with wooden back and arms, the lower portion used as a chest with hinged lid.

Cassone (It.). A chest or box with hinged lid.

Caster. Small wheel fastened to supporting legs of heavy furniture to facilitate moving. First used in early 19th century.

Catacombs. Underground chambers in Rome used by the early Christians as hiding places and for religious worship.

Catenary arch (arch.). An arch form that is in the shape that a chain takes when its ends are supported a distance apart.

Cavetto. A molding of concave form approximating a quarter-circle.

Cella (arch.). The interior chamber of a classical temple, in which usually stood the cult statue.

Cellaret. A portable chest, case, or cabinet, for storing bottles, decanters, and glasses.

Cellulose. An insoluble starchlike substance taken from plants to form the base of many synthetic materials.

Ceramics. The art of molding, modelling, and baking in clay. The products of this art.

Certosina (It.). An inlay of light wood, ivory, or other materials upon a dark background.

Chair rail (carp.). The topmost molding of a dado, sometimes known as the dado cap. It is placed on a wall at the height of a chairback to protect the plaster.

Chair table. A chair with a hinged back that may be dropped to a horizontal position as a table top.

Chalice. Cup or goblet used for the sacraments of the Church.

Chamfer. See Bevel.

Champlevé. A type of enamelware in which the pattern is grooved in a metal base and the grooves are filled with colored enamels.

Chandelier. A lighting fixture suspended from the ceiling. Branches support candles or electric bulbs.

Charger. A large dish.

Chasing. Ornamentation of any metal surface by embossing or cutting away parts.

Check (carp.). Small cracks which sometimes appear in lumber unevenly or imperfectly dried; perpendicular to the annual rings, and radiating away from the heart of the trunk.

Checkerboard (orn.). A pattern consisting of alternating light and dark squares.

Chest (cab.). A piece of furniture used as a box or container.

Chest-on-chest. A chest of drawers consisting of two parts, one mounted on top of the other.

Cheval glass. Literal meaning, "horse mirror." It is a large full-length mirror, usually standing on the floor.

Chevron (orn.). An ornamental motif composed of V-shapes. Also called zigzag.

Chiaroscuro. Literal meaning is "clear-obscure." Refers to a strong contrast of light and dark areas in painting.

China (pot.). The first European name for porcelain imported from the Orient.

Chroma. A term used to designate the degree of intensity, brilliance, luminosity, or saturation of a spectrum color. Yellow, near the center of the spectrum, is the most brilliant but has the least saturation and palest chroma. Red has a medium chroma; and blue, the darkest, with the greatest saturation. Sometimes the term "chromatic value" is used.

Churrigueresco (Sp.). The 17th century Spanish style introduced by Churriguero, the architect, characterized by elaborate ornamentation and curved lines.

Cinquecento (It.). The 16th century in Italy. The first 50 years was considered the high period of Renaissance production.

Cinquefoil (orn.). French "five leaves." A pattern resembling a five-leaved clover.

Cire-perdue (Fr., lost wax). An early method of making bronze castings, in which it was necessary to destroy the sculptor's original wax model as well as the mould, thereby allowing only one casting to be made.

Clapboard wall. A wall of planks laid horizontally, each one slightly overlapping the one below.

Classic. A term applying to a work of art of the first class or rank, or an established standard and acknowledged excellence.

Classical. A term referring to the arts of Greece and Rome or any work based on such forms.

Clavated. Club shaped. Applied to turnings used as furniture legs and stretchers, especially as seen in early Spanish furniture.

Clavichord. Seventeenth-century stringed instrument, ancestor of the piano. Known in the Carolean, William and Mary, and Queen Anne styles.

Claw-and-ball foot (cab.). A type of carved foot showing a bird's claw grasping a ball; used in conjunction with a cabriole furniture leg; introduced in the early 18th century in England, and possibly of Oriental origin.

Clerestory. A story above an adjoining roof. Clerestory windows in the nave wall of a church are those above the roof of the side aisles. In general a window placed near the top of a wall.

Cloche. Dome of glass that fitted over a wood base to protect artificial flowers and waxworks from dust.

Cloisonné. A type of enamelware in which the various colors are separated and held by delicate metal partition filaments.

Cloister. A covered passageway around an interior courtyard. Also the courtyard itself. Used particularly in medieval architecture.

Club foot. A foot used with the English cabriole furniture leg in the early years of the 18th century. The foot flares into a flat pad form that is round in shape.

Clustered columns. The system of placing several columns in close proximity or overlapping their shafts to form a support. Commonly seen in the European architectural styles of the Middle Ages.

Cobbler's bench. Shoemaker's bench with seat, last holder, bin, and compartments for pegs and tools.

Cockfight chair. Chair for reading and writing or viewing sports events used by straddling the seat and facing the back. The back had a small shelf. Popular from Queen Anne to Chippendale periods.

Coffer. An ornamental sunken panel in a ceiling, vault, or the lower surface of an arch, beam, or other architectural feature.

Collage. Composition made up of pieces of paper, photos, wallpaper, etc. glued together to a background surface to form a pattern or picture. Term sometimes used interchangeably with montage.

Colonnade. A row of columns usually supporting an entablature and forming a part of the architectural treatment of a corridor or passageway.

Colonnette. A small column.

Column (arch.). An elongated cylindrical structural support, usually having a base and a capital. May be isolated or attached to a wall.

Comb back. Windsor chair back, with a central group of spindles that extend above the back and are crowned with an additional rail.

Complementary color. An opposing color containing the primary color or colors not included in the original one; that is, red, blue, and yellow are complementary respectively to green, orange, and purple, and vice versa.

Composite order (arch.). A variant of the Corinthian order. The capital resembles the combination of an Ionic volute placed above rows of Corinthian acanthus leaves.

Composition. A term in design used to indicate a grouping of separate parts that produce the appearance of a co-ordinated whole and are esthetically related to each other by position, line, and form.

Composition ornament. An ornament made of putty, plaster, or other material, that is cast in a mould and applied to a surface to form a relief pattern. Also called "gesso" (It.) and "yeseria" (Sp.).

Connecticut chest. A type of Early American chest with double drawers, standing on four short legs; usually decorated with split spindles painted black.

Conventionalization. The reproduction of forms in nature with such changes as to make them more suitable to the particular mediums or materials in which they are reproduced. Simplifying or exaggerating natural forms in reproduction.

Conversation chair. S-shaped chair meant to seat two people facing in opposite directions. Used in the 18th and 19th centuries.

Conversation piece. Picture of a family group. See Genre.

Cool color. Blue and the hues that are near blue, such as blue-green and violet.

Corbel (arch.). A shoulder or bracket set in a wall to carry a beam; any stone, brick, or timber-work projecting as a shoulder to carry a burden.

Corinthian order. The most elaborate, slender, and graceful of the classical orders of architecture. The Romans standardized the column height at 10 diameters. The capital is enriched with two rows of acanthus leaves and four volutes.

Coromandel. An Eastern wood, used for furniture and often treated with a lacquered pattern.

Corner block (carp.). A square block of wood used to form a junction between the sides and head strip of door and window trim. Any block similarly used in cabinetmaking.

Cornice. The projecting, crowning portion of a classical entablature, consisting of bed moldings, fascia, and crown moldings; often used on interior walls without the frieze and architrave moldings.

Counter thrust (arch.). The opposing force or weight used to counterbalance the weight and thrust of a heavy arch.

Country-made (cab.). Cabinetmaking done by country cabinetmakers who are frequently less capable than those who are city-trained. Country-made furniture implies lower quality.

Cove. A concave surface often used to connect a wall and a ceiling. A cove-molding similar to the cavetto.

Creche. Miniature nativity scene with figures composed of wood, plaster, china, or composition, set up with stable and animals.

Crocket. Ornament used on the sides of pinnacles, usually leaf or bud shaped; commonly seen in Gothic art.

Cross-banding. A narrow band of wood veneer forming the frame or border of a panel; the grain of the wood is at right angles to the line of the frame.

Crotch veneer. A thin sheet of wood cut from the intersection of the main trunk and branch of a tree, showing an irregular effect of graining.

Crown molding. The topmost molding, particularly the fillets and cymas placed above the fascia in a classical cornice.

Crystal. A clear and transparent quartz, resembling ice; an imitation of this material made in glass.

Cubism. A development of painting and sculpture based largely on abstract design and geometric pattern. Being first and foremost an abstract expression, cubism has little to do with imitations of nature or natural objects. The cubist artist has thus created new forms which live within themselves, and he has sensitized and enhanced the values of forms, line, and color in their purest sense.

Cuneiform. Literally, wedge-shaped. A system of writing on clay tablets used in Sumeria, Babylonia, and Assyria, in which the characters were wedge-shaped.

Cusping (arch.). Pointed termination of a trefoil or quatrefoil in Gothic architecture.

Cyma curve. An S-shaped curve. In the *cyma recta* the curve starts and ends horizontally. In the *cyma reversa* the curve starts and ends vertically.

Dado. The lower portion of a wall, when treated differently from the surface above it. In the classical styles the dado usually has a base, shaft, and cap molding, and is often panelled or ornamented. A low wainscot.

Dado cap. The crowning or cap molding of a dado; sometimes called a chair rail.

Daguerreotype. First photographic process invented in 1839 by Louis Daguerre in France. Involved action of light on plate sensitized by a solution of iodine and silver salts. Produced a faint image, which had to be viewed at an angle to be clearly seen.

Dais. A low platform raised above the level of the floor and located at one side or at the end of a room.

Damascene work. A type of metal inlay. The design is incised by means of acid applications on a metal base, and the depressions are filled in with wires or different metals cut to fit.

Deal. Generic term for any member of the pine family when it is cut up into planks. Also applied to furniture made of such planks. English and Early American use.

Decalcomania. A process of decoration in which printed designs on thin paper are transferred to other materials.

Demotic. An abridged form of hieroglyphics, used by the Egyptians for ordinary correspondence conducted by the public scribes.

Dentil. A small square projecting block in a cornice.

Derbyshire chair. A popular name for a type of Jacobean chair of provincial origin.

Desornamentado (Sp.). The name applied to the severe style of architecture and decoration developed by the architect Herrera under the patronage of Phillip II of Spain. The word means "without ornament."

Diameter. A straight line drawn through the center of a circle and touching the perimeter in two places. The length of such a line. The unit for proportioning the classical orders of architecture. The dimension is taken from the diameter of the shaft at the base of the column of that order, and all other portions of the column and entablature are given in units or fractions of the diameter of the column shaft.

Diaper pattern. An all-over or repeating pattern without definite limits.

Dinanderie. 15th century metal alloy, the ancestor of pewter, being a combination of copper, tin, and lead. Used particularly in application to ornamental figures made in Dinant, Belgium.

Diorite. A type of dark-colored, hard stone much used in Egyptian sculpture.

Dip-dyeing. The process of dyeing textiles after they are woven by dipping whole pieces into the dye. Dip-dyeing is also known as piece-dyeing.

Disk-turning. Flat circular turning used to ornament furniture.

Distant colors. Colors which produce the feeling of space and appear to recede, particularly light tones of blue and purple.

Distemper. Opaque water color pigments.

Dome. A spherical vaulted roof similar to an inverted cup.

Donjon. The massive tower which was used as a final stronghold in medieval castles. Usually located in the interior of a courtyard.

Domino wallpaper. Wallpaper imitating marble graining, similar to that which was produced by the Dominotiers in France in the latter half of the 16th century.

Doric order. The oldest and simplest Greek order of architecture. The Romans standardized the proportions and made the columns 8 diameters high and the entablature 2 diameters.

Dormer window. A projecting upright window which breaks the surface of a sloping roof.

Double-hung sash. Window sash divided into two sliding sections, one lowering from the top and the other rising from the bottom.

Doublet (orn.). A pair, or the duplication of an outline in a surface pattern, usually in a reverse form.

Dovetail (carp.). Wedge-shaped projection on the end of a piece of wood used to interlock with alternating similar grooves or projections on another piece of wood. Joint used to join the front and sides of a drawer.

Dowel (carp.). Headless pin of metal or wood which is used to hold two pieces of wood together.

Draw curtain. A curtain that may be drawn along a rail or other support by means of a traverse arrangement of cords and pulleys.

Drawnwork. A pattern made by drawing threads from both the warp and weft of a fabric.

Dresser (cab.). A cabinet with drawers or shelves.

Drier. A chemical preparation added to paint which causes it to dry quickly.

Drop-lid. A top or front of a desk hinged at the bottom and arranged to fall back, forming a surface for writing.

Drum. Circular supporting wall for a dome. Also the cylindrical stones used to build up a column shaft. Any feature in cabinetmaking resembling this shape.

Dry-point. An etching made from a metal plate upon which a picture has been scratched with a sharp-pointed metal tool.

Earthenware. Pottery of coarse clay.

Ebéniste (Fr.). Term used to designate a high-grade cabinetmaker.

Echinus (shell-shaped). An ovoid shaped molding forming part of a classical capital. It springs from the shaft of the column, just under the abacus.

Eclecticism. The borrowing and combining of art forms of various past periods, adapting them to contemporary conditions.

Egg-and-dart (orn.). An ornament used as a molding decoration, consisting of ovoid forms separated by dartlike points.

Eggshell finish. A semiflat paint finish.

Electroplating. An electrical process of coating base metals with a very thin surfacing of a more valuable metal.

Elevation (arch.). The vertical projection of any object. The delineation of an object or surface from in front in which the dimensions are at specified scale, and not foreshortened as seen by the eye. Specifically, a drawing of a wall to scale to show its length, height, and various subdivisions and ornament.

Elgin marbles. The sculptures of the pediments and friezes of the Parthenon, named after Lord Elgin, who was responsible for having them removed to the British Museum in London.

Embossing. A process of stamping, hammering, or moulding a material so that a design protrudes beyond the surface.

Enamel. A colored glaze that is used to decorate metal and ceramic surfaces; it becomes hard and permanent after firing. A paint that imitates such a surface. Enamel ware refers to objects whose surfaces are treated with this material.

Encaustic painting. A method of painting with pigments mixed with hot wax. The wax mixture may be heated and applied with a spatula or brush, or it may be applied to the surface first, and the designs drawn with a stylus.

Engaged column (arch.). A column attached to a wall.

Engraving. The process whereby a design is incised with a sharp instrument upon a copper or steel plate; also, the impression printed from this plate.

Entablature. The surfaces and moldings of a classical order of architecture, consisting of the architrave, frieze, and cornice, and forming the upper portion of the order. The portion of the order supported by the column.

Entasis (arch.). The slight curve on a column shaft. In the Roman orders the entasis reduces the diameter of the shaft at the capital to five-sixths the dimension of the diameter at the base. The curve is limited to the upper two-thirds of the shaft.

Escabelle (Fr.). An early French Renaissance stool or chair.

Escritoire (O.F.). A desk with drawers and compartments.

Escutcheon. A shield with a heraldic device. In hardware it refers to a shaped plate for a keyhole or to a metal door fitting to which a handle or knob is attached.

Estrado (Sp.). Raised platform or dais at one end of main living room in 17th century Spanish houses.

Etchings. Prints from a copper plate upon which a drawing or design has been made by a metal tool or by "biting" with acid.

Etruscan. See Tuscan.

Exedra. Public room in Roman or Pompeian dwellings.

Faïence (Fr.). A type of pottery made originally at Faenza, Italy. It is a glazed biscuit ware, and the name is now popularly applied to many such decorated wares.

Famille noire, verte, jaune, rose, etc. (Fr.). French names which designate a particular type of Chinese pottery having a colored background. Translated, the words mean "black family," "green family," "yellow family," and "rose family."

Fasces (orn.). A bundle of rods enclosing an axe, a Roman symbol of power.

Fascia (arch.). A molding whose section consists of a vertical flat surface. Particularly the projecting crown molding of a cornice.

Fenestration. The arrangement of windows in a building.

Ferronerie velvet. Antique Venetian velvet made with patterns imitating delicate wrought iron forms.

Fiddle-back chair. An American Colonial rush-seated chair of the Queen Anne type, with the back splat silhouetted in a form approximating a fiddle-back or vase shape.

Filet lace. A lace produced by embroidering a pattern on a fine net usually in thread similar to that of the net.

Filigree. Ornamental openwork in a delicate pattern. Usually refers to the pattern made by fine gold or silver wires or plates formed in minute lacelike tracery.

Fillet (arch.). A molding whose section consists of a small vertical flat surface; usually used at the start or finish of a curved molding.

Finial. An ornament used as a terminating motif. A finial is usually in the form of a knob, pineapple, or foliage.

Firebacks. Metal linings, often ornamented and usually of cast iron, placed in a fireplace behind the fire to reflect heat and protect the masonry.

Fireside figures. Wooden silhouettes painted to resemble royal personages, guards, pages, etc. Used as fire screens and fireplace adornment in Europe during the 16th and 17th centuries.

Firing. The term used in pottery manufacture to describe the heating of the clay in the kilns to harden it.

Flamboyant (Fr., flame-like). A term that is used to designate the late Gothic style in France, because the window tracery was designed in reverse curved lines resembling conventional flamelike forms.

Flemish foot. Furniture foot used in Flanders, England, and France during the 17th century. The scroll design usually followed the line of an S- or C-curve.

Flemish scroll. An S- or C-curved ornamental form, probably of Spanish origin, but associated with Dutch and Flemish furniture design and used in England during the Carolean and William and Mary periods.

Fleur-de-lis. The conventionalized iris flower used by the former kings of France as a decorative motif symbolizing royalty.

Flock paper. Wallpaper imitating velvet and made by scattering powdered wool over a pattern printed in varnish on paper sheets.

Florentine arch. A semicircular arch that springs directly from a Renaissance column capital or pier and is trimmed with an architrave molding. Usually seen in series.

Fluid plan. Type of planning in modern architecture, in which one room opens into another with little division between them, and the whole may be thrown open into one large area, if desired.

Flush (arch.). A term referring to any surface that is on the same plane or level as the surface adjoining it.

Flutes or flutings. Parallel concave grooves that are used to ornament a surface. In classical architecture they are commonly seen on column shafts and run in a vertical direction. Spiral flutings are frequently used on furniture supports. Short flutings are used as a frieze ornament.

Flying buttress. In Gothic architecture, an arch springing from the wall of a building to an exterior stone pier, intended as a counterthrust weight to resist the thrust of the arched roof.

Form. A stool or long bench without a back.

Fractur painting. Decorative birth, marriage certificates, etc., made by Pennsylvania Germans during the 18th and 19th centuries.

French heading. A term used in curtain making to designate the gathering of a drapery or valance into folds at regular intervals near the top. The folds are sewed together in place so that they will have a more regular appearance.

Fresco. Method of painting on wet plaster with tempera colors. The plaster absorbs the pigment, and when dry, the painting becomes hard and durable and a part of the plaster.

Fret (orn.). A Greek geometric band or border motif, consisting of interlacing or interlocking lines; also known as the meander or key pattern.

Frieze. The central portion of the three main horizontal divisions of a classical entablature; usually a flat surface decorated with ornamental features or carving. Often used in decorative work without the architrave or cornice.

Full-tone. A color of which the hue is near its full chromatic value.

Gabon. Black ebony.

Gadroon (orn.). Elongated ovoid forms placed in a parallel series and projecting beyond the surface they enrich.

Gaine. An ornament or support in the form of a square post tapering toward the lower portion. It is usually crowned with a head or bust and has ornamental human or animal feet.

Gallery (cab.). A miniature railing placed along the edge of a shelf or table top. Specifically the *gallery-top* table.

Galloon or galon. A narrow close-woven braid used for trimming draperies and upholstery. A heavy guimpe.

Gargoyle. A projecting stone waterspout grotesquely carved in fantastic animal or bird form. Used in Gothic architecture.

Gazebo. Turret on a roof of a small garden shelter usually built of latticework.

Genie. A creature of ancient folklore fashioned like man but having supernatural powers. An imaginary form resembling this creature, used as an ornamental motif.

Genre (Fr.). Pictures that depict the activities of the comman man.

Gesso. A prepared plaster of chalk and white lead which may be cast to make repeating ornamental forms in relief to be applied to wood panels, plaster surfaces, etc.

Girandole. A type of branching chandelier or a wall mirror to which candle brackets are attached.

Girder. A heavy beam used over wide spans and often supporting smaller beams or heavy concentrated weights.

Gold size. An adhesive substance painted on a surface to which gold leaf is to be applied.

Gouache. An opaque water color pigment, or any picture painted in this medium.

Graffito ware. Ware of heavy pottery decorated with a rudely scratched design.

Graining. A painted imitation of the fiber lines of wood.

Granite. Granular crystalline rock of quartz, feldspar, and mica. The hardest and most durable building stone.

Great hall. The large, two-storied central hall of a medieval castle, used principally for dining and entertaining.

Greek cross. A cross formed of two bars of equal length meeting at right angles.

Grisaille (Fr.). Decorative painting in which objects are rendered in tones of one color. Often intended to give the effect of sculptured relief panels.

Groin vault. See Vault.

Gros-point (Fr.). Embroidery done in a cross-stitch on a double threaded net. Averages 64 to 256 stitches per square inch.

Grotesques (orn.). Fanciful hybrid human forms, animals, and plants.

Guadamacileria (Sp.). Decorated leather produced by the Moors in Cordova, Spain, and elsewhere.

Guilloche (orn.). A band or border running pattern having the appearance of overlapping or interlacing circular forms.

Guimpe. A narrow, flat, ornamental trimming, often having a wire or cord running through it. Used primarily to cover upholstery nails.

Hadley chest. A type of Early American, New England-made chest which stood on four feet, and usually had one drawer and was decorated with crude incised carving.

Half-timber. A type of house construction in which heavy wooden posts and beams form the skeleton of the structure. The area between them is filled in with brick, stone, or plaster.

Half-tone. A color that in tonal value is approximately halfway between white and black.

Hallmark. The mark or marks which designate that a piece of metalwork has received an official approval of quality, particularly the approval issued by Goldsmith's Hall, London.

Hammer-beam truss. A form of roof support used during the early English Renaissance. It consists of a Tudor arch form in wood, each end of which rests on a large wooden bracket.

Hard paste (pot.). Name used to identify hard-bodied or true porcelain, made of kaolin, or "China clay."

Hassock. A heavy cushion or thick mat used as a footstool.

Hausmalerei (Germ.). Pottery made in Germany by independent artists and amateurs, who decorated partially fired pieces, and returned them to the kiln for glazing and further firing.

Haut-relief (Fr.). See Relief.

Heddle. The bar of a loom which controls the warp threads.

Hellenistic. Period of Greek art under Alexander (3rd century B.C.) when the center of culture moved to Alexandria from Athens. Characterized by extreme realism and theatricalism. Lasted until Greece became a Roman colony.

Hennin. A high pointed headgear worn by medieval women.

Hex sign. A good luck symbol often placed on the exterior of buildings by the Pennsylvania Germans. It was usually in the shape of a circle, enclosing a six-pointed star or other motif.

Hieratic. An abridged form of hieroglyphics, used by the Egyptians, and reserved for religious writings.

Hieroglyphics. A system of writing used by the Egyptians, consisting of a combination of picture-writing and phonetic indications.

Highboy. A tall chest of drawers supported by legs and usually crowned with cornice moldings or a pediment.

Hispano-Mauresque. The term used to designate Spanish art productions that show an influence of both Moorish and Renaissance origin.

Hom. Assyrian tree-of-life pattern.

Honeysuckle. A decorative motif of Greek origin resembling a conventionalized fanlike arrangement of petals.

Hooked rug. A pile-surfaced rug made by pushing threads or strips of cloth through a canvas backing. By varying the colors of the pile, any pattern can be made.

Horseshoe arch. An arch whose total curve is greater than a semicircle. Used in Moorish and Spanish architecture.

Hue. A color itself, as red or blue. Many *tones* of the same hue are possible. A *tint* is a hue with white added, and a *shade* is a hue with black added.

Hutch. Another name for the chest, most common item of furniture in the Gothic household.

Hydria. Greek water jar with three handles that was used for carrying or pouring.

Icon. Portrait or image. In the Greek and Russian church it refers to the panels containing portraits or figures of sacred personages, as the Virgin, and the various saints. Also spelled *ikon*.

Idealism. The tendency in art to express universal or spiritual concepts.

Illumination. Hand decoration of manuscripts in color and gold and silver. Practiced to a great extent by monks in the monasteries in the Middle Ages.

Impost (arch.). A feature or structural member upon which an arch rests. The top of the impost is below the spring-line of the arch.

Impressionism. A late 19th century development in the French school of painting. Brilliant atmospheric effects were produced by using spectral colors in adjoining positions on the canvas instead of mixing the pigments on the palette before application. The paintings are best seen at a distance, as the broken pigments used to produce the effect of atmospheric realism are diffused under such a condition.

Incised. Cut into; said of a pattern or carving produced by cutting into a stone, wood, or other hard surface. The reverse of a *relief* carving, the pattern of which projects from the surface or background. Intaglio.

Ingrain. A flat-woven wool or wool-and-cotton carpet with a Jacquard design; usually reversible.

Inlay. Ornament or a pattern that is produced by inserting cut forms of one material into holes of similar shape previously cut in another material. The contrast of materials or colors produces the effect as well as the design of the cutting. Correctly speaking, marquetry is not inlay work, as both pattern and field are cut at the same time from a thin veneer.

Intaglio. Incised or countersunk decoration, as opposed to *relievo* decoration, which is in relief.

Intarsia (It.). See Inlay.

Ionic order. One of the classical orders of architecture. The characteristic feature of the capital of the column is the spiral-shaped volute or scroll. The standard proportion of the Roman column is 9 diameters high.

Jamb. The interior side of a door or window frame.

Japanning. A process, much used in the 18th century, by which furniture and metalwork were enamelled with colored shellac and the decoration raised and painted with gold and colors.

Jardinière velvet. Multi-colored velvet with a satin ground showing a floral design. Originally made in Genoa.

Jasper. An opaque variety of quartz which may be bright red, yellow, or brown.

Jasper ware. A name given by Wedgwood to a type of hard biscuit ware that was introduced in the late 18th century.

Joinery. The craft of assembling woodwork by means of mortise and tenon, dovetail, tongue and groove, dowels, etc.

Joist. A horizontal timber used to support a floor or ceiling.

Kakemono. A Chinese or Japanese painting, mounted on brocade and hung on the wall, without a frame.

Kakiyemon. A Japanese pottery artist who developed the use of colored enamel designs on Japanese porcelain. The name is also applied to decorations inspired by his works.

Kaolin. A white clay used in the manufacture of true porcelain; sometimes called *china-clay*.

Kapok. A filling material used for stuffing upholstery and pillows.

Keystone. The wedge-shaped central stone at the top of an arch.

Klismos. A Greek type of chair having a concave curved back rail and curved legs.

Kneehole desk. Desk with a solid lower portion but with an opening for the knees of the person seated at it.

Knotted rug. An Oriental rug weave in which the surface or pile is formed by the ends of threads knotted around the warps, the weft threads serving merely as a binder.

Krater. A wide-mouthed, two-handled bowl used by the Greeks for mixing wine and water.

Kylin. A chimerical beast often used in Chinese decoration.

Kylix. A flat-shaped Greek drinking cup on a slender center foot.

Lacquer. A varnish containing lac; or a hard varnish obtained from the sap of the lacquer tree. The latter is the base of Chinese and Japanese lacquer. Any varnish of shellac dissolved in alcohol.

Ladder back. A chair back having a ladder effect produced by the use of a series of horizontal back rails in place of a splat.

Lady-chapel. The most revered and elaborately decorated chapel at the east end of a cathedral. Dedicated to the Virgin.

Lantern (arch.). A small structure placed at the crowning point of a dome, turret, or roof, with openings for light to come through. Frequently its purpose is decorative only.

Latin cross. A cross form with one arm longer than the other.

Lavabo. A washstand or washbowl, often with a fountain or water supply. The support for same.

Lectern. A pedestal support for a large book or Bible.

Lekythos. A long narrow-necked flask used by the Greeks for pouring oil.

Letto (It.). Bed.

Linenfold. A carved Gothic panel enrichment which resembles folded linen or a scroll of linen.

Linoleum cut. A print made from blocks of linoleum which have been cut into grooves to form a picture or pattern.

Lintel. A horizontal beam, supported at each end, that spans an opening and usually supports a superstructure.

Loggia (It.). A room or area with an open arcade or colonnade on one side.

Louver. An opening in a wall or ceiling protected from the rain by slats placed at an angle.

Lozenge (orn.). An alternate name for the conventional diamond-shaped motif.

Lunette (orn.). A form resembling a crescent or half moon.

Luster. A thin metallic glaze used on pottery to produce a rich, iridescent color. Used in Persian ceramics, Spanish and Italian majolica, and English and American ware.

Macassar. A seaport city in the Dutch East Indies exporting a type of ebony to which its name is given—macassar ebony.

Machicolate. Literally, to furnish with a projecting gallery. In medieval castle architecture, machicolations were openings in the vault of a portal or passage or in the floor of a projecting gallery, for use in hurling missiles down on the enemy.

Maître-ébéniste (Fr.). Master cabinetmaker.

Majolica. Italian and Spanish pottery coated with a tin enamel and painted with bright colors.

Maltese cross. A cross in which the four similar arms are wedge-shaped with their points meeting.

Mantel. The projecting shelf surmounting a fireplace.

Maquette. Miniature or model room, usually furnished to show the appearance of a proposed scheme of decoration.

Marbling. A painted imitation of the veining of marble.

Marlborough leg. A heavy, straight-grooved furniture leg, with a block as a foot. Much used for English and American mahogany furniture in the mid-18th century.

Marquetry. A flush pattern produced by inserting contrasting materials in a veneered surface. Rare, grained, and colored woods are usually exclusively used for marquetry, but thin layers of tortoiseshell, ivory, mother-of-pearl, and metals are also occasionally seen.

Mastaba. An Arabic word meaning "bench." Applied to the early mound-shaped tombs of Egypt, and later to those built underground.

Meander. See Fret.

Medallion (orn.). A circular or oval frame having within it an ornamental motif.

Medium. The substance, material, or agency through which an artist expresses his ideas. In painting, the vehicle or liquid with which pigment is mixed or thinned, such as water, oil, wax, etc.

Mercerize. A process of treating cotton goods chemically to make them stronger, lustrous, and easier to dye.

Merino. Spanish sheep, the ancestor of nearly all the wool-growing sheep in the world.

Mesquita (Sp.). Mosque.

Metope. The space between the triglyphs of a Doric entablature.

Mezzanine. A low-ceilinged story between two high ones, especially one placed above the ground floor. Entresol (Fr.).

Mezzotint. A type of copper-plate engraving which produces an even gradation of tones, as in a photograph.

Mihrab. A prayer niche in a Mohammedan mosque located so that the worshipper faces in the direction of Mecca.

Millefleurs (Fr., a thousand flowers). A term particularly used to designate a 15th century Gothic tapestry pattern showing numerous small leaves, plants, and flowers.

Minaret. Tower on Mohammedan mosques, with one or more balconies from which the summons to prayer is given.

Miniature. A small painting in illuminated manuscripts, also any very small painting, or undersized object.

Minstrel gallery. The small balcony above the main entrance to the great hall of a medieval castle where the entertainers performed during the feasts.

Miter (carp.). A corner junction of two strips of wood or other material, the end of each piece being cut at a similar angle, as in the corner of a picture frame or door trim.

Mixing table. Small sideboard or butler's cabinet, with compartments at the end for bottles.

Modillion. The projecting bracket used to support the Corinthian cornice. Also frequently used as an independent decorative motif in architectural and furniture design.

Module. A measuring unit for an architectural order. The full diameter or half diameter of the lower portion of the shaft of the column.

Monochrome or monotone. Decoration in a single color or different tints of one color. See also Grisaille.

Monolithic. "One stone" or a structural mass of one solid piece, such as a concrete wall.

Montage. A composition made by fitting together parts of various drawings or photographs and attaching them to a background.

Moon gate. A circular opening in a wall large enough for human passage. Characteristic of Chinese architecture.

Mortise (carp.). A hole cut in a piece of wood and intended to receive a tenon projecting from another piece of wood.

Mosaic. Small squares of colored stone or glass (tesserae) set in cement and arranged in a picture or pattern. A popular and beautiful form of mural decoration used extensively in Early Christian and Byzantine art.

Mosque. Mohammedan place of worship.

Mounts. Ornamental or utilitarian metal work such as handles, drawer pulls, escutcheons, etc., used on cabinetwork.

Mozarabic (Sp.). The arts in the Moorish parts of Spain in which Christian elements were in evidence.

Mudejar (Sp.). A transitional style of art in the Christian parts of Spain in which Moorish and Italian Renaissance details were seen in the same design.

Mullion. A slender vertical or horizontal bar that acts as a division piece between windows or glass panels.

Multifoil. A pattern having many-lobed forms. An arch having more than five foils or arcuate divisions. Sometimes called a scalloped arch. See Arcuate.

Murrhine. Fragile opalescent glassware made by the Romans and used for ornamental and useful purposes.

Nanmu. A wood used in China for building houses. It is aromatic and turns a deep rich brown with age. Chinese name for Persian cedar.

Naturalism. The close imitation or representation in art of natural objects. Opposed to conventionalization.

Nave. The main or central part of a cruciform church; usually flanked by aisles and terminated by an apse.

Near colors. Colors that have an approaching tendency, therefore making a room appear smaller than it is actually. Dark tones, particularly those derived from red and yellow, are near colors.

Neutral colors. Colors that result from the mixture of several spectral hues. Pigments that have an admixture of white or black. Tints and shades. Hues that are at low chromatic values.

Newel. A heavy post placed at the termination of the handrail of a stairway.

Niche. A recessed or hollow space in a wall, intended to hold a statue or ornament.

Obverse. The side of any medal, coin, or medallion, upon which is the principle design. Opposite to "reverse."

Off-white. A color that is a pure white with a very slight admixture of a definite hue.

Ogee or ogive. A molding or an arch form composed of two opposing cyma curves whose convex sides meet in a point. A cyma curve.

Oinochöe. The Greek name for a wine pitcher.

On-the-glaze (pot.). A pattern produced by colors applied to the pottery after the glaze has been added to the biscuit.

Optical balance. An approach to symmetry obtained by making the two halves of a composition similar in general appearance but not identical in detail.

Order of architecture. A term used to designate a classical column and entablature. The pedestal and attic are sometimes included. There are three Greek orders, the Doric, Ionic, and Corinthian, and five Roman orders, the Tuscan, Doric, Ionic, Corinthian, and Composite.

Oriel window. A large projecting window which is supported by a corbeled brick or stone construction.

Ormolu (Fr. form, ormoulu). A type of cast bronze ornament, finished by hand-chasing and surfaced with gold. Particularly used as applied enrichment for furniture.

Ottoman. A backless low cushioned seat; or an upholstered foot-rest.

Ovolo (arch.). A convex molding with a section approximating a quarter circle.

Pagoda. In China and Japan, a tower, usually having several stories, built in connection with a temple or monastery.

Palampores. Printed East Indian cottons decorated with tree-of-life patterns. Imported into England in the 17th and 18th centuries and largely copied in English textiles and wallpapers.

Palisade construction. Wall construction of interlocking vertical planks of wood.

Palmette (orn.). A conventionalized motif derived from a fanlike branch of the palm tree.

Panel. A surface usually enclosed by a frame. Sometimes a surface of limited dimensions without a frame. In a *sunk* panel the frame is above or in front of the panel area. In a *bolection* panel, the panel area is above or in front of the frame.

Papelera (Sp.). A small cabinet intended to hold papers and writing materials.

Papier-mâché (Fr.). Pulped paper, moulded while wet into various ornamental forms or useful shapes.

Parcel. "Partly," as "parcel gilt," meaning partly gilded.

Pargework or pargetry. Ornamental plaster or stucco-work applied to a flat surface in relief.

Parquet. Flooring made of strips of wood laid in a pattern. The pattern of such a floor is sometimes known as *parquetry*.

Pastel. A crayon made of a color or colors ground and mixed with gum and water, and used for art work. Any drawing, etc., made with this crayon. Pastel colors are commonly associated with light shades.

Patera (orn.). A round or oval-shaped disk, often enriched by a rosette or other ornament.

Patina. Incrustation which forms on bronze and other materials through chemical action. Also the gloss on woodwork and the mellowing or softening in color that develops with age.

Patio (arch.). An inner court, open to the sky.

Pedestal. A supporting base or block for a statue, vase, or order of architecture. It usually is treated with moldings at the top and a base block at the bottom. Without moldings it is called a plinth.

Pediment. Originally the triangular space following the roof line at each exterior end of a Greek temple, accentuated by the moldings of the entablature. Later the same treatment was used as an ornamental feature and varied in shape, having segmental, scroll, and broken forms.

Peintures-vivantes. High reliefs of religious groups, modelled and colored in life-like reality, framed in fanciful architectural detail, and lighted by natural and artificial means that made them seem alive. Used extensively in Italy and Spain.

Pembroke table. A drop-leaf table.

Pendentive (arch.). The triangular concave masonry surface that transmits the weight of a circular dome to four isolated corner supports. It is shaped like a portion of the inside of a hemisphere. Originated in Byzantine architecture.

Peristyle. A continuous row of columns surrounding a building or a court.

Persiana (Sp.). Venetian blind used in Spain.

Petit-point. Embroidery done in a cross-stitch on a fine single net. The term is usually applied when there are more than 256 stitches to the square inch.

Pewter. An alloy of tin and lead which has a dull gray appearance and is used for the making of tableware and ornaments. Originally it was intended as a substitute for silver.

Pie-crust table. A small table having a top with its edge carved or moulded in scallops. Common in 18th century English furniture.

Piece-dyeing. A term used in textile manufacturing to indicate that the fiber of a cloth has been dyed after the completion of the weaving.

Pier. Heavy vertical masonry support for a superstructure. This type of support lacks the detail and proportions of a column or pilaster.

Pier glass. A glass or mirror designed to stand on the floor against a wall surface.

Pigment colors. Colors made from natural or synthetic materials and used to produce the various hues in common paints. Opposed to the spectral colors produced by the decomposition of light.

Pilaster. A flat-faced vertical projection from a wall, rectangular in plan but with the general proportions, capital, and base of a column.

Pile. In textile and carpet construction, the upright ends or loops (if uncut) of thread which are woven at right angles to the warp and weft. The nap generally has the appearance of velvet.

Pillar (arch.). The popular term used to designate a column. Also an isolated structure used for commemorative purposes.

Pinnacle. Small pyramidal or cone-shaped turret used in architecture to crown roofs and buttresses. In the decorative arts, any form resembling the architectural feature.

Piping. A method of applying and holding in place upholstery or padding to a curved surface by means of ribs resembling pipes.

Plain-sawing (carp.). The cutting of a plank of wood from the outside edge of a tree trunk. The grain appears in V-shapes opposed to *quarter-sawing* in which the plank is cut through or near the center of the trunk and causes the grain to appear in parallel lines.

Plan (arch.). The horizontal projection of any object. The delineation of an object or surface from above. The shape or internal arrangement of an object as indicated by a section cut parallel to the ground. Specifically, a drawing showing the arrangement and horizontal dimensions of the rooms of a building.

Plaque (Fr.). A plate or panel usually made of metal, glass, or pottery and treated with a surface enrichment. Used for decorative purposes.

Plateresco. The name given to the period of Spanish art during the first half of the 16th century. The word is derived from *platero,* meaning silversmith. The style of ornament often imitated the fine detail of the silversmith's work.

Plinth (arch.). Square member at the base of a column or pedestal. The *plinth-block* in carpentry is the small block of wood used at the bottom of door trim against which the baseboard butts.

Podium. A pedestal; also the enclosing platform of the arena of an amphitheater.

Pole screen. Adjustable panel mounted on a vertical pole.

Polychrome. An ornament or pattern in several colors.

Pomegranate. Decorative motif or ornament used in many periods. Symbol of fertility.

Pontil. An iron rod used in glass manufacturing to carry hot materials. *Pontil mark* is the permanent mark left by the pontil after the material has cooled.

Porcelain. A hard, vitreous, nonporous pottery. Opposed to earthenware, which, if unglazed, is absorptive. True porcelain is made of kaolin or china clay.

Porphyry. Rock composed of crystals of white or red feldspar in a red ground mass. A valuable stone for architectural or ornamental use.

Portland vase. Roman vase now in the British Museum, of blue-black glass with superimposed opaque white figures, having a cameo effect. It was copied in black porcelain by Josiah Wedgwood.

Post-impressionism. The development of the modern French school of painting which immediately followed Impressionism. It was a revolt against the principles of the color interpretation of the latter school. Instead of painting the colors of an object as they appear under different lights or in different atmospheres, the Post-impressionists returned to representation of the actual colors of the object itself without the atmospheric influence. This largely eliminated the effects of foreground and background by contrast-ing tonal values. It was less of a group movement than Impressionism.

Preclassic. The classification given to the arts and cultures of the Western peoples who preceded the civilizations of ancient Greece and Rome—Egypt, Babylon, Assyria, Chaldea, Persia, and Crete.

Pressed glass. Glass that is ornamented in relief by pressing into a mould.

Primary colors. The three pigment colors, red, yellow, and blue, which cannot be produced by any mixture of other pigments. Combinations of any two of the primaries are known as *secondaries.* The combination of any secondary with a primary is known as a *tertiary.* The spectral primaries are those seen in the rainbow.

Priming coat. A mixture used by painters for a first or preparatory coat.

Primitive. Early, simple, naïve. The term applied to the early artists of any school or period when they have not yet mastered the later and more highly developed principles.

Psyche. Upholstered sofa dating from about 1840, designed with Greek curves.

Pure design. The theory that all art and design is based on a set of universal, fundamental, and abstract principles that create the ideal of beauty.

Putto (It.). A young boy. A favorite subject in Italian painting and sculpture. Plural "putti."

Pylon. Monumental obelisk or the heavy mass of masonry pierced with an opening at the entrance of an Egyptian temple.

Quarter-round (carp.). A convex molding in the shape of a quarter circle. An *ovolo* molding.

Quarter-sawing (carp.). To saw wood planks toward or through the center of the tree trunk. See *plain-sawing.*

Quaternary. An intermediate hue in the pigment color-wheel, formed by a mixture of a tertiary color with either its adjoining primary or secondary. A fourth mixture of primary colors.

Quatrefoil. A four-lobed ornamentation.

Quattrocento (It.). The 15th century.

Rafter. A beam supporting a roof and usually following the pitch of the roof.

Rail (cab.). In panelling, any horizontal strip forming a portion of the frame; the vertical strips are called *stiles.*

Realism. The tendency in art to represent forms and objects as they actually are;

that is, detailed representation with photographic accuracy.

Reeding (orn.). A long, semicylindrical, stemlike form or a grouping of such used to enrich moldings.

Refectory. A dining hall, especially in ecclesiastical or collegiate buildings.

Relief. A type of decoration in which the design is made prominent by raising it from the surface or background of the material. *High relief* designates that the design is raised greatly; *low relief*, that the design is only slightly raised from the background.

Reliquary. A small receptacle designed to hold a sacred relic; usually made of ornamented precious metals enriched with jewels or enamel decoration.

Rep. A textile woven with a larger warp than weft thread or vice versa, producing a ribbed effect, as in poplin and corduroy.

Repoussé. Relief work on metal materials. The design is pushed out by hammering the material on the reverse side. Embossed.

Reredos (arch). A screen or wall-facing set behind a church altar, usually decorated with sculpture or carving. A retable.

Reticella (It.). Cutwork lace, similar to net work or filet.

Reverse. The side of a coin or medal, on which is placed the least important impression or design.

Rib. A projecting band on a ceiling, vault, or other surface.

Ribband back. Chair back designed with pattern of interlacing ribbons. Characteristic of Chippendale style.

Ribbed vault. See Vault.

Rinceau (Fr.). Scroll and leaf ornament sometimes combined with cartouches or grotesque forms and applied to friezes, panels, or other architectural forms. It is usually a symmetrical horizontal composition. Sometimes called an arabesque.

Rococo. A style in architecture and decoration. It is characterized by lightness and delicacy of line and structure, by asymmetry, and by the abundant use of foliage, curves, and scroll forms of decoration. The name is derived from the French words *rocaille* and *coquille* (rock and shell), prominent motifs in this decoration. The style often tended to the overornamentation of surfaces.

Roll. In the United States, a wallpaper trade and sales unit which designates 36 square feet of paper. Several rolls are usually included in a bundle or bolt or stick.

Romayne work. Carved medallion heads or knobs used as furniture ornaments or drawer pulls. Characteristic of Jacobean and Restoration periods.

Rondel. Round outline or object in a surface pattern.

Rope bed. Any bed with rope laced to the frame for holding the mattress.

Rose window. A circular window with tracery mullions radiating from a center in wheel form, the spaces between being filled with richly colored glass. Originally introduced in Gothic cathedrals, the form was later applied to wood panelling and furniture design.

Rosette (orn.). An ornamental motif formed by a series of leaves arranged around a central point. The leaves are usually conventionalized and may be arranged to form a circle, ellipse, or square.

Roundabout chair. A type of chair designed to fit into a corner; has a low back on two adjoining sides of a square seat.

Rustication (arch.). In stonework a type of beveling on the edges of each block to make the joints more conspicuous.

Sampler. A piece of needlework intended to show a beginner's skill. Specifically, a small piece of linen embroidered with alphabets and naïve patterns; made by children in the early 19th century in Europe and in North America and South America.

Sanguine drawing. A drawing in red crayon or chalk.

Sash bar. The strip of wood or metal which subdivides the individual panes of glass within the sash frame of a window.

Sash curtain. A lightweight curtain that is hung on or nearest the sash of a window. Also called glass curtain.

Sausage turning. Furniture turning resembling a string of sausages.

Scallop shell (orn.). A semicircular shell with ridges radiating from a point at the bottom. This motif was especially common in furniture design during the Queen Anne and Georgian periods in England and the United States. It was also extensively used in the early Spanish Renaissance.

Sconce. Ornamental wall bracket to hold candles or electric bulbs.

Scotia. A concave molding approximating a curve produced by two tangential curves of different radii.

Scratch carving. Shallow or deep scratching, to form a design, used in woodwork and pottery products.

Scribe (carp.). To fit one material to another, as the side of a wooden strip to an uneven surface of plaster or adjoining wood surface. A *scribe-molding* is a small strip of wood that can be easily cut or bent to fit an uneven surface or cover up an irregular joint or crack.

Scroll (orn.). A spiral line used for ornamental purposes, as in the arabesque and rinceau. A parchment roll used as an ornament.

Scroll pediment. Broken pediment with each half shaped in the form of a reverse curve, and ending in an ornamental scroll. Usually a finial of some sort is placed in the center between the two halves of the pediment.

Seaweed marquetry. Inlay of various woods in an arabesque design of small leaf and seaweed forms. Much used during the William and Mary period.

Secondary colors. Orange, purple, and green, each of which is produced by the combination of two primary colors.

Section (arch.). A term used to express the representation of a building, molding, or other object cut into two parts, usually by a vertical slice. The purpose of a sectional representation is better to show a silhouette shape or interior construction, showing vertical dimensions or heights.

Sedan chair. Enclosed chair, carried by four men, used for transportation in the 18th century.

Sedia (It.). Chair.

Segmental arch. An arch that is shaped as a part of a circle less than a semicircle.

Serpentine curve. An undulating curve used for the fronts of chests, desks, cupboards, and similar pieces. The curve is formed by two tangential cymas.

Sgabello (It.). A small wooden Renaissance chair, usually having a carved splat back, an octagonal seat, and carved trestle supports.

Sgraffito (It.). A method of decorating a surface. A pattern that is first scratched on a surface and then colored or reveals a colored ground beneath.

Shade. Something that serves to intercept light. A color or pigment that contains a percentage of black.

Shaft (arch.). Central portion of a column or pilaster between the capital and base.

Shaker furniture. A type of furniture made in the late 18th and early 19th centuries by the Shakers, a religious sect in New York State and later in New England. The designs were plain and functional; built-ins were characteristic.

Shed. In textile manufacture, an opening which is formed by the warp threads being lifted by a heddle; through this opening the shuttle holding the weft thread passes.

Shirring. Gathering a textile in small folds on a thread, cord, or rod.

Silhouette. A profile or outline drawing, model, or cut-out, usually in one color. The outline of any object. A shadow.

Sill (carp.). A horizontal board or strip forming the bottom or foundation member of a structure, especially the board at the bottom of a window that serves as a finishing member for the trim and casing. A door sill is usually called a *saddle*.

Singeries. Designs showing monkeys at play. Popular in France during the Louis XV period.

Size. Gelatinous solution used for stiffening textiles, glazing paper, and in other manufacturing processes. It is also often used as a first coat in painting.

Skeleton construction (arch.). Building construction of posts and beams assembled before the walls are erected. In steel construction the walls are nonbearing, being supported by the steel work, and are merely screens against the weather.

Skirt (cab.). Also called apron or frieze. The wooden strip that lies just below a shelf, window sill, or table top.

Slat-back chair. A type of Early American chair with wide horizontal ladder rails between the back uprights.

Slip (pot.). Clay and water of a creamlike consistency used as a bath for pottery, to produce a glaze or color effect.

Slipper chair. Any short-legged chair with its seat close to the floor.

Snake foot. In cabinet work, a foot carved to resemble a snake's head.

Socle. Plain, square and unmolded base or pedestal for a statue, or superstructure.

Soffit (arch.) The ceiling or underside of any architectural member.

Soft paste. Base of ceramics made before the introduction of kaolin, products of which lack the whiteness and extreme hardness of true porcelain.

Solar. A medieval term for an upper chamber in a castle. Usually the private room of the owner.

Spade foot (cab.). A square, tapering foot used in furniture design. It is separated from the rest of the leg by a slight projection.

Spandrel. The approximately triangular panel or wall space between two adjoining arches and a horizontal line above them.

Spanish foot. Foot in the shape of an inward curving scroll. Used in 18th century English and American furniture.

Spectral colors. The colors produced by a beam of white light as it is refracted through a prism. Although they are unlimited in number, they are usually designated as violet, indigo, blue, green, yellow, orange, and red. Commonly seen in the rainbow.

Spindle. A long slender rod often ornamented with turned moldings or bluster forms. See also Split spindle.

Spinet. Keyboard instrument, ancestor of the piano, in which the sound was produced by the action of quills upon strings.

Spiral leg (cab.). A furniture support carved in a twist, with a winding and descending groove or fluting. A rope twist.

Splat. A plain, shaped, or carved vertical strip of wood. Particularly that used to form the center of a chairback.

Splay. A line or surface that is spread out or at a slant. A bevel or chamfer.

Spline (cab.). A small strip of wood inserted between and projecting into two adjoining pieces of wood to form a stronger joint between them.

Split spindle. A long, slender, turned and moulded wooden rod that is cut in two lengthwise so that each half has one flat and one rounded side. Used as an applied ornament in 17th century English and American furniture.

Spring-line (arch.). The theoretical horizontal line in arch construction at which the upward curve of the arch proper starts.

Stalactite work (orn.). Small vertical polygonal or curved niches rising and projecting in rows above one another so that they resemble stalactite formations.

Statuary bronze. Bronze that has been surfaced with an acid application causing its color to become a dark brown. A finish usually given to bronze statues.

Stela. A stone slab or pillar used commemoratively, as a gravestone, or to mark a site.

Stencil. The method of decorating or printing a design by brushing ink or dye through a cut-out pattern.

Sterling. A term used in connection with silverware, indicating that the silver is 92½ per cent pure.

Stile. The vertical strips of the frame of a panel. The horizontal strips are termed *rails*.

Still-life. Paintings or decorative renderings of inanimate, motionless objects.

Stipple. Process of applying paint or ink to a surface in dot form, by means of a coarse brush or spray.

Stock-dyeing. A term used in textile manufacturing to indicate that a fiber is dyed before being spun into a thread.

Stone-jointing. The shaping or cutting of stones for walls and arches so that they will properly join each other; for use in the construction of walls and arches.

Stoneware. A heavy, opaque, nonporous and nonabsorbent pottery made from a silicous paste.

Strapwork. A term applied to carved wooden arabesque and rinceau patterns in which the section of the stem of the scroll is flat, resembling a pattern cut from a sheet of leather.

Stretcher. A brace or support which horizontally connects the legs of pieces of furniture.

String course (arch.). A molding or projecting horizontal motif running along the face of a building.

Stucco. Plaster or cement used as a coating for walls.

Stud. A small post, usually 2 x 4 inches, and of any height, used to form the wall construction in wooden dwellings or partitions. The studs support the joists and receive the lath or sheet material used for the finish.

Stumpwork. A type of embroidered picture worked in silk threads over padding, giving a relief effect.

Stylobate. The stone blocks or steps forming the lowest architectural feature of a

Greek temple and upon which the columns stand.

Sugi finish. A Japanese method for finishing woodwork. The surface is charred and then rubbed with a wire brush.

Summer beam. A large timber laid horizontally and used as a bearing beam. In Early American dwellings it was usually supported at one end by the masonry of the chimney and at the other end by a post, and it extended across the middle of the room. The name is derived from *sommier* (Fr.), meaning saddle or support.

Superimposed order. The placing of one order of architecture above another in an arcaded or colonnaded building; usually Doric on the first story, Ionic on the second, and Corinthian on the third. Found in the Greek stoas, used widely by the Romans, and later in the Renaissance.

Swag. Cloth draped in a looped garland effect; any imitation of same.

Swastika (fylfot or meander). A cross composed of four equal L-shaped arms placed at right angles. A good-luck symbol of ancient origin.

Symmetrical balance. Having the two halves of a design or composition exactly alike in mass and detail.

Tazza (It.). Large ornamental cup or footed salver.

Tempera. A paint composed of pigments that are soluble in water. Sometimes glue or the white of egg is also added to the solvent.

Tenon (carp.). A projection at the end of a piece of wood intended to fit into a hole (mortise) of corresponding shape on another piece of wood.

Terra cotta. A hard-baked pottery extensively used in the decorative arts and as a building material. It is usually made of a red-brown clay, but may be colored with paint or baked glaze.

Terrazzo. A concrete made of small pieces of crushed marble and cement. Used for surfacing floors and walls.

Tertiary color. A color that is formed by the combination of a primary and a secondary.

Tessera. A small cube of stone, glass, or marble, used in making mosaics.

Tester. Canopy framework over a four-poster bed.

Thimble foot. Same as spade or sabot foot.

Thrust (arch.). The outward force exerted by an arch or vault that must be counterbalanced by abutments.

Thuya wood. A rare African wood with rich graining, used for table tops and veneering of furniture.

Tie-beam. A horizontal beam which connects the rafters of a roof and prevents them from spreading. Used in truss construction to counteract the outward thrust of the slanting members.

Tilt-top. A table top that is attached to a hinge on a pedestal support so that the top may be swung to a vertical position.

Tinsel pictures. Decorative objects made from cut-out tinsel, paper, and pictures, mounted and pasted together.

Tint. A color made from a pigment that is mixed with white.

Toile-de-Jouy (Fr.). Cloth made in Jouy, France, particularly the printed cottons made by Oberkampf during the 18th and the 19th centuries.

Tole. Useful or decorative objects made of tin and ornamented with painted or enameled patterns.

Tonal value. One of the characteristics of a color. The relative strength of a color in contrast to white or black.

Tongue-and-groove (carp.). A type of wood joint in which a long, narrow, straight projection, known as the tongue, fits into a corresponding groove in the adjacent piece.

Torus (arch.). A convex semicircular-molding.

Trabeated construction (arch.). Construction in which the supporting members are the post and lintel, as distinct from arched construction.

Tracery. The stone mullions in a Gothic window.

Tracery pattern. A pattern in woodwork, textile, or other material imitating stone tracery.

Transept. In church architecture, that portion of the building that crosses the nave at right angles, near the apse or east end of the building.

Transitional. A style that shows evidence of two chronologically consecutive styles, possessing elements of both styles in its design.

Transom. The upper panel of a window or a window placed above a doorway.

Tree-of-life pattern. A pattern resembling a tree or vine, showing branches, leaves, flowers, and small animals. Originating in ancient Assyria, it was borrowed by the Persians, East Indians, and early English Renaissance designers. See also Hom and Palampores.

Trefoil. A three-lobed ornamentation resembling a clover.

Trencher. A large wooden platter upon which food is served.

Triclinium (Lat.). Dining room.

Triglyphs. Blocks with vertical channels which are spaced at intervals in the frieze of the Doric entablature.

Triptych. Any three-fold picture, in booklike form, usually of religious character.

Trumeau (Fr.). The decorative treatment of the space over a mantel, door, or window, consisting of a mirror and painting. Specifically, the overmantel panel treatment of the Louis XV and XVI periods.

Trumpet leg (cab.). A conical leg turned with flared end and shaped in the form of a trumpet.

Trundle bed. Child's or servant's bed on wheels, which was rolled under a full-sized bed when not in use. Of Gothic origin. Sometimes called "truckle-bed."

Truss. A support used for a wide span of roof or ceiling, consisting of beams or posts assembled in a triangular manner for greater strength.

Tudor arch. A flat, pointed arch characteristic of English Gothic and early Renaissance architecture and decoration.

Tudor rose. Decorative motif seen in English Renaissance work consisting of a conventionalized rose with five petals, with another smaller rose inside it. It was the royal emblem of England, symbolizing the marriage of Henry VII of Lancaster (red rose) to Elizabeth of York (white rose).

Turkey-work. A handmade textile imitating Oriental pile rugs, produced by pulling worsted yarns through a coarse cloth of open texture, then knotting and cutting them.

Turning (carp.). A type of ornamentation which is produced by rotating wood on a lathe and shaping it into various forms with cutting tools.

Turpentine. A resinous fluid used as a solvent and drying constituent in paint mixing.

Turret. A small tower superimposed on a larger structure.

Tuscan (Etruscan) order. A Roman variant of the Doric order of architecture. It is crude and heavy, and the standard proportion of the column is 7 diameters high.

Tympanum (arch.). The interior triangular surface of a pediment bounded by the sloping sides and the lower molding.

Underglaze (pot.). A term used to define a pattern that is applied to pottery before the final glazing is applied.

Unicorn. An imaginary animal often featured in the arts of the Middle Ages. The symbol of chastity.

Valance. A horizontal feature used as the heading of overdraperies and made of textile, wood, metal, or other material.

Value of a color. The relative amount of white or black in a color.

Vargueño (Sp.). A cabinet and desk with a drop-lid.

Vault. A roof constructed on the arch principle. A *barrel vault* is semicylindrical in shape. A *groin vault* is made by the intersection of two barrel vaults at right angles. In a *ribbed vault* the framework of arched ribs supports light masonry.

Velour-de-Gênes. Silk velvet. Made in Genoa and usually having a small all-over pattern.

Velvet carpet. A type of carpet closely resembling a Wilton, but without the wool backing and consequently without the wearing qualities of the Wilton.

Veneer. A thin sheet of finishing wood or other material that is applied to a body of coarser material.

Venetian blinds. Window shades made of small horizontal slats of wood strung together on tapes. The slats may be turned up or down to exclude or let in sunlight.

Venetian furniture. The name applied to the extravagantly curved and ornamented furniture of Baroque and Rococo influence, produced in Italy during the late Renaissance.

Verdure Tapestry. A tapestry design showing trees and flowers.

Vernis Martin (Fr.). Literally, Martin's varnish, but used as a term to describe the lacquer work done by a cabinetmaker named Martin during the 18th century in France in imitation of Oriental lacquer.

Vignettes. Ornamental motifs, patterns, or portraits centered in a large field.

Volute (orn.). A spiral, scroll-like form, as in the Ionic and Corinthian capitals.

Voussoir (arch.) A wedge-shaped block used in the construction of a true arch. The central voussoir is called the keystone.

Wag-on-wall. A weight-driven clock with exposed weights and pendulum, intended to hang on the wall.

Wainscot. A wooden lining for interior walls. Usually panelled. Any treatment resembling same.

Wainscot chair. An early 17th century wooden chair used in England and America.

Warm color. Red and the hues that approach red, orange, yellow, yellow-green.

Warp. In weaving, the threads that run lengthwise on a loom.

Waterleaf (orn.). A conventionalized leaf pattern of classical origin used to enrich a cyma reversa molding.

Wave pattern (orn.). A continuous pattern conventionally imitating a series of breaking wave crests.

Webbing. Strips of woven burlap used as a support for springs in upholstery.

Weft or woof. In weaving, the threads that run crosswise from selvage to selvage and are woven in and out of the warp threads by means of a shuttle or bobbin. These are now more commonly called the filler threads.

Welting. Strips of material sewn between upholstery seams to give a finished appearance.

What-not. A set of ornamental shelves used to hold bric-a-brac and china.

White lead. A heavy white substance that does not dissolve in water and is used as a base in paints when mixed with linseed oil.

Wilton carpet. A carpet with cut woolen pile and a cotton back.

Woodcut. A design engraved upon a block of wood in such a way that all the wood is cut away to a slight depth except the lines forming the design. For use in printing papers and textiles.

Yarn-dyeing. A process of dyeing the yarns before they are woven into a textile. Such a textile is called yarn-dyed.

Yesería (Sp.). Small lacelike patterns of plaster relief which were colored and used extensively on the walls of Moorish rooms.

Yoke. A cross-bar in the form of two S-curves used for the top rail of chairbacks. Typical of Georgian furniture.

Yorkshire chair. A popular name for a type of Jacobean chair of provincial origin.

QUESTIONS: PROBLEMS IN DESIGN

(+}{+}

Introduction

QUESTIONS

1. What is the difference between conventional and realistic ornament?
2. What is the difference between an ordinary post and an architectural column?
3. What are the three basic methods for supporting or constructing a roof or ceiling?
4. What is a period style of art and what were the basic influences in the development of each one?
5. Describe the following arches: semicircular, segmental, Gothic, Moorish, and Tudor.
6. What is an arabesque, a grotesque, and a rinceau?
7. Explain the following ornamental forms: lunette, volute, swastika, quatrefoil, Greek cross, and shield.
8. What are the three different methods for introducing contrasting effects for surface enrichment?
9. What is an all-over pattern? A border pattern?

PROBLEMS

Draw, sketch, or trace the following forms:
1. An all-over pattern; a panel pattern; a border pattern.
2. A segmental arch; a Gothic arch; an elliptical arch.
3. A natural object in a realistic manner and one in a conventionalized manner.
4. A triangular, a segmental, and a scroll pediment.

Chapter I

1. What is the difference between incised and relief carving?
2. What was the reason that the Greeks used many moldings on their buildings and the Egyptians used few?
3. Name the five Roman architectural orders.
4. Who was Vitruvius and what important contribution did he make to the design of buildings throughout the Roman Empire?
5. Name the following Greek ornamental motifs: two molding ornaments, one band or border pattern, and two additional ornamental motifs.
6. Describe briefly the character of Pompeian wall decoration.
7. What difference is apparent in the general shape and character of Greek and Roman moldings?
8. Name five classical moldings, and describe them.
9. What do the following architectural terms mean: entablature, cornice, shaft, pedestal, pediment, pilaster?
10. In what styles of art were the following decorative or structural motifs first used: sphinx, swan, acanthus leaf, lotus leaf, waterleaf, palm leaf, fret, winged vulture, arch, lintel?

PROBLEMS

Draw, sketch, or trace the following forms:

1. Greek Doric, Greek Ionic, and Roman Corinthian capitals.
2. Greek fret, Greek honeysuckle, and Egyptian lotus form.
3. The silhouettes of cyma recta, cyma reversa, ovolo, torus, and scotia moldings.
4. A human figure drawn in the Egyptian manner.
5. A wall treatment in the Pompeian manner.
6. Three examples of classical furniture.
7. Arabesque; acanthus leaf; amphora; antefix.
8. Two Greek columns supporting a lintel.
9. A Roman semicircular arched opening and a segmental arched opening.
10. A Roman Doric column and entablature.

Chapter II

QUESTIONS

1. Mention five of the important characteristics of Gothic architecture or design.

2. What were the principal causes for the decline of the Roman Empire?
3. Describe briefly the structural and ornamental forms used in the Romanesque style.
4. Name five of the minor arts of the Gothic period.
5. Name the principal wood used in the making of Gothic furniture and wall panelling. Describe the size, shape, and typical ornament of a Gothic panel.
6. Describe the general arrangement and decorative treatment of a "great hall."
7. Describe the general treatment of Romanesque column capitals.
8. In what styles was mosaic decoration extensively used?
9. What was the plan and what were the principal decorative forms used in Early Christian churches?
10. What were the causes of the decline of the Gothic period?
11. What influence did the Crusades have upon the arts of the Middle Ages?
12. How did the barbarian invasions affect the growth of the Christian church?

PROBLEMS

Draw, sketch, or trace the following forms:
1. Romanesque arch and column supports.
2. Gothic arch and clustered columns.
3. Linenfold panel ornament.
4. Trefoil pattern.
5. Gothic window showing tracery pattern.
6. Gothic chair or chest.
7. Finial motif.
8. Gothic fireplace with projecting hood.
9. Gothic sculptured figure.
10. Gothic molding, ornament, or surface pattern.

Chapter III

QUESTIONS

1. What were the principal causes of the Renaissance movement in Italy?
2. Name the subdivisions of the Italian Renaissance and give the principal influences of their development.
3. Name five of the great families that patronized the artists of the period. Name ten leading artists or craftsmen and tell what they are best known for.

4. Describe the general character of the Baroque and Rococo periods of decoration.
5. Why were the Jesuits influential in the expansion of the Rococo style of art?
6. Describe the character of Italian wall treatments of the 16th century.
7. What were some of the ornamental forms and motifs?
8. Explain the following words: bolection, gesso, cassone, sgabello, certosina, intarsia, Cinquecento, credenza.
9. Who were Vignola, Palladio, Bernini, Dante, Savonarola, della Robbia, Pinturicchio, Ghiberti, Michael Angelo, Raphael, Cellini? For what was each most noted?
10. What types of textiles were usually used in 16th century Italian rooms? What was the principal wood used in making early Renaissance furniture? What type of pottery was used in the Italian Renaissance interiors?

PROBLEMS

Draw, sketch, or trace the following forms:
1. Renaissance pilaster capital.
2. Cassone.
3. Credenza.
4. Candelabrum.
5. Arabesque ornament.
6. Sgabello and sedia.
7. Architectural picture frame.
8. Textile pattern.

Chapter IV

QUESTIONS

1. What were the two principal influences in early Spanish Renaissance art forms?
2. Describe the wall treatments of 16th century Spanish rooms.
3. What was the arch form introduced by the Moors?
4. What woods were used in Spanish furniture?
5. What types of supports were used for tables? Describe the shape of the turnings.
6. Describe the character of Spanish doors and ceilings.
7. Explain the following terms: vargueño, Plateresco, yeseria, artesenado, and Churrigueresco.
8. What were the principal minor decorative arts produced by the Moors?

9. What was the influence in the design of the Spanish 18th century furniture?
10. What important influence is seen in the art of Portugal that is not in the Spanish arts?

PROBLEMS

Draw, sketch, or trace the following forms:
1. Moorish tile pattern.
2. Spanish door.
3. Spanish table with turned leg.
4. Vargueño.
5. Horseshoe arch.

Chapter V

QUESTIONS

1. What were the principal influences affecting the introduction of the Renaissance movement in France?
2. Contrast the wall panel shapes and the character of the panel enrichments of the Rococo and Neo-classic styles.
3. Identify the following persons: Riesener, Oberkampf, Gouthière, Palissy, Houdon, Boulle, Goujon, Marot, David.
4. What are the differences between Rococo and Neo-classic furniture?
5. What were the principal characteristics of the Baroque style?
6. To what origin may be traced the fundamental forms and ornament of the furniture of the Empire period?
7. Mention the principal decorative motifs of the Neo-classic period, and describe their character.
8. Explain the following terms associated with the French decorative arts: chaise-longue, trumeau, chinoiserie, coiffeuse, toile-de-Jouy, grisaille, Sèvres, cabriole, Directoire.
9. What was the character of the color schemes in French late 18th century rooms?
10. What types of textiles were used in French decoration during the 18th century?

PROBLEMS

Draw, sketch, or trace the following ornamental forms:
1. Neo-classic natural flower ornament.
2. Classical figure of the Empire period.
3. Rococo cabriole furniture leg.

4. Neo-classic straight fluted furniture leg.
5. A piece of French Renaissance furniture.
6. A Rococo panel shape.
7. A Neo-classic panel shape.
8. An Empire ornamental motif.

Chapter VI

QUESTIONS

1. Who were Grinling Gibbons, Hepplewhite, Angelica Kauffmann, Josiah Wedgwood, Christopher Wren, Gainsborough?
2. In what English styles were the following motifs used: scallop shell, three ostrich feathers, romayne work, Greek fret, cabriole leg, inverted cup turning, seaweed marquetry?
3. What do the following terms mean: cross-banding, inlay work, Adam-Sheraton, Chinese-Chippendale, lion mask, club foot, Flemish scroll?
4. Describe the general character and wall treatment of a room of the early English Renaissance.
5. What periods were known as the Age of Oak, Age of Walnut, Age of Mahogany, Age of Satinwood?
6. Describe the following ornamental forms: strapwork carving, split-spindle, arcaded panel, bulbous leg, shield-back, patera, gadroon.
7. What were the principal differences between the Hepplewhite and Sheraton chairbacks?
8. What were the approximate dates of the English Regency style?
9. What borrowed forms are seen in Chippendale furniture?
10. When was the Oriental influence introduced in English furniture?

PROBLEMS

Draw, sketch, or trace the following forms:
1. Queen Anne, Hepplewhite, and Sheraton chairbacks.
2. Elizabethan, Jacobean, William and Mary, Queen Anne, Chippendale, and Sheraton chair legs.
3. Adam mantel.
4. Two Chippendale chairs.
5. Tudor arch.
6. Early Renaissance wall panelling.
7. Elizabethan cupboards.
8. Three Adam ornaments.
9. William and Mary highboy.
10. Grinling Gibbons ornament.

Chapter VII

QUESTIONS

1. When were the academic forms of classical architecture first used in American interiors?
2. Describe the general treatment of walls, floor, and ceiling in an Early American room, an American Georgian room, a Greek revival room.
3. What were the principal influences affecting the early industrial arts of the United States?
4. What woods were used in the making of Early American furniture?
5. Who were Savery, Goddard, Phyfe, Terry, McIntire, Affleck, Revere, and Stiegel?
6. Explain the system of construction of the Early American house. What was the summer beam?
7. What were the causes of the decline in esthetic appreciation during the Victorian period?
8. Describe the following objects: fiddle-back chair, Windsor rocker, butterfly table, Hitchcock chair, banister back, turkey-work, block-front, and Hadley chest.
9. Describe the principal characteristics of Duncan Phyfe furniture.
10. Contrast the principal differences in American and English furniture of similar periods.

PROBLEMS

Draw, trace, or sketch the following:
1. Early type of American panelled walls.
2. American late Colonial or Federal mantel treatment.
3. Carver chair.
4. Banjo clock.
5. American Windsor chair.
6. Colonial scroll pediment.
7. Butterfly table.
8. Early American fireplace.

Chapter VIII

QUESTIONS

1. Indicate five motifs of Chinese patterns and state the symbolism that is associated with each.
2. What were the arts for which the Persians of the Middle Ages were best known?

3. What is the general character of Dutch furniture of the 16th and 17th centuries and what were the influences in its design?
4. Name the characteristics of the Biedermeier style.
5. What types of artistic production are generally included in the peasant styles of Europe?
6. What were the ornamental motifs used by the Toltecs? The Aztecs? The Mayas?
7. Why is the study of African Negro sculpture of interest to Western art historians?
8. Describe a Chinese garden.
9. What pattern motifs are usually associated with the peasant arts?
10. Describe a typical Dutch interior of the 17th century.

PROBLEMS

Draw, sketch, or trace the following:
1. Several American Indian ornamental motifs.
2. Several pieces of peasant pottery.
3. An example of peasant furniture. A Biedermeier piece.
4. A piece of African Negro sculpture.
5. Three objects of Chinese art.
6. A Persian ornamental motif.

Chapter IX

QUESTIONS

1. Who were some of the early modern architects in the United States?
2. How does modern architecture differ from architecture in the past?
3. Discuss the effect of cast iron on modern architecture.
4. How has reinforced concrete influenced the modern architect?
5. Explain how the Arts and Crafts Movement and Art Nouveau fit into the growth of modern architecture.
6. Discuss the quality of early machine-made designs.
7. Discuss the influence of the Bauhaus.
8. Why was Richardson called both a traditionalist and a modernist?
9. What principles of design did Frank Lloyd Wright use?
10. What are some of the practical mechanical developments that have increased the comforts and conveniences of contemporary homes?

PROBLEMS

Draw, sketch or trace:
1. The plan of a modern house.

2. Art Nouveau ornamentation.
3. The side view of a cantilevered beam and its supports.

Chapter X

QUESTIONS

1. Outline the contributions of the Thonet family to furniture design.
2. Trace the development of the Arts and Crafts Movement.
3. Discuss the work of Charles Rennie Mackintosh.
4. Why was the work of Rietveld important to the furniture of the twenties?
5. In which ways were the Art Nouveau manifestoes of van de Velde misunderstood?
6. Discuss the use of the steel tube in furniture design.
7. Analyze the development of modern architecture and modern furniture as parallel sequences.
8. Explain what is meant by bentwood furniture.
9. State the importance of the work of Alvar Aalto.
10. State the characteristics of modern Scandinavian and Italian design.

PROBLEMS

Draw, sketch or trace:

1. A cantilevered steel tube chair.
2. A modern Scandinavian chair.
3. A machine-made American chair.

Chapter XI

QUESTIONS

1. Explain the three basic textile weaves.
2. Describe the weave and method of making a pile fabric, grospoint needlework, and handmade tapestry.
3. What do the following terms mean: shuttle, bobbin, warp thread, weft thread?
4. Describe the characteristics of the following textiles: toile-de-Jouy, damask, brocade, brocatelle, frisé, satin, rep, velvet, chintz.
5. What pattern motifs were used in fabrics of the following periods: Louis XV, Louis XVI, Adam, English Victorian, and Empire?
6. Name three materials suitable for each of the following purposes: heavy upholstery, glass curtains, lined draperies, and medium upholstery.

7. Who were Oberkampf and Jacquard?
8. In what periods were the following motifs used in textile patterns: tree-of-life, chinoiseries, classical figures, bow-knot?
9. What are the characteristic differences between a Gothic and a renaissance handmade tapestry?
10. What is the significance of the following words: moiré, strié, jaspé, broché, crewel, diaper, and rayon?

PROBLEMS

Draw, trace, or sketch a textile or wallpaper pattern from each of the following styles:

1. French Rococo.	5. Mohammedan.
2. French Neo-classic.	6. French Empire.
3. Chinese.	7. Italian Renaissance.
4. Persian.	8. Modern.

Chapter XII

QUESTIONS

1. What are the names of the three different types of draperies that may be used for a window and what are their purposes?
2. When is it best to let draperies hang straight to the floor, and when is it best to tie them back?
3. Describe the interior upholstery methods and materials used in the making of an all-upholstered chair.
4. Explain French heading, shirred heading, and box-pleating.
5. In a room where windows are of a different height, how may one create an appearance of greater regularity in the window heads?
6. What are the advantages in the use of a valance?
7. Name some of the useful textiles for sash curtains, draw curtains, and overdraperies.
8. What usually determines the choice of a figured or plain material for an overdrapery?
9. What are the advantages of Venetian blinds?
10. What is the difference between an imperial edge and a plain edge on a hair mattress?

PROBLEM

Draw a simple outline of draperies for several windows of different sizes and shapes. Show the type and proportion of the valances, the curve of the drapery, and the height of the tie-back, if used.

Chapter XIII

1. Name the six principal groups of Oriental rugs and briefly describe their principal pattern characteristics.
2. Describe the weave and pattern of Savonnerie and Aubusson rugs.
3. What is the difference between a Chenille and a Wilton carpet?
4. How is a hooked rug made? What is a hand-knotted rug?
5. In selecting a patterned rug for a home, what should be the first two considerations?
6. In what type of rooms are synthetic floor coverings suitable?
7. What is a "carved" rug, and where may one advantageously use it?

PROBLEM

Make a collection of sketches, tracings, or magazine pictures showing various types of patterned floor-coverings, including Oriental rugs, French Savonnerie and Aubusson, handmade domestic rugs, and linoleum.

Chapter XIV

QUESTIONS

1. Who were the Dominotiers?
2. Who were Papillon, Reveillon, Huet, and Jackson?
3. In what sizes were the first wallpapers made?
4. What is the usual width and height of a scenic wallpaper strip?
5. What is the difference in character of a pattern made by the hand-block process and one made by the roller press?
6. How many square feet in a "roll" of wallpaper?
7. How should expensive wallpaper be hung?
8. How does the use of wallpaper affect the selection of other surfaces and objects used in the same room?

PROBLEMS

1. Draw, sketch, or trace several period wallpaper patterns.
2. Design a small wallpaper repeat pattern in three colors, using crayons or paint in flat tones.

Chapter XV

1. Name the leading artists in the following schools of painting: Italian Primitive, Venetian, Roman and north Italian, Flemish, Dutch, and English.
2. Who were the leading early French exponents of Impressionism?
3. Explain the difference between the processes of making an etching and a dry-point.
4. What were Audubon prints, stumpwork, samplers, paper silhouettes, tinsel pictures?
5. Describe the influences in the development of Italian and Spanish 17th century painting and French 18th century painting.
6. What types of frames are suitable for modern pictures?
7. What types of pictures are suitable for a formal 18th century English room?
8. What types of pictures or wall decorations are suitable for an informal Early American room? For a room in the contemporary style?
9. Name the leading painters of the first 50 years of the 20th century.
10. When is it advisable to use a mat in framing a picture?

PROBLEMS

1. Identify in class the process by which each example in a collection of etchings, lithographs, pen or pencil drawings, crayon or pastel sketches, and other forms of reproductions was made. The collection may be added to by both student and instructor.
2. Make a small picture by a different process from those chosen by the other members of the class. The picture may be traced, cut out and pasted on a sheet, or sketched with a pencil or crayon. Suggestions: silhouettes, tinsel pictures, small samplers to be embroidered, and flowers or figures assembled from colored cut-outs.
3. Give "spot" tests by showing pictures of well-known paintings and have students identify the painters. These pictures should be shown by lantern slides if possible but examples may be torn from magazines and passed around the classroom.

Chapter XVI

QUESTIONS

1. From what ingredients is house paint mixed?
2. What is the effect of adding turpentine to paint? Of adding varnish?

3. What is known as an eggshell finish?
4. What is the value of stippling and how is it done?
5. How is a plaster wall prepared for painting?
6. How is old wallpaper removed?
7. What is the difference between oil paint and calcimine?
8. How does one "antique" a painted surface?
9. What do the terms "graining" and "marbling" mean?
10. How is metal leaf applied to a wall?

PROBLEM

Materials: Small, inexpensive tubes of oil paints—white, black, red, yellow, blue. Small bottles of turpentine, varnish, and linseed oil. Thin pieces of wood about 1 foot square, obtainable at any lumber yard. Two or three small brushes for oil painting.

Experiment in class with processes of painting. Observe the effect of oil, turpentine, and varnish when added to the paint. Experiment with antique effects, and observe the appearance of one, two, three, and four coats of paint. Compare surfaces coated with thin paint and those with thick paint.

Chapter XVII

QUESTIONS

1. What influence did the Chinese have on the development of European ceramics?
2. Explain the following terms: porcelain, stoneware, kaolin, glaze, and biscuit.
3. Name some of the leading potters of England and describe the types that each produced.
4. Name some of the leading types of French pottery.
5. What is the difference between Spanish and Italian majolica?
6. What type of glassware did Stiegel produce?
7. What are Waterford glass, Wistarberg glass, and Sandwich glass?

PROBLEMS

Draw, sketch, or trace the following types of pottery:
1. A wheel pattern of a Rouen plate.
2. A Staffordshire figure.
3. A typical Wedgwood ornament for jasper ware.
4. An English slip ware pattern.

5. A Chelsea figure.

6. A Sèvres vase.

Collect clippings from magazines and newspapers showing typical examples of period pottery.

Chapter XVIII

QUESTIONS

1. What is the difference in working qualities of cast iron and wrought iron?
2. How was old Sheffield plate made and in what years?
3. What is the difference between a door knob and a lever handle?
4. What type of drawer pulls were used on Jacobean furniture?
5. What metals are used to make pewter?
6. What is the difference between chiselling and repoussé work for metal ornamentation?
7. What is the difference between surface and mortise hardware?

PROBLEMS

Draw one example of each of the following pieces of hardware:

1. Butterfly hinge.
2. HL hinge.
3. Cocoon hinge.
4. Strap hinge.
5. Louis XVI lever handle.

Chapter XIX

QUESTIONS

1. Why must the lighting of rooms with electricity differ from former methods?
2. Name six special methods of arranging artificial illumination for modern interiors.
3. What are the most important locations for special light in the average living room?
4. What is the best height above the floor for the top of a shade for a standing lamp?
5. What general types of lighting are necessary in residential rooms?

1. Draw the plan of a room 16 × 22 feet, with mantel, two doors, and two windows. Locate the furniture and indicate the location of electric light bulbs, using modern methods of lighting.

2. Draw or trace a lighting fixture of each of the following period types: Louis XV, Louis XVI, English Georgian, American Colonial. A modern table lamp.

Chapter XX

QUESTIONS

1. Name six different basic types of decorative wall treatments.
2. What are the advantages of plain painted walls over other types?
3. What are the disadvantages of using stretched textiles for wall coverings?
4. What kinds of materials are being used by decorators to produce modern types of walls?
5. In what types of rooms are rough plaster walls suitable?
6. What is "embossed leather"?
7. What advantages are there in the use of mural decoration?
8. Describe some of the characteristics of a good mural painting.

PROBLEM

Discuss in class the advantages and disadvantages of the use of mural decorations in different types of rooms, basing the discussion on a collection of colored reproductions of antique and modern mural decorations. The collection may be added to by both pupils and teacher.

Chapter XXI

QUESTIONS

1. Explain the following terms: dado, chair rail, wainscot, mortise-and-tenon, dovetail, tongue-and-groove, butt joint, and sash bar.

2. Describe the following types of window: double hung, French window, and English casement.

3. What is a good proportion for the height of a room cornice in its relation to the total height of the room?

4. How is wood panelling constructed and what are the names of the component parts?

5. Name three woods used principally for structural purposes.
6. Name eight woods used for veneering, cabinetwork, and inlay.
7. What is veneer, marquetry, inlay, quarter-sawing, burl?

PROBLEMS

1. Draw five different types of cabinet joinery.
2. Draw a typical panel of each of the following styles: Louis XV, Colonial.
3. Draw the silhouette of a Colonial cornice.
4. Draw a typical panelled door of each of the following styles: Colonial, Louis XV, 16th century Italian, Spanish.
5. Draw a Colonial mantel of the late 18th century.

Chapter XXII

QUESTIONS

1. Name the five principal abstract components of room decoration.
2. Name five violations of good taste in the use of room accessories.
3. What is the difference between the terms "style" and "fashion"?
4. Name five different characteristics that may be expressed in the decorative treatment of a room.
5. Name several characteristics of room decoration that should be avoided.
6. Name several decorative features that would be particularly suitable in rooms expressive of the following types of people:
   a. An eight-year-old boy.
   b. A conservative old lady.
   c. A sophisticated young married couple.
   d. A bachelor who is fond of travel.
   e. A motion picture actress famous for her dancing.

Chapter XXIII

QUESTIONS

1. What is meant by the terms "symmetrical balance" and "optical balance"?
2. What are the principles usually followed in classical design for subdividing walls horizontally?
3. What produces the effects of vertical lines in room furnishings and decorations?
4. Why are square and circular forms usually inadvisable?
5. What do you understand by the word "scale" in reference to design?

1. The instructor should prepare some simple wall elevations pierced with various arrangements of windows, doors, mantel, etc., at a scale of 4 feet to the inch, and the student should study a composition for them by simple outline drawings of draperies and furniture similar to those presented in the illustrations on pages 762 and 763. For convenience in drawing, students may trace and use the furniture outlines shown on page 768. These pieces are shown at the scale of 4 feet to the inch, so that they will correspond to a wall elevation drawn at the same scale. Other furniture outlines may also be prepared by the instructor and copied in the students' notebooks.

2. Problems should be given for the study of walls of varying dimensions and types. It is helpful to take actual walls from rooms in the school, or from those in the students' own homes. These may be drawn in the same simple manner and studied on paper for wall composition. They may be assumed to be living rooms, bedrooms, libraries, offices, etc.

Chapter XXIV

QUESTION

Memorize the important suggestions for furniture arrangement given in the text and be prepared to write them in your own words.

PROBLEMS

Materials: Plans of several rooms of various dimensions are to be provided by the instructor, with architectural features indicated as in the simple plan shown on page 777.

1. Copy accurately one of the plans provided.

2. Cut out of thin cardboard duplicates of the pieces of furniture shown on page 786, and experiment with various possibilities for furniture location in the room plan you have made. When a final solution has been reached, outline each piece of furniture on the plan and indicate its name. The plans of the entire class should be exhibited and discussed.

Chapter XXV

QUESTIONS

1. What is the difference between spectral and pigment colors?

2. What are the general rules to follow in relation to the relative neutrality for colors in the different color areas of a room?

3. What are the psychological effects of different colors?
4. What wall colors are advisable for small rooms? What wall colors are permissible in large rooms? What are the cool colors?
5. What are the primary pigment colors; the secondary pigment colors?
6. Explain the words: hue, chroma, tint, shade, neutral color, and complementary color.
7. What effect has inadequate natural light upon the colors in a room?
8. What color change occurs when pigment is applied to a rough-textured surface?
9. Why are simple color compositions for room interiors preferable to schemes composed of many colors?
10. If a red surface adjoins an orange one, how does the red affect the orange? How would a blue surface affect an adjoining green surface?

PROBLEMS

Work out six different color schemes for rooms. Students should use poster or tempera pigments, fabrics, and wallpaper samples, if such are obtainable. Colors should be selected for walls, draperies, floor coverings, large upholstered pieces of furniture, and small accents if any. Specific problems may be composed by the instructor, or any of the following ones may be used:

1. A scheme for a woman's small bedroom with southern exposure.
2. A masculine living room with ample light to be done in dark tones.
3. A doctor's office with poor natural light.
4. An average-size Colonial bedroom with windows on two sides.
5. A large modern living room with high ceiling and a very large north window. The walls are lined in bleached oak plywood.
6. A small child's playroom with ample sunlight.

INDEX

Definitions of technical terms are given in the general glossary on page 811. French decorative art terms are given on page 231, textile terms on page 464, painters' pigments on page 626, ceramic terms on page 219, and cabinet woods on page 741. Lists of craftsmen and important decorative artists of each period will be found at the end of each chapter in Part One. Bibliographies are given at the end of each chapter.

Aalto, Alvar, 420, 421, 423, 425
A la, turque, 198; *grecque,* 211
Abacus, 41, 811
Abbaye-aux-Dames, -aux-Hommes, Caen, 82, 83
Abbey of Vezelay, France, 79
Abstract art and design, 591, 599, 811
Acanthus leaf, 45, 323, 811
Acapulco, Mexico, ceramics, 174
Accents, color, 799
Accessories, purpose of, 636; arrangement of in wall composition, 766; period with contemporary, 342, 348; peasant, 364. *See also* descriptions under country or style
Acropolis, in Athens, 38
Acroteria, 211, 811
Acts of the Apostles tapestries, 477
Adam, R. and J., 266–273, 653; book by, 263
Adam style, 266–273; influences, in Spain, 168, in France, 207, in America, 315; silverware, 671
Adams, W., 654
Affleck, T., 302, 335
African Negro sculpture, 376
Agate ware, 652, 654, 811
Agra, India, 350; Taj Mahal, 351
Aix, France, 593
Alabaster, 21, 811
Alamo, The, 333
Alaskan Indian arts, 375
Alba, Duchess of, 577
Alberti, L., 134

Alcazar, in Seville, 145, 146, 351; in Toledo, 157
Alcora, Spain, 640
Alexander, 35, 48
Alexandria, Egypt, 24
Alexandrian Age, in Greece, 37
Alfonso the Wise, 151
Alhambra, The, in Granada, 144–145; vases, 638
Aljubarrota, battle of, 160
Alken, sporting prints of, 613
Allah, 138
Alloys, 667, 811
Altamira, Spain, prehistoric painting in, 18
Aluminum, 667–668
Amboise, France, château, 562
America, Central, art influences in, 172; Indian arts of, 366–371
America, North, Indian arts of, 373–377
America, South, Indian arts of, 371–373
American styles of art, 268, 282–339; painting, 601–608; ceramics, 655–656; glassware, 661–664; Colonial silver and pewter, 671–672; metalwork, 674; Colonial and Georgian lighting fixtures, 694, 695; Colonial murals and stencil ornament, 702, 703, 707; wall treatments, 731
American-Oriental rugs, 518
Amherst, Mass., 323
Amorini, 61, 205, 811
Amphora, 46, 50, 811
Amsterdam, Holland, 358
Analogous color scheme, 799

i

Ancien regime, France, 181
Andalusia, Spain, 146, 576
Angelico, Fra, 109, 134, 561
Angelo, Michael. *See* Michael Angelo
Angers tapestries, 473
Anne, Queen, 235; style, in England, 238, 253–255, 257; of Cleves, 573
Annual rings in wood, 734
Anta, 811
Antefix, 46, 811
Anthemion, 45, 323, 811
Antimacassars, 328, 811
Antioch, mosaic from, 66
Antique, 332, 811; silverware, 670–672; woodwork, 698
Antiquing, 432–433, 635
Antiquity, styles of, 17–68
Antoinette, Marie. *See* Marie Antoinette
Antwerp, Belgium, 358; tapestries, 473; Cathedral, 569
Apollo, Temple of, 38
Applied moldings, 732
Applique, 812
Approaching colors. 791. 825
Apron, 252, 812
Apse, 812
Aquarelle, 609
Aquatints, 273, 611, 812
Arabesque, classical, 45, 59–61; development of, 148; origin of, 351; definition of, 812. *See also* descriptions under country or style for uses in later periods
Aragon, Spain, 139; Ferdinand of, 138, 144, 233; Catherine of, 233
Aranda, B., Count, 174, 640
Aranjuez, palace in, 159, 171; ceramic wall decorations, 640
Arca, 16, 812
Arcade, 812
Arcaded panels, 243, 812
Arcanum, 646
Archaic period, in Greece, 36–38; sculpture during, 47, 812
Arches, construction of, 6; comparative forms of, 8, 9; first use of, 21; origin of, 22; definition of, 812
Architects. *See* lists at end of each chapter in Part One.
Architect's table, 812
Architectural features, lighting of, 680; included in word "trim," 715; mantels, 724; built-ins, 725, 727, 778; dimensions of, 770
Architecture. *See* descriptions under country or style
Architrave, 42, 812
Arctic Indian arts, 375, 376
Arcuate, 812
Area effects in color, 801
Arequipa, Peru, 173
Arfe, or Arphe, 174
Argand lamp, 812
Arizona, Indians in, 373
Arkwright, R., 235

Arles, S. Trophime, 82
Arlington, Va., Lee Mansion, 323
Armada, Spanish, 140, 234
Armoire, 186, 225, 230
Armory Show, N. Y., 1913, 600, 607
Arms, 610
Arrangement, of pictures, 618–620; of furniture, 775–787
Arras, France, tapestries, 96, 242, 431; definition of, 812; ceramics, 644
Arrazzi, 812
Arris, 812
Art, styles of, methods for dividing, 11–14; books on, publication of, 262–263; objects, antique, uses in contemporary decoration, 342, 348; peasant, in contemporary decoration, 364; centers, in Italy, 559; museums of, establishment, 607; great, reasons for, 750
Art galleries. *See* Museums
Art Nouveau, 388, 389, 390, 394, 415, 417, 418
Artesonado, 812
Artifacts, 812; prehistoric, 19
Artistic integrity, definition of, 750
Artists. *See* lists at end of each chapter in Part One
Arts. *See* Decorative arts
Arts and Crafts Movement, 387, 388, 392, 393, 414, 415
Asbestos fiber, 435
Ash House, Charleston, S. C., 312
"Ashcan School," 607
Asheville, N. C., "Biltmore," 332
Ashlar, 712, 812
Asphalt tile, 529
Assisi, S. F. of, 559
Assyrian civilization, 21, 22
Astbury, J. and T., 652
Astragal molding, 812
Astral lamp, 812
Athena, statue of, 38
Athens, Ga., 323
Athens, Greece, 38–39; Parthenon, 37, 47
Atrium, 62, 812
Attic, 190, 812
Aubusson, tapestries, 481–482; rugs, 520–521. *See also* Tapestries, Floor coverings, and descriptions under country or style
Audubon, J. J., 336, 613
Augustus, King of Saxony, 646
Aurignacian period, 377
Austrian styles of art. *See* Germanic nations, Renaissance arts of
Avignon, Palace of the Popes, 95
Axminster carpets, 518, 812
Azay-le-Rideau, château, 184
Aztec Indian arts, 369–371; conception of Madonna in, 86; influence of, in Latin American architecture, 172
Azulejos, 160, 172, 640, 812

Babylonian civilization, 21
Bacchus, in painting, 576

Backgrounds and wall treatments, 696–714. *See also* Walls, and descriptions under country or style
Bagnell clocks, 309
Bahia, Brazil, 173
Balance, in wall composition, using pictures, 620; optical and symmetrical, 762–764; quantity, 772
Balboa, Vasco de, 139
Baldachino, 790; in S. Peter's, 119
Balkan States, peasant arts in, 362–365
Ball foot, 812; in Dutch furniture, 357
Ball-and-claw foot. *See* Claw-and-ball foot
Ballet, 107
Baltimore, Md., 657
Baluster, 124, 812
Bambino, 117, 813
Bamboo, style of Chippendale, 258; turnings, 813
Banding, 791; cross, 252, 255, 295
Bandy-legged, 813. *See* Cabriole
Banister, 813
Banister-back chair, 296, 813
Banjo clocks, 309
Baptistery, 77, 813; of Florence, 109
Barbarians, 76
Barbizon School, 581, 590, 591; influence of, in America, 605
Barcelona chairs, 163
Barchester tapestries, 474
Bargello, Florence, 559
Baroque style, painting in France, 585–586; definition of, 813. *See also* descriptions under country
Barrel vault, 6, 813
Basalt, 23, 813; ware, 654, 813
Base, of a column, 7, 56, 59; definition of, 813; molding, 813
Baseboard, 717, 718, 813
Bases of paint, 623
Basic hues, 791–792
Basilicas, Roman, 54; Early Christian, 76, 78; definition of, 813
Basket weave, 813
Basketry. *See* Indian arts, 366–377
Basle, Switzerland, 573
Basques, 137
Basra, 350
Bas-relief, 813. *See also* Low relief
Bastille, Paris, 181
Bataille, N., 476
Batalha, Portugal, 165
Baths of Caracalla, Rome, 55
Batik, 813
Battersea, England, 650; wallpapers, 543
Bauhaus, in Germany, 399, 400, 402
Bavarian interiors, 359, 362
Bay and bay window, 813
Baziotes, W., 608
Bead, molding, 45, 813; and shell pictures, 613
Beaker, 813
Beam, 5; definition of, 813; and lintel, *see* Lintel

Beauty, Line of, of Hogarth, 45, 580; contemporary concept of, 391
Beauvais tapestries, 189, 191. *See also* Tapestries
Beaux Arts, Ecole des, Paris, 332
Bedding. *See* Sleeping equipment
Bedrooms, arrangement of, 783
Beds, contemporary, 403; styles and location of, 783. *See also* Sleeping equipment
Behrens, P., 398
Belfast, Ireland, 661
Belgian Congo, arts of, 376
Bell turning, 813
Bellini, G. and J., 564
Bellows, G., 607, 611
Belter, J. H., 329–330, 335
Benard and Jacquemart, 227
Bench, Spanish, 166
Benedictine Order, 80
Beneman, G., 211, 228
Benin, Africa, arts of, 377
Benjamin, A., 334
Bennington ware, 649, 656
Benson, 610
Benton, T. H., 608
Berain, J., 188, 226
Berbers, 137
Bergère, 201, 230
Berlage, H. P., 398
Berlin, Germany, ceramics, 647
Bernadotte family, in Sweden, 216, 360
Bernini, G., 110, 118, 134; influence of, in France, 188
Bessemer process, 384
Bethlehem, Church of the Nativity, 77
Betty-lamp, 695
Bevel, in glass, 255, 300, 307; definition of, 813
Bible box, 245
Bibliographies. *See* list placed at end of each chapter.
Bibliothèque, 230
Biedermeier style, 216, 360–362, 614
"Biltmore," Asheville, N. C., 332
Binder, in paint, 623
Bird's beak molding, 27
Bird's-eye veneer, 736–737, 813
Biscuit, definition of, 636, 813; wares, 644, 648, 651
Bismarck, 389
Bisque. *See* Biscuit
Blackamoor statues, 328, 813
Blampied, 611
Bleach, 813
Bleu-du-roi, 644
Blinds, Venetian and woven wood, 502
Block printing, 814
Block-front furniture, 303, 813
Blois, château, fireplace, 98, 184; stairway, 178
Blue, and white ceramics, Staffordshire, 654; Chinese, 658; ware, old, 655
Blue period, of Picasso, 600
Boabdil, 138, 144

Boardman, T., 336
Boccaccio, G., 104, 106, 134
Body, 814
Body-support furniture, 402
Bogardus, James, 390, 391
Bohemian glass, 660–661
Boiserie, 191, 359
Bolection, moldings in Italian Renaissance, 115, 119; panelling in English Restoration style, 246–247, 249; in American Colonial style, 299, 724; definition of, 814
Bolivia, 371
Bolt. *See* Bundle
Bombé fronts, 200
Bonader, 814
Bonaparte. *See* Napoleon
Bonaparte, J., 169, 577
Bone, 589; porcelain, 637
Bonheur, M. R., 590
Bonington, R. P., 583
Bonnet top, 814
Book, covers, Gothic, 94; cases, 781; of Color, of Munsell, 796
Books, publication of art, 262–263; decorative effect of, 781; sample, of colors, 806
Borax furniture, 392
Border patterns, 14, 814; wallpaper, 532
Borghese, family, 109; P., 216
Bosch, 568
Boss, 814
Bossi, 271
Boston, Mass., Custom House, 323; Trinity Church, 326, 385
Boston-rocker, 305, 814
Bottger, K., 646
Botticelli, S., 134, 560, 561
Bottles and flasks, historical American, 663–664
Bouché, L., 608
Boucher, F., 197, 226, 585, 645
Boulard, J. B., 203, 228
Boulle, André Charles, 192–193, 228; André Charles, Jr., 228; Charles Joseph, 228
Boulle work, 193, 814. *See* Inlay
Bow ware, 648, 650
Box springs, 511
Box-plaiting, 495, 814
Bracket, 814; foot, 256, 814
Bradshaw, G. and W., 277
Bradwell Wood, England, 652
Braided rugs, 526
Bramante, D., 110, 118, 134
Braque, G., 600
Brass, 667, 669, 814; objects of, for decorative use, 673–675
Brasses, 814
Braziers, 55, 95, 814
Brazil, 139, 173
Breakfront, 814
Breuer, M., 399, 404, 405, 413, 420, 423, 425
Brewster chair, 814
Brick, use of, for walls, 397, 711, 712
Bristol, ceramics, 648, 649; glass, 661

British Museum, 654
British styles. *See* English styles
Broadloom rugs, 522, 814
Broken pediment, 7, 814
Bromley-on-Bow, England, interior, 241
Bromwich, 276
Bronze, 666, 670; statuary, 930
Brotherhood, Pre-Raphaelite, in England, 277, 383, 567, 683
Browne, R., 651
Brueghel, P., or Breughel, P., 568, 570
Bruges, Belgium, 567. *See also* Tapestries
Brunelleschi, F., 109, 134, 560
Brussels, carpets, 517, 814; tapestries, *see* Tapestries
Bucrania, 45
Buddhism, 342, 346; emblems of, used in Chinese ceramics, 658
Buen-Retiro ceramics, 171, 640
Buffet, 814
Built-in furniture and niches, 725, 727, 778; in Italian Renaissance, 117; Moorish, 150; in America, 315; Shaker, 322. *See also* Niche, Interior trim, Furniture, and descriptions under country or style
Bulbous forms, 243, 814
Bulbs and tubes, electric, 680–681
Bulfinch, C., 313, 334
Bun foot, 186, 252, 814
Bundle, 814. *See* Wallpaper
Burchfield, C., 678
Burette, C. M., 219, 228
Burgos, Spain, Cathedral, 151
Burl, 736, 814
Burnap, D., 309, 335
Burne-Jones, Sir E., 277, 583
Burslem, England, 653
Butt joint, 717, 814
Butterfly, hinge, 675; table, 294, 814
Buttress, 88–89, 814
Butt-wood veneer, 737–738, 814
Byzantine style, 69–76
Byzantium, 71

Cabinet woods, 734–744. *See* Woods
Cabinets-particuliers, 195
Cabochon, 94
Cabot, J. and S., 233
Cabral, P. de, 139
Cabriole leg, first use of, 165; French, 200, 201, 208; English, 254; in English Windsor chairs, 257; use of by Chippendale, 261; definition of, 814
Cadiz, 139
Caen, France, Abbaye-aux-Dames, aux-Hommes, 82
Caen stone, 196, 704–705, 815
Caffagiolo, Italy, 641
Caffieri, J. and P., 193, 228, 667
Cairo, Egypt, Pyramids, 25, 26; mosques in, 351
Calamine doors, 720
Calcimine, 624, 632, 700
Calderòn de la Barca, P., 174

Caldwell, 653
Calender, 815
California missions, 333
Callicrates, 38
Calligraphy, 815; Chinese, 348; Persian, Kufic, or cursive, 353, 354
Camber, 815. *See* Splay
Camel back, 815
Cameo, 815
Cameron, 610, 611
Camoens, or Camoës, L. V. de, 144, 174
Campaniform capital, 26
Canabas, J., 228
Candelabra, 67; ceiling types, 686, 815
Candle bulbs, 686–687
Canopy, 91, 815
Canterbury, 815; Cathedral of, 94
Cantilever construction, 815
Canton, china, 815; New, 649
Canvas wall coverings, 629
Cape of Good Hope, 139
Capistrano, S. Juan, 333
Capital, of a column, 7, 83, 815. *See also* descriptions under country or style
Capitol, in Richmond, Va., 313
Capo-di-Monte ceramics, 171, 639, 640, 641, 691
Caquetoire, 186, 187
Caracalla, Baths of, Rome, 55
Caravaggio, M., 134, 566–567, influence of in Spain, 574
Carcase or core of furniture, 736, 815
Carlin, M., 211, 228
Carolean period in England, 238
Carpets. *See* Floor coverings
Carthaginians, 137
Carthusian Order, 80
Cartoon, 815. *See* Tapestries
Cartouche, 115, 815
Cartuja, La, in Granada, 158
Carved rugs, 522, 523, 815
Carver chairs, 295, 815
Carving, ivory, 346, 353
Caryatid, 45, 815
Case furniture, 402, 815
Casein, use of in paint, 623
Casement windows, 721, 815
Cassapanca, 122, 124, 815
Cassat, M., 606
Cassino, Monte, 80
Cassone, 122, 124, 815
Cast iron, 667
Castel Durante, Italy, 641
Caster, 815
Castile, Spain, 139
Castles, in Spain, 153; Windsor, in England, 573
Catacombs, in Rome, 70, 815
Catalonia, Spain, ceramics, 640
Catenary arches, 333, 815
Cathedrals. *See* Churches, and descriptions under country or style
Catherine of Aragon, 233
Catholicism, 563

Caucasian rugs, 511
Cavetto molding, use of in Egypt, 27; definitions, 44, 815
Ceiling lights. *See* Lighting
Ceilings. *See* descriptions under country or style
Cella, 815
Cellaret, 815
Cellini, B., 11, 126, 134, 177, 667
Cellulose, 815
Centennial Exposition, Philadelphia, 1876, 285, 331
Central America. *See* America, Central
Ceramics, use of in furniture, 265; definitions of term, 636, 815; glossary of, 637. *See also* 636–665, and descriptions under country or style
Cerceau, J. de, 185, 186, 226
Certified lamps, 687–688
Certosina, 121, 815. *See also* Inlay, Intarsia, Marquetry
Cervantes Saavedra, M. de, 141, 144, 174
Cezanne, P., 590, 593
Chair legs, French, 200, 201, 209; English 254, 257, 262. For further descriptions, *see* country or style
Chair rail, 718, 815. *See also* Dado, Wainscot, and descriptions under country or style
Chair table, 815
Chairs. *See* descriptions under country or style
Chaise-longue, 196, 230
Chaldean civilization, 21
Chalice, 815
Chambers, Sir W., 268, 276, 313; influence of in France, 207
Chambord, château, 184
Chamfer, 815. *See* Bevel
Champlevé enamelware, 74, 815
Champollion, 30
Chandelier, 816
Chandos House, London, 267
Chansons-de-geste, 85
Chansons de Roland, 138
Chapels, Sistine, Vatican, 86, 111, 562; S. Chapelle, Paris, 92; Rosary, S. Domingo Puebla, Mexico; and S. Tomé, Toledo, 172
Characteristics, expressible in rooms, 755; of colors, 790–791
Chardin, J., 586, 587
Charger, 816
Charlemagne, 77, 79, 80, 138, 182
Charles I of England, 234, 237, 578; I of Spain, 355; II of England, 234, 238, 251, 358; II of Spain, 140; III of Spain, 640; IV of Spain, 555; V of Spain, 139, 177, 355; VIII of France, 177, 181; IX of France, 178, 182; X of France, 182
Charleston, S. C., 323; Ash House, 312; Steele House, 325
Charlotte, Queen, 654
Chartres Cathedral, 90, 94

Charts, color, use of, 789, 795–796; for presenting scheme, 807

Chasing, 677, 816

Châteaux, at Blois, 98, 178, 184; Langeais, 102; in Touraine, 184; Azay-le-Rideau, Chambord, Chaumont, Chenonceaux, 184; Vaux-le-Vicomte, 188; Compiegne, Malmaison, 216; Amboise, 562

Chaumont, château, 184

Check, 816

Checkerboard, 82, 816

Chelsea ware, 643, 648, 650

Chemical basis of paint, 794

Chenille carpets, 515–516

Chenonceaux, château, 184

Cheops, Pyramid of, 26

Cherry, 742

Chest-on-chest, 816

Chests, 99, 816. See also descriptions under country or style

Cheval glass, 816

Chevron, 82, 816

Chiaroscuro, 571–572, 816

Chicaneau, P., 644

Ch'ien Lung, Emperor, 658

Children's Crusade, 85

Children's rooms, treatment of, 771; arrangement of, 785

Chile, 371; Santiago de, 173

Chimera ornament, 45

China, definition of term, 638, 816. See Ceramics

Chinese, lacquer, 201, 255, 345, 357; Chippendale furniture, 258; art objects in contemporary rooms, 342, 348; dynasties, tables of, 343, 657, 658

Chinese styles of art, 341–349; rugs, 534–536; ceramics, 639, 645, 656–659. For influences on Western art, see descriptions under country or style, and chapters on ceramics, textiles, etc.

Ch'ing Dynasty in China, 342, 345, 657, 658

Chinoiseries, 198, 201, 205; in Spanish art, 168

Chippendale, Thomas I, 257, 278; Thomas II, 131, 257–262, 278; Thomas III, 263, 278; influences in Spanish art, 168; furniture, 257–262

Chirico, E. de, 600

Chivalry, 85

Chocolate drinking, 255, 670

Chopin, F., 182

Christian churches, Early, 78

Christianity, introduction of in Rome, 70

Chroma, or chromatic value, 630, 790, 816

Chromatic distribution, Law of, 799

Chromium, 667

Church, Early Christian, 76, 78; of the Ascension, Jerusalem, and of the Nativity, Bethlehem, 77; protests against authority of, 104; attitude of during Italian Renaissance, 107

Church, F. E., 605

Churches, Byzantine, 72; S. Mark's, S. Vitale, 75; Russian, 76; of the Ascension, of the Nativity, S. Apollinare-in-Classe, S. Appollinare Nuovo, S. Maria Maggiore, S. Paul's-Beyond-the-Walls, 77; Early Christian, 78; Abbey of Vezelay, 79, 83; Romanesque, 81; Abbaye-aux-Dames, and aux-Hommes, S. Trophime, Pisa Cathedral, 82, 83; Mont S. Michel, 82, 95; Durham and Peterborough Cathedrals, 83; Notre Dame, 86, 87, 92; Chartres, 90, 94; Canterbury and York Cathedrals, 94; Florence, 109; S. Peter's, 110, 111; Burgos, Leon, Salamanca, Seville, Toledo Cathedrals, 151, 152; Spanish, 152; Latin American, 172–173; Tepoztlan, Mexico, 173; Lincoln, Salisbury, Wells Cathedrals, 233; S. Paul's, London, 234; S. Patrick's Cathedral and Trinity, N. Y., 325; Trinity, Boston, 326; Antwerp, 569; Rouen, 594

Churrigueresco style, 142, 157–160, 726; influences of, in Latin America, 172

Churriguero, J., 144, 157, 174

Cicero, 106

Cid, El, 138

Cimabue, 109, 134, 559

Cinquecento period, in Italy, 111, 123, 816; in France, 177; frames of paintings, 615, 617

Cinquefoils, 91, 816

Cipriani, G. B., 133, 276

Cire-perdue process, 127, 128, 666–667, 816

Ciseleurs, 202, 219

Cistercian Order, 94, 151

Civil War, 330, 331

Clapboard walls, 290, 816

Classic, 816; Revival, see descriptions under country or style. See also Empire style, Regency, Adam, Neo-classic, etc.

Classical, 816; order, diagram of, 56; sculpture, examples of, 59; orders, proportioning of, 759–760. For revivals, see Classic

Classification of colors, 791

Clavated turnings, 162, 816

Clavichord, 816

Claw-and-ball foot, 255, 812, 816

Clerestory windows, 87, 88, 711, 816

Clews, J., 654

Clifford's Inn, interior in, London, 246

Cloche, 826

Clocks, American, 308–310

Clodion, 207, 226, 646

Cloisonné enamelware, 74, 348, 816

Cloister, 54, 816

Clouded wares, 652

Clouets, the 583

Club-foot, 254, 816

Cluny, Cistercian monks in, 151; Museum, tapestries in, 475–476

Clustered columns, 88, 816

Cnossus, Palace of, 33–34

Coaching print, English, 612

Coal, introduction of, as fuel, 696

Coalport, England, 652
Cobb, J., 278
Cobbler's bench, 816
Cochois, J. B., 228
Cockfight chair, 816
Cocoon hinge, 675
Code Napoleon, 181
Coffee drinking, 255, 670
Coffer, 816
Coffered ceilings, 115
Cole, T., 605
Collage, 600, 817
Collections and hobbies, use of in decoration, 756–757
Collectors' items, bottles, 664; list of common types, 756–757
Colleone, statue of in Venice, 561
Colombia, 173
Colonial painting. See American painting
Colonial style, American. See American styles of art
Colonna family, 109
Colonnade, 817
Colonnette, 817
Color and color schemes, 788–808; use of, in Impressionism, 591; from paintings, 618, 619; pigments, glossary of, 626; matching of, 630; complement of, 630; in Stiegel glass, 662; absorption of, light by, 689–690; and texture, in wall treatments, 764; wheel, use of, 791–792, 797, 799–800, and Frontispiece. See also descriptions under country or style
Colored engravings, 615
Colosseum, Rome, 22
Columbani, P., 276
Columbian Exposition of 1893. See Chicago World's Fair
Column, origin of, 7; entasis of, 42; use of diameter for proportioning, 58; definition of, 817. See also descriptions under country or style
Comb back, 817. See Windsor chair
Comfortables, 328, 507
Commercial, finishes in metal hardware, 670; interior designs, 752
Commode, 230
Compagnie des Indes, 197, 644
Compass curves. See Mechanical curves
Compiegne, château, 216
Complementary colors, 630, 791, 817; use of, in Impressionism, 591; schemes using, 799
Composite order, 58, 59, 817
Composition, ornament, 61, 817; of walls, 619, 620, 758–774; of paint, 621–622; in design, 758, 817
Compostela, Santiago de, 151
Concrete, use of in Roman construction, 56; blocks, use of in contemporary structures, 712
Concrete, reinforced, 397
Coney, J., 337, 671
Confidantes, 328

Confucianism, 342
Congo, Belgian, arts of, 376
Conic sections, curves of, 7
Connecticut chest, 295, 817
Conquistadors, 366
Conservatory of Music, Paris, 189
Consoles, French, 201, 230
Constable, J., 276, 581, 582
Constantine the Great, 71, 72, 76
Constantinople, 69, 71, 75, 95, 105, 137; S. Sophia, 72–74
Constitution mirror, 308
Construction, lintel, 5–6, 27, 823; truss, 6; trabeated, 27; of furniture, Spanish, 162–164; cantilever, 387–390, 815; of draperies, 495; of upholstered furniture, 507; details of wood panelling, 729, 732; skeleton, 829; see also descriptions under country or style
Contemporary styles of art, 381–408; in America, 286; in traditional backgrounds, 394; symmetry, lack of, in, 395, 764, 773; glassware, 664; lighting, 679–690; wall treatments, 710, 712, 713, 726; wall composition in, 759; beds, styles and arrangement of, 783. See also various chapters in Parts II and III
Contrast, and variety, 755; types of, 756; in line, 755–756, 766–767; in wall composition, 764; in color schemes, 769, 798; of floors and upholstery, 764–765
Conventionalization, 12, 817
Conversation, piece, 579, 817; chair, 817
Conversational groups, 777, 779
Convex mirror, 308
Cool colors, 791, 817
Cooper, J., 603
Copeland, book by, 262
Copeland, W. T., 654
Copley, J. S., 336, 602
Copper, 667, 669; luster plaque, Hispano-Mauresque, 149; objects for decorative use, 673–675
Coptic sect, Egypt, 350, 351
Coquille, 194
Corbel, 239, 817
Cordova, de, 139
Cordova, Spain, 350; Great Mosque in, 144, 351
Cordovan leather, 170
Corinthian order, Roman, 41–43, 58, 817
Cork, floor coverings, 529, 734; wall coverings, 713
Cork, Ireland, 660
Corneille, P., 179
Corner block, 717, 817; in upholstered furniture, 507
Cornice, 817; classical, 42, boards for draperies, 492; lighting, 685, 686; and cove details, 722–724. See also Interior trim, and descriptions under country or style
Corning, N. Y., 664
Cornucopia leg, 319
Coromandel, 742, 817; screen, 349

Corot, J., 588, 589
Corporation pictures, 569
Correggio, A., 563
Cortez, H., 139, 366, 369
Costa Rica, gold work, 369
Cotton fiber, 431
Council of Trent, 141
Counter Reformation, 108, 118, 563, 566
Counter thrust, 817; in Gothic construction, 89. *See* Thrust
Counterfeit porcelain, 641
Country-made, 817; furniture in America, 305
Courbet, G., 588, 589
Cove, 190, 781, 782; and valance lighting, 683; and cornice details, 722–724; in contemporary lighting layouts, 724; definition of, 817. *See also* Interior trim, and descriptions under country or style
Coverage of paint, 625
Coysevox, A., 188, 226
Craftsmen. *See* lists at end of each chapter in Part I
Cream ware, 649, 652
Creche, 817
Credence, or credenza, 97, 99, 123, 124, 186, 230
Cressent, C., 193, 228
Cresson, M., 203, 228
Cretan art, 33
Crewel embroidery, 242
Criard, or Criaerd, M., 203, 228
Crockets, 91, 817
Cro-Magnon Man, 17–19
Cromwell, O., 234
Cromwellian period, 237
Cross-banding, 252, 255, 295
Crotch veneers, 736, 817
Crown molding, 817
Crucifix, 92
Crucifixion tapestry, 472
Crusades, 80; effect of, 84, 85
Crystal, 818
Crystal Palace, London, 385, 386
Cubism, 591, 600, 818; Cezanne, forerunner of, 593
Cucci, D., 228
Cuneiform, 21, 818
Curie, Mme., 182
Currier and Ives, lithographs by, 330, 615
Curry, J. S., 608
Curves, classification of, 7, 8; mathematical and mechanical, 7–8, 44, 45; cyma recta and reversa, 44, 45; serpentine, 829
Cushions, for upholstery, 509
Cusping, 91, 818
Custom House, Boston, 323
Cuyp, A., 569
Cuzco, Peru, 173, 371
Cylinder printing, 440, 456; use of, in England, 235
Cyma curves, recta and reversa, 44, 45, 818
Czechoslovakia, peasant arts in, 362

Da Vinci, L., 109, 134, 177, 561, 562
Dadaism, 600
Dado, 726, 818; origin of, 42, 58; cap, 718
Dacron, 434
Daguerre, L., 330
Daguerreotypes, 330, 603, 818; cases of, 331
Dahomey, arts of, 376
Dais, 96, 818
Dale, 653
Dali, S., 578, 600
Damascening, 171, 355, 818
Damascus, 350
Dance, in Spain, 143
Danforth, S., 336
Dante, Alighieri, 104, 106, 134, 559
Dante chair, 122, 125, 163
Dark Ages, 69
Daubigny, C., 590
Daumier, H., 588, 589, 611
Davanzati Palace, Florence, 114, 116
David, J. L., 215, 226, 586, 587
Davies, A. B., 607
Davis, S., 607
Deal wood, 246, 742, 818
Decalcomania, 300, 321, 654, 818
Decameron, 107
Declaration of Independence, 313
Decorative artists. *See* lists at end of each chapter
Decorative Arts, Exposition of, in Paris, 1925, 390; taste in, 749–757; styles, development of, 753; terms, glossary of, 811–833
Decorative materials and accessories, Part Two, 429
Defects in rugs, 538
Degas, E., 590, 591, 592
Delacroix, E., 587, 588
Delanois, L., 228
Delftware, 311, 358, 641–643, 648
Delhi, India, 350
Della Robbia, family, 110, 134; work of, 117; plaques, 641; L., 641
Delorme, P., 185, 226
Demotic, 29, 818
Demuth, C., 608
Dentil, 44, 61, 818
Derain, 600
Derby ware, 648–651
Derbyshire chair, 244, 818
Deruta ware, 126
Descartes, R., 183
Design, definition of, 13–14 (*See* Ornament); Greek theories of, 39–40; contemporary concepts and standards of, 749–757; individuality in, 754, 755; of walls, 758, 774; interior, *see* Interior design
Desmalter, Jacob. *See* Jacob-Desmalter
Desornamentado style, 142–156, 818
De Stijl (also called Neo Plasticism), 397, 398, 401, 418
Deutsche Wërkbund, 398, 418

Diameter of column, used for proportioning, 58, 818
Diana, Temple of, Nimes, 81
Diane de Poitiers, 185, 585, 642
Diaper patterns, 14, 818. *See* Ornament
Diaz, 590
Dijon, France, interior in, 205
Dilettanti, Society of, 235
Dimensions, of furniture, in elevation, 768, in plan, 786; of architectural features, 770
Dinanderies, 774, 775, 818
Dinant, Flanders, 675
Dining rooms, arrangement of, 781–783
Diocletian's Palace, Spolato, 268
Diorite, 23, 818
Dip-dyeing, 818
Dipylons, 51
Direct, printing of textiles, 440; lighting, 681–682
Directoire style, 181, 212–214; lighting fixtures, 692
Directorate, French, 181
Disk-turnings, 48, 66, 162, 818
Distance effects of color, 801
Distant and receding colors, 791, 818
Distemper, 818. *See* Tempera
Divisions of walls, 760, 761, 766
Doccia ware, 639, 641, 645
Dolphin ornament, 59
Dom Manuel I, of Portugal, 160
Dome, 818; in Roman architecture, 55; S. Sophia, 72–73; S. Mark's, 75; Florence Cathedral, 109; S. Peter's, 111, 118; Taj Mahal, 351
Dominant, motif, importance of, 764, 765; color areas, 798
Dominican Order, 80, 172, 333
Domino wallpaper, 185, 818
Dominotiers, 541
Don Quixote, 141, 640
Donatello, 127, 135, 561
Donjon, 818
Doors, 715–720; hardware for, 675, 676. *See also* descriptions under country or style, and Interior trim
Dordogne, France, prehistoric painting in, 19
Doric order, 41–42, 43, 57, 59, 818
Dormer window, 819
Dou, 357
Double-duty rooms, arrangement of, 775
Double-hung windows, 721, 819
Doublet, 819
Doughty, T., 605
Douglas fir, 713, 742
Dovetail, 98, 717, 734, 819
Dowels, 98, 819
Down-lights, ceiling, 685
Drake, Sir Francis, 234
Draperies, 485–501; contrast of, with walls, 769
Drawings, 611

Dresden, Germany, 564, 646; ceramics, 211, 648, 650
Dressing and powder rooms, arrangement of, 785
Drop-lights, ceiling, 685
Drum, 119, 819
Dry points, 611
Drying, chemicals for paint, 624; of wood, kiln, 736
Du Barry, Countess, 180, 207
Du Bois, G. P., 608
Dual-purpose rooms, arrangement of, 775
Dublin, Ireland, 660
Dubois, 203, 228
Ducal Palace, Venice, 566
Duccio, 559
Duchamp, 600
Duchess of Alba, 577
Duesbury, 651
Dufour, J., 543; wallpapers by, 222, 552
Dufy, R., 600
Dummer, J., 337
Dupré, 590
Dürer, A., 573, 605, 610
Durham Cathedral, 83
Dutch styles of art, 355–356; furniture in America, 307; painting, 567, 573; ceramics, 641, 642
Dyeing of textiles, 441
Dyes in rugs, 537
Dynasties of China, 343, 657–658

Eakins, T., 605, 606
Eames, Charles, 408, 424, 425, 429
Early American style, 286–296. *See also* American styles of art
Early Christian period of art, 70, 76–77; churches, 78
Early Georgian style, in England, 238, 249–250, 254, 255, 257
Earthernware, definition of, 636. *See* Ceramics
East India, influence upon Portuguese arts, 165; Company, 197, 234, 569, 644, 651
East Indian rugs, 532–533
East Liverpool, O., 656
Eastern, church, influences of, 71; Roman Empire, 72
Eastlake, C. Jr., 276, 325
Ebéniste, 191, 211
Eby, 610
Ecce Homo, 152
Echinus, 41
Eclecticism, in Latin America, 174; in England, 275; in North America, 286, 326–327, 332, 753
Ecole des Beaux Arts, Paris, 332, 391–393
Ecran, 230
Ecuador, 173, 332
Edict of Nantes. *See* Nantes
Egas, E., 174
Egg-and-dart ornament, 44
Egg-crate louvers, 682
Eggshell finish, 625

Egypt, Ancient. *See* Egyptian styles of art
Egyptian styles of art, 22–33. For influences in later periods, *see* descriptions under country or style
Eight Immortals, 346, 657
El Greco. *See* Greco, El
Electricity, illumination by, 679, 680
Electroplating, 673, 819
Elevation, 819; indication of elements in, 768
Elgin Marbles, 47, 819
Elizabeth, Queen, 234; Furnace, Pa., 661
Elizabethan style, 237, 240, 243
Embossing, 819; of leather, 710
Embroideries, 613
Embuya wood, 173
Empire style, American, 320, 324; painting in France, 587; lighting, 692. *See* descriptions under country. *See also* Biedermeier and Regency
Enamel, definition of, in paint, 624; in ceramics, 637, 819
Enamelware, champlevé, 74; cloisonné, 74, 348, 369; Limoges, 102; Chinese, 348
Encaustic, 819
Engaged column, 819
Enghien tapestries, 473
England, Pre-Raphaelite Brotherhood, 277, 383, 567, 583; Gothic Revival, 382
English styles of art, 233–281; influence of in Spain and Portugal, 166–168; painting, 569, 578–583; ceramics, 647–648, 652, 655; glassware, 661; silverware, 670–671; metalwork, 673–674; lighting, 692–694; wood panelling, 697, 728; Baroque styles, *see* Jacobean and Restoration styles
Engravings, 273, by Dürer, 573; steel, 610; colored, 615; description of process of, 819
Entablature, 41, 42, 59, 819
Entasis, of columns, 42, 819
Epinal pictures, 614
Erasmus, 233, 573
Escabelle, 186, 819
Escorial, Spain, 142, 156
Escritoire, 819
Escutcheons, 677, 819
Eskimo arts, 375–376
Este family, 109
Estrado, 154, 820
Etagère, 230
Etchers, American and foreign, 610
Etchings, by Rembrandt, 572; by Whistler, 606; descriptions of, 610, 820; framing of 618
Etruria, sculpture in, 59; England, Wedgwood ware, 653
Etruscan, 820; arches, 22. *See also* Tuscan
Eugenie, Empress, 169, 216
European, peasant arts, 362–365; glassware, 662
Evalde, M., 228
Evelyn, J., 247, 251
Exedra, 67, 820

Exposed structure, 289–290
Extract printing of textiles, 440
Eyck, H. & J. van, 568, 569

Fabrics. *See* Textiles
Face-painting, 601
Faenza, Italy, 126, 641, 642
Faïence ware, 640, 820
Famille noire, verte, rose, jaune, 659, 820
Farnese Palace, Rome, 113
Fasces, 820
Fascia molding, 44, 820
Fashion, 753. *See* Taste
Fauteuil, 230
Fauves, 598
Featherwork of Indians, 371–372
Federal Style. *See* Post-Colonial
Fenestration, 820
Fenton, C., 336
Ferdinand of Aragon, 138, 144, 233
Ferronerie velvet, 820
Feudalism, remnants of, in Spain, 141
Fiber rugs, 527
Fiberglas, 435
Fibers, for textiles, 431; synthetic, 434; tests for, 432; use for rugs, 527, 537
Fiddle-back chair, 820
Field of the Cloth of Gold, 234
Fieldstone, 398
Fiestas, in Spain, 153
Filet lace, 820
Filigree ornament, 94, 171, 820
Filippo Lippi, Fra, 561
Filler threads, 437
Fillet molding, 44, 820
Filling materials in upholstery, 509
Fine Arts, French National School of, 189, 332
Finial, 88, 820
Finish, in paint, 625, 628, 700, 703, 790
Firebacks, 661, 673, 820; and fireplace equipment, 725–726
Fireplaces. *See* descriptions under country or style, and Mantels
Fireproof doors, 720
Fireside figures, 820
Firing of ceramics, 636, 637, 820
Fixed elements in wall design, 758, 759
Fixtures for lighting, 679, 695
Flamboyant style, 88, 820
Flamenco dancing in Spain, 143
Flanders, 355
Flaxman, J., 272, 276, 654
Fleeson, P., 547
Flemish, scroll, 251, 357, 820; foot, 186, 820
Flemish styles of art, 355–358; influence in France, 178; tapestries, 478; painting, 567, 573. *See also* Dutch
Fleur-de-lis, 647, 820
Fleury, A., 203, 228
Flint-glass, 662
Flock wallpaper, 199, 250, 820
Flood and spot lights, 684

Floor, construction, cantilever, 390; coverings, 513–540; patterns, 733, 734; composition and furniture arrangement, 758, 775; contrast of with upholstery, 769–770; plans, typical, 777, 785–787
Floors. See descriptions under country or style
Floral marquetry, 252
Florence, Italy, Cathedral and Baptistery of, 109; Hospital of the Innocents, 109; Palazzo Vecchio, 113; Bargello, 559; art center, 559; founding of ceramic works, 641
Florentine, arch, 113, 820; painting, 560
Flossa weave, 521
Fluid plans, 395, 405, 820
Fluorescent, paints, 625; lighting, 681
Flush, 820
Flutes or flutings, 820; origin of, 40
Flying buttress, 88, 89, 820
Foam rubber. See Latex
Folk arts, 363
Folk painting. See Primitive and Folk painting
Folwell, J., 302, 335
Fontaine. See Percier and Fontaine
Fontainebleau, Francis I rooms in, 184; Neo-classic room in, 204; School, of painting, 583
Forain, 610
Forbidden City in China, 343
Form, 820
Formal room, 773
Fossil Man, 17
Fouquet, N., 187, 783
Four-poster bed, 783
Foyers, 783–784
Fra, Angelico, see Angelico, Fra; Filippo Lippi, see Filippo Lippi, Fra
Fractur paintings, 307, 820
Fragonard, J. H., 197, 207, 226, 585, 587
Frames, of upholstery, 607; of pictures, see Pictures
Francis, I of France, 177, 181, 562; II of France, 181
Francis I style, 178, 181, 184; in America, 385
Francis, S. of Assisi, 559
Franciscan Order, 80, 172, 333, 559
Frankenthal, Germany, 647
Franklin, B., 182
Franks, 138
Frederick the Great, 647
Free curves, 8
Freer Art Gallery, Washington, "Peacock" room, 606
French Academy, Rome, 189; Guiana, arts of, 376; headings, 495, 821; Revolution, 587; prints, framing of, 617; East India Company, 644; doors and windows, 707, 721; burl, 742; beds, 783
French styles of art, 177–232; in Italian Renaissance, 126; influence of in Spain, 166–169; furniture and decorative art

terms, glossary of, 230; influences in English furniture, 263; tapestries, 478; painting, 583–601; ceramics, 642–646; lighting, 691–692, 693; wood panelling, 697, 729–730
Fresco work, 708, 821; Minoan and Mycenean, 33–34; Mayan, 369; revival of in Mexico, 601
Fret ornament, 45, 46, 821
Frieseke, F. C., 607
Frieze, 42, 821
Frisé, 439
Fueros Juzgos, 138
Fugitive pigments, 628
Full-tone, 821
Fulton, R., 336, 603
Functionalism, in Greek architecture, 41; in Gothic architecture, 90; in Shaker furniture, 322
Furniture, hardware for, 667; lighting of, 644; veneers, 736–739; indication of, in plan and elevation, 768, 777, 785; arrangement of, 775–787. See also descriptions under country or style
Furstenberg, Germany, 647
Futurism, 591, 600

Gabon, 821
Gabriel, J. A., 207, 226
Gadrooning, 186, 243, 821
Gaine, 821
Gainsborough, T., 276, 580, 581
Galérie des Glaces, Versailles, 189
Galleries, of art. See Museums
Gallery, 821
Galloon, 821
Gama, Vasco da, 139
Gambard, 228
Gardens, Moorish, 146; of Versailles, 188; English, 238; Chinese, 344
Gargoyle, 91, 821
Garner, R., 653
Garrick, D., 580
Gaudi, Antonio, 389, 390
Gaudreau, A. R., 228
Gauguin, P., 590, 595
Gavarni, 611
Gaw, G. and R., 304
Gazebos, 250, 821
Gazette, N. Y., quotation from, 302
General Grant style in America, 326
Genghis Khan, 349
Genie, 21, 821
Genre, painting, 567, 568, 587, 821
Genuine leather, 435
Geometrical ornament, Moorish, 148; Islamic, 352
George I, of England, 235; II, of England, 235; III, of England, 235, 652, 654; IV, of England, 236
Georgian style, in England, 238, 246; in America, 286, 297, 299, 300
German silver, 669

German styles of art, 216, 358–362; painting, 573; ceramics, 646–647; Bohemian glassware, 660–661
Germanic nations, Renaissance arts of, 355–362
Germantown, Pa., 305
Gesso ornament, 121, 821
Ghengis Khan, 349
Ghent, Belgium, 567, 568
Ghiberti, L., 109, 127, 135
Ghiordes knot, 537
Gibbons, G., 247, 276; mirror by, 248
Gibbs, J., 276
Gillow, Richard, and Robert, 265, 278
Gillow and Shearer, 265
Gimson, Ernest, 416
Giorgione da Castelfranco, 135, 564, 565
Giotto di Bondone, 109, 135, 560
Giralda tower, Seville, 152
Girandole, 308, 821
Girder, 289, 821
Gizeh, Egypt, Pyramid of Cheops, 25, 26
Glackens, W., 605, 607
Glass, windows, first use of, in Europe, 95; structure of, 384; paintings on, 614, 615; production of, in antiquity, 660; methods of ornamentation of, 660; walls of, 710
Glassware, 659–664
Glaze, in ceramics, 638
Glazing, 632, 633; and antiquing of walls, 700
Glossaries, of French furniture, 230; of textiles, 464; ceramics, 637; cabinet-woods, 741; decorative art terms, 811
Goa, India, 165
Gobelins tapestries, 189, 191
Goddard, J., 301, 303, 335
Goddess of Mercy, 346
Gold, 667; leaf, use of, in tooled leather, 710; size, 635, 821
Gold Coast, arts of, 376
Golden Age, in Greece, 37; sculpture during, 47; in England, 234
Golden oak, 392
Good Hope, Cape of, 139
Goodison, B., 278
Gooseneck lamps, 687
Gothic Revival, in America, 325
Gothic style, 70, 80–102; revival of, in America, 325; tapestries, 475; painting in France, 583. See also descriptions under country
Goths, 80
Gottlieb, A., 608
Gouache, 609, 821. See Tempera
Goujon, J., 185, 226
Gouthiére, P., 220, 226, 667
Goya Y. Lucientes, F. de, 144, 174, 577, 579
Graeme Park, Philadelphia, 297
Graffito ware, 821
Graining, 269, 821; and marbling, 634, 733–734
Granada, Spain, 350; Alhambra, 144–146;

La Cartuja, 158; center of Spanish ceramics, 638
Grand Condé of France, 140
Grandfather and grandmother clocks, 310
Granite, 821; use in Egypt, 23, 26
Grass rugs, 528
Grays, 793
Great, hall, 96–97, 821; Fire of London, 234
Great Britain. See English styles of art
Greatbach, D., 336, 656; W., 653
Greco, El, 144, 155, 174, 574, 575
Greece, Ancient. See Greek styles of art
Greek, cross, 72, 821; Revival style in America, 286, 323
Greek styles of art, 34–52. For influences in later periods, see descriptions under country or style
Greenough, H., 323, 336
Gregg, F., 607
Gregorian chants, 85
Grendey, G., 278
Greuze, 586
Griffin ornament, 45, 59
Grisaille painting, 94, 206, 706, 708, 821
Groin vault, 821
Gropius, Walter, 398, 399, 400, 402, 404, 405, 406
Gros-point needlework, 439, 821
Grosz, G., 608
Grotesques, 59, 821
Growth rings in wood, 734, 735
Guadalete River, battle of, 138
Guadamacileria, 170, 821
Guas, E. and J., 175
Gubbio Majolica ware, 645
Guernica, 600
Guilds, 569; of S. Luke, 641
Guilford, Conn., 308
Guillemart, F., 228
Guilloche, 30, 45, 821
Guimpe, 821
Gunpowder, 184

H-L hinge, 675
Hadley chest, 294, 295, 821
Hadrian, Emperor, 56
Hagia Sophia. See S. Sophia
Haida Indians of British Columbia, 375
Haig, T., 278
Halfpenny, W., 277
Half-timber, 238, 240, 821
Half-tone, 821
Hall, of Justice, Alhambra, 144; of Ambassadors, Alcazar, Seville, 145; of Mirrors, Versailles, 189
Hallett, W., 278
Hallmark in silver, 670, 822
Halls, arrangement of, 783–784
Hals, F., 571, 572
Hamilton, Lady, portraits of, 581
Hamlet of Marie Antoinette, 208
Hammer-beam truss, 241, 822
Hampton Court Palace, 234, 248

Hand knotted rugs (contemporary), 521
Handmade rugs and carpets, 519
Hanging gardens in Babylonia, 21
Hanging of pictures, 616, 618, 620
Hanover, N. H., room in, 316
Hanseatic League, 567
Hard paste ceramics, 637, 638, 646, 822
Hardware, 675, 678; Gothic, 102
Hardwood, 734
Harland, T., 310, 335
Harmony, color, principles of, 788–810
Harrodsburg, Ky., 323
Hassam, C., 607
Hassocks, 328, 822
Hatshepsu, Temple of, 29
Hatton Garden, room from, 249
Hausmalerei, 647, 822
Haut-relief, 822
Havana, Cuba, 172
Havell, 613
Haverhill, Mass., house in, 314
Hawthorn jar, 658
Headings, for draperies, 495
Heartwood, 736
Heating, contemporary, 404
Hebrews, architectural style of, 22
Heddles, 436, 822
Hellas, 35
Hellenic Age, in Greece, 47
Hellenistic, 822; Age in Greece, 37, 47, 48
Hemp, 435
Hennin, 822
Henri, R., 607
Henry, II of France, 178, 181; III of France,
    182; IV of France, 178; VIII of England,
    233, 573, 578
Henry II style, 181–182, 185
Hepplewhite, G. & A., 263–265, 278
Herat, 350
Hermits, 75
Hernandez, G., 175
Herodotus, 23, 24, 37
Herold and Kandler, 646
Herrera, J. de, 142, 144, 156, 175
Herring, 613
Hesselium, G., 602
Het Loo, palace at, 253
Hex-signs, 306, 822
Hieratic, 29, 822
Hieroglyphics, 822; Egyptian, 29; Mayan,
    366, 367
High Baroque style, in Italy, 111–119; de-
    cline, 128
High relief, 12
Highboy, 252, 822
Hindu craftsmen, influence of, 165
Hinges. *See* Hardware
Hispania, 137
Hispanic periods. *See* Spanish styles of art
Hispano-Mauresque, 822; period, 142; ware,
    638
Historical schools of painting, 559
Hitchcock, 320–321
Hoadley, S., 310, 335

Hoban, J., 313, **334**
Hobbema, H., 569
Hobbies. *See* Collections
Hofmann, H., 608
Hogarth, W., 578–580; Line of Beauty of,
    45, 580
Holbein, H., 234, 573, 595
Holland, 139, 569. *See* Dutch styles of art
Holland, H., 277
Hom pattern, 441, 822. *See* Tree-of-life
Home, change in attitude toward, 698
Homemade rugs, 523
Homer, 34
Homer, W., 604, 605
Honeysuckle ornament, 45, 46, 822
Hooch, P. de, 569
Hooded fireplaces, 724
Hooked rugs, 523, 822
Hope, T., 278
Hopi Indians, 373
Hopper, E., 608
Hoppner, 581
Horizontal, divisions of walls, 759; and
    vertical contrasts, 766–767
Horseshoe arch, 145, 147, 351, 822
Hospital of the Innocents, Florence, 109
Houdon, J. A., 207, 226; work in America,
    311
House plans, American, 287, 288, 289
Howard, Admiral, 140
Hubener, G., 336
Huchiers-menuisiers, 191
Hudson River School, 604
Hue, 790, 822
Huet, C., 226; J. B., 227, 456
Huffelé, L., 228
Hugo, V., 328, 383
Huguenots, 180; immigrants in England,
    251
Hull, J., 337
Humanists, 104
Humor, in Chinese art, 346
Huns, 80
Hunt, W. H., 277, 583
Hunting tapestry, 472
Hutch, 99, 822
Hydria, 50, 822
Hypostyle Hall, at Karnak, 277

Iberian Peninsula, arts of. *See* Portuguese
    and Spanish styles of art
Icon, 86, 822
Ictinus, 38
Idealism, 822
Identification of colors, systems for, 795–
    797
Ikon. *See* Icon
Il Furioso, 566
Il Riccio, 127
Illuminated manuscripts, 74, 353, 354
Illumination, by electricity, *see* Lighting;
    definition of, 822
Images of Virgin, 85
Images populaires, 614

Imagination, in the decorative arts, 754
Imitation, limits of, in the decorative arts, 703, 704; wood panelling, 732
Impost, 822
Impressionism, 822; French, 567, 590, 591; reaction against, 598. *See also* Post-impressionism
Inca Indians, arts of, 371
Ince, W., 278
Incandescent bulb. *See* Bulbs, electric
Incised ornament, 12, 28, 29, 822
India, 139; influence in English arts, 242
Indian arts, American, 365–376
Indian (East) rugs, 532
Indication of elements, in elevation, 768; in plan, 786
Indiennes, 444, 458
Indirect lighting, 681–682
Individuality in design, 754, 755
Industrial Revolution, 383, 384, 387, 413; In England, 236; effect of, on art, 587
Industrialization, of France, 215; effect of in Chinese art, 348; influence in peasant art, 364
Infanta, of Spain, 575
Ingrain carpets, 517, 822
Ingres, J., 487, 588
Inlay, 12, 113, 275, 822; Boulle work, 193, 792. *See also* Intarsia, and Marquetry
Innes, G., 604, 605
Inquisition, 141, 234
Intaglio, 823
Intarsia, 113, 271, 823
Intensity, in color, 790
Interest in color compositions, attainment of, 798
Interior design, definitions of, 3, 4; influence of roof forms in, 5; use of metals in, 667; purpose of, 750
Interior trim and woodwork, 715–745
Ionic order, 41–43, 58, 823
Iran, 349
Irish Chippendale furniture, 262; glassware, 661
Iron, 384, 385, 666, 667
Irving, W., 144, 604
Isabella of Castile, 138
Isabellina period in Spain, 142, 154
Islamic arts, 349–355
Ispahan, 350–351; Royal Palace at, 352; carpets, 531
Istanbul. *See* Constantinople
Italian styles of art, 104–136; influences in Spain, 153; Empire style, 216; painting, 559–567; ceramics, 640–642; lighting, 691; mural decoration, 705
Italy, art centers in, 559
Ives, Currier and, lithographs by, 330, 614, 615
Ivory, carvings, 346, 353; Coast, arts of, 378

Jacarandá, 173, 743
Jackson, J. B., 543

Jacob, G., 203, 211, 228
Jacob-Desmalter, F. H., 219, 229
Jacobean style, 237, 240–244
Jacquard, J. M., 227, 457; loom, 517
Jacquemart and Benard, 227
Jade and jadeite, 346, 370
Jamb, 823
James I of England, 234
Japanese influence in English ceramics, 651, 652
Japanese prints, influence of, on Degas, 593; on Toulouse-Lautrec, 598; on Whistler, 606
Japanning, 300, 823
Jardinière velvet, 823
Jarves, D., 663
Jasper, 823; ware of Wedgwood, 271, 649, 653–654, 823
Jaune, famille, 659, 820
Jeanneret, C. E. *See* Le Corbusier
Jefferson, T., 183, 284, 334
Jehan, Shah, 351
Jerez de la Frontera, battle of, 138
Jersey City, N. J., 656
Jersey glass, 663
Jerusalem, Temple of Solomon, 22; Church of the Ascension, 77
Jesse-tree, 94
Jesuit Order, 108, 563
Jews, 139, in Spain, 351
Jigsaw ornament, 328
Joan of Arc, 177
John of Padua, 234
Johnson, T., 278
Joinery, 717, 823
Joint, butt, 717
Joist, 723
Jones, I., 234, 237, 245, 277; W., 262
Josephine, Empress, 271; bedroom of, 218
Joubert, G., 229
Juhl, Finn, 424, 426
Jumma Musjid Mosque, Delhi, 351
Jute, 435

Kakemono, 823
Kakiyemon, 651, 823
Kalsomine. *See* Calcimine
Kandler. *See* Herold and Kandler
K'ang Hsi, Emperor, 658
K'ang Hsi Dynasty in China, 343
Kaolin, 823; discoveries of, 637, 646, 656; South Carolina, 656
Kapok, 509, 823
Karnak, Hypostyle Hall in, 27, 28
Kas, 357
Kauffmann, A., 265, 272, 277
Kearsley, Dr. J., 334
Kent, W., 131, 256, 277, 671
Keystone, 823
Khorsabad, Palace of Sargon, 21, **22**
Kierstead, C., 337, 671
Kiln, drying of wood, 736
King of Rome, 134
Klee, P., 600

Klismos chair back, 48, 213, 220, 221, 274, 823
Kneehole desk, 823
Knights Templars, 80
Knots in rug weaving, 535
Knotted rug, 823
Knotty pine panelling, 250; informal, 698
Koran, 138, 147–148, 349
Krater, 50, 51, 823
Kuan-yin, 346
Kufa, 350
Kuhn, W., 608
Kuniyoshi, Yasuo, 608
Kylin, 657, 823
Kylix, 46, 50, 823

La Farge, J., 326
La Fontaine, 179
La Salle, Philippe de, 227, 453
Labrouste, Henri, 385, 386
Lacquer, 624, 823; use in France, 201–202; in England, 255; in China, 345–347, 357; in Holland, 357
Ladder-back, 823; in Barcelona, 163
Lady-chapel, 86, 823
Lahore, India, 350
Lake, 653
Lalique, 664
Laminated products, 329
Lamps, portable, 685; shade design and material of, 688; base materials, 687; heights of, 688; Betty-type, 695; Argand and astral, 812. See also Lighting, and descriptions under country or style
Lancaster, Pa., 305
Lancret, 585
Landscape painting, beginnings of, 581; in England, 583; in France, 588, 590; in America, 605
Landsdowne House, London, 267
Langeais, bedroom in château, 102
Langley, B., 256, 263, 277
Langlois, P., 278
Language of color, 800–801
Lannuier, H. L., 335
Lantern, 823
Latex, 509
Latin America, art influences in, 172–173
Latin cross, 82, 87, 823
Latour, Q., 587
Latrobe, B. H., 313, 334
Laurencin, M., 600
Lavabo, 823
Law of chromatic distribution, 799
Lawrence, Sir T., 277, 581
Le Brun, V., 586
Le Corbusier, 182, 398, 400, 401, 402, 405, 413, 420
Le Nain, 585
Le Roux family, 337
Le Vau, L., 188
Lead, 670
Leaders in the arts. See end of each chapter in Part One

Leaning Tower of Pisa, 82
Leather, Spanish embossed and tooled, 169–170; artificial and upholstery, 435; use of, as wall covering, 709–710
Lebrun, C., 188, 277, 473; appointed Director of Fine Arts, 585
Lectern, 823
Lee Mansion, Arlington, Va., 323
Leedy, J., 336
Lefèvre, 188
Leger, 600
Lekythos, 50, 823
Lelarge, J. B., 229
Leleu, F., 229
L'Enfant, P. C., 334
Leno weave, 438
Lenôtre, A., 188, 227
Leon Cathedral, 151
Lepautre, J., 188, 227
Lescot, P., 185, 227
Letto, 125, 823
Levasseur, E., 229
Lewis, 610
Liberty cap, 213
Libraries, arrangement of, 784
Lie, J., 607
Light, color absorption of, 689–690, 788; effects of on color, 803–804
Lighting and lighting fixtures, 679–695. See also descriptions under country or style
Lignereux, M. E., 219, 229
Lille, France, 644
Lima, Peru, 173
Limestone, use in Egypt, 23, 27, 29, 32; use in Greece, 40–41
Limners, 601
Limoges, France, enamelware, 102
Lincoln Cathedral, 233
Line, contrasts, 755–756, 766–767; in character and direction, 766–767
Line of Beauty of Hogarth, 45, 580
Linen, fiber, 432; rugs, 528
Linenfold panelling, 98, 240, 244, 823
Linings for draperies, 499
Linnell, J. and W., 278
Linoleum, 528, 734; cuts, 611, 823
Linseed oil, 623, 624
Lintel construction, 5–6, 27, 823
Lion-mask period, 256
Lippi, Fra Filippo, 561
Lisbon, 139, 166
Lit, 231
Lithographs, 611; by Currier and Ives, 330, 614, 615
Little Dutch Masters, 572
Liverpool, England, 649, 652
Living rooms, arrangement of, 777–782
Lock, M., 278
Locks, tumbler and cylinder, 677
Loggia, 823; of the Lanzi, Florence, 111
Loire Valley, tapestries, 473
London, Great Fire of, 234, 246; S. Paul's Cathedral, 234; Hampton Court Palace, 234, 248; Banqueting House, Whitehall,

and Clifford's Inn, 246; Early Georgian and Hatton Garden rooms, 249; room by A. Swan, 250; Chandos House, Lansdowne House, 267; Houses of Parliament, 325, 383; Crystal Palace, 384

Longfellow, H. W., 671

Longton Hall, England, 652

Lorrain, C., 584, 585

Lost wax. *See Cire-perdue*

Louis XII of France, 181, 184; XIII of France, 178, 182; XIV of France, 179, 182, 187, 194; XV of France, 180, 182, 194, 644; XVI of France, 180, 182, 586; XVIII of France, 182

Louis XIII style, interiors, 185; XIV style, *see* Baroque style, painting, 585; XV style, *see* Rococo style; XVI style, *see* Neoclassic style

Louis Napoleon, 216, 326, 328, 385

Louis-Philippe, of France, 182, 328

Lorenzo the Magnificent. *See* Medici, L. de'

Louver, 823; egg-crate, 682

Louvre, Paris, 561, 566, 569, 577, 591

Low Countries, 567. *See also* Dutch and Flemish styles of art

Low relief, 12

Lowestoft ware, 645, 651

Loyola, 159

Lozenge, 823

Ludwigsburg, 647

Luks, G., 607

Lull, R., 144, **175**

Lulli, 179

Lunette, 823

Lurçat, J., 482

Lurex thread, 435

Luster, 638, 823; ware, 639, 653; type rugs, 518

Lustres, 211

Luther, M., 107, 573

Lyons, France, silk industry, 457

Macassar, 824

McBey, 610

McComb, J., **313**, 334

Macedonians, 35

Machicolate, 184, 824

Machine production, beginnings of, in America, 327; influence of on peasant arts, 364. *See also* Industrialization

Machine-made floor coverings, 514

McIntire, S., 313, 316, 317, 334

MacKintosh, Charles Rennie, 389, 417, 418

Macret, P., 229

Madonna, influence of in art, 85

Madrid, Spain, Prado Museum, 143, 575, 578; Royal Palace interior, 167, 171; Provincial Hospital, 159; ceramic wall treatments, 640

Magellan, 139

Magnesium, 667–668; oxide flooring, 401

Mahogany, 161, 173, 210, 257, 739, 743; Age of, 237, 238, 262; first use, in America, 296

Maiano, B. da, 126–127

Maintenon, Mme. de, 180

Maison Carré, Nimes, 54, **313**

Maître-ébénistes, 191, 824

Majolica ware, Italian, 126, 640–643; Spanish, 149; derivation of name, 638; definition of, 824. *See also* Ceramics, and Italian and Spanish styles

Majorca, Island of, 149

Malabar Coast, 165

Malaga, Spain, 598

Malmaison, château, 216

Maltese cross, 824

Mamelukes, 350

Manchu Dynasty in China, 342, 346. *See also* Ch'ing Dynasty

Mandarin red, 343

Manet, E., 590, 591, 592

Manheim, Pa., 661

Manor houses, Georgian American, 297

Mansart, J. H., 227, 253

Mantels, 723–724, 824. *See also* descriptions under country or style, and Fireplaces

Manuel, I, Dom, 160

Manuelino style, in Portugal, 142, 154, **165**

Manuscripts, illuminated, 74, 353, 354

Manwaring, R., 278; book by, 263

Maple, 740, 743

Maquette, 824

Marathon, 35

Marble, use of, in Greece, 40–41, 46–47

Marbled wares, 652

Marbling and graining, in Adam style, 269; in America, 299; *also* 634, 824

Marco Polo, 104, 341

Marcoussis, 610

Marie Antoinette, 180, 207, 586

Marie Louise, of Austria, 216

Marin, J., 608

Marlborough, campaign of, 355; leg, 261, 302, 824

Marmion, Va., interior, 299

Marot, D., 188, 227, 235, 253, 358

Marquetry, 12, 824; seaweed and floral, 252, 829; in Dutch furniture, 357; in veneers, 739. *See also* Inlay and Intarsia, and descriptions under country or style

Mars, Temple of, 58

Marseilles, ceramics, 643

Marsh, R., 608

Martel, C., 138

Martin, H., 605

Martin brothers, 229; *Vernis-Martin*, 202, 229, 832

Martinez, A., **175**

Martini, S., 559

Mary, Queen, of England, 235; Princess, of England, 355

Masaccio, T. G., 135, 560

Masonry, exposed, in wall treatments, **712**

Mastaba tombs, 24, 824

Masters, Little Dutch, 572

Mat finish, 790

Matching of colors, 630

Mathematical curves, 7–8, 44
Mathsson, Bruno, 421, 423
Matisse, H., 598, 599, 610, 611
Mats, use of, 617
Mattresses, 510. See Sleeping equipment
Mayan art, 366; influences, 172
Mayhew, T., 279; book by, 263
Mazarin, Cardinal, 179
Meander ornament, 45, 824
Measurements for draperies, 501
Mecca, 138, 349, 350
Mechanical curves, 7, 44
Medallion, 115, 824
Medford, Mass, Isaac Royall House, 297
Medici, L. de', 105, 561; family, 108; C.
    de', 177; M. de', 178; ceramics, 641
Medium, 824
Medium color areas, 798
Medullary rays, 734
Meissen ware, 646, 647
Memling, H., 568
Ménagère, 225, 363
Mennecy ceramics, 637, 644
Mennonites, 305
Menuisiers, 191
Mercerize, 824
Mercy, Goddess of, 346
Merino wool, 433, 824
Merton tapestries, 474
Mesopotamia and Palestine, early arts, 20–22
Mesquita, 824
Mesz, J., 336
Metal, structures of, 384; leaf, use of, in
    wall decoration, 635
Metals and hardware, 666–678; precious,
    see Gold, and Silver. See also descriptions
    under country or style
Metalwork, 666–678. See also descriptions
    under country or style
Metope, 824
Metropolitan Museum, founding of, 331
Mexican styles of art, 139, 172, 173; Indian,
    366; work of Rivera and Orozco, 601
Mezzanine, 824
Mezzotints, 273, 611, 824
Michael Angelo, B., 109, 110, 118, 119, 135,
    156, 562, 563
Michelangelo. See Michael Angelo
Michel. C. See Clodion
Middle Ages, art periods of, 69–103
Midwestern glass, 663
Mihrab, 352, 824
Milanese school of painting, 560
Milk glass, 663
Millbach, Pa., interior, 306
Millefleurs tapestries, 474, 824
Miller, G., 335
Millet, J. F., 590
Minaret, 152, 824
Ming Dynasty in China, 342, 344; ceramics
    of, 657, 658
Miniature painting, 824; Persian, 353, 354
Minoan art, 33

Minor arts. See description under country or
    style
Minstrel gallery, 96, 824
Minton, 654
Miro, J., 600
Mirrors, Venetian, 125; by G. Gibbons, 248;
    by Chippendale, 261; Colonial American,
    307; Constitution type, 308. See also de-
    scriptions under country or style
Mission furniture, Spanish, 334
Missions. The Alamo, 333; California, 333
Miter, 98, 824
Mitla, 366, 369
Mixing of paint colors, suggestions for, 625,
    629, 631
Mixing table, 824
Modern. See Contemporary
Modillion, 824
Module, 58, 824
Mogul dynasty, 349
Mohammed, 138, 349
Mohammedan arts, 349; patterns, 352
Moldings, classical, 44–45, 62; of doors and
    windows, 717
Molière, 179
Monasteries, Monte Cassino, 80; S. Maria of
    Victory, 160
Monet, C., 590, 594
Mongols, 349
Monks, 74–75, 79–80
Monochromaticism, use of by Daumier, 590
Monochrome or monotone, 824
Monolithic, 56, 824
Monotypes, 611
Mont S. Michel, 82, 95
Montage, 824
Montaigne, F. de, 183
Monte Cassino, Italy, 80; Alban, Mexico, 369
Montfort, S. de, 85
Montgolfier, 207
Monticello, Va., 313
Montigny, P. C., 229
Montmartre, 598
Mood of a room, 689
Moon-gates, 344, 824
Moorish styles of art, 144–151; arch, 161,
    351; ceramics, 639. See also Islamic arts
Moors, 138
Moquette carpets, 521
More, Sir T., 573
Morisco art, 142
Morisot, 590
Morland, 611
Morris, William, 276, 277, 325, 388, 398,
    414, 415, 416, 417, 420, 421, 422,
    423, 426, 428
Morse, S. F. B., 336, 602, 603
Mortise, 824; type hardware, 677
Mortlake tapestries, 474, 477
Mosaics, Pompeian, 62, 64–66; at Antioch,
    66, in S. Sophia, 74; Early Christian, 77;
    Mayan, 367; Byzantine, 457
Mosque, 80; at Cordova, 144, 351; at
    Ispahan, 350; Jumma Musjid, Delhi, 351

Mosul, 350
Mother of pearl inlay, 275
Motherwell, R., 608
Mount Lebanan, N. Y., 321
Mounts, 825
Moustiers ware, 643
Movable elements, in wall design, 759
Mozarabic art, 142–150, 825
Mudejar art, 142–150, 825
Mullions, 88, 825
Multifoil, 825
Multi-purpose rooms, arrangement of, 775
Munsell System of color, 795–797
Mural decoration, use of, 701; in country house, 704; informal, 708; examples of, 705, 709. See also descriptions under country or style, Walls and Painting.
Murano, Italy, 660
Murillo, B. E., 144, 175, 576, 577
Murrhine ware, 67, 825
Museums of art, Prado, Madrid, 143, 575, 578; Metropolitan, N. Y., 331; Cluny, 475–476; Freer, Washington, 606; establishment of, 607; British, 654
Musical instruments, placing of, 781
Mycenean art, 34
Myron, 47
Mythology, Norse and Germanic, 359

Nailheads, use of in Spain, 163, 165
Nailsea, England, 661
Names of colors, 794–797
Nanmu, 343, 743, 825
Nantes, Edict of, 178, 180–182, 235, 251, 358; ceramics, 642
Nantgarw, England, 652
Naples, Italy, ceramics, 641
Napoleon I, 134, 169, 181, 182, 587
Napoleonic code, 181
Natchez, Miss., 323; interior in, 326
National School of Fine Arts, Paris, 189, 332
Nattier, 856
Natural and synthetic wall coverings, 710–713
Naturalism, 825; in painting, 565
Naturalistic ornament, 12
Navajo Indians, 373; rugs and blankets, 526
Nave, 82, 87, 825
Nealeolo, V., 653
Near or approaching colors, 791, 825
Nebuchadnezzar, hanging gardens of, 21
Needlepoint rugs, 523
Needlework used with French furniture, 225, gros- and petit-point, 439
Nefretete, Queen, 31
Negro sculpture, African, 376
Nelson, Lord, 581
Neo-classic style, painting in France, 586; ceramics, 646. See also descriptions under country
Nephrite, 368
Neutral or gray, 793, 825; use of, in decoration, 798, 799

Neutrality, degree of, 793–794
Neutralization of colors, 630, 631, 790, 793; by complement, 793–794; analysis of, 794
Nevers, France, ceramics, 642
Nevinson, 611
New Canton, 649
New England, early settlers of, 282
New Jersey glass, 661
New Mexico, Indians in, 373
New York City, drawing room, 19th century, 314; Washington Square houses, 323; S. Patrick's Cathedral, Trinity Church, 325; Roosevelt house, 327; Metropolitan Museum, 331; Armory Show of 1913, 600
N.Y.S.I.D. color charts, 796
Newel, 825
Newport, R. I., furniture, 303
Niche, 825; Italian, 117; Spanish, 150; Adam, 268; prayer, 352; in period styles, 726
Nicomedes, King, 48
Nigeria, arts of, 376
Nimes, France, Maison Carré, 54, 313; Temple of Diana, 81
Nine Worthies, tapestry, 473
Nineveh, 21
Noblesse oblige, 236
Noire famille, 659, 820
Nootka Indians of Vancouver, 375
Norman style, 77; in England, 70. See also Romanesque
Normandy, peasant arts in, 363
North American Indian arts, 373–377
Northwest coast of America, Indian arts of, 375
Norton, J., 656
Notre Dame, Paris, 86, 87, 92
Nouveaux-riches, in France, 181
Numdah rugs, 527
Nuremburg, Germany, 573
Nurseries, arrangement of, 785
Nylon fiber, 434
Nymphenburg, Germany, 360; ceramics, 647

Oak, Age of, 237, 243; uses of, in flooring, 734; in furniture, 739; description of, 743
Oaxaca, Mexico, 173, 366, 369
Oberkampf, C. P., 199, 227, 382, 455, 543
Obverse, 825
Odiot, 219, 667
Odoacer, 71
Oeben, J. F., 203, 229
Off-black, 790
Off-white, 790, 825
Ogee or ogive, 825; arch, 88, 351; moldings, 269
Oil, as painters' medium, 567; paintings, framing of, 615, 617; paint, 623, 624; linseed, 623, 624
Oinochoë, 50, 825
Old blue ware, 655
On-the-glaze colors, 638
One-hue scheme, 799
Opera, origin of, 107

Optical balance, examples of, 763, 765; definition, 764, 825
Orders, of architecture, 41–43, 56, 59; religious, 80
Oriel windows, 239, 825
Oriental arts, 341–355; influence in English fruniture, 256; objects in America, 311; influence in Dutch art, 357; in French painting, 593, 596, 598, 606; ceramics, influence in Europe, 642, 644, 646, 648. See also Chinese, Japanese, Islamic
Oriental rugs, 530; use of, 538
Oriental-Lowestoft, 651
Original pictures, use of in decoration, 609
Orleans, France, ceramics, 644
Orlon fiber, 434
Ormolu, 193, 670, 825
Ornament, forms used, 11, 13; character and classification of, 12; common terms used, 13. See also descriptions under country or style
Ornamental hardware, 676, 677
Orozco, M., 600
Orrefors glass, 664
Orsini family, 109
Ostwald color system, 795
Otis, E., 384
Ottoman, 328, 825
Ourique, battle of, 160
Outlets, electrical, 680
Overlaid glass, 663
Overmantel treatments, 725. See also Mantels
Ovid, 106
Ovolo molding, 44, 825
Oxides, uses of in paint, 624
Ox-skull ornament, 45

Padua, John of, 234
Paestum, Italy, temples in, 38
Pagodas, 343, 825
Painted wall decoration. See Mural decoration painting, prehistoric, 18, 19; Chinese, 347; Persian, 353, 354; historic styles of, 558, 622; of walls, 623, 635. See also Pictures, Walls
Paints, 623–635. See also Pigment colors
Palaces of Sargon, 21, 22; Cnossus, Crete, 33; of the Popes, Avignon, 95; Italian, 112–113; Farnese, Vecchio, 113, 114; Davanzati, 114, 116; Dos Aguas, Valencia, 159; Versailles, 187; Hampton Court, 235, 248; Het Loo, 253; Diocletian's, Spalato, 268; Summer, in Peiping, 342; Royal at Ispahan, 352; Schönbrun, 360; Ducal, Venice, 566
Palampores, 242, 444, 825
Palazzo. See Palaces
Palestine, early arts of, 20, 22
Palestrina, 107
Palisade walls, 290, 825
Palisander, 743
Palissy, B., 194, 227, 642; ware, 642, 645

Palladio, A., 110, 111, 117, 135; influence in England, 245
Palmette, 21, 30, 45, 825
Palomino y Velasco, A., 175
Panama, Indian gold work, 369
Panel, 825; lights, ceiling, 686
Panelling, elimination of, 696; period designs of, 727, 732. See descriptions under country or style, and Interior trim
Panels. See Panelling
Panels, arcaded, 243, 812
Panetière, 225
Pantheon, Rome, 55, 56
Pantomime, 107
Papelera, 164, 165, 825
Paper, invention of, in China, 347
Papier maché products, 275, 327, 826
Papillon, J., 199, 227, 543
Papyrus ornament, 26, 27
Parcel, 826
Pargework or pargetry, 241, 242, 826
Parian ware, 656
Paris, Notre Dame, 86, 87, 92; S. Chapelle, 92; allure of, 183; Bastille, 181; Conservatory of Music, 189; streets named for famous persons, 223; École des Beaux Arts, 332; Exposition of 1925, 390; early tapestries, 472; Louvre, 561, 566, 569, 577, 591; Salon of 1824, 581; Montmartre, 598
Parmele, E., clocks by, 308
Parquet, examples of patterns, 734; definition of, 826
Parthenon, 37, 38, 39, 47
Paste, in ceramics, 638
Pastels, 617, 826
Patching of walls, 628
Pater, W., 585
Paterae ornaments, 269, 271, 826
Patina, 826
Patio, Spanish, 173; definition of, 826
Patrons of arts in Italy, 108
Pattern interest, in painting, 598; contrasts with plain surfaces, 769; in wall composition, 770; limitation of, 771
Patterns, composition and character of, 11, 13–14; of period textiles, 441, 459; of wallpapers, 549; of Stiegel glass, 662. See also Ornament and Design
Pavia, Italy, 177
Pax Romana, 52
Peabody, Mass., McIntire interior, 317
Peacock, throne in Delhi, 351; room by Whistler, 606
Peale family, 311, 336; C. W., 602, 603; children of, Raphaelle, Titian, and Rembrandt, 603
Peasant arts, of Europe, 362–365; rugs, 520; wall hanging, Swedish, 612; paintings and folk art, 613; ceramics, Spanish, 640
Pedestal, 42, 58, 826
Pediment forms, 7, 40, 43; definition of, 826
Peintures-vivantes, 119, 826
Peiping, 343, 346

Peking. *See* Peiping
Pelham, P., 602
Pembroke table, 265, 826
Pencil sketches, framing of, 617
Pendentives, 72, 826; in S. Sophia, 73; S. Mark's, 75
Pène du Bois, G., 608
Penn, W., 305
Pennell, 610
Pennsylvania, Academy of Fine Arts, 603
Pennsylvania Dutch. *See* Pennsylvania German
Pennsylvania German, crafts, 305, 307; ceramics, 655
Penshurst, Kent, England, 97
Percier C., and Fontaine, 216, 218, 226, 227, 456
Pergolesi, M. A., 133, 272, 277
Pericles, 35, 47
Period decorations and furniture, Part One, 15
Period styles, definition of, 9; methods of dividing, 10; basic external influences, 10; objects from, use of in contemporary settings, 342, 343, 753–754; textile patterns, 441–459; lighting and lighting fixtures, 685, 686, 690–695; floors in, 734; development of, 753; rooms in, wall composition of, 760, 762; room arrangement in, 776; uses of color, 805. *See also* description in Part One
Peristyle, 62, 826
Permanent pigments, 628
Perret, Auguste, 397
Persane, 444
Persepolis, 34
Persian styles of art, 353–355; ancient, 25, 32, 34; rugs, 530–532; ceramics, 639
Persiana, 151, 826
Perspective, principles of, Italian, 112
Personality, expression of, in decoration, 754–755
Peru, 139, 173, 371
Peterborough Cathedral, 83
Petit Trianon, 195
Petit-point needlework, 439, 826
Petrarch, F., 104, 106, 135
Pewter, 242, 667, 672–673, 826
Phidias, 37, 38, 47
Philadelphia, W. Penn House, 288; Graeme Park, 297; Samuel Powel House, 298; Exposition of 1876, 331; Academy of Art, 605
Philadelphia furniture, 301, 302
Philip II of Spain, 139, 156, 355; IV of Spain, 140, 575; V of Spain, 159
Philosophy, Mohammedan and Christian, 138
Phoenicians, 137
Photographs, framing of, 617
Photo-murals, 552, 553
Photo-reproductions, 615
Phrygian cap, 213
Phyfe, D., 318, 335

Pianos, placing of, 779–781
Picabia, 600
Picasso, P., 144, 175, 182, 578, 598, 599, 600
Picture moldings, 718
Pictures, 558–622; use of in Colonial America, 312; miscellaneous types, 609; framing, selection, and hanging of, 615–620
Pie-crust table, 255, 826
Piece-dyeing, 441, 826
Pier, 826; glass, 221, 826. *See* Psyche
Pigment colors, 623, 826; glossary of, 626; characteristics of, 626–628, 790; neutralization of, 630, 631, 790, 793, 794
Pilaster, 7, 58, 826
Pile, 826; fabrics, 438
Pillar, 826
Pillement, J., 197, 207, 227
Pillows, 512, *See* Sleeping equipment
Pine, knotty, 250, 698; descriptions of, 743–744
Pingree House, Salem, Mass., 318
Pinnacle, 88, 826
Pinturicchio, B., 135
Pinxton, England, 652
Pinzon, 139
Piping in upholstery, 503, 509, 826
Piranesi, G. B., 133, 204, 277; book by, 270, 586
Pisa, Cathedral and Leaning Tower of, 82
Pissarro, 590, 594
Pizarro, 139, 366, 371
Plain walls, painting of, 628; rough plaster effects, 633, 634; treatment of, 700–703; pattern interest with, 769, 770
Plain weave, 437
Plain-sawing, 735, 826
Plan, 826; indication of furniture in, 777, 785
Planning, and backgrounds, contemporary, 395–401; of color schemes, 789, 798–799, 803, 806–809
Plans, of Early American houses, 287–289; of rooms, for study of arrangement, 785
Plaque, 827
Plaster, patching of, 628; rough effects, 633, 634
Plastics, 404; as wall coverings, 397, 713; as floor coverings, 734
Plate, 100; Sheffield, 673; glass, 722
Plateresco style, in Spain, 142, 154, 827
Platero, 154
Plato, 27
Pleinairists, 594, *See also* Impressionism
Plinth, 717, 827
Plywood, use of in furniture, 402; sheets, 713; as wall coverings, 726; use of in veneers, 739. *See also* Woods and Veneers
Podium, 827
Pointed arches, 89–91, 351
Pointillism, 596
Poitiers, Diane de, 185, 585, 642; France, battle at, 350
Pole screen, 827

Pollard veneer, 738
Polychrome, 121, 161, 827; decoration in Chinese ceramics, 658–659
Polyclitus, 47
Pombal, Marquez de, 166
Pombalino, 166
Pomegranate, 827
Pompadour, Mme. de, 180, 197, 207, 543, 644
Pompeian styles of art, 62–68; influence in Italy, 133; in Spain, 168; in France, 196, 586; in England, 266
Pompeii, 62–68
Pontil and pontil mark, 659, 827
Poole, 653
Poor, H., 608
Poor man's silver, 672. See Pewter
Popayan, Colombia, 173
Popularization of decorative arts in France, 212
Porcelain, 827. See Ceramics and descriptions under country or style
Porphyry, 73, 827
Portable lamps, 685
Portici, Italy, ceramics, 641
Portland Vase, 67; reproduction of by Wedgwood, 654, 827
Portuguese styles of art, 142, 160, 165–166, 168–169
Post-Colonial American styles of art, 286, 313–320
Post-Impressionism, 573, 591
Poster paints. See Tempera
Poterat, E., 643–644
Pottery. See Ceramics, and descriptions under country or style
Poudreuse, 231
Poussin, N., 585
Powder rooms, arrangement of, 785
Powel, Samuel, house of, 298
Prado Museum, Madrid, 143, 575, 578
Praxiteles, 37, 47, 48
Prayer niche, 352
Preclassic, 827
Pre-Columbian art, 365
Prehistoric art, 17–19
Prendergast, M., 607
Preparation of walls for painting, 628
Pre-Raphaelite Brotherhood, 277, 388, 415, 567, 583
Pressed glass, American, 663; definition of, 827
Primary colors, 128, 792, 827
Primaticcio, 177, 583
Primavera, 744
Priming coat, 629, 827
Primitive, 559, 827
Primitive and folk painting, in America, 603. See also Folk arts
Printing, invention of, 104, 347; and dyeing of textiles, 440
Prints. See Pictures
Prints, Japanese, influence of on Western artists, 593, 598, 606. See also Pictures

Procedure, in color schemes, 808, 809
Proportion, and scale, 770–772
Protestantism, 108
Provençal style in France, 223
Provincial styles in France, 222–226
Psyche, 221, 827
Psychological effects of colors, 801–803
Psychology of color, 799–800
Publications, art, 262–263
Puebla, Mexico, potters, 173
Pueblo Indian arts, 373, 376
Pueblos, 373
Pugin, A. W. N., 325
Pure design, 5; application of rules, 750, 827
Puritan Protectorate, 234
Purity of silver, 671
Putto, 827
Pylon, 827
Pyramids of Egypt, 25, 26, 32

Quantity balance, 772
Quarter round, 44, 827; sawing, 734–735, 827
Quartered oak flooring, 734
Quarternary colors, 792, 793, 827
Quatrefoils, 91, 827
Quattrocento period in Italy, 111, 827
Queen Anne, 235; style, 238, 253–255, 257; silverware, 670–671
Queen Elizabeth, 234
Queen's ware, 654
Quito, Ecuador, 173

Rabelais, 182
Racine, J., 179
Radios, placing of, 781
Raeburn, Sir H., 277, 581
Rafter, 827
Rag rugs, 525, 526
Rails, 98, 827
Ramie fiber, 434
Randolph, B., 302, 335
Raphael Sanzio, 86, 111, 118, 135, 563, 564, 641; tapestries by, 477
Rare woods, 741
Rascalon, B., 219, 229
Ravenna, S. Vitale, 75; S. Apollinare Nuovo, 77
Ravrio, A. A., 219, 227
Ready-made paints, 625, 626
Realism, 827; in French painting, 588; in American painting, 608
Realistic ornament, 12
Recamier, Mme., portrait of, 215
Receding colors, 791, 818
Recessed ceiling lights, 682–684
Reconquest of Spain, 138
Recreation rooms, arrangement of, 785
Red gum, 740–741, 744
Reeding, 264, 828
Refectory, 828; table, 125
Reformation, 108, 141, 355; Counter, see Counter Reformation

Regency style, in France, 182, 193–194; in England, 233, 274–275; silverware, 671
Regent in France, 180
Regina Coeli, 86
Relics, sale forbidden, 85
Relief ornament, 12; Greek, 41
Religious ecstasy of Middle Ages, 80
Reliquaries, 85, 828
Rembrandt v. R., 357, 571, 572, 611
Renaissance, 105; patrons of arts in Italian, 108; styles of, *see* descriptions under country
Renoir, P. A., 590, 594, 595
Rep, 828
Repoussé metalwork, 171, 369, 828; in silver, 671, 677
Reproductions, use and avoidance of, 609, 754
Reredos, 828
Resist printing of textiles, 440
Restoration style, in England, 233, 238, 246–251, 615; in France, 182
Restraint in use of accessories, 403
Reticella, 828
Reveillon, J. B., 227, 543
Revere, P., 337, 671, 673
Reverse, 828
Revolution, French, 181, 182, 317; art during French, 212, 587; American, 313, 315
Reynolds, Sir J., 277, 580
Rhythm in wall composition, 766
Rib, 828; construction, 90
Ribband back, 828
Ribera, J. de, 175, 574
Riccardi family, 108
Richardson, H. H., 326, 334, 391, 392, 393
Richelieu, Cardinal, 179
Richmond, Va., Capitol at, 313; Victorian interior in, 324
Riesener, J. H., 211, 229
Rietveld, Gerrit, 418, 420, 421
Rinceau, 45, 59, 828
Rio de Janeiro, Brazil, 173
Rittenhouse, D., 335
Rivera, D., 600, 601
Robert, H., 207, 208, 227, 586, 587
Rocaille, 194
Rock Crystal, 691
Rocking chairs, 305; Shaker types, 322
Rockingham ware, 652, 653
Rococo style, painting in France, 585; definition of, 828. *See also* descriptions under country
Rocroy, battle of, 140
Rodin, P., 611
Rodrigue, V., 175
Roentgen, D., 229
Rogers, J., 330
Roi Soleil, Le, 179
Roland and Oliver, 138
Roll, 828
Roller printing of textiles, 440
Roman Empire, introduction of Christianity in, 70; split, 71; fall of, 79; Eastern, 72

Roman styles of art, 52–68
Romanesque style, 70, 77–83; revival of in America, 325–331, 385. *See also* descriptions under country
Romantic painting in France, 587; color names, 795–796
Romanticists, 578
Romayne work, 245, 251, 828
Rome, Ancient, 17; Pompeii, 62–68
Rome, Italy, Colosseum, 22; Baths of Caracalla, 55; Pantheon, 55, 56; Temple of Mars, 58; S. Maria Maggiore, S. Paul's-Beyond-the-Walls, 77, 78; Farnese Palace, 113; French Academy, 189; S. Peter's, 118, 563
Romney, G., 277, 580–581
Roncesvalles, battle of, 138
Rondel, 828
Roof forms, 5, 6
Room arrangement. *See* Furniture arangement and under specific rooms
Roosevelt, T., house in N. Y., 327
Rope bed, 828
Rose, period of Picasso, 600; du Barry, Pompadour, 644; Tudor, 832
Rose, famille, 659, 820
Rosetta Stone, 29
Rosette, 21, 828
Rose-window, 87, 88, 828
Rosewood, 329, 739, 744
Rossetti, D. G., 277, 583
Rotary veneers, 736
Rouault, G., 598
Rouen, France, Cathedral, painted by Monet, 594; ceramics, 637, 639, 642–643
Rough plaster effects, 703
Roundabout chairs, 300, 828
Rousseau, J. J., 180; T., 590; H., 595
Rovira, H., 175
Roxbury, Mass., 309
Royal Academy, 580, 602
Royal Worcester, 652
Royall, I., House in Medford, Mass., 297
Rubaiyat of Omar Khayyam, 354
Rubber, foam, for upholstery. *See* Latex
Rubber tile, 529
Rubens, P., 569, 570; tapestries by, 478; work of, in England, 578
Rug-knots, 535
Rugs. *See* Floor coverings
Rush rugs, 528
Ruskin, J., 276, 277, 325, 382, 583
Russia, churches in, 76; icons, 86
Rustic pottery of Palissy, 642
Rustication, 158, 828
Ruysdael, J., 569
Rya weave, 521
Ryder, A., 606

Saarinen, Eero, 407, 408, 424, 425, 426
Sacrifices, human, 370
Sadler, J., 654
Saint. All words meaning "Saint" are spelled "S.," and listed as though spelled "Sai."

S. Antonio, Texas, 333
S. Apollinare, Nuovo and in-Classe, 77
S. Barbara, 333
S. Bartholomew's, Massacre of, 178
S. Carlos Borromeo del Rio Carmelo, 333
S. Caystano, Mexico, 173
S. Chapelle, Paris, 92
S. Cloud, ceramics, 189, 211, 637, 644
S. Domingo Puebla, Mexico, 172
S. Francis, Xavier, 165, of Assisi, 559
S.-Gaudens, A., 336
S. Helena, 85
S. Ignatius, 159
S. José, 333
S. Juan Capistrano, 333
S. Luis Rey, 333
S. Maria Maggiore, Rome, 77
S. Maria of Victory, monastery in Portugal, 160
S. Mark's, Venice, 75
S.-Memin, C.B.J.F. de, 207, 36; work in America, 311
S. Paul's Cathedral, London, 234
S. Paul's-Beyond-the-Walls, 77, 78
S. Peter's, Rome, 110, 111, 118, 563; Baldachino, 119
S. Porchaire, France, ceramics, 642
S. Sophia, Constantinople, 72–74
S. Trophime, Arles, 82
S. Vitale, Ravenna, 75
Saintes, Brittany, ceramics of Palissy, 642
Saitic period in Egypt, 25
Salamanca Cathedral, Spain, 151
Salamander, use of, 184–187
Salem, Mass., Pingree House, 318
Salisbury cathedral, 233
Salle, Philippe de la, 227, 454
Salon, The, in Paris, 588, 591; des Refusés, 591
Salt, 653; -box house, 289; glaze, 638; glaze wares, 652
Samarkand, 350
Sambin, H., 186, 227
Samothrace, Victory of, 47
Sample books of color, 806
Samplers, 460, 613, 828
San, Santa, Santo. See Saint
Sanderson, R., 337
Sandwich glass, 663
Sanguine drawings, 211, 828
Sanitas, 629
Sansovino, J., 127, 135, 667
Santiago, de Compostela, 151; scallop shell of, 156; de Chile, 173
Saone, Sir J., 268, 275, 277, 323
Sapwood, 736
Saracens, 80
Sarcillo, F., 175
Sardis, capital from, 43
Sargon, Palace of, 21, 22
Sarto, A. del, 177
Sartorious, 613
Sash bars, 721, 828; curtains, 828
Saskia, 571

Satin weave, 437
Satinwood, 744; Age of, 237, 238, 263
Satire, in painting, 579, 588, 598
Sausage turning, 828
Savery, W., 302, 335
Savonarola, G., 105, 107, 135, 561; cell of, 116; chair, 125
Savonnerie rugs, 519
Sawing, plain- and quater-, 734, 735, 826, 827
Scallop shell ornament, 156, 255, 827
Scale and proportion, 770, 772
Scandinavian arts, 358, 362; rugs, 521
Sceaux ceramics, 639, 644
Scenic papers, 542
Schemes, color. See Color and color schemes
Schönbrun Palace, Vienna, 360
Schools of painting, 558–622. See also descriptions under country or style
Sconces, 273, 828; electrical, 686–689
Scopas, 47
Scotch, Chippendale furniture, 262; carpets, 517
Scotia molding, 45, 829
Scott, Sir W., 328, 383
Scratch-carved ornament, 655, 829; patterns in ceramics, 647
Screen printing of textiles, 440
Scribe, 829; The, Egyptian statue, 32
Scroll, 829; pediment, 7, 829; paintings, Chinese, 347
Sculpture, prehistoric, 20; African Negro, 376–378. See also descriptions under country or style
Sculptured rugs, 522
Seasoning of wood, 736
Seaweed marquetry, 252, 829
Secondary colors, 792, 829
Secondary rooms, arrangement of, 784–785
Secret rooms, 195
Section, 829
Sedan chairs, 202, 829
Sedia, 124, 829
Segmental pediment, 7; arch, 829
Segonzac, 600, 610
Sehna knot, 537
Selection, arrangement and harmony, Part III, 747
Semi-direct lighting, 681–682
Semi-permanent pigments, 628
Seneca, 106
Sense, color, 798
Serigraphs, 615
Serpentine, fronts, 200; curves, 829
Serra, Fra J., 333
Sert, 578
Setauket, N. Y., 703
Seurat, G., 590, 596, 597
Seville, Spain, 350, 575, 576; Alcazar, 145–146, 351; Cathedral, 151–152; Giralda Tower, 152; ceramics, 640
Sèvres ware, 637, 643–644, 647–649
Sforza family, 108; L., 562
Sgabello, 122, 124, 362, 829

Sgraffito, ceramics, 655; ornament, 829
Shackleton, T., 279
Shades, 768, 829; for windows, 501
Shaft, 42, 829
Shaker furniture, 320–322, 829
Shearer, Gillow and, 265
Shearer, T., 265, 279
Shed, in weaving, 436, 829
Sheeler, C., 608
Sheffield plate, 583
Shelf, clock, 310
Shell and bead pictures, 613
Shelton, England, 652
Sheraton, T., 265–266, 279; designs for draperies, 487–488
Shi'a Sect, 148, 352
Ship pictures, wool, 613
Shirring for draperies, 495, 829
Sideboards, location of, 781
Sierra Leone, arts of, 376
Silhouettes, 330, 613, 614, 829
Silk fiber, 432
Sill, 717, 829
Siloe, D., 175
Silver, 667; American, 312; antique, 670–672
Simultaneity in art, 600
Singeries, 198, 201, 829
Sisley, 590, 594
Sistine Chapel, Vatican, 86, 111, 562
Size, 829
Sizes of wallpaper, 547
Skeleton construction, 829
Sketches, framing of, 617
Skirt, 829
Slat-back chairs, 295, 829
Sleeping, chair, 251; equipment, 510
Sleigh bed, 303
Slers, D. and J., 652
Slip, 638, 829; ware, 645, 646, 655
Slipcovers, 503
Slipper chair, 829
Sloan, J., 605, 607, 608
Small color areas, 799
Smibert, J., 602
Smith, G., 486; designs by, 275; Captain J., 287
Snake foot, 829
Socle, 829
Socrates, 37
Sofas, placing of, 779
Soffit, 829
Soft paste ceramics, 637, 638, 644, 651, 830
Softwood, 734
Solar, 830
Solomon, temple of, 22
Solutrian period, 377
Sorel, A., 583
Sorolla, 578
Source of color, 788
South Amboy, N. J., 656
South American Indian arts, 371–373
South Jersey glass, 663
Spade foot, 830

Spain, Jews in, 351; Infanta of, 575; Catalonia, ceramics, 640. For styles of art, *see* Spanish styles
Spandrel, 830
Spanish, foot, 296, 830; missions in California, 333–334; provinces, arts in, 355. Baroque style, *see* Churrigueresco style. Armada, *see* Armada, Spanish
Spanish styles of art, 137–176; paintings, 574; ceramics, 638, 640
Sparta, 36, 47
Spatter finish, or glaze, 633
Spectral colors, 830
Spectrum, 788
Sphinx, The, 26; ornament, 45
Spindle, 830; split, 245, 830
Spinets, 202, 830
Spinner, D., 336
Spiral ornament, 31, 45; leg, 252, 357, 830
Splat, 124, 300, 830
Splay, 98, 830
Spline, 717, 830
Split spindle ornament, 245, 830
Spode, J., 653, 654; blue and white ceramics, 654
Spolato, Dalmatia, Diocletian's palace, 268
Sporting prints, 612, 613
Spot lights, 686
Spray painting, 701
Spring-line, 7, 830
Springs, in upholstery work, 508
Staffordshire, England, 652; ceramics, 643, 652, 656
Stained-glass, 92–94, 95; influence of, in work of Rouault, 598
Stainless steel, 669
Stains, 625
Stairways, in Alcazar, 157; Château de Blois, 178; English, 242
Stalactite ornament, 144, 147, 351, 830
Standards of taste in design, 749–757
Stangers, the, 663
Stanton Hall, Natchez, Miss., 326
Stanza and Logi in Vatican, 563
Statuary bronze, 830
Steel (*See* Iron), 397, 668–669; engravings, 610; stainless, 669
Steele House, Charleston, S. C., 325
Steen, J., 357, 569
Stelae, 48, 830
Stencil, ornament, 300, 321, 707, 708, 830; printing of textiles, 440
Sterling, in silver, 671, 830
Steuben glass, 664
Stick. *See* Bundle
Stiegel, H. W., 336, 661–663, 673
Stiles, 98, 830
Still-life, Pompeian, 63; painting, 573, 830
Stippling, 629, 700, 830
Stock, hardware, 677; dyeing, 441, 830
Stoic philosophies, 106
Stoke-on-Trent, 653
Stone Age in China, 341
Stone-jointing, 830

Stoneware, 637, 830
Straight and curved lines, 767–768
Strapwork carving, 244–246, 830
Strasbourg, ceramics, 644–645
Stravinsky, I., 182
Strawberry Hill, 250
Strength of wood, 739
Stretcher, 125, 830
String course, 830
Striped glass, 663
Structural, glass products, 664; wood glossary, 741
Stuart, G., 311, 336, 602
Stuart and Revett, 266
Stuart period in England, 238
Stucco, 703, 830
Stud, 830
Student color charts, 796, 797
Stumpwork, 615, 830
Style, definitions of, 753–754. See Taste
Styles of art, method of dividing, 11–14
Stylobate, 42, 830
Subtle colors, 791
Sugi finish, 831
Suites, of furniture, 392, 752
Sullivan, L., 335, 393, 394
Sully, T., 603
Sumerian civilization, 20
Summer beam, 831
Sung Dynasty, 347
Sunni sect, 148, 352
Sunrooms, arrangement of, 784
Superimposed order, 831
Supports, isolated, 88; for draperies, 492
Surface contrasts, 768–770
Surrealism, 600
Susa, 34
Swag, 248, 831
Swan, A., 256, 263, 277; room by, 250
Swansea, England, 652
Swastika, 45, 831
Sweden, Empire style in, 216
Swedish, peasant wall hanging, 612; glass, 664
Switzerland, peasant arts in, 362
Symbolism, of colors, 800–801; in Chinese art, 346; in Indian art, 374, 375
Symmetrical balance, examples of, 762; definition, 764, 830; division by architectural motifs, 767
Symmetry, avoidance of in contemporary design, 395, 764, 773. See also Balance
Synthetics, for wall coverings, 713; for floor coverings, 528, 734. See also Plastics
Syria, Early Christian style in, 77
Systems of color, 795–796

Table, manners, Gothic, 99; silver, 670–672; of light and color absorption, 690
Table, types to use, 779; chair-, 815. See also descriptions under country or style
Tableware, 31, 99. See Silver
Tabriz, 350
Taffeta or plain weave, 437

Taj Mahal, at Agra, 351
Talavera de la Reina, 640; potters, 173
Tambour, 231
Tamerlane, 349
Tang Dynasty, 347
Taoism, 342
Tapestries, 471–483; Arras, 96, 242, 431; Beauvais and Gobelins, 189, 191; handmade, 439; Verdure, 832
Taste, in decorative arts, 749–757
Taxco, Mexico, 173
Tazza, 831
Tea drinking, 255, 670
Teakwood, furniture, 345
Technical terms, location of glossaries for, 811
Teheran, 351
Television sets, placing of, 781
Teltihuacan, Mexico City, 369
Tempera paint, 348, 567, 609, 831. See also Gouache, Distemper
Temple, style of architecture in America, 323
Temples, of Solomon, 22; at Karnak, 27; of Hatshepsu, 29; of Zeus, Selinus and Olympia, of Apollo, Corinth, Paestum, Italy, 38; Maison Carré, Nimes, 54, 313; of Mars, 58; of Diana, Nimes, 81; Toltec, Mexico, 368
Teniers, 357, 569; tapestries by, 478
Tenon, 831
Tent bed, 303
Tepoztlan, Mexico, church, 173
Terminology of colors, 794–797
Terra cotta, use of, in Greece, 51; della Robbia plaques of, 117; statues by Clodion, 646; use of, by Wedgwood, 654; use of, in Vermont, 656; definition of, 831
Terrariums, 55
Terrazzo, 115, 831
Terry, E., 335; clocks by, 309
Tertiary colors, 792, 793, 831
Tessera, 831
Tester, 125, 831
Tests for fibers, 435
Textiles, 431–485; glossary of, 464; period patterns of, 441–459; use of as wall coverings, 206, 217, 629, 708–709. See also descriptions under country or style
Texture, in walls, 703; effect of on color, 804–805
Theodosius III, 72
Theotocopoulos, Domenikos, 174. See also Greco, El
Thermoplastics and thermosets, 404
Thimble foot, 831
Thomas, S., 335; clocks by, 309
Thomire, P., 219, 227, 667
Thonet Industries, 413, 414, 420, 421
Thonet, Michael, 413, 420
Thornton, Dr. W., 335
Thousand and One Nights, 145, 350
Thread and thrum rugs, 528
Threaded glass, 663

Three-color, ware, Ming, 658
Three-way bulbs, 681
Thrust and counter thrust, 89, 831
Thuỳa wood, 66, 744, 831
Tie-beam, 831
Tie-backs, for draperies, 500
Tiepolo, G., 567, 568
Tiffany, L., 664
Tile stoves in Europe, 696
Tile work. See Ceramics
Tilt-top tables, 255, 831
Tin, 670; glazes, 638
Tinsel pictures, 614, 831
Tinting values of pigments, 629
Tintoretto, Il, 135, 566
Tints, 790, 831
Titanïum oxide, use of in paint, 624
Titian, 135, 564–566
Tivoli, Villa d'Este, 113
Tlaxcala, Mexico, 173
Tlinkit Indians of Alaska, 375
Toby jugs, 653, 655
Toft, T., 647
Toiles-de-Jouy, 199, 203, 455, 831
Toledo, Spain, 137, 574, 575; Cathedral,
    151; Alcazar, Holy Cross Hospital, 157;
    Transparente, 159; Chapel of Santo Tomé,
    575; ceramics, 640
Toltec Indians of Yucatan, 369
Tomar, 165
Tone, or tonal value, 630, 790, 831
Tongue and groove, 734, 831
Top-grain leather, 435
Torus molding, 45, 831
Totonacan Indians in Mexico, 369
Toulouse-Lautrec, H., 596, 598
Touraine, 178; châteaux in, 184
Tournai, tapestries, 473; ceramics, 644
Townsend, J., 303
Trabeated construction, 27, 831
Tracery, 88, 831
Transept, 82, 87, 831
Transfer printing, 638; in ceramics, 648,
    651–652, 654–655. See also Decalcomania
Transitional, 831
Transom, 831
Transparente, in Toledo Cathedral, 159
Travertine stone, 704
Treaty of Versailles, 189
Tree-of-life pattern, 21, 242, 441, 831
Trefoils, 94, 832
Trencher, 100, 832
Trent, Council of, 141
Trenton, N. J., 656
Triangular pediment, 7
Trianon, Petit, 195, 207; interior, 208
Triclinium, 62, 66, 832
Triglyphs, 832
Trim, 715–745; disguise of, 700. See also
    descriptions under country or style
Trimmings, for draperies, 499
Trinity Church, Boston, 326; N. Y., 325
Triptych, 832

Tropical decorations, 404. See Contemporary
    styles
Troy, art in ancient, 34
Troyon, 590
Trumbull, J., 311
Trumeau, 199, 832
Trumpet leg, 252, 832
Trundle bed, 99, 832
Truss, 832; construction, 6
Tubes, fluorescent, 681
Tudor arch and rose, 832; period in Eng-
    land, 237, 240, 243
Tufft, T., 302
Tufted rugs, 523
Tufting in upholstery, 509
Turkey work, 296, 525, 832
Turkish rugs, 533
Turkoman rugs, 533
Turner, 654
Turner, J., 277, 582, 583; Impressionist
    methods of, 591
Turnings, 832; disk, 48, 66, 162, 818;
    clavated, 162, 816; bamboo and bell, 813;
    sausage, 828
Turpentine, 623, 823
Turquoise, use by Indians, 375
Turret, 832
Tuscan, 832. See also Etruscan
Tussah silk, 433
Tut-ankh-Amen, tomb of, 24
Twentieth century trends in the arts, 381.
    See also Contemporary styles, and de-
    scriptions under country
Twill weave, 437
Twyford, 652
Tympanum, 832
Types of hardware, listed, 677–678
Tyre, art in ancient, 34
Tz'u Hsi, Empress of China, 343

Ucello, P., 561
Umbrian School of painting, 560
Underglaze color, 638, 642 832
Unicorn tapestries, 475, 832
United States. See America
U. S. Plywood Corporation, 713
Unity, in design, attainment of, 758; in color
    schemes, 798
Upholstery, 505–510; contrast of, with floor
    coverings, 769–770
Urbino, Italy, 126, 563; Majolica ware, 643,
    645
Utrecht, Treaty of, 235
Utrillo, 598

Vaisselier, 225
Valances, 492, 832; lighting of, 684. See
    also Cornices, and chapters on lighting
    and draperies
Valdevira, P., 175
Valencia, ceramics, 638
Valmy, battle of, 181
Value of a color, 790, 832
Van de Velde, Henri, 388, 417, 418

Van der Rohe, M., 398, 402, 403, 405, 405, 406, 413, 417, 418, 420, 426
Van der Weyden, R., 568
Van Dyck, Sir A., 234, 569, 571, 578; P., 337
Van Gogh, V., 573, 596
Vandals, 80
Vandergoten, J., 175
Vargueño, 161, 164, 832
Variety. See Contrast
Varnishes, 624, 625
Vasari, 83
Vase, forms, Grecian, 50
Vase and urn lights, 685
Vatican, Sistine Chapel, 86; Stanza and Logi, 563
Vault, 832; Gothic, 87–88; ribbed, 828
Vaux-le-Vicomte, château, 188, 227
Vecchio, Palazzo, 113, 114
Velasquez de Silva, D., 114, 175, 575–577
Velours-de-Gênes, 448, 449, 832
Velvet carpets, 517, 832; paintings, 613
Veneers, 832; in Dutch furniture, 357; as wall coverings, 552, 711, 713, 726; for furniture, 736–739. See also Marquetry, and descriptions of use under country or style
Venetian, ornament, 121; 18th century styles, 122, 131–132, 832; glass, 127, 660; blinds, 151, 502, 832; influence in Spain, 168; School of painting, 564
Venice, Italy, S. Mark's, 75; influence in Spanish art, 168; art center, 559; statue of Colleone, 561; Ducal Palace, 566; founding of ceramics works, 641
Venus of Willendorf, prehistoric statue, 19
Vera Cruz, Mexico, 369
Verdure tapestries, 478, 832
Vermeer, J., 357, 572–573
Vernis-Martin, 202, 229, 832
Verona, Italy, 566
Veronese, P., 135, 566, 567
Verrocchio, A., 127, 561
Versailles, Hamlet in, 181; Palace of, 187; Gardens of, 188; Galérie des Glaces, Treaty of, 189; bedroom of Louis XIV, 190; Petit Trianon, 207
Verte, famille, 659, 820
Vertical, divisions of walls, 761–764; and horizontal contrasts, 766–767
Verticality, Gothic accentuation of, 90
Vesuvius, Mt., 62
Vezelay, Abbey of, 79, 83
Victoria, Queen, 236, 275
Victorian style, influences in Spanish art, 169; in Latin America, 174; in England, 238, 275–276; in America, 286, 325–330. See descriptions under country for other influences
Vienna, 647; Schönbrun Palace, 360
Vieux Paris ware, 646
Vignettes, 832
Vignola, G. B., 110, 111, 117, 135, 177
Vile, W., 279

Villapando, F. C. de, 75
Villas, in Italy, 108; d'Este, Tivoli, 113; Moorish, 146
Vincennes, ceramics, 643, 644, 651
Vinci, Leonardo da. See Da Vinci, L.
Viollet-le-duc, 325
Virgin, portrayed as human, 561. See Madonna
Virginia, early settlers in, 282; William and Mary College, 298
Visconti family, 108
Visigothic arch, 147
Visigoths, 80, 137
Vista Alegre ceramics, 160
Vitruvius, standards of, 56–59, 73, 111, 156, 158
Vittoria, 127, 667
Vlaminck, 600
Voltaire, 180
Volutes, 42, 832
Vorticism, 600
Voussoir, 79, 833
Vues d'optiques, 614

Wag-on-wall, 833
Wagner, O., 389
Wainscot, origin of, 42, 58; Gothic, 97; chairs, English and American, 243, 294, 833; descriptions of, 726, 833. See also Dado
Wall hanging, Swedish, 612
Wallpapers, 541–557; domino, 185; flock, 199; by Dufour, 222; removal of, 631, 632; antiquing of, 635; spot pattern, 699. See Walls, and descriptions under country or style
Walls, coverings for, textiles, 217, 629, 708–709; clapboard, 290, 816; composition and treatments of, 395, 397, 619, 620, 758–774; use of veneers on, 552, 711, 713, 726. See also Painting, Mural decoration, Wallpaper and Panelling. For specific descriptions see country or style
Walnut, Age of, 237, 238, 252; wood, 251, 739, 744
Walpole, H., 250
Walton, 653
War, of 1812, 654; God of, 657
Warm colors, 791, 833
Warp, 833; threads, 436
Washington, D. C., White House, 286; Capitol in, 313; Freer Art Gallery, "Peacock" room, 606
Washington, G., 182; portraits of by Peale, 603
Water colors, 609; framing of, 617
Waterford glass, 661
Waterleaf ornament, 45, 833
Waterloo, 216, 236
Watkins, F., 608
Watt, 235
Wattage, of bulbs, 687
Watteau, A., 194, 197, 227, 584, 585
Waugh, S., 664

Wave pattern, 31, 833
Wax silhouettes, 614
Weaves, 437–438; methods of making, 436; in rugs, 535
Webbing, for upholstery, 507, 833
Weber, M., 608
Wedgwood, J., 265, 271, 277, 653–654; wares, 211, 643, 647, 649, 653–654
Weir, A., 607
Weft threads, 436. *See also* Filler
Wegener, Hans, 424, 426
Weisweiler, A., 211, 229
Wellington, Duke of, 236
Wells Cathedral, 233
Welsh dressers, 245
Welting, 503, 833
West, 610; Indies, arts in, 172; India Company, 569
West, B., 336, 602
Western culture, styles of, 9
Westover, Va., 297
Whatnots, 328, 833
Wheel, color, 791–792, 796, 797, 799–800
Whieldon, T., 645, 653, 654
Whistler, J. Mc., 336, 590, 605, 606, 610
White House, Washington, D. C., Oval room, 286
White lead, 623, 833
Whitehall, London, Banqueting House, 246
Willard clocks, 309; family, 336
Willendorf, Venus of, 19, 378
William, the Conqueror, 77, 82, 233; of Orange, 235, 252, 355
William and Mary, of England, 235; style, 238, 252–253; College, Va., 298
Willow pattern, 654
Wilson, 653
Wilton carpets, 516, 833
Windows, 720; glass for, 95, 722; shades for, 501; trim of, 715–718; casement, 721, 815
Windsor, chairs, English, 245, 257; American, 304–305; tapestries, 474; Castle, in England, 573
Winslow, E., 337
Wiring, electrical, 680
Wistar, C. and R., 663
Wistarberg ware, 663
Wolstenholme, 613

Women during Middle Ages, 85
Wood, G., 608; R., 649, 653; A., 653; E., 653, 654; and Caldwell, 653
Woodcuts, 610; by Holbein, 572
Woods, painting and staining of, 632; trim, examples of, 716; joinery of, methods, 717; flooring, 733; grain in, 734; cabinet, 737–744; glossary of, 741–744. *See also* veneers, Plywood, and descriptions under country or style
Woodwork. *See* Interior trim, Panelling, and descriptions under country or style
Woof threads, 436, 833. *See also* Weft and Filler
Wool fiber, 436; ship pictures, 613
Worcester, England, 654; ceramics, 649, 651–652
World War I, 236; II, 80
World's Fair of 1893, 386
Wren, C., 235, 247, 256, 277, 313, 671; influence in America, 298
Wright, F. L., 335, 394, 395, 396, 398, 405
Wrought iron, 163, 667, 668
Wyant, A., 605

Xavier, S. F., 175

Yardage, for slipcovers, 504
Yarn dyeing, 833
Yesería ornament, 145, 147, 833
Yoke, 833; chair back, 256, 257
York, Pa., 305
York Cathedral, 94
Yorkshire chair, 244, 245, 833
Yuan or Mongol period, 347
Yucatan, paintings in, 368

Zanesville, O., 662
Zapotec Indians, 369
Zeus, Temple of, 38
Zinc, 667; oxide, use in paint, 624
Zola, E., 182
Zorn, 610
Zuber, J., 543
Zucchi, A. P., 133, 272, 277
Zuloaga, 478
Zuñi Indians, 373
Zurbaran, F., 175, 574

18th c. culture came
down from The Palace
—

20th c. culture comes
up from The street —